A TASTE OF
AMERICA

A TASTE OF
AMERICA

THE COMPLETE BOOK OF
AMERICAN REGIONAL COOKING

Edited and adapted by
MARIAN HOFFMAN

GALLERY BOOKS

A Macdonald Orbis BOOK

Created and manufactured by arrangement with
Ottenheimer Publishers, Inc.

Copyright © 1988, Ottenheimer Publishers, Inc.

First published in Great Britain in 1988
by Macdonald & Co (Publishers) Ltd
London & Sydney

A member of Maxwell Pergamon Publishing Corporation plc

British Library Cataloging in Publication Data

Hoffman, Marian
    A taste of America.
1. Food: American dishes—Recipes
    I. Title
    641.5973

ISBN 0-8317-8652-3

Text edited by Marian Hoffman

Printed in the United States of America

Macdonald & Co (Publishers) Ltd
Greater London House
Hampstead Road
London NW1 7QX

Contents

Symbols

The symbols will enable you to see at a glance how easy a recipe is, the preparation and cooking times, and from which region of the United States the recipe originated.

 easy

 more difficult

 for experienced cooks

 preparation time

 cooking time

 region

When using the recipes in this book remember the following points:

Cooking and preparation times are approximate and will vary according to the type of equipment used, the experience of the cook, and the number of convenience foods used.

Use only one set of measurements for the recipes, since American, imperial, and metric measurements are not exact equivalents.

In the text of the recipes, American quantities and ingredients are listed first, with the British equivalents in brackets. The British equivalent to an American ingredient only appears after the first mention of that ingredient.

Introduction

Just what constitutes American cuisine is difficult to define. Many "American" recipes are versions of traditional dishes brought over from the Old World, reflecting the ethnic heritage of many Americans. Other recipes reflect the foods and innovations of the New World. Each region of the United States has its own specialties depending on which crops grow in that climate, how close it is to the coast, and which ethnic groups have settled in that area.

A Taste of America is a comprehensive collection of over 1,000 recipes culled from the different regions of the United States. Each recipe has been labeled according to region; there are recipes from New England, the Mid Atlantic, the South, the Midwest, the Pacific Southwest, and the Pacific Northwest. Some recipes, however, are found so commonly throughout the country that they have simply been labeled "United States."

The recipes, many of which are illustrated by full color photographs, include preparation and cooking times and are ranked according to degree of difficulty. These features, plus step-by-step instructions, make this book an easy-to-use as well as comprehensive collection of American cookery.

Appetizers and First Courses

Stuffed Mushrooms

Stuffed Mushrooms

	00:20	Serves 4	United States 
	00:40		

American	Ingredients	Metric/Imperial
4	Large (or 8 smaller mushrooms)	4
4 tbsp	Margarine	50 g/2 oz
1	Small onion, chopped	1
1 tbsp	Flour	1 tbsp
½ cup	Milk	125 ml/4 fl oz
½	Small red pepper	½
¼ cup	Cooked ham, chopped	50 g/2 oz
1 tbsp	Parsley, chopped	1 tbsp
	Salt and pepper	
5 tbsp	Fresh bread crumbs	4 tbsp

1. Preheat oven to 350°F/180°C/Gas Mark 4.
2. Wipe the mushrooms, remove the stalks, and reserve. Put mushroom caps, upside down, in a shallow, greased, ovenproof dish. Dot with 2 tablespoons [25g/1oz] of margarine and bake in oven for 10 minutes.
3. Meanwhile, heat the remaining margarine in a saucepan and fry the onion until softened. Stir in the flour and cook, stirring, for 2 to 3 minutes. Blend in the milk and bring to a boil, stirring all the time. Boil for 2 minutes.
4. Chop the reserved mushroom stalks and half the pepper (slice remainder of the pepper for garnish). Add the pepper, mushroom stalks, ham, parsley, salt, pepper, and bread crumbs to the sauce. Pile some stuffing into each mushroom cap.
5. Return to the oven and bake for a further 15 to 20 minutes. Serve hot, garnished with strips of red pepper.

Stuffed Artichokes

	00:30	Serves 4	Pacific Southwest
	00:50		

American	Ingredients	Metric/Imperial
4	Medium globe artichokes	4
¾ cup	Dry bread crumbs	40 g/1½ oz
3 tbsp	Parmesan cheese, grated	2 tbsp
1 tbsp	Parsley, chopped	1 tbsp
½ tsp	Garlic salt	½ tsp
¼ tsp	Dried oregano, crumbled	¼ tsp
¼ tsp	Pepper	¼ tsp
2 tbsp	Butter	25 g/1 oz
2 tbsp	Olive oil	1½ tbsp
1 cup	Boiling water	250 ml/8 fl oz

1. Remove stems from the artichokes. Cut about ½ inch from the tips of the leaves, using kitchen scissors. Drop into boiling salted water: cook 5 minutes. Drain; shake to remove water; cool.
2. Combine the bread crumbs, cheese, parsley, garlic salt, oregano, and pepper. Mix well.
3. Tap the base of the artichokes on a flat surface to spread the leaves. Stuff each artichoke with one quarter of the bread-crumb mixture; spoon it between the leaves. Put the artichokes into a saucepan or stove-top [flame-proof] casserole; place them close together so they do not tip over. Top each artichoke with ½ tablespoon [7½ g/¼ oz] butter and ½ tablespoon oil. Pour in boiling water and cover. Cook over low heat 35 to 45 minutes or until the artichokes are tender.

Stuffed Tomatoes

	02:15	Serves 4	United States
	00:00		

American	Ingredients	Metric/Imperial
4	Medium tomatoes, peeled	4
	Cream-Cheese Stuffing	
4 oz	Cream cheese, softened	100 g/4oz
2 tbsp	Light [single] cream	1½ tbsp
1 tsp	Chopped chives	1 tsp
	Dressing	
2 tbsp	Wine vinegar	1½ tbsp
6 tbsp	Vegetable oil	5 tbsp
¼ tsp	Salt	¼ tsp
	Pepper to taste	
1 tsp	Chopped chives	1 tsp

1. Cut a thin slice from the bottom of each tomato. Reserve the slices. From stem ends, scoop out the seeds and pulp with a spoon. Mix the cream cheese, cream, and 1 teaspoon chives. Fill the tomatoes with cream-cheese stuffing.
2. Mix the vinegar, oil, salt, pepper, and 1 teaspoon chives. Pour the dressing over the tomatoes. Chill up to 2 hours. Serve on salad greens. Use reserved tomato slices as hats for tomatoes.
3. Note: To peel tomatoes, dip in boiling water 30 seconds, then rinse with cold water. Skins will slip off.

Sweet-Potato Fingers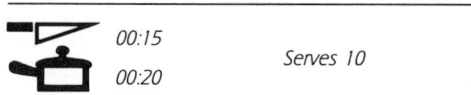

	00:15				
	00:20		Serves 10		South

American	Ingredients	Metric/Imperial
4-6	Cooked sweet potatoes	4-6
¼ cup	Flour	25 g/1 oz
	Fat for deep frying	
½ cup	Brown [demerara] sugar	100 g/4 oz
1 tsp	Salt	1 tsp
½ tsp	Nutmeg	½ tsp

1. Cut the sweet potatoes into strips or fingers. Score lightly with a fork. Dip each finger into flour until well coated.
2. Heat the fat in a medium frying pan. Fry the potato fingers until golden brown. Drain on paper towels [kitchen paper]. Sprinkle with a mixture of brown sugar, salt, and nutmeg. Makes about 40 fingers.

Toasted Pecans

	00:05				
	01:30		Serves 24		South

American	Ingredients	Metric/Imperial
12 cups	Pecans	1.5 kg/3¼ lb
¼ lb	Butter	100 g/4 oz
	Salt	

1. Preheat oven to 250°F/130°C/Gas Mark ½.
2. Place the pecans in a rectangular oven dish. Toast in the oven 30 minutes. Add butter over all by slicing or dotting it over nuts. Stir once or twice, until the pecans and butter have mixed well. The nuts will be greasy at this point.
3. Sprinkle with salt to taste. Toast the pecans 1 hour; salt again several times. Stir as you go. When done, the butter will be completely absorbed and nuts crisp.

Roasted Chestnuts

	00:15				
	00:30		Serves 4		New England

American	Ingredients	Metric/Imperial
24	Chestnuts	24

1. Using a sharp knife, make two diagonal slits on the flat side of each chestnut.
2. Heat charcoal grill. If you don't have a charcoal grill, cook the chestnuts in an open fire.
3. Put 6 chestnuts on a square of foil and wrap up into a neat parcel—one for each person. Put directly on the hot coals and leave for about 30 minutes.
4. Remember to let the nuts cool a little before eating.

Vegetable Fritters

Vegetable Fritters

	01:00				
	00:20		Serves 6		United States

American	Ingredients	Metric/Imperial
1	Small eggplant [aubergine]	1
	Salt	
1	Large zucchini [courgette]	1
½	Small cauliflower	½
¾ cup	Flour	75 g/3 oz
2	Eggs	2
4 tbsp	Milk	3½ tbsp
	Oil for deep-frying	

1. Slice the eggplant into thin rounds. Place the slices in a colander and sprinkle with salt. Cover with a plate and put aside for 30 minutes. Slice the zucchini. Divide the cauliflower into flowerets.
2. Sift the flour into a mixing bowl with a pinch of salt. Make a well in the center and add the eggs. Mix the eggs into the flour; gradually add milk, beating well until the batter is smooth. Rinse then drain the eggplant and pat dry with paper towels [kitchen paper]. Fill a deep frying pan half full of oil. When the fat is hot, dip the vegetables into batter and fry individual pieces until golden all over. Drain on paper towels [kitchen paper] and serve as soon as possible.

Avocado Cream

Potato Skins

| | 00:30 | Serves 8 | New England |
| | 01:15 | | |

American	Ingredients	Metric/Imperial
8	Medium-sized potatoes	8
¼ cup	Flour	50 g/2 oz
	Cooking oil	
	Seasoned salt	

1. Preheat oven to 400°F/200°C/Gas Mark 6.
2. Scrub the potatoes and pierce with a fork. Rub lightly with oil and bake for about 50 to 60 minutes, or until tender. Cool.
3. Cut the potatoes in half lengthwise and scoop out most of the white part, leaving about a ¼-inch shell. Cut the shells in half lengthwise, then in half cross-wise, which will give you eight pieces from each potato. Dip in flour and shake off excess, then deep fry in oil heated to 375°F [190°C] for about 2 minutes or until lightly browned.
4. Drain on a paper towel [kitchen paper]. Sprinkle with seasoned salt, and serve. Makes about 64 potato skins.
5. These may be made ahead of time and reheated by placing on baking sheet in 375°F/190°C/Gas Mark 5 oven for about 10 minutes.

Avocado Cream

| | 01:15 | Serves 4 | Pacific Southwest |  |
| | 00:00 | | | |

American	Ingredients	Metric/Imperial
2	Ripe avocado	2
1 tbsp	White wine vinegar	1 tbsp
4	Anchovy fillets, finely chopped	4
2 tsp	Finely chopped onion	2 tsp
	Salt	
	Cayenne pepper	
1 tsp	Sugar	1 tsp
½ cup	Heavy [double] cream, whipped	125 ml/4 fl oz
	Paprika	

1. Cut the avocados in half and remove the seed.
2. Scrape out all the flesh, being careful not to break the skin. Reserve the empty shells, adding lemon juice to prevent discoloring. Put the flesh into a bowl and mash well. Add vinegar, anchovy, and onion. Season with salt, cayenne pepper, and sugar.
3. Chill for at least an hour; just before serving, fold in the whipped cream. Fill the avocados shells and sprinkle with paprika.

Quiche Lorraine

| | 01:40 | Serves 6 | South |
| | 00:50 | | |

American	Ingredients	Metric/Imperial
1	Recipe Pâte Brisée (see Index)	1
6 oz	Gruyère cheese	175 g/6 oz
4 slices	Bacon	4 rashers
3	Eggs	3
¾ cup	Light [single] cream	175 ml/6 fl oz
1	Small onion, peeled and finely chopped	1
¼ tsp	Nutmeg	¼ tsp

1. Preheat oven to 450°F/230°C/Gas Mark 8.
2. Line a deep 8-inch pie plate with the pastry, and refrigerate while preparing the filling. Rest for 1 hour.
3. Cut the cheese into thin slices, or use packaged cheese slices, and cut into 2-inch strips.
4. Cut the bacon into small pieces. Fry until crisp and then drain.
5. Arrange alternate layers of cheese and bacon in the pie shell and sprinkle with chopped sautéed onion.
6. Beat the eggs lightly. Combine with the cream, nutmeg, and seasoning and pour over the bacon and cheese.
7. Bake for 10 minutes; then reduce heat to 300°F/150°C/Gas Mark 2 and bake for 30 minutes, or until the custard is set and pastry is cooked.

Cucumber Boats

Cucumber Boats

	00:30		
	00:00	Serves 8	United States

American	Ingredients	Metric/Imperial
1	Cucumber	1
1 (4½-oz) can	Sardines	1 (125 g/4½ oz) tin
½ cup	Mayonnaise	125 ml/4 fl oz
2 tsp	Lemon juice	2 tsp
1 tbsp	Parsley, chopped	1 tbsp
2	Hard-boiled eggs	2
1 tsp	Salt	1 tsp
½ tsp	Pepper	½ tsp
1	Lettuce	1
½	Head celery	½
2	Large carrots	2

1. Cut the cucumber into 2½-inch lengths. Cut in half lengthwise, remove ½ inch strip of skin underneath cucumber pieces to make them stand up. Cut each strip into 2 triangles to make sails. Remove the soft center from each piece of cucumber.

2. Drain the sardines and mash them in a bowl with mayonnaise and lemon juice. Chop the parsley and hard-boiled eggs; add them to the sardine mixture with salt and pepper. Fill the cucumber pieces with the mixture.

3. Arrange the cucumbers on a serving plate. Shred the lettuce; cut the celery into 1-inch pieces and the carrot into wedges. Arrange these vegetables on a serving plate in between the cucumber boats. Secure sails by pushing the narrow end of the sail into the filling and propping it up with a cocktail stick if necessary.

Party Croissant

Party Croissant

| | 01:30 | Serves 8 | United States |
| | 00:20 | | |

American	Ingredients	Metric/Imperial
1 oz	Yeast	25 g/1 oz
5 tbsp	Butter or margarine	65 g/2½ oz
⅔ cup	Lukewarm water	150 ml/¼ pt
	Salt	
½ tsp	Sugar	½ tsp
2	Eggs	2
1 tbsp	Sesame seeds, without skins, plus more to sprinkle over croissant	1 tbsp
2 cups	Flour	225 g/8 oz
	Filling	
5 oz	Garlic cheese	150 g/5 oz
¼ lb	Smoked ham, in thin slices	100 g/4 oz
18-20	Pimento-filled olives	18-20

1. Crumble the yeast in a large bowl. Melt the butter in a pan and add water. Pour a little of the warm liquid over the yeast and stir. Pour in the rest of the liquid. Add salt, sugar, 1 egg, and sesame seeds. Add nearly all of the flour and work until the dough becomes smooth and shiny. Let it rise under a cloth for about 30 minutes.

2. Place the dough onto a lightly floured baking board and knead it until it stops sticking to the board. Roll out the dough into a triangle. Lay the filling in an even strip across the widest part of the triangle. Roll together toward the point. Form into a croissant.

3. Preheat oven to 400°F/200°C/Gas Mark 6.

4. Place the croissant on a prepared baking sheet and let it rise for approximately 20 minutes. Brush with second egg and sprinkle some sesame seeds over croissant. Bake on the lowest rack in the oven for about 20 minutes. Test with a toothpick.

Mushroom Rolls

| | 00:30 | Serves 15-20 | United States |
| | 00:15 | | |

American	Ingredients	Metric/Imperial
½ lb	Mushrooms	225 g/8oz
¼ cup	Butter	50 g/2oz
3 tbsp	Flour	2 tbsp
¾ tsp	Salt	¾ tsp
1 cup	Light [single] cream	250 ml/8 fl oz
2 tsp	Chives, minced	2 tsp
1 tsp	Lemon juice	1 tsp
1	Family-sized loaf sliced fresh white bread	1

1. Clean and finely chop the mushrooms. Sauté for 5 minutes in butter. Blend in flour and salt. Stir in the light cream. Cook until thick.

2. Add the chives and lemon juice; cool. Remove the crust from the white bread. Roll slices thin and spread with the mixture. Roll up. Pack and freeze, if desired.

3. When ready to serve, defrost, cut each roll in half, and toast on all sides in 400°F/200°C/Gas Mark 6 oven. Makes 3½ dozen.

Cheese and Anchovy Snack

| | 00:15 | Serves 4 | United States  |
| | 00:15 | | |

American	Ingredients	Metric/Imperial
¼	Loaf French bread	¼
	Bel Paese or Cheddar cheese	
1 can (2 oz)	Anchovy fillets	1 tin (50 g/2 oz)
½ cup	Butter	50 g/2 oz

1. Preheat oven to 400°F/200°C/Gas Mark 6.

2. Cut the bread into slanting slices about ¼ inch thick. Place a slice of cheese on each and arrange in a baking pan, slightly overlapping. Put into a moderately hot oven until the cheese has melted and the bread is crisp.

3. Mash the anchovy fillets and mix with the butter. Spread over the bread and return to the oven for a few minutes to heat through.

4. If you find anchovies a little too salty for your taste, soak them for 10-15 minutes in a little milk and then pat dry before using.

Stuffed Eggs

	00:25			
	00:15	Serves 4	United States	

American	Ingredients	Metric/Imperial
4	Eggs	4
½ tsp dried or ½ tbsp fresh	Parsley	½ tsp dried or ½ tbsp fresh
	Salt and pepper	
4 tbsp	Mayonnaise	3½ tbsp

1. Hard-boil the eggs in boiling water to cover for 10-15 minutes. Stir cooking eggs for the first 2 minutes to help keep the yolks in the middle. Drain and cool the eggs in cold water.
2. Shell and cut each egg in half lengthwise. Scoop out the yolks into a bowl; add parsley, salt and pepper, and mayonnaise. Beat until smooth. Pile the yolks back into the whites or pipe them with a large star pipe.

Swiss Cheese Snack

	00:05		
	00:10	Serves 4	Midwest

American	Ingredients	Metric/Imperial
8	Slices bread	8
	Butter	
	Prepared mustard	
4	Slices Swiss cheese	4
4	Thin slices cooked ham	4

1. Cut the crusts from the bread and spread with butter.
2. Spread a little mustard on half the slices; put a slice of cheese and a slice of ham on top. Cover with the remaining slices of bread and press down firmly.
3. Cut in half crosswise and fry in hot butter, turning once.

Cheese Fingers

	00:15		
	00:15	Serves 9	Midwest

American	Ingredients	Metric/Imperial
9	Bread slices	9
	Butter	
½ cup	Grated cheese	50 g/2 oz
2	Eggs	2
2 tbsp	Milk	1½ tbsp

1. Remove the crusts from the bread, spread with butter, and make into sandwiches with the grated cheese. (Spread a little prepared mustard or chopped pickle on one side of the bread if desired.)
2. Cut into neat fingers.
3. Beat the eggs; add milk and seasoning.
4. Dip the fingers quickly in and out of the egg and fry in hot butter until crisp and golden.

Stuffed Eggs

Cheese Pastries

	01:30			
	00:15	Serves 4	United States	

American	Ingredients	Metric/Imperial
	Pasta Pastry	
2 cups	Flour	225 g/8 oz
½ tsp	Salt	½ tsp
¼ cup	Butter or margarine	50 g/2 oz
	Lukewarm water to mix	
	Filling	
¼ cup	Butter or margarine	50 g/2 oz
1½ cups	Grated cheese	175 g/6 oz
1	Egg	1

1. To make the pastry, sift the flour and salt, rub in the butter, and add enough water to make a soft but not sticky dough. Knead into a ball, cover, and leave for about 1 hour.
2. To make the filling, beat the butter until soft. Then beat in most of the cheese, beaten egg, and seasoning.
3. Roll out the dough very thinly, cut into rounds with a serrated cutter, about 2½ inches in diameter.
4. Put a little of the cheese mixture on each round of dough, dampen the edge and fold over, pressing the edges well together.
5. Fry in deep fat until well browned. Drain and serve sprinkled with the remaining cheese.

Melon Shrimp

Cheese Straws

 00:50
00:10
Serves 4   Mid Atlantic

American	Ingredients	Metric/Imperial
½ cup	Butter or 1 stick	100 g/4 oz
1 cup	All-purpose [plain] flour	100 g/4 oz
1 cup	Grated cheese	100 g/4 oz
1 tsp	Dry mustard	1 tsp
	Cayenne pepper and salt to taste	

1. Cut the butter into the flour, which has been sifted into a bowl. Blend well. Add the grated cheese, dry mustard, pepper, cayenne pepper, and salt if necessary. Shape the paste into a ball, wrap well, and refrigerate for at least 30 minutes.
2. Preheat oven to 400°F/200°C/Gas Mark 6.
3. Roll out paste on a floured board and cut into strips or rounds. Bake in an oven for 6–10 minutes or until golden brown and crisp.

Melon Shrimp

 00:15
00:00
Serves 4-6   Pacific Southwest

American	Ingredients	Metric/Imperial
1	Honeydew melon (or watermelon)	1
1 can (4½ oz)	Shrimp [prawns]	1 tin (125 g/4½ oz)
	A little mayonnaise, tomato purée and cream	

1. Using a vegetable ball cutter, cut some balls from a honey-dew or watermelon and mix with the shrimp.
2. Put into dishes and coat with mayonnaise to which a little tomato purée and cream has been added.

Peaches Filled with Cheese

 00:15
00:00
Serves 4-5   Midwest

American	Ingredients	Metric/Imperial
1 can (about 30 oz)	Peach halves	1 tin (850 g/ 30 oz)
3 tbsp	Grated Cheddar cheese	2 tbsp
1 tbsp	Grated Parmesan cheese	1 tbsp
1 tbsp	Softened butter	15 g/½ oz
	Cayenne pepper	
	Lettuce	
3 oz	Cream cheese	75 g/3 oz
5-6 tbsp	Light [single] cream	4-5 tbsp
	Paprika	

1. Drain the peaches.
2. Mix the cheese with the butter, season to taste with salt and cayenne pepper, and fill the peach halves.
3. Arrange them on a platter, or on individual dishes, on a bed of lettuce.
4. Beat the cream cheese and cream together, and spoon over the peaches. Sprinkle with paprika.

Piroshki

 00:40
00:55
Serves 4   Pacific Northwest

American	Ingredients	Metric/Imperial
2 tbsp	Butter	25 g/1 oz
1	Small onion, finely chopped	1
4–6	Mushrooms	4-6
2–3 tbsp	Cooked rice	1½–2 tbsp
2 tbsp	Cooked chopped ham	1½ tbsp
1 tbsp	Chopped parsley	1 tbsp
1 (8-oz)	Package frozen flaky pastry, thawed	1 (225 g/8 oz)
1	Beaten egg	1

1. Melt the butter and cook finely chopped onion for 2–3 minutes to soften; then add the mushrooms and cook for 4 more minutes. Add the cooked rice and ham. Season with salt and pepper, and add chopped parsley. Cool before using.
2. Roll out the puff pastry into a long strip about 1½ inches in width or wider if larger piroshki are desired. Using a 1½-inch cutter, cut out as many rounds as possible.
3. Put a teaspoon of the cooled filling into the center of each pastry circle. Moisten the edges and press together to form a crescent-shaped pie. Brush the top with a beaten egg and bake in a hot oven for 10–15 minutes until golden brown and crisp. Serve hot.
4. Other ingredients can be used in piroshki such as smoked salmon, diced chicken, or small quantities of leftover meat.

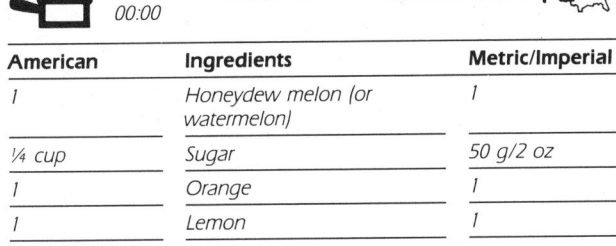

Peaches Filled with Cheese

Meatball Appetizers 👨‍🍳

| | 00:20 | | |
| 🍳 | 00:20 | Serves 4 | Midwest 🗺️ |

American	Ingredients	Metric/Imperial
1 lb	Ground [minced] beef	450 g/1 lb
5 tbsp	Dry bread crumbs	4 tbsp
1	Egg	1
⅓ cup plus 2 tbsp	Steak sauce	75 ml/3 fl oz plus 1½ tbsp
2 tbsp	Oil	2 tbsp
2 tbsp	Light brown sugar	2 tbsp
2 tbsp	Butter	25 g/1 oz

1. Combine the beef, bread crumbs, egg, and 2 tablespoons [1½ tbsp] steak sauce. Mix and shape into 1-inch meatballs. Brown in the oil in a frying pan. Drain fat from the pan.
2. Add ⅓ cup [75 ml/3 fl oz] steak sauce, brown sugar, and butter to the meatballs in the pan. Simmer for 15 minutes until done. Makes 2 dozen meatballs.

Melon and Grape Cocktail 👨‍🍳👨‍🍳

| | 00:15 | | |
| 🍳 | 00:00 | Serves 4-6 | Pacific Southwest 🗺️ |

American	Ingredients	Metric/Imperial
1	Honeydew melon (or watermelon)	1
¼ cup	Sugar	50 g/2 oz
1	Orange	1
1	Lemon	1
1	Small bunch of grapes	1
1	Sprig mint	1

1. Using a vegetable ball cutter, cut some balls from a honeydew or watermelon. Half fill some glasses with the melon balls.
2. Dissolve sugar in juice of 1 orange and 1 lemon, and pour over melon.
3. Peel and seed some grapes, and put them on top of the melon. Do not mix them at this stage. Cover and leave for several hours.
4. When ready to serve, mix the fruit and garnish with a sprig of mint.

Beef Tartare

Baked Spareribs

| | 12:00 | | |
| 01:30 | | Serves 4-6 | Pacific Southwest |

American	Ingredients	Metric/Imperial
3–4 lb	Pork spareribs	1.25–1.75 kg/ 3–4 lb
½	Clove garlic	½
¼ cup	Soy sauce	60 ml/2 fl oz
¼ cup	Sherry	60 ml/2 fl oz
3 tbsp	Honey	2 tbsp
¼ tsp	Ginger	¼ tsp

1. Preheat oven to 350°F/180°C/Gas Mark 4.
2. Crush the garlic. Mix the ingredients together and add seasoning. Pour this mixture over the spareribs. Leave to marinate overnight or longer, turning as often as possible.
3. Bake the spareribs for 1¼–1½ hours, basting every 15 minutes with marinade. The ribs should be well browned and the meat tender.
4. Serve with rice and salad.

Beef Tartare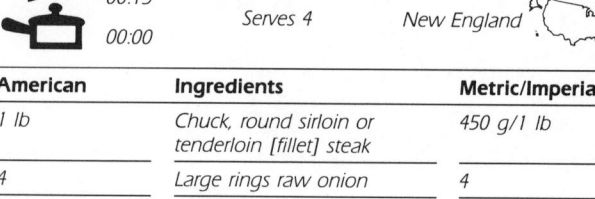

| | 00:15 | | |
| 00:00 | | Serves 4 | New England |

American	Ingredients	Metric/Imperial
1 lb	Chuck, round sirloin or tenderloin [fillet] steak	450 g/1 lb
4	Large rings raw onion	4
4	Raw egg yolks	4
4	Anchovy fillets	4
2 tsp	Capers	2 tsp
	Fresh horseradish, if available (optional)	
4	Quarters lemon	4
	Freshly ground black pepper	

1. Buy and grind [mince] the steak as near to serving time as possible, as the meat becomes dark in color if left standing. Only add pepper to the meat.
2. Shape the meat into 4 equal-sized cakes and make a depression in the center of each with a spoon. Place an onion ring around this depression and put an egg yolk into the center of each. Sprinkle a few capers on top of the egg yolk and lay one curled anchovy fillet on top of each yolk. Garnish with a few chives or fresh horseradish if available.
3. Serve with rye bread and butter, or French bread and lemon quarters.

Sausage Biscuits

| | 00:15 | | |
| 00:15 | | Serves 12 | South |

American	Ingredients	Metric/Imperial
8 oz	Sharp Cheddar cheese, grated	225 g/8 oz
1 lb	Hot [spicy] pork sausage meat	450 g/1 lb
2 cups	Biscuit mix [biscuit dough]	225 g/8 oz

1. Preheat oven to 400° F/200°/C Gas Mark 6.
2. Mix everything together in a bowl, working in the sausage and cheese well. Drop onto ungreased cookie [baking] sheets; shape slightly with your fingers if you wish. Bake about 15 minutes or until nicely browned.
3. Serve the biscuits piping hot. Makes about 3 dozen biscuits.

Herb Cheese Dip

| | 00.05 | | |
| 00.00 | | About 1½ cups [375 ml/12 fl oz] | Mid Atlantic |

American	Ingredients	Metric/Imperial
3 pkg (3 oz each)	Cream cheese	250 g/9 oz
4 tbsp	Heavy [double] cream	3½ tbsp
2 tsp	Lemon juice	2 tsp
½	Clove garlic, crushed	½
1–2 tbsp	Milk	1–2 tbsp
2 tbsp	Freshly chopped parsley	2 tbsp

1. Mix all the ingredients well, adding seasoning to taste.
2. Serve slightly chilled.

Ham Appetizer

Mexican Dip

	00:10		
	00:15	Serves 4	Southwest

American	Ingredients	Metric/Imperial
3 tbsp	Ground or very finely chopped onion	2 tbsp
3 tbsp	White wine vinegar	2 tbsp
½ cup	Tomato ketchup	125 ml/4 fl oz
1 tsp	Worcestershire sauce	1 tsp
	Juice of ½ lemon	
½ tsp	Paprika pepper	½ tsp
	Black pepper, salt, sugar	
6–8	Frankfurters	6–8

1. Put the onion and vinegar into a pan, and simmer for 5 minutes.
2. Add tomato ketchup, Worcestershire sauce, and lemon juice. Simmer for a few minutes longer, then add paprika, pepper, salt, and sugar to taste.
3. Cut some frankfurters into 2–3 pieces and heat in the dip.
4. Serve with crusty bread.

Ham Appetizer

	00:20		
	00:00	Serves 4	Mid Atlantic

American	Ingredients	Metric/Imperial
2 tbsp	Finely chopped green pepper	1½ tbsp
2 tbsp	Finely chopped celery	1½ tbsp
2 tbsp	Finely chopped pimento	1½ tbsp
¼ tsp	Dijon mustard	¼ tsp
2 tsp	Lemon juice	2 tsp
2 tsp	Olive oil	2 tsp
4	Slices cooked ham	4
	Stuffed olives or gherkins for garnish	

1. Mix the green pepper, celery, and pimento together.
2. Mix the mustard with the lemon juice and oil. Add salt and pepper to taste. Pour over the vegetables, and mix well.
3. Divide equally between the four slices of ham, fold over, and secure with toothpicks.
4. Arrange on a serving dish, and garnish with stuffed olives or gherkins cut into fan shapes.

Shrimp Dip

| | 00:05 | About 1¾ cups | South |
| | 00:00 | [425 ml/14 fl oz] | |

American	Ingredients	Metric/Imperial
¼ cup	Chili sauce	60 ml/2 fl oz
2 tsp	Lemon juice	2 tsp
1 tsp	Prepared horseradish [relish]	1 tsp
¼ tsp	Salt	¼ tsp
4	Drops hot-pepper sauce	4
1 cup	Sour cream	250 ml/8 fl oz
1 (4½-oz) can	Shrimp [prawns], drained and chopped	1 (125g/4½ oz) tin

1. Combine the chili sauce, lemon juice, horseradish, salt, and hot-pepper sauce. Fold in sour cream; add chopped shrimp. Chill.
2. Serve dip with crisp vegetables.

Garlic Butter Chips

| | 00:10 | Serves 8 | United States |
| | 00:08 | | |

American	Ingredients	Metric/Imperial
¾ cup	Butter or margarine	175 g/6 oz
2–3 cloves	Garlic, cut into slivers	2–3
1 bag (7½ oz)	Potato chips [crisps]	1 bag (200 g/7½ oz)

1. Preheat oven to 350°F/180°C/Gas Mark 4.
2. Heat the butter with the garlic for a few minutes, then remove the garlic.
3. Brush the potato chips with the garlic butter and place on baking sheets lined with paper towels [kitchen paper]. Heat for 5 minutes, then drain on clean paper towels.

Avocado Spread

| | 00.05 | About ½ cup | Pacific Southwest |
| | 00.00 | [125 ml/4 fl oz] | |

American	Ingredients	Metric/Imperial
4 oz	Mashed avocado	100 g/4 oz
2 tsp	Ground onion	2 tsp
1 tbsp	Lemon juice	1 tbsp
1 tbsp	Mayonnaise	1 tbsp
	Pinch of cayenne pepper	
	Dash of Tabasco	

1. Combine all the ingredients and beat until smooth.

Avocado Dip

| | 00.10 | About 1 cup | Pacific Southwest |
| | 00.00 | [250 ml/8 fl oz] | |

American	Ingredients	Metric/Imperial
1	Cut clove garlic	1
3	Ripe avocado pears	3
	Pinch of cayenne pepper	
1 tbsp	Finely chopped onion	1 tbsp
1 tbsp	Olive oil	1 tbsp
1 tbsp	Lemon juice	1 tbsp
	A few drops of Tabasco sauce	

1. Rub the sides of a bowl with the garlic.
2. Remove the seeds and scoop out all the flesh from the pears and put it into the bowl.
3. Add all the other ingredients and mix well. Season to taste and chill before serving.

Chili Dip

| | 00:05 | About 2½ cups | South |
| | 00:00 | | |

American	Ingredients	Metric/Imperial
4 pkg (3 oz each)	Cream cheese	350 g/12 oz
½ cup	Mayonnaise	125 ml/4 fl oz
½ cup	Chili sauce	125 ml/4 fl oz
3 tbsp	Prepared horseradish	2 tbsp
2 tbsp	Pickle relish	1½ tbsp

1. Beat the cream cheese with the mayonnaise until smooth and creamy.
2. Add the other ingredients and mix well.

Mustard Dip

| | 00:10 | About 1 cup | Midwest  |
| | 00:00 | [250 ml/8 fl oz] | |

American	Ingredients	Metric/Imperial
4 tbsp	Prepared mustard	3½ tbsp
1 tbsp	Vinegar	1 tbsp
2 tsp	Ketchup	2 tsp
2 tsp	Prepared horseradish	2 tsp
1	Small onion, peeled and finely chopped	1
½ cup	Heavy [double] cream, whipped	125 ml/4 fl oz

1. Combine the mustard, vinegar, ketchup, horseradish, and onion.
2. Whip the cream lightly, and mix with the other ingredients.

Cream Cheese and Orange Spread

	00.05	About ½ cup	
	00.00	[125 ml/4 fl oz]	Pacific Southwest

American	Ingredients	Metric/Imperial
3 oz	Cream cheese	75 g/3 oz
2 tbsp	Finely chopped crystallized or preserved ginger	1½ tbsp
2 tsp	Grated orange rind	2 tsp
3 tbsp	Orange juice	2 tbsp

1. Beat the cream cheese until soft and smooth.
2. Add the ginger and orange rind, and mix in the orange juice.

Blue Cheese Spread

	00:10	About 1 cup	
	00:10	[250 ml/8 fl oz]	Midwest

American	Ingredients	Metric/Imperial
¼ lb	Blue cheese	100 g/4 oz
2 pkg (3 oz)	Cream cheese	175 g/6 oz)
2 tbsp	Mayonnaise	1½ tbsp
2 tbsp	Crisply cooked diced bacon	1½ tbsp

1. Combine the cheeses, and blend until creamy and smooth.
2. Add the mayonnaise and bacon.

Cheese and Pimento Spread

	00.05	About 1¼ cups	
	00.00	[300 ml/10 fl oz]	Pacific Southwest

American	Ingredients	Metric/Imperial
1 cup	Grated Cheddar cheese	100 g/4 oz
1 jar (4 oz)	Pimento, drained and chopped	1 jar (100 g/4 oz)
3–4 tbsp	Mayonnaise	2–3½ tbsp
	Pinch of paprika	

1. Blend the ingredients together to form a spreadable paste.

Garlic Butter Chips and Chili Dip

Cheese and Chive Dip

	01:05	About 2 cups	
	00:00	[450 ml/¾ pint]	Midwest 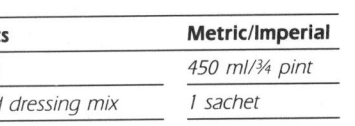

American	Ingredients	Metric/Imperial
2 cups	Sour cream	450 ml/¾ pint
1 envelope	Garlic salad dressing mix	1 sachet
1 tbsp	Vinegar	1 tbsp
½ cup	Crumbled blue cheese	100 g/4 oz
4 tbsp	Finely chopped chives	3½ tbsp

1. Combine all the ingredients and let chill for at least 1 hour before using. The flavors will then be well blended.

Onion Dip

	01:10	3 cups	
	00:00	[750 ml/1¼ pints]	United States

American	Ingredients	Metric/Imperial
1 cup	Sour cream or yogurt	250 ml/8 fl oz
2 cups	Cottage cheese	450 g/1 lb
½ cup	Mayonnaise	125 ml/4 fl oz
1	Package onion soup mix	1
2 tbsp	Chopped parsley	1½ tbsp

1. Combine the sour cream or yogurt with the cottage cheese and beat until smooth.
2. Stir in the mayonnaise. When well mixed, add the onion soup mix and parsley. Blend well, and chill before serving.

Curried Cheese Dip

	00:05	2½ cups	
	00:00	[600 ml/1 pint]	South

American	Ingredients	Metric/Imperial
2 cups	Cottage cheese	450 g/1 lb
¼ cup	Evaporated milk	4 tbsp
1 tbsp	Worcestershire sauce	1 tbsp
	A few drops of hot pepper sauce	
½ tsp	Salt	½ tsp
1 tbsp	Curry powder	1 tbsp
1 tbsp	Minced onion	1 tbsp

1. Beat the cheese with the evaporated milk until smooth and creamy.
2. Add the other ingredients, and taste for seasoning.

Apple-Nut Horseradish Dip

	00:10	1 cup	
	00:00	[250 ml/8 fl oz]	New England

American	Ingredients	Metric/Imperial
2	Apples, peeled and cored	2
1 tbsp	Lemon juice	1 tbsp
¼ cup	Yogurt	125 ml/4 fl oz
1 tbsp	Prepared horseradish	1 tbsp
2 tbsp	Walnuts, minced or ground	1½ tbsp

1. Grate the apples; immediately combine with lemon juice to prevent discoloration. Blend in the remaining ingredients.
2. Serve the dip at once with chips [crisps], crackers, or vegetable dippers.

Creamy Curry Dip

	00:15		
	00:05	Serves 8	United States

American	Ingredients	Metric/Imperial
1 tbsp	Margarine	15 g/½ oz
1	Onion, finely chopped	1
1 tsp	Curry powder	1 tsp
½ cup	Cheddar cheese, grated	50 /2 oz
½ cup	Cottage cheese, sieved	100 g/4 oz
2 tbsp	Lemon juice	2 tbsp
4 tbsp	Milk	3½ tbsp

1. Heat the margarine in a frying pan. Add the onion and fry until soft (about 5 minutes). Stir in the curry powder, then put aside to cool.
2. Stir the grated cheese into the cottage cheese with a tablespoon, then beat in the lemon juice, milk, and cold onion mixture until all are thoroughly combined.

Blue Cheese Dip

	00:05	About 1 cup	
	00:00	[250 ml/8 fl oz]	Midwest

American	Ingredients	Metric/Imperial
3 tbsp	Blue cheese	2 tbsp
2 tbsp	Chili sauce	1½ tbsp
1 tbsp	Dry vermouth	1 tbsp
½ cup	Sour cream	125 ml/4 fl oz

1. Soften the cheese. Add the other ingredients and beat until smooth and creamy.

Appetizer Franks

	00:10		
	00:25	Serves 10	Midwest

American	Ingredients	Metric/Imperial
1 cup	Tomato ketchup	250 ml/8 fl oz
¼ cup	Steak sauce	60 ml/2 fl oz
¼ cup	Brown [demerara] sugar, packed	50 g/2 oz
2 tbsp	Vinegar	1½ tbsp
1 lb	Hot dogs, cut in 1-inch pieces	450 g/1 lb

1. In a medium saucepan, combine all the ingredients except the hot dogs; simmer 10 minutes. Add hot dogs; simmer 15 minutes longer.
2. To serve, keep warm in a chafing dish or fondue pot. Makes about 50.

Creamy Curry Dip

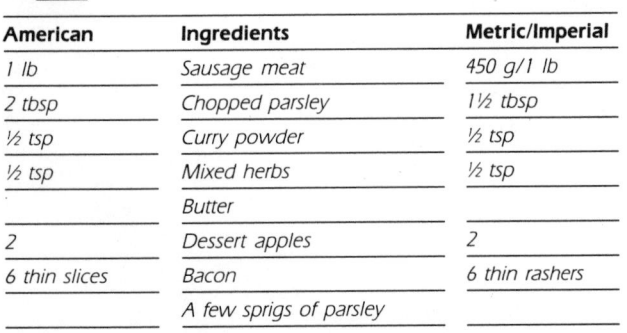

Sausage and Apple Snack

Pigs in Blankets

	00:30	Serves 6	United States
	00:20		

American	Ingredients	Metric/Imperial
6	Frankfurters	6
	Prepared mustard	
6	Thin fingers cheese	6
	Flaky pastry (see Index)	
	Egg or milk to glaze	

1. Preheat oven to 450°F/230°C/Gas Mark 8.
2. Split the frankfurters, spread very lightly with mustard, and insert a finger of cheese in each.
3. Roll the pastry thinly and cut into 6-inch squares. Place 1 frankfurter diagonally on each square, and bring together the other two diagonal corners of the pastry, so that the ends of the frankfurters are exposed.
4. Put onto a baking sheet, glaze with egg or milk, and bake for 20 minutes.
5. Serve hot with broiled [grilled] tomatoes or cold with salad.

Chicken Liver Paté

	08:30	Serves 8-10	United States
	00:10		

American	Ingredients	Metric/Imperial
1 lb	Chicken livers (fresh or frozen)	450 g/1 lb
1 cup	Butter	225 g/8 oz
2	Onions	2
1	Large clove garlic (optional)	1
1	Small glass sherry or brandy	1
1 tbsp	Fresh mixed herbs: parsley, lemon thyme, basil, marjoram, and summer savory (or 2 tsp dried herbs)	1 tbsp
	Pinch of dried mace (optional)	
	Garnish	
1 can (14 fl oz)	Consomme, chilled	1 tin (400 ml/14 fl oz)
1 cup	Button mushrooms	125 g/4 oz
1	Bunch watercress	1

1. Fry the finely chopped onions and crushed garlic gently in ⅓ cup [75 g/3 oz] of butter for a few minutes. Do not allow it to brown. Remove garlic. Add the chicken livers and cook for 3–4 minutes. Then add the mixed herbs, mace, and seasoning. Cook for 1 minute. Remove from the stove and let cool.
2. Mash the livers to a soft pulp in a electric blender, stirring in ⅓ cup [75 g/3 oz] of melted butter. Add the sherry or brandy. Put the pâté into a serving dish or a lightly oiled mold so that it can be turned out after chilling. It can be made several days before a party if kept in the refrigerator, and should be a delicate pink inside when cut.
3. Make the garnish: Chop the chilled consomme and place it around the pâté. Cook the mushrooms gently for a few minutes in the remaining melted butter until completely absorbed. Drain on paper towel [kitchen paper]. Let cool. Garnish the top of the pâté with mushrooms and surround with watercress.

Sausage and Apple Snack

	00:25	Serves 6	Mid Atlantic
	00:20		

American	Ingredients	Metric/Imperial
1 lb	Sausage meat	450 g/1 lb
2 tbsp	Chopped parsley	1½ tbsp
½ tsp	Curry powder	½ tsp
½ tsp	Mixed herbs	½ tsp
	Butter	
2	Dessert apples	2
6 thin slices	Bacon	6 thin rashers
	A few sprigs of parsley	
	Toast	

1. Combine the sausage meat, parsley, curry powder, herbs, and seasoning. Shape into 6 patties.
2. Sauté for about 5 minutes on each side. Remove from the pan and keep hot.
3. Core but do not peel the apples, cut each into three slices and sauté for about 2 minutes on each side.
4. Roll up the bacon, put onto a skewer, and fry or broil [grill].
5. Put the sausage patties on a serving dish with an apple ring on the bottom. Arrange the bacon rolls in the center and garnish with parsley. Serve with hot toast.

Duck Paté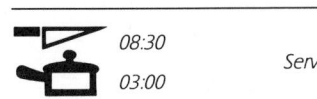

08:30
03:00

Serves 6-8

South

American	Ingredients	Metric/Imperial
4 cups	Cooked duck	900 g/2 lb
1 cup	Chopped duck and lamb liver	225 g/8 oz
1 cup	Chopped lean raw pork or veal	100 g/4 oz
1 cup	Chopped fat bacon, blanched	175 g/6 oz
1	Onion	1
½	Clove garlic	½
4 tbsp	Bread crumbs soaked in cream	3 tbsp
1	Small egg	1
1 tbsp	Chopped parsley and thyme	1 tbsp
2 tsp	Grated orange rind	2 tsp
¼–½ cup	Brandy	60–125 ml/ 2–4 fl oz
	Pinch of mace	
10–12 slices	Fat bacon	10-12 rashers
4	Slices orange	4
½ can (7 fl oz)	Consomme	½ tin (200 ml/7 fl oz)
3 tsp	Gelatin [gelatine]	3 tsp
1–2 tbsp	Brandy (or sherry)	1-2 tbsp

1. Preheat oven to 325°F/160°C/Gas Mark 3.

2. Grind the livers, pork or veal, fat bacon, finely chopped onions, and crushed garlic together. Mix in the bread crumbs, beaten egg, chopped herbs, orange rind, and brandy (or sherry). Add seasoning and mace.

3. With a knife, stretch the bacon slices by scraping them; line a loaf or pâté pan completely with them. Cut cooked duck into strips and sprinkle half into the loaf pan; season, then cover with half the meat mixture. Put in the rest of the duck, then the remaining mixture. Fold over any overlapping pieces of bacon. Cover the whole pan carefully with foil. Put in a baking pan of water [bain-marie] and bake in the oven for 2–3 hours.

4. Half an hour before the pâté is done, remove the foil and place 4 slices of orange down the center; recover and continue cooking. When done, remove from the oven and let cool. Put a double layer of greaseproof paper on top, then weights to press the pâté and make it firm.

5. Dissolve 3 teaspoons of gelatin in half a can of consomme; let cool and add 1–2 tablespoons of brandy (or sherry). When nearly set, turn the pâté out onto a wire rack and spoon jelly consomme over it. Let set. Serve on a salad-lined plate with orange segments for flavor and color.

Duck Paté

Tuna Fish Paté

08:30
00:00

Serves 8

Pacific Southwest

American	Ingredients	Metric/Imperial
2 cans (about 7 oz)	Tuna fish	2 tins (200 g/7 oz)
1 cup	Butter	225 g/8 oz
4 tbsp	Olive oil	3½ tbsp
2 tbsp	Lemon juice	1½ tbsp
1 tsp	Dijon mustard	1 tsp
2 tbsp	Grated onion	1½ tbsp
2 tbsp	Brandy	1½ tbsp

1. Drain the fish, soften the butter, and then pound all the ingredients together, seasoning to taste with salt and freshly ground black pepper.

2. Pack into dishes and chill well before serving.

Grapefruit with Crab

1. Preheat the broiler [grill].
2. Remove the crusts from the bread and toast on one side only. Lightly butter the untoasted side.
3. Flake the crabmeat, combine with the mayonnaise and onion, and spread on the buttered side of the toast. Sprinkle generously with cheese.
4. Put under a hot broiler [grill] for 1–2 minutes until the cheese melts and is lightly browned. Serve at once.

Party Crabmeat

 00:20 / 00:10 — Serves 50 — Mid Atlantic

American	Ingredients	Metric/Imperial
1 cup	Butter	225 g/8 oz
1½ cups	Flour	175 g/6 oz
2 qts	Milk	2 l/3½ pint
3 lb	Crabmeat, picked over	1.25 kg/3 lb
1 lb	Mushrooms, sliced and sautéed	450 g/1 lb
1 cup	Dry sherry	250 ml/8 fl oz
	Hearty dash lemon juice	
	Hearty dash Worcestershire sauce	
	Dash nutmeg	
	Parsley	

1. In a large pan, melt the butter, stir in the flour, and then add the milk. Stir constantly until the white sauce is thick.
2. Add all the remaining ingredients and heat until the mixture is hot. (Be careful the mixture does not scorch). Serve from the chafing dish with toast rounds or favorite crackers.

Grapefruit with Crab

 00:15 / 00:00 — Serves 4 — Pacific Southwest

American	Ingredients	Metric/Imperial
2	Grapefruit	2
1 cup	Crabmeat	225 g/8 oz
	A little mayonnaise	
	Parsley or lemon slices for garnish	

1. Mix the flesh from the grapefruit with the crabmeat.
2. Bind with a little mayonnaise, season to taste, and serve in the grapefruit shells, garnished with parsley or lemon slices.

Clam Puffs

00:20 / 00:04 — Serves 4-6 — South

American	Ingredients	Metric/Imperial
½ lb	Minced clams, drained and chopped	225 g/8 oz
¼ cup	Swiss cheese, freshly grated	25 g/1 oz
1	Clove garlic, mashed or put through garlic press	1
1 tbsp	Mayonnaise	1 tbsp
	Salt	
	White pepper	
	Cayenne pepper	

1. Mix all the ingredients, adding enough mayonnaise to bind. Add salt and white pepper to taste and a light dash of cayenne. All this may be mixed together ahead of time.
2. Preheat the broiler [grill]. Spread the mixture, forming a crown, on toasted rounds of white bread. Broil [grill] for 3-4 minutes, watching carefully so they don't burn. Remove when golden and serve hot. Makes 16 to 18.

Crabmeat Nippies

 00:10 / 00:04 — Serves 4 — Mid Atlantic

American	Ingredients	Metric/Imperial
4	Slices bread	4
	Butter	
1 can (6 oz)	Crabmeat	1 tin (175 g/6 oz)
2 tsp	Mayonnaise	2 tsp
1 tsp	Grated onion	1 tsp
½ cup	Grated Cheddar or American cheese	50 g/2 oz

Clam Savory

Clam Savory

00:10
00:05

Serves 4-5

New England

American	Ingredients	Metric/Imperial
3 tbsp	Butter	40 g/1½ oz
1	Small onion, peeled and finely chopped	1
½	Green pepper, finely chopped	½
1 can (7½ oz)	Clams, drained and chopped	1 tin (200 g/7½ oz)
1 cup	Grated cheese	100 g/4 oz
1 tbsp	Tomato purée	1 tbsp
1 tbsp	Worcestershire sauce	1 tbsp
1 tbsp	Sherry	1 tbsp
⅛ tsp	Cayenne pepper	⅛ tsp
	Dill pickle (optional)	
4-5	Slices hot buttered toast	4-5

1. Heat the butter in a sauté pan, add onion and green pepper, and sauté for 3 minutes.
2. Add the clams, cheese, tomato purée, Worcestershire sauce, sherry, and cayenne pepper. Cook for a few minutes until the cheese has melted, stirring all the time.
3. Put a thin slice of dill pickle on each slice of toast and serve the clam mixture on top.

Fish and Mushroom Bundles

Fish and Mushroom Bundles

| | 00:45 | | |
| | 01:00 | Serves 4 | United States |

American	Ingredients	Metric/Imperial
¼ lb	White fish	100 g/4 oz
	Salt and pepper to taste	
½ cup	Milk	125 ml/4 fl oz
3 tbsp	Margarine	40 g/1½ oz
2 tbsp	Flour	1½ tbsp
2 tbsp	Mushrooms, chopped	1½ tbsp
1 tbsp	Parsley, chopped	1 tbsp
1 tsp	Lemon juice	1 tsp
1 (8-oz)	Package frozen puff pastry, thawed	1 (225 g/8 oz)
	Extra milk for glazing	

1. Put the fish into a saucepan, season well with salt and pepper, then add the milk. Bring to a boil, then simmer for 15 to 20 minutes or until the fish flakes easily. Drain and reserve the cooking liquid.
2. Heat 2 tablespoons [25 g/1 oz] of margarine in a saucepan, stir in flour and cook, stirring, for 2 minutes. Add the reserved cooking liquid and bring to a boil, stirring all the time. Cook for 2 minutes.
3. Melt the remaining margarine in a frying pan and fry the mushrooms until cooked. Flake the cooked fish, removing all skin and bones. Add the fish to the sauce with mushrooms, parsley, and lemon juice. Allow the mixture to become cold.
4. Preheat oven to 450°F/230°C/Gas Mark 8.
5. Roll out the pastry on a lightly floured surface. Cut into 8, 5-inch circles. Place each pastry circle in a muffin tin (the pastry should stand well above the edges of the tin). Put a spoonful of fish mixture into each circle. Dampen the inside edges of the pastry, bring them to the center, and press them firmly together to seal. Make a small slit in the top of each bundle. Brush with milk and bake for 20 to 25 minutes or until golden. Serve the hot bundles, 2 per person, with salad.

Oysters Baltimore

| | 00:10 | | |
| | 00:20 | Serves 4-6 | Mid Atlantic |

American	Ingredients	Metric/Imperial
4 slices	Bacon	4 rashers
18	Oysters	18
3 tbsp	Chili sauce	2 tbsp
1 tbsp	Worcestershire sauce	1 tbsp
6 tbsp	Heavy [double] cream	5 tbsp
½ tsp	Tarragon	½ tsp
2 tbsp	Lemon juice	2 tbsp
1 tsp	Salt	1 tsp
¼ tsp	Pepper	¼ tsp

1. In a medium-sized frying pan, fry the bacon until crisp. Set the bacon aside to drain, then crumble into bits for garnish. Pour off all but 1 tablespoon of fat from the pan. Add the oysters with their liquid. Cook uncovered over medium heat until most of the pan juices are absorbed.
2. Mix the remaining ingredients; add to the oysters. Simmer no more than 5 minutes to blend all flavors. Add extra seasonings if desired. These oysters are delicious served over hot buttered toast. Garnish with crumbled bacon.

Shrimp Mold

| | 08:30 | | |
| | 00:00 | Serves 12-16 | South |

American	Ingredients	Metric/Imperial
¼ cup	Water	60 ml/2 fl oz
1 envelope	Gelatin [gelatine]	1 sachet
1 can (10¾ oz)	Tomato soup	1 tin (300 g/10¾ oz)
8 oz	Cream cheese	225 g/8 oz
½ cup	Onion, chopped	100 g/4 oz
1 cup	Celery, chopped	225 g/8 oz
1 cup	Mayonnaise	250 ml/8 fl oz
1 lb	Cooked shrimp [prawns], chopped	450 g/1 lb

1. Soften the gelatin in water. Warm the soup and add gelatin and cream cheese. Mix well. Add the other ingredients.
2. Pour into an oiled 6-cup [1.5 l/2½ pint] mold. Refrigerate until firm. Unmold to serve. Serve with light and dark cocktail rye bread.

Marinated Clams

Marinated Clams

03:00
00:00
Serves 8-10   Pacific Northwest

American	Ingredients	Metric/Imperial
2 lb	Shelled clams	900 g/2 lb
2	Onions, minced	2
2	Cloves garlic, crushed	2
⅓ cup	Oil, preferably olive oil	5 tbsp
5 tbsp	Parsley, chopped	4 tbsp
2 tbsp	Lemon juice	1½ tbsp
½ tsp	Salt	½ tsp
1 tsp	Pepper	1 tsp

	Garnish	
2-3	Hard-boiled eggs	2-3
1	Small head of lettuce	1
2-3	Tomatoes	2-3
	Sprigs of dill	

1. Drain the clams well and place them in a bowl. Mix the onion, garlic, oil, parsley, lemon juice, salt, and pepper and pour over the clams. Refrigerate for 2-3 hours.

2. Rinse the lettuce. Tear the larger leaves in half and place on a large plate. Place the marinated clams with most of the marinade on the lettuce.

3. Place wedges of egg and tomatoes around the clams. Garnish with sprigs of dill.

Soups

Game Stock

 00:20 / 02:00 — About 2 quarts [2 1/3½ pints] — United States

American	Ingredients	Metric/Imperial
1	Game carcass with any meat attached	1
2	Onions, sliced	2
2	Carrots, sliced	2
2–3	Stalks celery	2–3
6	Sprigs parsley	6
1	Sprig thyme (or ¼ tsp dried thyme)	1
1	Bay leaf	1
6–8	Peppercorns	6–8

1. Put the carcass of the game bird into a pan with the sliced vegetables, herbs and seasoning. Cover with water, and bring slowly to a boil. Then skim off any scum that rises to the surface, and simmer until well flavored and reduced in quantity.
2. Strain and use, or freeze for later use.

White Bone Stock

 00:20 / 02:30 — About 2 quarts [2 1/3½ pints] — United States

American	Ingredients	Metric/Imperial
2 lb	Raw veal knuckle bones	900 g/2 lb
1	Chicken carcass and giblets	1
2	Onions, peeled and sliced	2
2	Carrots, peeled and sliced	2
3	Stalks celery	3
1	Bay leaf	1
6	Sprigs parsley	6
1	Small sprig thyme (or ¼ tsp dried thyme)	1
2 tsp	Salt	2 tsp
6	Peppercorns	6
1	Small piece mace	1
3 qts	Water	3 1/5¼ pints
	Rind of ½ lemon	

1. Have the butcher chop the raw veal bones and chicken carcass into small pieces. Put these into a pan of water with vegetables, herbs and seasoning. Bring to a boil and skim frequently for about half an hour. Add 1 cup [250 ml/8 fl oz] cold water and skim again. Then add lemon rind and simmer for 2 hours.
2. Strain through a muslin cloth and sieve. Then let cool. Remove the fat from the top. Store the stock in the freezer.

Fish Stock

 00:20 / 00:40 — About 1 quart [1 1/1¾ pints] — United States

American	Ingredients	Metric/Imperial
½–1 lb	White fish back-bones and skins	225–450 g/ 8 oz–1 lb
1	Onion, sliced	1
2	Small carrots, sliced	2
2	Stalks celery	2
6	Sprigs parsley	6
1	Bay leaf	1
1	Sprig thyme	1
6–7 cups	Water	1.25–1.75 l/ 2¼–2½ pints
1½ cups	White wine or cider (optional)	350 ml/12 fl oz
	Salt and pepper	

1. Use the backbones from white fish—sole, turbot, or halibut preferably—and the skins, if available. Put these in a pan with the sliced onion, carrot, celery, herbs, and water. Add the white wine or cider, if available. Then add salt and pepper. Bring very slowly to a boil and simmer for 30–40 minutes, until the liquid has reduced and is well flavored.
2. Strain and cool. Use at once or freeze for later use.

Mixed Household Stock

 00:15 / 06:00 — About 2 quarts [2 1/3½ pints] — United States

American	Ingredients	Metric/Imperial
2 lb	Mixed raw or cooked beef, veal and/or chicken bones and possibly a ham bone	900 g/2 lb
1½ lb	Onions, carrots, and celery, chopped	575 g/1¼ lb
	A little oil (optional)	
1	Bay leaf	1
6	Sprigs parsley	6
1	Sprig thyme	1
	A few mushroom stalks or peelings	
6–8	Peppercorns	6–8

1. Brown the raw bones and the vegetables in a little hot oil. Then add the cooked bones, herbs, and mushroom peelings. Add water to cover and bring to a boil. Then simmer for 4–6 hours until reduced and well flavored.
2. Strain and cool, allowing the fat to set in a solid crust on top. Use this stock quickly or keep in a freezer. If keeping in a refrigerator for a day or two, reboil every day to keep it from becoming sour.

Vegetable Stock

00:15
02:00

About 1 quart
[1 1/1¾ pints]

United States

American	Ingredients	Metric/Imperial
3	Medium onions, unpeeled	3
3	Medium carrots, peeled	3
2	Leeks, white part only	2
4–5	Stalks celery	4–5
1	Small turnip, peeled	1
1 tbsp	Butter	15 g/½ oz
2–3 quarts	Water	2–3 l/ 3½–5¼ pints
6	Peppercorns	6
1	Bay leaf	1
4–6	Sprigs parsley	4–6
1	Sprig thyme (or ¼ teaspoon dried thyme)	1

1. Cut up the vegetables and brown these until golden in a little butter. Add the water, herbs, and seasoning. Bring to a boil, and simmer for 1½–2 hours, by which time the stock should be well flavored.
2. Strain and cool. Use for soups or sauces calling for vegetable stock.

Ordinary Chicken Stock

Chicken Stock for Consomme

00:25
02:00

About 2 quarts
[2 1/3½ pints]

United States

American	Ingredients	Metric/Imperial
1	Boiling chicken with giblets	1
2	Onions, peeled and sliced	2
4	Stalks celery	4
2–3	Carrots	2–3
1	Thin sliver lemon rind	1
1	Bay leaf	1
6–8	Parsley sprigs	6–8
1	Sprig tarragon (or ¼ tsp dried tarragon)	1
1	Small sprig thyme (or ¼ tsp dried thyme)	1
6	Peppercorns	6
1 tsp	Salt (or more if needed)	1 tsp

1. Put a cleaned and cut-up boiling chicken into a large pot with the sliced vegetables. Add the herbs and seasoning. Cover with water, and bring slowly to a boil. Then cover the pan and simmer for 2 hours.
2. Strain and let cool. When cold, skim the fat from the top and use the stock for chicken consomme or other soups requiring strong chicken stock. The stock can also be stored in the freezer, or covered in the refrigerator for 2–3 days.

Ordinary Chicken Stock

00:25
04:00

About 2 quarts
[2 1/3½ pints]

United States

American	Ingredients	Metric/Imperial
1	Cooked chicken carcass	1
	Giblets, if available	
1	Onion, sliced	1
2	Carrots, sliced	2
2	Stalks celery	2
1	Bay leaf	1
1	Sprig thyme (or ¼ tsp dried thyme)	1
6	Sprigs parsley	6
6	Peppercorns	6
	Salt	
1	Chicken bouillon [stock] cube (if necessary)	1

1. Put the broken-up chicken carcass and bones into a pan with any available giblets and any leftover chicken meat or skin. Add the vegetables and herbs. Cover with water, and add pepper and salt. Bring to a boil slowly, and simmer for 3–4 hours, or until well flavored. If not sufficiently well flavored, add a chicken cube and cook for a few more minutes.
2. Strain and let cool. If not using at once, store in the freezer.

Beef Vegetable Soup

Rich Brown Beef Stock

 00:20
03:00

About 2½ quarts [2½ 1/4 pints]

United States

American	Ingredients	Metric/Imperial
2–3 lb	Veal bones	900 g–1.25 kg/ 2–3 lb
2–3 lb	Meaty beef bones (including a bone with marrow)	900 g–1.25 kg/ 2–3 lb
2 lb	Lean beef—in one piece for boiled beef or cut into pieces	900 g/2 lb
3–4	Onions, unpeeled	3–4
4	Carrots	4
4	Stalks celery	4
	Salt	
10	Peppercorns	10
	A few mushroom stalks or peelings	
2	Bay leaves	2
8–10	Sprigs parsley	8–10
1	Sprig thyme (or ¼ tsp dried thyme)	1
5 quarts	Water	5 1/8 pints

1. Get the butcher to break the bones. Put them into a pan with the beef and a little beef marrow or good drippings. Heat the pan, and as the bones and meat brown, stir and keep from burning. Remove and keep warm while browning the vegetables. Return the bones and meat to the pan, and cover with water. Add herbs, salt, pepper, and mushroom peelings or stems, if available.
2. Bring to a boil. Skim frequently during the first hour. Then cover the pan and simmer for 2–3 hours, by which time the stock should be well flavored and a good brown color. (If the meat is a large piece and is to be used as boiled beef, this can be removed after 2 hours, and the stock simmered without it for remaining cooking time.)
3. Strain the stock and let cool. Then skim off the fat, which will form a crust on top. If the stock is not required for a day or two, do not remove the fat until just before using, as it acts as a protective seal. Keep in the refrigerator or freezer.

Vegetable Soup

 00:20
00:55

Serves 4

New England

American	Ingredients	Metric/Imperial
2 tbsp	Oil	1½ tbsp
2 slices	Bacon	2 rashers
3–4	Carrots, peeled and chopped	3–4
2	Onions, peeled and chopped	2
3	Tomatoes, peeled and chopped	3
2	Stalks celery, chopped	2
½	Small head cabbage, shredded	½ small head
5 cups	Stock or water	1.2 1/2 pts
	Bouquet garni	
½ cup	Elbow macaroni [macaroni]	50 g/2 oz
	Chopped parsley	
	Grated cheese	

1. Heat the oil in a large saucepan. Add the chopped bacon and vegetables, and sauté all together for about 5 minutes.
2. Add the stock, seasoning, and bouquet garni. Cover and simmer for about 30 minutes.
3. Add the macaroni and cook for 20 minutes, or until the macaroni is tender.
4. Remove the bouquet garni. Adjust the seasoning, sprinkle with parsley, and serve grated cheese separately.

Beef Vegetable Soup

 10:30
02:15

Serves 8

United States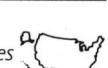

American	Ingredients	Metric/Imperial
¾ cup	Dried green peas	175 g/6 oz
12 cups	Water	3 1/5¼ pints
3 tbsp	Salt	2 tbsp
3	Onions, peeled and cut into wedges	3
10	Black peppercorns	10
2	Bay leaves	2
2¾–3 lb	Beef, for example shoulder roast	1.25 kg/2¾–3 lb
8	Potatoes	8
4	Carrots	4
½ lb	Wedge cabbage	225 g/8 oz
	Snipped parsley	

1. Soak the peas in 4 cups [1 l/1¾ pints] of the water and 1 tablespoon of the salt for 8–10 hours. Pour away the water. Place the peas in a pot with the remaining 8 cups [2 l/3½ pints] of water. Cook the peas together with the onions and spices for about 45 minutes. Skim away all the pea skins.
2. Rinse the meat under running water. Stick a meat thermometer into the beef so that the point of the thermometer comes to the middle of the thickest part of the meat. The entire stick of the thermometer should be in the meat. Place the meat in the pot. Boil over low heat for 1¼ to 1½ hours.
3. Peel the potatoes and carrots about 30 minutes before the meat is done. Cut the vegetables into chunks and cook them in the soup. Add shredded cabbage about 10 minutes before the meat is done. Season to taste.
4. When the meat is done, remove the pot from the stove. Let it stand, covered, for about 20 minutes. Remove the meat from the soup, cut it into slices, and serve it on a plate with the soup. Or cut pieces of the meat into the soup. Garnish with parsley and serve.

Curried Vegetable Soup

00:25
00:35
Serves 4–5
New England

American	Ingredients	Metric/Imperial
¼ cup	*Margarine or other cooking fat*	*50 g/2 oz*
1	*Onion, peeled and sliced*	*1*
1	*Carrot, peeled and sliced*	*1*
1	*Stalk celery, diced*	*1*
1	*Green pepper, seeded and diced*	*1*
1	*Apple, peeled, cored and sliced*	*1*
⅓ cup	*Flour*	*40 g/1¼ oz*
2 tsp	*Curry powder*	*2 tsp*
⅛ tsp	*Powdered mace*	*⅛ tsp*
1	*Chicken bouillon [stock] cube*	*1*
2 cups	*Water*	*450 ml/¾ pint*
2	*Cloves*	*2*
1 cup	*Canned or cooked tomatoes*	*225 g/8 oz*
1 tbsp	*Chopped parsley*	*1 tbsp*

1. Heat the fat in a large saucepan; add the onion and sauté it for 3 minutes. Add the carrot, celery, green pepper, and apple. Stir all together over low heat for a few minutes.
2. Mix the flour, curry powder, mace, and crumbled bouillon cube together; stir in the water and pour the mixture into the pan. Add the cloves, tomatoes, and a little salt and pepper. Cover and simmer for about 30 minutes.
3. Add the chopped chicken, adjust the seasoning, and sprinkle with parsley before serving.

Country Vegetable Soup

Country Vegetable Soup

00:30
00:40
Serves 4–5
United States

American	Ingredients	Metric/Imperial
3 tbsp	*Bacon or other cooking fat*	*2 tbsp*
½ cup	*Diced carrot*	*50 g/2 oz*
½ cup	*Diced onion*	*50 g/2 oz*
½ cup	*Diced celery*	*50 g/2 oz*
½ cup	*Diced turnip*	*50 g/2 oz*
3 cups	*Stock or water*	*700 ml/1¼ pints*
1 cup	*Canned tomatoes*	*275 g/10 oz*
½ cup	*Diced potato*	*50 g/2 oz*
1 tbsp	*Chopped parsley*	*1 tbsp*

1. Heat the fat in a large kettle and sauté the carrot, onion, celery, and turnip for about 5 minutes.
2. Add the stock or water, tomatoes, potato, and a little seasoning. Cover and simmer for 35 minutes.
3. Add the parsley and adjust the seasoning before serving.

Vegetable Soup with Garlic

 00:30 / 00:20   Serves 6–8   Mid Atlantic

American	Ingredients	Metric/Imperial
4 tbsp	Butter	50 g/2 oz
1	Large onion (or 3 leeks, sliced)	1
3	Potatoes, sliced	3
2–3	Large ripe tomatoes, peeled and chopped (or ¾ cup canned [tinned] tomatoes)	2–3
6–7 cups	Stock	1.25–1.75 l/ 2½–3 pints
	Chopped parsley	
	A pinch of oregano	
1 cup	Sliced green beans	100 g/4 oz
2–3 tbsp	Vermicelli	1½–2 tbsp
2–3 cloves	Garlic	2–3
	Several sprigs of fresh basil (or 2 tsp dried basil)	
2	Slices tomato, grilled or fried	2
	Garnish	
	Grated cheese	

1. Melt the butter, and cook the onion or leeks and potatoes for 5–6 minutes without browning. Add the tomatoes. Pour on the stock and bring to a boil. Add the herbs, seasoning, beans, and vermicelli. Cook over a low heat until all are tender.
2. Meanwhile, prepare a garlic paste. Crush the garlic and mix with the basil and 2 slices of grilled or fried tomato. Pound all together to make a smooth paste, adding a little of the juice from the soup to moisten.
3. Add this mixture to the soup just before serving and mix well. Serve hot, with grated cheese in a separate dish.

Eastern Avocado Soup

 01:15 / 00:00   Serves 6   Pacific Southwest

American	Ingredients	Metric/Imperial
2–3	Avocados, rather over-ripe	2–3
4 cups	Tomato juice	1 l/1¾ pints
3–4 tsp	Curry powder (or paste)	3–4 tsp
2–3 tsp	Lemon juice	2–3 tsp
1 cup	Chicken stock	250 ml/8 fl oz
⅔ cup	Yogurt	150 ml/5 fl oz
	Salt and pepper	
1 cup	Heavy [double] cream	250 ml/8 fl oz
	Garnish	
1 tbsp	Chopped chives (or 1 tbsp chopped nuts)	1 tbsp
	Lemon quarters	
	Brown bread and butter or crackers	

1. Peel and remove the seeds from the avocados. Put in an electric blender, adding a can of tomato juice, 3–4 teaspoons of curry powder, according to taste, and stock. When blended, add the lemon juice, yogurt, and salt and pepper to taste. Blend again.
2. Chill in the refrigerator until just before serving, when lightly whipped cream should be stirred into the soup, leaving a streaky appearance.
3. Sprinkle with chopped chives or chopped nuts, and serve with lemon quarters and brown bread and butter or crackers.

White Vegetable Soup

 00:20 / 00:40   Serves 4–6   United States

American	Ingredients	Metric/Imperial
1	Onion (or the white part of 2 leeks, well washed)	1
2	Young carrots	2
2	Stalks celery	2
3 tbsp	Butter	40 g/1½ oz
2 tbsp	Flour	1½ tbsp
4–5 cups	Milk	900 ml– 1.2 l/ 1½–2 pints
1 tbsp	Chopped parsley	1 tbsp
	Pinch of dried thyme	
2	Bay leaves	2
¼ tsp	Mace	¼ tsp
½ cup	Peas (fresh or frozen)	50 g/2 oz
¼ cup	Green beans	50 g/2 oz
¼ cup	Corn	25 g/1 oz
	Liaison	
2	Egg yolks	2
½ cup	Cream	125 ml/4 fl oz
	Garnish	
1 tbsp	Chopped parsley	1 tbsp
	Fried bread croutons (see Index)	

1. Peel and cut the root vegetables into short strips or dice. Melt the butter and cook these vegetables until tender without browning, about 5–6 minutes. Sprinkle in flour and mix well; add the milk and blend well. Slowly bring to a boil. Then reduce heat and simmer for 10–12 minutes. Add herbs and seasoning.
2. Meanwhile, cook the peas, beans, and corn in boiling salted water until just tender, 7–10 minutes. Drain and rinse under cold water. Add to the soup. Heat together for 5 minutes. Adjust seasoning and add liaison.
3. Make liaison: Mix the egg yolks and cream well. Add a few spoonfuls of hot soup and stir well. Then strain back into the hot soup, stirring constantly. Reheat the soup but do not boil, or the egg will curdle.
4. Serve the soup hot, sprinkled with chopped parsley and with fried bread croutons.

Hot Avocado and Prawn Soup

Hot Avocado and Prawn Soup

	00:25		
	00:20	Serves 4–6	Pacific Southwest

American	Ingredients	Metric/Imperial
1	Small onion, finely chopped	1
2	Stalks celery, finely chopped	2
3–4 cups	Well-flavored chicken stock	700 ml–1 l/ 1¼–1¾ pts
1	Small bay leaf	1
	Blade or pinch of mace	
3–4	Sprigs parsley	3–4
2–3	Avocados (according to size)	2–3
½ cup	Peeled shrimp [prawns]	50 g/2 oz
	Garnish	
1 cup	Heavy [double] cream	250 ml/8 fl oz
	Chopped chives or paprika	
	Slivers of fresh avocado	

1. Put the onion and celery into the stock with the bay leaf, mace, sprigs of parsley, and a little seasoning. Simmer for about 15 minutes to flavor the stock. Strain and reserve the stock.

2. Peel and remove the seeds from the avocados, and chop the flesh roughly. Put into an electric blender and blend slowly while adding the stock. When quite smooth, return to the pan and heat very gently, adding the shrimp. Do not allow to boil, as this will spoil the flavor and texture of the soup. Adjust the seasoning.

3. Whip the cream slightly and add a spoonful of cream to each soup cup. Sprinkle the top with paprika or chopped chives, and add a few thin slivers of another avocado as a garnish.

Iced Avocado Soup

01:30
00:00
Serves 6   Pacific Southwest

American	Ingredients	Metric/Imperial
2–3	Ripe avocados	2–3
4 tsp	Lemon juice	4 tsp
1 tsp	Onion juice	1 tsp
	A dash of Tabasco	
3 cups	Chicken stock	700 ml/1¼ pints
1 (6–8 oz)	Small carton natural yogurt	1 (6–8 oz)
	Salt and pepper	
¼ tsp	Nutmeg	¼ tsp
¾ cup	Heavy [double] cream	175 ml/6 fl oz
1–2 tsp	Chopped fresh dill (or a few fresh tarragon leaves)	1–2 tsp
	Garnish	
	Cheese straws (see Index)	
	Rolls of brown bread and butter, sprinkled with chopped walnuts	

1. Peel the avocados. Reserve a quarter of one avocado to use as garnish; sprinkle it with lemon juice and cover it with a plastic wrap [clingfilm] to prevent browning. Mash the remaining avocado with 2–3 teaspoons lemon juice. Make onion juice by crushing small pieces of onion in a garlic press or squeezing through a fine sieve. Add this juice and a dash of tabasco to the avocado.
2. Put all these ingredients into an electric blender and add the chicken stock by degrees, blending slowly. When smooth, add the natural yogurt. Blend again, and when thoroughly mixed add salt, pepper, and nutmeg to taste.
3. Add half the cream to the soup, stirring it in only partially to give a marbled appearance to the soup. Pour into soup bowls and chill.
4. Just before serving, beat the remaining cream and cut the reserved piece of avocado into thin slivers. Slide these into soup bowls. Put a spoonful of whipped cream into each bowl and sprinkle the top with chopped fresh dill or a few tarragon leaves.
5. Serve with hot cheese straws or rolls, or brown bread and butter sprinkled with chopped walnuts.

Jerusalem Artichoke Soup

00:25
00:25
Serves 4–6   United States

American	Ingredients	Metric/Imperial
2 cups	Water	500 ml/¾ pint
1 tsp	Lemon juice	1 tsp
1	Bay leaf	1
3–4	Sprigs parsley	3–4
1 tsp	Salt	1 tsp
	Pepper and mace to taste	
3 cups	Jerusalem artichokes, peeled and sliced	450 g/1 lb
3 tbsp	Butter	40 g/1½ oz
1	Onion, finely sliced	1
1	Stalk celery, finely sliced	1
2 tbsp	Flour	1½ tbsp
2 cups	Milk	450 ml/¾ pint
	Liaison	
2	Egg yolks	2
½ cup	Cream	125 ml/4 fl oz
	Garnish	
1 tbsp	Chopped parsley	1 tbsp
	Fried bread croutons (see Index)	

1. Put the water, lemon juice, bay leaf, parsley sprigs, and seasoning into a pan and add the finely sliced artichokes. Bring to a boil, and simmer until tender, about 10–15 minutes.
2. Melt the butter and cook the finely sliced onion and celery slowly, covered, until soft. Do not allow to brown. Sprinkle in the flour, and blend well.
3. When the artichokes are tender, strain the liquid onto the onion mixture and blend well. Remove the bay leaf and parsley sprigs, and add these to the soup. Mix in the artichokes and bring to a boil, stirring constantly. Put the soup through a food grinder or fine sieve, or blend thoroughly in an electric blender until creamy.
4. Return the soup to the pan and reheat. At the same time, in another pan, heat the milk to just below boiling point. Pour into the artichoke soup and whisk together (adding hot rather than cold milk makes the soup lighter and more delicate).
5. Make the liaison by mixing the egg yolks and cream thoroughly. Add a few spoonfuls of hot soup; mix well. Then strain the liaison into the soup, stirring constantly.
6. Reheat the soup, being careful not to boil it or the egg will curdle. Sprinkle with chopped parsley and serve with fried bread croutons.

Baked Bean and Tomato Soup

00:10
00:10
Serves 4–6   New England

American	Ingredients	Metric/Imperial
1 can (8-oz)	Baked beans in tomato sauce	1 (225 g/8 oz)
1 can (10¾ oz)	Condensed tomato soup with 1 can of water	1 tin (300g/10¾ oz)
1 can (12 fl oz)	Tomato juice	1 tin (350 ml/12 fl oz)
1 tbsp	Tomato purée	1 tbsp
½ tsp	Sugar	½ tsp
1 tbsp	Chopped parsley	1 tbsp
	Garnish	
2–3 slices	Bacon	2–3 rashers

1. Put half a can of baked beans in a pan with tomato soup, tomato juice, water, tomato purée, and seasonings. Heat together gently, adding the chopped parsley. When well mixed and hot, put the soup into an electric blender and blend until smooth.
2. Return to the pan and heat, adding the remaining beans. Serve hot with the bacon, which has been fried until crisp and sprinkled on top.

Cabbage Soup

00:25
00:45
Serves 4–6
Mid Atlantic

American	Ingredients	Metric/Imperial
2 cups	Shredded green cabbage	275 g/10 oz
1	Large onion, chopped	1
2	Small leeks, white part only, sliced	2
2	Carrots, sliced	2
1	Potato, sliced	1
2 slices	Fat bacon	2 rashers
1 tbsp	Flour	1 tbsp
4 cups	Brown stock (or water and cubes—ham stock can be used, if not too salt)	1 1/1¾ pints
2 tbsp	Chopped parsley	1½ tbsp
1	Bay leaf	1
	A pinch of nutmeg	
2 tsp	Chopped dill or 1 tsp dill seeds	2 tsp

	Garnish	
3–4	Frankfurters	3–4
	Fat for frying	
	Fried bread and bacon croutons (see Index)	

1. Slice and wash the green cabbage. Put it into a pan of boiling salted water, and cook for 5 minutes. Then drain and rinse under cold water.

2. Meanwhile, chop the bacon and heat over gentle heat until the fat runs. Then add the onion, leeks, carrots, and potato; stir over heat for a few minutes. Sprinkle in flour and blend well before adding the stock. Add parsley, bay leaf, salt, and pepper. Bring to a boil. Then reduce the heat, and simmer for 10 minutes before adding the cabbage. Cook for 20 minutes more, or until the vegetables are tender but not mushy.

3. Adjust the seasoning, and add nutmeg and chopped dill, or a few dill seeds. Remove the bay leaf.

4. For garnish, either fry the frankfurters and cut them in slices, putting a few slices into each serving, or prepare fried bread and bacon croutons to serve separately.

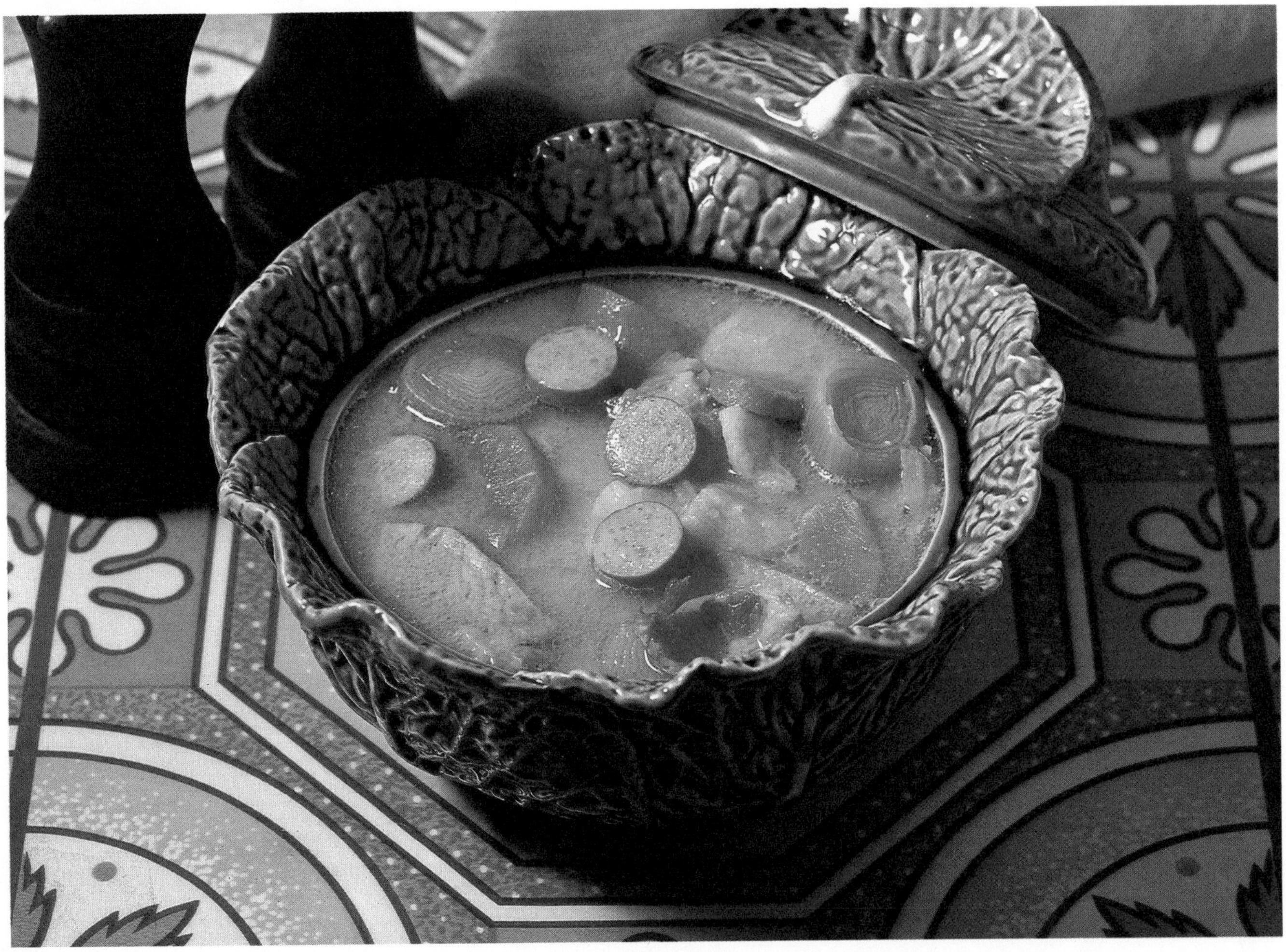

Cabbage Soup

Cream of Asparagus Soup

 00:15 / 00:30   Serves 4   United States

American	Ingredients	Metric/Imperial
1 lb	Asparagus, green or white (or equivalent amount of canned asparagus)	450 g/1 lb
1	Onion, finely chopped	1
3–4	Sprigs parsley	3–4
3–4 cups	Chicken stock (or water and chicken stock cubes)	700 ml–1 l/ 1¼–1¾ pints
3 tbsp	Butter	40 g/1½ oz
2 tbsp	Flour	1½ tbsp
¼ tsp	Mace	¼ tsp
	A little green coloring, if necessary	
	Liaison	
2	Egg yolks	2
½ cup	Heavy [double] cream	125 ml/4 fl oz
	Garnish	
	Fried bread croutons (see Index)	

1. If using fresh asparagus, wash, scrape, and trim them. Remove the tips for garnish. If using canned asparagus, merely remove the tips and drain off the liquid, reserving it for making soup.

2. Chop the asparagus stalks and put them in a pot with the chopped onion. Add parsley sprigs, chicken stock and the liquid from the can if canned asparagus are used. Add a little salt and pepper. Cover the pan and simmer for 10–15 minutes, or until the asparagus is tender.

3. Put into an electric blender and blend until smooth, or through a food mill or fine nylon sieve.

4. Melt the butter and add the flour. Stir until smooth, and cook for a minute or two. Remove from the heat and strain into the asparagus soup. Blend until smooth, bring to a boil, stirring constantly, then simmer for a few minutes. Adjust seasoning to taste and add some mace.

5. Meanwhile, in a small pan cook the reserved tips for about 5–7 minutes, until tender, in a little hot stock or water. Strain the liquid into the soup and divide the tips equally into the soup cups.

6. Make the liaison. Mix the egg yolks and cream well. Add a few spoonfuls of hot soup and mix well before straining into the soup; stir constantly. Reheat the soup gently without allowing it to boil.

7. If the soup is not a good color, a little green coloring can be added, but great care must be exercised as it can easily be overdone. Serve the soup hot with fried bread croutons.

Black Bean Soup

12:20 / 03:30   Serves 4–6   New England

American	Ingredients	Metric/Imperial
1–1½ cups	Dried black beans	225–350 g/ ½–¾ lb
1	Ham bone or some ham meat minus fat	1
5–6 cups	Water	1.25 l/2–2¼ pints
2	Medium onions, sliced	2
4–5	Stalks celery, sliced	4–5
2–3	Carrots, sliced	2–3
	1 bay leaf, 5–6 sprigs parsley, 1 sprig thyme, tied together	
2	Cloves	2
½ tsp	Mustard powder	½ tsp
	A pinch of cayenne pepper	
	Stock or milk	
	Garnish	
2	Hard-boiled eggs	2
4–6	Slices lemon or ½ cup [100 g/4 oz] chopped ham	4–6
	Fried bread croutons (see Index)	

1. Wash the beans in several changes of cold water, then cover with cold water and soak overnight. Drain and put the beans into a large thick pan. Add the water, ham bone, or pieces of ham, cover the pan, and cook for 2 hours. Add the onions, celery, and carrots, the herbs, cloves, mustard, and cayenne pepper. Recover the pan and cook for another 1–1½ hours or until the beans are tender.

2. Remove the bone and herbs. Put the soup through a fine sieve or blend in an electric blender. Reheat the soup and if too thick add enough stock or milk to make a good texture. Adjust the seasoning.

3. Serve hot. Garnish with slices of hard-boiled egg and lemon slices or chopped ham and fried bread croutons.

Brown Bean Soup

12:20 / 02:00   Serves 4   New England

American	Ingredients	Metric/Imperial
⅔ lb	Brown beans/red kidney beans, dried	325 g/11 oz
6 cups	Water	1.3 l/2¼ pints
1 tbsp	Salt	1 tbsp
1	Large leek, peeled and finely chopped	1
1	Green pepper, finely chopped	1
1 can (1 lb)	Tomatoes, strained	1 tin (450 g/1 lb)
1	Garlic clove, crushed (optional)	1
¼ tsp	Chili powder	¼ tsp

American	Ingredients	Metric/Imperial
4 cups	Vegetable broth (use the cooking water)	1 1/1¾ pints
⅔ lb	Lean salted pork/corned beef	325 g/11 oz
1 tbsp	Butter or margarine	15 g/½ oz
⅓ cup	Watercress, snipped	8 g/⅓ oz

1. Place the beans in a generous amount of water. Let them stand overnight. Then pour off the water.
2. Place the beans in the water; add salt and boil for 1½ hours. Pour off the water, but save it for the broth.
3. While the beans are boiling, prepare and rinse the vegetables. Stir all the ingredients, except the pork, butter, and watercress into the bean stew. Boil the soup over low heat for about 20 minutes. Stir the soup vigorously so that the beans break up. If you use a blender, the bean pieces will become too small.
4. Cut the pork into strips and brown them in butter. Serve the soup hot, garnished with the pork and watercress.

Green Bean Soup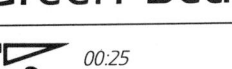

 00:25
00:40   Serves 4–6   Midwest

American	Ingredients	Metric/Imperial
2–3 tbsp	Butter	25–40 g/ 1–1½ oz
1	Medium onion (or 3–4 shallots) finely chopped	1
1	Clove garlic, crushed	1
2 tbsp	Flour	1½ tbsp
4 cups	Chicken or veal stock	1 1/1¾ pints
1 lb	Green beans	450 g/1 lb
1 tsp	Chopped or dried summer savory	1 tsp
	A little green coloring if required	
	Garnish	
4–6 tbsp	Heavy [double] cream	3½–5 tbsp
2 slices	Bacon	2 rashers

1. Melt the butter and cook the onon and garlic for 5–6 minutes in a covered pan. Add the flour and blend in smoothly. Pour on the stock and mix well. When smooth, bring to a boil, stirring constantly. Add salt and pepper.
2. String the beans and cut in slanting slices, or break them in half depending on their size. Add to the soup, with dried savory, and cook for 25 minutes or until the beans are tender.
3. Strain the soup, reserving a few pieces of bean for garnish (keep warm). Put the remaining soup and beans through a food mill or blend until smooth in an electric blender.
4. Reheat the soup, adjust the seasoning to taste, and add a little green coloring if required.
5. Serve hot with a spoonful of whipped cream on each bowl and sprinkle with finely crumbled, crispy fried bacon and the reserved green beans.

Brown Bean Soup

Beet Soup

00:25
00:45   Serves 4–6   Pacific Northwest

American	Ingredients	Metric/Imperial
3	Medium beets [beetroot]	3
1	Onion, sliced	1
2	Carrots, shredded	2
½	Small turnip, shredded	½
½	Small parsnip, shredded	½
2	Stalks celery, sliced	2
6 cups	Well-flavored brown or household stock	1.3 l/2¼ pints
1	Bay leaf	1
3–4	Sprigs parsley	3–4
½	Small cabbage, shredded	½
1–2 tbsp	Tomato purée	1–1½ tbsp
2 tsp	Lemon juice	2 tsp
1–2 tbsp	Mixed chopped parsley, dill, and basil	1–1½ tbsp
	Garnish	
6 tbsp	Sour cream	5 tbsp
3–4	Cooked frankfurters or other sausages	3–4

1. Peel and cut two of the beets into thin, short strips. Place in a soup pot with the onion, carrots, turnip, parsnip, and celery. Cover with stock, and add herbs and seasoning. Cook gently without boiling for 30–35 minutes.
2. Meanwhile, wash the cabbage and drain thoroughly. Add cabbage and tomato purée to the soup. Simmer until the cabbage is tender but not over-cooked.
3. While the soup cooks, grate the remaining beet into a small pan, cover with a cup of hot stock, and add the lemon juice to make the beet juice run. Heat gently for a few minutes but do not boil, as this will ruin the good red color. Strain this juice into the soup, adjust the seasoning, and add the chopped herbs.
4. Serve hot with a spoonful of sour cream and hot slices of frankfurter or other cooked sausage in each soup plate. (This soup improves by being made a day before being served and reheated carefully.)

Cream of Brussels Sprout Soup

00:20
00:35   Serves 4–6   New England

American	Ingredients	Metric/Imperial
4 tbsp	Butter	50 g/2 oz
1	Onion, chopped	1
1	Potato, chopped	1
1 lb	Washed and trimmed Brussels sprouts, chopped	450 g/1 lb
1½ tbsp	Flour	1¼ tbsp
4 cups	White stock (or water and chicken cubes)	1 l/1¾ pints
2	Bay leaves	2
3–4	Sprigs parsley	3–4
¼ tsp	Mace	¼ tsp
1 cup	Light [single] cream	250 ml/8 fl oz
	Garnish	
1 cup	Cooked chestnuts, broken into pieces	100 g/4 oz
2–3 tbsp	Butter	25–40 g/ 1–1½ oz
	Seasoning	

1. Melt the butter, and cook the onion and potato for 2–3 minutes. Then add the chopped sprouts and cook for a further 5 minutes, stirring constantly. Sprinkle in the flour and blend well. Then pour on the stock. Stir until well mixed and smooth. Then bring to a boil, stirring constantly. Reduce the heat, add the bay leaves, parsley sprigs, and seasoning. Cover and simmer soup for about 20 minutes, or until the vegetables are tender but not overcooked.
2. Remove the bay leaves. Then put the soup through a food mill or into an electric blender, and blend until smooth. Adjust seasoning, and reheat the soup, adding a cup of hot cream at the last moment.
3. Sprinkle with pieces of cooked chestnut, fried in butter until golden brown.

Cream of Barley Soup

02:15
02:00   Serves 4   United States

American	Ingredients	Metric/Imperial
1 cup	Pearl barley	225 g/8 oz
1	Onion, sliced	1
1	Carrot, sliced	1
2	Stalks celery, sliced	2
1	Bay leaf	1
3–4	Sprigs parsley (or 1 tbsp chopped parsley)	3–4

4–5 cups	Chicken or veal stock	1–1.25 l/ 1¾–2 pints
	Chicken carcass or ham bone, if available	
½ cup	Cream	125 ml/4 fl oz
	Garnish	
1–2 tbsp	Chopped parsley	1–1½ tbsp
	Fried bacon croutons (see Index)	

1. Wash the pearl barley and soak it overnight if possible; otherwise, cover it with boiling water and soak for 2 hours.
2. Put the vegetables into a pan with the drained barley, herbs, and stock. If a chicken carcass or a ham bone is available, it can be added to the soup at this stage. Cover the pan and cook gently until the barley is tender, about 1½–2 hours.
3. Discard the bones and herbs. Then set aside the barley and strain the soup through sieve, or blend the soup and barley in an electric blender, food processor, or food mill.
4. Reheat the soup and adjust seasoning. Add the cream just before serving. Sprinkle with chopped parsley and serve with bacon-flavored croutons.

Cauliflower Soup

00:20
00:25   Serves 4–6   United States

American	Ingredients	Metric/Imperial
1	Medium cauliflower	1
1	Bay leaf	1
1	Onion, chopped	1
1	Medium potato, sliced	1
3 tbsp	Butter	40 g/1½ oz
1 tbsp	Flour	1 tbsp
5 cups	Milk	1.25 l/2 pints
½ cup	Cream	125 ml/4 fl oz
¼ tsp	Mace	¼ tsp
	Garnish	
1 tbsp	Chopped chervil	1 tbsp
	Grated cheese	

1. Divide the well-washed cauliflower into flowerets, and cut the hard stalk and leaves into small pieces. Cook the cauliflower in boiling salted water with a bay leaf for 4–5 minutes to lightly cook and to remove any strong flavor. Drain and rinse under cold water. Reserve one quarter of the small flowerets for garnish.
2. Meanwhile, melt the butter, add the onion and potato, and cook gently for 5–6 minutes, stirring to prevent browning. Sprinkle in flour and blend smoothly. Then pour in milk, and mix well before bringing to a boil. Add the cauliflower, then reduce the heat and simmer gently until the potatoes and cauliflower are just tender.
3. Put the soup into an electric blender and blend until smooth, or put through a fine food mill. Return to the pan and reheat, adding the reserved cauliflower flowerets. Add the seasoning and the cream.
4. Sprinkle with chopped chervil and serve grated cheese separately.

Cream of Carrot Soup

Cream of Carrot Soup 🥬🥬🥬

00:20
00:50

Serves 4–6

United States

American	Ingredients	Metric/Imperial
4 tbsp	Butter	50 g/2 oz
1½ cups	Sliced young carrots	225 g/8 oz
1	Large onion, finely sliced	1
½	Clove garlic	½
2 tbsp	Rice	1½ tbsp
3–4	Sprigs parsley (or 1 tbsp dried parsley)	3–4
	Thinly peeled rind from ½ orange	
4 cups	Chicken or white stock	1 1/1¾ pints
¼ tsp	Sugar	¼ tsp
	Juice of ½ orange	

	Liaison	
2	Egg yolks	2
¼ cup	Cream	60 ml/2 fl oz
	Garnish	
	Finely grated rind of ½ orange	
2 tsp	Chopped parsley	2 tsp

1. Melt the butter and add the vegetables, crushed garlic, and rice. Mix well over gentle heat for 5 minutes without browning. Add the parsley, orange rind, stock, sugar, and seasonings. Bring the soup to a boil. Then lower the heat, and simmer for 30–40 minutes, or until the vegetables are tender.

2. Put the soup into an electric blender and blend until smooth, or put through a food mill. Return to the pot and reheat, adding orange juice.

3. If the soup is not thick enough, add the cream and egg yolk liaison: mix the egg yolks and cream well. Put a few spoonfuls of hot soup into the liaison. Then strain it back into the soup, stirring constantly. Reheat the soup without allowing it to boil.

4. Serve in soup bowls, sprinkled with grated orange rind and parsley.

Curried Corn Soup

Curried Corn Soup

 00:15
00:20
Serves 4–6
Mid Atlantic

American	Ingredients	Metric/Imperial
3 tbsp	Butter	40 g/1½ oz
2 tsp	Curry powder	2 tsp
1	Onion, chopped	1
1	Medium potato, finely sliced	1
1½ cups	Fresh or canned [tinned] sweetcorn	175 g/6 oz
3½ cups	Milk	850 ml/1½ pints
1	Bay leaf	1
3–4	Sprigs parsley	3–4
	Salt and pepper	
¼ tsp	Mace	¼ tsp
1	Chicken bouillon [stock] cube	1
	Paprika	

1. Melt the butter, and cook the curry powder, onion, and potato gently with a lid on the pan for 5 minutes, shaking the pan occasionally to prevent sticking. Add 1 cup [100 g/4 oz] of the corn. Stir well. Then add the milk, bay leaf, parsley, salt, pepper, and mace. Bring to simmering heat, add a chicken stock cube, and cook until the vegetables are tender.
2. Put the soup into an electric blender and blend until smooth, or put through a fine food mill.
3. Return the soup to the pan with the remaining corn (which if fresh should be simmered until tender in salted water). Reheat the soup until nearly boiling, and adjust the seasoning.
4. Serve in soup bowls with paprika sprinkled on top.

Creole Soup

 00:15
00:35
Serves 4
Southwest

American	Ingredients	Metric/Imperial
3 tbsp	Butter, oil or bacon fat	40 g/1½ oz
½ cup	Chopped green and red peppers	100 g/4 oz
1	Onion, chopped	1
2 tbsp	Flour	1½ tbsp
2 tsp	Tomato purée	2 tsp
4	Large ripe tomatoes, chopped and seeded	4
4 cups	Stock	1 l/1¾ pints
	1 bay leaf, 4 sprigs of parsley, 1 sprig of thyme, tied together	
	A pinch of cayenne pepper	
¼ tsp	Paprika pepper	¼ tsp
¼ tsp	Sugar	¼ tsp
1 tsp	Vinegar	1 tsp
2–3 tsp	Grated fresh horseradish (or 1 tsp dried horseradish)	2–3 tsp
	Garnish	
1 tbsp	Chopped parsley	1 tbsp
	Garlic croutons (see Index)	

1. Melt the butter, oil, or bacon fat. Cook the peppers and onions gently for 5–6 minutes without browning. Stir in the flour and blend well; add the tomato purée, fresh or canned tomatoes, stock, bay leaf, herbs, and seasoning. Bring to a boil, stirring constantly. Then reduce the heat and simmer for 25–30 minutes.
2. Remove the bay leaf and herbs, and adjust the seasoning. Add freshly grated or dried horseradish and vinegar. If the soup is not a good enough color, a little more tomato purée can now be added. Serve hot, sprinkled with chopped herbs and garlic croutons.

Chervil Soup

 00:15
00:25
Serves 4–6
United States

American	Ingredients	Metric/Imperial
2	Young carrots, finely sliced	2
1	Small potato, finely sliced	1
4–5 cups	Chicken or white stock	1–1.25 l/ 1¾–2 pints
3	Sprigs parsley	3
3 tbsp	Butter	40 g/1½ oz
2 tbsp	Flour	1½ tbsp
¼ tsp	Mace or a pinch of nutmeg	¼ tsp
4 tbsp	Chopped fresh chervil	3½ tbsp
½ cup	Cream	125 ml/4 fl oz
	Garnish	
	Fried bread croutons (see Index)	

Cream of Celery Soup

1. Put the carrots and potato in a pan with stock and parsley sprigs, and simmer until tender, 15–20 minutes.

2. Melt the butter and stir in the flour. When smooth, strain the stock onto the flour and butter; mix well.

3. Blend the potato and carrots in an electric blender and add to the soup. Mix well. Then bring to a boil, stirring constantly. Simmer for a few minutes, adding salt, pepper, and mace or nutmeg.

4. Just before serving, add the chopped chervil and cream. Reheat but do not boil, as this destroys the delicate flavor of chervil.

5. Serve with fried bread croutons.

Cream of Celery Soup

	00:20	
	00:45	Serves 4–6	Mid Atlantic

American	Ingredients	Metric/Imperial
1 slice	Bacon	1 rasher
3–4 tbsp	Butter	40–50 g/ 1½–2 oz
2 cups	Chopped celery	225 g/8 oz
1	Large onion, chopped	1
1	Potato, sliced	1
1 tbsp	Flour	1 tbsp
2 cups	Water (or white stock)	450 ml/¾ pint
1	Bay leaf	1
	Several sprigs of parsley	
	A pinch of thyme	
3 cups	Milk	700 ml/1¼ pints
	Garnish	
4–6 tbsp	Cream	3½–5 tbsp
	Paprika	
	Fried bread croutons or bacon croutons (see Index)	

1. Chop the bacon and put it in a pan with the butter. Cook gently for a few minutes. Then add the celery, potato, and onion. Cook together for 4–5 minutes, stirring constantly to prevent browning. Sprinkle in the flour and blend smoothly. Add the stock or water, mix well, and bring to a boil. Reduce the heat; add the bay leaf, parsley sprigs, and thyme. Simmer for 20–30 minutes, or until the vegetables are tender.

2. Put the soup through a fine food mill or into an electric blender and blend until smooth. Reheat gently. In another pan, heat the milk; when it is nearly boiling, add the milk to the soup pan with seasoning to taste.

3. Serve with a spoonful of cream and a dusting of paprika in each soup bowl, and fried bread croutons or bacon croutons separately.

Lemon Soup

Lemon Soup

	00:10			
	00:25	Serves 4–6	Midwest	

American	Ingredients	Metric/Imperial
5 cups	Strong chicken stock	1.25 1/2 pints
2–3 tbsp	Rice	1½–2 tbsp
2	Eggs	2
1	Large lemon	1
4–6 tbsp	Heavy [double] cream	3½–5 tbsp
	Chopped parsley	

1. Heat the strongly flavored chicken stock in a pan. When boiling, add the rice and cook for 12 minutes, or until the rice is cooked.

2. Meanwhile, beat the eggs well with the lemon juice, until frothy. Take the soup pan off the heat and let it cool slightly before adding 4–5 tablespoons [3½–4 tbsp] of hot stock to the egg mixture. Stir in well.

3. Pour the stock and rice into the top of a double boiler. Strain the egg mixture into the stock, and stir in well. Stir over gentle heat while the soup thickens. Do not boil, or the eggs will curdle.

4. When the soup is creamy, add the lemon rind and adjust the seasoning. If serving hot, pour into soup bowls, put a spoonful of cream into each, and sprinkle with chopped parsley. If serving cold, allow the soup to cool, add the slightly whipped cream, then chill before serving.

Jellied Gazpacho

	12:15			
	00:05	Serves 6–7	New England	

American	Ingredients	Metric/Imperial
1 (14-oz) can	Tomato juice	1 (400 g/14 oz) tin
2 envelopes	Unflavored gelatin [gelatine]	2 sachets
4	Tomatoes, peeled, seeded and chopped	4
1	Cucumber, peeled, seeded and chopped	1

½	Green pepper, seeded and cut into dice	½
¼ cup	Grated onion	25 g/1 oz
4 tbsp	Olive oil	3½ tbsp
4 tbsp	Wine vinegar	3½ tbsp
1 clove	Garlic, crushed	1
6–8 drops	Hot pepper sauce	6–8
	Freshly ground black pepper	

1. Heat the tomato juice. Add the gelatin and stir until dissolved. Set aside to cool.

2. Combine the tomatoes, cucumber, green pepper, and onion; add to the tomato juice.

3. Stir in the oil and vinegar; add garlic, hot pepper sauce, and salt and black pepper to taste. Mix well and chill thoroughly, preferably overnight.

4. Serve in small bowls set in a bed of crushed ice.

Gazpacho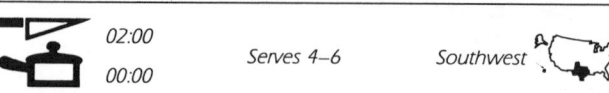

	02:00			
	00:00	Serves 4–6	Southwest	

American	Ingredients	Metric/Imperial
4–6	Large ripe tomatoes	4–6
4–6	Scallions [spring onions] or 1 medium onion	4–6
1–2	Cloves garlic	1–2
1	Medium cucumber	1
1	Green pepper	1
1	Thick slice brown bread	1
1½ cups	Iced water	350 ml/12 fl oz
4 tbsp	Good quality olive oil	3½ tbsp
2 tbsp	Wine vinegar	1½ tbsp
1 tbsp	Lemon juice	1 tbsp
2 tbsp	Chopped mixed parsley, basil, marjoram	1½ tbsp
	A few ice cubes	
Garnish		
	Fried garlic croutons (see Index)	

1. Remove the skins from the tomatoes by dipping them in boiling water for a count of 10, then in cold water. Chop the tomatoes coarsely, removing the hard cores. Reserve 2–3 tbsp for garnish. Slice the white parts of the spring onions or chop a medium onion. Crush the garlic and mix with the onions and tomatoes. Peel and dice the cucumber, sprinkle it with salt, and let it stand for 20–30 minutes; then wash it well and drain. Add half to the tomato mixture and reserve the remainder for garnish. Remove the stalk, pips, and veins from the green pepper and slice finely. Add three-quarters to the soup and reserve the rest for garnish. Soak the bread in half the iced water until really soft.

2. Put the tomato mixture into an electric blender. Add olive oil, vinegar, lemon juice, the softened bread, and some salt and pepper. Blend until smooth and strain if necessary through a coarse sieve.

3. Add the reserved vegetables to the soup, and chill thoroughly. Just before serving, add enough of the remaining iced water to thin the soup to a desired consistency. Adjust the seasoning and sprinkle with herbs. Serve with a few small ice cubes and with fried garlic croutons in each soup bowl.

Creamy Cucumber Soup

Serves 4–6 United States

00:45
00:30

American	Ingredients	Metric/Imperial
2–3	Medium cucumbers	2–3
4–5	Spring onions (or 3 shallots) chopped finely	4–5
3 tbsp	Butter	40 g/1½ oz
2 tbsp	Flour	2 tbsp
4 cups	Chicken stock or white stock (or water and cubes)	1 l/1¾ pints
¼ tsp	Mace	¼ tsp
	A pinch of sugar	
1 tbsp	Chopped parsley	1 tbsp
1 tsp	Chopped dill	1 tsp
	A little green coloring (if necessary)	
2	Egg yolks	2
½ cup	Heavy [double] cream	125 ml/4 fl oz

	Garnish	
2 tsp	Chopped dill	2 tsp
	Fried bread croutons (see Index)	

1. Peel and quarter the cucumbers; remove and discard the seeds. Cut into small dice. Reserve 4–5 tablespoons [3½–4 tbsp] of cucumber dice to use as garnish: sprinkle these with salt, and let them stand for 20 minutes before washing and draining. Melt the butter and cook the onions (or shallots) very gently for 5 minutes to soften without browning. Add the larger amount of cucumber dice and cook gently for 2–3 minutes, stirring frequently.

2. Sprinkle in the flour, blending smoothly before adding the stock. Bring to a boil, stirring constantly. Add herbs and seasonings, then simmer gently for 15 minutes or until the vegetables are tender.

3. Put the soup into an electric blender and blend until smooth, or put through a food mill. Return to the pot and reheat. Add a little green coloring and adjust the seasoning to taste.

4. Make the liaison: mix the egg yolks and cream well; add a few spoonfuls of hot soup, and mix well before straining the mixture into the soup, whisking constantly. Heat the soup gently, but do not boil, as this causes the egg yolk to curdle.

5. Just before serving, add the raw, drained cucumber dice, and sprinkle each soup bowl with a little chopped dill. Serve with fried bread croutons.

Creamy Cucumber Soup

Soup with Red and Green Lentils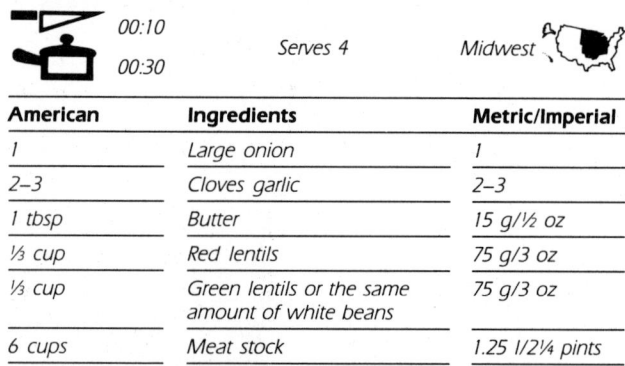

00:10
00:30
Serves 4
Midwest

American	Ingredients	Metric/Imperial
1	Large onion	1
2–3	Cloves garlic	2–3
1 tbsp	Butter	15 g/½ oz
⅓ cup	Red lentils	75 g/3 oz
⅓ cup	Green lentils or the same amount of white beans	75 g/3 oz
6 cups	Meat stock	1.25 l/2¼ pints
	Sour cream	

1. Chop the onion into large pieces and crush the garlic cloves. Melt the butter in a large pot and brown the onion and garlic.
2. Stir in the lentils and stock. Let the soup simmer over low heat for 20–30 minutes, or until the lentils feel soft. Serve with a dab of sour cream in the soup.

Leek and Potato Soup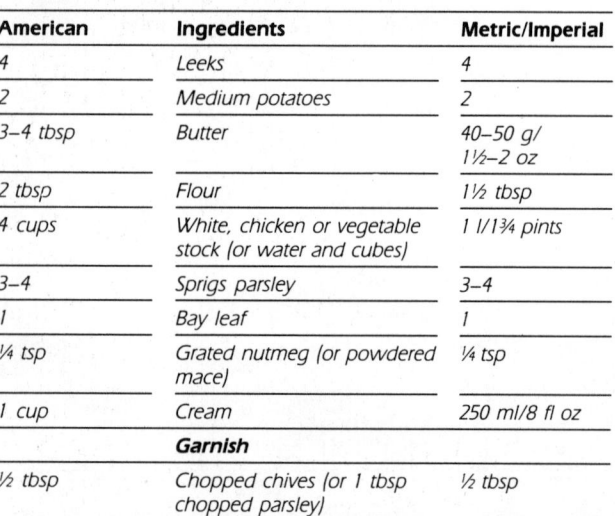

00:20
00:35
Serves 4–6
New England

American	Ingredients	Metric/Imperial
4	Leeks	4
2	Medium potatoes	2
3–4 tbsp	Butter	40–50 g/ 1½–2 oz
2 tbsp	Flour	1½ tbsp
4 cups	White, chicken or vegetable stock (or water and cubes)	1 l/1¾ pints
3–4	Sprigs parsley	3–4
1	Bay leaf	1
¼ tsp	Grated nutmeg (or powdered mace)	¼ tsp
1 cup	Cream	250 ml/8 fl oz
	Garnish	
½ tbsp	Chopped chives (or 1 tbsp chopped parsley)	½ tbsp
	Cheese croutons (see Index)	

1. Slice the white parts of the leeks and wash well in salted cold water. Peel and slice the potatoes finely. Melt the butter and add the potato and drained leeks. Cook gently for 5–6 minutes, stirring to prevent sticking and browning. Sprinkle in flour. When thoroughly mixed, add the stock (or water and cubes). Add herbs and seasoning. Bring to a boil, stirring constantly. Then lower the heat and simmer for 25–30 minutes, or until the vegetables are tender.
2. Blend the soup in an electric blender or put through a fine food mill. Reheat and adjust the seasoning. Put the cream into a separate pan, and bring to just below boiling point before adding it to the soup.
3. Sprinkle each soup bowl with chives or chopped parsley, and serve the cheese croutons separately.

Lentil Soup

12:10
03:30
Serves 4–5
Midwest

American	Ingredients	Metric/Imperial
¾ cup	Dried lentils	175 g/6 oz
1	Onion, peeled and chopped	1
¼ cup	Cubed salt pork	25 g/1 oz
1 cup	Chopped celery	100 g/4 oz
½ cup	Diced carrots	50 g/2 oz
1	Bay leaf	1
1	Clove	1
1	Beef bouillon [stock] cube	1
2 cups	Water	450 ml/¾ pint
1–2 tbsp	Vinegar	1–1½ tbsp

1. Pick over and wash the lentils, cover completely with cold water, and let soak overnight.
2. Pour off the water. Put 3 cups [1¼ pints] of water and the soaked lentils into a saucepan.
3. Put the onion and salt pork into a pan, and sauté until the onion is translucent. Put into the pan with the lentils and add all the other ingredients except the vinegar. Cover and simmer for about 3–3½ hours, or until the lentils are tender.
4. Before serving, remove the bay leaf, add vinegar, and adjust the seasoning.

Parsnip Soup

00:20
00:40
Serves 4
New England

American	Ingredients	Metric/Imperial
3 tbsp	Butter	40 g/1½ oz
1½ cups	Peeled and finely sliced parsnips	350 g/12 oz
1	Onion, chopped	1
1 tbsp	Flour	1 tbsp
3–4 cups	Vegetable or white stock (or water and cube)	700 ml–1 l/ 1¼–1¾ pints
3–4	Sprigs parsley	3–4
1	Small bay leaf	1
	A pinch of thyme	
	A pinch of nutmeg	
½ cup	Cream	125 ml/4 fl oz
	Garnish	
1 tbsp	Chopped parsley	1 tbsp
	Fried bread croutons (see Index)	

1. Melt the butter, and cook the onion and parsnips gently for 5–6 minutes with a lid on the pan, to soften without browning. Remove from the heat, and sprinkle in the flour. Then blend well. Pour on the stock, mix well, and add the herbs and seasonings. Bring to a boil, and simmer for 20–30 minutes until the parsnips are tender. Remove the bay leaf.
2. Put the soup into an electric blender, and blend until smooth, or put through a food mill. Return the soup to the pan, adjust the seasoning, and reheat, adding the cream.
3. Serve in soup bowls sprinkled with chopped parsley and with fried bread croutons.

Soup with Red and Green Lentils

Lentil and Ham Soup

 06:15 / 02:00   Serves 4–6   Midwest

American	Ingredients	Metric/Imperial
1 cup	Red lentils	225 g/8 oz
1	Large or 2 small onions, chopped	1
2	Small carrots, chopped	2
2	Stalks celery, chopped	2
2 tbsp	Butter or bacon fat	25 g/1 oz
1	Ham bone	1
	1 bay leaf, 4–5 sprigs of parsley, 1 sprig thyme, tied together	
	Pepper	
	A little sugar	
1 tsp	Tomato purée	1 tsp
	Garnish	
	Fried bread croutons (see Index)	
½ cup	Chopped cooked sausages or chopped ham	50 g/2 oz
2 tbsp	Chopped parsley	1½ tbsp

1. Wash the lentils several times. Then cover with cold water and soak for 4–6 hours or overnight. If used unsoaked, the cooking time has to be considerably increased as does the amount of water used, as it evaporates during cooking.
2. Sauté the onion, carrots, and celery in the melted butter for 5–6 minutes to soften. Then add the drained lentils and the ham bone. Add the bay leaf, parsley sprigs, thyme, pepper, and a little sugar. Bring to a boil. Then cover and simmer until tender. This will take at least 2 hours or longer, depending on the type of lentils.
3. Remove the herbs, and put the soup through a fine food mill or into the electric blender and blend until smooth, adding tomato purée. If the soup is too thick at this stage, thin it with stock or water. Adjust the seasoning, adding salt if necessary.
4. Serve hot with fried bread croutons, chopped cooked sausages, or chopped ham. Sprinkle with chopped parsley.

Cream of Mushroom Soup

 00:15 / 00:25   Serves 4–6   United States

American	Ingredients	Metric/Imperial
4 tbsp	Butter	50 g/2 oz
1	Onion, chopped	1
2–3 cups	Sliced mushrooms	225–350 g/ 8–12 oz
3 tbsp	Flour	2 tbsp
3 cups	Chicken or white stock (or water and cube)	700 ml/1¼ pints
1	Bay leaf	1
3–4	Sprigs parsley	3–4
¼ tsp	Mace	¼ tsp
2 cups	Heavy [double] cream	450 ml/¾ pint
	Garnish	
	Chopped parsley or chives	
	Fried bread croutons (see Index)	

1. Melt the butter and cook the onion for 4–5 minutes to soften. Then add the mushrooms, cover the pan, and cook for 5 more minutes. Sprinkle in the flour, and stir until smooth. Pour on the stock, and mix well. Add the bay leaf, parsley, and mace. Season with salt and pepper. Bring to a boil, and simmer for 10–15 minutes.
2. Remove the bay leaf. Put the soup through a fine food mill or into an electric blender and blend until smooth. Reheat, adding the heated cream. Adjust the seasoning to taste.
3. Sprinkle with chopped parsley or chives, and serve with fried bread croutons.

Onion Soup

00:20 / 01:00   Serves 4–6   New England

American	Ingredients	Metric/Imperial
3–4 tbsp	Butter	40–50 g/ 1½–2 oz
4–5	Medium onions, peeled and finely sliced	4–5
1–2	Cloves garlic, crushed	1–2
½ tsp	Sugar	½ tsp
2 tbsp	Flour	1½ tbsp
5 cups	Vegetable stock (or water)	1.25 l/2 pints
½ cup	White wine (optional)	125 ml/4 fl oz
1	Bay leaf	1
3–4	Sprigs parsley	3–4
1	Sprig thyme	1
	A pinch of nutmeg	
4–6	Slices French bread	4–6
4–6 tbsp	Grated mixed Gruyere or Emmenthal and Parmesan cheese or other strong hard cheese	3½–5 tbsp

1. Melt the butter; add the onions and garlic and a sprinkling of sugar. Brown slowly, stirring constantly to prevent burning. Sprinkle in the flour and brown this slightly. Add the stock or water and the wine, if using any; otherwise, add the equivalent amount of water. Bring to a boil, stirring constantly. Add herbs and seasoning, and simmer for 20–30 minutes.
2. Meanwhile, cut the French bread into slices and put them into the oven to dry and brown slightly.
3. Remove the bay leaf from the soup. Put the slices of bread into the ovenproof soup bowls or a large tureen. Pour the soup over the bread and sprinkle thickly with cheese. Put into a hot oven for 15–20 minutes or under a broiler [grill] for 7–10 minutes to brown the cheese.

Onion Soup

White Onion Soup

	00:15		
	00:55	Serves 4–6	South

American	Ingredients	Metric/Imperial
5 tbsp	Butter	65 g/2½ oz
3–4	Onions, finely sliced	3–4
3 tbsp	Flour	2 tbsp
5 cups	Hot milk	1.25 l/2 pints
1	Bay leaf	1
4	Sprigs parsley	4
	Pepper	
½ tsp	Mace	½ tsp
	Liaison	
2	Egg yolks	2
½ cup	Cream	125 ml/4 fl oz
	Garnish	
	Fried bread croutons (see Index)	

1. Melt 2 tablespoons [25 g/1 oz] of the butter and cook the onions *very gently* until tender, stirring frequently to prevent browning, about 30 minutes. Remove from the heat. Sprinkle in flour and remaining butter, cooking 3–5 minutes. When well mixed in, add the milk and blend well. Bring to a boil, stirring constantly. Add the bay leaf, parsley, pepper, and mace. Simmer the soup for 15–20 minutes, stirring frequently to prevent sticking.

2. Make the liaison: mix the egg yolks into the cream. Add several spoonfuls of hot soup to this mixture and, when blended, strain back into the soup, stirring constantly. Reheat without boiling or the egg will curdle.

3. Serve hot with fried bread croutons.

Parsley Soup

	00:15		
	00:35	Serves 4–6	United States

American	Ingredients	Metric/Imperial
2½ cups	Fresh chopped parsley	75 g/3 oz
3 tbsp	Butter	40 g/1½ oz
1	Onion, chopped	1
1	Stalk celery, chopped	1
2 tbsp	Flour	1½ tbsp
5 cups	Vegetable or white stock	1.25 l/2 pints
	A pinch of nutmeg	
½	Bay leaf	½
	Garnish	
4–6 tbsp	Heavy [double] cream	3½–5 tbsp
	A sprinkling of paprika	
	Fried bread or bacon croutons (see Index)	

1. Coarsely chop the parsley including the stems, which are full of flavor.

2. Melt the butter, and cook the onion and celery gently for a few minutes without browning. Sprinkle in flour and mix well. Pour on the stock and bring slowly to a boil, blending smoothly. Add the chopped parsley and salt, pepper, nutmeg, and bay leaf. Simmer for 25 minutes. Remove the bay leaf.

3. The soup can be served as it is, blended in an electric blender, or put through a food mill.

4. Reheat the soup and pour into soup bowls. Serve with a spoonful of cream in each bowl, a sprinkling of paprika, and fried bread or bacon croutons.

Pea Soup with Bacon

Pea Soup with Bacon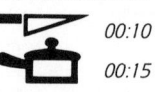

	00:10	Serves 4–6	South
	00:15		

American	Ingredients	Metric/Imperial
1 can (10½ oz)	Condensed pea soup or 2 cans of ordinary pea soup	1 tin (300 g/10¾ oz)
¾ can	Milk	¾ tin
2 slices	Bacon	2 rashers
4 tbsp	Cooked peas	3½ tbsp
4 tbsp	Heavy [double] cream	3½ tbsp
1 tbsp	Chopped mint	1 tbsp
	Garnish	
	Fried bread croûtons (see Index)	

1. Chop the bacon slices, and cook gently until crisp. Add the pea soup and a can of water or milk. Stir over gentle heat until smooth. Then add the cooked peas. Heat to boiling point.
2. Pour into heated soup bowls and put a spoonful of heavy cream into the center of each one. Sprinkle with chopped mint and serve at once with fried bread croutons.

Green Pea Soup

	00:20	Serves 4–6	Midwest
	00:35		

American	Ingredients	Metric/Imperial
2 tbsp	Butter	25 g/1 oz
1	Small onion (or several young green onions), finely chopped	1
1	Head lettuce, washed and sliced	1
2 cups	Fresh or frozen peas	250 g/8 oz
4 cups	Chicken stock	1 l/1¾ pints
	Sugar to taste	
1	Sprig mint (or 1 teaspoon dried mint)	1
	Garnish	
4–6 tbsp	Heavy [double] cream	3½–5 tbsp
2 tsp	Fresh (or dried chopped) mint	2 tsp
	Fried bread or bacon croutons (see Index).	

1. Melt the butter and soften the onion and lettuce for 4–5 minutes without browning.
2. Add three quarters of the peas to the soup pan, reserving the remainder as garnish. Add the stock, salt, pepper, sugar to taste, and mint. Cover the pan and cook gently until tender, about 20 minutes.
3. Put the soup into an electric blender, first removing the mint stalk, and blend until smooth; or put through a food mill or fine sieve.
4. Meanwhile, cook the remaining peas in a little boiling salted and sugared water. Drain and divide among the soup bowls.
5. Reheat the soup and adjust the seasoning to taste. Pour into soup bowls. Add a tablespoon of cream to each bowl, sprinkle with chopped mint, and serve with fried bread croutons or bacon croutons.

Ham Flavored Pea Soup

	08:20	Serves 4–6	South
	02:10		

American	Ingredients	Metric/Imperial
1 cup	Split peas	200 g/7 oz
5–6 cups	Water	1.25 l/2–2¼ pints
1	Ham bone	1
1	Onion, chopped	1
2	Stalks celery, chopped	2
1	Bay leaf	1
4–5	Sprigs parsley (or 1 large tbsp dried parsley)	4–5
½ tsp	Sugar	½ tsp
¼ tsp	Ground pepper	¼ tsp
2 tbsp	Butter	25 g/1 oz
1 tbsp	Flour	1 tbsp
	A little mint	
	Garnish	
4–6 tbsp	Cream	3½–5 tbsp
½–1 cup	Chopped ham (or 2–3 slices [rashers] of bacon chopped and fried crisply)	50–100 g/2–4 oz
	Fried bread croutons (see Index)	

Pea Pod Soup

1. Start making this soup the day before it is required, as the split peas need to be soaked for 6–8 hours in cold water after being washed in several changes of cold water.

2. The next day, wash the ham bone, and remove and discard any surplus fat. Put into a large pan with the split peas and the water in which they have been soaking. Add the onion, celery, bay leaf, parsley sprigs, sugar, black pepper, and a little salt, remembering that the ham bone is likely to be salty. Cover and bring the soup to a boil, then simmer gently, until the peas are tender. Stir from time to time to prevent the peas from sticking. This may take 1–2 hours.

3. Remove the bay leaf and bones. Then put the soup into an electric blender and blend until smooth, or put through a food mill.

4. Melt the butter in the rinsed-out pan, then stir in the flour. When blended, pour on the soup. Stir until smoothly blended, then bring to a boil, stirring constantly, Simmer for a few minutes. Adjust the seasoning and add mint and a little more water if soup is too thick.

5. Serve hot with a spoon of cream on top of each serving and a garnish of chopped ham or fried bacon bits, or fried bread croutons.

Pea Pod Soup

00:15
00:45   Serves 4   Midwest

American	Ingredients	Metric/Imperial
2 lb	Young, unopened pea pods	900 g/2 lb
1	Onion, peeled and sliced	1
2–3	Sprigs mint	2–3
2–3	Sprigs parsley	2–3
4 cups	Stock or 2 bouillon [stock] cubes and 4 cups water	1 I/1¾ pints
2 tbsp	Margarine	25 g/1 oz
1½ tbsp	Flour	1 tbsp
	Sugar	
4 tbsp	Cooked green peas (optional)	3½ tbsp
	Chopped mint	

1. Wash the pods and put them into a large saucepan with the onion, mint, parsley, and stock. Bring to a boil, cover, and simmer for about 40 minutes.

2. When the outer flesh of the pods is tender, rub all through a sieve or food mill.

3. Melt the margarine in a pan, stir in the flour, and cook for 2 minutes. Add the purée and stir until boiling. Add salt, pepper, and sugar to taste.

4. Add whole, cooked peas, and serve sprinkled with a little chopped mint.

Lettuce Soup

 00:25 / 00:30   Serves 4–6   Mid Atlantic

American	Ingredients	Metric/Imperial
2–3	Heads lettuce	2–3
3 tbsp	Butter	40 g/1½ oz
1	Small onion, finely chopped	1
2 tbsp	Flour	1½ tbsp
4 cups	Chicken stock (or water and cubes)	1 l/1 ¾ pints
½ tsp	Sugar	½ tsp
3–4	Sprigs parsley (or 1 tbsp dried parsley)	3–4
2	Sprigs mint (or 1 tsp chopped mint)	2
1 cup	Heavy [double] cream	250 ml/8 fl oz
	Garnish	
4–6 tbsp	Heavy [double] cream	3½–5 tbsp
2 tsp	Finely chopped mint or parsley	2 tsp
	Fried bread croutons (see Index) or brown bread and butter.	

1. Coarsely chop the well-washed lettuce. Melt the butter and soften the lettuce and onion gently in a covered pan for 5–6 minutes without browning. Sprinkle in the flour and blend smoothly before adding the stock and seasoning. When smooth, bring to a boil, stirring constantly. Reduce the heat and simmer for 15 minutes, having added salt, pepper, sugar, parsley, and mint.
2. Put the soup into an electric blender and blend until smooth, or put through a food mill or fine sieve.
3. Reheat the soup in a clean pan. Meanwhile, heat the creamy milk in another pan and add to the soup when on the point of boiling—this lightens the texture of the soup. Adjust seasoning to taste.
4. If serving hot, pour into soup bowls and put a large spoonful of cream on top of each bowl. Sprinkle with chopped parsley or mint. If serving cold, chill thoroughly, adding a little more seasoning. Serve in soup bowls with a spoonful of whipped heavy [double] cream on top, and sprinkle with chopped herbs as above.
5. If serving hot, serve with fried bread croutons; if cold, with brown bread and butter.

Mushroom Soup

 00:15 / 00:20   Serves 4–6   Midwest

American	Ingredients	Metric/Imperial
2–3 tbsp	Butter	25–40 g/1–1½ oz
1	Onion, finely sliced	1
2 cups	Sliced white mushrooms	225 g/8 oz
2 tbsp	Flour	1½ tbsp
4 cups	Clear beef stock or 2 cans [tins] consomme	1 l/1¾ pints
1 tbsp	Chopped parsley	1 tbsp
1 tsp	Chopped tarragon	1 tsp
½ cup	Cream	125 ml/4 fl oz
4 tbsp	Sherry	3½ tbsp

1. Melt the butter, and cook the onion gently with lid on pan for 3–5 minutes, without browning. Add mushrooms, and cook for a minute or two more. Sprinkle in the flour. When blended, add the stock or canned consomme. Bring slowly to a boil, stirring constantly, and simmer for 10–15 minutes. Add seasoning.
2. Just before serving add herbs, cream, and sherry. Serve at once.

Potato Soup

 00:15 / 00:35   Serves 3–4   Mid Atlantic

American	Ingredients	Metric/Imperial
2 tbsp	Margarine	25 g/1 oz
2 tbsp	Onion, finely chopped	1½ tbsp
1 cup	Potato, diced	100 g/4 oz
4 tbsp	Water	3½ tbsp
½	Clove garlic, crushed	½
	Salt and pepper	
1 cup	Milk	250 ml/8 fl oz
1 tbsp	Chopped parsley	1 tbsp
	A pinch of nutmeg	

1. Heat the margarine in a pan, add the onion and potato, and sauté for about 5 minutes.
2. Add water, garlic, and a little salt and pepper. Cover and cook over low heat until the potato is quite soft.
3. Add the milk and stir until the soup boils. Then mash through a sieve.
4. Return to the pan. Adjust the seasoning, add parsley and a pinch of nutmeg, and reheat before serving.

Sauerkraut Soup

 00:10 / 00:50   Serves 4–6   Pacific Northwest

American	Ingredients	Metric/Imperial
1	Onion, sliced	1
2	Small carrots, sliced	2
3–4 tbsp	Butter	40–50 g/1½–2 oz
1	Potato, peeled and sliced	1
2 tbsp	Flour	1½ tbsp
1 tsp	Tomato purée	1 tsp
¾ lb	Sauerkraut	350 g/12 oz
4–5 cups	Brown or household stock	1–1.25 ml/1¾–2 pints
1 tbsp	Chopped parsley	1 tbsp
1 tsp	Chopped chervil	1 tsp

Sour cream

1. Melt the butter, and cook the onion and carrots until golden. Then add the potato. Stir in the flour and, when smooth, add the tomato purée and sauerkraut. Cook for a few minutes, stirring constantly. Then add the stock and the herbs.

2. Bring to a boil, and simmer for about 40 minutes. Season to taste, and serve hot with a spoonful of sour cream in each soup bowl.

Cream of Potato Soup

Yellow Pea Soup

| | 00:25 | | |
| | 00:50 | Serves 4–6 | New England |

American	Ingredients	Metric/Imperial
3 tbsp	Butter	40 g/1½ oz
3–4	Medium potatoes, finely sliced	3–4
2	Medium onions, finely sliced	2
1–2	Stalks celery, finely sliced	1–2
2½ cups	Boiling water	600 ml/1 pint
1	Bay leaf	1
3–4	Sprigs parsley	3–4
	A pinch of thyme	
	Salt and pepper	
¼ tsp	Mace or nutmeg	¼ tsp
2 cups	Milk	450 ml/¾ pint
	Garnish	
4–6 tbsp	Heavy [double] cream	3½–5 tbsp
1 tbsp	Chopped chives or parsley	1 tbsp
	Fried bread croutons or cheesy croutons (see Index)	

1. Melt the butter and cook the potatoes, onions, and celery very gently, stirring frequently, without allowing them to brown, for about 5–6 minutes. Add the boiling water and stir well. Add the herbs, salt and pepper, mace or nutmeg. Bring to a boil. Then reduce heat, and simmer gently with lid on pan for about 30–40 minutes, or until the vegetables are tender. Stir from time to time to keep the vegetables from sticking and browning.

2. Remove the bay leaf. Then put soup through a fine food mill or into an electric blender, and blend until smooth. Reheat. Then add the milk, which has been heated until nearly boiling in a separate pan (this lightens the texture of the soup). Adjust seasoning.

3. Serve with a spoonful of cream, a sprinkling of chopped chives or parsley, and fried bread croutons or cheesy croutons in each bowl.

Yellow Pea Soup

| | 12:20 | | |
| | 02:00 | Serves 6–8 | South |

American	Ingredients	Metric/Imperial
1 cup	Split yellow peas	225 g/8 oz
5 cups	Water	1.25 l/2 pints
1	Ham bone	1
2	Onions, sliced	2
1 cup	Chopped celery or celeriac	100 g/4 oz
2	Carrots, sliced	2
1	Small potato, sliced	1
	1 bay leaf, several sprigs of parsley, a sprig thyme, tied together	1
½–1 cup	Chopped ham	50–100 g/2–4 oz
2 tbsp	Parsley	1½ tbsp
	Garnish	
	Fried bread croutons (see Index)	

1. Wash and soak the split peas in cold water overnight if not using a quick cooking variety. Drain and put into a pan, with the water, the ham bone, vegetables, bay leaf, parsley sprigs and some salt and pepper. Bring to a boil. Then simmer for 1½–2 hours or until peas and vegetables are tender.

2. Remove the ham bone and herbs, and put the soup into an electric blender and blend until smooth. Measure soup and bring it up to the required quantity with water or stock. Taste and adjust seasoning. Reheat, adding the chopped ham.

3. Sprinkle with chopped parsley, and serve with fried croutons.

Squash Soup

	00:20		
	00:35	Serves 4	South

American	Ingredients	Metric/Imperial
1	Large squash [marrow]	1
6 tbsp	Margarine	75 g/3 oz
1	Onion, peeled and sliced	1
1 cup	Water	250 ml/8 fl oz
	Bouquet garni	
	Salt and pepper	
3 tbsp	Flour	2 tbsp
1 cup	Milk	250 ml/8 fl oz
1	Egg yolk	1
2 tbsp	Light [single] cream or evaporated milk	1½ tbsp

1. Peel the squash, cut it into pieces, and remove the seeds.
2. Melt the margarine in a pan. Put in the squash and onion and cook for about 5 minutes, stirring well.
3. Add the water, bouquet garni, and a little salt and pepper and cook until the squash is quite soft. Remove the bouquet garni.
4. Strain through a sieve, then mash the squash until smooth. Add the squash to the liquid and return all to the pan.
5. Blend the flour smoothly with the milk; add to the squash purée and stir until boiling. Then reduce the heat and simmer for 5 minutes.
6. Mix the egg yolk with the cream, stir into the soup, and reheat but do not allow it to boil. Adjust the seasoning, and serve with croutons of fried or toasted bread.

Spring Soup

	00:30		
	00:30	Serves 4–6	Mid Atlantic

American	Ingredients	Metric/Imperial
4	Young carrots	4
2–3	Young leeks according to size (or 8–10 scallions/spring onions)	2–3
3 tbsp	Butter	40 g/1½ oz
1½ tbsp	Flour	1¼ tbsp
4 cups	Chicken stock (or water and chicken cubes)	1 l/1¾ pints
½ cup	Cauliflower flowerets	125 g/4 oz
2–3 tbsp	Peas	1½–2 tbsp
2–3 tbsp	Young green beans	1½–2 tbsp
	A little sugar	
2 tbsp	Mixed parsley, chervil, mint and thyme	1½ tbsp
	Liaison	
½ cup	Cream	125 ml/4 fl oz
2	Egg yolks	2

1. Peel and dice the carrots. Wash the leeks or scallions thoroughly and cut the white part into slices. Melt the butter and cook these vegetables gently in a covered pan for 5–6 minutes

without allowing to brown. Sprinkle in flour, mix thoroughly, then add the stock. Blend well until smooth and bring to a boil, stirring constantly. Cook for a few minutes before adding the cauliflower flowerets, peas, sliced beans, and sugar. Simmer for 15 minutes. Add the herbs, and cook for a few more minutes to draw out the flavor of the herbs. Season to taste.
2. Make the liaison by mixing the cream with the egg yolks. Take a few spoonfuls of the hot soup and mix well with the cream and egg yolk mixture before straining it back into the soup, stirring constantly. Reheat, being very careful not to allow the soup to boil as this causes the egg to curdle and spoils the texture of the soup.

Cream of Tomato Soup

	00:25		
	00:40	Serves 4–6	South

American	Ingredients	Metric/Imperial
3 tbsp	Butter	40 g/1½ oz
1	Large onion, chopped	1
1	Carrot, chopped	1
1	Stalk celery, sliced	1
2 tbsp	Flour	1½ tbsp
1 tbsp	Tomato purée	1 tbsp
1 lb	Fresh ripe tomatoes	450 g/1 lb
1½ cups	Vegetable stock (or chicken stock)	350 ml/12 fl oz
1 tsp	Sugar	1 tsp
¼ tsp	Paprika	¼ tsp
	Salt and pepper	
1	Bay leaf	1
3–4	Sprigs parsley	3–4
	A sprig of thyme	
2 cups	Milk	450 ml/¾ pint
	Garnish	
4–6 tbsp	Heavy [double] cream (or sour cream)	3½–5 tbsp
1 tbsp	Chopped parsley (or chives)	1 tbsp
	Cheesy croutons (see Index)	

1. Melt the butter and cook the onion, carrot, and celery gently for 5–6 minutes to soften without browning, stirring frequently. Sprinkle in the flour, and mix well. Then stir in the tomato purée and the chopped tomatoes. Add the stock, sugar, salt, pepper, paprika, and herbs. Bring to a boil, stirring constantly. Reduce heat, and simmer for about 30 minutes. Remove the bay leaf.
2. Put the soup through a fine food mill, or blend until smooth in an electric blender. Reheat the soup. In a separate pan, heat the milk to just below boiling point and add to the soup, mixing thoroughly. Adjust seasoning to taste.
3. Serve with a spoonful of cream, a sprinkling of herbs, and cheesy croutons on top of each soup bowl.

Tomato Soup

	00:15		
	00:30	Serves 4–6	South

American	Ingredients	Metric/Imperial
2 slices	Bacon, chopped	2 rashers
1 tbsp	Butter	15 g/½ oz
2	Large onions, finely sliced	2
4–6	Ripe tomatoes, chopped	4–6
1 tbsp	Tomato purée	1 tbsp
2–3	Strips lemon rind	2–3
4 cups	Chicken stock	1 l/1¾ pints
	Salt and pepper	
1 tsp	Sugar	1 tsp
1 tbsp	Parsley	1 tbsp
¼ tsp	Thyme	¼ tsp
1 tsp	Basil	1 tsp
	Garnish	
1 tbsp	Chopped mixed parsley and basil	1 tbsp
	Fried garlic croutons (see Index)	

1. Heat the bacon pieces in a pan. When the fat has run, add the butter. When it has melted, add the onions and cook gently for 5–6 minutes until tender and golden brown. Add the tomatoes and tomato purée, lemon rind, stock, salt, pepper, sugar, and herbs. Bring to a boil. Then simmer for 20 minutes, or until the tomatoes are tender.

2. Put the soup through a food mill or blend in an electric blender. Adjust the seasoning and serve hot, sprinkled with chopped parsley and basil, and with fried garlic croutons.

Iced Tomato Soup Louise

	01:10		
	00:00	Serves 4–6	South

American	Ingredients	Metric/Imperial
1 can (10¾ oz)	Condensed tomato soup	1 tin (300 g/ 10¾ oz)
1½ cups	Evaporated milk	350 ml/12 fl oz
1 cup	Ricotta (or cottage) cheese	225 g/8 oz
	A little grated onion	
1–2 tsp	Grated horseradish	1–2 tsp
	Lemon juice to taste	
	A little sugar	
	Garnish	
4–6 tbsp	Whipped cream	3½–5 tbsp
	Chopped chives or paprika	

1. Blend the canned soup with the milk and cheese. Add the grated onion, horseradish, lemon juice, sugar, and seasoning. Blend again until smooth.

2. Chill well. Serve in soup cups with a spoonful of whipped cream in the center of each bowl and sprinkled with chopped chives or paprika.

Tomato Soup

Iced Tomato and Cucumber Soup

	00:45		
	00:00	Serves 4–6	South

American	Ingredients	Metric/Imperial
1	Cucumber, peeled and diced	1
2 cans (about 14 oz each)	Tomato juice	2 tins (about 400 g/14 oz each)
1–2 tsp	Onion juice	1–2 tsp
1–1½ tsp	Worcestershire sauce	1–1½ tsp
½ tsp	Sugar	½ tsp
2–3 tsp	Lemon juice	2–3 tsp
	Salt and pepper	
	A dash of tabasco	
	Garnish	
4–6 tbsp	Sour cream	3½–5 tbsp
4–6	Slices lemon	4–6
1 tbsp	Chopped chives	1 tbsp
	Brown bread and butter	

1. Peel and dice the cucumber. Sprinkle with salt and leave covered for at least 20–30 minutes. Drain and rinse with cold water.

2. Put the tomato juice into a bowl and add the onion juice (made by crushing small pieces of onion in a garlic press). Add Worcestershire sauce, sugar, lemon juice, salt and pepper, and a dash of tabasco.

3. Add the diced cucumber to tomato soup and ladle into soup bowls. Chill thoroughly.

4. Garnish with a spoonful of sour cream and a thin slice of lemon or a sprinkling of chopped chives in each bowl. Serve brown bread and butter separately.

Spinach Soup

Spinach Soup

| | 00:25 | Serves 4–6 | Midwest |
| | 00:25 | | |

American	Ingredients	Metric/Imperial
1 lb	Fresh spinach (or 1 package frozen spinach)	450 g/1 lb
3 tbsp	Butter	40 g/1½ oz
1	Onion, finely chopped	1
1½ tbsp	Flour	1¼ tbsp
4 cups	White or vegetable stock (or water and chicken cube)	1 l/1¾ pints
3–4	Sprigs parsley (or 1 tbsp dried parsley)	3–4
1	Bay leaf	1
	A squeeze or two of lemon juice	
¼–½ tsp	Powdered mace	¼–½ tsp
½ cup	Cream	125 ml/4 fl oz
	Garnish	
2	Hard-boiled eggs, sliced	2
	Paprika or fried bread croutons or bacon croutons (see Index)	

1. Wash the spinach thoroughly if using fresh spinach; drain and shake off excess water. Melt the butter and cook the onion and spinach gently until the spinach has softened and become limp, without browning. If using frozen spinach, allow block to unfreeze completely during this process. Sprinkle in flour and blend smoothly. Add the stock (or water and cubes). Bring the soup to a boil, stirring constantly. Then add the parsley, bay leaf, and seasoning. Reduce the heat and simmer for 10–12 minutes. Do not overcook as this spoils the green color and fresh flavor.
2. Put the soup through a fine food mill, or blend until smooth in an electric blender. Reheat, adding a little lemon juice. Adjust the seasoning and add the mace. Stir in the cream just before serving.
3. Garnish with slices of hard-boiled egg sprinkled with paprika, or alternatively with fried bread or bacon croutons.

Tomato and Horseradish Soup

| | 00:10 | Serves 4 | South |
| | 00:05 | | |

American	Ingredients	Metric/Imperial
1 can (10¾ oz)	Condensed tomato soup	1 tin (300 g/10¾ oz)
1½ cups	Beef stock (or water)	350 ml/12 fl oz
1–1½ tsp	Fresh horseradish (or ¼–½ tsp dried horseradish)	1–1½ tsp
2 tsp	Tomato purée	2 tsp
1 tbsp	Chopped parsley	1 tbsp
2 tsp	Basil	2 tsp
1 tsp	Sugar	1 tsp
	Salt and pepper	
	Garnish	
4 tbsp	Heavy [double] cream	3½ tbsp
1 tbsp	Chopped parsley	1 tbsp
	Cheese croutons (see Index)	

1. Pour the soup into a pan and add stock or water. Add the horseradish, tomato purée, parsley, basil, sugar, salt, and pepper. Bring to a boil and serve with a spoonful of cream in each bowl and a sprinkling of chopped parsley on top.
2. Serve with cheese croutons.

Potage Solferino

| | 00:30 | Serves 4–6 | New England |
| | 00:40 | | |

American	Ingredients	Metric/Imperial
3	Leeks, sliced	3
2	Small young carrots, thinly sliced	2
2	Medium potatoes, peeled and sliced	2
3 tbsp	Butter	40 g/1½ oz
1	Small clove garlic, crushed (or shake of garlic powder)	1
4	Ripe tomatoes	4
1 tbsp	Chopped parsley	1 tbsp
¼ tsp	Chopped basil	¼ tsp
½	Bay leaf	½
½ tsp	Sugar	½ tsp
4–5 cups	Stock or water	1–1.25 l/1¾–2 pints
2 tsp	Tomato purée	2 tsp

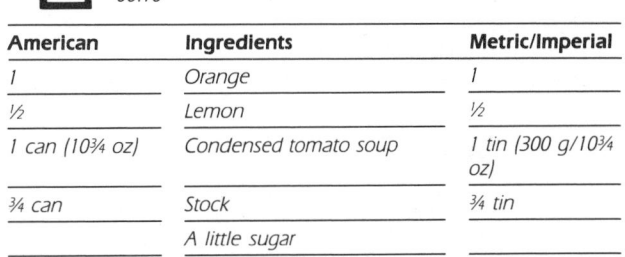

Orange and Canned Tomato Soup

	Garnish	
1	Ripe tomato, peeled, seeded and chopped (or 3–4 tbsp potato dice cooked in boiling salted water)	1 tomato (or 2–3½ tbsp diced potato)
1 tbsp	Chopped parsley	1 tbsp

1. Melt the butter and cook the leeks, carrots, and potatoes gently for 5–6 minutes, stirring constantly to prevent browning. Add the garlic.
2. Dip the tomatoes into boiling water for 10 seconds, then into cold water. Peel and chop the tomatoes, and add to the soup with herbs and seasoning. Pour on the stock or water, and bring the soup to a boil. Then reduce the heat and simmer for 20–30 minutes, or until the vegetables are tender. Remove the bay leaf.
3. Put the soup through a fine food mill or an electric blender, and blend until smooth. Reheat, adding the tomato purée, and adjust the seasoning to taste.
4. Serve hot, garnished with the chopped flesh of one peeled and seeded tomato or potato dice cooked in a little boiling water. Sprinkle with chopped parsley.

Orange and Canned Tomato Soup

00:15
00:10
Serves 4
South

American	Ingredients	Metric/Imperial
1	Orange	1
½	Lemon	½
1 can (10¾ oz)	Condensed tomato soup	1 tin (300 g/10¾ oz)
¾ can	Stock	¾ tin
	A little sugar	
	Salt and pepper	

1. Remove the rind from the orange and lemon with a potato peeler. Cut into match-like strips. Put these into boiling water for 1 minute, then drain and rinse with cold water.
2. Put the can of soup in a pan with the stock; add sugar, salt, and pepper and heat, stirring until smooth. For the last few minutes, add the orange and lemon rind and lastly the juice of the orange and ½ lemon.

Almond Cream Soup

Purée of Turnip Soup

	00:25	Serves 4–6	New England
	00:50		

American	Ingredients	Metric/Imperial
2 cups	Sliced young turnips	225 g/8 oz
2	Medium sliced potatoes	2
1	Small sliced onion	1
3 tbsp	Butter	40 g/1½ oz
1½ tbsp	Flour	1 tbsp
3 cups	White or chicken stock	700 ml/1¼ pints
1 cup	Milk	250 ml/8 fl oz
1 tbsp	Chopped parsley (or 1 tsp paprika)	1 tbsp
	Garnish	
	Bacon croutons (see Index)	

1. Melt the butter and cook the turnips, potatoes, and onion gently until they are tender, 20–30 minutes. Sprinkle in a little flour and blend thoroughly. Pour on the stock and mix well before bringing to a boil. Reduce the heat and simmer for 15 minutes.
2. Put the soup into an electric blender and blend until smooth. Reheat, adding more seasoning, if necessary, and the milk.
3. Sprinkle with parsley or paprika on top, and serve bacon croutons separately.

Almond Cream Soup

	00:30	Serves 4	United States
	00:50		

American	Ingredients	Metric/Imperial
1	Small potato, finely sliced	1
3–4	Spring onions, finely sliced (or 2–3 slices of ordinary onion)	3–4
3–4	Stalks celery, finely sliced	3–4
3 cups	Chicken or white stock	700 ml/1¼ pts
½–¾ cup	Almonds	50–75 g/2–3 oz
1	Small bay leaf	1
3–4	Sprigs parsley	3–4
2 tbsp	Butter	25 g/1 oz
1 tbsp	Flour	1 tbsp
	Salt and pepper	
	A pinch of mace	
4–5 tbsp	Heavy [double] cream	3½–4 tbsp

1. Put the potato, onions, and celery in a pan with the stock, bay leaf, and sprigs of parsley. Simmer gently with lid on until the potato slices are tender.
2. Meanwhile, pour boiling water over the almonds, let stand for a few minutes, then drain and pop almonds out of their skins. Reserve 10–12 whole almonds for garnish, and chop or finely grind the remainder. This can be done in an electric blender but a little stock should be added to liquify it slightly. Add this paste to the pan, and cook for another 20 minutes.
3. Remove the bay leaf and sprigs of parsley. Pour the soup into an electric blender and blend slowly until smooth. Strain through a fine sieve.
4. Melt the butter, add the flour, and stir until smooth off the heat. Add the strained soup slowly, stirring until smooth. Bring to a boil, stirring constantly. Add salt, pepper, and mace, being careful not to overpower the light almond flavor.
5. Cut the remaining almonds into slivers, brown lightly in a cool oven, and sprinkle with a little salt.
6. Add a spoonful of cream to each soup bowl, and at the last moment sprinkle with the crisp brown almonds. The soup can also be served chilled.

Curried Chicken Soup

	00:10	Serves 4–5	South
	00:15		

American	Ingredients	Metric/Imperial
2 tbsp	Margarine or cooking fat	25 g/1 oz
2 tsp	Curry powder	2 tsp
1½ tbsp	Flour	1 tbsp
3 cups	Chicken stock	700 ml/1¼ pints
	Paprika	
	Salt	
1	Egg yolk	1
4 tbsp	Light [single] cream or milk	3½ tbsp
¼–½ cup	Chopped cooked chicken meat or 1–2 tbsp chopped chutney	50–100 g/ 2–4 oz (or 1–1½ tbsp chopped chutney)
2–3	Chives, chopped	2–3

1. Melt the fat in a saucepan. Add the curry powder and flour. Blend well and stir over low heat for about 3 minutes.
2. Gradually add the stock; stir until boiling, and season carefully with paprika and salt to taste.
3. Reduce the heat. Add the egg yolk and cream mixed together and stir until slightly thickened.
4. Add the chicken or chopped chutney and serve sprinkled with chopped chives.

Watercress Soup

00:25
00:35   Serves 4–6   New England

American	Ingredients	Metric/Imperial
2 bunches	Fresh watercress	2 bunches
3 tbsp	Butter	40 g/1½ oz
1	Potato, sliced	1
1	Small onion, finely chopped	1
1 tbsp	Flour	1 tbsp
3 cups	White or chicken stock (or water)	700 ml/1¼ pints
3–4 sprigs	Parsley	3–4
1	Bay leaf	1
2 cups	Milk	450 ml/¾ pints
¼ tsp	Mace	¼ tsp
	A little green coloring (optional)	

	Garnish	
	Watercress sprigs	
4–6 tbsp	Cream	3½–5 tbsp
	Fried bread croutons (see Index)	

1. Wash and pick over the watercress, discarding any yellow leaves. Reserve enough green top-sprigs to make the final garnish, and chop the remaining cress roughly. Melt the butter and cook the potato and onion together for 2–3 minutes before adding the chopped watercress. Continue cooking for 3–4 minutes, stirring constantly to prevent browning. Sprinkle in the flour and blend well. Add the stock and blend together before bringing to a boil. Add the herbs and some seasoning; reduce the heat and simmer until the potato is tender, about 20 minutes.
2. Remove the bay leaf. Put the soup into an electric blender and blend until smooth, or put through a fine food mill or sieve. Return the soup to the pan and reheat gently. At the same time, heat the milk in a separate pan. When almost at boiling point, pour into the watercress mixture—this makes texture of the soup lighter and more delicate. Adjust the seasoning, adding mace and a little green coloring if desired.
3. Serve with a spoonful of cream in each bowl and the reserved watercress sprigs on top. Fried bread croutons are also excellent with this soup.

Watercress Soup

Cream of Curry Soup

00:20
00:30　　Serves 4–6　　South

American	Ingredients	Metric/Imperial
3 tbsp	Butter	40 g/1½ oz
1	Large onion, chopped	1
1	Cooking apple, peeled and cored	1
½ tbsp	Curry powder or paste (or more if desired)	½ tbsp
1 tbsp	Flour	1 tbsp
2 tbsp	Rice	1½ tbsp
4–5 cups	Chicken stock	1–1.25 l/ 1¾–2 pints
1 tsp	Sweet chutney	1 tsp
2 tsp	Coconut	2 tsp
1	Bay leaf	1
3–4	Sprigs parsley	3–4
1	Slice lemon	1
½ cup	Cream	125 ml/4 fl oz
Garnish		
1 tbsp	Chopped parsley (or paprika)	1 tbsp
	Lemon wedges	
½–1 cup	Plain boiled rice	100–225 g/ 4–8 oz

1. Melt the butter, and cook the onion and apple gently for 5–6 minutes to soften without browning. Stir in curry powder or paste and cook for 1 minute. Remove from the heat and sprinkle in the flour. Blend well. Then add the rice, stock, chutney, and coconut. Bring to a boil, stirring constantly. Reduce the heat. Add the seasonings, herbs, and a slice of lemon. Cover the pan and simmer for 15–20 minutes to cook the rice.
2. Remove the bay leaf and lemon. Put the soup into an electric blender and blend until smooth. Reheat and adjust the seasoning. Just before serving, stir in the cream.
3. Sprinkle with chopped parsley or paprika, and serve lemon wedges and plain boiled rice separately.

Cream of Chestnut Soup

00:50
01:00　　Serves 4–6　　United States

American	Ingredients	Metric/Imperial
1 lb	Fresh peeled chestnuts (buy 2 lb to produce this amount) or a 450 g/1 lb can [tin] chestnut purée (unsweetened)	450 g/1 lb
3 tbsp	Butter	40 g/1½ oz
1	Large onion, sliced	1
2	Small carrots, sliced	2
1	Stalk celery, sliced	1

4–5 cups	Ham, chicken or brown stock (or water and bouillon [stock] cubes)	1–1.25 l/ 1¾–2 pints
1 tbsp	Chopped parsley (or 3–4 sprigs parsley)	1 tbsp
	A pinch of thyme	
1	Bay leaf	1
	A pinch of nutmeg	
1 cup	Cream	250 ml/8 fl oz
Garnish		
2–3	Cooking apples	2–3
4 tbsp	Butter	50 g/2 oz
1–2 tsp	Sugar	1–2 tsp
1 tbsp	Chopped parsley	1 tbsp

1. If using fresh chestnuts, prepare as follows: Make a small slit in the top of each nut and place in a well-greased pan in a moderate oven for 10–15 minutes to loosen both the outer and inner skin. Remove both skins. If using canned chestnut purée, add to the soup after the vegetables have been cooked.
2. Melt the butter, and add the onion, carrots, and celery. Mix well over gentle heat before adding the chestnuts. Cover the pan, and cook for 3–4 minutes, shaking the pan occasionally. Add the stock, herbs, and seasoning and simmer for 20–30 minutes, or until the chestnuts and vegetables are tender.
3. Remove the bay leaf. Put the soup into an electric blender and blend until smooth, or put it through a fine food mill. Return the soup to the pan and reheat. Season to taste. Add the cream just before serving or put a spoonful of cream in each soup bowl.
4. Make the apple-ring garnish by peeling and coring 2–3 cooking apples and cutting them into rings. Melt the butter and fry the apple slices until golden brown on each side, sprinkling the slices with a little sugar.
5. Float 1–2 slices of apple in each soup bowl and sprinkle with chopped parsley.

Cream of Chicken Soup

00:25
00:40　　Serves 4–6　　Mid Atlantic

American	Ingredients	Metric/Imperial
1	Small onion, chopped	1
2	Stalks celery, sliced	2
4–5	Button mushrooms, sliced	4–5
3 tbsp	Butter	40 g/1½ oz
2 tbsp	Flour	2 tbsp
5 cups	Well-flavored chicken stock	1.25 l/2 pints
	1 small bay leaf, 2–3 sprigs of parsley tied together	
¼ tsp	Mace	¼ tsp
¼–½ cup	Chopped cooked white chicken meat	75–100 g/3–4 oz

Chinese Chicken Soup

	Liaison	
2	Egg yolks	2
½ cup	Cream	125 ml/4 fl oz
	Garnish	
1 tbsp	Chopped tarragon (or 2 tbsp chopped parsley)	1 tbsp

1. Wash the chicken giblets, removing the livers. Reserve these for garnish.

2. Peel and slice the onion, carrots, and celery. Put these into a pan and sauté with the giblets. Add the stock, herbs, and peppercorns. Bring slowly to a boil. Reduce the heat, and simmer for 1–1½ hours until the vegetables are tender and the giblets well cooked.

3. Melt the butter and blend in the flour; cook 3–5 minutes. Strain onto the chicken stock; blend thoroughly and bring to a boil, stirring constantly. Cook for a few minutes. Taste for seasoning.

4. Cook the chicken livers gently in 1 tablespoon butter [25 g/1 oz] for about 5–8 minutes, depending on their size. Chop the livers roughly and divide among the soup bowls before adding the hot soup. Sprinkle with chopped parsley.

Chinese Chicken Soup

00:20
00:10
Serves 4–6
Midwest

American	Ingredients	Metric/Imperial
4–5	Spring onions	4–5
6	Small mushrooms, finely sliced	6
5 cups	Strongly flavored clear chicken stock	1.25 l/2 pints
2 cups	Shredded white chicken meat	225 g/8 oz
2	Beaten eggs	2
	Salt and pepper	
2–3 tsp	Soy sauce	2–3 tsp

1. Finely slice the white part of the spring onions and reserve the green part for garnish. Heat the chicken stock until boiling. Add the mushrooms and onions, and cook for 2–3 minutes. Add the shredded white chicken meat.

2. Beat the eggs until frothy with a little salt and pepper.

3. Stir the soup well. Then pour the beaten egg steadily into the soup, stirring constantly, so that it remains in shreds. Allow to cook for a minute or two to set the egg. Add soy sauce to taste and serve in soup bowls, sprinkled with the finely chopped green parts of the spring onions.

Chicken Giblet Soup

	00:20			
	01:50	Serves 4–6	Mid Atlantic	

American	Ingredients	Metric/Imperial
2 sets	Chicken giblets	2 sets
1	Large onion	1
2–3	Carrots	2–3
2–3	Stalks celery	2–3
4 cups	Chicken stock	1 1/1¾ pints
	4–5 parsley stalks, 1 sprig of thyme, 1 bay leaf tied together	
6	Peppercorns	6
2 tbsp	Butter	25 g/1 oz
2 tbsp	Flour	1½ tbsp
	Garnish	
1 tbsp	Butter	15 g/½ oz
2	Chicken livers	2
2 tbsp	Chopped parsley	1½ tbsp

1. Wash the chicken giblets, removing the livers. Reserve these for garnish.
2. Peel and slice the onion, carrots, and celery. Put these into a pan and sauté with the giblets. Add the stock, herbs, and peppercorns. Bring slowly to a boil. Reduce the heat, and simmer for 1–1½ hours until the vegetables are tender and the giblets well cooked. (Remove the skin and carcass, or strain the soup into another pan.)
3. Melt the butter and blend in the flour; cook 3–5 minutes. Strain onto the chicken stock; blend thoroughly and bring to a boil, stirring constantly. Cook for a few minutes. Taste for seasoning.
4. Cook the chicken livers gently in 1 tablespoon butter [25 g/1 oz] for about 5–8 minutes, depending on their size. Chop the livers roughly and divide among the soup bowls before adding the hot soup. Sprinkle with chopped parsley.

Chicken Noodle Soup

	00:05			
	00:20	Serves 4–6	Mid Atlantic	

American	Ingredients	Metric/Imperial
4–5 cups	Well-flavored clear chicken stock	1–1.25 1/ 1¾–2 pints
8 oz	Fine egg noodles	225 g/8 oz
2 tbsp	Finely chopped parsley	1½ tbsp

1. Bring the stock to a boil. Add the noodles, stirring constantly, and boil slowly for about 15 minutes, or for the time stated on the package of noodles. Stir frequently to prevent the noodles from sticking. Add seasoning to taste.
2. Serve hot in soup bowls and sprinkle liberally with finely chopped parsley.

Chicken Gumbo

	00:20			
	00:40	Serves 4–6	Southwest	

American	Ingredients	Metric/Imperial
1	Large onion, chopped	1
2 tbsp	Butter or bacon fat	25 g/1 oz
1½ cups	Canned [tinned] tomatoes	425 g/15 oz
½	Green pepper, seeded and chopped	½
¾–1 cup	Canned [tinned] okra (or ready-cooked okra)	275 g/10 oz
½ cup	Rice	100 g/4 oz
4–5 cups	Strongly flavored chicken stock	1–1.25 1/ 1¾–2 pints
1–2 cups	Chopped cooked chicken	100–225 g/ 4–8 oz
1 tbsp	Chopped parsley	1 tbsp
1 tsp	Chopped tarragon	1 tsp
½ cup	Cooked corn (optional)	50 g/2 oz
	Garnish	
	Fried bread croutons (see Index)	

1. Melt the butter or bacon fat in a soup pot and cook the onion gently for 5–6 minutes until tender but not brown. Add the chopped tomatoes, chopped pepper, okra, and rice. Pour in the stock and mix thoroughly. Add salt and pepper if necessary. Simmer until the vegetables are tender, about 20–30 minutes.
2. Adjust the seasoning and add the chopped cooked chicken and herbs. If available, cooked corn can also be added. Reheat and serve hot.
3. This soup can be served on its own as a main course, with fried bread croutons or thick bread and butter.

Chicken and Ham Soup

	00:10			
	00:08	Serves 4–6	New England	

American	Ingredients	Metric/Imperial
4–5 cups	Clear chicken stock (or consomme)	1–1.25 1/ 1¾–2 pints
½ cup	White wine	125 ml/4 fl oz
2	Slices mild ham	2
½ cup	Lightly cooked fresh peas	50 g/2 oz
1 tsp	Chopped tarragon (or ½ tsp dried)	1 tsp
1 tbsp	Chopped parsley	1 tbsp
1 tbsp	Gelatin [gelatine] for cold soup	1 tbsp

1. If serving hot, heat the clear chicken stock, adding at the last minute a glass of white wine, the shredded ham which has had all the fat removed, the lightly cooked green peas, and herbs. Serve hot. Sprinkle with chopped parsley.

2. If serving cold and using chicken stock that is not already jellied, put the gelatin to soak in ½ cup [125 ml/4 fl oz] of stock. When it has swollen, heat gently and add to the heated stock. Skim off any grease carefully, add the white wine and let it cool in a bowl. When it is on the point of setting, add the shreds of ham and the peas, and spoon into soup bowls. Chill well and serve garnished with chopped parsley or watercress leaves.

Turkey and Chestnut Soup

	00:20		
	01:45	Serves 4–6	Mid Atlantic

American	Ingredients	Metric/Imperial
	Carcass of one cooked turkey	
3–4 tbsp	Chestnut stuffing (see Index)	2–3½ tbsp
2	Onions, sliced	2
2–3	Carrots, sliced	2–3
2–3	Stalks celery, sliced	2–3
	Several sprigs of parsley	
1	Bay leaf	1
5–6 cups	Water	1.25–1.5 l/ 2–2¼ pints
1 tbsp	Butter	15 g/½ oz
¾ tbsp	All-purpose [plain] flour	¾ tbsp
	Garnish	
5–6	Chestnuts	5–6
1 tbsp	Chopped parsley	1 tbsp

1. Remove the remaining chestnut stuffing from the cold turkey and reserve. Take off any pieces of turkey meat which can be used as a garnish. Break up the turkey carcass and put it into a large pan with the sliced onions, carrots, celery, and herbs. Cover with water and simmer until well flavored. Avoid boiling hard as this makes the stock cloudy. Strain.

2. Put the chestnut stuffing into an electric blender with a cup [250 ml/8 fl oz] of turkey stock and blend until smooth. Turn into a pan and add the remaining stock, seasoning, and the turkey meat. Cook together for a few minutes. If the soup is too thin, blend the butter and flour together to make a paste, add to the soup in small pieces, and stir until thickened.

3. Bring to a boil. Serve the soup hot with a few cooked chestnuts, fried in butter and broken into pieces. Sprinkle chopped parsley on top.

Turkey and Chestnut Soup

Chicken Chowder

00:25
01:45
Serves 5–6
New England

American	Ingredients	Metric/Imperial
1	*Chicken carcass and giblets*	*1*
7½ cups	*Cold water*	*2 l/3 pints*
1	*Onion, peeled and sliced*	*1*
3	*Celery stalks (with leaves), chopped*	*3*
1	*Carrot, peeled and diced*	*1*
1 tsp	*Salt*	*1 tsp*
1 lb	*Cream-style corn*	*450 g/1 lb*
2	*Eggs (1 hard-boiled, 1 beaten)*	*2*
1 cup	*Flour*	*100 g/4 oz*
¼ tsp	*Salt*	*¼ tsp*

1. Break up the carcass and put it with the giblets into a large kettle. Add the water, onion, celery, carrot, and salt. Cover and simmer for about 1½ hours. Skim the fat and scum off the top.
2. Remove the pieces of carcass and giblets, cut off all the meat, and return it to the pan.
3. Add the corn and simmer for 10 minutes. Then add the finely chopped hard-boiled egg. Adjust the seasoning.
4. Sift the flour and salt together; stir in the beaten egg with a fork until the mixture looks like cornmeal. Drop in spoonfuls into the hot soup a few minutes before serving.

Okra Chowder

00:20
01:05
Serves 5–6
New England

American	Ingredients	Metric/Imperial
4 cups	*Okra*	*1 kg/2¼ lb*
¼ cup	*Bacon or other cooking fat*	*25 g/1 oz*
2 cups	*Diced celery*	*225 g/8 oz*
1	*Green pepper, seeded and diced*	*1*
1	*Small onion, peeled and chopped*	*1*
2	*Large tomatoes, peeled, and seeded and chopped*	*2*
1 tsp	*Brown sugar*	*1 tsp*
¼ tsp	*Paprika*	*¼ tsp*
4 cups	*Boiling water*	*1 l/1¾ pts*
	Bacon to garnish (optional)	

1. Cut the stems from the okra and cut into slices.
2. Heat the bacon fat in a saucepan; add the okra, celery, green pepper, and onion. Sauté for about 5 minutes.
3. Add the tomatoes, sugar, paprika, and boiling water. Cover and simmer for about 1 hour, or until the vegetables are tender. Add seasoning to taste.
4. A little diced, crisply cooked bacon sprinkled on top is a pleasant addition.

Game Soup

00:20
00:25
Serves 4–6
New England

American	Ingredients	Metric/Imperial
5 cups	*Well-flavored game stock (made from carcass and meat of any game available)*	*1.25 l/2 pints*
1	*Onion, diced*	*1*
2	*Small carrots, diced*	*2*
2	*Stalks celery, sliced*	*2*
	1 bay leaf, 1 sprig of thyme, 3–4 sprigs of parsley, tied together	
1 tbsp	*Red currant or other sharp jelly*	*1 tbsp*
¼ cup	*Port (or sherry)*	*60 ml/2 fl oz*
½ cup	*Diced cooked game (if available)*	*100 g/4 oz*
	A dash of lemon juice	
	Garnish	
1 tbsp	*Chopped parsley*	*1 tbsp*
	Fried bread croutons (see Index)	

1. Put strained stock into a soup pot, having first skimmed off the fat. Add the herbs and diced raw vegetables, and cook these in the simmering stock until they are tender. Avoid boiling the soup as this makes the stock cloudy. Add the red currant or other sharp jelly, and let it dissolve. Remove the herbs and add port (or sherry) and the diced cooked game, if available. Heat through. Season to taste, and add a dash of lemon juice.
2. Sprinkle with chopped parsley, and serve with fried bread croutons.

Fresh Corn Chowder

00:30
00:25
Serves 4–6
New England

American	Ingredients	Metric/Imperial
2	*Potatoes, peeled and diced*	*2*
1½ cups	*Fresh corn*	*350 g/12 oz*
3 cups	*Salted water*	*700 ml/1¼ pints*
½	*Green pepper, seeded and chopped*	*½*
3 tbsp	*Butter or bacon fat*	*40 g/1½ oz*
1	*Onion, chopped*	*1*
2	*Stalks celery, chopped*	*2*
2 tbsp	*Flour*	*1½ tbsp*
2 cups	*Milk*	*450 ml/¾ pint*
	1 bay leaf, 3–4 sprigs of parsley, tied together	
	Salt and pepper	
¼ tsp	*Mace or nutmeg*	*¼ tsp*
½ cup	*Cream*	*125 ml/4 fl oz*

	Garnish	
2 tbsp	Chopped parsley	1½ tbsp
	Fried bread croutons or cheesy croutons (see Index)	

1. Pre-cook the diced potatoes together with the fresh corn in the lightly salted water until tender, or about 6–8 minutes. Then strain carefully, reserving 2 cups [450 ml/¾ pint] of the water for chowder.

2. Melt the butter or bacon fat and cook the green pepper, onion, and celery for 6–7 minutes, until golden brown. Sprinkle in the flour and blend thoroughly, then add the reserved potato water. Mix this in thoroughly and add the milk, bay leaf, parsley sprigs, salt, pepper, and mace or nutmeg. Bring to a boil and add the green pepper. Cook for 2–3 minutes.

3. Add the potato and corn, remove from the heat, and allow the flavors to blend for at least 10–15 minutes. Then remove the herbs. Reheat the chowder and adjust the seasoning. At the last minute, add the cream and reheat without boiling.

4. Sprinkle with chopped parsley or paprika, and serve with fried bread croutons or cheesy croutons.

Canned Corn Chowder

 00:05 / 00:08　　Serves 4　　New England

American	Ingredients	Metric/Imperial
1 small can (8 oz)	Corn and pimento mixed	1 small tin (225 g/8 oz)
1 can (10¾ oz)	Condensed chicken or celery soup	1 tin (300 g/10¾ oz)
1 tsp	Onion powder or dehydrated onion	1 tsp
	Salt and pepper	
	A pinch of sugar	
1 tsp	Curry powder (optional)	1 tsp
1½–2 cups	Milk	375–450 ml/½–¾ pint
½	Chicken cube	½
¼–½ cup	Cream	60–125 ml/2–4 fl oz
1 tbsp	Butter	15 g/½ oz
	Garnish	
1 tbsp	Chopped parsley	15 g/½ oz

1. Mix the can of soup with the can of mixed corn and pimento. Add the onion powder or dehydrated onion, salt, pepper, a pinch of sugar and, if desired, 1 teaspoon curry powder.

2. Heat together, adding the milk and the chicken cube. Cook gently for 5–6 minutes without boiling. Just before serving, add a little cream and put a small lump of butter on top of each soup bowl. Sprinkle with chopped parsley, and serve with plain crackers.

Cod Soup with Orange

Cod Soup with Orange

 00:25 / 00:20　　Serves 4　　New England

American	Ingredients	Metric/Imperial
⅔ lb	Cod fillets (frozen or fresh)	300 g/11 oz
4 cups	Fish stock	1 l/1¾ pts
5–6	Potatoes, cut into cubes	5–6
1	Whole fennel, cut into cubes	1
1	Leek, shredded	1
1 can (8 oz)	Crushed tomatoes	1 tin (225 g/8 oz)
2	Cloves garlic	2
	Salt and pepper	
	Juice from ½ orange or 2–3 tbsp juice concentrate	
2 tbsp	Chopped parsley	2 tbsp

1. Allow the fish to partially thaw, if frozen, and cut it into 1– to 1½–inch cubes.

2. Bring the stock to a boil in a pot. Add the vegetables and garlic. Season with salt and pepper, and let the soup simmer for 10–12 minutes until the vegetables feel soft. Add the orange juice and simmer the soup for another 3–4 minutes.

3. Serve the soup piping hot with snipped parsley sprinkled on top.

Lobster Bisque

	00:45			
	01:00	Serves 6	New England	

American	Ingredients	Metric/Imperial
1 large	Freshly boiled lobster	1 large
5–6 cups	Fish stock	1.25 l/2–2¼ pts
1	Small onion, sliced	1
1	Carrot, sliced	1
2	Stalks celery, sliced	2
	1 bay leaf, 3–4 sprigs of parsley, tied together	
	Salt and pepper	
5 tbsp	Butter	65 g/2½ oz
2½ tbsp	Flour	1¾ tbsp
¼ tsp	Mace or nutmeg	¼ tsp
1 cup	Cream	250 ml/8 fl oz
3–4 tbsp	Sherry (or brandy)	2–3½ tbsp

1. Split the freshly boiled lobster down the back with a sharp knife and remove the intestine, which looks like a long black thread down the center of the back. Also remove the stomach sac from the head and the tough gills. Crack the claws, remove the meat, and add this to the back meat. If the lobster is female and there is red coral or roe, save this for garnish. Also reserve the greenish curd from the head.
2. Break up all the lobster shells and put them into a pan with the fish stock. Add the onion, carrot, celery, herbs, salt, and pepper. Cover the pan and simmer for 30–45 minutes.
3. Meanwhile, cut the lobster meat into chunks. Pound the coral roe with 2 tablespoons butter [25 g/1 oz] to use as garnish and to color the soup.
4. Melt 3 tablespoons [40 g/1½ oz] butter in a pot, and stir in the flour until smoothly blended. Cook for a minute or two before adding the strained lobster stock. Blend until smooth and then bring to a boil, stirring constantly. Reduce heat, and simmer for 4–5 minutes before adding the lobster meat. Remove herbs. Add the mace or nutmeg, and adjust the seasoning. Lastly, add the cup of hot cream and the sherry (or brandy).
5. Serve in soup bowls with a piece of the coral butter in each bowl; sprinkle with paprika.

1½–2 lb	Haddock or cod	675–900 g/ 1½–2 lb
1 (2-oz)	Piece of fat salt port	1 (50 g/2 oz)
1	Onion, peeled and chopped	1
8	Medium potatoes, diced	8
2 cups	Boiling water	450 ml/¾ pint
1 qt	Milk, scalded	1 l/1¾ pints
6	Crackers [dry biscuits] crumbled	6
2 tbsp	Margarine	25 g/1 oz

1. Wash the fish, put it into a pan, and just cover with cold salted water. Cover the pan, bring slowly to a boil, and simmer for 5 minutes. Drain and reserve the stock. Remove the skin and any bone from the fish.
2. Cut the pork into small pieces, put it into a saucepan, and fry until the fat renders. Remove the crackling, and drain on paper towels [kitchen paper].
3. Put the onion into the pan with the pork fat, and sauté until soft. Add the potato and boiling water, and boil for 5 minutes. Then add the fish and the reserved fish stock. Bring to a boil, and simmer for 15 minutes.
4. Add the milk, and adjust the seasoning to taste. Reheat, and add the crackers and margarine. (If the chowder is too thick, add a little more milk.)
5. Serve hot, with the pork crackling sprinkled on top.

Clam Chowder

	00:45			
	00:45	Serves 4	New England	

American	Ingredients	Metric/Imperial
3–4 qt	Clams in shells, preferably hard backs (or 1½–2 cups chopped canned clams)	350–450 g/ ¾–1 lb
2 cups	Water	450 ml/¾ pint
1–1½ inch cube	Fat salt pork (or 2 slices of fat bacon)	2.5–3.75 cm cube (or 2 rashers)
1	Onion, finely sliced	1
1 cup	Diced potato	100 g/4 oz
1	Bay leaf	1
1 tbsp	Parsley	1 tbsp
¼ tsp	Thyme	¼ tsp
1–1½ cups	Chicken stock if using canned clams; reduce to ¾ cup (175 ml/6 fl oz if using raw clams)	250–375 ml/8–12 fl oz
2 cups	Canned [tinned] tomatoes	450 g/1 lb
½	Green pepper, seeded and diced	½
2 tbsp	Butter	25 g/1 oz
	Paprika	

1. If using fresh clams, scrub the shells well and wash carefully in several changes of cold water. Put into a soup pot and add 2 cups [450 ml/¾ pint] of water. Cover the pot tightly and bring to a boil slowly. When the boiling point is reached, remove the pot from the heat and leave for a minute. Strain through muslin (to catch any sand) and reserve the juice. Cool the clams, remove from their shells, and chop. If using canned clams, merely chop, drain, and reserve liquid.
2. Chop the fat salt pork or fat bacon, and heat gently until the fat melts and the bacon is crisp. Remove any crisp pieces of pork or bacon and reserve.
3. Cook the onion gently in fat for 4–5 minutes without browning. Add the potato, bay leaf, parsley, and thyme. Pour on the stock, heat gently to boiling point, and cook for 10 minutes, adding seasoning to taste. Add the tomatoes and green peppers. Cook for 5–7 minutes.
4. Add the chopped clams and their liquid, and cook for long enough to heat through thoroughly without boiling. Add crispy pieces of bacon. Just before serving, stir in the butter. Place in soup plates and sprinkle with paprika.
5. Serve with plain crackers [dry biscuits], which can be crumbled into the chowder if desired.

Shrimp Bisque

Shrimp Bisque

🔻 00:45
🍲 00:50   Serves 4–6   Pacific Southwest

American	Ingredients	Metric/Imperial
2 lb	Shrimp [prawns]	900 g/2 lb
3 cups	Chicken stock	700 ml/1¼ pts
3 tbsp	Butter	40 g/1½ oz
1	Onion, sliced	1
1	Carrot, sliced	1
1	Stalk celery, sliced	1
3 tbsp	Rice	2 tbsp
1	Bay leaf	1
3–4	Sprigs parsley (or 1 tbsp dried parsley)	3–4 sprigs
	A squeeze of lemon juice	
¼ tsp	Ground mace	¼ tsp
1 cup	Heavy [double] cream	250 ml/8 fl oz
3 tbsp	Brandy or sherry	2 tbsp

1. Remove the shells from the shrimp, and wash in cold water. Reserve ½ cup [100 g/4 oz] shrimp for garnish. Put the shells into a pan with the stock, and simmer gently for 20 minutes.
2. Melt the butter, and cook the onion, carrot, and celery for 4–5 minutes to soften. Add the rice, the shrimp (roughly chopped), the herbs, lemon juice, and seasoning. Cook together for a minute. Then strain the stock over. Bring to a boil and simmer for 20 minutes.
3. Remove the bay leaf. Put the soup into an electric blender and blend until smooth, or put through a fine food mill or sieve.
4. Return the soup to the pan; add the reserved shrimp. Reheat and adjust the seasoning. Add the heated cream and, just before serving, add the brandy or sherry.

Mock Bouillabaisse

Fine Fish Soup

	00:30	Serves 4	New England
	00:30		

American	Ingredients	Metric/Imperial
1 (2–3 lb)	Whole white fish (cod, haddock, hake)	1 (900 g–1.25 kg/ 2–3 lb)
1–2	Leeks	1–2
1½ qts	Water	1.5 l/2½ pts
1 tbsp	Salt	1 tbsp
½ tsp	White peppercorns	½ tsp
2	Bay leaves	2
1	Sprig thyme	1
	Several sprigs parsley	
2	Potatoes, sliced	2
3	Tomatoes, peeled and cut in pieces	3
1–2	Cloves garlic, crushed	1–2
2 tbsp	Butter or margarine	25 g/1 oz
½–¾ lb	Raw shrimp [prawns], shelled and deveined	225–350 g/ 8–12 oz
½ cup	White wine	125 ml/4 fl oz
	Parsley and dill	

1. Fillet the fish or ask your fish dealer to do so, saving the head, skin, and bones. Put all trimmings in a pot. Wash the leeks carefully and put the green part in the pot. Add water, salt, peppercorns, bay leaves, thyme, and parsley. Let it boil, covered, for 20 minutes.
2. Sauté the potatoes, tomatoes, and garlic in the butter or margarine for 5 minutes over low heat. Add the fish stock, which has been strained. Cut the fish fillets in pieces and let them simmer with the shrimp and white wine for about 5 minutes.
3. Sprinkle with parsley and dill and serve with crisp, warm, white bread.

Mock Bouillabaisse

	00:30	Serves 6–8	Pacific Southwest
	00:35		

American	Ingredients	Metric/Imperial
½ cup	Olive oil	125 ml/4 fl oz
2	Medium onions, chopped	2
2	Leeks, chopped	2
2	Carrots, chopped	2
1–2	Cloves garlic, crushed	1–2
2 lb	Mixed fish: red snapper, flounder, whiting, halibut, perch, red mullet, haddock, eel	900 g/2 lb
4 fresh or ½ cup canned	Tomatoes	4 fresh or 150 g/ 5 oz tinned
1	Bay leaf	1
1 tbsp	Chopped fennel	1 tbsp
	A pinch of saffron soaked in boiling water	
1	Sprig thyme	1
4–5	Parsley stalks, chopped	4–5
2–3	Thinly peeled pieces of orange zest	2–3
3 cups	Fish stock	700 ml/1¼ pts
	Salt and pepper	
1 cup	Shrimp [prawns], clams, and lobster meat	225 g/8 oz
1 tsp	Lemon juice	1 tsp
1 cup	White wine	250 ml/8 fl oz
6–8	Slices French bread	6–8
	Garnish	
2 tbsp	Butter	25 g/1 oz
1	Clove garlic, crushed	1
2 tbsp	Chopped parsley	1½ tbsp

1. Heat the oil in a large pan. Add the onions, leeks, carrots, and garlic. Cook slowly until golden brown, stirring frequently to prevent burning.
2. Add the fish, which should be boneless and cut into chunks. Add the peeled, chopped tomatoes (or canned tomatoes), bay leaf, fennel, saffron, thyme, parsley, orange zest, fish stock, salt, and pepper. Cover the pan and cook for 15–20 minutes.
3. Then add the shellfish, leaving the shrimp whole but cutting the clam or lobster meat into chunks (canned minced clams and canned lobster meat can be used). Bring to a boil and cook for 6–8 minutes. Then add lemon juice and wine. Reheat for a few more minutes, and adjust the seasoning.
4. While the soup is cooking, cut the French bread into ½-inch slices and put into a warm oven to bake until hard. Mix the softened butter with a crushed clove of garlic; add pepper and salt. Spread this paste onto the bread slices.
5. Put a slice of bread into the bottom of each soup bowl. Carefully spoon the pieces of fish and shellfish into the soup bowls, dividing equally; then spoon over the broth, sprinkle with chopped parsley, and serve at once.

Fine Fish Soup

White Fish Chowder

White Fish Chowder

 00:25
01:00

Serves 4–6   New England

American	Ingredients	Metric/Imperial
1 lb	Fresh cod, haddock or halibut, filleted	450 g/1 lb
	Head, skin and bones of fish	
2 cups	Water	450 ml/¾ pt
2	Onions (1 sliced, 1 chopped)	2
1	Carrot, sliced	1
1	Bay leaf	1
3–4 sprigs	Parsley (or 1 tbsp dried parsley)	3–4 sprigs (or 1 tbsp dried)
	Salt and pepper	
1 cube	Fat salt pork (about 1 inch) or 2–3 slices of fat bacon	1 cube
1 cup	Diced potatoes	225 g/8 oz
2 cups	Milk	450 ml/¾ pt
⅛ tsp	Ground mace or nutmeg	⅛ tsp
1 tbsp	Chopped fennel	1 tbsp
1 tbsp	Chopped parsley	1 tbsp
2 tbsp	Butter	25 g/1 oz

1. Wash the fish skin, head, and bones in cold water, and put into a pan with the water. Add 1 onion, carrot, bay leaf, parsley sprigs, salt, and pepper. Bring slowly to a boil, skimming as necessary. Reduce the heat, and simmer for 15–20 minutes. Strain and reserve the liquid for the chowder.

2. Chop the fat salt pork or bacon, and cook slowly until the fat melts. Remove the crispy pieces of bacon, and reserve for garnish.

3. Chop the second onion and add to the hot fat. Cook gently until tender. Then add the diced potatoes and the fish stock. Cook for 5–6 minutes before adding the fish chunks. Then simmer until the potatoes are tender and the fish cooked, about 10 minutes.

4. Bring the milk to nearly boiling point and add to the fish mixture with the seasoning and herbs. Stir in the butter and serve at once.

Moules Marinière

 01:15
00:25

Serves 4   United States

American	Ingredients	Metric/Imperial
40–50	Mussels, fresh and unopened	40–50
1	Onion (or 4–5 shallots)	1
1	Carrot	1
1	Stalk celery	1
1	Clove garlic	1
1 cup	White wine	250 ml/8 fl oz
1 cup	Water	250 ml/8 fl oz
2 tbsp	Chopped parsley	1½ tbsp
1	Bay leaf	1
	A pinch of thyme	
	Pepper	
3 tbsp	Butter	40 g/1½ oz
3 tbsp	Flour	2 tbsp

1. Wash the mussels and scrub thoroughly to remove any weed or sand. Knock or scrape off barnacles. Remove the beards. Examine mussels carefully and, if any are not tightly closed, discard immediately, as they are poisonous if not alive when cooked. Soak the mussels in plenty of cold water.

2. Meanwhile, chop the onion or shallots, peel and chop the carrot, and slice the celery. Crush the garlic and add to the pan with wine, water, 1 tablespoon of chopped parsley, the bay leaf, thyme, and ground black pepper. Bring to a boil and then simmer for 6–8 minutes.

3. Drain the mussels and add to the pan. Cover tightly with a lid and simmer for 6–8 minutes, shaking the pan frequently to make sure that all mussels are covered by liquid. Remove from heat as soon as the mussels open their shells.

4. Strain off the liquid and reserve. Remove the mussels from the pan and carefully remove half of each shell. If serving for a party, carefully remove the inner part of beard; otherwise, each diner can do this for himself at the table. Put the half shells holding the fish into a deep dish and keep warm.

5. Put the cooking liquid into a pan. Blend the butter and flour into a paste, and add to the liquid a little at a time. Bring slowly to a boil, whisking constantly. Add the second tablespoon of chopped parsley. Adjust seasoning, and pour over the mussels.

6. Serve in deep soup plates.

Pink Fish Soup

| | 00:35 | | |
| 01:10 | | Serves 6 | United States |

American	Ingredients	Metric/Imperial
1 lb	Filleted white fish	450 g/1 lb
	Stock	
	Skin, bones and heads of several fish	
5 cups	Water	1.25 l/2 pints
2	Onions	2
1	Carrot	1
	Several sprigs of parsley (or 1 tbsp chopped parsley)	
1	Bay leaf	1
1 sprig fresh (or ¼ tsp dried)	Chopped thyme	1 sprig fresh (or ¼ tsp dried)
6	Peppercorns	6
½ tsp	Salt	½ tsp
	Soup	
3 tbsp	Butter	40 g/1½ oz
1	Onion, finely chopped	1
2	Small carrots, finely sliced	2
2	Leeks, sliced	2
1	Stalk celery, sliced	1
1	Clove garlic, crushed	1
2 tbsp	Flour	1½ tbsp
2 tbsp	Tomato purée	1½ tbsp
1 cup	Canned tomatoes, sieved	275 g/10 oz
	Sugar and mace or nutmeg to taste	
1 tbsp	Chopped parsley and fennel	1 tbsp
½ cup	Peeled fresh (or canned) shrimp [prawns] or flaked, cooked (or canned) salmon	100 g/4 oz
	Garnish	
	Paprika	
	Garlic croutons (see Index)	

1. Skin and fillet the fish if not already prepared. Cut the fish into bite-sized chunks, and put in the refrigerator while making the stock.

2. Wash the skin, head and bones of fish and put it in a pan with 5 cups [1.25 l/2 pts] of water, peeled and quartered onions, the carrot, herbs, peppercorns, and salt. Bring to a boil. Then lower the heat, and simmer gently for 20–30 minutes. Strain and reserve the stock.

3. Melt the butter. Add the onion, carrots, leeks, celery, and garlic, and cook gently for 5–6 minutes covered, until they are tender. Sprinkle in the flour and blend well. Add the tomato purée and tomatoes, stirring until well mixed. Add the seasoning and herbs; cover the pan and cook gently for 10–15 minutes. Pour in the fish stock, add the fish chunks, bring the soup to a boil, and simmer for 10 minutes.

4. Add the shrimp, flaked cooked salmon, or canned salmon. Heat through and adjust the seasoning. Sprinkle with paprika, and serve with garlic croutons.

Consomme Madrilene

Consomme Madrilene

| | 00:30 | | |
| 00:50 | | Serves 4–6 | South |

American	Ingredients	Metric/Imperial
1 lb	Ripe tomatoes	450 g/1 lb
5 cups	Well-flavored, clear jellied chicken stock	1.25 l/2 pts
1 cup	Chopped lean beef	225 g/8 oz
¼ cup	Sherry (or white wine)	60 ml/2 fl oz
1 tbsp	Parsley	1 tbsp
1 tsp	Basil	1 tsp
	A pinch of sugar	
2	Egg whites and shells of 2 eggs	2
	Garnish	
1	Large tomato, peeled and cut into strips, if hot	1
	Lemon quarters and cheese straws (see Index), if cold	

1. Chop the tomatoes and put into an enamel or heat-proof glass pan. Add well-flavored, jellied chicken stock, which has been skimmed to remove fat. Add chopped lean raw beef, sherry or white wine, herbs, sugar, and seasoning.

2. Beat the egg whites until frothy but not stiff. Add to the soup pan with the finely crushed egg shells. Bring the soup very slowly to a boil, whisking thoroughly the whole time. When the soup is just reaching the boiling point and is rising up in the pan, stop whisking. Remove the pan from the heat to allow the egg white crust to subside, then leave the pan on a very low heat for 30–40 minutes.

3. Put a piece of clean cloth over a fine sieve and strain the soup carefully, allowing the egg white crust to slide onto the cloth. Pour the soup through this filter again, by which time it should be clear. Adjust the seasoning.

4. Prepare the garnish: Dip 1 large tomato into boiling water for 10 seconds, and then in cold water. Remove the skin and seeds, and cut the tomato flesh into strips. Add to the soup just before serving. If serving cold, let it cool and set in the refrigerator. Then stir with a fork. Serve in chilled soup bowls with lemon quarters and cheese straws.

Clear Beet Consomme

Maryland Crab Soup

 00:30 / 01:00   Serves 4–6   Mid Atlantic

American	Ingredients	Metric/Imperial
6 cups	Strong beef stock	1.25 l/2¼ pts
3 cups	Mixed vegetables (fresh, leftover or frozen—include chopped onions and celery, diced carrots, peas, lima [broad] beans, cut string beans, corn, okra and tomatoes, not squash, [marrow] cabbage or potatoes)	350 g/12 oz
1 tbsp	Crab seasoning	1 tbsp
1 lb	Crabmeat (claw or white meat)	450 g/1 lb
	Claws and pieces of whole crab if available (either raw or cooked)	

1. Heat the stock in a large soup pot. Add the vegetables and seasoning, and simmer for 1 hour.
2. Add the crabmeat and the crab claws and pieces (if available) 30 minutes before serving. Simmer gently, to heat through and allow the flavors to blend.
3. Serve hot in large soup bowls, with bread and butter or hard crusty rolls and butter as accompaniment.

Consomme a La Princesse

 00:10 / 00:20   Serves 4–6   United States

American	Ingredients	Metric/Imperial
2–3 tbsp	Asparagus tips	1½–2 tbsp
1	Small cooked chicken breast	1
4–5 cups	Clear chicken or beef consomme	1–1.25 l/ 1¾–2 pints
	A little sherry (optional)	
1 tbsp	Finely chopped parsley	1 tbsp

1. Cook the asparagus tips, if fresh, in boiling salted water; if canned, rinse and heat in a little of the liquid from the can. Dice the white chicken meat.
2. Heat the clear chicken or beef consomme. Add a little sherry if desired, the asparagus tips, and the chicken dice; heat through.
3. Serve hot with the asparagus and chicken divided among soup bowls. Sprinkle with finely chopped parsley.

Clear Beet Consomme

 00:10 / 00:45   Serves 4–6   Pacific Northwest

American	Ingredients	Metric/Imperial
4–5 cups	Clear jellied chicken consomme	1–1.25 l/ 1¾–2 pints
2–3	Small well-colored cooked red beets [beetroot]	2–3
1–2 tsp	Onion juice	1–2 tsp
	Juice of half a lemon	
	Garnish	
4–6 tbsp	Sour cream	3½–5 tbsp
	Piroshki (see Index)	
1	Lemon, cut in quarters or sixths	1

1. First prepare the clear jellied stock. Either chicken or brown stock may be used, or use canned jellied consomme to make an equivalent quantity. Put the stock or consomme into a pan with the grated peeled beets, the onion juice (made by squeezing small pieces of cut onion in a garlic press), and some seasoning if necessary, although the stock should be well flavored.
2. Bring the soup slowly to a moderate heat and let it cook very gently for 30–40 minutes, or until the soup is well flavored and colored by the beets. Do not let it boil, as this makes the soup a muddy brown color instead of a rich red.
3. Strain the soup through a double layer of clean cloth. Add enough lemon juice to sharpen the flavor and adjust the seasoning. If serving hot, reheat to just below the boiling point and serve with a garnish of sour cream, served separately, and with piroshki. If serving cold, put into a clean bowl and chill in the refrigerator. Mix with a fork before serving with lemon quarters and sour cream.

Poor Millionaire's Consomme I

Poor Millionaire's Consomme I

	02:00		
	00:05	Serves 4–6	United States

American	Ingredients	Metric/Imperial
2 (10½-oz) cans	Condensed consomme	2 (300 g/10½ oz) tins
1–2 tbsp	Sherry	1–1½ tbsp
	A squeeze of lemon juice	
1 (4-oz)	Small jar caviar (black or red)	1 (100 g/4 oz)
1	Carton sour cream or fresh thick [double] cream made sour with lemon juice	1 (250 ml/8 fl oz)
	Salt and pepper	
	A pinch of onion or garlic powder (optional)	
	Paprika or 1–2 tsp chopped chives	
	Garnish	
	Cheese straws (see Index)	
	Lemon quarters	

1. Heat the consomme very slightly until it just dissolves. Add the sherry and a few drops of lemon juice to sharpen the flavor. Pour into soup bowls, allowing space at the top for the garnish; then chill until thoroughly set.
2. Place a large teaspoon of caviar in a mound on top of each bowl of jellied soup.
3. Mix salt, pepper, onion or garlic powder (if desired), and paprika into the sour cream, and spoon this mixture over the caviar.
4. Sprinkle the top with paprika or chopped chives, and serve with cheese straws and lemon quarters.

Poor Millionaire's Consomme II

	02:00		
	00:30	Serves 4–6	United States

American	Ingredients	Metric/Imperial
2 (10½-oz) cans	Chicken consomme or 3–4 cups [700 ml–1 l/1¼–1¾ pints] clear chicken jellied stock	2 (300 g/10½ oz) tins
3–4	Ripe red tomatoes, peeled, seeded and chopped	3–4
2	Thin strips finely pared lemon rind	2
	A little red vegetable coloring (if needed)	
1 tsp	Lemon juice	1 tsp
24–36	Peeled freshly boiled shrimp [prawns]	24–36
4–6	Thin slices lemon	4–6

1. Heat the jellied chicken stock or canned consomme gently with the peeled, seeded, chopped tomatoes, seasoning (if necessary), and lemon rind. Simmer for 20–30 minutes, or until the soup is well flavored and colored. Strain and cool.
2. If the soup is not a clear red, add a little food coloring. Add lemon juice and adjust the seasoning.
3. Chill in a bowl in the refrigerator. When set, break up slightly with a fork and spoon into soup bowls.
4. Garnish with freshly cooked shrimp. Canned or frozen shellfish can be used, but may need to be soaked in a little French dressing to improve the flavor. Decorate with lemon curls.

Quick Tomato Consomme

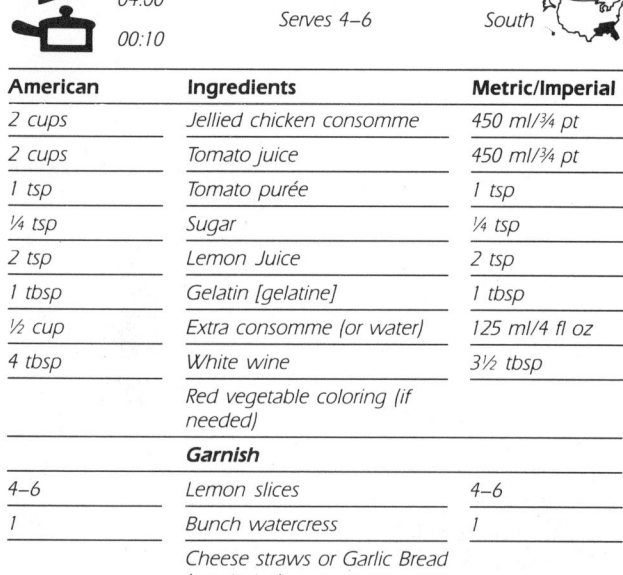

04:00
00:10
Serves 4–6
South

American	Ingredients	Metric/Imperial
2 cups	Jellied chicken consomme	450 ml/¾ pt
2 cups	Tomato juice	450 ml/¾ pt
1 tsp	Tomato purée	1 tsp
¼ tsp	Sugar	¼ tsp
2 tsp	Lemon Juice	2 tsp
1 tbsp	Gelatin [gelatine]	1 tbsp
½ cup	Extra consomme (or water)	125 ml/4 fl oz
4 tbsp	White wine	3½ tbsp
	Red vegetable coloring (if needed)	
	Garnish	
4–6	Lemon slices	4–6
1	Bunch watercress	1
	Cheese straws or Garlic Bread (see Index)	

1. Put the canned consomme, tomato juice, tomato purée, and sugar into a pot with the lemon juice and bring slowly to a boil.
2. Put the gelatin into a small pan with a little water. When it has swelled, dissolve over gentle heat. Remove the hot soup from the heat and add the gelatin.
3. Strain the soup through muslin and a fine sieve. Adjust the seasoning. When almost cold, add the white wine and the additional consomme or water. If the color is not good, add a little vegetable coloring.
4. Pour into soup bowls and let chill. Garnish the top of each bowl with a lemon slice or a little watercress. Serve with cheese straws or garlic bread.

Consomme Julienne

00:15
00:20
Serves 4–6
United States

American	Ingredients	Metric/Imperial
4–5 cups	Clear beef consomme	1–1.25 l/ 1¾–2 pints
2	Small carrots	2
2–3	Sticks celery, white part only	2–3
1	Leek, white part only	1
1 cup	Stock	250 ml/8 fl oz
2–3 tbsp	Sherry	1½–2 tbsp

1. Prepare the vegetables by cutting into even, match-like strips. Put into a pan, and cover with a little stock and seasoning. Cook gently until just tender. Drain, reserving the stock for use in another soup or sauce.
2. Heat the clear consomme and add a little sherry. Add the julienne of vegetables, and serve hot.

Beef Consomme

03:15
00:55
Serves 4–6
Midwest

American	Ingredients	Metric/Imperial
1 lb	Lean beef	450 g/1 lb
10 cups	Rich beef stock made from raw bones and meat	2½ 1/4 pints
2	Egg whites	2
	Egg shells of 2 eggs	
4–5 tbsp	Sherry	3½–4 tbsp

1. Cut the lean beef into small pieces and put into a pot with the rich brown stock, which has been specially made with bones, vegetables, herbs, and seasonings.
2. Beat the egg whites until frothy but not stiff. Wash the egg shells, crumple them into the whites, and add all this mixture to the soup pan. Heat the soup gently while stirring the egg-white mixture into it with a wire whisk, using a backward beating movement. When just reaching the boiling point, remove the whisk and allow the soup to rise in the pan. Then remove it quickly from the heat; when it subsides again, continue to cook on a very low heat for 35–45 minutes to allow the meat juices and flavor to blend into the soup.
3. Put a piece of cheese cloth or a clean cloth over a fine sieve and strain the soup through this, allowing the egg-white crust to slide onto the cloth. Pour the soup back through this filter and, if necessary, repeat a second time to make the soup completely clear. Add the sherry and seasoning, if necessary, and serve hot or chilled.

Tomato Consomme Madras

01:10
00:05
Serves 4–6
South

American	Ingredients	Metric/Imperial
2 (10½-oz) cans	Jellied condensed consomme	2 (300 g/10½ oz) tins
3 cups	Small bottle of tomato juice cocktail, with tabasco or Worcestershire sauce added	700 ml/1¼ pints
2 tsp	Curry powder (or paste)	2 tsp
	A few drops lemon juice	
3 tbsp	Fresh mayonnaise	2 tbsp
	Grated lemon rind to taste	
1–2 tsp	Lemon juice	1–2 tsp
1 tbsp	Heavy [double] cream, whipped	1 tbsp
2 tsp	Chopped chives	2 tsp

1. Heat the consomme very slightly to dissolve it. Add the tomato juice and the curry powder (or paste). Mix in thoroughly. Add a little lemon juice.
2. Pour into soup bowls and let chill.
3. Mix the mayonnaise with grated lemon rind and juice. Add the whipped cream. Put a spoonful of this mayonnaise onto the center of each bowl of jellied soup and sprinkle with chopped chives. Serve with brown bread and butter.

Tomato Consomme Madras

Consomme Royale

| | 02:10 | | | |
| | 00:25 | Serves 4–6 | United States | |

American	Ingredients	Metric/Imperial
4–5 cups	Clear beef consomme or canned consomme	1–1.25 ml/ 1¾–2 pints
2–3 tbsp	Sherry	1½–2 tbsp
	Royale Garnish	
1	Whole egg	1
2	Egg yolks	2
½ cup	Cream	125 ml/4 fl oz
4–5 tbsp	Consommé	3½–4 tbsp
	Salt and pepper	
	A pinch of mace	
⅛ tsp	Chopped chervil	⅛ tsp

1. First make the Royale Garnish. Beat the whole egg and the egg yolks together well. Mix the cream with 4–5 tablespoons [3½–4 tbsp] of consomme. Add a good pinch of salt, pepper, mace, and the chervil if available. Add the eggs to this creamy mixture, and mix well together. Butter the sides of a baking pan or a fire-proof dish or bowl and pour in the custard. Cover tightly with foil and stand it in a pan of hot water, which should reach halfway up the sides of the baking pan or dish. Cook in a slow oven (300°F/150°C/Gas Mark 2) until the custard is set, 15–20 minutes or more. Let it cool. Turn out the cold custard and cut it into slices. Cut the slices into small shapes—diamonds, crescents, stars, etc.—and use as garnish for the soup.
2. Heat the clear consomme; add seasoning to taste and sherry. Pour into soup bowls. Add the Royale Garnish and serve hot.

Consomme Philadelphia

| | 04:00 | | | |
| | 00:05 | Serves 4–6 | Mid Atlantic | |

American	Ingredients	Metric/Imperial
2 (10-oz) cans	Condensed consomme	2 (250 ml/10 oz) tins
1 (8-oz) pkg	Cream cheese	1 (225 g/8 oz) pkt
	A few drops Tabasco	
	A few drops onion juice (or garlic juice, or powder)	
	Salt and pepper	
1–2 tbsp	Cream	1–1½ tbsp
1–2 tbsp	Sherry	1–1½ tbsp
	Garnish	
2–3 tsp	Chopped chives or a sprinkling of paprika	2–3 tsp
	Hot garlic bread (see Index)	

1. Reserve just over a quarter of one can of consomme for garnish. Put the remainder into an electric blender with the cream cheese, tabasco, onion or crushed garlic, salt, and pepper to taste. Blend gently until smooth, adding a little cream if necessary.
2. Taste and adjust the seasoning. Pour into soup bowls and chill, covered.
3. Heat the remaining consomme until just melted but not hot. Add sherry. Let cool. When the soup is set, spoon a thin layer of this garnishing mixture onto each bowl and chill again. When set, sprinkle with chopped chives or a little paprika.
4. Serve cold with hot garlic bread.

Cranberry and Orange Soup

Cranberry and Orange Soup

	01:15		
	00:10	Serves 4–6	New England

American	Ingredients	Metric/Imperial
1 lb	Fresh cranberries (or canned equivalent)	450 g/1 lb
2 cups	Light chicken stock (or water)	450 ml/¾ pt
1½ cups	White wine	375 ml/12 fl oz
2–3	Pieces lemon rind	2–3
	Pared orange rind	
½	Cinnamon stick	½
¼–½ cup	Sugar to taste	50–100 g/2–4 oz
	Juice of two oranges	
	Juice of ½ lemon	
2 envelopes	Gelatin [gelatine] (if soup is to be jellied)	2 sachets
	Garnish	
4–6	Slices orange	4–6

1. Wash the cranberries if fresh. Put them into a pan with the chicken stock (or water) and white wine. Add the pieces of lemon and orange rind and the cinnamon stick. Simmer for about 10 minutes, until the cranberries have softened.
2. Put the fruit and juice through a fine nylon sieve or the fine food mill after removing the cinnamon stick. Sweeten to taste and add the orange and lemon juice. (If using canned cranberries, it may not be necessary to add any sugar as these are usually sweetened.)
3. This soup can also be serve jellied if two envelopes of gelatin are softened in a little stock or water and then added after the soup has been sieved. It will then be necessary to reheat the soup for a few minutes while blending in the gelatin.
4. Serve chilled or jellied with a thin slice of orange as a garnish.

Apple Soup

	00:30		
	00:30	Serves 4–6	Mid Atlantic 

American	Ingredients	Metric/Imperial
1½ lb	Cooking apples	675 g/1½ lb
5 cups	Water	1.25 l/2 pints
6–8	Strips thinly pared lemon rind	6–8
	Juice of half a lemon	
½ cup	Granulated sugar	100 g/4 oz
1–1½ tbsp	Cornstarch [cornflour]	1–1¼ tbsp
½ cup	Heavy [double] cream	125 ml/4 fl oz
	Garnish	
	Grated lemon rind, if hot	
	Thin slices of lemon, if cold	

1. Wash and quarter the apples, removing the cores, and peel. Put into a pan with water and thinly pared lemon rind. Cook, covered, until the apples are soft, about 20–25 minutes.
2. Strain the liquid from the pan. Put the apple pulp through a fine sieve or food mill, or blend until smooth in an electric blender, adding the liquid gradually and mixing well with the sugar and lemon juice.
3. Mix the cornstarch with a little cold water. Add a few spoonfuls of hot soup, and mix well before adding to the soup. Bring the soup to a boil, and cook for 4–5 minutes to cook cornstarch.
4. Stir in cream just before serving, and sprinkle top of each soup bowl with finely grated lemon rind. If serving cold, add the cream when the soup is cold and serve with a thin slice of lemon on top of each soup bowl.

Cold Buttermilk Soup

	01:15		
	00:00	Serves 4–6	Mid Atlantic 

American	Ingredients	Metric/Imperial
2	Large eggs	2
	Grated rind and juice of 1 lemon (or vanilla extract)	
¼ cup	Sugar	50 g/2 oz
4 cups	Buttermilk	1 l/1¾ pints
½ cup	Heavy [double] cream	125 ml/4 fl oz
	Garnish	
	Grated rind of half a lemon or	
2 tbsp	Chopped and lightly browned almonds	1½ tbsp

1. Beat the egg yolks, lemon rind, and juice (or vanilla) with the sugar until light and frothy. Beat the buttermilk, and stir into the egg-yolk mixture.
2. Beat the egg whites until stiff, adding a pinch of salt. Then whip the cream. Carefully fold the egg whites into the cream. Add this to the egg yolk and buttermilk. Do not blend too thoroughly, but leave it rather lumpy in texture.
3. Ladle into soup bowls. Then chill thoroughly, garnish with finely grated lemon rind or chopped almonds, and serve plain crackers separately.

Yogurt, Shrimp, and Cucumber Soup

Yogurt, Shrimp, and Cucumber Soup

02:00
00:00   Serves 4-6   United States

American	Ingredients	Metric/Imperial
½	Large cucumber, peeled and diced	½
1 cup	Natural yogurt	250 ml/8 fl oz
1½ cups	Chicken stock	375 ml/12 fl oz
1 cup	Tomato juice	250 ml/8 fl oz
1	Clove garlic, crushed	1
1-2 tsp	Lemon juice	1-2 tsp
2 tsp	Chopped dill or fennel	2 tsp
½ cup	Cooked shrimp [prawns]	100 g/4 oz
1	Large tomato, peeled and diced	1
2 tbsp	Diced green pepper	1½ tbsp
1 cup	Cream	250 ml/8 fl oz

	Garnish	
2 tsp	Chopped dill or fennel, or paprika	2 tsp
	French bread and butter, or garlic bread (see Index)	

1. Peel and dice the cucumber. Sprinkle with salt and leave covered for at least 20–30 minutes. Then drain and rinse with cold water. Put the yogurt, stock, tomato juice, and crushed garlic into an electric blender. Blend slowly until smooth, adding pepper, lemon juice, and chopped dill or fennel when the soup is well mixed.

2. Add the drained diced cucumber and shrimp, the diced tomato, and diced pepper. Stir in the cream, adjust the seasoning, and chill thoroughly.

3. Sprinkle with chopped dill or fennel or paprika, and serve with French bread or garlic bread.

Cherry Soup

	00:30		
	00:25	Serves 4–6	Mid Atlantic

American	Ingredients	Metric/Imperial
1½ lb	Sweet red cherries (or canned equivalent)	675 g/1½ lb
4 cups	Water	1 l/1¾ pints
½	Cinnamon stick (or ¼ tsp ground cinnamon)	½
3–4	Slivers orange or lemon rind and juice of half an orange or lemon	3–4
1 cup	Red wine	250 ml/8 fl oz
1 tbsp	Cornstarch [cornflour]	1 tbsp
	Sugar to taste	

1. Pit [stone] the cherries and put about three-quarters of them into a pan. Cover with the water and add the cinnamon and lemon or orange rind, which must be very finely pared, and the juice of half an orange or lemon. Cover the pan and simmer gently until the cherries are tender.
2. Put the soup through a fine food mill or into an electric blender, and blend until smooth. Add the red wine.
3. Add the cornstarch to the cold water and mix until smooth. Add a little hot soup to the cornstarch mixture and pour this back into the soup. Stir in well, then bring to a boil and cook for 4–5 minutes. Add the reserved cherries for the last few minutes to heat through.
4. Add sugar to taste and serve hot with crackers, which can be crumbled into the soup if desired.

Tripe Soup

	00:15		
	01:25	Serves 6	Mid Atlantic

American	Ingredients	Metric/Imperial
½ lb	Cooked honeycomb tripe	225 g/8 oz
3-4 cups	Chicken or white stock	700 ml-1 l/ 1¼-1¾ pints
2	Potatoes, chopped	2
2	Onions, chopped	2
2-3	Stalks celery, chopped	2-3
3 tbsp	Butter	40 g/1½ oz
1½ tbsp	Flour	1¼ tbsp
1 tbsp	Chopped parsley	1 tbsp
1 tsp	Marjoram	1 tsp
	A pinch of thyme	
	A pinch of cayenne pepper	
	Garnish	
2 tbsp	Butter	25 g/1 oz
½ cup	Cream	125 ml/4 fl oz
	Fried bread croutons (see Index)	

1. Buy ready-cooked tripe or canned tripe, and cut into small cubes. Cook gently in the chicken or white stock for about 1 hour, adding pepper and salt if necessary.
2. Meanwhile, sauté the potatoes, onions, and celery in melted butter until tender, shaking to prevent sticking and burning, about 5-10 minutes. Then blend in the flour until smooth.
3. When the tripe is cooked, strain the liquid into the vegetables and stir to mix in well. Bring slowly to a boil, stirring until smooth. Add the tripe and the chopped herbs and cayenne pepper. Simmer together for a few minutes. Adjust the seasoning. Add some butter and cream just before serving.
4. Serve hot with fried bread croutons.

Kidney Soup

	00:30		
	01:10	Serves 4-6	United States

American	Ingredients	Metric/Imperial
3	Lamb kidneys (or 225 g/½ lb ox kidneys)	3
	Salted water to cover kidneys for soaking	
2-3 tbsp	Butter	25-40 g/1-1½ oz
2	Onions, chopped	2
2	Carrots, sliced	2
2	Stalks celery, sliced	2
1½ tbsp	Flour	1¼ tbsp
1 tbsp	Tomato purée	1 tbsp
5 cups	Beef or brown stock	1.25 l/2 pints
1 tsp	Worcestershire sauce	1 tsp
	Several sprigs of parsley, 1 sprig thyme, 1 bay leaf, tied together	
1 cup	Sliced mushrooms	100 g/4 oz
	A dash of Tabasco or chili sauce	
	A little gravy mix, beef bouillon, or soy sauce	
2-3 tbsp	Sherry	1½-2 tbsp
2 tbsp	Chopped parsley	1½ tbsp
	Garnish	
	Fried bread croutons (see Index)	

1. Remove the skin and cores from the kidneys and cut into small pieces. Put to soak for a few minutes in cold, slightly salted water to remove any strong flavor. Drain.
2. Melt the butter and cook the onions, carrots, and celery for a few minutes, stirring well. Add the kidney and cook for 6–7 minutes to brown all the ingredients lightly. Sprinkle in flour and mix well. Add the tomato purée, stock, and Worcestershire sauce. Bring to a boil slowly, stirring constantly. Add herbs and seasoning. Then cover the pan and simmer for about 45 minutes, or until the kidney and vegetables are tender. Remove the herbs.
3. Just before the end of the cooking time, add the sliced mushrooms and a dash of tabasco or chili sauce. Adjust the seasoning and, if soup is not a good color, add a little gravy mix, beef bouillon, or soy sauce.
4. Just before serving, add the sherry and sprinkle with chopped parsley. Serve with fried croutons.

Curry Soup

Curry Soup

	00:25		
	01:00	Serves 4-6	United States

American	Ingredients	Metric/Imperial
1	Large onion, chopped	1
1	Carrot, chopped	1
1-2	Stalks celery, chopped	1-2
1	Medium cooking apple	1
3-4 tbsp	Butter	40-50 g/ 1½–2 oz
1 tbsp	Curry powder (or paste)	1 tbsp
1½ tbsp	Flour	1¼ tbsp
1 tbsp	Tomato purée	1 tbsp
4-5 cups	Stock	1–1.25 l/ 1¾–2 pints
1	Bay leaf	1
3-4 sprigs	Parsley	3-4
	A pinch of thyme	
2 tbsp	Shredded coconut	1½ tbsp
1 tsp	Sugar	1 tsp
2 tsp	Lemon juice	2 tsp
4-6 tbsp	Cooked rice	3½–5 tbsp
	Garnish	
4-6	Slices lemon	4-6
	Paprika	

1. Melt the butter and add the onion, carrot, celery, and apple. Stir well and cook gently for 5-6 minutes. Add the curry powder or paste, and cook for a few minutes. Add the flour, mixing well, and cook for a few minutes to brown slightly. Add the tomato pureé and the stock. Blend well before bringing slowly to a boil. Reduce the heat. Add the herbs, seasoning, coconut, and sugar. Simmer for 30–45 minutes.
2. Remove the bay leaf, then blend the soup in an electric blender or put through a fine food mill. Return to the pan, add rice, and adjust seasoning. Reheat, adding lemon juice just before serving. (If preferred, the rice can be served separately.)
3. Serve hot with a slice of lemon and sprinkled with paprika.

Hearty Meat and Vegetable Soup

Hearty Meat and Vegetable Soup 🍳🥦

08:00
02:00   Serves 6-8   South

American	Ingredients	Metric/Imperial
3-4 tbsp	Pearl barley	2–3½ tbsp
1½–2 lb	Neck or breast of mutton or lamb	675-900 g/ 1½–2 lb
6-8 cups	Water	1.25–2 l/ 2¼–3 pints
1 tsp	Salt	1 tsp
¼ tsp	Pepper	¼ tsp
1	Bay leaf	1
2	Large onions, 1 to add whole, the other diced for garnish	2
1	Clove	1
3	Carrots (1 sliced for the soup, 2 diced for garnish)	3
4	Celery stalks (2 whole for the soup, 2 diced for garnish)	4
½	Small turnip, diced for garnish	½
1	Leek, sliced for garnish	1
2 tbsp	Chopped parsley	1½ tbsp

1. Soak the barley for several hours, preferably overnight, in cold water.
2. Remove as much fat as possible from the lamb or mutton and put into a soup pot with the water and the drained barley. Add the salt and pepper, bay leaf, herbs, a whole onion stuck with a clove, a sliced carrot, and 2 stalks of celery. Bring slowly to a boil and simmer for 1½ hours, skimming off the fat and scum occasionally.
3. If time allows, let the soup cool and skim off the fat; if not, skim carefully while hot, removing the bay leaf and celery and carrot as far as possible.
4. Add the diced vegetables and cook for 20–30 minutes, or until they are tender. Adjust the seasoning; if too much liquid has evaporated, add a little extra to make up quantity. Remove the bones, leaving the meat in the soup. Reheat and serve hot, sprinkled with chopped parsley.

Pot-Au-Feu 🍳

00:15
03:30   Serves 4-6   Mid Atlantic

American	Ingredients	Metric/Imperial
1	Ham bone	1
1	Veal knuckle or lamb bone	1
1 tbsp	Dried navy [haricot] beans	1 tbsp
¼ cup	Dried baby lima [broad] beans	50 g/2 oz
¼ cup	Dried split peas	50 g/2 oz
1 tbsp	Rice	1 tbsp
1	Onion, peeled and finely chopped	1
½ cup	Finely chopped celery	50 g/2 oz
1 tbsp	Finely chopped parsley	1 tbsp
½ cup	Tomato puree	100 g/4 oz
6 cups	Water	1.25 l/2¼ pints
	Chopped chives or scallions, [spring onions] for garnish	

1. Put all the ingredients, except the garnish, into a large saucepan. Cover and simmer for 3–3½ hours.
2. Remove the bones, cut off any meat and return it to the pan. Skim off any excess fat and adjust the seasoning.
3. Reheat and serve sprinkled with the chopped chives.

Oxtail Soup 🍳

02:10
03:30   Serves 4-5   South

American	Ingredients	Metric/Imperial
1	Oxtail	1
2 tbsp	Cooking fat	1½ tbsp
1	Clove garlic, crushed	1
3	Onions	3
6 cups	Water	1.25 l/2¼ pints
1	Bay leaf	1
1 tsp	Salt	1 tsp
6	Peppercorns	6
2-3	Carrots, peeled and chopped	2-3
¼	Small head cabbage, shredded	¼
½ cup	Peeled and chopped tomatoes	350 g/12 oz
1 tsp	Worcestershire sauce	1 tsp

1. Have the oxtail disjointed. Heat the fat in a saucepan; add the pieces of oxtail, garlic, and 1 onion, peeled and sliced. Sauté until the oxtail is well browned.
2. Add the water, bay leaf, salt, and peppercorns. Cover, bring to a boil, and simmer over low heat for about 3 hours. Set aside to cool.
3. When cold, skim off the fat and strain the liquid back into the pot.
4. Add the pieces of oxtail and the remaining 2 onions, peeled and chopped. Cover and simmer until the onion is tender, about 20–30 minutes. Add Worcestershire sauce and check the seasoning before serving.

Cheese and Spinach Soup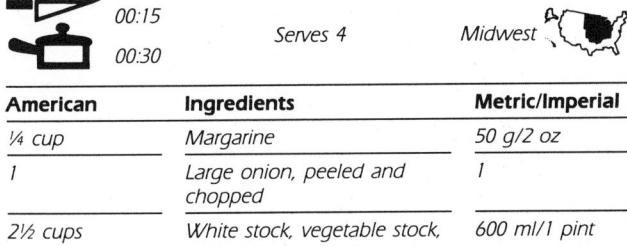

	00:15	Serves 4	Midwest
	00:30		

American	Ingredients	Metric/Imperial
¼ cup	Margarine	50 g/2 oz
1	Large onion, peeled and chopped	1
2½ cups	White stock, vegetable stock, or water	600 ml/1 pint
1 cup	Milk	250 ml/8 fl oz
3 tbsp	Flour	2 tbsp
	Salt and pepper	
	Nutmeg	
2 tsp	Chopped parsley	2 tsp
½ cup	Grated cheese	50 g/2 oz
4 tbsp	Chopped cooked spinach	3½ tbsp
	Few chives or scallions [spring onions]	
	Graham cracker [digestive biscuit] crumbs	

1. Heat the fat in a saucepan; add the onion and sauté until translucent but not brown.
2. Add hot stock or water and simmer for 10 minutes. Then add milk.
3. Mix the flour to a smooth paste with a little extra milk, add gradually to the liquid in the pan. Stir until boiling.
4. Add salt, pepper, and a little nutmeg to taste, and stir over low heat 5 minutes.
5. Add parsley, cheese, and spinach; bring to a boil again, and adjust the seasoning. Serve very hot, with a sprinkling of chopped chives and crushed graham cracker crumbs.

Cheese and Spinach Soup

Cheese Soup

 00:15
00:20   Serves 4   Mid Atlantic

American	Ingredients	Metric/Imperial
1	Onion, finely chopped	1
1 tbsp	Margarine	15 g/½ oz
3 tbsp	Flour	2 tbsp
4 cups	Stock	1 l/1¾ pints
1¼ cups	Grated cheese	150 g/5 oz
1	Egg yolk	1
⅓ cup	Crème fraîche or sour cream	5 tbsp
	Shredded celery	
	Chopped parsley	

1. Sauté the onion in margarine. Stir in the flour when the onion has become transparent. Cover with stock, stirring constantly, and simmer for 5-6 minutes.
2. Stir in the cheese and let it melt. It should not, however, be allowed to boil. Remove the pan from the heat; stir in the egg yolk and crème fraîche or sour cream.
3. Serve immediately, garnished with celery and parsley.

Cheese Croutons

 00:08
00:08   Serves 4   Mid Atlantic

American	Ingredients	Metric/Imperial
2–3	Slices white bread	2–3
2 tbsp	Butter (approximately)	25 g/1 oz
	A little mustard or vegetable extract	
4–6 tbsp	Grated Parmesan cheese	3½–5 tbsp
	Salt and pepper	
	Cayenne pepper	

1. Toast the bread slices on one side only. Let cool. Then butter the reverse side and spread with a little mustard. Sprinkle thickly with the grated cheese, and with a little salt and pepper.
2. Broil [grill] until the cheese is melted and browned. Sprinkle with cayenne pepper. When slightly cooled, cut into squares or fingers. Serve hot.

Garlic Croutons

 00:10
00:05   Serves 4   United States

American	Ingredients	Metric/Imperial
1	Clove garlic or ¾ tsp dried or powdered garlic	1
3	Slices white bread	3
	Oil	
	Salt and pepper	
	Cayenne pepper (optional)	

1. Crush the garlic. Cut the crusts off the bread slices and cut into cubes. Heat the oil. When hot, add the bread cubes and cook, stirring constantly. When the cubes start to turn color, add the garlic and mix well. When the cubes are golden brown, remove and drain.
2. Sprinkle with salt and pepper and a touch of cayenne pepper, and serve hot.

Fried Bread Croutons

 00:10
00:05   Serves 4   United States

American	Ingredients	Metric/Imperial
2	Large slices white bread	2
	Oil	
1 tbsp	Butter	15 g/½ oz
	Salt and pepper	
	Onion powder (as desired)	

1. Remove the crusts from the slices of bread and cut the bread into small cubes. Heat enough oil in a frying pan to come at least halfway up the sides of the bread cubes while cooking. When the oil is hot, add the butter. When this has melted and is foaming, add all the bread cubes at once.
2. Cook over a moderate-to-hot flame, stirring constantly to ensure that the cubes brown evenly. When golden brown, place on paper towels [kitchen paper] to drain. Remove from the pan when slightly less brown than the final color you want, as they continue to cook for a few seconds because of the hot oil.
3. Season with salt, pepper, and onion powder, if this will improve the soup for which the croutons are intended. Keep hot and serve separately.

Bacon Croutons

 00:10
00:10   Serves 4   United States

American	Ingredients	Metric/Imperial
2 slices	Bacon	2 rashers
2	Large slices white bread cut into cubes	2
	Oil	
	Pepper	

1. Remove the rinds from the bacon slices and chop the bacon finely. Put into a dry frying pan and cook slowly to extract fat, then cook until crisp and golden. Remove bacon bits and reserve.
2. Add enough oil to the bacon fat to cook the diced bread in the same way as Fried Bread Croutons (see above). When golden brown, remove and drain. Add the bacon bits with pepper and serve hot.

Cheese Soup

Salads

Mixed Green Salad

Wilted Lettuce Salad

00:15
00:12   Serves 4   Midwest

American	Ingredients	Metric/Imperial
1	Large head Boston [cabbage] lettuce	1
6	Radishes, thinly sliced	6
1	Hard-boiled egg	1
5–6 slices	Bacon	5–6 rashers
1 tsp	Sugar	1 tsp
¼ cup	Red wine vinegar	60 ml/2 fl oz
¼ tsp	Prepared horseradish	¼ tsp
⅛ tsp	Black pepper	⅛ tsp
5–6	Scallions [spring onions], chopped	5–6

1. Wash and drain the lettuce and break it up into a salad bowl. Add the sliced radishes.
2. Remove the yolk carefully from the hard-boiled egg and set it aside. Chop the white of the egg and sprinkle it over the lettuce.
3. Cook the bacon in a frying pan until crisp. Remove, and drain on paper towels [kitchen paper].
4. Add sugar, vinegar, horseradish, and pepper to the bacon drippings in the pan. Mix well, add scallions, and heat until the mixture bubbles; then pour at once over the lettuce. Toss lightly. Add the crumbled bacon and sprinkle with the sieved, hard-boiled egg yolk.

Mixed Green Salad

00:20
00:00   Serves 4   United States

American	Ingredients	Metric/Imperial
1	Head Bibb lettuce (or ½ head iceberg lettuce)	1
2	Green peppers, cleaned, seeded, and cut into strips	2
4	Small tomatoes, sliced	4
2	Small onions, sliced and separated into rings	2
2	Hard-boiled eggs, sliced	2
½ cup	Stuffed green olives, sliced	50 g/2 oz
½	Medium cucumber, peeled, seeded, and cut into chunks	½
Salad Dressing		
4 tbsp	Olive oil	3½ tbsp
3 tbsp	Tarragon vinegar	2 tbsp
½ tsp	Salt	½ tsp
¼ tsp	Freshly ground pepper	¼ tsp
1	Clove garlic, crushed	1
¼ tsp	Crushed oregano	¼ tsp
1 tbsp	Fresh parsley, chopped	1 tbsp

1. Wash the lettuce; clean, dry, and tear into bite-sized pieces. Place in a salad bowl; add the peppers, tomatoes, onions, eggs, olives, and cucumber. Refrigerate.
2. Combine all the dressing ingredients; mix well. At serving time, toss the salad at the table with the prepared dressing.

Avocado Salad with Bacon

00:20
00:10   Serves 4   United States

American	Ingredients	Metric/Imperial
1 lb	Bacon	450 g/1 lb
3–4	Ripe avocados [avocado pears]	3–4
4	Tender stalks celery	4
	A piece of leek	
3–4	Hard-boiled eggs	3–4
2	Tomatoes, cut in wedges	2
Dressing		
5 tbsp	Oil	4 tbsp
2 tbsp	Tarragon vinegar	1½ tbsp
1	Clove garlic, crushed	1
2 tsp	Light French mustard	2 tsp
1–2 tsp	Italian salad spices, or 1 tsp herb salt	1–2 tsp

1. Fry the bacon in a dry pan until crisp. Place the bacon on a paper towel [kitchen paper] so that the fat drains off. Divide the avocados in half and remove the pits [stones]. Peel the halves and cut them into slices.
2. Alternate the sliced avocado, celery, leek, bacon, egg slices, and tomato wedges in a salad bowl.
3. Mix the dressing ingredients together and adjust the seasonings. Shake up the dressing and pour it over the salad.

Avocado Salad with Bacon

Green Salad with Croutons

	00:15		
	00:10	Serves 4–6	United States

American	Ingredients	Metric/Imperial
	Croutons	
1	Clove garlic, peeled and sliced	1
1 cup	Stale Italian bread, with the crust removed [save for bread crumbs], cubed	100 g/4 oz
2 tbsp	Olive oil	1½ tbsp
	Salad	
1	Medium head iceberg lettuce	1
1	Medium head Romaine [cos] lettuce or endive	1
¼ cup	Parmesan cheese, grated	25 g/1 oz
	Dressing	
½ cup	Olive oil	125 ml/4 fl oz
¼ cup	Red wine vinegar	60 ml/2 fl oz
½ tsp	Dried oregano, crumbled	½ tsp
½ tsp	Salt	½ tsp
¼ tsp	Pepper	¼ tsp

1. First, prepare the croutons. Heat the olive oil in a small frying pan and sauté the garlic in oil over moderate heat until lightly browned. Remove the garlic with a slotted spoon and discard. Add the bread cubes and sauté stirring frequently, until golden brown. Drain on paper towels [kitchen paper].

2. Combine the dressing ingredients in a bottle or screwtop jar and shake well. Allow to stand at room temperature. Clean the lettuce and pat dry. Tear into bite-sized pieces and place in a salad bowl. Refrigerate until serving time.

3. To serve, sprinkle the salad with cheese and croutons. Shake the dressing well and pour it over the salad. Toss well and serve immediately.

Caesar Salad

	00:15		
	00:20	Serves 4–5	New England

American	Ingredients	Metric/Imperial
2	Small heads Romaine [cos] or other lettuce	2
2 tbsp	Butter	25 g/1 oz
1	Clove garlic, crushed	1
2	Slices bread, cut into ½-inch [1.25-cm] cubes	2
2 slices	Bacon, chopped	2 rashers
	Grated Parmesan cheese	
	Chopped parsley	
	Dressing	
1	Coddled egg	1
⅔ cup	French dressing	150 ml/¼ pint
1 tsp	Salt	1 tsp
1 tsp	Prepared mustard	1 tsp

1. To make the dressing, coddle the egg first by putting it into boiling water for 1 minute and then removing the shell. Then mix well with all the other ingredients.

2. Remove any tough outer leaves from the lettuce, wash and dry well. Break up into pieces and put them into a salad bowl; add the dressing and toss lightly.

3. Heat the butter in a frying pan, add crushed garlic and cubes of bread, and cook until crisp and golden brown. Fry the bacon until crisp, then drain on paper towels [kitchen paper].

4. Scatter the bacon and croutons over the salad, and sprinkle generously with grated cheese and parsley.

Hot Bean Salad

	00:15		
	00:25	Serves 8	New England

American	Ingredients	Metric/Imperial
2 lb	Green or yellow beans, cut up or left whole	900 g/2 lb
8	Strips of bacon [streaky]	8
2	Large onions, finely chopped	2
4 tbsp	Wine or cider vinegar	3½ tbsp
	Lemon juice	
2 tsp	Sugar	2 tsp

1. Boil the beans until they are almost done but not quite. Reserve and keep hot.

2. Chop the bacon and fry until crisp. Drain and keep warm.

3. Fry the onions in the bacon fat until transparent. Then add the vinegar, lemon juice, sugar, and seasonings to the frying pan.

4. Pour the sauce over the beans, and sprinkle the bacon bits on top. This looks most effective if the beans are cooked whole, except for their ends, and arranged in a row on a platter with the sauce and the bacon bits running down the middle.

Cauliflower and Avocado Salad

	03:15		
	00:00	Serves 6	Pacific Southwest

American	Ingredients	Metric/Imperial
1	Medium-sized cauliflower	1
½ cup	French dressing	125 ml/4 fl oz
1	Ripe avocado	1
½ cup	Sliced stuffed olives	50 g/2 oz
2–3	Tomatoes, peeled and cut into eighths	2–3
½ cup	Crumbled cheese (Roquefort or blue)	100 g/4 oz
	Lettuce or endive	

1. Divide the cauliflower into flowerets, cover with iced water, and chill for 1 hour.

2. Drain and dry the cauliflower. Then chop coarsely, and put into a bowl. Pour over the French dressing, and leave for 2 hours.

3. Just before serving, add the peeled and diced avocado, olives, tomatoes, and cheese.

4. Serve on a bed of lettuce.

Coleslaw

 00:25 / 00:00 Serves 7–8 Mid Atlantic

American	Ingredients	Metric/Imperial
2 small or 1 large	White cabbage, shredded	2 small or 1 large
½ cup	Chopped green pepper	50 g/2 oz
8 tbsp	Shredded pimento	7 tbsp
½ cup	Chopped celery stalks	50 g/2 oz
3 tbsp	Vinegar	2 tbsp
½ cup	Salad oil	125 ml/4 fl oz
¼ tsp	Sugar	¼ tsp
1 tsp	Salt	1 tsp
¼ tsp	Pepper	¼ tsp
¼ cup	Chopped dill pickle	25 g/1 oz

1. Put all the vegetables in a bowl.
2. Combine the vinegar and the pickle, sugar, salt, and pepper; shake well. Add oil and shake again.
3. When ready for use, pour the dressing over the vegetables, and toss lightly.

Peanut Crunch Slaw

 01:15 / 00:08 Serves 6–7 Southwest

American	Ingredients	Metric/Imperial
1	Small white cabbage, shredded	1
1 cup	Diced celery	100 g/4 oz
	Dressing	
½ cup	Sour cream	125 ml/4 fl oz
½ cup	Mayonnaise	125 ml/4 fl oz
¼ cup	Chopped scallions [spring onions]	25 g/1 oz
¼ cup	Green chopped pepper	25 g/1 oz
¼ cup	Chopped cucumber	25 g/1 oz
	Topping	
½ cup	Salted peanuts, coarsely chopped	50 g/2 oz
1 tbsp	Butter	15 g/½ oz
2 tbsp	Grated Parmesan cheese	1½ tbsp

1. Combine the cabbage and celery. Sprinkle with a little salt and pepper and set aside to chill.
2. Combine all ingredients for the dressing, season and chill.
3. When required for use, brown the peanuts in the butter and stir in the cheese.
4. Toss the vegetables and dressing together and sprinkle the nuts and cheese on top.

Cauliflower and Avocado Salad

Pasta Slaw

 00:25 / 00:00 Serves 4–5 Mid Atlantic

American	Ingredients	Metric/Imperial
¼ cup	Mayonnaise	60 ml/2 fl oz
1 tbsp	Sour cream	1 tbsp
1 tbsp	Vinegar	1 tbsp
2 tsp	Sugar	2 tsp
1 cup	Pasta, cooked (any kind)	100 g/4 oz
1 cup	Finely shredded white cabbage	100 g/4 oz
3 tbsp	Grated carrot	2 tbsp
3 tbsp	Diced green pepper	2 tbsp

1. Make a dressing with the mayonnaise, sour cream, vinegar, and sugar.
2. Add the pasta and vegetables and toss lightly, but be sure all the ingredients are well coated with the dressing.

Raw Mushroom Salad

 00:45 / 00:00 Serves 5–6 United States

American	Ingredients	Metric/Imperial
1 lb	Button mushrooms	450 g/1 lb
	Juice of 1 lemon	
8 tbsp	Olive oil	7 tbsp
	Salt and freshly ground black pepper	
1 tsp	Finely chopped chives	1 tsp
1 tsp	Finely chopped parsley	1 tsp

1. Remove the stalks from the mushrooms, wash and dry the caps, and cut into slices. Arrange in a shallow salad bowl.
2. Blend the lemon juice and oil, add salt and pepper to taste, and pour over the mushrooms. Toss carefully and set aside to chill for at least ½ hour.
3. Before serving, sprinkle with the chives and parsley.

Coleslaw with Almonds

 00:25 00:00   Serves 4–5   Mid Atlantic

American	Ingredients	Metric/Imperial
½	Medium-size white cabbage	½
2	Stalks celery, chopped	2
½	Cucumber, thinly sliced	½
½	Green pepper, shredded	½
1	Onion, peeled and finely chopped	1
⅔ cup	Mayonnaise	150 ml/¼ pint
1 tbsp	Vinegar	1 tbsp
¼ cup	Toasted browned almonds	25 g/1 oz

1. Wash and drain the cabbage; discard the outer leaves and hard stalk.
2. Shred the cabbage finely and mix with the celery, cucumber, green pepper, and onion.
3. Mix the mayonnaise and vinegar; add salt and pepper to taste and pour over the vegetables. Toss with two forks until the vegetables are evenly coated.
4. Put into a serving dish and sprinkle with toasted almonds.

Pepper Salad

01:20 00:10   Serves 6   New England

American	Ingredients	Metric/Imperial
2	Red peppers	2
2	Green peppers	2
6	Firm tomatoes, peeled and thickly sliced	6
6	Hard-boiled eggs	6
	Anchovy fillets	
	Black olives	
	Herb dressing [see Index]	

1. Wash and dry the peppers, then broil [grill] them quickly, turning frequently until the skin has charred on all sides. Remove the skin under cold water, then cut the peppers lengthwise into 6 or 8 pieces. Wash off the seeds and remove excess fiber, then pat dry.
2. Arrange the slices of tomato in the bottom of a large, flat serving dish. Sprinkle with some of the dressing, cover with the pieces of green pepper, then sprinkle with more dressing; add the pieces of red pepper and sprinkle again with dressing.
3. Shell and slice the hard-boiled eggs and put on top of the red pepper. Add the rest of the dressing.
4. Arrange anchovy fillets in a lattice pattern on top and place an olive in the center of each square. Chill before serving.

Potato and Cauliflower Salad

02:30 00:45   Serves 5–6   Mid Atlantic

American	Ingredients	Metric/Imperial
3 cups	Diced cooked potatoes	350 g/12 oz
1 cup	Diced celery	100 g/4 oz
¼ cup	Finely chopped onion	25 g/1 oz
½	Small cauliflower, divided into small flowerets	½
2	Hard-boiled eggs	2
6 slices	Bacon, fried until crisp	6 rashers
1 cup	Mayonnaise or salad dressing	250 ml/8 fl oz
1 tsp	Caraway seeds [optional]	1 tsp

1. Mix the potatoes, celery, onion, and cauliflower together. Add the chopped hard-boiled eggs and crumbled bacon.
2. Add the mayonnaise, toss lightly, and add a little salt if required. Set aside to chill before serving.
3. Arrange on a platter or in a salad bowl, and sprinkle with caraway seeds.
4. If time permits, the eggs can be separated, the whites chopped and mixed with the other ingredients, and the yolks sieved on top.

Potato and Frankfurter Salad

02:15 00:20   Serves 4   Mid Atlantic

American	Ingredients	Metric/Imperial
1 lb	Potatoes	450 g/1 lb
6–8	Scallions [spring onions], chopped	6–8
1 tsp	Chopped parsley	1 tsp
	Cream Dressing [see Index]	
1	Lettuce	1
4	Frankfurters	4
4	Slices cooked ham	4
2	Hard-boiled eggs, quartered	2
3–4	Tomatoes	3–4

1. Cook, peel, and dice the potatoes. Add sautéed onion and parsley; while the potatoes are still warm, add 3–4 [2–3½] tablespoons cream dressing. Toss lightly and set aside to chill.
2. Put the potato in the center of a platter lined with lettuce leaves.
3. Put a frankfurter on each slice of ham and roll up. Arrange the ham rolls around the dish and garnish with hard-boiled eggs and tomatoes.

Potato Salad with Frankfurters

	00:30	Serves 4	Midwest
	00:45		

American	Ingredients	Metric/Imperial
3	Large potatoes	3
2 tbsp	Vinegar	1½ tbsp
1 tsp	Salt and pepper	1 tsp
½ lb	Bacon, chopped	225 g/8 oz
3	Eggs	3
¼ cup	Chopped scallions [spring onions]	25 g/1 oz
	Lettuce	
4	Frankfurters	4

Provençal Salad

	01:00	Serves 4–6	South
	01:30		

American	Ingredients	Metric/Imperial
4 tbsp	Oil	3½ tbsp
2	Onions, peeled and chopped	2
2	Cloves garlic, crushed	2
2	Small eggplants [aubergines], cubed	2
4	Zucchini [courgettes], sliced	4
2	Green peppers, seeded and chopped	2
3–4	Stalks celery, choppped	3–4
1 lb	Tomatoes, peeled, seeded, and chopped	450 g/1 lb
½ tsp	Dried or 1 teaspoon chopped fresh basil	½ tsp dried (or 1 tsp fresh)

1. Heat the oil in a frying pan, add onion and garlic, and sauté until the onion is transparent. Add the eggplant, zucchini, green pepper, and celery. Mix well and cook for 5 minutes.
2. Add the tomatoes, seasoning, and basil; cover and cook over low heat for about 1 hour, stirring occasionally.
3. Uncover and continue cooking until most of the liquid has evaporated. Set aside to cool before serving.

Potato Special

Potato Special

	02:25	Serves 6–8	Mid Atlantic
	00:20		

American	Ingredients	Metric/Imperial
6 cups	Diced cooked potatoes	675 g/1½ lb
3–4	Scallions [spring onions], chopped	3–4
4	Hard-boiled eggs, chopped	4
1 tsp	Celery seed	1 tsp
1½ tsp	Salt	1½ tsp
¼ tsp	Pepper	¼ tsp
1 tsp	Curry powder	1 tsp
1 cup	Sour cream	250 ml/8 fl oz
½ cup	Mayonnaise	125 ml/4 fl oz
2 tbsp	Vinegar	1½ tbsp
	Chopped parsley	

1. Mix the potatoes, onions, chopped eggs, and seasoning (except curry powder) together in a bowl. Set aside to chill.
2. Mix the curry powder with the sour cream. Add the mayonnaise and vinegar.
3. When ready to serve, add to the potato mixture. Toss all lightly together and sprinkle with parsley.

Ratatouille Salad

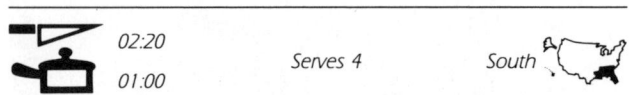

	02:20 01:00	Serves 4	South 

American	Ingredients	Metric/Imperial
2	Eggplants [aubergines]	2
	A little coarse salt	
½ cup	Olive oil	125 ml/4 fl oz
1	Onion, peeled and chopped	1
1	Large red pepper, seeded and cut into small pieces	1
4	Tomatoes, peeled and chopped	4
2	Cloves garlic, crushed	2
12	Coriander seeds	12
	Chopped basil or parsley	

1. Wipe the eggplants, cut into ½-inch [1.25 cm] squares and put into a colander. Sprinkle with coarse salt and leave to drain.
2. Heat some of the oil in a frying pan and sauté the onion for about 10 minutes, or until it begins to soften. Add a little more oil, put in the eggplant and red pepper, cover, and simmer for 30–40 minutes.
3. Add tomatoes, garlic, and coriander; continue to cook until the tomatoes are soft and mushy, adding a little more oil if necessary. Adjust the seasoning, then chill.
4. Drain off any excess oil and sprinkle with basil or parsley.

Tomato and Rice Salad

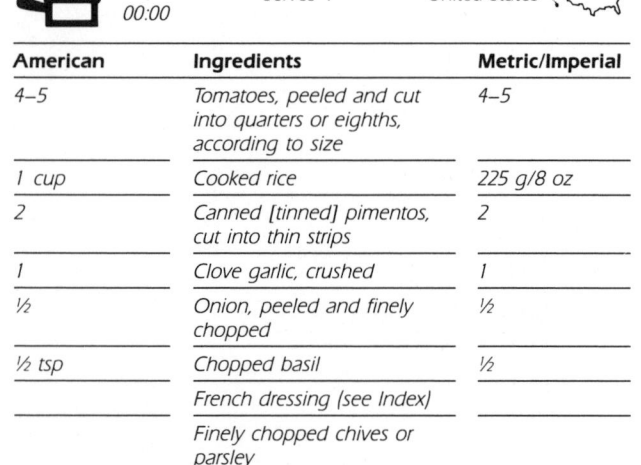

	02:10 00:00	Serves 4	United States

American	Ingredients	Metric/Imperial
4–5	Tomatoes, peeled and cut into quarters or eighths, according to size	4–5
1 cup	Cooked rice	225 g/8 oz
2	Canned [tinned] pimentos, cut into thin strips	2
1	Clove garlic, crushed	1
½	Onion, peeled and finely chopped	½
½ tsp	Chopped basil	½
	French dressing (see Index)	
	Finely chopped chives or parsley	

1. Combine the tomatoes, rice, pimentos, garlic, and onion. Sprinkle with chopped basil.
2. Add enough French dressing to coat all the ingredients, but avoid adding too much.
3. Chill and serve sprinkled with chopped chives or parsley.

Stuffed Tomatoes

	02:30 00:00	Serves 4	United States

American	Ingredients	Metric/Imperial
8	Firm ripe tomatoes	8
2	Ripe avocados	2
	Juice of 1 lemon	
1 tbsp	Onion juice	1 tbsp
	Salt and black pepper	
	A pinch of chili powder	
4 tbsp	Finely chopped celery or green pepper	3½ tbsp
1 tbsp	Finely chopped parsley	1 tbsp

1. Peel the tomatoes after plunging them into boiling water for 1 minute and then in cold water.
2. Cut in half crosswise and remove the seeds and pulp. Cover loosely with foil and chill in the refrigerator until required.
3. Peel the avocados, remove the seed, and mash well with a wooden spoon. Add lemon juice, salt, pepper, chili powder, and celery or green pepper. Set aside to chill.
4. When ready to use, fill the tomato halves with the avocado mixture and sprinkle with parsley.

Zucchini and Blue Cheese Salad

	00:15 00:00	Serves 5–6	Midwest

American	Ingredients	Metric/Imperial
1	Lettuce or other salad greens	1
2 cups	Zucchini [courgette], sliced thinly	225 g/8 oz
3–4	Scallions [green onions], sliced	3–4
½ cup	Sliced raw mushrooms	50 g/2 oz
½ cup	Radishes, sliced	50 g/2 oz
2	Tomatoes, peeled and quartered	2
	Salt and pepper	
	French Dressing (see Index)	
½ cup	Crumbled blue cheese	100 g/4 oz

1. Break up the lettuce into bite-sized pieces, and put it into a bowl with all the other ingredients. Season with salt and pepper.
2. Add the dressing and toss lightly. Then sprinkle the cheese on top.

Ratatouille Salad

Tomato and Herb Salad

| | 02:10 | Serves 4–6 | New England |
| | 00:00 | | |

American	Ingredients	Metric/Imperial
4	Firm tomatoes	4
	Salt	
	Olive oil	
	Wine vinegar or lemon juice	
	Chopped herbs	

1. Peel some firm tomatoes, cut them into fairly thick slices, and arrange them on a platter. Sprinkle with a little salt, a few drops of olive oil and wine vinegar or lemon juice.
2. Sprinkle thickly with chopped herbs as available—parsley, chives, dill, basil, tarragon, etc.
3. Chill before serving.

Hot Potato Salad

| | 08:20 | Serves 6 | Mid Atlantic |
| | 00:50 | | |

American	Ingredients	Metric/Imperial
1 cup	Butter	225 g/8 oz
1 tbsp	Flour	1 tbsp
½ cup	Milk	125 ml/4 fl oz
6	Medium potatoes	6
½ cup	French dressing	125 ml/4 fl oz
½ cup	Mayonnaise	125 ml/4 fl oz
1	Onion, finely chopped	1

1. Preheat the oven to 400°F/200°C/Gas Mark 6.
2. Make the white sauce with butter, flour, and milk.
3. Boil the potatoes; peel and cut them into slices or cubes. Cover with French dressing and leave them in it all day.
4. Half an hour before you eat, mix the white sauce and mayonnaise with the onion. Then add the potatoes.
5. Bake in a greased casserole, uncovered, for about 30 minutes. Can be served lukewarm.

Macaroni and Sausage Salad

Hot Macaroni Salad

 00:10
00:20   Serves 5–6   United States

American	Ingredients	Metric/Imperial
7 oz	Macaroni	200 g/7 oz
6 slices	Bacon, diced	6 rashers
2 tbsp	Vinegar	1½ tbsp
1 tbsp	Finely chopped onion	1 tbsp
½ tsp	Salt	½ tsp
¼ tsp	Pepper	¼ tsp
⅓ cup	Salad Cream (see Index)	5 tbsp
½ cup	Sliced radishes	50 g/2 oz
¼ cup	Green chopped pepper	25 g/1 oz
4 tbsp	Chopped parsley	3½ tbsp

1. Cook the macaroni in boiling salted water.
2. While the macaroni is cooking, fry the bacon until crisp. Remove bacon from the pan and drain off excess fat from the pan, leaving about 1 tablespoon. Add vinegar, onion, and seasoning and bring to boiling point.
3. Add drained macaroni and all the other ingredients; toss lightly.
4. Serve hot with a green salad, if desired.

Macaroni and Sausage Salad

01:30
00:15   Serves 4   United States

American	Ingredients	Metric/Imperial
7 oz	Macaroni	200 g/7 oz
4 tbsp	Oil	3½ tbsp
1½ tbsp	Vinegar	1¼ tbsp
½ tsp	Salt	½ tsp
1 tsp	Thyme	1 tsp
¼ lb	Smoked sausage, cubed	50 g/2 oz
1 cup	Cheese, cubed	225 g/8 oz
½	Cucumber, cubed	½
	Part of 1 leek, shredded	
	Tomatoes	
	Lettuce	

1. Boil the macaroni according to the directions on the package. Combine the oil, vinegar, salt, and thyme. Pour the dressing over the hot macaroni. Let cool.
2. Mix the sausage, cheese, cucumber, and leek with the cold macaroni. Season. Serve with tomatoes and lettuce.

Salad Andalouse

00:10
00:00   Serves 4   Pacific Southwest

American	Ingredients	Metric/Imperial
1 cup	Cooked rice	100 g/4 oz
4	Tomatoes, peeled and cut into quarters	4
2	Canned pimentos, cut into thin strips	2
1	Clove garlic, crushed	1
½	Onion, peeled and finely chopped	½
	French Dressing (see Index)	
	Finely chopped parsley	

1. Combine the rice, tomatoes, pimento, garlic, and onion. Add seasoning if required.
2. Add enough French dressing to coat all the ingredients well, but avoid adding excess dressing.
3. Sprinkle with parsley before serving.

Macaroni Salad

02:10
00:15   Serves 6   United States

American	Ingredients	Metric/Imperial
2 cups	Shell or ring macaroni	225 g/8 oz
2 tbsp	Butter	25 g/1 oz
1 cup	Cubed Cheddar cheese	100 g/4 oz
1 cup	Sliced gherkins	100 g/4 oz
½ cup	Very finely chopped onion	50 g/2 oz
2 cups	Cooked peas	225 g/8 oz
½ cup	Mayonnaise	125 g/4 fl oz
	Seasoning	
	Lettuce	

1. Cook the macaroni in boiling salted water; drain well, add the butter, and toss lightly.
2. Add cheese, gherkins, onion, and peas.
3. Stir in the mayonnaise and blend carefully, making sure the macaroni is well mixed with the mayonnaise.
4. Check the seasoning and set aside to chill.
5. Serve individually in lettuce leaves or on a bed of shredded lettuce.

Macaroni Salad

Turkey Salad in Curried Mayonnaise 🥦🥦

01:15
00:40

Serves 4–6

South

American	Ingredients	Metric/Imperial
3 cups	Turkey meat	450–675 g/ 1–1½ lb
3 cups	Mixed cooked vegetables, peas, beans, corn, celery and pimento	350 g/12 oz
4	Tomatoes	4
1	Bunch watercress	1
1 tbsp	Butter	15 g/½ oz
1	Shallot (or 1 tbsp chopped onion)	1
½ tbsp	Curry powder	½ tbsp
1 tsp	Flour	1 tsp
½ cup	Stock	125 ml/4 fl oz
2 tsp	Coconut	2 tsp
2 tsp	Chutney	2 tsp
3 tsp	Lemon juice	3 tsp
1–1½ cups	Mayonnaise	250–375 ml/ 8–12 fl oz
	A pinch of paprika	
1–2	Lemons	1–2

1. Cook the vegetables separately, and let cool. Shred the cold turkey. Quarter the tomatoes, remove the seeds, strain, and reserve juice for thinning the mayonnaise. Wash the watercress and dry throroughly.

2. Make the curry flavoring: Melt the butter and cook the chopped shallot or onion until tender. Add curry powder or paste and cook for a minute or two. Sprinkle in the flour and cook for 3–5 minutes. Add the stock and blend well. Then bring to a boil, stirring all the time. Sprinkle on the coconut, add chutney and lemon juice, and cook for 10–15 minutes. Then strain and let cool. Add the lemon juice, salt, and pepper.

3. Add the cooled curry mixture to the mayonnaise to taste. Add as much of the strained tomato juice as will make spooning consistency.

4. Mix all the vegetables together; season with salt and pepper and sprinkle with lemon juice. Put into a dish or salad bowl. Arrange the turkey shreds in the center, spoon mayonnaise carefully over the top allowing the vegetable salad to show around the edges. Sprinkle the top with paprika. Arrange the tomato quarters and small sprigs of watercress alternately around the edge of dish, and serve with lemon quarters separately.

Luncheon Salad

 00:20
00:00   Serves 4–5   United States

American	Ingredients	Metric/Imperial
2 cups	Chopped cooked meat or poultry	350 g/12 oz
2 cups	Grated raw carrot	225 g/8 oz
2 tbsp	Finely chopped onion	1½ tbsp
2	Unpeeled dessert apples, cored and chopped	2
3–4	Stalks celery, chopped	3–4
2 tsp	French mustard	2 tsp
½ cup	Mayonnaise	125 ml/4 fl oz
	Lettuce	
1 tbsp	Chopped parsley	1 tbsp
	Cranberry or apple jelly	

1. Combine the meat, carrot, onion, apple, and celery in a bowl.
2. Mix the mustard with the mayonnaise, add to the ingredients in the bowl, and toss lightly together. Add a little salt to taste.
3. Arrange "cups" of lettuce on individual dishes. Pile the mixture in the center, sprinkle with parsley, and top with a spoonful of jelly.

Smoked Turkey Salad

 00:25
00:15   Serves 4–6   Midwest

American	Ingredients	Metric/Imperial
1 lb	Smoked turkey breast	450 g/1 lb
½ lb	Noodles	225 g/8 oz
3–4 tbsp	Cream	2–3½ tbsp
2–3	Lettuce hearts	2–3
3–4	Tomatoes	3–4
½ cup	Cooked corn and pimento	50 g/2 oz
	Mayonnaise	
¾ tsp	Salt	¾ tsp
¼ tsp	pepper	¼ tsp
1 tsp	Dried mustard	1 tsp
1½ tsp	Sugar	1½ tsp
1	Egg	1
¾ cup	Salad oil	175 ml/6 fl oz
1 tsp	Lemon juice	1 tsp
1 tsp	Wine vinegar	1 tsp

1. Make mayonnaise: Put salt, pepper, mustard and sugar into liquidizer. Add egg. Mix thoroughly at low speed. Add a few drops of oil. Mix well. Then add remaining oil in steady stream until it has been absorbed and mayonnaise is very thick. Add lemon juice, vinegar and 1–2 tablespoons boiling water, which thins it and helps to make it keep.
2. Boil noodles until tender in salted water, drain and let cool. Add beaten cream to mayonnaise, mix two-thirds with the cold noodles and season to taste.
3. Cut smoked turkey into very thin slices and place on top of noodle mayonnaise in a neat row. Garnish dish with lettuce hearts, peeled tomato quarters, and corn and pimento mixed with a little of remaining mayonnaise.

Turkey, Celery, Grape and Nut Salad

 00:15
00:02   Serves 4   Pacific Southwest

American	Ingredients	Metric/Imperial
2 cups	Chopped turkey	350 g/12 oz
½ cup	Grapes	50 g/2 oz
½ cup	Sliced celery	50 g/2 oz
3–4 tbsp	Almonds	2–3½ tbsp
	Juice of ½ lemon	
	Grated rind of ½ orange	
1 cup	Mayonnaise	250 ml/8 fl oz
	Lettuce or endive leaves	
½ tsp	Paprika	½ tsp

1. Chop the turkey into medium-sized pieces. Peel the grapes after dipping into boiling, then cold, water. Slice the celery. Dip the almonds in boiling water, remove the skins, and brown halved nuts in a moderate oven for 2 minutes.
2. Add extra lemon juice and grated orange rind to the mayonnaise, to flavor. Mix the turkey and other ingredients into the mayonnaise. Arrange on lettuce or endive leaves and sprinkle with a little paprika.

Turkey Stuffed Tomatoes

 00:35
00:00   Serves 4   United States

American	Ingredients	Metric/Imperial
1 cup	Cooked chopped turkey	175 g/6 oz
4	Large red tomatoes	4
½	Cucumber	½
2	Stalks celery	2
3–4 tbsp	Cooked corn	2–3½ tbsp
½ cup	Mayonnaise (approx.)	125 ml/4 fl oz
4	Slices lemon or chopped parsley	4

1. Chop the cold turkey. Cut off the tops of the tomatoes, remove the seeds, and reserve the juice. Peel the cucumber, dice and salt it, and leave for 20 minutes. Then wash and drain. Chop the celery and mix with the corn.
2. Combine the mayonnaise and the juice from the tomatoes.
3. Mix the vegetables and turkey with enough mayonnaise to make a creamy mixture. Fill into the tomatoes, and garnish with sliced lemon or chopped parsley. Serve with brown bread and butter.

Turkey, Celery, Grape, and Nut Salad

Turkey and Pomegranate Salad

	00:10	Serves 5–6	Mid Atlantic
	00:00		

American	Ingredients	Metric/Imperial
2 cups	Cooked turkey, cut into cubes	350 g/12 oz
2–3	Stalks celery, chopped	2–3
	Seeds from 1 large ripe pomegranate	
1 cup	Blanched chopped almonds	100 g/4 oz
	Salt and black pepper	
	Mayonnaise	
	Lettuce	
2	Slices pineapple, cut into wedges	2

1. Combine the turkey, celery, pomegranate seeds, and almonds. Season carefully with salt and freshly ground black pepper.
2. Add enough mayonnaise to moisten and toss all lightly together.
3. Serve on a bed of lettuce and garnish with wedges of pineapple.

Chicken Salad

	01:15	Serves 5–6	New England
	00:00		

American	Ingredients	Metric/Imperial
¼ lb	Mushrooms	100 g/4 oz
½ cup	French dressing (see Index)	125 ml/4 fl oz
1	Large iceberg lettuce	1
1½ cups	Diced cooked chicken	500 g/18 oz
1 can	Artichoke hearts, drained and cut in halves	1 tin
1	Small red pepper, seeded and cut into strips	1
½ lb	Cooked green beans, sliced	225 g/8 oz
1 cup	Grapes, halved and seeded	175 g/6 oz
¼ cup	Toasted flaked almonds	25 g/1 oz

1. Wash and slice the mushrooms and place in a shallow bowl. Pour the French dressing over them and set aside for 1 hour, stirring occasionally.
2. Wash the lettuce, discarding the outer leaves, and line a deep salad bowl or large platter.
3. Combine the chicken, artichoke hearts, red pepper, and beans. Add the mushrooms and the dressing, season to taste, and toss all lightly together. Refrigerate until ready to serve, then spoon the chicken mixture over the lettuce.
4. Sprinkle with grapes and toasted almonds.

Waldorf Chicken Salad

Avocado and Chicken Salad

| | 00:15 | Serves 6 | Pacific Southwest  |
| | 00:00 | | |

American	Ingredients	Metric/Imperial
3	Ripe avocado	3
2 tbsp	Orange juice	1½ tbsp
1 cup	Diced cooked chicken	175 g/6 oz
1–2	Stalks celery, diced	1–2
3	Oranges	3
¼ cup	Mayonnaise	60 ml/2 fl oz
	A pinch of paprika pepper	
1 tbsp	Chopped pimento	1 tbsp
	Salad greens	

1. Peel the avocados, remove the stones, and scoop out some of the flesh. Brush the avocados with orange juice.
2. Cut the scooped-out avocado flesh into small pieces and place in a bowl with the chicken and celery.
3. Peel and section 2 of the oranges, removing the seeds and white pith. Cut into small pieces and add to the chicken and celery mixture.
4. Combine the mayonnaise with the paprika, add salt to taste, and blend with the chicken.
5. Fill the avocado halves and sprinkle with chopped pimento. Serve on a bed of salad greens and garnish with sections of the remaining orange.

Waldorf Chicken Salad

| | 00:15 | Serves 4 | Mid Atlantic  |
| | 00:00 | | |

American	Ingredients	Metric/Imperial
4	Dessert apples	4
	Juice of ½ lemon	
½ cup	Mayonnaise	125 ml/4 fl oz
	Salt and pepper	
1 cup	Cooked chicken, diced	175 g/6 oz
2	Sticks celery, chopped	2
1 tbsp	Walnuts, chopped	1 tbsp
	Lettuce leaves for serving	

1. Peel, core, and dice apples. Mix apple with lemon juice to prevent it discoloring. Season mayonnaise with salt and pepper and put it in a bowl with diced apple, chicken, celery, and walnuts. Mix lightly.
2. Arrange lettuce on a serving plate. Place prepared salad in the middle and serve.

Chicken Salad with Lychees

| | 01:40 | Serves 5–6 | South |
| | 00:00 | | |

American	Ingredients	Metric/Imperial
3 cups	Cooked diced chicken	500 g/18 oz
2–3	Stalks celery, chopped	2–3
1	Green pepper, chopped	1
¾ cup	French Dressing (see Index)	175 ml/6 fl oz
	Salad greens	
1 can (8 oz)	Lychees	1 tin (225 g/8 oz)
1 can (10½ oz)	Mandarins	1 tin (300 g/10½ oz)
	Dressing	
¾ cup	Mayonnaise	175 ml/6 fl oz
¼ cup	Sour cream	60 ml/2 fl oz
2 tsp	Curry powder	2 tsp
2 tbsp	Grated onion	1½ tbsp
2 tbsp	Chopped parsley	1½ tbsp

1. Combine the chicken, celery, and green pepper. Add salt, pepper, and the French dressing. Toss lightly together and chill for about 30 minutes.
2. Arrange some salad greens around a large platter and pile the chicken mixture in the center.
3. Drain the lychees and mandarins. Place a mandarin segment in each lychee and arrange around the edge or down the center.
4. Blend all the ingredients for the dressing together, chill well, and serve the dressing separately.

Chicken Stuffed Apples

🕐 00:20
00:00

Serves 4

Mid Atlantic

American	Ingredients	Metric/Imperial
2 cups	White cooked chicken meat	350 g/12 oz
1¼ cups	Mayonnaise	300 ml/½ pint
½ cup	Pineapple chunks	50 g/2 oz
1 cup	Grapes	100 g/4 oz
2	Stalks celery	2
4	Large apples	4
1 tsp	Grated lemon rind	1 tsp
2 tbsp	Slivered almonds	1½ tbsp

1. Dice the chicken finely and mix with the drained pineapple chunks, peeled seeded grapes, and chopped celery. Mix with the mayonnaise.
2. Polish the apples and cut them in half. Scoop out the flesh with a grapefruit knife or spoon. Remove the core and dice the remaining apple; add to the mayonnaise.
3. Fill the apple halves with chicken mayonnaise. Sprinkle the top with grated lemon rind and lightly browned almonds.

Cheese and Lettuce Salad

🕐 03:10
00:00

Serves 5–6

Midwest

American	Ingredients	Metric/Imperial
1	Large firm lettuce	1
1 pkg (3 oz)	Cream cheese	75 g/3 oz
8 oz	Cottage cheese	225 g/8 oz
2 tbsp	Sour cream	1½ tbsp
2 tbsp	Very finely chopped or minced onion	1½ tbsp
¼ cup	Chopped green pepper	25 g/1 oz
½ cup	Grated raw carrots	50 g/2 oz
¼ cup	Chopped nuts	25 g/1 oz
	French dressing (see Index)	

1. Wash, drain, and dry the lettuce. Remove the hard central stalk, making a cavity large enough to hold the cheese mixture.
2. Beat the cream cheese, cottage cheese, sour cream, and onion together until soft and creamy; add all the other ingredients and blend well.
3. Stuff the lettuce and chill for several hours. Cut into wedges and serve with French dressing.

Chicken Salad with Lychees

Turkey and Grape Aspic

 08:00 / 00:05   Serves 4–6   United States

American	Ingredients	Metric/Imperial
1–1½ lb	Turkey meat	450–675 g/ 1–1½ lb
1½ tbsp	Gelatin	1¼ tbsp
2¾ cups	Clear, well-flavored turkey stock	600 ml/1 pint
4 tbsp	White wine	3½ tbsp
1 lb	White grapes (or ½ lb, and 1 can [tin] of mandarin oranges)	450 g/1 lb
	Juice of ½ lemon	
	A few tarragon leaves	
	Lettuce and watercress	

1. Make the aspic: Melt gelatin in ¾ cup [6 fl oz] clear hot turkey stock. When melted, add the white wine and the remaining stock. Let cool thoroughly.
2. Meanwhile, dip the white grapes into boiling water for 10 seconds, then into cold. Remove the skins and seeds and put the grapes in a bowl with a little lemon juice to prevent browning. Cut the turkey meat into neat small slices and cubes.
3. Pour a layer of aspic into a round mold. Arrange a decorative pattern of grapes with tarragon leaves and leave in refrigerator to set. Pour over another layer of aspic. Now put in a layer of turkey and repeat. Continue making layers of grapes, meat, and aspic until all is used, allowing enough aspic to cover the top completely.
4. Put in the refrigerator and leave until set. Then dip in a bowl of hot water to loosen the jelly and turn out onto a salad-lined plate. Canned mandarin oranges can be added or used in place of grapes.

Swiss Ham Salad

 01:10 / 00:00   Serves 4–5   Midwest

American	Ingredients	Metric/Imperial
¾ lb	Cooked ham, cut in thick slices and diced	350 g/12 oz
¾ lb	Gruyère cheese, diced	350 g/12 oz
6 tbsp	Olive oil	5 tbsp
2 tbsp	White wine vinegar	1½ tbsp
	Salt and freshly ground black pepper	
	Romaine lettuce [cos] or curly endive	
	Finely chopped parsley or fresh herbs	

1. Combine the ham and cheese in a bowl.
2. Make a dressing with the oil, vinegar, salt, and pepper; pour over the ham and cheese and toss lightly. Refrigerate and leave about 1 hour to marinate.
3. Arrange the lettuce in a salad bowl, pile the ham and cheese in the center, and sprinkle with parsley or herbs.

Cheese and Fruit Salad

 00:15 / 00:00   Serves 4   Mid Atlantic

American	Ingredients	Metric/Imperial
1 cup	Cream or cottage cheese	225 g/8 oz
⅓ cup	Chopped walnuts	40 g/1½ oz
2	Rings canned or fresh pineapple, chopped	2
1	Iceberg or Romaine [cos] lettuce	1
1	Large grapefruit	1
2	Bananas	2
	Juice of ½ lemon	
	French dressing (see Index)	

1. Combine the cheese with the nuts and pineapple.
2. Arrange the lettuce on a platter, reserving some of the heart for garnish. Pile the cheese in the center.
3. Arrange segments of grapefruit and slices of banana brushed with lemon juice around the cheese, and tuck pieces of lettuce heart in between.
4. Pour the dressing over the top. If canned pineapple is used, 1 tablespoon pineapple juice can be substituted for 1 tablespoon of the oil in the French dressing.

Ham and Pineapple Salad

 02:00 / 00:08   Serves 4   United States

American	Ingredients	Metric/Imperial
½ cup	Shell or other small pasta	50 g/2 oz
3 tbsp	Mayonnaise	2 tbsp
1	Green pepper, seeded and chopped	1
4	Large slices cooked ham	4
	Lettuce	
4	Rings pineapple	4
2	Tomatoes	2

1. Cook the pasta in boiling salted water for 5–8 minutes. Drain well.
2. While still warm, add the mayonnaise, green pepper, and seasoning; then set aside until quite cold.
3. Place a spoonful of the mixture on half of each slice of ham; fold the other half over.
4. Arrange on a bed of lettuce and place a ring of pineapple on each slice of ham. Garnish with wedges of tomato.

Beef Salad Nicoise

Beef Salad Nicoise 🖐️🖐️

⏱️ 01:30
00:00

Serves 8

South 🗺️

American	Ingredients	Metric/Imperial
8	Slices rare cold roast beef	8
1	Small cucumber	1
	Salt	
8	Ripe tomatoes	8
2	Green peppers	2
2	Small chopped onions or 24 scallions [spring onions]	2
3	Lettuce hearts	3
3	Stalks white celery	3
3	Hard-boiled eggs (optional)	3
16	Anchovy fillets	16
12	Green olives	12
12	Black olives	12

	Dressing	
4 tbsp	Best wine vinegar or lemon juice	3½ tbsp
12 tbsp	Best olive oil	11 tbsp
1 tsp	French mustard	1 tsp
¼ tsp	Sugar	¼ tsp
2	Cloves crushed garlic	2

1. Prepare the ingredients for the salad. Cut the slices of beef into thin strips. Slice the cucumber, salt it and allow it to stand for 10 minutes; then wash and drain it in cold water. Quarter and seed the tomatoes. Seed and slice the peppers. Wash and chop the onions or top the spring onions. Break up and wash the lettuce and discard the outer leaves; hard-boil eggs. Soak the anchovies in milk for 10 minutes to remove salt, then drain. Pit [stone] the olives.

2. Arrange lettuce leaves around a large salad bowl or dish. Put the ingredients into the bowl in layers, reserving the anchovies and olives for the top. Arrange the top layer carefully with an eye to color. Then make a lattice design with the anchovies over the whole top, putting an olive in the center of each lattice (alternating the colors).

3. Mix all the ingredients for the dressing together and spoon over the whole salad. Serve cold with garlic bread or French bread and butter.

Rainbow Salad

| | 00:15 | Serves 4 | United States |
| | 00:00 | | |

American	Ingredients	Metric/Imperial
¼ lb	Cooked ham, diced	100 g/4 oz
1 cup	Cottage cheese	225 g/8 oz
	A pinch of cayenne pepper	
¼ tsp	Salt	¼ tsp
½	Cucumber	½
4	Stalks celery, chopped	4
2	Red dessert apples, cored and chopped but not peeled	2
2	Carrots, grated	2
2 tbsp	Lemon juice	1½ tbsp
	Lettuce	
2	Hard-boiled eggs	2
	Parsley or watercress	
	Dressing	
½ cup	Yogurt	125 ml/4 fl oz
1 tsp	Lemon juice	1 tsp
	A pinch of garlic salt	
1 tsp	Prepared mustard	1 tsp
	Black pepper, paprika pepper	

1. Combine the ham, cottage cheese, pepper, and salt.
2. Arrange some thin slices of cucumber around the edge of a large platter and cut the rest into ¼-inch dice.
3. Put the diced cucumber, celery, apples, and carrots into a bowl, add the lemon juice, and mix well. Arrange on the platter, put some lettuce leaves in the center, and place the ham and cheese mixture on top.
4. Cut the eggs in halves lengthwise and arrange on top. Place a sprig of parsley or watercress in the center.
5. Combine the dressing ingredients and serve with the salad.

Luncheon Salad Bowl

| | 00:15 | Serves 5–6 | United States |
| | 00:00 | | |

American	Ingredients	Metric/Imperial
1	Cut clove of garlic	1
1 cup	Shredded lettuce	100 g/4 oz
1 cup	Shredded Romaine [cos]	100 g/4 oz
1 cup	Shredded escarole	100 g/4 oz
1	Small bunch watercress	1
½	Green pepper, seeded and cut into rings	½
½ can (4 oz)	Luncheon meat, shredded	½ tin (100 g/4 oz)
¼ lb	American cheese, cut into strips	100 g/4 oz
3	Hard-boiled eggs, cut into wedges	3
½ cup	French dressing (see Index)	125 ml/4 fl oz

1. Rub a wooden salad bowl with the cut clove of garlic.
2. Arrange all the ingredients in the bowl. Add the dressing and toss lightly until all the ingredients are coated.

Russian Salad

| | 01:30 | Serves 4–6 | Pacific Northwest |
| | 00:00 | | |

American	Ingredients	Metric/Imperial
½–¾ lb	Cooked veal or ham	225–350 g/ 8–12 oz
½	Small cucumber	½
2	Cooked beets [beetroot]	2
2	Cooked medium potatoes	2
2	Cooked carrots	2
1	Apple	1
½ cup	Cooked peas (or beans)	50 g/2 oz
12	Scallions [spring onions] (optional)	12
¼ tsp	Salt	¼ tsp
¼ tsp	Pepper	¼ tsp
½ tsp	French mustard	½ tsp
	A pinch of sugar	
6 tbsp	Olive oil	5 tbsp
2 tbsp	Vinegar (or lemon juice)	1½ tbsp
1	Clove garlic	1
1	Crisp lettuce	1
1 cup	Thick mayonnaise	250 ml/8 fl oz
4	Tomatoes, peeled and quartered	4

1. Shred the meet and dice the lightly salted cucumber half. Put in a bowl with the diced beets, potatoes, carrots, apple, peas (or beans); if desired, chop the scallions, and add to the meat mixture.
2. Make French dressing: Mix salt, pepper, mustard, and sugar together with 1 tablespoon oil. Then beat in oil and vinegar alternately. Adjust the seasoning. Put in a whole clove of garlic until read to use, then remove it. Moisten the meat and vegetables with French dressing. Leave for an hour or so.
3. Just before serving, arrange the washed lettuce leaves around the outside of the salad bowl. Spoon the meat mixture into the center. Squeeze the tomatoes through a sieve and add the juice to the mayonnaise. Spoon the mayonnaise over the salad and garnish with tomato quarters.

Rainbow Salad

Seafood Medley

Seafood Medley

| | 00:20 | Serves 5–6 | Mid Atlantic  |
| | 00:00 | | |

American	Ingredients	Metric/Imperial
1 can (6½ oz)	Tuna fish	1 tin (175 g/ 6½ oz)
1 can (6½ oz)	Crabmeat	1 tin (175 g/ 6½ oz)
1 can (4¼ oz)	Shrimp [prawns]	1 tin (125 g/ 4¼ oz)
½ cup	French dressing (see Index)	125 ml/4 fl oz
1 cup	Diced celery	100 g/4 oz
½ cup	Diced cucumber	50 g/2 oz
6–8	Radishes, chopped	6–8
1 tbsp	Capers	1 tbsp
2 tbsp	Lemon juice	1½ tbsp
½ cup	Mayonnaise	125 ml/4 fl oz
	Salt, pepper, and paprika pepper	
	Lettuce	

1. Drain the tuna and break up into flakes. Add flaked crabmeat and shrimp. Stir in the French dressing and set aside to chill for about 15 minutes.
2. Add celery, cucumber, radishes, and capers.
3. Blend lemon juice with the mayonnaise, add seasoning to taste, and toss all ingredients lightly together.
4. Serve on crisp lettuce.

Crab Mayonnaise

| | 02:00 | Serves 5–6 | Mid Atlantic |
| | 00:15 | | |

American	Ingredients	Metric/Imperial
1 lb	Fresh, canned, or frozen crab meat	450 g/1 lb
1 tbsp	Oil	1 tbsp
1	Small onion, peeled and chopped	1
2 tsp	Curry powder	2 tsp
2 tsp	Tomato purée	2 tsp
1 tbsp	Clear honey	1 tbsp
6 tbsp	Red wine	5 tbsp
4 tbsp	Water	3½ tbsp
	Juice of ½ lemon	
1 cup	Mayonnaise	250 ml/8 fl oz
½	Red or green pepper, cut into strips	½
	Black olives	
2–3	Tomatoes	2–3
	Lettuce	

1. Arrange the crabmeat in a shallow oval dish.
2. Heat the oil in a frying pan, sauté the onion for 3–5 minutes; then add curry powder and fry for another 2 minutes.
3. Add tomato purée, honey, wine, and water. Bring to the boiling point; add seasoning and lemon juice. Simmer until the mixture becomes thick and syrupy, then strain and leave to cool.
4. Stir this dressing into the mayonnaise and spoon it over the crab.
5. Arrange the strips of pepper in a lattice pattern over the top; put an olive into each square and slices of tomato around the edge. Chill and serve with crisp lettuce.

Crab Salad

| | 00:10 | Serves 4 | Mid Atlantic |
| | 00:12 | | |

American	Ingredients	Metric/Imperial
1 cup	Rice	225 g/8 oz
	Nutmeg	
	Lemon juice	
	Olive oil	
1 lb	Fresh white crabmeat	450 g/1 lb
6	Black olives, pitted	6
1	Red or green pepper, seeded and cut into strips	1
½	Clove garlic, crushed	½
3–4	Raw mushrooms, sliced	3–4
	A few walnuts	

1. Cook the rice in boiling salted water until just tender (about 12 minutes). Drain well and while still warm add a good pinch of nutmeg, squeeze of lemon juice, and enough oil to moisten.
2. Add crabmeat, olives, red or green pepper, garlic, and mushrooms. Mix lightly together.
3. Arrange in a bowl or on a platter, and sprinkle chopped walnuts on top.

Egg and Shrimp Mayonnaise

 01:10
00:00   Serves 6   United States

American	Ingredients	Metric/Imperial
½ cup	Mayonnaise	125 ml/4 fl oz
½ cup	Sour cream	125 ml/4 fl oz
1 tsp	Curry powder	1 tsp
6	Hard-boiled eggs	6
	Lettuce	
1 cup	Fresh or frozen shrimp [prawns]	225 g/8 oz
	Paprika pepper	
	Brown bread or rolls	

1. Combine the mayonnaise, sour cream, and curry powder, chill for 1 hour.
2. Shell and cut the hard-boiled eggs in halves and arrange rounded side up on crisp lettuce.
3. Fold the shrimp into the mayonnaise and spoon over the eggs. Sprinkle with paprika.
4. Serve with rolls or thinly sliced buttered brown bread.

Shrimp and Rice Salad

 00:25
00:08   Serves 4–5   United States

American	Ingredients	Metric/Imperial
2 tbsp	Butter	25 g/1 oz
2	Small onions, peeled and chopped finely	2
1 cup	Sliced mushrooms	100 g/4 oz
2 cups	Cooked rice	450 g/1 lb
1 cup	Cooked peas	100 g/4 oz
1	Small red pepper, seeded and cut into strips	1
2 tbsp	Chopped parsley	1½ tbsp
4 oz	Cooked ham, cut into strips	100 g/4 oz
1 lb	Shrimp [prawns]	450 g/1 lb
	French dressing (see Index)	
	Lettuce	
	Slices of tomato and cucumber for garnish	

1. Heat the butter and sauté the onions until lightly browned. Remove from the pan. Add a little more butter, if required, and fry the mushrooms for 3 minutes.
2. Mix the onion, mushroom, and any pan juices with the rice. Add the peas, red pepper, parsley, ham, and shrimp, saving a few for the garnish. Mix lightly and add enough dressing to moisten.
3. Arrange the rice mixture in a ring on a serving dish. Surround with shredded lettuce and put the rest of the lettuce in the center.
4. Top with the reserved shrimp and arrange alternate slices of tomato and cucumber on the ring of lettuce.

Shrimp and Rice Salad

Molded Tuna Salad

 06:00
00:00   Serves 5–6   Pacific Southwest

American	Ingredients	Metric/Imperial
1 envelope	Unflavored gelatin [gelatine]	1 sachet
¼ cup	Cold water	60 ml/2 fl oz
¾ cup	Hot water	175 ml/6 fl oz
2 tbsp	Lemon juice	1½ tbsp
1 tsp	Prepared mustard	1 tsp
¼ tsp	Paprika pepper	¼ tsp
2 cans (6½ oz each)	Tuna fish	2 tins (175 g/6½ oz each)
1 cup	Chopped celery	100 g/4 oz
½ cup	Heavy [double] cream, whipped	125 ml/4 fl oz
	Lettuce	
	Dressing	
½ cup	Mayonnaise	125 ml/4 fl oz
¼ cup	Finely diced cucumber	25 g/1 oz
1 tbsp	Chopped green pepper	1 tbsp
1 tsp	Tarragon vinegar	1 tsp
	A dash of cayenne pepper	

1. Soften the gelatin in cold water for 5–10 minutes, add hot water, and stir until the gelatin has melted. Add lemon juice, mustard, paprika, and salt to taste. Set aside to chill until partially set.
2. Add drained and flaked tuna and celery and fold in the whipped cream.
3. Spoon into individual molds and chill until set.
4. Turn out on a bed of lettuce. Combine all the ingredients for the dressing, and serve separately.

Tuna in Lemon Baskets

Anchovy and Tuna Salad

| | 00:15 | | | |
| 00:00 | | Serves 4 | Pacific Southwest |  |

American	Ingredients	Metric/Imperial
4	Tomatoes, peeled and quartered	4
2	Small green peppers, seeded and sliced thinly	2
4	Stalks celery, chopped	4
1	Small cooked beet [beetroot]	1
2	Hard-boiled eggs, cut into quarters	2
1 can (3 oz)	Anchovy fillets	1 tin (75 g/3 oz)
1 can (6½ oz)	Tuna fish, drained and flaked	1 tin (175 g/6½ oz)
	Green and black olives	
	Dressing	
2 tbsp	White wine vinegar	1½ tbsp
6 tbsp	Olive oil	5 tbsp
	Salt and freshly ground black pepper	
½ tsp	Prepared mustard	½ tsp
1 tsp each	Finely chopped tarragon, chives, chervil, and parsley	1 tsp each

1. Arrange the tomatoes, green peppers, celery, beet, and eggs in a salad bowl or on a large platter.
2. Combine all the ingredients for the dressing together and blend well.
3. Arrange the anchovy fillets, tuna, and olives attractively on top and pour the dressing over.

Smoked Fish Salad

Tuna in Lemon Baskets

| | 00:15 | | | |
| 00:00 | | Serves 6 | Pacific Northwest | |

American	Ingredients	Metric/Imperial
3	Large lemons	3
1 can (7–9 oz)	Tuna fish	1 tin (200–250 g/7–9 oz)
3 tbsp	Dry white wine	2 tbsp
6	Scallions [spring onions]	6
1 tsp	Grated lemon rind	1 tsp
	Salt, black pepper, tarragon vinegar, and mayonnaise	
	Parsley stalks, capers, or gherkins	

1. Cut the lemons in half lengthwise and cut a small piece from the underside so that they will stand firmly. Scoop out the flesh, leaving the skins clean, and strain off the lemon juice.
2. Put the tuna fish into a bowl, add the lemon juice, and pound well.
3. Add the white wine, finely chopped scallions, grated lemon rind, and salt and pepper. Check the seasoning and add a little tarragon vinegar if required. Bind with mayonnaise and pile into the lemon skins.
4. Arrange a parsley stalk across the top to form a handle and garnish with capers or a gherkin.

Anchovy and Tuna Salad

Smoked Fish Salad

02:00
00:15   Serves 10–12   United States

American	Ingredients	Metric/Imperial
2 lb	Smoked fish or white fish	900 g/2 lb
1	Large cucumber	1
12	Radishes	12
1	Head celery	1
6	Spring onions	6
1 cup	Mayonnaise	250 ml/8 fl oz
	Lettuce leaves	

1. Place the fish in a large saucepan; add sufficient water to cover. Bring to a boil, cover, and simmer over low heat for 10–15 minutes or until the fish flakes easily. Set aside to cool, then flake coarsely.

2. Dice the unpeeled cucumber. Slice the radishes into thin rounds. Chop the celery into ½-inch [1.25 cm] pieces. Chop the spring onions.

3. Mix the fish and vegetables together in a large bowl. Gently mix in the mayonnaise. Line a serving dish with lettuce leaves and pile salad on top. Serve chilled.

Cheese and Macaroni Salad Ring

03:30
00:10   Serves 6–9   United States

American	Ingredients	Metric/Imperial
1 cup	Elbow macaroni	100 g/4 oz
¼ cup	French dressing (see Index)	60 ml/2 fl oz
2 cups	Cottage cheese	450 g/1 lb
4 tbsp	Diced pimento	3½ tbsp
¼ cup	Diced green pepper	25 g/1 oz
2 tbsp	Very finely chopped onion	1½ tbsp
2 tbsp	Chopped parsley	1½ tbsp
	Lettuce	
	Radishes and stuffed green olives for garnish	

1. Cook the macaroni in boiling salted water for about 10 minutes. Drain well and, while still warm, add the French dressing and mix well. Set aside to chill.

2. Add the other ingredients except the lettuce, radishes, and olives; mix lightly but thoroughly and press into a 9-inch ring mold. Chill for several hours.

3. When ready to serve, arrange some lettuce on a platter. Loosen the mixture from the side of the mold with a knife and turn out on the lettuce.

4. If the salad is to accompany poultry or meat, cut the meat into neat dice, bind with a little mayonnaise, season, and pile in the center of the macaroni ring.

5. Garnish with radish flowers and slices of olive.

Tomato Jellied Ring

Tomato Jellied Ring

08:00
00:10
Serves 4–6
United States

American	Ingredients	Metric/Imperial
4 cups	Tomato juice	1 l/1¾ pints
2 tsp	Salt	2 tsp
¼ tsp	Freshly ground black pepper	¼ tsp
¼ tsp	Finely chopped basil	¼ tsp
1	Onion, peeled and finely chopped	1
2 envelopes	Flavored gelatin [gelatine]	2 sachets
¼ cup	Cold water	60 ml/2 fl oz
2 tsp	Prepared horseradish	2 tsp
2 tbsp	Sugar	1½ tbsp
2 tbsp	Lemon juice	1½ tbsp
¼ lb	Elbow macaroni, cooked (or noodles)	100 g/4 oz
	Lettuce	

1. Put the tomato juice, seasoning, basil, and onion into a frying pan, heat to boiling point, and simmer for 10 minutes. Then strain.
2. Soak the gelatin in the cold water for 5 minutes, add to the hot tomato juice, and stir until dissolved.
3. Add horseradish, sugar, and lemon juice; adjust the seasoning to taste, and set aside to chill until the mixture begins to thicken.
4. Stir in the cooked macaroni, and pour into a lightly oiled, 9-inch ring mold. Chill until set.
5. Unmold onto the shredded lettuce, and fill the center as desired.

Ham Mousse

06:00
00:00
Serves 4–5
United States

American	Ingredients	Metric/Imperial
1 envelope	Unflavored gelatin [gelatine]	1 sachet
2 tbsp	Cold water	1½ tbsp
¼ cup	White wine vinegar	60 ml/2 fl oz
2 cups	Finely cubed cooked ham	350 g/12 oz
1 cup	Finely diced celery	100 g/4 oz
1 tbsp	Sugar	1 tbsp
1 tbsp	Pickle relish	1 tbsp
1 tsp	Prepared mustard	1 tsp
½ cup	Heavy [double] cream, whipped	125 ml/4 fl oz
	Lettuce	
	Stuffed olives	
Horseradish Cream		
3 tsp	Well-drained horseradish	3 tsp
½ tsp	Salt	½ tsp
¾ cup	Heavy [double] cream, whipped	175 ml/6 fl oz

1. Soften the gelatin in the cold water for about 5 minutes. Add the vinegar and heat over hot water until dissolved.
2. Combine ham, celery, sugar, pickle relish, and mustard. Stir in the melted gelatin and whipped cream. Check the seasoning and pour into a mold rinsed in cold water. Chill until set.
3. Unmold on a bed of lettuce and garnish with slices of stuffed olives.
4. Fold the horseradish and salt into the whipped cream, and serve separately.

Molded Chicken Salad

12:00
00:00
Serves 5–6
Mid Atlantic

American	Ingredients	Metric/Imperial
1 envelope	Unflavored gelatin [gelatine]	1 sachet
¼ cup	Cold water	60 ml/2 fl oz
1 cup	Hot chicken stock	250 ml/8 fl oz
2 tbsp	Chopped red pepper	1½ tbsp
2 tbsp	Chopped green pepper	1½ tbsp
2 cups	Diced cooked chicken	350 g/12 oz
1 tbsp	Finely chopped onion	1 tbsp
1 cup	Chopped celery	100 g/4 oz
1 cup	Cooked rice	225 g/8 oz
½ tsp	Salt	½ tsp
¼ cup	French dressing (see Index)	60 ml/2 fl oz
⅛ tsp	Paprika pepper	⅛ tsp
½ cup	Mayonnaise	125 ml/4 fl oz
	Lettuce	

1. Combine the gelatin and cold water and leave for about 10 minutes to soften. Add hot chicken stock and stir until the gelatin has melted.

2. Rinse a 6-cup [1.5 l/2½ pint] mold with cold water, then put in the red and green peppers. Cover with 2 tablespoons [1½ tbsp] of the melted gelatin and refrigerate until set.

3. Mix all the ingredients except the lettuce, and add the remaining gelatin.

4. When the gelatin in the mold is quite firm, spoon the chicken mixture on top and leave until set.

5. Unmold and serve on a bed of lettuce.

Salad Nicoise

	00:15		
	00:00	Serves 4	South

American	Ingredients	Metric/Imperial
2	Lettuce hearts	2
4	Tomatoes, peeled, seeded and quartered	4
½	Spanish onion, peeled and thinly sliced	½
1	Green pepper, seeded and cut into strips	1
8	Small radishes	8
4	Stalks celery, sliced	4
1 can (6½ oz)	Tuna fish	1 tin (175 g/6½ oz)
8	Anchovy fillets	8
2	Hard-boiled eggs	2
8	Black olives	8
	Dressing	
2 tbsp	White wine vinegar or lemon juice	1½ tbsp
6 tbsp	Olive oil	5 tbsp
	Few leaves fresh basil, chopped	

1. Place the fish in a large saucepan; add sufficient water to cover. Bring to a boil, cover, and simmer over low heat for 10–15 minutes or until the fish flakes easily. Set aside to cool, then flake coarsely.

2. Dice the unpeeled cucumber. Slice the radishes into thin rounds. Chop the celery into ½-inch pieces. Chop the spring onions.

3. Mix the fish and vegetables together in a large bowl. Gently mix in the mayonnaise. Line a serving dish with lettuce leaves and pile salad on top. Serve chilled.

Molded Chicken Salad

Cucumber and Cranberry Mold

Cucumber and Cranberry Mold

 06:00
00:00
Serves 8–10   New England

American	Ingredients	Metric/Imperial
3 cups	Peeled and chopped cucumber	350 g/12 oz
5 cups	Cranberry juice	1¼ l/2 pints
1 tsp	Onion juice	1 tsp
1 tsp	Garlic juice	1 tsp
1 tsp	Lemon juice	1 tsp
1 tsp	Salt	1 tsp
	A few drops chili sauce	
4 envelopes	Unflavored gelatin [gelatine]	4 sachets
1½ cups	Water	375 ml/12 fl oz
2	Eggs whites	2
Garnish		
	Watercress Thinly sliced cucumber	

1. Put 2 cups [225 g/8 oz] of the chopped cucumber into a blender or food mill, then pass through a fine sieve. Mix this with cranberry juice, onion juice, garlic juice, and lemon juice. Add salt and chili sauce.
2. Dissolve the gelatin in water, add to the cucumber and cranberry mixture. Chill until it begins to set; then beat until frothy, but be careful not to overbeat—the mixture should be thick and syrupy.
3. Fold in a stiffly beaten egg white and the remaining 1 cup [100 g/4 oz] of chopped cucumber. Season to taste, spoon into a mold, and chill until set.
4. Turn out and garnish with watercress and thinly sliced cucumber.

Molded Apricot Ring

 12:00
00:05
Serves 4   Pacific Southwest

American	Ingredients	Metric/Imperial
1 can (1¼ lb)	Apricots	1 tin (575 g/1¼ lb)
1 cup	Pineapple juice	250 ml/8 fl oz
1 envelope	Unflavored gelatin [gelatine]	1 sachet
2 tbsp	Water	1½ tbsp
3 oz	Cream cheese	75 g/3 oz
1 tbsp	Heavy [double] cream, whipped	1 tbsp
½	Small green pepper, blanched and finely chopped	½
	A pinch of paprika pepper	
	A pinch of salt	
	Watercress or lettuce	

1. Drain the apricots, finely chop enough to make ¼ cup [50 g/2 oz] and reserve the rest.
2. Mix 1 cup [8 fl oz] apricot syrup with the pineapple juice and heat to boiling point.
3. Soften the gelatin for 5 minutes in the water. Then dissolve it in the hot fruit juice.
4. Add the chopped apricots to half the gelatin and pour into a 4-cup [1 l/1¾ pint] ring mold. Refrigerate until set.
5. Chill the remaining gelatin until it begins to thicken.
6. Blend the cream cheese with the cream; add the green pepper, paprika, and salt, and spread on top of the firm gelatin.
7. Cover with the remaining thickened gelatin and set aside until firm.
8. Unmold and fill the center with watercress or lettuce and the remaining apricots.

Molded Grapefruit Salad

 08:00
00:00
Serves 4   Pacific Southwest

American	Ingredients	Metric/Imperial
1 can (about 16 oz)	Grapefruit	1 tin (about 450 g/1 lb)
2 envelopes	Unflavored gelatin [gelatine]	2 sachets
2 tbsp	Lemon juice	1½ tbsp
1	Dessert apple, peeled, cored and chopped	1
2–3	Stalks celery, chopped	2–3
	Lettuce	

1. Drain the syrup from the grapefruit, and add sufficient water to make 1 cup [250 ml/8 fl oz].
2. Soften the gelatin in a little of the syrup for 5–10 minutes. Then stir over hot water until melted. Add the rest of the syrup and lemon juice, and leave in a cold place until it begins to thicken.
3. Stir in the grapefruit, apple, and celery, Pour into a prepared mold or into individual molds, and refrigerate until set.
4. Serve on a bed of lettuce.

Jellied Tomato and Apple

06:00
00:05
Serves 4
Mid Atlantic

American	Ingredients	Metric/Imperial
1 envelope	Unflavored gelatin [gelatine]	1 sachet
½ cup	Water	125 ml/4 fl oz
1½ cups	Tomato juice	350 ml/12 fl oz
1 tbsp	Worcestershire sauce	1 tbsp
	Seasoning	
1	Large apple, peeled, cored and chopped	1
¼ cup	Chopped cooked ham	25 g/1 oz
	Lettuce	

1. Soften the gelatin in the water for 5–10 minutes.
2. Put it into a pan with the tomato juice and melt over low heat.
3. Remove from the heat, add Worcestershire sauce and seasoning, and set aside until it begins to thicken.
4. Add the apple and ham, adjust the seasoning, and pour into 4 prepared individual molds.
5. Refrigerate until set, then serve on a bed of lettuce.

Jellied Tongue and Potato Salad

12:00
00:05
Serves 6
Mid Atlantic

American	Ingredients	Metric/Imperial
1½ envelopes	Unflavored gelatin	1½ sachets
¼ cup	Cold water	60 ml/2 fl oz
1½ cups	Stock	350 ml/12 fl oz
¼ tsp	Dry mustard	¼ tsp
	A pinch of cayenne pepper	
1 tsp	Worcestershire sauce	1 tsp
1½ cups	Diced cooked tongue	225 g/8 oz
1½ cups	Diced cooked potato	225 g/8 oz
½ cup	Diced celery	50 g/2 oz
¼	Green pepper, diced	¼
¼ cup	Mayonnaise	60 ml/2 fl oz
2 tbsp	Vinegar	1½ tbsp
½ tsp	Salt	½ tsp
⅛ tsp	Pepper	⅛ tsp

1. Soften the gelatin in the cold water for about 10 minutes. Add boiling stock, stir until the gelatin has melted, then divide in half and leave to cool.
2. Mix the mustard and cayenne smoothly with the Worcestershire sauce and add to one half of the melted gelatin.
3. Put the tongue into the bottom of a 6-cup mold rinsed out with cold water and pour the seasoned gelatin on top. Refrigerate until set.
4. Combine all the other ingredients with the rest of the gelatin and when the meat layer is set, pour it on top.
5. Leave until set. Then unmold and garnish as desired.

Molded Grapefruit Salad

Stuffed Pears

00:20
00:00
Serves 6
Mid Atlantic

American	Ingredients	Metric/Imperial
3	Large ripe pears	3
	Lemon juice	
2	Red-skinned dessert apples, cored and diced but not peeled	2
2–3	Stalks celery, diced	2–3
1 can (6½ oz)	Crabmeat	1 tin (175 g/ 6½ oz)
1 tbsp	Finely chopped onion	1 tbsp
1 tbsp	Chopped parsley	1 tbsp
	French dressing (see Index)	
	Lettuce	

1. Wipe the pears but do not peel them. Cut in halves, remove the cores, and scoop out some of the flesh. Brush the pear halves with lemon juice.
2. Put the scooped-out flesh into a bowl and add apple, celery, crabmeat, onion, and parsley. Add enough French dressing to moisten, mix well, and check the seasoning.
3. Spoon into the pear halves, arrange on a bed of lettuce, and garnish with thin slices of unpeeled apple brushed with lemon juice.

Florida Salad

Florida Salad

	00:10	Serves 4–5	South
	00:00		

American	Ingredients	Metric/Imperial
1 can (8 oz)	Grapefruit sections	1 tin (225 g/8 oz)
1 cup	Sour cream	250 ml/8 fl oz
1 tsp	Salt	1 tsp
1 tsp	Dry mustard	1 tsp
½	Head cabbage, shredded	½

1. Drain the grapefruit.
2. Mix 2 tablespoons [1½ tbsp] of the grapefruit juice with the cream, salt, and mustard. Pour over the cabbage and toss lightly.
3. Add the grapefruit sections, and mix in lightly.

Honeyed Salad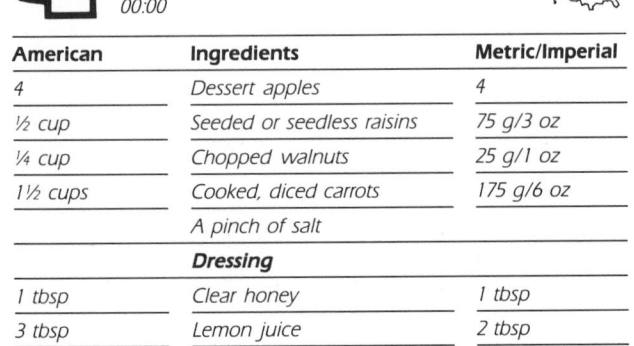

	00:15	Serves 4–5	Mid Atlantic
	00:00		

American	Ingredients	Metric/Imperial
4	Dessert apples	4
½ cup	Seeded or seedless raisins	75 g/3 oz
¼ cup	Chopped walnuts	25 g/1 oz
1½ cups	Cooked, diced carrots	175 g/6 oz
	A pinch of salt	
	Dressing	
1 tbsp	Clear honey	1 tbsp
3 tbsp	Lemon juice	2 tbsp

1. Peel, core, and dice three of the apples and combine with the raisins, nuts, and carrots. Add a pinch of salt.
2. Add the honey and lemon juice blended together, toss lightly, and set aside in a cool place for about 1 hour.
3. Arrange in a salad bowl or on a platter; garnish with the remaining apple (unpeeled, cut into slices, and brushed with lemon juice).

Frozen Fruit Salad

	04:00	Serves 6–8	United States
	00:00		

American	Ingredients	Metric/Imperial
3 oz	Cream cheese	75g/3 oz
3 tbsp	Mayonnaise	2 tbsp
	A pinch of salt	
1 cup	Heavy [double] cream, whipped	250 ml/8 fl oz
¼ cup	Chopped dates (seeded)	25 g/1 oz
¼ cup	Maraschino cherries	25 g/1 oz
¼ cup	Crushed pineapple	25 g/1 oz
¼ cup	Chopped kumquats (seeded)	25 g/1 oz
1 tbsp	Finely chopped preserved ginger	1 tbsp
½ cup	Chopped blanched almonds	50 g/2 oz
	Lettuce	

1. Blend the cheese and mayonnaise, add a pinch of salt, and fold in the whipped cream, fruits, and ginger.
2. Pour into refrigerator trays, sprinkle with almonds, and freeze until firm.
3. Cut into squares and serve on lettuce.

Orange and Onion Salad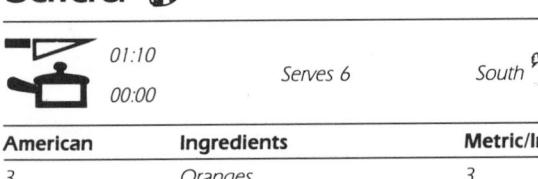

	01:10	Serves 6	South
	00:00		

American	Ingredients	Metric/Imperial
3	Oranges	3
1	Spanish onion	1
2 tbsp	Tarragon or white wine vinegar	1½ tbsp
4 tbsp	Salad oil	3½ tbsp
	Salt and pepper	
	A pinch of paprika	
	A pinch of sugar	
	Chopped parsley	

1. Peel the oranges, removing all the white pith, and cut into thin slices.
2. Peel the onion and slice thinly. Then separate the slices into rings.
3. Arrange the orange and onion slices alternately in a serving dish.
4. Combine the vinegar and oil, and add seasoning of salt, black pepper, and a pinch each of paprika and sugar. Shake well, and pour over the orange and onion.
5. Marinate for at least one hour, and before serving sprinkle with chopped parsley.

Pear and Grape Salad

| | 00:15 | | |
| | 00:00 | Serves 4 | Mid Atlantic  |

American	Ingredients	Metric/Imperial
4	Ripe dessert pears	4
1 cup	Cream cheese	225 g/8 oz
1–2 tbsp	French dressing (see Index)	1–1½ tbsp
½ lb	Black grapes	225 g/8 oz
	Crisp lettuce	

1. Peel the pears, cut in half, and scoop out the core with a teaspoon.
2. Blend the cream cheese with enough French dressing to make it spreadable and coat the rounded side of each pear half.
3. Halve and seed the grapes and press them into the cheese; close together so that each pear half resembles a small bunch of grapes.
4. Serve on crisp lettuce leaves.

Pear and Cheese Salad

| | 00:20 | | |
| | 00:00 | Serves 3 | Midwest |

American	Ingredients	Metric/Imperial
3	Large ripe pears	3
4 oz	Gorgonzola cheese	100 g/4 oz
2–3 tbsp	Heavy [double] cream, whipped	1½–2 tbsp
	Seasoning	
	Curly endive or lettuce	
	Paprika pepper	

1. Peel, halve, and core the pears.
2. Combine the cheese, whipped cream, and a little seasoning, beat until smooth and creamy.
3. Put into a pastry bag with a rose nozzle and pipe some cheese mixture into the center of the pears. Press the two halves together, and pipe the remaining cheese where the pears join.
4. Arrange on a bed of endive or lettuce and sprinkle lightly with paprika.

Orange and Onion Salad

Pear and Grape Salad

Brandied Fruit Salad

| | 03:15 | | |
| | 00:00 | Serves 5–6 | United States |

American	Ingredients	Metric/Imperial
3	Apples, peeled, cored and thinly sliced	3
3	Pears, peeled, cored and sliced	3
2	Oranges, peeled, all white pith removed, then sliced	2
1	Melon, cut into balls	1
1 cup	Seeded cherries	225 g/8 oz
½ cup	Sugar	100 g/4 oz
¼ cup	Brandy	60 ml/2 fl oz
1¼ cups	White wine	300 ml/½ pint

1. Combine all the fruit; sprinkle with sugar. Mix the brandy and wine and pour over the fruit.
2. Mix lightly but thoroughly, and chill for at least 3 hours to blend the flavors.

Waldorf Salad

| | 02:10 | | |
| | 00:00 | Serves 3–4 | Mid Atlantic  |

American	Ingredients	Metric/Imperial
½ cup	Mayonnaise	125 ml/4 fl oz
½ cup	Sour cream	125 ml/4 fl oz
1 tbsp	Honey	1 tbsp
2–3	Tart [sharp] apples, peeled, cored, and diced	2–3
1 cup	Diced celery	100 g/4 oz
½ cup	Coarsely chopped walnuts	50 g/2 oz
1 cup	Halved, seeded grapes	100 g/4 oz

1. Combine the mayonnaise, sour cream, and honey.
2. Add the apple and mix well to prevent the apple discoloring.
3. Add celery, walnuts, and grapes. Mix again lightly and chill well before serving.

Lettuce and Orange Salad

 00:15
00:00   Serves 4   Pacific Southwest

American	Ingredients	Metric/Imperial
2	Oranges	2
1	Iceberg lettuce	1
	Sugar	
¼ cup	Roasted and salted almonds	25 g/1 oz
	Dressing	
2 tbsp	Butter	25 g/1 oz
¼	Clove garlic, crushed very finely	¼
1 tsp	Lemon juice	1 tsp

1. Cut the oranges in half lengthwise, and each half into four pieces. Remove the pulp with a sharp knife, then remove the seeds and any white pith.
2. Arrange the lettuce in a salad bowl, put the orange pieces on top, sprinkle with a little sugar, and add the almonds.
3. For the dressing, melt the butter with the garlic; add lemon juice, mix well, and pour into the bowl.
4. Toss the ingredients very lightly.

Californian Salad

 00:15
00:00   Serves 4–6   Pacific Southwest

American	Ingredients	Metric/Imperial
1	Lettuce or other salad greens	1
2–3	Stalks celery, chopped diagonally	2–3
½	Cucumber, peeled and diced	½
2	Tomatoes, peeled and sliced	2
1	Dessert apple, cored, sliced and brushed with lemon juice	1
1	Banana, peeled, sliced and brushed with lemon juice	1
2–3 tbsp	Mayonnaise or salad dressing	1½–2 tbsp

1. Wash and dry the lettuce, break it up into small pieces, and arrange around the edge of a salad bowl or platter.
2. Put the celery, cucumber, tomatoes, apple, and banana into a bowl. Season lightly with salt and pepper, add the mayonnaise, and toss lightly together.
3. Pile in the center of the lettuce, and decorate as desired.

All-Purpose Salad

 02:00
00:00   Serves 6–8   United States

American	Ingredients	Metric/Imperial
6 cups	Cooked diced potatoes	675 g/1½ lb
4	Hard-boiled eggs, chopped	4
3–4	Scallions [green onions], chopped	3–4
1 tsp	Celery seed	1 tsp
	Dressing	
1 cup	Sour cream	250 ml/8 fl oz
½–1 tsp	Curry powder	½–1 tsp
½ cup	Mayonnaise	125 ml/4 fl oz
2 tbsp	Vinegar	1½ tbsp
1 tsp	Sugar	1 tsp

1. Combine the potatoes, eggs, onions, and celery seed. Season with salt and pepper, and set aside to chill.
2. Mix all the ingredients for the dressing, and pour over the potato mixture. Toss all lightly together just before serving.

Green Sauce

 00:15
00:00   About 1 cup [250 ml/8 fl oz]   South

American	Ingredients	Metric/Imperial
1	Slice white bread	1
½ cup	Water	125 ml/4 fl oz
1 cup	Parsley, blanched	25 g/1 oz
4 tbsp	Drained capers	3½ tbsp
4	Anchovy fillets	4
2	Cloves garlic	2
2 tbsp	Chopped onion	1½ tbsp
1	Small gherkin	1
½ cup	Olive oil	125 ml/4 fl oz
½ tsp	Salt	½ tsp
¼ tsp	Freshly ground black pepper	¼ tsp
1 tbsp	White wine vinegar	1 tbsp

1. Soak the bread in the water, drain, and mash smooth.
2. Put all except the last four ingredients into a blender and blend into a paste. If a blender is not available, chop the ingredients very finely, or put through a mincer and work into a paste.
3. Turn the mixture into a bowl and work in 2 teaspoons of the oil, salt, and pepper. Then add the remaining oil gradually, stirring all the time until the mixture is smooth.
4. Stir in the vinegar and adjust the seasoning to taste.

Herb Dressing

| | 00:05 | About 1 cup | United States |
| | 00:00 | [250 ml/8 fl oz] | |

American	Ingredients	Metric/Imperial
1	Clove garlic, crushed	1
1 tbsp each	Finely chopped parsley, tarragon, chervil and chives	1 tbsp each
8 tbsp	Olive oil	7 tbsp
3 tbsp	White wine vinegar	2 tbsp
	Salt and freshly ground black pepper	

1. Combine garlic and herbs with oil and vinegar. Add salt and pepper to taste.

Mayonnaise

| | 00:10 | About 1 cup | South |
| | 00:00 | [250 ml/8 fl oz] | |

American	Ingredients	Metric/Imperial
2	Egg yolks	2
½ tsp	Salt	½ tsp
¼ tsp	Dry mustard	¼ tsp
1½ tsp	Wine vinegar	1½ tsp
1 cup	Olive oil	250 ml/8 fl oz
½ tsp	Lemon juice	½ tsp

1. Rinse a bowl with hot water and dry well.
2. Put in the egg yolks, salt, mustard, and 1 teaspoon of the vinegar. Beat vigorously or at low speed with an electric mixer.
3. Add half the oil, drop by drop, and then the remaining vinegar.
4. Beat in the rest of the oil in a steady stream.
5. Add lemon juice.
Note: If the mayonnaise curdles, break an egg yolk into a clean basin and gradually beat the curdled mixture into it.

Chiffonade Dressing

| | 00:10 | About 1¼ cups | United States |
| | 00:00 | [300 ml/½ pint] | |

American	Ingredients	Metric/Imperial
1 cup	French dressing (see Index)	250 ml/8 fl oz
1	Hard-boiled egg, chopped	1
1 tsp	Finely chopped parsley	1 tsp
1 tbsp	Finely chopped pimento	1 tbsp
1 tsp	Finely chopped chives	1 tsp
⅛ tsp	Paprika	⅛ tsp

1. Combine all ingredients.

Californian Salad

Cottage Cheese Dressing

| | 00:05 | About 1¼ cups | United States |
| | 00:00 | [300 ml/½ pint] | |

American	Ingredients	Metric/Imperial
1 cup	French dressing (see Index)	250 ml/8 fl oz
3 tbsp	Cottage cheese	2 tbsp
2 tbsp	Chopped parsley	1½ tbsp
1 tbsp	Finely chopped chutney	1 tbsp

1. Combine all ingredients and chill before serving.

Aïoli

| | 00:10 | About 1¼ cups | South  |
| | 00:00 | [300 ml/½ pint] | |

American	Ingredients	Metric/Imperial
1	Slice French bread	1
	Milk	
3	Cloves garlic, crushed very finely	3
2	Egg yolks	2
⅛ tsp	Salt	⅛ tsp
1 cup	Olive oil	250 ml/8 fl oz
½ tsp	Cold water	½ tsp
1 tsp	Lemon juice	1 tsp

1. Remove the crust from the bread, and discard it. Soak the bread in a little milk, then squeeze it out.
2. Add the garlic, egg yolks, and salt, and beat well.
3. Add the oil very slowly and, as the dressing thickens, beat in the water and lemon juice.

Cream Dressing

	01:05 00:00	About 1 cup [250 ml/8 fl oz]	United States

American	Ingredients	Metric/Imperial
½ tsp	Prepared mustard	½ tsp
1 tsp	Sugar	1 tsp
2 tsp	Tarragon vinegar	2 tsp
½	Clove garlic, crushed	½
1	Hard-boiled egg	1
1 tsp	Chopped tarragon or chives	1 tsp
½ cup	Light [single] cream	125 ml/4 fl oz

1. Mix the mustard, sugar, and vinegar together; add the garlic and yolk of the hard-boiled egg. Mix well, then stir in the cream and chopped tarragon or chives. If the vinegar makes the cream too thick for pouring, add a few drops of water or milk.
2. Chill thoroughly, then pour over crisp lettuce hearts and sprinkle with the chopped egg white.

French Dressing

	00:05 00:00	About ½–¾ cup [125–175 ml/4–6 fl oz]	South

American	Ingredients	Metric/Imperial
1 tsp	Dijon mustard	1 tsp
2 tbsp	White wine vinegar	1½ tbsp
	Salt	
	Freshly ground black pepper	
6-8 tbsp	Olive oil	5-7 tbsp

1. Mix the mustard and vinegar with salt and pepper to taste.
2. Add good olive oil and beat with a whisk until the mixture thickens.

Russian Dressing

	00:05 00:00	About 1 cup [250 ml/8 fl oz]	Pacific Northwest

American	Ingredients	Metric/Imperial
1 cup	Mayonnaise	250 ml/8 fl oz
1 tbsp	Chili sauce	1 tbsp
1-2 tsp	Chopped chives	1-2 tsp
2 tsp	Chopped red pepper or canned [tinned] pimento	2 tsp

1. Combine all ingredients.
Note: Chili sauce varies considerably in strength. It is advisable to add about ½ teaspoon, then taste and increase the quantity as necessary. The quantity given is for a mild chili sauce.

Green Goddess Dressing

	00:05 00:00	About 2 cups [400 ml/¾ pint]	Midwest

American	Ingredients	Metric/Imperial
1 cup	Mayonnaise	250 ml/8 fl oz
1	Clove garlic, crushed	1
¼ cup	Finely chopped parsley	2 tbsp
2 tbsp	Chopped chives	1½ tbsp
1 tbsp	Lemon juice	1 tbsp
1 tbsp	Tarragon vinegar	1 tbsp
½ tsp	Salt and black pepper	½ tsp
2 tsp	Anchovy paste	2 tsp
2 tbsp	Cream	1½ tbsp

1. Combine all ingredients and stir until dressing is smooth.

Salad Cream

	00:20 00:10	About 1½ cups [375 ml/12 fl oz.]	United States

American	Ingredients	Metric/Imperial
2	Eggs	2
2 tsp	Sugar	2 tsp
1 tbsp	Butter	1 tbsp
1 cup	Milk	250 ml/8 fl oz
¾ cup	Vinegar	175 ml/6 fl oz
1 tsp	Salt	1 tsp
	A small pinch of cayenne pepper	
1 tsp	Dry mustard	1 tsp
2 tsp	Cornstarch [cornflour]	2 tsp

1. Separate the eggs and put the yolks, sugar, butter, ⅔ of the milk, vinegar, and seasonings into the top of a double boiler. Stir over boiling water until the ingredients are well blended.
2. Blend the cornstarch with the remaining milk, add to the other ingredients, and stir until the mixture thickens.
3. When cold, fold in the stiffly beaten egg whites.

Thousand Island Dressing

	00:05 00:00	About 1 cup [250 ml/8 fl oz]	United States

American	Ingredients	Metric/Imperial
1 cup	Mayonnaise	250 ml/8 fl oz
1 tbsp	Chili sauce	1 tbsp
1 tbsp	Chopped green olives	1 tbsp
2 tsp	Finely chopped chives	2 tsp

1. Combine all ingredients.

French Dressing

Fruit Salad Dressing

	01:00	About 1¾ cups	United States
	00:05	[425 ml/14 fl oz]	

American	Ingredients	Metric/Imperial
¼ cup	Currant jelly	25 g/1 oz
1 cup	Mayonnaise	250 ml/8 fl oz
½ cup	Sour [soured] cream	125 ml/4 fl oz
¼ cup	Chopped toated almonds	25 g/1 oz

1. Melt the jelly and leave to get cold.
2. Combine with the other ingredients and chill before using.

Cucumber Cream Dressing

	00:05	About 2 cups	United States
	00:00	[400 ml/¾ pint]	

American	Ingredients	Metric/Imperial
2 tbsp	Vinegar	1½ tbsp
2 tbsp	Sugar	1½ tbsp
1 cup	Peeled, diced cucumber	100 g/4 oz
1 cup	Heavy [double] cream, whipped	250 ml/8 fl oz

1. Mix the vinegar, sugar, and cucumber and fold into the whipped cream.

Eggs and Cheese

Breakfast Special

	00:20			
	00:20	Serves 4	United States	

American	Ingredients	Metric/Imperial
8	Eggs	8
2 tbsp	Butter or margarine	25 g/1 oz
1 lb	Chicken livers	450 g/1 lb
½ cup	Milk	125 ml/4 fl oz
	A pinch of nutmeg	
	Chopped parsley or chives	

1. Preheat the oven to 325°F/160°C/Gas Mark 3.
2. Heat the butter in a frying pan and cook the chicken livers for about 7 minutes, then divide into 4 lightly buttered small casseroles.
3. Beat the eggs; add milk, seasoning, and a good pinch of nutmeg. Pour over the livers and bake for 20 minutes, or until the eggs are set.
4. Sprinkle with chopped parsley or chives before serving.

Eggs and Cheese with Cream

	00:05			
	00:10	Serves 6	Midwest	

American	Ingredients	Metric/Imperial
6	Eggs	6
1 cup	Grated cheese	125 g/4 oz
½ cup	Cream	125 ml/4 fl oz
1 tsp	Finely chopped parsley	1 tsp
2 tbsp	Butter	25 g/1 oz

1. Preheat the oven to 375°F/190°C/Gas Mark 5.
2. Break the eggs carefully into a buttered, ovenproof dish and sprinkle with salt and pepper. Cover with half the cheese.
3. Pour the cream on top and sprinkle with the remaining cheese and parsley.
4. Dot with butter and put into a moderately hot oven until the eggs are just set, about 7 to 10 minutes.

Cottage Eggs

	00:05			
	00:05	Serves 4–5	New England	

American	Ingredients	Metric/Imperial
6	Eggs	6
½ tsp	Salt	½ tsp
¼ tsp	Pepper	¼ tsp
2 tbsp	Light [single] cream	1½ tbsp
½ cup	Cottage cheese	100 g/4 oz
2 tbsp	Butter	25 g/1 oz
4–5	Slices hot buttered toast	4–5

1. Beat the eggs lightly; season with salt and pepper.
2. Blend the cream with the cottage cheese and stir in the eggs.
3. Heat the butter in a frying pan, pour in the egg mixture, and cook lightly as for scrambled eggs.
4. Serve on hot toast.

Egg and Corn Savory

	00:10			
	00:08	Serves 4	Mid Atlantic	

American	Ingredients	Metric/Imperial
4	Eggs	4
1 can (12 oz)	Corn	1 tin (350 g/ 12 oz)
	Milk	
¼ cup	Butter	50 g/2 oz
3 tbsp	Flour	2 tbsp
	Cayenne pepper	
1 cup	Grated cheese	125 g/4 oz
2 tbsp	Bread crumbs	1½ tbsp
	A little extra butter	

1. Boil the eggs for 5 minutes.
2. Drain the corn, measure the liquid, and add sufficient milk to make 1½ cups [350 ml/12 fl oz].
3. Make a sauce with the butter, flour, milk, and corn liquid. Add the seasoning, most of the cheese, and corn.
4. Put half this sauce into a buttered baking dish. Shell the eggs and arrange on top. Cover with the remaining sauce.
5. Mix the remaining cheese with bread crumbs, sprinkle on top, and dot with butter.
6. Brown under a hot broiler [grill].

Golden Buck

	00:05			
	00:10	Serves 4	Mid Atlantic	

American	Ingredients	Metric/Imperial
2 tbsp	Butter	25 g/1 oz
1½ cups	Grated cheese	175 g/6 oz
4 tbsp	Beer or ale	3½ tbsp
1 tsp	Worcestershire sauce	1 tsp
1 tsp	Lemon juice	1 tsp
	Cayenne pepper	
	A pinch of celery salt	
4	Eggs	4
4	Slices buttered toast	4

1. Melt the butter in a small frying pan. Add cheese, beer, Worcestershire sauce, lemon juice, and seasoning. Stir over low heat until smooth and creamy.
2. Beat the eggs lightly and stir into the mixture. Stir until the eggs are lightly set; then spoon onto the hot toast.

Curry Spiced Egg

American	Ingredients	Metric/Imperial
8	Eggs	8
1	Large onion	1
1 tbsp	Margarine	15 g/½ oz
1 tbsp	Curry powder	1 tbsp
1¼ cups	Chicken stock	300 ml/10 fl oz
½ tsp	Salt	½ tsp
¼ tsp	Black pepper	¼ tsp
2½ tsp	Arrowroot	2½ tsp
5 tbsp	Crème fraîche	4 tbsp
	Juice from ½ lemon	

00:10 / 00:25 — Serves 4 — United States

1. Hard-boil the eggs for 10 minutes.
2. Peel the onion and finely chop it. Melt the margarine in a saucepan; add curry and onion. Cook the onion so that it slowly softens over low heat for several minutes. Add chicken stock salt, and pepper and simmer for about 10 minutes.
3. Mix the creme fraîche with arrowroot and lemon juice and fold into the sauce. Bring to a boil quickly, then pour the sauce over the eggs, which have been shelled and cut in half. Sprinkle a little parsley on top, if desired.

Scrambled Eggs with Oysters

American	Ingredients	Metric/Imperial
6	Eggs	6
	Dash of Tabasco	
2 tbsp	Butter	25 g/1 oz
1 tsp	Anchovy paste	1 tsp
1 can (8 oz)	Oysters	1 tin (225 g/8 oz)
	Freshly ground black pepper	
1 tbsp	Finely chopped parsley	1 tbsp
	Croutons of fried bread	

00:05 / 00:08 — Serves 4 — New England

1. Whisk the eggs very lightly with the Tabasco (avoid overbeating).
2. Put the butter and anchovy paste into a small frying pan and, when hot, pour in the eggs. Stir until just beginning to set, then add the drained and chopped oysters. Season with salt and black pepper.
3. Finish scrambling the eggs but avoid over-cooking.
4. Put onto hot serving dishes, sprinkle with parsley, and serve with croutons of fried bread or with toast.

Curry Spiced Egg

Eggs in Snow

American	Ingredients	Metric/Imperial
2	Slices bread	2
	Butter	
2	Eggs	2
	Nutmeg	
	Grated cheese	

00:05 / 00:06 — Serves 2 — New England

1. Toast the bread on one side; turn and toast the under side very lightly. Butter the lightly toasted side and keep hot.
2. Separate the eggs, add seasoning and a pinch of nutmeg to the egg whites, and beat until stiff.
3. Spread the egg white over the buttered toast. Make a slight indentation in the middle and drop in the egg yolk.
4. Sprinkle with grated cheese and put under a hot broiler [grill] for a few minutes until the egg yolk has set.

Fried Eggs

American	Ingredients	Metric/Imperial
2 tbsp	Olive oil	1½ tbsp
1	Onion, peeled and thinly sliced	1
1	Green pepper, seeded and cut into strips	1
4 slices	Bacon, cut into pieces	4 rashers
4	Eggs	4

00:05 / 00:05 — Serves 4 — Midwest

1. Heat the oil in a frying pan. Add onion, green pepper, and bacon, and cook over medium heat until the onion is transparent.
2. Break the eggs into the pan carefully; cover with the lid of the pan or with foil and continue to cook for 2–3 minutes, or until the eggs are just firm. Add a dash of salt and pepper, if desired.
3. Slide carefully onto a hot serving dish.

Eggs With Green Peppers

| | 00:05 | | | |
| | 00:10 | Serves 4 | United States | |

American	Ingredients	Metric/Imperial
2	Green peppers, seeded and chopped	2
½ cup	Light [single] cream	125 ml/4 fl oz
½ tsp	Salt	½ tsp
3 tsp	Tabasco	3 tsp
4	Eggs	4
½ cup	Grated Parmesan cheese	50 g/2 oz

1. Preheat the oven to 375°F/190°C/Gas Mark 5.
2. Blend the peppers and cream in an electric mixer; add salt and Tabasco, and pour into a buttered, ovenproof baking pan.
3. Break each egg carefully on top, sprinkle with the cheese, and cook in a moderate oven until the eggs are set, about 10 minutes.

Egg Plate Pie

| | 00:25 | | | |
| | 00:35 | Serves 4–5 | United States | |

American	Ingredients	Metric/Imperial
	Pie Crust	
1½ cups	All-purpose [plain] flour	175 g/6 oz
¾ tsp	Salt	¾ tsp
½ cup	Shortening	100 g/4 oz
3 tbsp	Cold water	2 tbsp
	Filling	
2 tbsp	Margarine	25 g/1 oz
1	Onion, peeled and chopped	1
½ lb	Tomatoes, peeled, seeded, and chopped	225 g/8 oz
1 tbsp	Chopped parsley	1 tbsp
2	Hard-boiled eggs, chopped	2
2	Eggs, beaten	2
3 tbsp	Milk	2 tbsp
⅛ tsp	Dried (or ½ tsp fresh) Chopped chervil (optional)	⅛ tsp dried

1. Preheat the oven to 400°F/200°C/Gas Mark 6.
2. Make the pie crust in the usual way, and use half to line a 7-inch pie plate. Prick the base with a fork.
3. Heat the fat in a pan; sauté the onion until soft but not browned. Then add tomatoes, and cook for 2 minutes.
4. Remove from the heat, and add all the other ingredients.
5. Put into the pie crust, moisten the edges, and cover with the remaining pastry. Press the edges well together, decorate as desired, and make two slits in the top. Brush with milk to glaze and let cool if possible. Then bake for about 30 minutes, or until golden brown.

Egg and Bacon Pie

| | 00:30 | | | |
| | 00:40 | Serves 6 | Mid Atlantic |  |

American	Ingredients	Metric/Imperial
1	Recipe Pastry for 8–9 Inch, 1-Crust Pie (see Index) plus ½ cup [50 g/2 oz] grated cheese	1
2 tbsp	Butter or margarine	25 g/1 oz
2–3	Onions, peeled and chopped	2–3
6 slices	Bacon, chopped	6 rashers
3	Eggs	3
2 cups	Milk	450 ml/¾ pint
½ tsp	Dry mustard	½ tsp
2 tsp	Chopped parsley	2 tsp

1. Preheat the oven to 375°F/190°C/Gas Mark 5.
2. Line a deep 8-inch pie plate with pastry.
3. Heat the butter in a frying pan, add the onion and bacon, and fry for 3–4 minutes.
4. Beat the eggs in a bowl; add the warmed milk, drained onion, and bacon, salt, pepper, mustard, and parsley.
5. Pour into the pastry shell, and cook for 35–40 minutes. If desired, extra slices of rolled bacon can be broiled [grilled] and used as garnish.

Egg and Mushroom Casserole

| | 00:20 | | | |
| | 00:25 | Serves 4 | United States | |

American	Ingredients	Metric/Imperial
½ lb	Mushrooms, sliced thinly	225 g/8 oz
4	Hard-boiled eggs, sliced	4
3 tbsp	Butter or margarine	40 g/1½ oz
2 tbsp	Flour	1½ tbsp
1½ cups	Milk	350 ml/12 fl oz
	Salt and pepper	
	A pinch of nutmeg	
2	Tomatoes, peeled and sliced	2
	Cracker [biscuit] crumbs	
	Chopped parsley	

1. Preheat the oven to 400°F/200°C/Gas Mark 6.
2. Make a sauce with 2 tablespoons [25 g/1 oz] of the butter, the flour, and milk. Add salt, pepper, and a good pinch of nutmeg. Add the mushrooms and simmer for 10 minutes.
3. Arrange the slices of egg and tomato in a casserole, pour over the sauce, and sprinkle with cracker crumbs. Dot with the remaining 1 tablespoon [15 g/½ oz] of butter and cook for about 20–25 minutes, until the top is crisp and brown.
4. Sprinkle with parsley before serving.

Curried Eggs

00:10
00:25
Serves 4
South

American	Ingredients	Metric/Imperial
1	Medium-sized onion, peeled and chopped	1
2–3 tbsp	Oil	1½–2 tbsp
2 tbsp	Flour	1½ tbsp
1 tbsp	Curry powder	1 tbsp
2 cups	Stock	450 ml/¾ pint
1	Large apple, peeled, cored and diced	1
1 tbsp	Worcestershire sauce	1 tbsp
4	Hard-boiled eggs	4
2 cups	Freshly cooked rice	450 g/1 lb
	Chutney	

1. Sauté the onion in the oil until soft but not browned. Add flour, curry powder, and a little salt; and stir over low heat until the mixture forms a smooth paste.
2. Add the stock gradually; stir until boiling. Add the apple and Worcestershire sauce; cover and simmer gently for 15–20 minutes. Add the eggs, and heat through.
3. Put the rice on a large platter, and arrange the eggs and sauce on top. Serve with chutney and a tossed green salad.

Scrambled Eggs with Anchovies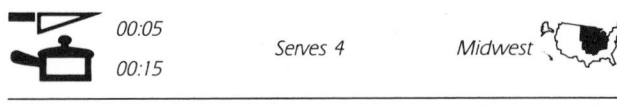

00:05
00:15
Serves 4
Midwest

American	Ingredients	Metric/Imperial
¼ cup	Butter	50 g/2 oz
4	Slices of bread	4
	Anchovy paste	
6	Eggs	6
8	Anchovy fillets	8
	Capers	
	Cayenne pepper	

1. Heat half the butter in a pan and fry the bread until crisp. Remove from the pan, spread very lightly with anchovy paste, and keep hot.
2. Put the rest of the butter into the pan; add the eggs, beaten very slightly with pepper and a small pinch of salt. Stir until just set.
3. Spoon the scrambled egg onto the fried bread and arrange 2 anchovy fillets across each piece. Put a caper into each section, sprinkle sparingly with cayenne, and serve at once.

Curried Eggs

Eggs With Vegetables

 00:10 / 00:20 — Serves 4 — South

American	Ingredients	Metric/Imperial
3 tbsp	Olive oil	2 tbsp
1	Green pepper, seeded and thinly sliced	1
1	Onion, peeled and finely chopped	1
1	Tomato, peeled, seeded, and chopped	1
1	Clove garlic, crushed	1
1 tsp	Salt	1 tsp
⅛ tsp	Freshly ground black pepper	⅛ tsp
6	Eggs	6

1. Heat the oil in a frying pan, add the green pepper and onion, and sauté until the vegetables begin to soften.
2. Add tomato, garlic, and seasoning; simmer until the ingredients are soft and mushy.
3. Add the lightly beaten eggs and stir just enough to mix with the vegetables. Cook for a few minutes until the eggs are just set.
4. Serve with toast or on thin sautéed slices of ham.

Bacon and Kidney Scramble

 00:10 / 00:10 — Serves 4 — Mid Atlantic

American	Ingredients	Metric/Imperial
2	Lamb kidneys	2
3–4 tbsp	Butter	40–50 g/1½–2 oz
4 slices	Bacon	4 rashers
3	Eggs	3
1 tbsp	Cream	1 tbsp
	Black pepper	
	A pinch of mixed herbs	
4	Slices hot buttered toast	4

1. Skin the kidneys, remove the cores, and cut into thin slices.
2. Heat the butter in a small frying pan; add the kidney, fry for a few minutes, then add the chopped bacon. Cook together until the kidney is tender.
3. Beat the eggs lightly; add cream, seasoning, and herbs and pour over the kidneys. Stir over low heat until the eggs are lightly set.
4. Serve on hot buttered toast.

Egg and Shrimp Pie

 00:45 / 00:12 — Serves 4 — United States

American	Ingredients	Metric/Imperial
6	Eggs	6
1 (8-inch)	Baked pie shell	1 (8-inch)
1 tbsp	Butter	15 g/½ oz
1 tsp	Prepared mustard	1 tsp
1½ cups	Shrimp [prawns]	350 g/12 oz
½ cup	Cream sauce	125 ml/4 fl oz
1 tbsp	Chopped parsley	1 tbsp
2 tbsp	Grated cheese	1½ tbsp

1. Preheat the broiler [grill].
2. Boil the eggs for 7 minutes, then shell and slice carefully. Arrange the slices in the pie shell and sprinkle with a little salt and pepper.
3. Heat the butter in a small pan, add mustard and shrimp, and sauté for a few minutes. Stir in the cream sauce and parsley. Check the seasoning and pour the sauce over the eggs.
4. Sprinkle with cheese and brown under a hot broiler [grill].

Californian Omelette

 00:05 / 00:08 — Serves 2 — Pacific Southwest

American	Ingredients	Metric/Imperial
3	Eggs	3
1 tbsp	Milk	1 tbsp
1 tbsp	Water	1 tbsp
½ tsp	Salt	½ tsp
⅛ tsp	Black pepper	⅛ tsp
¼ cup	Diced avocado	25 g/1 oz
3–4 tbsp	Very finely chopped cooked chicken	2–3½ tbsp
1 tbsp	Finely chopped chives	1 tbsp
1 tbsp	Butter	15 g/½ oz
1 tbsp	Oil	1 tbsp
1 tbsp	Cream	1 tbsp

1. Beat the eggs lightly; add the milk, water, seasoning, avocado, chicken, and chives.
2. Heat the butter and oil in a frying pan, pour in the egg mixture, and stir lightly with a fork until the mixture just begins to set.
3. Pour on the cream; cook a minute longer, then fold over and serve at once.

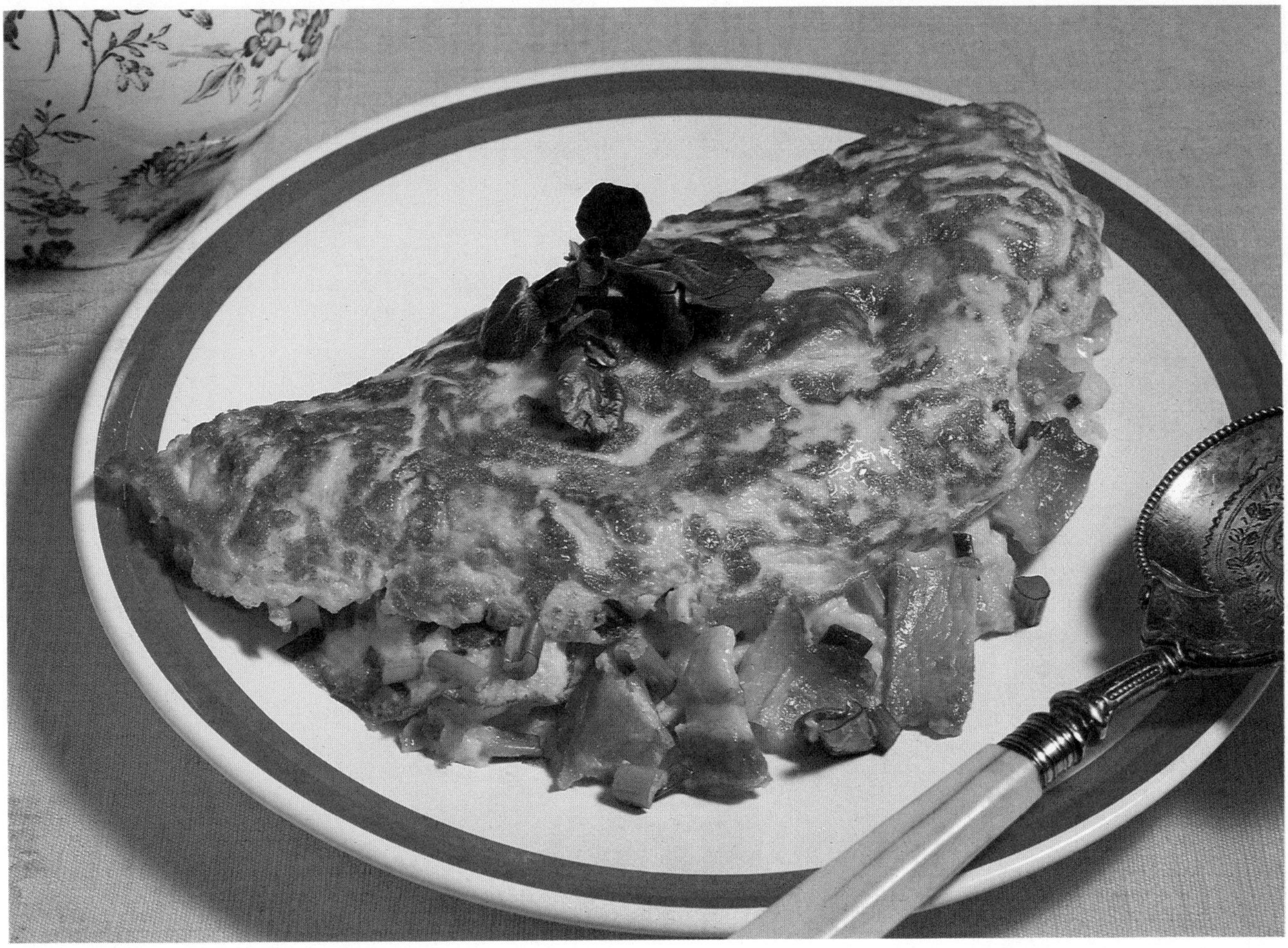

Bacon Omelette

Bacon Omelette

	00:05		
	00:10	Serves 2–3	Mid Atlantic

American	Ingredients	Metric/Imperial
3 tbsp	Butter	40 g/1½ oz
4	Scallions [spring onions], sliced	4
4	Eggs	4
2 tbsp	Heavy [double] cream, whipped	1½ tbsp
½ tsp	Salt	½ tsp
¼ tsp	Pepper	¼ tsp
1 tsp	Prepared mustard	1 tsp
6 slices	Crisply fried bacon	6 rashers

1. Melt half the butter in a frying pan and sauté the onion for 3 minutes. Then remove from the pan.
2. Beat the eggs, cream, salt, pepper, and mustard until the mixture is just blended. Add the onion and bacon.
3. Heat the remaining butter in the pan; pour in the egg mixture and cook over low heat, stirring lightly with a fork and lifting the eggs to allow the uncooked mixture to run underneath.
4. When the eggs are just set, fold over and turn out onto a hot dish.

Deviled Omelette

	00:05		
	00:10	Serves 2–3	United States

American	Ingredients	Metric/Imperial
3	Eggs	3
	Cayenne pepper	
¼ tsp	Dry mustard	¼ tsp
	A pinch of curry powder	
2 tbsp	Light [single] cream	1½ tbsp
¼ cup	Chopped cooked ham	75 g/3 oz
1 tbsp	Butter	15 g/½ oz

1. Beat the eggs lightly; add seasoning, mustard, and curry powder. Stir in the cream and chopped ham.
2. Heat the butter in a small frying pan. Pour in the egg mixture and cook quickly, stirring occasionally with a fork and loosening the omelette from the side of the pan.
3. When the omelette is lightly set on the under side, put the skillet under a hot broiler [grill] to brown the top.
4. Fold over and serve at once.

Fried Egg and Cheese Sandwich

Omelette With Ham and Vegetables

| | 00:15 | | |
| | 00:25 | Serves 4 | Midwest  |

American	Ingredients	Metric/Imperial
1 cup	Diced ham (or any cold cooked meat or garlic sausage)	175 g/6 oz
2 tbsp	Oil	1½ tbsp
1	Large potato	1
1	Onion	1
3–4	Tomatoes	3–4
1	Small green or red pepper	1
6	Eggs	6
3 tsp	Chopped mixed herbs	3 tsp
3–4 tbsp	Butter	40–50 g/ 1½–2 oz
1	Clove garlic (optional)	1

1. Heat the oil and cook the diced potato and finely chopped onion in a covered pan until tender. Shake the pan to prevent sticking. Dice the ham (or meat); peel, seed, and chop the tomatoes and pepper. Add to the potato mixture and heat through. (Any leftover cooked vegetables can be substituted or added to the mixture at this stage).
2. Mix the eggs well with 3 tablespoons [2 tbsp] water and chopped herbs and seasoning. Heat 2 tablespoons [25 g/1 oz] of butter in a large omelette or frying pan. When foaming, pour the egg mixture into the pan and stir in the ham and vegetable mixture. Stir gently for 1 minute to mix the egg and mixture well. Then leave over moderate heat for 2–3 minutes, until fairly well set.
3. Place a large plate over a frying pan and turn the omelette onto it. Heat the remaining butter in the pan and return the omelette with cooked side uppermost. Cook for 2 minutes to brown the other side, and serve at once.

Fried Egg and Cheese Sandwich

| | 00:10 | | |
| | 00:05 | Serves 4 | United States  |

American	Ingredients	Metric/Imperial
8	Slices bread	8
	Butter	
¼ lb	Cheese, grated	100 g/4 oz
2	Eggs, beaten	2
	Salt and pepper	
	Oil for frying	

1. Make the sandwiches with bread, butter, and cheese. Beat the eggs well and season. Dip the sandwiches into the egg.
2. Heat the oil in a frying pan and fry the sandwiches quickly until golden.
3. Drain on paper towels [kitchen paper] and serve very hot.

Chicken Liver Omelette

| | 00:10 | | |
| | 00:15 | Serves 2–3 | United States |

American	Ingredients	Metric/Imperial
	Filling	
3 tbsp	Butter	40 g/1½ oz
2 tbsp	Minced onion	1½ tbsp
¼ cup	Chopped mushrooms	50 g/2 oz
¼ lb	Chicken livers	100 g/4 oz
1 tbsp	Flour	1 tbsp
¾ cup	Chicken stock	175 ml/6 fl oz
1 tsp	Tomato purée	1 tsp
⅛ tsp	Thyme	⅛ tsp
	Omelette	
4	Eggs	4
¼ tsp	Salt	¼ tsp
⅛ tsp	Black pepper	⅛ tsp
2 tbsp	Cold water	1½ tbsp
1 tbsp	Butter	50 g/½ oz

1. Heat the butter in a frying pan. Sauté the onion, mushrooms, and chicken livers until the livers are browned, then remove them from the pan and keep hot.
2. Add the flour to the pan and mix with the pan juices. Add the stock and stir until boiling. Add the tomato paste, seasoning, and thyme and cook for 5 minutes.
3. Return the livers to the pan and reheat.
4. Prepare the omelette in the usual way and spread with the liver mixture just before serving.

Mimosa Eggs

Mimosa Eggs 👨‍🍳👨‍🍳

	01:30		
	00:00	Serves 6	South

American	Ingredients	Metric/Imperial
6	Firm tomatoes	6
6	Hard-boiled eggs	6
2–3 tbsp	Grated Pamesan cheese	1½–2 tbsp
	Salt and black pepper	
	Mayonnaise	
3–4	Chives, finely chopped	3–4
	Olives and watercress for garnish	

1. Cut a slice from the top of each tomato, remove the pulp carefully, and strain off the juice.

2. Cut a slice from the broad end of the eggs, scoop out the yolks, and rub through a sieve. Reserve a little of the yolk. Add the grated cheese and seasoning to the rest and bind with a little mayonnaise. Fill the egg cases with this mixture and put cut side down into the tomato cases.

3. Thin down a little more mayonnaise to a coating consistency with some of the tomato juice and pour over the eggs. Sprinkle the reserved sieved yolk over half of them and sprinkle the rest with finely chopped chives.

4. Garnish with olives and watercress, and chill before serving.

Cheese and Ham Omelette 👨‍🍳

	00:05		
	00:06	Serves 2–3	Midwest

American	Ingredients	Metric/Imperial
4	Eggs	4
1 tbsp	Water	1 tbsp
½ tsp	Salt	½ tsp
¼ tsp	Freshly ground black pepper	¼ tsp
½ cup	Cooked ham, cut into fine strips	75 g/3 oz
½ cup	Cottage cheese, well drained	100 g/4 oz
1 tbsp	Butter	15 g/½ oz
1 tbsp	Oil	1 tbsp

1. Beat the eggs, water, salt, and pepper until just blended. Add the ham and cheese.

2. Heat the butter and oil in a 9-inch frying pan. Pour in the egg mixture and cook over medium heat, stirring with a fork, for a few seconds, then lift the eggs to allow the uncooked mixture to run underneath.

3. Fold over and roll out onto a hot dish.

Southwest Omelette

 00:10
00:05   Serves 4   Southwest

American	Ingredients	Metric/Imperial
6	Eggs	6
¼ cup	Light [single] cream	60 ml/2 fl oz
1	Red pepper, chopped	1
1	Green pepper, chopped	1
1	Onion, chopped	1
1	Clove garlic, chopped	1
½ cup	Ham, cut into julienne-strips	75 g/3 oz
3	Sprigs fresh parsley, chopped	3
4 tbsp	Butter	50 g/2 oz
	Salt to taste	

1. In a large bowl, stir the eggs with a fork; add the cream and salt.
2. In a large frying pan, melt the butter over medium heat. Add the egg mixture, stirring often with a wooden spoon. Immediately add the chopped vegetables and ham. Continue stirring until the eggs are cooked; remove from the heat.
3. Add the chopped parsley, and serve.

Tomato Omelette

 00:05
00:15   Serves 2–3   United States

American	Ingredients	Metric/Imperial
	Filling	
2 tbsp	Olive Oil	1½ tbsp
4 tbsp	Minced onion	3½ tbsp
⅛ tsp	Minced garlic	⅛ tsp
1½ cups	Peeled, seeded and chopped tomatoes	350 g/12 oz
½ tsp	Salt	½ tsp
¼ tsp	Black pepper	¼ tsp
1 tbsp	Chopped parsley	1 tbsp
	Omelette	
4	Eggs	4
¼ tsp	Salt	¼ tsp
⅛ tsp	Pepper	⅛ tsp
2 tbsp	Cold water	1½ tbsp
1 tbsp	Butter	15 g/½ oz

1. Heat the oil in a frying pan, sauté the onion and after 3 minutes, sauté the garlic for 2 minutes. Stir in the tomatoes, salt, and pepper and cook over low heat until the tomato is soft. Then add parsley.
2. Prepare the omelette in the usual way. When the eggs are just set, put the tomato mixture in the center and fold over.
3. Turn out onto a hot dish and serve at once.

Chicken and Pineapple Omelette

 00:15
00:10   Serves 1   Pacific Northwest

American	Ingredients	Metric/Imperial
2	Eggs	2
1 tbsp	Water	1 tbsp
	Salt and pepper	
1 tbsp	Butter	15 g/½ oz
¼ cup	Cooked chicken, chopped	25 g/1 oz
1 cup	Pineapple, fresh or canned, chopped	225 g/8 oz
2 tsp	Chopped chives	2 tsp
½	Fresh tomato	½
	Watercress	

1. Whisk the eggs, water, and seasoning together.
2. Melt the butter in an omelette pan and pour in the egg mixture. As it begins to set, pull in the edges of the omelette to the center with a fork, allowing the liquid egg to run to the side of the pan.
3. Spoon the chicken, pineapple, and chive filling into the center and cook until set. Carefully fold the omelette in half, and slide onto a warm plate.
4. Garnish with tomato and watercress.

Mexican-style Cheese

 00:15
00:25   Serves 4–5   Southwest

American	Ingredients	Metric/Imperial
2 tbsp	Oil	1½ tbsp
1	Green pepper, seeded and chopped	1
½ cup	Finely chopped onion	50 g/2 oz
1 tbsp	Flour	1 tbsp
½ cup	Milk	125 ml/4 fl oz
3 cups	Grated American cheese	350 g/12 oz
1 cup	Drained, canned [tinned] tomatoes	225 g/8 oz
1	Canned [tinned] pimento, cut into strips	1
3 tbsp	Chopped black olives	2 tbsp
	Cayenne pepper	
3	Egg yolks	3
	Toast or cooked rice	

1. Heat the oil in a pan. Add the green pepper and onion; sauté for about 10 minutes.
2. Stir in the flour and milk; stir until boiling.
3. Add the cheese and tomatoes and cook over low heat for about 10 minutes. Add pimento, olives, and seasoning and cook another few minutes.
4. Add the beaten egg yolks gradually; stir with a fork until the mixture thickens. It should not boil at this stage.
5. Serve on toast or with cooked rice.

Chicken and Pineapple Omelette

Cheese and Bacon Slices

 00:08 / 00:10   Serves 4   Mid Atlantic

American	Ingredients	Metric/Imperial
2 cups	Grated cheese	225 g/8 oz
1	Egg, beaten	1
1 tsp	Worcestershire sauce	1 tsp
⅛ tsp	Prepared mustard	⅛ tsp
	Cayenne pepper	
1 tbsp	Butter	15 g/½ oz
4 slices	Bread	4
4 slices	Bacon	4 rashers
4	Black olives	4

1. Preheat the oven to 400°F/200°C/Gas Mark 6.
2. Combine the cheese with the beaten egg, Worcestershire sauce, and seasonings. Spread on the bread and top with a slice of bacon.
3. Put into a buttered baking pan and bake in a moderately hot oven for 10 minutes.
4. Place an olive on top and serve at once.

Melted Cheese on Toast

00:05 / 00:06   Serves 4   Midwest

American	Ingredients	Metric/Imperial
1 cup	Milk	250 ml/8 fl oz
1 cup	Bread crumbs	50 g/2 oz
1 cup	Grated Cheddar or American cheese	100 g/4 oz
½ tsp	Salt	½ tsp
¼ tsp	Paprika pepper	¼ tsp
⅛ tsp	Dry mustard	⅛ tsp
1 tsp	Worcestershire sauce	1 tsp
1	Egg	1
4	Slices hot buttered toast	4

1. Put the milk, bread crumbs, and cheese into the top of a double boiler. Stir over hot water until the cheese has melted.
2. Add the seasoning, Worcestershire sauce, and beaten egg. Cook for 1 minute, stirring all the time, then pour over the toast.

Toasted Cheese and Bacon Sandwich

 01:15 / 00:20   Serves 4   Mid Atlantic

American	Ingredients	Metric/Imperial
12	Prunes	12
8	Slices bread	8
	Butter	
8 slices	Bacon	8 rashers
4	Slices Gouda or processed cheese	4
	Watercress for garnish	

1. Preheat the broiler [grill].
2. Cover the prunes with boiling water and let stand about 1 hour.
3. Remove the crusts from the bread, and butter one side of each slice.
4. Broil [grill] the bacon until crisp; set aside 2 slices and chop the rest coarsely.
5. Remove the seeds from the prunes; set aside 4 and chop the remainder.
6. Cover half the slices of buttered bread with the chopped prunes and bacon. Top with the remaining slices.
7. Toast the sandwiches on one side; turn over and cover the untoasted side with a slice of cheese. Broil [grill] until the cheese bubbles and browns.
8. Top each sandwich with half a slice of bacon and a prune. Serve hot garnished with watercress.

Cheese and Tomato Sandwich

 00:12 / 00:07   Serves 4   Southwest

American	Ingredients	Metric/Imperial
¾ cup	Grated cheese	75 g/3 oz
2 tbsp	Softened butter	25 g/1 oz
1 tsp	Prepared mustard	1 tsp
1 tsp	Worcestershire sauce	1 tsp
2	Tomatoes	2
4	Slices buttered toast	4
4 slices	Bacon	4 rashers

1. Preheat oven to 475°F/240°C/Gas Mark 9.
2. Combine the cheese, butter, mustard, and Worcestershire sauce.
3. Peel the tomatoes; cut across in halves and then cut each half through again, making 8 slices. Place 2 tomato slices on each slice of bread and sprinkle with salt and pepper. Cover with the cheese mixture and top with a slice of bacon.
4. Arrange on a baking tray and cook in a fairly hot oven for 5 to 7 minutes, or until the bacon is crisp and the cheese has melted.

Monte Cristo Sandwich

⏱ 00:15
00:10   Serves 4   Southwest

American	Ingredients	Metric/Imperial
8	Slices bread	8
2	Eggs	2
½ cup	Milk	125 ml/4 fl oz
½ tsp	Salt	½ tsp
	A pinch of pepper	
	Sliced breast of chicken or turkey	
4	Slices cooked ham	4
4	Slices Swiss cheese	4
	Prepared mustard	
	Butter for frying	

1. Cut the crusts from the bread.
2. Beat the eggs, milk, salt, and pepper together. Dip the slices of bread in the mixture and allow them to soak well; drain.
3. Arrange some thin slices of chicken on 4 of the slices of bread. Cover with a slice of ham and top with a slice of cheese. Spread lightly with mustard and cover each with another slice of bread. Press down well and cut across diagonally.
4. Heat the butter in a frying pan and fry the sandwiches until brown and crisp, turning once. Serve while hot.

Cheese and Bacon Supper Pie

⏱ 00:40
00:20   Serves 4   Mid Atlantic

American	Ingredients	Metric/Imperial
2 tbsp	Butter	25 g/1 oz
1	Small onion, peeled and chopped	1
4 slices	Bacon, diced	4 rashers
2 cups	Cottage cheese	450 g/1 lb
2	Eggs	2
1 tsp	Mustard	1 tsp
1 (8-inch)	Baked pie shell	1 (8-inch)
	Chopped parsley	
1	Tomato	1

1. Preheat oven to 375°F/190°C/Gas Mark 5.
2. Heat the butter and sauté the onion until just soft. Add the bacon and fry until crisp.
3. Sieve the cheese. Add the beaten eggs, bacon, onion, and mustard. Season carefully with a little salt and pepper, and mix well.
4. Turn into the pie shell and bake for about 20 minutes, or until the filling is firm and golden brown.
5. Sprinkle with parsley, and garnish with wedges of tomato.

Cheese Puff

⏱ 00:10
00:05   Serves 4   Midwest

American	Ingredients	Metric/Imperial
2	Egg whites	2
½ tsp	Baking powder	½ tsp
¼ tsp	Salt	¼ tsp
¼ tsp	Paprika	¼ tsp
1 cup	Grated sharp Cheddar cheese	125 g/4 oz
4	Slices hot buttered toast	4

1. Beat the egg whites until stiff. Stir in the baking powder and salt, sifted together. Add the paprika and grated cheese, and fold in lightly.
2. Spread on the toast about ¼-inch thick and brown under a hot broiler [grill]. Serve at once.

Cheese Pie I

⏱ 01:20
00:20   Serves 4   Midwest

American	Ingredients	Metric/Imperial
	Pastry	
1 cup	All-purpose [plain] flour	100 g/4 oz
¼ tsp	Salt	¼ tsp
	A pinch of cayenne pepper	
¼ cup	Butter	50 g/2 oz
1–2 tbsp	Water	1–1½ tbsp
	Filling	
1	Clove garlic	1
½ cup	Cottage cheese	100 g/4 oz
½ cup	Grated Gruyère cheese	50 g/2 oz
2 tbsp	Grated Parmesan cheese	1½ tbsp
3	Scallions [spring onions]	3
3	Eggs	3
½ cup	Heavy [double] cream	125 ml/4 fl oz
	A pinch of nutmeg	
	A pinch of cayenne pepper	

1. Preheat the oven to 400°F/200°C/Gas Mark 6.
2. Sift the flour, salt and cayenne. Make a well in the center. Add softened butter and 1 tablespoon of water, and blend with the fingers, adding a little more water if required. Chill for at least 1 hour before using, then roll out and line an 8-inch pie plate.
3. Rub the bottom of the pastry shell very lightly with cut garlic.
4. Sieve the cottage cheese, add the Gruyère, Parmesan and onions. Add beaten eggs, cream and seasoning, and stir the ingredients together until smooth.
5. Pour into the pastry shell, and bake for about 20 minutes.

Cheese Pie II

| | 00:10 | Serves 6 | Midwest |
| | 00:45 | | |

American	Ingredients	Metric/Imperial
	Pastry	
1¾ sticks	Butter	200 g/7 oz
1⅔ cups	Flour	200 g/7 oz
3 tbsp	Water	2 tbsp
	Filling	
⅔ cup	Light [single] cream	150 ml/¼ pint
⅔ cup	Sour cream	150 ml/¼ pint
4	Eggs	4
5 tbsp	Grated Parmesan cheese	4 tbsp
¼ tsp	Black pepper	¼ tsp
1 tsp	Salt	1 tsp
½ tsp	Paprika	½ tsp
1 cup	Aged [mature] Cheddar cheese, cubed	225 g/8 oz
1 cup	Swiss cheese, cubed	225 g/8 oz
5 tbsp	Onion, minced	4 tbsp

1. Combine all the pastry ingredients in a bowl. Mix the dough together using your fingertips until it is well blended. Let stand in a cool place for about ½ hour.
2. Preheat the oven to 425°F/220°C/Gas Mark 7. Flatten the dough with the palm of your hand into a thin baking dish, with a detachable bottom and a diameter of 11 inches, so that the bottom and sides of the dish are evenly covered. Make sure that the dough goes all the way up to the edge of the baking dish and that there are no holes in the dough. Place the dish in the oven and bake the pie shell for about 10 minutes.
3. Meanwhile, mix together the cream, sour cream, and eggs; beat well. Season with the grated Parmesan cheese, salt, pepper, and paprika. Combine and lay out the 2 kinds of cheese in the pie shell. Sprinkle the minced onion on top. Finally, pour the egg mixture over the cheese cubes.
4. Place the pie on a rack in the middle of the oven. Bake for 35 minutes. If the pie gets too dark, cover the top with a piece of aluminum foil.

Cheese and Ham Toast

| | 00:05 | Serves 4 | United States |
| | 00:05 | | |

American	Ingredients	Metric/Imperial
4	Slices cooked ham	4
4	Slices buttered toast	4
	A little chopped chutney	
4	Slices Gruyère cheese	4
2	Tomatoes, peeled and sliced	2

1. Put a slice of ham on each piece of toast. Spread lightly with chutney and cover with a slice of cheese.
2. Arrange slices of tomato on top and put under a hot broiler [grill] to heat through.

Cheese, Bacon and Tomato Pie

| | 00:30 | Serves 4–5 | United States |
| | 00:40 | | |

American	Ingredients	Metric/Imperial
	Pastry for an 8–9 inch, 2-crust pie (see Index)	
6 oz	Bacon slices [rashers], blanched	175 g/6 oz
2–3	Tomatoes, peeled and sliced	2–3
½ lb	Cheddar cheese (cut into thin slices or slices of processed cheese)	225 g/8 oz
	Cayenne pepper	
1	Egg or milk to glaze	1

1. Preheat the oven to 450°F/230°C/Gas Mark 8.
2. Line an 8–9 inch pie plate with half the pastry and prick the bottom.
3. Trim the bacon, cut the slices into two or three pieces, and put half in the bottom of the pie shell.
4. Cover with half the sautéed tomatoes; sprinkle generously with cayenne pepper. Cover with half the slices of cheese, and repeat the layers.
5. Dampen the edge of the pastry and cover with the remaining pastry. Press the edges together neatly, make a hole in the center, and decorate the pie with pastry leaves made with the trimmings.
6. Glaze with beaten egg or milk, bake for 30–40 minutes, and serve hot with tomato sauce, or cold with salad.

Sweetcorn and Cheese Pie

| | 00:30 | Serves 4–5 | Mid Atlantic |
| | 00:15 | | |

American	Ingredients	Metric/Imperial
1 cup	Cottage cheese	225 g/8 oz
½ cup	Grated Parmesan cheese	50 g/2 oz
1 can (12 oz)	Corn	1 tin (350 g/12 oz)
¼ tsp	Paprika	¼ tsp
1	Canned [tinned] pimento, chopped	1
1 cup	Cooked peas	100 g/4 oz
1 (8-inch)	Baked pie shell	1 (8-inch)
2	Tomatoes, peeled and sliced	2

1. Preheat the oven to 375°F/190°C/Gas Mark 5.
2. Combine the cottage cheese, Parmesan, and drained corn. Season with salt, pepper, and paprika; add pimento and peas. If the mixture is a little stiff, add some of the liquid drained from the corn.
3. Pour into the pie shell and arrange slices of tomato around the edge.
4. Bake for about 15 minutes in a moderate oven.

Cheese Pie II

Puffed Cheese Rarebit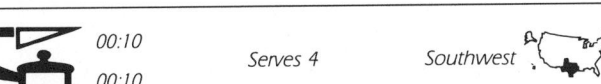

🔪 00:10		
🍳 00:10	Serves 4	Southwest

American	Ingredients	Metric/Imperial
4	Slices bread	4
	Butter	
3	Eggs	3
1 cup	Grated cheese	125 g/4 oz
¼ tsp	Prepared mustard	¼ tsp
1–2 tbsp	Cream	1–1½ tbsp

1. Preheat the oven to 400°F/200°C/Gas Mark 6.
2. Toast the bread, spread with butter, and arrange the slices in an ovenproof dish.
3. Separate the eggs, then beat the yolks. Add cheese, mustard, seasoning, and cream.
4. Beat the egg whites stiffly and fold into the mixture. Pile onto the slices of toast and put into a moderately hot oven for about 7 minutes, or until brown and puffy.

Cheese Custard Pie

🔪 00:30		
🍳 00:45	Serves 4	Midwest

American	Ingredients	Metric/Imperial
1 (8-inch)	Baked pie shell	1 (8-inch)
1	Egg white	1
1¼ cups	Milk	300 ml/½ pint
½ cup	Light [single] cream	125 ml/4 fl oz
1 cup	Grated cheese	100 g/4 oz
¼ tsp	Paprika	¼ tsp
½ tsp	Grated onion	½ tsp
	A small pinch of cayenne pepper	
3	Eggs	3

1. Preheat the oven to 325°F/160°C/Gas Mark 3.
2. Brush the baked pie shell with lightly beaten egg white.
3. Scald the milk and cream, remove from the heat, add cheese, and stir until it has melted. Add salt, paprika, onion, and cayenne pepper.
4. Beat in the eggs, one at a time, then pour into the pastry shell.
5. Bake for about 45 minutes, or until the custard is firm.

Roquefort Soufflé

Cheese and Bacon Mousse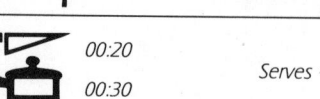

| | 08:00 | Serves 6–8 | Mid Atlantic |
| | 00:05 | | |

American	Ingredients	Metric/Imperial
1 envelope	Gelatin	1 sachet
4 tbsp	Water	3½ tbsp
2 tbsp	Butter	25 g/1 oz
2 tbsp	Flour	1½ tbsp
1 cup	Milk	250 ml/8 fl oz
½ tsp	Salt	½ tsp
¼ tsp	Cayenne pepper	¼ tsp
¼ tsp	Prepared mustard	¼ tsp
	A few drops of Worcestershire sauce	
¾ cup	Grated cheese	75 g/3 oz
4 oz	Bacon, cooked and chopped	100 g/4 oz
½ cup	Cream cheese	100 g/4 oz
2	Eggs, separated	2
2 tbsp	Milk	1½ tbsp

1. Soften the gelatin in the water. Then dissolve over hot water. Make a sauce with the butter, flour, and milk; add the seasonings, Worcestershire sauce, grated cheese, bacon, and the dissolved gelatin.
2. Mix the cream cheese with the egg yolks and milk, and stir into the sauce mixture. Beat together until smooth. Beat the egg whites until stiff, and fold in lightly. Pour into a 4 × 8 × 4-inch loaf pan, and refrigerate until set.
3. When required, turn out and serve with a salad.

Roquefort Soufflé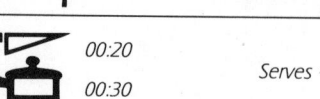

| | 00:20 | Serves 4 | South |
| | 00:30 | | |

American	Ingredients	Metric/Imperial
¼ lb	Roquefort cheese	100 g/4 oz
4 tbsp	Butter	50 g/2 oz
5 tbsp	Flour	4 tbsp
5 tbsp	Milk	4 tbsp
5	Eggs, separated	5
1 tsp	Potato flour	1 tsp
½ tsp	Salt	½ tsp
1/16 tsp	Cayenne pepper	1/16 tsp
1½ tbsp	Armagnac	1¼ tsp

1. This soufflé is made best if the Roquefort is so dry that it can be grated. If this is not the case, freeze it for a short while so that it is easy to grate.
2. Melt the butter, add the flour, then the milk, a little at a time, stirring constantly until the mixture becomes creamy. Remove from the heat and allow to cool for a few minutes.
3. Beat the egg yolks, one at a time, into the batter. Blend in the grated cheese, potato flour, cayenne pepper, and the Armagnac.
4. Preheat the oven to 425°F/220°C/Gas Mark 7. Beat the egg whites into very stiff peaks and fold them extremely carefully into the soufflé batter without stirring too much. Grease and flour a soufflé dish and fill it with the batter. Flatten the surface of the soufflé with a knife.
5. Bake in the middle of the oven on a rack for about 25–30 minutes, or until the soufflé has risen to almost double its original height and has become a golden brown.

Tomato Fondue with Frankfurters

| | 00:10 | Serves 2-3 | Midwest |
| | 00:15 | | |

American	Ingredients	Metric/Imperial
1	Clove garlic	1
2 cups	Grated Cheddar or American cheese	225 g/8 oz
½ cup	Grated Gruyère cheese	50 g/2 oz
½ cup	Condensed tomato soup	125 ml/4 fl oz
1 tsp	Worcestershire sauce	1 tsp
3 tbsp	Dry sherry	2 tbsp
1 small can	Cocktail frankfurters	1 small tin
	French bread	

1. Rub the inside of the fondue pot with the cut clove of garlic.
2. Put in the cheeses, tomato soup, and Worcestershire sauce. Stir continuously over a low heat until the cheese has melted and the mixture is creamy. Stir in the sherry, and cook 2–3 minutes. Adjust the seasoning before serving.
3. The frankfurters are then speared onto the fondue forks and dipped into the fondue.
4. Serve with plenty of French bread.

Herb and Cottage Cheese Pie

Herb and Cottage Cheese Pie

02:00
00:30
Serves 6
United States

American	Ingredients	Metric/Imperial
	Pie Crust	
5 tbsp	Butter	65 g/2½ oz
	Salt	
1½ cups	Flour, sifted	175 g/6 oz
1	Egg yolk	1
1 tbsp	Cold water	1 tbsp
	Filling	
2	Leeks	2
2 tbsp	Butter	25 g/1 oz
1½ lb	Fresh spinach	675 g/1½ lb
2 tbsp	Chopped parsley	1½ tbsp
2 tbsp	Chopped chives	1½ tbsp
	Salt	
	Pepper	
3	Eggs, separated	3
⅓ lb	Cottage cheese	150 g/5 oz

1. First make the pie crust. Place the butter in a warm bowl, and soften the butter with a wooden spoon. Add the salt to the flour and shape it into a pyramid in the bowl. Make a hole in the middle and fill it with the butter, egg yolk, another dash of salt, and the water. Stir with a spoon. Dip your fingers in a small amount of flour and knead the dough. Add more water, if needed. Place the dough in a piece of waxed paper so that it is totally covered. Refrigerate for at least an hour. Remove the dough from the refrigerator 15 minutes before it is to be rolled out.

2. Cut the white part of the leeks into thin rings. Melt the butter in a frying pan, and place the leek rings in the butter. Stir until they have become soft. Add the spinach and the herbs. Season well and mix. Add more melted butter if the mixture seems too dry. Let cool.

3. Roll out the dough and line a pie tin with detachable sides or 4 individual tart pans [flan rings] with it. Cut away any extras around the edge with a sharp knife.

4. Preheat the oven to 375°F/190°C/Gas Mark 5. Cover a baking sheet with foil and place it in the oven. Place the herb mixture in the bottom of the pans.

5. Separate the egg yolks and the whites. Strain the cottage cheese through a sieve; beat the egg yolks and the cottage cheese together and season well. Beat the whites into stiff peaks and fold them carefully into the cheese mixture. Pour into the tart pans.

6. Bake for about 30 minutes, until the pie has risen and become golden brown. Serve warm or cold.

Cheese and Ham Soufflé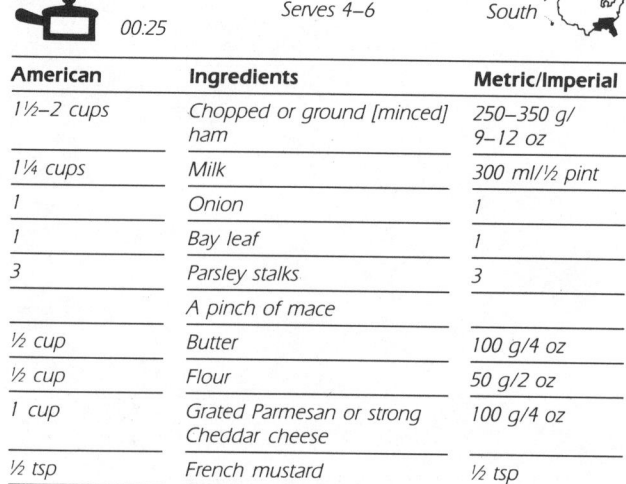

| | 00:30 | | |
| | 00:25 | Serves 4–6 | South |

American	Ingredients	Metric/Imperial
1½–2 cups	Chopped or ground [minced] ham	250–350 g/ 9–12 oz
1¼ cups	Milk	300 ml/½ pint
1	Onion	1
1	Bay leaf	1
3	Parsley stalks	3
	A pinch of mace	
½ cup	Butter	100 g/4 oz
½ cup	Flour	50 g/2 oz
1 cup	Grated Parmesan or strong Cheddar cheese	100 g/4 oz
½ tsp	French mustard	½ tsp
3	Large eggs	3
	A little cayenne pepper (optional)	

1. Preheat the oven to 375°F/190°C/Gas Mark 5.
2. Heat the milk with the onion, bay leaf, parsley, and mace. Melt the butter, remove from the heat, and stir in flour. Strain the milk into the pan and stir over gentle heat until smooth. Then bring to a boil, stirring all the time. Remove from the heat, and add ham, cheese, mustard, and seasoning.

3. Separate the eggs carefully and mix in the yolks one at a time. (At this point, the mixture can be left covered, the whites beaten and added just before the soufflé is due to be cooked.) Beat the whites with a pinch of salt, until they stand up in peaks. Add 1 tablespoon of whites to the mixture and mix in well. Then carefully fold in the remainder with a spoon without over mixing.
4. Pour the mixture into a soufflé dish and bake in the oven until well risen and brown on top, 20–25 minutes. Sprinkle the top with a little grated cheese or a dusting of red pepper, and serve at once.

Mushroom Rarebit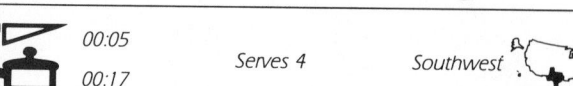

| | 00:05 | | |
| | 00:17 | Serves 4 | Southwest |

American	Ingredients	Metric/Imperial
¼ cup	Butter	50 g/2 oz
4 cups	Sliced mushrooms	450 g/1 lb
2 tbsp	Tomato purée	1½ tbsp
3 tbsp	Stock or water	2 tbsp
4 tbsp	Grated Parmesan cheese	3½ tbsp
4	Slices toast or English muffins	4

1. Heat the butter in a pan. Add the mushrooms and sauté slowly for about 10 minutes.
2. Add seasoning and tomato purée mixed with the stock. Add the cheese and continue to cook slowly until the mushrooms are tender, about 5 to 7 minutes.
3. Serve on hot buttered toast or English muffins.

Cheese Crisp

![Sunday Double Decker Sandwich](sunday-double-decker-sandwich.jpg)
Sunday Double Decker Sandwich

Cheese Crisp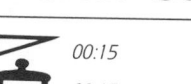

01:15
00:00   Serves 4   Midwest

American	Ingredients	Metric/Imperial
6	Graham crackers (digestive biscuits)	6
2 oz	Potato chips [crisps]	50 g/2 oz
6 tbsp	Butter	75 g/3 oz
½ cup	Cooked rice	100 g/4 oz
1 cup	Cream cheese	225 g/8 oz
2 tbsp	Chopped gherkins	1½ tbsp
4 tbsp	Mayonnaise	3½ tbsp
	Salt and pepper	
	A few thin slices cucumber	
	Paprika	

1. Put the crackers and potato chips between waxed paper and crush with a rolling pin. Add the melted butter, mix well, and press into an 8-inch pie plate. Set aside to chill.
2. Mix the rice, cream cheese, and gherkins; add mayonnaise and season to taste.
3. Fill the pie dish. Then garnish with twists of cucumber and sprinkle with paprika.

Sunday Double Decker Sandwich

00:15
00:15   Serves 4   United States

American	Ingredients	Metric/Imperial
8 slices	Cooked bacon	8 rashers
8	Slices white bread	8
½ cup	Butter	100 g/4 oz
2 tsp	Mustard	2 tsp
4	Large tomatoes	4
1 cup	Chopped onion	100 g/4 oz
8	Slices processed cheese	8

1. Preheat the broiler [grill].
2. Remove the crusts and toast the bread on one side only. Spread the untoasted side with butter. Spread with mustard, if desired.
3. Halve the bacon slices and lay on the bread. Slice the tomatoes and place them on top of the bacon. Brush with a little melted butter and onion; broil [grill] for 3–5 minutes.
4. Cover the tomato with process cheese. Broil until the cheese bubbles. Pile one on top of another to make 4 sandwiches and broil again until the top layer of cheese is well browned. Serve at once.

Fish and Shellfish

Easy-to-Bake Fish with Cheese and Tomatoes

Barbecued Fish

01:00
00:15
Serves 4   United States

American	Ingredients	Metric/Imperial
4	Thick steaks of halibut or other firm white fish	4
	Marinade	
2 tbsp	Chopped onion	1½ tbsp
2 tbsp	Chopped green pepper	1½ tbsp
2 tbsp	Oil	1½ tbsp
2 tbsp	Lemon juice	1½ tbsp
½ cup	Dry white wine	125 ml/4 fl oz
¼ cup	Soy sauce	60 ml/2 fl oz
½ cup	Peeled, chopped tomatoes	100 g/4 oz
1 tsp	Powdered ginger	1 tsp
1	Clove garlic, crushed	1

1. Heat the coals in an outdoor grill until hot, about 30 minutes, or preheat the broiler [grill].
2. Heat the oil, and sauté the onion and green pepper until soft. Then add all the other ingredients. Bring to a boil and simmer for 1 minute.
3. When cool, pour over the fish, and leave for at least 30 minutes, longer if possible.
4. A hinged wire broiler [grill] is useful for cooking the fish—otherwise put it on the rack of the barbecue or the broiler pan and cook, turning once, until the fish flakes easily, about 10–15 minutes.
5. Serve the fish with the remaining marinade, heated, or with Tartare Sauce (see Index).

Easy-to-Bake Fish with Cheese and Tomatoes

00:15
00:20
Serves 4–6   New England

American	Ingredients	Metric/Imperial
1½ lb	Haddock or cod fillets	675 g/1½ lb
½ tbsp	Butter	10 g/¼ oz
1 tbsp	Flour	1 tbsp
¾ tsp	Salt	¾ tsp
1 tbsp	Squeezed lemon juice	1 tbsp
2 tbsp	Dill, chopped	1½ tbsp
¾ cup	Cheese, grated	75 g/3 oz
¼ cup	Milk	60 ml/2 fl oz
2–3	Tomatoes	2–3

1. Preheat the oven to 425°F/220°C/Gas Mark 7.
2. Rinse the fish and let the water totally drain off. Grease a baking dish with low sides and sprinkle flour on the bottom. Place the fish in the dish. Salt and sprinkle with lemon juice. Add dill and grated cheese. Cover with milk.
3. Bake in the middle of the oven for about 20 minutes, or until the fish has a nice color. Cut the tomatoes into cubes and spread them over top of the fish.

Fish au Gratin on a Bed of Broccoli

00:15
00:45
Serves 4–6   New England

American	Ingredients	Metric/Imperial
1 (½-lb) pkg	Frozen broccoli	1 (225 g/ 8 oz) pkt
1½ lb	Fresh or frozen fish fillets— cod or haddock	675 g/1½ lb
1 tsp	Salt	1 tsp
	Au Gratin	
1¼ cups	Cheese, coarsely grated	150 g/5 oz
3 tbsp	Bread crumbs	2 tbsp
5 tbsp	Leek, finely shredded, or snipped chives	4 tbsp
2-3 tbsp	Milk, cream or sour cream	1½-2 tbsp

1. Preheat the oven to 425°F/220°C/Gas Mark 7.
2. Prepare the broccoli according to directions on the package. Place in a greased, ovenproof dish. Cut the fish fillets in slices. Place the fish over the broccoli. Sprinkle with salt.
3. Mix the grated cheese with the bread crumbs and leek or chives. Pull the mixture together with milk, cream, or sour cream.
4. Dab the cheese mixture over the fish. Bake in the oven for 20–30 minutes, or until the fish is done. Serve with sliced or mashed potatoes.

Fish Kebabs

	00:45		
	00:10	Serves 4	United States

American	Ingredients	Metric/Imperial
2 lb	Firm fish—Halibut, swordfish, cod, etc.	900 g/2 lb
	Cucumber	
	Stuffed olives	
	Marinade	
¾ cup	Oil	175 ml/6 fl oz
½ cup	Lemon juice	125 ml/4 fl oz
1	Bay leaf	1
4	Drops soy sauce	4

1. Preheat the broiler [grill].
2. Combine the marinade ingredients.
3. Cut the fish into 1-inch cubes, put into a shallow pan, pour the marinade over, and leave for 30 minutes, stirring occasionally.
4. Thread onto skewers with alternate slices of cucumber and stuffed olives.
5. Broil [grill] for about 10 minutes, basting frequently with the marinade, and serve with Tartare Sauce (see Index).

Fish Curls

	00:45		
	00:10	Serves 4–6	New England

American	Ingredients	Metric/Imperial
1 lb	Fish fillets	450 g/1 lb
2 tbsp	Oil	1½ tbsp
2 tsp	Vinegar	2 tsp
1 tsp	Lemon juice	1 tsp
1 tsp	Parsley, chopped	1 tsp
½	Small onion, chopped	½
	Salt	
	Pinch of cayenne pepper	
¼ cup	Flour	25 g/1 oz
1	Egg	1
2 tbsp	Milk	1½ tbsp
	Oil for deep-frying	

Fish au Gratin on a Bed of Broccoli

Fish Curls

1. Cut the fillets into ½-inch wide strips. Mix 1 tablespoon of oil, the vinegar, lemon juice, parsley, onion, salt, and cayenne pepper together in a bowl. Add the fish strips and marinate for 30 minutes. Drain and dry the fillets thoroughly on absorbent paper towels [kitchen paper].
2. Sift the flour and a pinch of salt into a mixing bowl. Beat in the egg, milk, and remaining 1 tablespoon of oil. Coat fish in the batter.
3. Fill a deep frying pan one third to one half full of oil and heat it until a cube of bread will brown. Fry pieces of fish until golden, placing them in the pan one by one to prevent them sticking together. Drain well before serving.

Baked Fish

	00:10		
	00:40	Serves 2–4	New England

American	Ingredients	Metric/Imperial
1 lb	Fish fillets (sole, flounder, or red snapper)	450 g/1 lb
1 tbsp	Parsley, chopped	1 tbsp
1 tbsp	Lemon juice	1 tbsp
¾ tsp	Seasoned salt	¾ tsp
3 tbsp	Olive oil	2 tbsp
1	Medium onion, thinly sliced	1
1	Clove garlic, minced	1
1	Large tomato, chopped	1
3	Slices lemon	3
2 tbsp	White wine	1½ tbsp

1. Preheat the oven to 350°F/180°C/Gas Mark 4.
2. Arrange the fish in an 8- or 9-inch square baking dish. Sprinkle with parsley, lemon juice, and seasoned salt.
3. Heat the oil in a small frying pan; fry the onion and garlic until limp. Top the fish with the onion mixture, including the oil from the pan. Arrange the tomatoes on top of the onion mixture; place lemon slices on top of the fish. Pour wine over all.
4. Bake 30 to 35 minutes, or until the fish flakes with a fork.

Herbed Fish Parcels

Herbed Fish Parcels

 00:30
00:30   Serves 4–6   New England

American	Ingredients	Metric/Imperial
1 lb	White fish	450 g/1 lb
1	Small onion, finely chopped	1
4 tbsp	Oil	3½ tbsp
4 tsp	Lemon juice	4 tsp
4 tsp	Parsley, chopped	4 tsp
	Salt and pepper	

1. Preheat the oven to 400°F/200°C/Gas Mark 6.
2. Skin the fish and cut into 4 or 6 portions. Place each piece of fish on a lightly oiled square of foil. Sprinkle with onion, oil, lemon juice, parsley, salt, and pepper. Fold up the foil to make 4 to 6 parcels. Fold the edges together.
3. Cook in the oven for 30 minutes, or until the fish is cooked. Serve very hot.

Fish Fillets on Spinach

 00:25
00:30   Serves 6   New England

American	Ingredients	Metric/Imperial
1½ lb	Fish fillets	675 g/1½ lb
	Juice of 1 lemon	
2 lb	Fresh spinach	900 g/2 lb
2 tbsp	Vegetable oil	1½ tbsp
1	Medium onion, chopped	1
1 tsp	Margarine	1 tsp
½ tsp	Salt	½ tsp
⅛ tsp	White pepper	⅛ tsp
½ tsp	Fresh nutmeg, grated	½ tsp
2	Tomatoes, peeled	2
¼ cup	Mozzarella cheese, grated	25 g/1 oz

1. Preheat the oven to 350°F/180°C/Gas Mark 4.
2. Wash the fish; pat it dry. Sprinkle with lemon juice; let it stand 10 minutes. Wash the spinach well; chop it coarsely.
3. Heat the oil in a frying pan. Add the onion; sauté until soft. Fry the fish in the pan with the onions for a few minutes on each side until golden brown. Remove the fish and onions; reserve. Add the spinach to the pan; stir-fry 4 to 5 minutes.
4. Grease a casserole dish with margarine. Add the spinach. Arrange the fish fillets on top of the spinach; sprinkle with salt, pepper, and nutmeg. Place peeled and sliced tomatoes on top of the fish. Sprinkle with grated chese. Bake in the oven 15 minutes.

Fish Steaks with Shrimp Sauce

 00:20
00:22   Serves 4   New England

American	Ingredients	Metric/Imperial
4	Fish steaks (each 125–225 g/6–8 oz)	4
	Juice of 1 lemon	
½ tsp	Salt	½ tsp
¼ tsp	White pepper	¼ tsp
2 tbsp	Butter	25 g/1 oz
1	Medium onion, sliced	1
1 tbsp	Parsley, chopped	1 tbsp
½ cup	Dry white wine	125 ml/4 fl oz
½ cup	Beef bouillon [stock]	125 ml/4 fl oz
6 oz	Fresh mushrooms, sliced	175 g/6 oz
¼ lb	Frozen cooked shrimp [prawns]	100 g/4 oz
1 tbsp	Lemon juice	1 tbsp
¼ cup	Plain yogurt	60 ml/2 fl oz
	Lemon slices and parsley for garnish	

1. Wash the fish; pat it dry. Sprinkle the fish with the juice of 1 lemon, salt, and pepper. Heat the butter in a frying pan; add the fish and onion. Brown the fish 5 minutes on each side. Sprinkle with parsley. Pour in white wine and simmer 5 minutes. Remove the fish to a heated platter; keep it warn.
2. Add bouillon to the frying pan; bring to a boil. Add the mushrooms; simmer slowly 8 minutes, stirring often. Add the shrimp; simmer 2–3 minutes. Season the sauce with 1 tablespoon of lemon juice and stir in the yogurt. Heat thoroughly, but do not boil. Adjust the seasonings.
3. Pour the sauce over the fish steaks; garnish with lemon slices and parsley.

Fish in Foil with Tomato-Filled Zucchini

Fish in Foil with Tomato-Filled Zucchini 🐷🐷

00:45
01:00
Serves 4
New England

American	Ingredients	Metric/Imperial
1	Whole haddock, cod, pike, or perch	1
2 tsp	Salt	2 tsp
	Dill	
	Parsley stalks	
2	Large zucchini (courgettes)	2
2 tsp	Salt per quart of water	2 tsp
1 lb	Tomatoes	450 g/1 lb
1	Small carrot, finely grated	1
2	Onions, finely chopped	2
2 tbsp	Tomato paste	1½ tbsp
½ tsp	Black pepper	½ tsp
½ tsp	Salt	½ tsp
½ tsp	Tarragon	½ tsp
4 tbsp	Chopped parsley	3½ tbsp

1. Preheat the oven to 350°F/180°C/Gas Mark 4.
2. Clean the fish, but let the head and fins remain. Rub salt into the fish and fill the stomach with dill and parsley. Place the fish on a sheet of aluminum foil. Place a ruler next to the fish and measure the back at the thickest spot.
3. Make a tight package with the foil around the fish and place in a roasting pan in the oven. If the fish is 1½ inches thick, it will take 30 minutes to bake; 2½ inches thick, 40 minutes; and 3 inches thick, 50 minutes. Increase or decrease by 5 minutes for every ¼ inch.
4. Peel the zucchini along 4 lines with spaces in between, so that the peel remains on the spaces in between. Cut lengthwise into halves and take out the seeds. Place in salted, boiling water and boil for 10 minutes. Remove from the water, then drain well.
5. Scald the tomatoes in the same water and peel them. Cut the tomatoes into 4 pieces and place them in a saucepan together with the carrot, onions, tomato paste, pepper, salt, and tarragon. Boil for about 5 minutes.
6. Place the zucchini halves on an ovenproof plate and pour the tomato mixture into the zucchini. Place a plate over the fish and let it sit there during the last 20 minutes of the fish baking time.
7. Serve the fish in foil, surrounded by tomato-filled zucchini. Sprinkle with parsley.

Fish Kebabs, Two Different Ways

Fish Kebabs, Two Different Ways

00:20
00:10 — Serves 4 — South

American	Ingredients	Metric/Imperial
1 lb	Fillets of fish with firm meat	1 lb
	Salt	
	Pepper	
¼ lb	Mushrooms	100 g/4 oz
6 slices	Bacon, cut in squares	6 rashers
5	Tomatoes	5
	Oil	
	Crayfish Kebabs	
25	Grapes	25
12	Crayfish tails or clams from a can	12
4	Tomatoes	4
	Oil	
	Salt	
	Black or white pepper	

1. Preheat the broiler [grill] or the coals on an outdoor grill.
2. Cut the fish into 1 × 1 × ½-inch cubes. Lightly salt and pepper the fish cubes. Divide each tomato into 8 pieces.
3. Alternate the fish, mushrooms, bacon, and tomato pieces on a skewer, making 4 skewers in all. Baste with oil before grilling for 10–15 minutes. Turn the skewers several times.
4. To make 4 skewers of crayfish kebabs, take the seeds out of the grapes without cutting them in two. Cut each tomato into 8 pieces. Alternate the grapes, crayfish tails or clams, and tomatoes on a skewer. Baste with oil, salt and pepper lightly, and grill until slightly brown (4–8 minutes). Turn several times.

Fish Pie

00:30
00:40 — Serves 4 — Pacific Northwest

American	Ingredients	Metric/Imperial
1½ lb	Fillets of haddock, flounder or other fish	675 g/1½ lb
1 tsp	Grated lemon rind	1 tsp
2	Hard-boiled eggs, chopped	2
¼ cup	Medium Cream Sauce (see Index)	60 ml/2 fl oz
	Flaky Pastry (see Index)	
	Egg to glaze	

1. Preheat the oven to 425°F/220°C/Gas Mark 7.
2. Remove any skin from the fish and cut into small pieces.
3. Add the seasoning, lemon rind, and chopped eggs and bind with the sauce.
4. Roll the pastry into a square and put the fish mixture in the center.
5. Dampen the edges of the pastry and fold each corner to the center, keeping the square shape.
6. Garnish the center with pastry leaves, brush with beaten egg, and bake for 30–40 minutes.

Fish with Potato Crust

00:15
01:05 — Serves 4–5 — South

American	Ingredients	Metric/Imperial
1 lb	Potatoes, peeled	450 g/1 lb
4 tbsp	Butter or margarine	50 g/2 oz
2 tbsp	Light [single] cream or milk	1½ tbsp
1	Egg	1
1½ lb	Cod fillets	675 g/1½ lb
2 tbsp	Dry white wine	1½ tbsp
2 tsp	Lemon juice	2 tsp
2 tbsp	Flour	1½ tbsp
1 (8-oz)	Package frozen shrimp [prawns]	1 (225 g/8 oz)
½ cup	Grated Gruyère cheese	50 g/2 oz
	Milk	

1. Preheat the oven to 450°F/230°C/Gas Mark 8.
2. Cook the potatoes in boiling salted water, drain thoroughly, and dry over low heat. Add 2 tablespoons [25 g/1 oz] butter, the cream, and beaten egg; whip until fluffy.
3. Put the fish into a frying pan with the wine, lemon juice, and enough salted water to barely cover. Poach for 15 minutes. Drain carefully and retain the stock. Flake the fish coarsely, removing any skin.
4. Make a sauce with the remaining 2 tablespoons [25 g/1 oz] butter, flour, and 1 cup [250 ml/8 fl oz] of the fish stock. Add the shrimp and cheese and season to taste.
5. Put the fish into an oven dish; add enough sauce to moisten and cover with the potatoes. Brush with a little milk and bake for about 30 minutes, or until the potato crust is brown.
6. Serve any remaining sauce separately, thinning it down if necessary with a little of the fish stock.

Fish Pie

Fish and Oyster Pie

	00:25		
	00:25	Serves 5–6	New England

American	Ingredients	Metric/Imperial
12	Oysters	12
6 tbsp	Dry white wine	5 tbsp
¾ lb	Poached fish	350 g/12 oz
	Nutmeg	
1 cup	Medium Cream Sauce (see Index)	250 ml/8 fl oz
1 tsp	Finely chopped onion	1 tsp
2 tbsp	Heavy [double] cream	1½ tbsp
2 tbsp	Finely chopped parsley	1½ tbsp
1 tbsp	Butter or margarine	15 g/½ oz
	Pastry for an 8–9 inch, 1-crust pie (see Index)	
	Egg or milk to glaze	

1. Preheat the oven to 425°F/220°C/Gas Mark 7.
2. Remove the oysters from their shells and cook in their liquid and the wine until the edges begin to curl. Drain, and save the liquid.
3. Remove any skin and bone from the fish, flake, and put into a deep 8–9 inch pie plate with the oysters. Season with salt, pepper, and nutmeg.
4. Make the sauce; add the oyster liquid and wine, onion, cream, and parsley. Correct the seasoning and pour over the fish. Dot with butter.
5. Moisten the edge of the pie plate. Cover with the pastry, pressing the edges well down. Make one or two slits in the top to allow the steam to escape. Glaze with a little egg or milk, and bake about 20 minutes or until the pastry is well browned.

Fish, Onion, and Tomato Pie

	00:30		
	00:55	Serves 4–6	Pacific Southwest

American	Ingredients	Metric/Imperial
	Pastry for a 9-inch, 2-crust pie (see Index)	
4 tbsp	Olive oil	3½ tbsp
2–3	Onions, peeled and chopped	2–3
1½ lb	Fillets of sole	675 g/1½ lb
2–3	Tomatoes, peeled and chopped	2–3
1	Clove garlic, crushed	1
2 tbsp	Finely chopped parsley	1½ tbsp
	Salt and black pepper	
6	Stuffed olives, chopped	6
2	Hard-boiled eggs, chopped	2

1. Preheat the oven to 400°F/200°C/Gas Mark 6.
2. Line a 9-inch pie plate with half the pastry.
3. Heat 3 tablespoons [2 tbsp] of the oil in a frying pan. Sauté the onion for about 10 minutes. Add the fish, cut into strips, tomato, garlic, and parsley. Cook over low heat about 10 minutes, stirring frequently. Add the seasoning, olives, and chopped eggs.
4. Turn into the pastry shell and cover with the rest of the pastry, pressing the edges well together. Make a small hole in the top and brush the top of the pie with the remaining 1 tablespoon oil.
5. Bake for about 35 minutes, or until the pastry is golden brown. Serve cut in wedges.

Fish Rolls with Sesame Seeds

Island Fish Stew

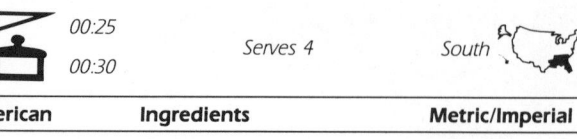

	00:25		
	00:30	Serves 4	South

American	Ingredients	Metric/Imperial
1 lb	Cod or haddock	450 g/1 lb
1 (7½ oz) can	Clams in water	1 (200 g/7½ oz) tin
4 cups	Fish stock	1 1/1¾ pints
1 (8 oz) can	Whole peeled tomatoes	1 (225 g/8 oz) tin
	Salt	
	Freshly ground pepper	
4–6	Potatoes, peeled and boiled	4–6
¼ lb	Fresh shrimp [prawns], shelled	100 g/4 oz
	Dill	

1. Cut the fish into large cubes. Drain the clams, reserving their juice. Mix the clam juice, fish stock, and the juice from the can of tomatoes and simmer together for about 10 minutes. Add the fish cubes and simmer in the broth for several minutes. Season with salt and freshly ground pepper.
2. Add the boiled potatoes, clams, shrimp, and tomatoes, and simmer for several more minutes. Chop the dill and sprinkle it over the stew.
3. Serve with crispy, warm French bread and a good cheese.

Fish Rolls with Sesame Seeds

	00:15		
	00:40	Serves 5–6	United States

American	Ingredients	Metric/Imperial
1½ lb	Fillets of fish, hake, flounder, cod, fresh haddock etc.	675 g/1½ lb
1½ cups	Milk	350 ml/12 fl oz
3 tbsp	Butter	40 g/1½ oz
3 tbsp	Flour	2 tbsp
4 tbsp	Sesame seeds, toasted	3½ tbsp
1 cup	Grated cheese	100 g/4 oz
3 tbsp	Lemon juice	2 tbsp
	Paprika	

1. Preheat the oven to 350°F/180°C/Gas Mark 4.
2. Roll up the fillets and fasten with toothpicks. Arrange in a shallow buttered casserole. Sprinkle with salt and pepper, pour the milk over, cover, and cook for 20–30 minutes. Then carefully pour off the milk and reserve. Remove the toothpicks from the fish.
3. To toast the sesame seeds, put them in a frying pan and toss over medium heat until they begin to color, or spread them out on a baking sheet and toast in the oven.
4. Melt the butter in a pan, stir in the flour and sesame seeds, and cook for 2 minutes. Gradually add the milk in which the fish has been cooked, and stir until boiling. Add cheese and lemon juice. Stir until the cheese has melted. Adjust the seasoning, and pour over the fish.
5. Sprinkle with paprika, brown under a hot broiler [grill] for a few minutes, and serve with riced potatoes, carrots, and a green vegetable.

Barbecued Haddock Fillets

	00:30		
	00:05	Serves 4	United States

American	Ingredients	Metric/Imperial
4	Haddock fillets	4
	Oil	
1 tsp	Salt	1 tsp
¼ tsp	Pepper	¼ tsp
⅛ tsp	Oregano	⅛ tsp
¼ cup	Mayonnaise	60 ml/2 fl oz
2 tbsp	Lemon juice	1½ tbsp
2 tbsp	Prepared mustard	1½ tbsp
2–3 tbsp	Chopped parsley	1½–2 tbsp

1. Heat the coals in an outdoor grill until hot, about 30 minutes, or preheat the broiler [grill].
2. Brush the fish well with oil, and sprinkle with salt, pepper, and oregano.
3. Cook on the rack of the barbecue or in the broiler for 3–4 minutes, turning once.
4. Mix the mayonnaise, lemon juice, mustard, and parsley together, and spread generously over the fillets.
5. Cook for 1–2 minutes, and serve at once with a salad.

Island Fish Stew

Fish Steaks in Foil

1. Preheat the oven to 350°F/180°C/Gas Mark 4.
2. Heat the butter in a frying pan, and sauté the almonds until they just begin to color. Add the mustard, vinegar, 1 tablespoon water, and olives. Stir well for a few minutes.
3. Arrange the fish in a shallow buttered casserole, pour the sauce over, cover, and cook for 25–30 minutes.
4. Serve with rice, cooked in chicken stock, a tomato salad, and some French bread.

Fish Steaks in Foil

00:30
00:20   Serves 6   Midwest

American	Ingredients	Metric/Imperial
6	Cod steaks, or any other suitable white fish	6
6	Lemons	6
½ cup	Butter, melted	125 g/4 oz
6 tbsp	Dry white wine	5 tbsp
1	Clove garlic, crushed	1
2 tbsp	Chopped parsley	1½ tbsp

1. Heat the coals in an outdoor grill until hot, about 30 minutes, or preheat the broiler [grill].
2. Season the fish with salt and pepper.
3. Peel the lemons, removing all the white pith, and cut into thin slices.
4. Cut 6 pieces of heavy duty aluminum foil into squares, about 10–12 inches each. Arrange half the lemon slices down the center of each square of foil. Place a steak of fish on top, and cover with the rest of the lemon slices.
5. Mix the melted butter with the wine, crushed garlic, and parsley, and spoon over the fish. Fold over the foil, and seal each parcel as securely as possible.
6. Grill, allowing about 20 minutes, and serve in the foil with Tartare Sauce (see Index).

Casserole of Halibut with Almonds

00:05
00:35   Serves 4   United States

American	Ingredients	Metric/Imperial
½ cup	Butter or margarine	100 g/4 oz
3 tbsp	Blanched slivered almonds	2 tbsp
2 tsp	Dry mustard	2 tsp
1 tbsp	Tarragon vinegar	1 tbsp
2 tbsp	Sliced green olives	1½ tbsp
4 small or 2 large	Halibut steaks	4 small or 2 large

Steamed Haddock with Mediterranean Sauce

00:20
01:20   Serves 5–6   New England

American	Ingredients	Metric/Imperial
6	Medium tomatoes, peeled and coarsely chopped	6
½ tsp	Dried oregano	½ tsp
½ tsp	Thyme	½ tsp
½ tsp	Basil	½ tsp
1 tsp	Chives	1 tsp
2	Scallions [spring onions], finely minced	2
5 tbsp	Vermouth	4 tbsp
2 lb	Haddock or cod fillets	900 g/2 lb
	Salt and freshly ground pepper	
1 tbsp	Olive oil	1 tbsp

1. Combine the tomatoes, herbs, green onions, and vermouth in a medium-sized saucepan. Simmer for 30 minutes while preparing haddock.
2. Place the haddock on a large piece of aluminum foil. Season with salt and pepper. Fold the foil around the haddock securely. Place the haddock in a steamer over boiling water. Steam about 20 minutes, or until the fish begins to flake.
3. Pour the juice from the foil packet into the tomato sauce. Rewrap the foil packet; keep the haddock warm in a very slow oven. Add the olive oil to the sauce; simmer about 30 minutes longer, or until thickened and considerably reduced in volume. Arrange the haddock on a heated platter. Pour the sauce over the haddock; serve.

Haddock and Tomato Pie

01:30
00:30   Serves 4   New England

American	Ingredients	Metric/Imperial
	Pastry	
1½ cups	All-purpose [plain] flour	175 g/6 oz
	Pinch salt	
6 tbsp	Butter	75 g/3 oz
2 tbsp	Vegetable shortening	1½ tbsp
1	Egg yolk	1
1–2 tbsp	Water	1–1½ tbsp

	Filling	
2 tbsp	Butter or margarine	25 g/1 oz
1 cup	Finely sliced onion	100 g/4 oz
1 tbsp	Flour	1 tbsp
½ cup	Milk	125 ml/4 fl oz
	Nutmeg	
2	Eggs	2
3	Tomatoes, peeled, seeded, and halved	3
1½ cups	Cooked flaked haddock	250 g/9 oz
	Grated cheese	

1. Preheat the oven to 375°F/190°C/Gas Mark 5.
2. Sift the flour and salt, cut in the butter and shortening, and mix with the beaten egg yolk and water, if required. Set aside to chill as long as possible (at least 1 hour), then line a deep 7-inch pie plate. Bake 'blind' (see Index: Pastry for 9-Inch, 1-Crust Pie).
3. Heat the butter; add the onion and sauté until soft. Stir in the flour, add milk, and stir until boiling. Remove from the heat; add the seasoning and beaten eggs.
4. Arrange the fish and tomatoes, cut side down, in the pastry shell. Season, pour over the sauce, and sprinkle with cheese.
5. Bake for 20–25 minutes, and serve with a plain tossed green salad.

Flounder with Oyster Sauce

00:15 00:55	Serves 4	New England

American	Ingredients	Metric/Imperial
1	Small onion, peeled and chopped	1
1	Carrot, peeled and chopped	1
1½ cups	Dry white wine	350 ml/12 fl oz
	Peppercorns	
1	Bay leaf	1
1½ lb	Flounder (plaice) fillets	675 g/1½ lb
1½ tbsp	Butter or margarine	20 g/¾ oz
1½ tbsp	Flour	1¼ tbsp
½ cup	Heavy [double] cream	125 ml/4 fl oz
	Paprika	
18	Fresh oysters	18
½ cup	White seeded grapes	50 g/2 oz

1. Preheat the oven to 350°F/180°C/Gas Mark 4.
2. Put the onion and carrot into a pan with the wine; add a little salt, about 6 peppercorns, and a bay leaf. Simmer for 15 minutes.
3. Put in the fish and poach gently for 7–10 minutes. Remove the fish carefully, drain, and arrange in a shallow casserole.
4. Strain the fish stock and, if there is less than 1 cup [250 ml/8 fl oz], make up the quantity with a little more wine.
5. Make a sauce with the butter, flour, and stock. Add cream and paprika to taste, and stir over low heat until the sauce is smooth and thick. Add the oysters, adjust the seasoning, and pour over the fish.
6. Arrange the grapes on top, cover, and cook for about 20 minutes.
7. Serve with baked potatoes and sliced cucumber, dressed with a little tarragon vinegar.

Fish Sticks

Fish Sticks

03:20 00:06	Serves 2	Mid Atlantic

American	Ingredients	Metric/Imperial
1 lb	Cod, haddock, or snapper fillets	450 g/1 lb
1	Egg	1
1 tsp	Water	1 tsp
½ tsp	Curry powder	½ tsp
¼ tsp	Celery salt	¼ tsp
¼ tsp	Onion salt	¼ tsp
¼ cup	Flour	25 g/1 oz
½ cup	Dried bread crumbs	25 g/1 oz
	Oil for frying	

1. Prepare the fish sticks the day before or at least 2 to 3 hours in advance. Cover and keep in a cool place—the coating will be firmer.
2. Cut the fish into rectangles (½×3 inches), removing any bones at the same time. Break the egg into a bowl; whisk in the water, curry powder, celery, and onion salts. Coat the fish with flour, the egg mixture, and then bread crumbs. Press the coating on firmly.
3. Heat a little oil in a frying pan. Add the fish sticks, and fry on each side for 2–3 minutes. Drain on paper towels [kitchen paper].

Cod with Tomatoes and Onions

| | 00:40 | | |
| | 00:35 | Serves 4–5 | Pacific Northwest  |

American	Ingredients	Metric/Imperial
2 tbsp	Butter	25 g/1 oz
4	Large potatoes, peeled and sliced thinly	4
1½ lb	Cod steaks or fillet	675 g/1½ lb
4–5	Onions, peeled and sliced thinly	4–5
1 large can (about 20 oz)	Tomatoes	1 large tin (about 575 g/20 oz)
1 tbsp	Corn oil	1 tbsp
½ cup	Fish stock	125 ml/4 fl oz
1	Green pepper, seeded and chopped	1
	Bread crumbs	
	Cole Slaw	
1	Small head of white cabbage, finely shredded	1
4–5 tbsp	Heavy [double] cream	3½–4 tbsp
3–4 tbsp	White vinegar	2–3½ tbsp
4 tbsp	Sugar	3½ tbsp

1. Preheat the oven to 350°F/180°C/Gas Mark 4.
2. Use half the butter to grease a deep casserole. Arrange half the potatoes, fish, onion, and tomatoes in alternate layers in the casserole. Sprinkle with oil, salt, and pepper. Then repeat the layers in the same order.
3. Pour in the stock, sprinkle with chopped green pepper and bread crumbs, and dot with the remaining butter.
4. Cook, uncovered, for 35 minutes.
5. For the cole slaw, mix the cream, vinegar, and sugar together well; toss the cabbage in the cream mixture.

Salmon Pie

| | 00:20 | | |
| | 00:40 | Serves 4 | Pacific Northwest 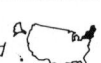 |

American	Ingredients	Metric/Imperial
2 tbsp	Butter	25 g/1 oz
2 tbsp	Flour	1½ tbsp
½ cup	Milk	125 ml/4 fl oz
4 tbsp	Light [single] cream	3½ tbsp
1	Egg	1
½ cup	Cottage cheese	100 g/4 oz
1 tsp	Dried chives	1 tsp
1 (7-oz) can	Salmon	1 (200 g/7 oz) tin
1 (8-inch)	Baked pastry shell	1 (8-inch)
2–3	Tomatoes, peeled and sliced	2–3

1. Preheat the oven to 375°F/190°C/Gas Mark 5.
2. Make a thick sauce with the butter, flour, and milk. Remove from the heat; stir in the cream, egg yolk, cheese, chives, and drained and flaked salmon. Season to taste.
3. Beat the egg white stiffly and fold into the mixture after it has cooled.
4. Turn into the baked pastry shell, and bake for 20 minutes. Arrange slices of tomato around the edge, and bake for 10 minutes.

Smoked Salmon Pie

| | 00:25 | | |
| | 00:35 | Serves 5–6 | Pacific Northwest |

American	Ingredients	Metric/Imperial
	Pâte Brisée (see Index)	
4	Whole eggs	4
2	Egg yolks	2
2 cups	Heavy [double] cream	450 ml/¾ pint
¼ lb	Smoked salmon	100 g/4 oz
	Freshly ground pepper	
2 tbsp	Butter	25 g/1 oz

1. Preheat the oven to 375°F/190°C/Gas Mark 5.
2. Line a 9-inch pie plate with the pastry, prick the bottom, and bake for 10 minutes. Let cool.
3. Beat the eggs, egg yolks, and cream together and season carefully.
4. Pour about two-thirds of the mixture into the cooled pastry shell. Cut the salmon into pieces and arrange on top, then pour the rest slowly on top.
5. Dot with butter, and bake for about 25 minutes.

Kedgeree

| | 00:10 | | |
| | 00:35 | Serves 4 | New England |

American	Ingredients	Metric/Imperial
1 cup	Rice	225 g/8 oz
1 lb	Smoked haddock	450 g/1 lb
6 tbsp	Butter	5 tbsp
3	Hard-boiled eggs	3
	Lemon juice	
	Milk	
2 tbsp	Chopped parsley	1½ tbsp

1. Cook the rice in boiling salted water until tender, about 9–10 minutes. Drain well.
2. Poach the haddock in boiling water (or milk and water) for 10–15 minutes. Drain and remove all skin and bone. Flake finely.
3. Melt the butter in the pan; add the rice, fish, and 2 of the hard-boiled eggs, chopped. Mix well, and cook over very low heat for about 10 minutes. Season carefully with salt, pepper and a little lemon juice. (More salt will be required if fresh fish is used.) Add a little milk if the mixture seems too dry.
4. Put onto a serving dish, garnish with the remaining hard-boiled egg, cut in slices, and sprinkle with chopped parsley.

Pike with Tomato and Anchovy

Pike with Tomato and Anchovy

 00:25
00:20
Serves 4
New England

American	Ingredients	Metric/Imperial
3 lb	Pike fillets	1.25 kg/3 lb
½ tsp	Salt	½ tsp
	Freshly ground white pepper	
1 cup	Sieved tomatoes	225 g/8 oz
¼ cup	Onion, finely chopped	25 g/1 oz
1 (2-oz) can	Anchovy fillets, chopped	1 (50 g/2 oz) tin
1 tsp	Chervil or thyme	1 tsp
¾ cup	Mild Cheddar cheese, grated	75 g/3 oz
2 tbsp	Grated Parmesan	1½ tbsp
1 cup	Fish stock	250 ml/8 fl oz
4 tbsp	Butter	50 g/2 oz
4 tbsp	Chopped parsley	3½ tbsp

1. Preheat the oven to 450°F/230°C/Gas Mark 8.
2. Grease an ovenproof dish and place the fish on it with the flesh side facing up and the belly parts slightly overlapping. Season well with salt and a few turns of the pepper mill.
3. Combine the tomatoes, onion, anchovies, and thyme or cher-·vil in a bowl. Divide the tomato mixture evenly over the fish. Blend the 2 cheeses and sprinkle over the tomato mixture.
4. Bring the stock to a boil and pour it carefully around the fish. Place the dish in the oven for 15–20 minutes. Then carefully pour off most of the liquid into a saucepan and beat in 3–4 table-spoons [40–50 g/1½–2 oz] butter and the chopped parsley.
5. Heat the sauce and pour around the fish on a serving dish. Serve with freshly boiled potatoes or boiled rice.

Salmon and Spaghetti Casserole

00:15
00:45
Serves 5–6
Pacific Northwest

American	Ingredients	Metric/Imperial
½ cup	Butter	100 g/4 oz
½ cup	Flour	50 g/2 oz
2 cups	Hot chicken stock	450 ml/¾ pint
	A pinch of nutmeg	
¼ cup	Dry sherry	60 ml/2 fl oz
1 can (about 15 oz)	Salmon	1 tin (about 425 g/15 oz)
¼ cup	Light [single] cream	60 ml/2 fl oz
2 cups	Sliced mushrooms	225 g/8 oz
½ lb	Spaghetti, cooked	225 g/8 oz
½ cup	Grated Parmesan cheese	50 g/2 oz
½ cup	Bread or cereal crumbs	25 g/1 oz

1. Preheat the oven to 350°F/180°C/Gas Mark 4.
2. Make a sauce with half the butter, the flour, and the chicken stock. Season with salt, pepper, and a good pinch of nutmeg.
3. Add the sherry and the liquid from the salmon, and simmer over a low heat for 5 minutes. Stir in the cream and adjust the seasoning. Sauté the mushrooms in the remaining butter and add to the sauce.
4. Mix half the sauce with the cooked spaghetti, and put into a shallow casserole. Flake the salmon, mix with the remaining sauce, and pour over the spaghetti.
5. Sprinkle with cheese and bread crumbs, mixed together, and cook for about 20 minutes, or until well browned.

Sea Fish Pie

00:40
01:00   Serves 4–5   United States

American	Ingredients	Metric/Imperial
	Pastry for an 8–9 inch, 2-crust pie (see Index)	
2 tbsp	Butter	25 g/1 oz
2 tbsp	Cornstarch [cornflour]	1½ tbsp
½ cup	Milk	125 ml/4 fl oz
½ cup	Light [single] cream	125 ml/4 fl oz
1	Egg	1
½ tsp	Anchovy paste	½ tsp
1 tsp	Lemon juice	1 tsp
1 tsp	Chopped capers	1 tsp
½	Small onion, very finely chopped	½
1 tsp	Chopped parsley	1 tsp
3 cups	Cooked flaked fish	500 g/18 oz
	Egg or milk to glaze	
	Cucumber, tomato, radishes	

1. Preheat the oven to 400°F/200°C/Gas Mark 7.
2. Line an 8-inch pie plate with half the pastry.
3. Make a sauce with the butter, cornstarch, milk, and cream. Remove from the heat; add the lightly beaten egg and all the other ingredients. Season to taste.
4. Turn into the pastry shell. Dampen the edges of the pastry, cover with the pastry lid, pressing the edges well together, and decorate the edge.
5. Mark a small circle in the center of the pastry (a 2–3 inch cookie [biscuit] cutter is best to do this). Cut the circle across in four and turn the pointed ends back to expose the filling.
6. Glaze the pie with beaten egg or milk, and bake for ¾–1 hour. Garnish with radish roses and thin overlapping slices of tomato and cucumber.

Crab-Stuffed Red Snapper

00:20
00:30   Serves 4   Midwest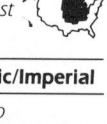

American	Ingredients	Metric/Imperial
5 tbsp	Minced onion	4 tbsp
3 tbsp	Butter	40 g/1½ oz
1 cup	Crabmeat, picked over	225 g/8 oz
½ cup	Fresh bread crumbs	25 g/1 oz
4 tbsp	Fresh chopped parsley	3½ tbsp
¼ cup	Heavy [double] cream	60 ml/2 fl oz
¼ tsp	Thyme	¼ tsp
1 (4-lb)	Red snapper, (or substitute sea bass), dressed for stuffing	1 (1.75 kg/4 lb)
	Salt and pepper	
¼ cup	Dry white wine	60 ml/2 fl oz
¼ cup	Butter, melted	50 g/2 oz

1. Preheat the oven to 400°F/200°C/Gas Mark 6.
2. Sauté the onion in butter until golden. Remove from the heat and mix in the crabmeat, bread crumbs, parsley, cream, and thyme. Sprinkle the cavity of the fish lightly with salt and pepper. Stuff the fish and skewer edges securely.
3. Place the fish in a greased baking pan. Mix the wine with the butter; pour the wine-butter mixture over the fish. Bake in the oven, uncovered, for 30 minutes, or just until the flesh is opaque. Baste frequently with the wine sauce.

Salmon Supper Ring

00:20
00:20   Serves 4   Pacific Northwest

American	Ingredients	Metric/Imperial
1 tbsp	Butter	15 g/½ oz
1 tbsp	Cornstarch [cornflour]	1 tbsp
½ cup	Milk	125 ml/4 fl oz
	Salt and pepper	
1 (7 oz) can	Salmon, drained and flaked	1 (200 g/7 oz) tin
1 tsp	Chopped capers	1 tsp
1 tsp	Lemon juice	1 tsp
1	Package biscuit mix	1
	Egg or milk to glaze	

1. Preheat the oven to 450°F/230°C/Gas Mark 8.
2. Make a sauce with the butter, cornstarch, milk, and seasoning. Add the salmon, capers, and lemon juice; mix all well.
3. Roll the biscuit dough thinly into an oblong shape, spread with the filling, moisten the edges of the dough, and roll up. Then move carefully onto a greased baking sheet and twist into a horseshoe shape.
4. Using kitchen scissors or a sharp knife, make some cuts about two-thirds of the way into the roll. Turn each section onto its side, so that the filling is exposed a little.
5. Glaze with egg or milk, bake for 15–20 minutes, and serve with salad.

Casserole of Sole

00:15
00:40   Serves 6   Pacific Southwest

American	Ingredients	Metric/Imperial
2 cups	Milk	450 ml/¾ pint
2½ lb	Fillets of sole	1.25 kg/2½ lb
2½ cups	Sliced mushrooms	275 g/10 oz
½ cup	Butter	100 g/4 oz
2 cups	White seedless or seeded grapes	225 g/8 oz
4 tbsp	Flour	3½ tbsp
	Lemon juice	
4 tbsp	Bread crumbs	3½ tbsp
2 tbsp	Grated cheese	1½ tbsp

1. Preheat the oven to 375°F/190°C/Gas Mark 5.

2. Heat the milk in a frying pan. When just below boiling point, put in the fish, and poach very gently for 5 minutes.

3. Sauté the mushrooms in half the butter for 3 minutes. Then put into a lightly buttered casserole with the grapes. Arrange the drained fish on top.

4. Make a sauce with the remaining butter, flour, and the milk in which the fish was cooked. Season with salt, pepper, and lemon juice; pour over the fish.

5. Sprinkle with bread crumbs and cheese, mixed together; dot with butter. Cook for 25–30 minutes, or until the top is golden brown.

6. Serve with parsley-buttered potatoes, buttered green peas, and a tomato salad.

Salmon Supper Ring

Red Snapper in Foil

 00:30 / 00:40   Serves 4–5   United States

American	Ingredients	Metric/Imperial
1	Red snapper (or substitute sea bass)	1
	Corn oil	
4 tbsp	Butter	50 g/2 oz
½ cup	Finely chopped celery	50 g/2 oz
¼ cup	Finely chopped green pepper	25 g/1 oz
2	Scallions [spring onions], chopped	2
1 cup	Bread crumbs	50 g/2 oz
2 tbsp	Finely chopped parsley	1½ tbsp
¼ cup	Coarsely chopped toasted almonds	25 g/1 oz
1	Large tomato, peeled and sliced	1
6	Thin slices onion	6
6	Thin slices orange	6
6	Thin slices lime	6
	Salt and pepper	
	Juice of ½ lime	

1. Heat the coals in an outdoor grill until hot, about 30 minutes, or preheat the broiler [grill].

2. Rub the fish lightly with oil, and sprinkle inside and out with salt and black pepper.

3. Heat the butter. Add the celery, green pepper, and onions, and sauté for a few minutes. Add the bread crumbs, parsley, almonds, and seasoning. Press the mixture together, and stuff the fish. Secure with string.

4. Brush a sheet of foil lightly with oil, place the fish on it, and arrange slightly overlapping slices of tomato, onion, orange, and lime down the length of the fish. Sprinkle with salt, black pepper, and lime juice. Fold the foil over to make a parcel, and secure tightly.

5. Cook on the rack of the barbecue or in the broiler [grill] for 30–40 minutes, and serve with Tartare Sauce (see Index).

Tuna Pie

00:25 / 00:50   Serves 6   Pacific Northwest

American	Ingredients	Metric/Imperial
	Pastry for an 8–9 inch, 2-crust pie (see Index)	
1 small can (about 7 oz)	Tuna fish	1 small tin (about 200 g/7 oz)
½ cup	Finely chopped onion	50 g/2 oz
1 small can (about 3 oz)	Sliced mushrooms	1 small tin (about 75 g/3 oz)
1 (10¾ oz) can	Cream of mushroom soup	1 (300 g/10¾ oz) tin
2 tbsp	Grated Parmesan cheese	1½ tbsp
2 tsp	Lemon juice	2 tsp
1 tsp	Finely chopped parsley	1 tsp
⅛ tsp	Celery seed	⅛ tsp
⅛ tsp	Thyme	⅛ tsp
6	Hard-boiled eggs, sliced	6

1. Preheat the oven to 450°F/230°C/Gas Mark 8.

2. Line an 8–9 inch pie plate with half the pastry.

3. Drain the oil from the tuna fish and put 1 tablespoon of it into a sauté pan. Add the onion; sauté until transparent, then add mushrooms and continue cooking until the onion and mushrooms begin to color. Add the mushroom soup; stir until smooth, then remove from the heat. Add cheese, lemon juice, and flavorings.

4. Arrange the flaked fish and eggs in the pastry shell. Pour the sauce over and cover with the remaining pastry. Crimp the edges and make one or two slits in the top to allow the steam to escape.

5. Bake for 10 minutes. Then reduce the heat to 350°F/180°C/Gas Mark 4, and bake for 30–35 minutes, or until the pastry is well browned.

6. Before serving, garnish with slices of dill pickle [gherkins].

Baked Stuffed Fish

| | 00:15 | Serves 5–6 | Midwest |
| | 00:35 | | |

American	Ingredients	Metric/Imperial
2 lb	Fish fillets	900 g/2 lb
	Stuffing	
2 tbsp	Bacon fat	1½ tbsp
2 tbsp	Finely chopped onion	1½ tbsp
2 tbsp	Finely diced celery	1½ tbsp
1½ cup	Dry bread crumbs	40 g/1½ oz
	A pinch of thyme	
	A pinch of marjoram	
	Sauce	
2 tbsp	Butter	25 g/1 oz
2 tbsp	Flour	1½ tbsp
1 cup	Milk	250 ml/8 fl oz
1 cup	Grated sharp Cheddar or American cheese	100 g/4 oz

1. Preheat the oven to 350°F/180°C/Gas Mark 4.
2. Grease a shallow baking dish, and arrange half the fillets in the bottom. Sprinkle with salt and pepper.
3. Heat the bacon fat in a pan, add the onion and celery, and cook until the onion is soft. Add bread crumbs, thyme and marjoram, a little salt and a dash of pepper, and mix well. If the mixture is a little stiff, add 1–2 tablespoons hot water.
4. Spoon the stuffing over the fish, and arrange the remaining fillets on top.
5. Make a roux with the butter, flour, and milk. Add seasoning and most of the cheese. Pour over the fish, sprinkle with the remaining cheese, and bake for about 30 minutes.

Baked Fish in Tomato Sauce

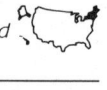

| | 00:15 | Serves 4–5 | New England |
| | 01:00 | | |

American	Ingredients	Metric/Imperial
1¼ lb	Fish fillets	575 g/1¼ lb
1 tbsp	Oil	1 tbsp
1	Onion, peeled and thinly sliced	1
½	Clove garlic, crushed	½
2	Medium potatoes, peeled and thinly sliced	2
½ cup	Sliced stuffed olives (optional)	50 g/2 oz
½ cup	Green peas	50 g/2 oz
	Sauce	
1 (8 oz) can	Tomato sauce	1 (225 g/8 oz) tin
¼ tsp	Chopped fennel or dill	¼ tsp
	A dash of cayenne pepper	
1 cup	Hot water	250 ml/8 fl oz

1. Preheat the oven to 350°F/180°C/Gas Mark 4.
2. Cut the fish into serving pieces, and season with salt and pepper.
3. Heat the oil in a small pan, and sauté the onion and garlic until the onion is golden brown.
4. Arrange layers of fish and the other ingredients in a shallow greased casserole, finishing with potatoes.
5. Combine the ingredients for the sauce, and pour over the fish. Cover and cook for 40 minutes. Then uncover and cook for 15–20 minutes longer.

Fish au Gratin

| | 00:15 | Serves 4–5 | United States |
| | 00:25 | | |

American	Ingredients	Metric/Imperial
1½ lb	Fillets of white fish	675 g/1½ lb
4–5	Slices processed Cheddar cheese	4–5
¼ tsp	Dried fennel or dill	¼ tsp
½ tsp	Oregano	½ tsp
2 tbsp	Chopped parsley	1½ tbsp
1 tbsp	Oil	1 tbsp
1	Onion, peeled and chopped	1
1 tbsp	Flour	1 tbsp
½ cup	Milk	125 ml/4 fl oz
	Tarragon (to garnish)	

1. Preheat the oven to 400°F/200°C/Gas Mark 6.
2. Prepare the fish, and place half in a greased baking dish. Cover with half the cheese. Arrange the rest of the fish on top, and add the remaining slices of cheese. Sprinkle with herbs.
3. Heat the oil in a small pan, and sauté the onion until transparent. Stir in the flour, and cook for 1 minute. Then gradually add the milk, and stir until boiling. Add seasoning. Cook for 2 minutes, then pour over the fish, and bake for 20–25 minutes.
4. Garnish with a little tarragon, if available.

Fish and Batter

| | 00:15 | Serves 4 | United States |
| | 00:35 | | |

American	Ingredients	Metric/Imperial
¼ cup	Butter	50 g/2 oz
4	Fillets cod, haddock or flounder	4
	Juice of ½ lemon	
	Batter	
1 cup	Flour	100 g/4 oz
¼ tsp	Salt	¼ tsp
1	Egg	1
1 cup	Milk and water (½ and ½)	250 ml/8 fl oz
½ cup	Grated dry cheese	50 g/2 oz

1. Preheat the oven to 425°F/220°C/Gas Mark 7.
2. Grease a deep ovenproof dish or casserole with some of the butter. Wash and dry the fish, and arrange in the dish, skin side downwards. Melt the remaining butter and pour it over the fish. Add lemon juice and seasoning. Cover and bake for 15 minutes.
3. While the fish is cooking, make the batter. Sift the flour and salt into a bowl, make a well in the center, and drop in the egg. Add half the liquid, and stir until smooth. Add the rest of the liquid and, when quite smooth. beat very thoroughly. Add the cheese and beat for another minute.
4. When fish has baked for 15 minutes, pour the batter over it, and bake for 20 minutes longer, or until the batter is well risen and brown.

Sole Fillets in Orange Sauce

| | 00:15 | | |
| | 00:08 | Serves 4 | Pacific Southwest |

American	Ingredients	Metric/Imperial
¼ cup	Soy sauce	60 ml/2 fl oz
½ tsp	Ground ginger	½ tsp
1 tsp	Salt	1 tsp
	Juice of 2 oranges	
1 lb	Sole fillets	450 g/1 lb
1	Large onion, chopped	1
1 tbsp	Butter	15 g/½ oz
4	Leaves Chinese cabbage, finely shredded	4
¼ cup	Water	60 ml/2 fl oz
½ tbsp	Arrowroot or cornstarch [cornflour]	½ tbsp
	Pepper	

1. Mix the soy sauce, ginger, salt, and orange juice in a bowl. Cut each fillet into 3 strips lengthwise and place in the mixture.
2. Fry the onion in the butter in a wide pan, then add the cabbage. Lift out the fish. Combine the water and arrowroot or flour, and add it to the soy-sauce mixture; pour this over the fish. Cover and allow to come to a boil while shaking the pan.
3. Season with pepper and serve with boiled rice.

Broiled [Grilled] Lake Trout

| | 00:20 | | |
| | 00:15 | Serves 2 | Pacific Northwest |

American	Ingredients	Metric/Imperial
1	Whole lake trout (brown or rainbow)	1
¼ cup	Oil	60 ml/2 fl oz
¼ tsp	Pepper	¼ tsp
	Butter	
	Lemon slices	
	Parsley	

Sole Fillets in Orange Sauce

1. Split the trout into 2 fillets; remove the backbone. Wash thoroughly; remove all traces of blood or membrane. Place in a salt solution made in the proportion of 2 tablespoons [1½ tbsp] salt to 1 cup [250 ml/8 fl oz] water; let stand 8 to 10 minutes.
2. Preheat the broiler [grill] about 10 minutes. Oil the heated broiler pan.
3. Brush the fish with oil mixed with pepper. Amount of oil required will be about ¼ cup [60 ml/2 fl oz] with ¼ teaspoon pepper. Place the trout on the broiler pan, skin side up, about 2 inches below the heat. After 5 minutes, the skin should be turning brown; baste. Cook until the skin is well browned, then turn the fish flesh side up. Baste again; cook until the flesh side is well browned. Remove to a hot platter; butter the top of the fish.
4. Garnish with lemon slices and parsley. Allow up to 225 g/8 oz of fish per person.

Sweet-Sour Tuna Snack

| | 00:10 | | |
| | 00:10 | Serves 4 | Pacific Southwest |

American	Ingredients	Metric/Imperial
4	Slices bread	4
	Butter	
1 can (about 7 oz)	Tuna fish	1 tin (about 200 g/7 oz)
2–3 tbsp	Mayonnaise	1½–2 tbsp
4	Slices drained canned pineapple	4
4	Slices Cheddar or Swiss cheese	4

1. Preheat the broiler [grill].
2. Toast the bread on one side only and lightly butter the untoasted side.
3. Drain and flake the tuna, and add enough mayonnaise to make it spreadable. Spread on the buttered side of the toast, cover with a slice of pineapple, and top with a slice of cheese.
4. Put under a hot broiler until the cheese has melted.

Fish Mousse

Fish Mousse

06:30
00:10

Serves 6

South

American	Ingredients	Metric/Imperial
2½–3 lb	Fillets of fish (haddock, flounder, cod etc.)	1-1.25 kg/ 2½–3 lb
2	Slices of lemon	2
2	Slices of onion	2
1 tsp	Salt	1 tsp
¼ tsp	Pepper	¼ tsp
2 cups	Mayonnaise	450 ml/¾ pint
4 tbsp	Lemon juice	3½ tbsp
2 tbsp	Wine or tarragon vinegar	1½ tbsp
1 tbsp	Grated onion	1 tbsp
1 tsp	Curry powder	1 tsp
1 tsp	Worcestershire sauce	1 tsp
⅛ tsp	Hot pepper sauce	⅛ tsp
2 tbsp	Finely chopped parsley	1½ tbsp
2 envelopes	Unflavored gelatin [gelatine]	2 sachets

1. Put the fish into a pan with 1½ cups [350 ml/12 fl oz] water, lemon and onion slices, salt and pepper. Poach for 5–10 minutes, or until barely cooked. Drain and reserve the stock. Remove any skin from the fish and flake finely.
2. Mix ½ cup [125 ml/4 fl oz] of the fish stock with the mayonnaise; add lemon juice, vinegar, grated onion, curry powder, Worcestershire sauce, hot pepper sauce, and parsley. Add the fish. Adjust the seasoning to taste and beat until thoroughly mixed.
3. Soften the gelatin in a little cold water. Then dissolve over hot water and stir into the fish mixture. Pour into a large mold or into individual ones, and refrigerate until firm.
4. When required, turn out on a bed of salad greens, and garnish as desired.

Casserole of Fish

00:20
01:00

Serves 4–5

United States

American	Ingredients	Metric/Imperial
1 lb	Fish (flounder, cod, etc.)	450 g/1 lb
1 cup	Fine noodles	225 g/8 oz
2 tbsp	Butter	25 g/1 oz
2 tbsp	Flour	1½ tbsp
1 cup	Milk	250 ml/8 fl oz
2 cups	Grated American or Cheddar cheese	225 g/8 oz
1 tsp	Worcestershire sauce	1 tsp
2 tbsp	Lemon juice	1½ tbsp
¼ cup	Buttered bread crumbs	15 g/½ oz

1. Preheat the oven to 300°F/150°C/Gas Mark 2.
2. Poach the fish for 10–15 minutes. Drain, remove the skin and bone, and break up into flakes.
3. Cook the noodles in boiling salted water for about 10 minutes; drain and save 1 cup [250 ml/8 fl oz] of the water.
4. Make a sauce with the butter, flour, milk, and water from the noodles. Add seasoning, half the cheese, Worcestershire sauce, and lemon juice. Stir until the cheese has melted and the sauce is smooth.
5. Sprinkle half the remaining cheese into a greased casserole. Arrange the fish, noodles, and sauce in layers. Top with the remaining cheese and buttered crumbs, and cook in the oven for about 30 minutes.

Fish and Vegetable Casserole

00:25
00:40

Serves 6

United States

American	Ingredients	Metric/Imperial
¼ cup	Vegetable oil	60 ml/2 fl oz
6	Slices fish	6
1 cup	Peeled diced tomatoes	225 g/8 oz
½ lb	Green beans, sliced	225 g/8 oz
½ lb	Green peas, shelled	225 g/8 oz
1 cup	Shredded cabbage	100 g/4 oz
1 lb	Lima beans, shelled	450 g/1 lb
3	Medium potatoes, peeled and sliced	3
2	Onions, peeled and sliced	2
1	Clove garlic, crushed	1

1. Preheat the oven to 425°F/220°C/Gas Mark 7.
2. Heat half the oil in a large casserole. Sprinkle the fish with a little salt and pepper; arrange in the casserole.
3. In a large bowl, combine all the vegetables and garlic, and add a little salt and pepper. Arrange the vegetable mixture over the fish, and sprinkle with the remaining oil.
4. Reduce the heat of the oven to 350°F/180°C/Gas Mark 4. Cover the casserole tightly, and cook for 25 minutes. Uncover and cook for 15–20 minutes longer.

Mussel Risotto

Mussel Risotto

00:20
00:30

Serves 4–6

New England

American	Ingredients	Metric/Imperial
1 quart	Mussels	1 1/1¾ pints
	Salt	
	Pepper	
1	Onion, chopped	1
2	Stalks celery, sliced	2
1 tbsp	Margarine	1 tbsp
3 tbsp	Dry white wine	2 tbsp
½ cup	Water	120 ml/4 fl oz
½ lb	Shrimp	225 g/½ lb
1 cup	Long-grained rice	225 g/8 oz
2 tbsp	Parsley, chopped	1½ tbsp

1. Scrub mussels in cold water and remove any beard. Discard any that are open. Place mussels in a large saucepan with salt, pepper, onion, celery, margarine, white wine, and water. Cover and cook quickly until mussels open.
2. Strain off liquid and reserve. Remove mussels from shells. Save a few for garnish. Discard any mussels that have not opened.
3. Peel and devein shrimp. Poach gently in mussel liquid until cooked.
4. Put rice in a saucepan with 1½ cups [350 ml/12 fl oz] water. Bring to a boil, cover pan tightly, and cook gently for 20 minutes or until rice is tender and liquid is absorbed.
5. Combine mussels with shrimp and pour over rice. Sprinkle with chopped parsley.

Haddock with Spinach

00:25
00:25

Serves 4–5

New England

American	Ingredients	Metric/Imperial
1 lb	Haddock fillets	450 g/1 lb
1½ cups	Milk	350 ml/12 fl oz
1	Slice onion	1
	A small piece of bay leaf	
3–4	Peppercorns	3–4
4 tbsp	Butter	50 g/2 oz
3 tbsp	Flour	2 tbsp
1 tbsp	Prepared mustard	1 tbsp
2	Hard-boiled eggs	2
1½ lb	Spinach	675 g/1½ lb
¼ tsp	Grated nutmeg	¼ tsp
	Grated cheese	

1. Preheat the oven to 425°F/220°C/Gas Mark 7.
2. Poach the fish in ½ cup [125 ml/4 fl oz] milk and ½ cup [125 ml/4 fl oz] water with the onion, bay leaf, and peppercorns. Strain off, and reserve the stock. Remove the onion, bay leaf, and peppercorns; flake the fish finely.
3. Make a sauce with the butter, flour, 1 cup [250 ml/8 fl oz] of the fish stock and 1 cup [250 ml/8 fl oz] milk. Season with salt, pepper, and mustard. Add the eggs, cut into slices, and the fish.
4. Cook the spinach in the water that clings to the leaves after washing, until just wilted. Drain well, chop, and add a little salt, pepper, and nutmeg.
5. Put the spinach into a greased casserole, cover with the fish and sauce mixture, sprinkle with grated cheese, and bake for 15 minutes.

Fillet of Turbot with Wine-Onion and Tomato-Butter

Fillet of Turbot with Wine-Onion and Tomato-Butter

00:25		
01:00	Serves 4	South

American	Ingredients	Metric/Imperial
	Wine-Onion Sauce	
1	Large onion	1
1 cup	Red wine	250 ml/8 fl oz
¼ cup	Red wine vinegar	60 ml/2 fl oz
2 tbsp	Butter	25 g/1 oz
	Salt	
	Pepper	
1 tbsp	Honey	1 tbsp
	Tomato Butter	
7–8	Medium-large tomatoes	7–8
⅓ cup	Heavy [double] cream	75 ml/3 fl oz
4 tbsp	Butter	50 g/2 oz
	Salt	
	Pepper	
	Fish	
4	Turbot fillets	4
1 tbsp	Oil	1 tbsp
	Salt	
	Pepper	
	Cayenne pepper	
	Snipped parsley	

1. Shred or finely chop the onion. Place in a pot with the wine and vinegar, cover, and simmer for 10 minutes. Then simmer, uncovered, so that all the liquid evaporates. Add the butter and seasonings and stir until the butter has melted. Add the honey and mix well. This may be done in advance and then reheated.
2. Boil and peel the tomatoes; remove the seeds from 3 of the tomatoes. Cut the 3 seeded tomatoes into small pieces, cover, and refrigerate. Strain the other tomatoes into a tomato juice and bring it to a boil together with the cream. Simmer, uncovered, until ⅔ of the original amount of liquid remains. Add the butter and season carefully.
3. Dredge the fish fillets in the oil; add salt, pepper, and a dash of cayenne pepper. Heat up the tomato butter and the wine-onion sauce. Broil [grill] the fish 2 to 3 minutes on each side.
4. Carefully warm up the refrigerated tomatoes in the tomato sauce. Divide the wine-onion up onto 4 warm plates. Place a fish fillet on each bed of onions, and pour the decorative tomato sauce around the onion. Sprinkle with parsley and serve immediately.

Spicy Shellfish Stew

00:15		
00:25	Serves 6	South

American	Ingredients	Metric/Imperial
1 tbsp	Curry	1 tbsp
2 tbsp	Oil	1½ tbsp
2 (1-lb) pkgs	Frozen crayfish or shrimp [prawns]	2 (450 g/1 lb) pkts
2	Green peppers, finely shredded	2
2	Cloves garlic, crushed	2
2 tbsp	Chili sauce	1½ tbsp
½ tsp	Salt	½ tsp
1 (8 oz) can	Crushed tomatoes	1 (225 g/8 oz) tin
⅛ tsp	Cayenne pepper	⅛ tsp
¾ cup	Crème fraîche or sour cream	175 ml/6 fl oz

1. Sauté the curry in hot oil while stirring constantly. Sauté the crayfish or shrimp on all sides in the curry fat, but only for a short time so that the meat does not become tough; it should be just cooked through. Remove the fish from the pan and place on a plate.
2. Sauté the shredded peppers in the same oil. Add the garlic, chili sauce, salt, and crushed tomatoes. Stir and season with cayenne pepper, a few grains at a time, constantly testing the stew. Cover and allow the mixture to simmer until the green peppers feel soft. Blend in the crayfish and the crème fraîche or sour cream. Bring the mixture to a slow boil and check the seasoning.
3. Serve with rice or freshly boiled noodles, salad, and warm, crisp bread.

Seafood Pie

Seafood Pie

00:40
00:50
Serves 6–8
Mid Atlantic

American	Ingredients	Metric/Imperial
	Pastry for a 9-inch, 1-crust pie (see Index)	
3 tbsp	Butter or margarine	40 g/1½ oz
3 tbsp	Very finely chopped green onions or chives	2 tbsp
1½ cups	Diced cooked seafood— shrimp [prawns], lobster, scallops etc. as available	350 g/12 oz
1 tbsp	Tomato paste	1 tbsp
	Cayenne pepper	
3 tbsp	Sherry	2 tbsp
4	Eggs	4
1½ cups	Heavy [double] cream	350 ml/12 fl oz
¼ cup	Grated Gruyère cheese	25 g/1 oz

1. Preheat the oven to 375°F/190°C/Gas Mark 5.
2. Line a 9-inch pie plate with the pastry, prick the bottom, and bake for 15 minutes. Remove from the heat and let cool.
3. Melt the butter in a frying pan, add the onion, and sauté for about 2 minutes. Add the seafood, and stir over low heat for 2 minutes. Add the tomato paste, seasoning, and sherry. Stir until boiling.
4. Beat the eggs; add the cream and stir in the cooled seafood mixture. Season to taste and pour into the pastry shell. Sprinkle with cheese, and bake for 25–30 minutes.
5. Serve cut into wedges.

Seafood Jambalaya

00:25
01:00
Serves 6
Southwest

American	Ingredients	Metric/Imperial
3 tbsp	Margarine	40 g/1½ oz
¾ cup	Chopped green pepper	75 g/3 oz
¼ cup	Chopped celery	25 g/1 oz
5 tbsp	Chopped onion	4 tbsp
½ cup	Fresh parsley, chopped	25 g/1 oz
1 (16-oz can)	Tomatoes, chopped, with juice	1 (450 g/1 lb) tin
2 cups	Chicken stock	450 ml/¾ pint
½ tsp	Salt	½ tsp
⅛ tsp	Pepper	⅛ tsp
½ tsp	Chili powder	½ tsp
2	Bay leaves	2
2 cups	Cooked rice	450 g/1 lb
1 pint	Oysters, drained	450 ml/¾ pint
½ lb	White fish, cut in chunks	225 g/8 oz
1 lb	Regular [undressed] crabmeat, cartilage removed	450 g/1 lb

1. Sauté the green pepper, celery, and onion in margarine 5 minutes in a large saucepan. Add the parsley, tomatoes, stock and seasonings; simmer over medium heat 30–40 minutes.
2. Add the rice, oysters, and fish and simmer 10 minutes. Add the crabmeat and simmer 5 more minutes.

Shellfish Rice Feast

Shellfish Rice Feast

00:30		
00:35	Serves 5–6	South

American	Ingredients	Metric/Imperial
1–1¼ cups	Long-grain rice	225–275 g/ 8–10 oz
1	Minced onion (optional)	1
1 tbsp	Butter	15 g/½ oz
2½ cups	Fish stock	600 ml/1 pint
5 tbsp	Snipped dill	4 tbsp
1 tsp	Crushed tarragon (optional)	1 tsp
Mushrooms		
¼–½ lb	Fresh mushrooms	100–225 g/ 4–8 oz
1–1½ tbsp	Butter	15–20 g/½–¾ oz
½ tbsp	Squeezed lemon juice	½ tbsp
	Salt	
1 (4-oz)	Jar black caviar	1 (100 g/4 oz)
½ cup	Crème fraîche or sour cream	125 ml/4 fl oz
Curry Shrimp		
1¼ lb	Shrimp [prawns]	575 g/20 oz
1 tbsp	Butter	15 g/½ oz
1–1½ tsp	Curry	1–1½ tsp
Garlic Clams		
1 (8-oz) can	Clams in water	1 (225 g/8 oz) tin
1 tbsp	Butter	15 g/½ oz
1	Clove garlic, crushed	1

1. Sauté the rice and the onion, if desired, lightly in butter. Cover with the stock. Boil the rice for 20 to 25 minutes, according to the directions on the rice package. Mix the dill and perhaps the tarragon with the rice. Transfer to a heated bowl.
2. While the rice is cooking, rub the mushrooms clean and sauté in butter over rather low heat for 5 to 8 minutes. Season with the salt and lemon. If you wish, you can place the mushrooms in a warm bowl and cover them with aluminum foil.
3. Place the caviar and the crème fraîche in separate bowls, or in a bowl together. Shell the shrimp. Drain the clams. Melt butter for the shrimp and the clams in separate pots right before serving. Add the curry for the shrimp and crush the garlic for the clams. Add the shrimp and clams to their individual pots. Sauté lightly and place them in warm bowls.
4. Place all the dishes on the table and let guests help themselves to whichever side dishes they want.

Seafood Casserole

00:30		
00:35	Serves 6–7	South

American	Ingredients	Metric/Imperial
6 tbsp	Olive oil	5 tbsp
2	Cloves garlic, crushed	2
2–2½ lb	Firm fish, rock bass, flounder, snapper etc.	900 g–1.25 kg/ 2–2½ lb
12	Mussels, well scrubbed	12
½ lb	Shelled shrimp [prawns]	225 g/8 oz
	Salt and pepper	
½ cup	Finely chopped parsley	50 g/2 oz

1. Preheat the oven to 350°F/180°C/Gas Mark 4.
2. Heat the oil and garlic in a casserole. Put the large fish in first, then the mussels and shrimp. Add salt and pepper, and sprinkle with the parsley.
3. Cover tightly with foil. Then put the lid on the casserole—it should be well fitting—and cook about 30 minutes, or until the fish is tender and the mussels have opened. Baste from time to time with the juices.
4. Serve in hot deep dishes with rice, tossed green salad, and plenty of French bread.

Seafood Casserole

Fish Puff

	00:25		
	00:40	Serves 6	Midwest

American	Ingredients	Metric/Imperial
3 tbsp	Butter	40 g/1½ oz
1–2	Stalks celery, chopped	1–2
1 tbsp	Finely chopped green pepper	1 tbsp
1 tbsp	Finely chopped onion	1 tbsp
2 cups	Flaked cooked fish	225 g/8 oz
2 cups	Mashed potato	450 g/1 lb
1 tbsp	Lemon juice	1 tbsp
	A few drops of Tabasco	
3	Eggs	3
2 tbsp	Chopped parsley	1½ tbsp

1. Preheat oven to 350°F/180°C/Gas Mark 4.
2. Heat the butter in a pan; add celery, green pepper, and onion. Sauté until the onion is soft.
3. Combine the fish, potato, lemon juice, Tabasco, and parsley in a bowl with salt and pepper. Add the onion and celery mixture.
4. Separate the eggs; add the beaten yolks to the fish mixture, and beat well until light. Whip the egg whites until stiff, and fold into the mixture.
5. Turn into a greased baking dish and bake for 30–40 minutes, or until set and lightly browned.

Seafood Newburg

	00:25		
	00:15	Serves 6–8	New England

American	Ingredients	Metric/Imperial
4 tbsp	Butter or margarine	50 g/2 oz
4 cups	Fresh or frozen uncooked seafood (lobster, shrimp [prawns], crabmeat, or fish fillets, all in 1-inch pieces)	900 g/2 lb
3 tbsp	Lemon juice	2 tbsp
1 tbsp	Flour	1 tbsp
1 tsp	Salt	1 tsp
½ tsp	Paprika	½ tsp
⅛ tsp	Cayenne pepper	⅛ tsp
2 cups	Light [single] cream	450 ml/¾ pint
3	Egg yolks	3
2 tbsp	Sherry	1½ tbsp
6 cups	Hot cooked rice	1.25 kg/3 lb
	Parsley for garnish	

1. Melt the butter in a large frying pan. Sauté the seafood about 5 minutes, stirring constantly. Sprinkle with lemon juice. Mix the flour, salt, paprika, and pepper; add to the seafood. Remove from the heat. Gradually stir in 1½ cups [350 ml/12 fl oz] of cream. Return to the heat until the sauce comes to a simmer.
2. Combine the egg yolks with the remaining ½ cup [125 ml/4 fl oz] of cream; blend ¼ cup [60 ml/2 fl oz] of hot liquid mixture with this. Return this to the pan; stir until slightly thickened. Add the sherry last.
3. Serve over rice, garnished with parsley.

French Style Clams

French Style Clams

00:15
00:10
Serves 4
South

American	Ingredients	Metric/Imperial
2 (8-oz) cans	Clam meats in water	2 (225 g/8 oz) tins
7 tbsp	Melted butter	75 g/3 oz
1 (3-ounce) can	Herrings or anchovies	1 (75 g/3 oz) tin
5 tbsp	Finely chopped parsley	4 tbsp
⅔ cup	Sour cream	150 ml/¼ pint
3–4	Small cloves garlic, crushed	3–4
½ tsp	Salt	½ tsp
¼ tsp	Black pepper	¼ tsp
5 tbsp	Fresh bread crumbs	4 tbsp
5 tbsp	Grated cheese	4 tbsp

1. Preheat the oven to 475°F/240°C/Gas Mark 9.
2. Drain the clams. Spread them out in a deep ovenproof dish. Mix the melted butter with drained, mashed herrings, parsley, sour cream, garlic, salt, and pepper. Divide the mixture up evenly over the clams.
3. Mix the grated bread and cheese together and sprinkle over the dish. Bake for about 10 minutes, or until the top has become nicely brown. Serve with crisp warm bread and butter.

Clam Pie

00:40
00:40
Serves 4–5
New England

American	Ingredients	Metric/Imperial
	Pastry	
3 cups	All-purpose [plain] flour	350 g/12 oz
¾ tsp	Salt	¾ tsp
¾ cup	Butter	100 g/4 oz
¾ cup	Water	175 ml/6 fl oz
	Filling	
2 (8-oz) cans	Minced clams	2 (225 g/8-oz) tins
2	Large potatoes	2
1	Small onion	1
2 tbsp	Butter	25 g/1 oz
1 tsp	Flour	1 tsp
2 tbsp	Heavy [double] cream	1½ tbsp
2 tbsp	Chopped parsley	1½ tbsp

1. Preheat the oven to 425°F/220°C/Gas Mark 7.
2. Make the pastry according to the instructions for Pâté Brisée (see Index) and refrigerate as long as possible, at least 1 hour.
3. Drain the clams and retain 2 tablespoons [1½ tbsp] of the liquid.
4. Peel the potatoes and onion and cook until just tender in boiling salted water; drain and cut into fine dice.
5. Melt the butter; stir in the flour. Add the cream, parsley, salt, clams, and 2 tablespoons [1½ tbsp] of their liquid. Mix well; add the potatoes and onion.
6. Line an 8-inch pie plate with half the pastry; put in the clam mixture and cover with the remaining pastry. Press the edges well together and crimp. Cut one or two slits in the top of the pastry and bake for about 25 minutes, or until the pastry is well browned.

Stuffed Clams

00:45
00:35
Serves 4–6
New England

American	Ingredients	Metric/Imperial
24	Clams, littleneck or rock	24
¾ cup	Dry white wine	175 ml/6 fl oz
¼ cup	Water	60 ml/2 fl oz
½ tsp	Salt	½ tsp
3 tbsp	Olive oil	2 tbsp
½ cup	Onion, chopped	50 g/2 oz
½ cup	Raw long-grain rice	100 g/4 oz
¼ tsp	Pepper	¼ tsp
½ tsp	Allspice	½ tsp
¼ tsp	Cinnamon	¼ tsp
3 tbsp	Currants	2 tbsp
3 tbsp	Pine nuts	2 tbsp
2 tbsp	Parsley, chopped	1½ tbsp

1. Scrub the clams; soak them in several changes of cold water to remove sand. Place in a frying pan with wine, water, and salt. Cover and steam 10 minutes, until shells open. Discard any clams that do not open. Cool; remove the clams from their shells. Save the shells; strain the pan juices.
2. In a medium-sized saucepan, heat the oil and sauté the onion until golden. Add the rice and 1 cup [250 ml/8 fl oz] pan juices. Bring to a boil. Cover; reduce heat to low. Cook 15 minutes. Add pepper, spices, currants, pine nuts, and parsley. Cook 5 minutes. Cool. Dice the clams; add to the pilaf.
3. Stuff the shells with the rice mixture; chill.

Clam Pie

Pilgrims' Clam Pie

00:45
00:50   Serves 6   New England

American	Ingredients	Metric/Imperial
36	Shell clams (or 3 225 g/8 oz cans minced clams)	36
1½ cups	Water	350 ml/12 fl oz
¼ cup	Butter	50 g/2 oz
½ cup	Fresh mushrooms, sliced	50 g/2 oz
2 tbsp	Onion, minced	1½ tbsp
¼ cup	All-purpose [plain] flour	25 g/1 oz
¼ tsp	Dry mustard	¼ tsp
⅛ tsp	Liquid hot pepper sauce	⅛ tsp
¼ tsp	Salt	¼ tsp
⅛ tsp	White pepper	⅛ tsp
1 cup	Reserved clam liquid	250 ml/8 fl oz
1 cup	Half-and-half cream [top of the milk]	250 ml/8 fl oz
1 tbsp	Lemon juice	1 tbsp
2 tbsp	Parsley, chopped	1½ tbsp
2 tbsp	Pimento, chopped	1½ tbsp
	Pastry for a 1-crust 9-inch pie (see Index)	
1	Egg, beaten	1

1. Preheat the oven to 375°F/190°C/Gas Mark 5.
2. Wash the clam shells thoroughly. Place the clams in a large pot with water. Bring to a boil; simmer 8–10 minutes, or until the clams open. Remove the clams from their shells; cut into quarters. Reserve 1 cup [250 ml/8 fl oz] of clam liquid. (If using canned clams, drain and reserve 1 cup liquid).
3. In a frying pan, melt the butter. Add the mushrooms and onion; cook until tender. Stir in the flour, mustard, liquid hot pepper sauce, salt, and pepper. Gradually add the clam liquid and half-and-half. Cook, stirring constantly, until thick. Stir in lemon juice, parsley, pimento, and clams.
4. Pour the mixture into a 9-inch round, deep-dish pie plate (about 2 inches deep). Roll out the pastry dough; place on top of the mixture in the pie plate. Secure the dough to the rim of the pie plate by crimping. Vent the pastry. Brush with a beaten egg.
5. Bake 25–30 minutes, or until the pastry is browned.

Soft-Shelled Crabs

00:10
00:10   Serves 4–6   Mid Atlantic

American	Ingredients	Metric/Imperial
4 tbsp	Butter	50 g/2 oz
2 tbsp	Lemon juice	1½ tbsp
6–8	Soft-shelled crabs, cleaned	6–8
1 tbsp	Cornstarch [cornflour] or flour	1 tbsp
¼ cup	Water	60 ml/2 fl oz

1. Heat the butter and lemon juice in a medium-sized frying pan. Cook the crabs over medium heat until browned, 5 minutes per side. Remove the crabs to a heated platter.
2. Mix the cornstarch and water; add to the pan juices, stirring until slightly thickened. Pour the sauce over the crabs. Serve at once.

Crab Cakes

00:15
00:10   Serves 4–6   Mid Atlantic

American	Ingredients	Metric/Imperial
1 lb	Crabmeat	450 g/1 lb
1	Egg yolk	1
1½ tsp	Salt	1½ tsp
	Healthy dash of black pepper	
1 tsp	Dry mustard	1 tsp
2 tsp	Worcestershire sauce	2 tsp
1 tbsp	Mayonnaise	1 tbsp
1 tbsp	Parsley, chopped	1 tbsp
½ tsp	Paprika	½ tsp
1 tbsp	Melted butter	15 g/½ oz
	Bread crumbs for coating cakes	
	Liquid shortening for frying	

1. Lightly toss the crabmeat and all the ingredients (except the bread crumbs) in the order listed. When well blended, shape into cakes. Roll each cake in bread crumbs, until coated on all sides.
2. Heat the shortening in a frying pan. Fry the crab cakes quickly in hot fat until golden brown.

Crabmeat Kebabs

00:15
00:15   Serves 4   Mid Atlantic

American	Ingredients	Metric/Imperial
2 cups	Canned [tinned] (or fresh) crabmeat	500 g/1 lb
1 cup	Bread crumbs	56 g/2 oz
2 tbsp	Dry sherry	2 tbsp
1 tsp	Dry mustard	1 tsp
1 tsp	Chopped tarragon	1 tsp
	Slices of bacon	

1. Combine the crabmeat, bread crumbs, sherry, mustard, and tarragon. Roll into small balls.
2. Wrap ½ slice bacon around each, and impale on skewers. Cook about 15 minutes.

Crabmeat Kebabs

Imperial Crab

	00:25			
	00:20	Serves 8	Mid Atlantic	

American	Ingredients	Metric/Imperial
1	Green sweet pepper, minced	1
1	Medium onion, minced	1
2 tsp	Dry mustard	2 tsp
2 tsp	Prepared horseradish	2 tsp
2 tsp	Salt	2 tsp
½ tsp	Freshly ground white pepper	½ tsp
2	Eggs, beaten	2
1 cup	Mayonnaise	250 ml/8 fl oz
3 lb	Lump crabmeat	1.25 kg/3 lb
	Paprika	

1. Preheat the oven to 350°F/180°C/Gas Mark 4.
2. Combine the green pepper, onion, mustard, horseradish, salt, white pepper, and eggs; mix well. Blend in mayonnaise thoroughly; fold in the crabmeat. Spoon crabmeat mixture into 8 large cleaned crab shells or ramekins. Coat with additional mayonnaise, sprinkle generously with paprika.
3. Arrange the crab shells in a shallow, oblong baking pan. Bake in the oven 15–20 minutes, or until heated through.

Crab Norfolk

	00:15			
	00:07	Serves 8	Mid Atlantic	

American	Ingredients	Metric/Imperial
2 tbsp	Clarified butter	25 g/1 oz
3 oz	Country or prosciutto ham, cut into julienne strips	75 g/3 oz
4	Scallions [spring onions], without tops, finely chopped	4
¾ cup	Madeira	175 ml/6 fl oz
3 lb	Crabmeat picked clean of shells	1.25 kg/3 lb
	Chopped parsley	
¼ lb	Butter	50 g/2 oz
8	Parsley sprigs	8

1. Preheat the oven to 400°F/200°C/Gas Mark 6.
2. Heat a large frying pan; season it with clear butter. Drop in the ham and scallions. Roll once. Add the Madeira. The pan temperature is right if the Madeira flames. If the alcohol is not burned off in flame, allow the Madeira to reduce for a minute. Add the crabmeat.
3. Bring the ham and scallions to the top of the pan. Sprinkle with chopped parsley; dot with cold butter. Place the pan in the oven for 2 minutes until the butter melts and the mixture is hot.
4. Spoon carefully into 8 ramekins. Garnish with parsley sprigs.

Grilled Scallops

Scallops with Mushrooms

	00:15	Serves 6	Pacific Southwest
	00:30		

American	Ingredients	Metric/Imperial
1½ lb	Scallops	675 g/1½ lb
½ cup	Butter	125 g/4 oz
1 cup	Dry white wine	250 ml/8 fl oz
½ tsp	Salt	½ tsp
⅛ tsp	Pepper	⅛ tsp
1	Scallion [spring onion], minced	1
2 tbsp	Flour	1½ tbsp
2 cups	Heavy [double] cream	450 ml/¾ pint
½ lb	Fresh mushrooms, sliced	225 g/8 oz
	Drops of lemon juice	
	Salt and pepper to taste	
1 tbsp	Cognac	1 tbsp
2 tbsp	Butter	25 g/1 oz
6	Scallop shells	6
	Roe for garnish (optional)	

1. Wash the scallops well in slightly salted water to remove all grit. Drain; dry on paper towels [kitchen paper]. Cut the scallops in half or in fourths to make them bite-sized.
2. In a medium saucepan, bring ½ cup [125 g/4 oz] butter, wine, 1 teaspoon salt, ⅛ teaspoon pepper, and onion to simmer. Add the scallops; return to simmer. Cover; simmer slowly 3–5 minutes. Remove the scallops with a slotted spoon and set aside.
3. Boil the pan liquids; reduce to just butter. Add flour; cook, stirring, 3–5 minutes. Stir in the cream, mushrooms, lemon juice, and salt and pepper to taste. Over medium heat, cook until thickened, stirring frequently. Add cognac. Blend two-thirds of the sauce with the scallops. Season to taste.
4. Grease the shells. Divide the scallop mixture between them. Cover with the rest of the sauce. Dot with 2 tablespoons [25 g/1 oz] of butter.
5. Just before serving, place in a preheated 400°F/200°C/Gas Mark 6 oven; heat about 10 minutes or until the sauce is bubbling. Garnish with roe, if available.

Grilled Scallops

	01:00	Serves 6	Pacific Southwest
	00:05		

American	Ingredients	Metric/Imperial
2½ lb	Scallops	1.25 kg/2½ lb
	Corn oil	
½ cup	Melted butter	125 g/4 oz
	Juice of 1 large lemon	
3–4 tbsp	Finely chopped scallions [spring onions]	2–3½ tbsp

1. Heat the coals in an outdoor grill until hot, about 30 minutes, or preheat the broiler [grill].
2. Prepare the scallops, and marinate in enough oil to coat all sides. Let stand for about 1 hour.
3. Drain, and put into a preheated shallow pan. Sprinkle with salt and pepper.
4. Mix the melted butter with the lemon juice and onions, and baste the scallops continuously while they are cooking. They should only take about 5–7 minutes.
5. Serve with Tartare Sauce (see Index) or with Cheese and Chive Dip (see Index).

Scallops with Honey

	00:05	Serves 6	Pacific Southwest
	00:16		

American	Ingredients	Metric/Imperial
1½ lb	Fresh or frozen scallops, defrosted	675 g/1½ lb
2 tbsp	Honey	1½ tbsp
2 tbsp	Prepared mustard	1½ tbsp
1 tsp	Curry powder	1 tsp
1 tsp	Lemon juice	1 tsp
	Lemon slices	
	Salt and pepper	

1. Preheat the broiler [grill].
2. Rinse the scallops; pat dry with paper towels [kitchen paper]. Combine honey, mustard, curry, and lemon juice. Place the scallops on a broiler pan; season and brush with honey mixture and melted butter. Broil [grill] 4 inches from flame, 8 minutes or until lightly browned.
3. Turn the scallops; brush with remaining sauce. Cook 8 minutes longer. Garnish with lemon slices.

Crayfish-Perch

Crayfish-Perch 🧑‍🍳

	01:00		
	00:50	Serves 10	South

American	Ingredients	Metric/Imperial
3 (9-oz) pkgs	Frozen crayfish or small lobsters	3 (250 g/9 oz) pkts
1½ lb	Perch fillet	675 g/1½ lb
	Broth	
	Crayfish shells and trimmings from the fish	
2 tbsp	Butter	25 g/1 oz
2 tbsp	Brandy	1½ tbsp
2	Small carrots	2
2	Shallots	2
¼ lb	Celery root [celeriac]	100 g/4 oz
4	Sprigs parsley	4
1	Bay leaf	1
½ tsp	Thyme	½ tsp
1	Bottle dry white wine	1
4 cups	Water	1 l/1¾ pint
	Fish Pâté	
3	Egg whites	3
2½ cups	Heavy [double] cream	600 ml/1 pint
1 tsp	Salt	1 tsp
¼ tsp	White pepper	¼ tsp
⅛–¼ tsp	Ground nutmeg	⅛–¼ tsp
	Sauce	
	Broth [see above]	
1⅔ cups	Heavy [double] cream	400 ml/13 fl oz
⅛–¼ tsp	Cayenne pepper	⅛–¼ tsp
	Salt, if needed	

1. Thaw and shell the crayfish carefully. Carefully remove the "stomach," which is situated behind the eyes, and throw it away. The upper part of the shell and the tail meats should be in one piece. Try also to retain the long antennae. The claws, legs, and rest of the shell are to be saved for the broth. (See the picture. The upper shells/heads are pâté-filled.)

2. Rinse the upper shells well, and place them in the refrigerator, together with the tails.

3. Clean the perch and cut into fillets. Save the trimmings for the broth. Place the fillets in the refrigerator.

4. Crush or coarsely chop the crayfish shells, claws, etc., and the scrapings from the fish. Sauté these in butter in a large pan. Add the brandy and ignite.

5. Peel and finely chop the carrots, shallots, and celery root. Sauté them together with the shells for several minutes. Add the sprigs of parsley, the bay leaf, the thyme, white wine, and water. Cover and boil for about 20 minutes. Strain and then allow the broth to thicken, uncovered, until slightly more than half the original amount of liquid remains. You may prepare in advance up to this step.

6. Make the fish pâté. Run the fish fillets through a food processor or 3 times through a meat grinder. Then add the egg whites, one at a time, while beating constantly, and add the cream, a small amount at a time. Season with salt, white pepper, and nutmeg.

7. Spoon the pâté into the clean, cold upper crayfish shells, and place them closely together in a wide pan. Cover with the broth and let simmer for 5 to 7 minutes, until the pâté has become white. Then remove the shells from the pan, and keep them warm under a sheet of aluminum foil.

8. To make the sauce, add the cream to the stock and let it simmer until it becomes somewhat thick. Thicken with ½ tablespoon [5 g/¼ oz] butter mixed with ½ tablespoon flour, if necessary. Season with cayenne pepper and salt, if needed.

9. Place the tails in the bottom of a copper pan or serving dish with sides. Place the filled upper shells on top, with the antennae sticking up. Carefully pour the hot sauce over the dish. Heat well on the stove or in a very hot oven for about 5 minutes.

Mussels Aurora

Mussels Aurora

 00:20
00:10
Serves 4–6   New England

American	Ingredients	Metric/Imperial
50	Mussels	50
	Salt	
2 tbsp	Margarine	25 g/1 oz
1	Onion, finely chopped	1
1	Clove garlic, crushed (optional)	1
¾ cup	Canned tomatoes	175 g/6 oz
	Freshly ground black pepper	
	Chopped parsley for garnish	

1. Wash the mussels in several changes of water and remove any beard. Discard any mussels that are open. Put the mussels in a large saucepan with 1 cup [250 ml/8 fl oz] salted water. Heat rapidly; shaking the pan occasionally until all shells have opened. Keep warm.
2. Melt the margarine in a saucepan and fry the onion and garlic until softened. Add the tomatoes; bring to a boil. Season to taste.
3. Put the mussels into a serving dish, spoon the sauce over top, and serve sprinkled with chopped parsley.

Marinated Mussels

 04:00
00:12
Serves 4   New England

American	Ingredients	Metric/Imperial
48	Mussels (10-12 per person)	48
1	Onion, minced	1
¾ cup	Dry white wine	175 ml/6 fl oz
¼ cup	Water	60 ml/2 fl oz
5 tbsp	Snipped parsley	4 tbsp
	Pinch thyme	
2 tbsp	Butter	25 g/1 oz

American	Ingredients	Metric/Imperial
	Marinade	
4 tbsp	Olive oil	3½ tbsp
2 tbsp	Dry white vermouth or white wine	1½ tbsp
2 tbsp	Shallot, finely minced	1½ tbsp
1 tbsp	Snipped parsley	1 tbsp
2 tbsp	Mixed herbs; tarragon, thyme, basil, etc.	1½ tbsp
	Salt	
	Pepper	
	Salad	
1	Tomato per person	1
1	Leek	1
	Lettuce	
	Snipped parsley	

1. Place the onion, wine, water, parsley, thyme, and butter in a thick-bottomed pot. Bring to a boil. Place the mussels in the pot and stir well. Cover the pot and shake well so the mussels move around. Boil for several minutes, until all the mussels have opened. Cool. Remove the mussels from their shells.
2. Mix the marinade ingredients together. Add the mussels and mix well. Let stand for several hours.
3. Cut the tomatoes into 4 wedges, then slice into thin pieces. Cut the leek into thin rings; sprinkle with snipped parsley. Sprinkle the rest of the marinade over the salad. Serve with marinated mussels.

Lobster Boats

 00:15
00:15
Serves 4   New England

American	Ingredients	Metric/Imperial
½ lb	Cooked lobster meat	225 g/8 oz
24	Fresh mushrooms, approximately 1½ inches in diameter	24
¼ cup	Condensed cream of mushroom soup	60 ml/2 fl oz
2 tbsp	Fine soft bread crumbs	1½ tbsp
2 tbsp	Mayonnaise or salad dressing	1½ tbsp
¼ tsp	Worcestershire sauce	¼ tsp
⅛ tsp	Liquid hot pepper sauce	⅛ tsp
	Dash pepper	
	Grated Parmesan cheese	

1. Preheat the oven to 400°F/200°C/Gas Mark 6.
2. Drain the lobster meat; remove any remaining shell or cartilage. Chop the lobster meat. Rinse the mushrooms in cold water; dry them and remove their stems.
3. Combine the soup, crumbs, mayonnaise, seasonings, and lobster. Stuff each mushroom cap with a tablespoon of the lobster mixture. Sprinkle with cheese.
4. Place the mushrooms in a well-greased 15 × 10 × 1-inch baking pan. Bake in the oven 10–15 minutes, or until lightly browned.

Marinated Mussels

Shrimp with Tomatoes and Cheese

Lobster Thermidor

00:45
00:40

Serves 4   New England

American	Ingredients	Metric/Imperial
4	Lobsters (675 g/1½ lb each) or 6 lobster tails	4
1½ sticks	Butter or margarine	175 g/6 oz
½ lb	Mushrooms, washed and sliced	50 g/2 oz
1 tbsp	All-purpose [plain] flour	1 tbsp
1 tbsp	Worcestershire sauce	1 tbsp
1 tbsp	Parsley, chopped	1 tbsp
½ cup	Brandy	125 ml/4 fl oz
2 cups	Heavy [double] cream	450 ml/¾ pint
4	Egg yolks	4
	Salt and white pepper to taste	
	Parmesan cheese	

1. Simmer the lobsters in heavily salted water 15–20 minutes, until a leg detaches easily from the body. Drain; cool. Crack claws; remove the meat. Cut into small pieces. Remove everything from the body and tail; reserve the tomalley [coral] and meat. Cut the meat into small pieces. Place the clean shells on a rack in an open broiling [grilling] pan; tuck tails under the grid to keep from curling.
2. Heat 1 stick [125 g/4 oz] butter in a frying pan. Sauté the mushrooms 2 minutes, stirring frequently. Add flour; stir until it disappears, cooking at least 5 minutes. Add lobster meat, Worcestershire, parsley, brandy, and cream; stir until it barely reaches boiling point.
3. Stir a little sauce into egg yolks beaten with tomalley; pour the eggs into the sauce. Heat well, but do not boil. Season with salt and pepper.
4. Fill the shells with the mixture. Sprinkle with Parmesan and dot with the remaining butter. Bake in a preheated 350°F/180°C/Gas Mark 4 oven until bubbling.

Shrimp with Tomatoes and Cheese

08:00
00:25

Serves 4   Mid Atlantic

American	Ingredients	Metric/Imperial
1 (8 oz) can	Tomatoes (whole tomatoes)	1 (225 g/8 oz) tin
7 tbsp	Oil	6 tbsp
½ cup	Snipped parsley	15 g/½ oz
15	Large shrimp [prawns]	15
½ lb	Soft whipped cheese, cream or soft Cheddar	225 g/8 oz
3½ tbsp	Butter	45 g/1¾ oz
	Black pepper	
	Tabasco sauce	
	Salt (optional)	

1. Prepare the sauce at least 8 hours in advance so that it has time to pull together. Pour off the juice from the tomatoes. Chop the tomatoes into large pieces; mix pieces with the juice and 2 tablespoons [1½ tbsp] of the oil in a pot. Simmer uncovered for 15 minutes. Let cool.
2. Remove the shells from the shrimp but let outer tip of the tail remain.
3. Grease a shallow; ovenproof dish; pour in the tomato sauce, and place the shrimp in the sauce with tails facing upward. Cover with parsley, the soft cheese, and the butter in small dabs. Grind a fair amount of pepper over the dish and add a few drops of Tabasco sauce. No extra salt is needed if the cheese is salted. Drip the rest of the oil over the dish and place under the broiler [grill] until the shrimp are cooked and the dish has become golden brown. Serve with rice.

Baked Stuffed Shrimp

00:30
00:40

Serves 5   Midwest

American	Ingredients	Metric/Imperial
1 lb	Extra jumbo or lobster shrimp [king prawns]	450 g/1 lb
¼ cup	Milk	60 ml/2 fl oz
1	Egg	1
½ cup	Bread crumbs	25 g/1 oz
½ tsp	Paprika	½ tsp
1 lb	Lump crabmeat	450 g/1 lb
1 tsp	Worcestershire sauce	1 tsp
	Salt and pepper to taste	
1 tsp	Tabasco sauce	1 tsp
1 tsp	Mustard	1 tsp
1 tbsp	Mayonnaise	1 tbsp
2	Slices white bread, cubed into small pieces	2
1	Medium onion	1
½	Green pepper, finely chopped	½
½ cup	Butter or margarine, melted	125 g/4 oz

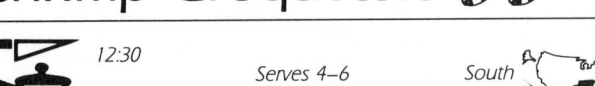

Shrimp Croquettes

1. Preheat the oven to 400°F/200°C/Gas Mark 6.
2. Shell the uncooked shrimp; leave the tail shell on. Split the shrimp down the back; spread apart, butterfly fashion. Dip the uncooked shrimp into the milk and egg mixture. Next dip in the bread crumbs and paprika mixture.
3. Combine the crabmeat, Worcestershire sauce, salt, pepper, Tabasco sauce, mustard, mayonnaise, and bread cubes.
4. Sauté the onion and green pepper in 2 tablespoons [25 g/1 oz] melted butter; add to the crabmeat mixture.
5. Firmly stuff the breaded shrimp with the crabmeat mixture. Place the shrimp, tail-side-up, on a greased, shallow baking dish. Baste with butter. Bake in the oven 30–40 minutes, until brown.

Shrimp Croquettes 🍳🍳

	12:30		
	00:25	Serves 4–6	South

American	Ingredients	Metric/Imperial
½ lb	Fresh shrimp [prawns], shelled and chopped	225 g/8 oz
1 cup	Thick béchamel sauce (see below)	250 ml/8 fl oz
3	Egg yolks	3
	Pepper	
	Salt (optional)	

1. Make a thick béchamel sauce and mix in the chopped shrimp. Let it boil for just a second, and remove from the heat. Stir in the egg yolks and season with pepper and perhaps a small amount of salt. Season with dash of nutmeg.
2. Pour the mixture onto an oiled plate and let it cool. It is best to allow the mixture to sit in the refrigerator overnight. The mixture should be really cold, or it will be difficult to form croquettes.
3. Divide the mixture into small piles and shape them into croquettes the size of wine bottle corks. Roll them in flour. Then dip them in beaten egg. Roll in bread crumbs. Fry them in smoking oil until golden brown in color. Remove with a spoon with holes in it, and drain on paper towels [kitchen paper].
4. Serve the croquettes piled on top of each other in a pyramid shape on a plate, and serve with lemon and a bunch of deep-fat fried parsley.
5. *Béchamel Sauce:* Melt 3 tablespoons [40 g/1½ oz] butter in the top of a double boiler over boiling water; stir in 3 tablespoons [2 tbsp] flour with a wooden spoon until smooth. Add 2 cups [450 ml/¾ pint] milk gradually; stirring constantly; cook until the sauce is thick. Stir in salt and pepper. Remove the top of the double boiler from the water.
6. Strain the sauce through a fine sieve; use as desired. Pour any remaining sauce into a small bowl. Cover the top of the sauce with a circle of wet waxed [greaseproof] paper; refrigerate for future use.

Shrimp and Rice Casserole

Shrimp and Rice Casserole

   00:30   Serves 4   United States

01:00

American	Ingredients	Metric/Imperial
4 slices	Bacon	4 rashers
1	Small onion, peeled and chopped	1
1 cup	Rice	225 g/8 oz
1 large can (about 30 oz)	Tomatoes	1 large tin (about 850 g/30 oz)
	Salt and pepper	
1	Bay leaf	1
½ lb	Fresh shrimp [prawns] or scampi, peeled and deveined	225 g/8 oz

1. Preheat the oven to 350°F/180°C/Gas Mark 4.
2. Dice the bacon and fry slowly until crisp. Remove from the pan and drain on a paper towel [kitchen paper].
3. Add the onion and rice to the bacon fat and stir over low heat for about 5 minutes. Transfer to a casserole.
4. Add tomatoes, 1 cup [250 ml/8 fl oz] water, seasoning, and bay leaf. Cover and cook for about ½ hour.
5. Add the bacon and shrimp and cook for another 10 minutes.

Deep-Fried Shrimp with Rhode Island Sauce

00:35
00:15   Serves 4   New England

American	Ingredients	Metric/Imperial
	Batter	
¼ cup	Beer, slightly warm	60 ml/2 fl oz
¼ cup	Water, slightly warm	60 ml/2 fl oz
2 tbsp	Oil	1½ tbsp
5 tbsp	Flour	4 tbsp
1 tsp	Salt	1 tsp
1	Egg white, stiffly beaten	1
	Shrimp	
2½ lb	Extra large, unshelled shrimp [king prawns]	1.25 kg/2½ lb
4 cups	Oil for deep-frying	1 l/1¾ pints
	Rhode Island Sauce	
⅔ cup	Mayonnaise	150 ml/5 fl oz
1 tbsp	Tomato paste	1 tbsp
1 tbsp	Dry sherry	1 tbsp
¼ tsp	Garlic powder	¼ tsp
½ tsp	Salt	½ tsp
3–6	Dashes Tabasco	3–6
⅓ cup	Sour cream	75 ml/3 fl oz
	Parsley	
	Lemon wedges	

1. Mix all the batter ingredients except the egg white. Beat until smooth. Let it stand and soak while you shell the shrimp. Beat the egg white into stiff peaks and fold it carefully into the batter. Stir only as much as is necessary. This is so the shrimp will be as crispy as possible.
2. Heat the oil so that it is about 350°F/180°C, or until a little cube of white bread quickly becomes golden brown. Another sign that the oil is at the right temperature is if you can just see small smoke rings.
3. Mix the shrimp in frying batter and put them carefully, one by one, into the oil. Do not put too many shrimp in the oil at one time. They easily bunch together and cause the oil to lose its heat. It is, therefore, best to deep fry in several batches. Drain the shrimp by placing them on folded paper towels [kitchen paper].
4. Make Rhode Island Sauce by mixing together the mayonnaise, tomato paste, sherry, garlic powder, salt, and Tabasco sauce. Mix until smooth, then add sour cream.
5. Finally, when everything else is done, deep-fry the parsley. The parsley should be dry and well drained, and all the stems should be removed. Carefully drop a fistful of parsley in hot oil and fry it for several seconds, until it becomes dark green in color. Serve the shrimp with the sauce, parsley, and lemon wedges.

Deep-Fried Shrimp with Rhode Island Sauce

Meat

Roast Rump of Beef

2. Peel and quarter the carrots and turnips lengthwise. Remove the herbs and the single onion from the pot; add the carrots, turnips, celery, and small onions. Simmer for another hour.

3. Make the dumplings: Sift the flour with a pinch of salt. Mix in finely shredded suet, herbs, and pepper. Mix in water to make a light dough. Divide into pieces about the size of a small walnut, rolling between your hands. Drop the dumplings into the boiling liquid around the meat, cover the pot, and cook them for about 15–20 minutes.

4. Serve on a large dish with the vegetables and dumplings, and serve the gravy in a sauceboat separately.

Roast Rump of Beef

| | 00:15 | Serves 6 | New England |
| | 01:35 | | |

American	Ingredients	Metric/Imperial
1 (3 lb)	Rump roast	1 (1.25 kg/3 lb)
1 lb	Potatoes	450 g/1 lb
1 lb	Parsnips or pumpkin	450 g/1 lb
	Salt	
4 tbsp	Drippings or lard	3½ tbsp

1. Preheat the oven to 350°F/180°C/Gas Mark 4.

2. Wipe the meat all over with a clean, damp cloth. Peel the potatoes and parsnips or pumpkin, cut into pieces, and parboil in boiling salted water for 10 minutes. Drain well.

3. Put the drippings or lard in the roasting pan and put it in the oven until hot. Add the vegetables and stir so that all pieces are coated in fat. Put the meat in the center of the pan and arrange the vegetables around it.

4. Baste the meat with some fat, then roast in the oven for 20 minutes per pound plus 20 minutes over.

Boiled Beef and Carrots

| | 00:15 | Serves 6 | Mid Atlantic |
| | 02:30 | | |

American	Ingredients	Metric/Imperial
3–4 lb	Round [topside] beef roast	1.25–1.75 kg/ 3–4 lb
1	Large onion stuck with 2 cloves	1
8–10	Medium carrots	8–10
2	Small turnips	2
3	Celery stalks	3
4–6	Small whole onions	4–6
6	Peppercorns	6
1	Bay leaf	1
	Some parsley stems	
	A sprig of thyme	
8 tbsp	Suet or butter	125 g/4 oz
2 cups	All-purpose [plain] flour	225 g/8 oz
3 tbsp	Chopped parsley	2 tbsp
½ tbsp	Thyme	½ tbsp
½ tbsp	Marjoram	½ tbsp

1. In a large pot, put the beef, the large onion, the peppercorns, herbs, enough water to cover the meat, and a little salt. Bring to a boil slowly. Remove any scum that rises to the surface, put a lid on the pot, and simmer for 1 hour.

Barbecued Beef

| | 00:30 | Serves 4–5 | Southwest |
| | 01:00 | | |

American	Ingredients	Metric/Imperial
2 lb	Round steak [boned and rolled rib roast]	900 g/2 lb
	Corn oil	
4	Medium-sized onions	4
4	Medium-sized carrots	4
	Tangy Barbecue Sauce (see Index)	

1. Heat the coals in an outdoor grill until hot, about 30 minutes.

2. Brush the meat on both sides with corn oil, and brown on both sides over the hot coals.

3. Put the meat on a sheet of heavy duty aluminum foil, large enough to fold over the roast. Sprinkle with salt and pepper. Add the onions and carrots, cut into quarters, and coat generously with Tangy Barbecue Sauce.

4. Fold the foil over the meat and cook over the hot coals for about 1 hour, or until the meat is cooked to your taste. This can also be cooked in a 350°F/180°C/Gas Mark 4 oven.

Stock-Cooked Roast Beef

Stock-Cooked Roast Beef

	00:20		
	00:30	Serves 6–8	New England

American	Ingredients	Metric/Imperial
2 qt	Strong beef stock	2 l/3½ pints
6	Carrots, cut into pieces	6
6	Medium onions, peeled	6
12	Leeks (white part only)	12
2	Fresh fennels, well trimmed and sliced	2
12	Potatoes, all the same size, peeled	12
	Cauliflower	
24	Brussels sprouts	24
1	Tenderloin [fillet] of beef, about 2½ lb [1.25 kg]	1
	Pepper	
	Parsley	

1. Place the stock in a large pot. Add the carrots and onions when it starts to boil. Cook for several minutes, then add the leeks and fennels.

2. Boil the potatoes and cauliflower separately in salted water. Do the same with the Brussels sprouts.

3. Bind the roast beef up well, leaving a long piece of string hanging from the meat. Season with salt and pepper. When all the vegetables are cooked, remove them with a slotted spoon and keep them warm. Place the meat in the simmering stock, and let it simmer until it feels done, about 7–10 minutes per pound. Pick up the meat and cut a slice to see if it is pink inside. Add more stock, if necessary. The meat should be pink on the inside.

4. When the meat is done, take it out of the stock and remove the string. Cut into thin slices.

5. Meanwhile, place the vegetables in the stock, and make sure that they become well heated. Place the ingredients in a large, deep, serving bowl, and pour broth over them. Serve immediately. On the table, you should have different kinds of mustard, pickles, grated horseradish, a pepper mill, and coarse salt.

6. Leftover stock makes an excellent soup for the next day.

Beef Burgundy

Beef Burgundy

	00:10	Serves 4–6	South
	02:10		

American	Ingredients	Metric/Imperial
1½–2 lb	Braising beef	675–900 g/ 1½–2 lb
2 tbsp	Oil or shortening	1½ tbsp
4–5 slices	Fat bacon	4–5 rashers
8–12	Pickling onions	8–12
12	Button mushrooms	12
	A pinch of sugar	
1 tbsp	Flour	1 tbsp
3–4 tbsp	Brandy	2–3½ tbsp
½ cup	Burgundy or red wine	125 ml/4 fl oz
1 cup	Beef stock	250 ml/8 fl oz
	Parsley, sprig of thyme, or bay leaf	

1. Preheat the oven to 325°F/160°C/Gas Mark 3.
2. Cut the meat into large pieces. Melt the shortening or oil in a thick casserole. Brown the meat quickly on both sides. Take out and keep warm. Cut the bacon into small pieces and put into the hot fat with the onions, mushrooms, and a pinch of sugar. Brown all over. Remove the onions and mushrooms, and put in a serving dish to keep warm. Add flour to the bacon and brown slightly. Return the meat to the casserole.
3. Heat the brandy and wine together and bring to a boil. Light with a match, pouring over the meat while flaming. Add enough stock almost to cover the meat. Add a few bits of parsley, sprig of thyme, or bay leaf, and season. Cover the casserole and cook for about 2 hours. After 1 hour, add the onions and mushrooms, and cook for another hour.
4. Add the meat to the vegetables in the serving dish. Boil up the sauce to reduce the quantity a little, and pour it over the meat. Serve with mashed potatoes and large croutons of fried bread.

Roast Beef and Yorkshire Pudding

	00:40	Serves 8	New England
	01:05		

American	Ingredients	Metric/Imperial
4 lb	Rolled rib roast	1.75 kg/4 lb
1 cup	All-purpose [plain] flour	100 g/4 oz
¾ tsp	Salt	¾ tsp
2	Large eggs	2
1 cup	Milk	250 ml/8 fl oz
1 cup	Shortening for roasting	225 g/8 oz
2 lb	Potatoes	900 g/2 lb
1 cup	Stock	250 ml/8 fl oz
½ cup	Grated fresh horseradish	50 g/2 oz

1. Preheat the oven to 450°F/230°C/Gas Mark 8.
2. Prepare the batter. Sift the flour into a mixing bowl; add salt. Make a hollow in the center, then add eggs and a little milk. Stir and draw the flour into the center gradually until smooth. Add the remaining milk. Beat well. Let stand for 30 minutes.
3. Melt the shortening in the roasting pan. Place the unfrozen roast in the pan, baste well, and roast for 15 minutes per pound, basting every 15 minutes.
4. Peel the potatoes. Boil for 5 minutes, drain, and scratch with fork to make crisp. After 15 minutes, put the potatoes in the pan with the meat to cook for about 45 minutes. After 30 minutes, pour off about 1 tablespoon of the fat drippings from the meat into a small open pan. Reheat, add the batter, and place at the top of the oven until well risen and brown, about 30 minutes.
5. When the roast is cooked, place it on a heated platter with the potatoes and Yorkshire pudding and keep warm. Pour off all clear fat, and make a gravy with the juices in the roasting pan, adding stock. Stir and scrape well to loosen all meaty brown bits, and season to taste.
6. Serve with grated horseradish.

Beef with Sauerkraut

	00:10	Serves 6	Midwest
	02:30		

American	Ingredients	Metric/Imperial
2½–3 lb	Brisket of beef	1.25 kg/2½–3 lb
3 tbsp	Bacon fat	2 tbsp
1	Large onion, peeled and sliced	1
2 lb	Sauerkraut	900 g/2 lb
2 cups	Boiling water	450 ml/¾ pint
	A few caraway seeds	

1. Heat the fat in a pan; add the onion and sauté until lightly browned.
2. Put in the meat and arrange the sauerkraut on top. Add boiling water, cover, and simmer over low heat for 2–2½ hours or until the meat is tender. Add salt and pepper to taste and a few caraway seeds.
3. Serve with boiled potatoes.

Beef Stew with Pastry Crust

| | 00:45 | Serves 6 | Mid Atlantic  |
| | 01:45 | | |

American	Ingredients	Metric/Imperial
2½ lb	Stew meat [stewing steak]	1.25 kg/2½ lb
	Butter for frying	
1½ tbsp	Flour	1¼ tbsp
1 tsp	Salt	1 tsp
¼ tsp	Black pepper	¼ tsp
1	Large onion, chopped	1
1	Large eggplant [aubergine], sliced and peeled	1
¼ lb	Fresh mushrooms	100 g/4 oz
1 can (8 oz)	Crushed tomatoes	1 tin (225 g/ 8 oz.)
1¼ cups	Beef stock	300 ml/½ pint
2	Cloves garlic, crushed	2
2 tsp	Marjoram	2 tsp
3–4 tbsp	Red wine	2–3½ tbsp
2–3 tsp	Arrowroot, mixed with a little water	2–3 tsp
	Pimento-filled olives, cut in half	
	Snipped parsley	
1	Egg, beaten	1

1. Cut meat into 1¼-inch cubes, dredge them in flour, and brown them in butter in a frying pan. Season with salt and pepper. Place the meat in a stew pot. Brown the onion, eggplant, and mushrooms, each separately, in the frying pan, and place them in the stew pot. Add the crushed tomatoes and broth. Bring to a boil and season with garlic and marjoram.

2. Simmer the stew for about an hour, or until the meat feels very tender. Season with red wine toward the end of the simmering time. Thicken with arrowroot, which has been mixed with a little water, so that stew has a fine consistency. Pour the stew into an ovenproof dish. Garnish with sliced olives and snipped parsley.

3. Preheat the oven to 400°F/200°C/Gas Mark 6.

4. Place the pastry crust patties together and roll them out into a ¼-inch thick crust. Brush the edges of the pan with a beaten egg. Place the crust over the stew. Press well around the edges of the pan; make a hole in the crust for the steam to escape. Place in the oven for about 20–25 minutes.

Beef Stew with Pastry Crust

Caribbean Style Corned Beef Kebabs

Beef Braised in Beer

	00:25		
	02:00	Serves 4	Midwest

American	Ingredients	Metric/Imperial
1½ lb	Beef suitable for braising, cut into large pieces	675 g/1½ lb
2 tbsp	Oil	1½ tbsp
2–3	Medium onions	2–3
1	Clove garlic	1
1 tbsp	Flour	1 tbsp
1 cup	Brown ale or beer	250 ml/8 fl oz
	Parsley, thyme, bay leaf	
	A pinch of nutmeg, sugar	
4–6	Slices of French bread	4–6
	French mustard	

1. Preheat the oven to 325°F/160°C/Gas Mark 3.
2. Heat the oil and brown the meat on both sides quickly. Remove and add sliced onions and brown these. Pour off any excess fat. Add crushed garlic and then flour. Pour 1 cup [250 ml/8 fl oz] of hot water onto the beer or ale and add to the pot. Bring to a boil, adding herbs, nutmeg, sugar, and seasoning.
3. Return the meat to the casserole. Cover with a tightly fitting lid. Cook slowly for 1½–1¾ hours.
4. Before serving, put in the slices of bread, which have been spread thickly with French mustard. Allow to soak up the oil from the top of the casserole and some gravy.
5. Return the casserole to the oven without the lid for another 15 minutes, when the bread should be well browned.

Creole Beef Stew

	00:15		
	02:10	Serves 4	South 

American	Ingredients	Metric/Imperial
2 tbsp	Oil	1½ tbsp
1½–2 lb	Chuck steak [brisket] or shoulder of beef	675–900 g/ 1½–2 lb
2	Onions, peeled and thinly sliced	2
1	Clove garlic, crushed	1
	Black pepper	
⅛ tsp	Thyme	⅛ tsp
⅛ tsp	Marjoram	⅛ tsp
	A dash of cayenne pepper	
1	Small bay leaf	1
1 tsp	Wine vinegar	1 tsp
1 (8-oz) can	Tomato sauce	1 (225 g/8 oz) tin
1 cup	Water	250 ml/8 fl oz
½ tsp	Sugar	½ tsp

1. Heat the oil in a heavy frying pan; put in the meat, cut into cubes, and brown on all sides. Remove the meat from the pan.
2. Add the onions to the fat remaining in the pan, and sauté until browned. Add all the other ingredients, and stir until boiling.
3. Return the meat to the pan, and simmer over very low heat for about 2 hours.
4. Remove the bay leaf, adjust the seasoning, and serve with potatoes (or rice) and a green vegetable.

Pot Roast

	00:15		
	02:40	Serves 6	Mid Atlantic

American	Ingredients	Metric/Imperial
1	Clove garlic	1
3–4 lb	Shoulder, blade of beef, or chuck steak [brisket or silverside]	1025–1.75 kg/ 3–4 lb
	Flour	
2 tbsp	Oil	1½ tbsp
1–2	Carrots, peeled and chopped	1–2
1–2	Stalks celery, chopped	1–2
2–3 tbsp	Chopped green pepper	1½–2 tbsp
1	Small turnip, peeled and diced	1
1	Onion, peeled and stuck with 3 cloves	1
2 cups	Boiling stock or water	450 ml/¾ pint
	Cooked rice or noodles	

1. Cut the clove of garlic and rub it over the meat. Sprinkle the meat liberally with flour to which some salt and pepper has been added.
2. Heat the oil in a large heavy pan, put in the meat, and brown well on one side. Turn it over; add the carrots, celery, green pepper, and turnip, and cook until the meat is browned on the underside.

3. Pour off any excess fat, add the onion and stock. Cover tightly, and cook over low heat for 2–2½ hours, turning the meat occasionally and adding stock or water as required. Adjust seasoning.

4. Serve with rice or noodles and the pot liquid, thickened with 1 tablespoon flour mixed to a smooth paste with 2 tablespoons [1½ tbsp] cold water. Add to the hot liquid and stir until thickened. (Any leftover meat is very good served cold.)

Caribbean Style Corned Beef Kebabs 🧑‍🍳🧑‍🍳

	00:25		
	01:05	Serves 4	South

American	Ingredients	Metric/Imperial
4	Thick slices canned corned beef	4
2	Medium onions	2
2 tbsp	Oil	1½ tbsp
1 cup	Rice	225 g/8 oz
3 cups	Beef stock	700 ml/1¼ pints
1	Orange	1
2–3 tbsp	Butter	25–40 g/ 1–1½ oz
¼ cup	Pineapple juice	60 ml/2 fl oz
1 tsp	Worcestershire sauce	1 tsp
1 tsp	Cornstarch [cornflour]	1 tsp
8 strips	Bacon, blanched	8 rashers
2	Bananas	2
12	Pineapple chunks (fresh or canned)	12
8	Button mushrooms	8
4	Bay leaves	4

1. Preheat the oven to 350°F/180°C/Gas Mark 4.
2. Cook 1 finely chopped onion in oil for 5 minutes without browning. Add the rice and cook for another 5 minutes. Now add 2 cups [450 ml/¾ pint] of stock and seasoning, and stir well.
3. Cook in the oven for about 30 minutes, until all the stock is absorbed. Grate about half the orange rind over the rice, and mix in the juice of the orange with 1 teaspoon of melted butter. Turn into a buttered cake tin and keep warm in the oven.
4. For the gravy, cook 1 finely chopped onion in 1 cup [250 ml/8 fl oz] of stock for about 15 minutes. Add the pineapple juice, Worcestershire sauce, and the remaining grated orange rind, without pith. Mix the cornstarch with 1 tablespoon cold water until smooth; add to the gravy and boil for 1 minute to thicken.
5. Cut each slice of corned beef into 4 chunks and wrap each in half a slice of bacon. Arrange on 4 skewers alternately with banana and pineapple chunks, mushrooms, and half bay leaves. Brush well with melted butter and broil [grill] for 10 minutes, turning all the time.
6. Turn the rice mold onto a warmed serving dish. Lay the kebabs on top or alongside and serve the gravy separately.

Cornish Style Pasties

Cornish Style Pasties 🧑‍🍳🧑‍🍳

	00:45		
	00:35	Serves 4–6	Midwest 

American	Ingredients	Metric/Imperial
1 lb	Chopped cooked beef steak	450 g/1 lb
½ lb	Chopped cooked liver	225 g/8 oz
3 cups	Flour	350 g/12 oz
1 cup	Beef drippings or shortening	250 ml/8 fl oz
3	Medium potatoes	3
2	Onions	2
1	Small turnip	1
2	Carrots	2
1	Egg	1

1. Preheat the oven to 400°F/200°C/Gas Mark 6.
2. Sift the flour into a bowl with the salt. Mix in the drippings or shortening with a knife or pastry blender. Then rub in lightly with the fingers, and mix with ½ cup [125 ml/4 fl oz] cold water to make a firm dough. Put into the refrigerator in a plastic bag for at least 15 minutes. Remove, cut into 6–8 equal pieces, and roll into squares about ¼ inch thick.
3. Mix the chopped beef and liver together, with salt and pepper. Peel and dice the vegetables, and mix together. Sauté in butter for 4–5 minutes; drain and let cool. Put a heaping spoonful of the vegetable mixture on half of each square; top this with a spoonful of meat mixture.
4. Brush the edges of each pastry square with an egg white beaten with a pinch of salt. Fold over and press the ends together. Crimp with fingers to make a scalloped edge and the traditional crescent shape. Bake the pasties for 30 minutes in the oven.

Beef and Rice Casserole

00:15
02:20

Serves 4–5

New England

American	Ingredients	Metric/Imperial
½ lb	Bacon slices [rashers]	225 g/8 oz
2 lb	Boneless beef chuck [stewing steak]	900 g/2 lb
2	Onions, peeled and sliced	2
¾ cup	Rice, uncooked	175 g/6 oz
1 cup	Dry red wine	250 ml/8 fl oz
1½ cups	Beef consomme	350 ml/12 fl oz
1	Clove garlic, crushed	1
1 sprig fresh or ½ tsp dried	Thyme	1 sprig fresh or ½ tsp dried
1 tsp	Chopped parsley	1 tsp
¼ tsp	Saffron	¼ tsp
3–4	Tomatoes, chopped	3–4
½ cup	Grated Parmesan cheese	50 g/2 oz

1. Preheat the oven to 325°F/160°C/Gas Mark 3.
2. Cut the bacon into strips and sauté in a frying pan until crisp. Then remove the bacon to a large casserole.
3. Cut the meat into cubes and brown in the bacon fat. Remove to the casserole.
4. Add the onions and rice to the remaining fat; stir until the rice begins to color, then set aside.
5. Put the wine, consomme, garlic, herbs, and saffron into the casserole. Cook for 1 hour.
6. Remove the casserole from the oven, skim off any excess fat and stir in the rice and onion mixture and tomatoes. Cover, and return to the oven for another hour, checking occasionally to see if any extra liquid is required.
7. Before serving, adjust the seasoning and stir in the cheese.

Hearty Beef Casserole

00:15
02:45

Serves 6

New England

American	Ingredients	Metric/Imperial
1½–2 lb	Beef chuck [skirt of beef], cut into 1½-inch cubes	675–900 g/ 1½–2 lb
2 tsp	Salt	2 tsp
¼ tsp	Pepper	¼ tsp
3 tbsp	Flour	2 tbsp
6 tbsp	Bacon fat	5 tbsp
1	Large onion, peeled and sliced	1
2 cups	Beef stock	450 ml/¾ pint
1 tsp	Marjoram	1 tsp
1 tsp	Basil	1 tsp
1 large can (20 oz)	Whole tomatoes	1 large tin (575 g/20 oz)
6	Carrots, sliced	6
6	Small potatoes, quartered	6

1. Preheat the oven to 325°F/160°C/Gas Mark 3.
2. Trim any excess fat from the meat.
3. Heat the fat in a frying pan and brown the meat on all sides. Sprinkle with flour and cook for 5 minutes. Add the onion and cook until golden. Remove the meat and onion to a casserole.
4. Add 2 cups [450 ml/¾ pint] stock. Stir until simmering. Add the herbs; cook for a few more minutes, then pour over the meat.
5. Add the vegetables and cook for about 2½ hours at a slow simmer.

Daube of Beef

12:00
02:50

Serves 6–8

Pacific Southwest

American	Ingredients	Metric/Imperial
3 lb	Top round [topside] beef	1.25 g/3 lb
¼ lb	Carrots, peeled and sliced lengthwise	100 g/4 oz
1 tbsp chopped fresh or 1 tsp dried	Oregano	1 tbsp chopped fresh or 1 tsp dried
1 tbsp chopped fresh or 1 tsp dried	Basil	1 tbsp chopped fresh or 1 tsp dried
3 slices	Bacon	3 rashers
3	Tomatoes, peeled and chopped	3
Marinade		
1 cup	Salad oil	250 ml/8 fl oz
1	Onion, peeled and chopped	1
4	Shallots, peeled and chopped	4
1	Stalk celery, cut into pieces	1
1	Carrot, peeled and coarsely chopped	1
½ cup	Dry red wine	125 ml/4 fl oz
6	White peppercorns	6
2	Cloves garlic, crushed	2
1	Bay leaf	1
1 tbsp fresh or 1 tsp dried	Thyme	1 tbsp fresh or 1 tsp dried
1 tbsp fresh or 1 tsp dried	Marjoram	1 tbsp fresh or 1 tsp dried
2	Sprigs parsley	2

1. Put all the ingredients for the marinade into a frying pan and simmer gently for 15–20 minutes. Cool, then pour over the meat in a large bowl. Leave for 12–24 hours, piercing the meat and turning it over occasionally.
2. Transfer the meat to a casserole; add 1 cup [250 ml/8 fl oz] of the liquid from the marinade. Arrange the carrots and herbs around the meat and cover with slices of bacon.
3. Cover the casserole tightly and cook for about 2½ hours. Add the tomatoes and cook for another ½ hour.
4. Adjust the seasoning, and serve with buttered noodles and a green vegetable.

Cottage Pie

Cottage Pie

	00:20			
	01:00	Serves 4–6	Midwest	

American	Ingredients	Metric/Imperial
1–1½ lb	Diced or ground [minced] cooked beef or lamb	450–675 g/ 1–1½ lb
2	Medium onions	2
1–2 tbsp	Oil	1–1½ tbsp
½–¾ cup	Beef stock	125–175 ml/ 4–6 fl oz
1 tbsp	Chopped mixed herbs, mainly parsley	1 tbsp
	Nutmeg	
	Worcestershire sauce	
4–6	Medium-sized potatoes	4–6
1 tbsp	Butter	15 g/½ oz
	Milk	

1. Preheat the oven to 375°F/190°C/Gas Mark 5.
2. Cook the chopped onions in oil until golden brown. (Do not overbrown or this will make dish bitter.) Add the meat, stock, seasoning, herbs, a grating of nutmeg, and a dash of Worcestershire sauce.
3. Peel the potatoes and boil until tender in salted water. When soft, drain and dry off in a saucepan. Mash, and beat in butter and then a little milk. Season to taste.
4. Put the meat mixture into an ovenproof dish, smooth down, and pile hot potato on top to make a slightly domed cover. Rough the surface evenly with a fork, and sprinkle with small pieces of butter. Bake in the oven for 30–40 minutes, by which time the top should be crisp and brown. (As a variation, chopped mushrooms may be added to the meat mixture.)

Croquettes

	00:30			
	00:25	Serves 4	Midwest	

American	Ingredients	Metric/Imperial
2–3 cups	Cooked ground [minced] meat	350–500 g/ 12–18 oz
1 lb	Peeled potatoes	450 g/1 lb
1	Small onion	1
1 tbsp	Chutney	1 tbsp
1 tbsp	Chopped herbs	1 tbsp
	Tomato purée (optional)	
2–3 tbsp	Flour	1½–2 tbsp
2	Eggs	2
	Dry white crumbs	
	Fat for deep frying	
	A bunch of parsley	

1. Boil and mash the potatoes. Finely chop the onion and mix with the meat, chutney, herbs, and seasoning, adding a little tomato purée if the mixture is too dry.
2. Put the mixture on a floured board. Make into a long roll, and cut into sections about 1 inch thick and 3 inches long. Roll these in seasoned flour. Then brush with beaten egg all over and roll in bread crumbs.
3. Deep-fry in smoking hot fat until well browned. Drain and serve with parsley fried in deep fat for a few seconds and a well-flavored sauce.

Caserole of Beef with Walnuts

| | 00:15 | | |
| | 02:10 | Serves 4–5 | Pacific Southwest |

American	Ingredients	Metric/Imperial
2 tbsp	Drippings or peanut oil	1½ tbsp
1½–2 lb	Beef chuck [skirt or stewing steak]	675–900 g/ 1½–2 lb
12	Small white onions, peeled	12
1 tbsp	Flour	1 tbsp
¼ cup	Red wine	60 ml/2 fl oz
	Bouquet garni	
1	Clove garlic	1
2 cups	Beef stock	450 ml/¾ pint
1	Small bunch celery	1
1 tbsp	Butter or margerine	15 g/½ oz
¼ cup	Walnut meats	25 g/1 oz
	Rind of ½ orange, shredded and blanched	

1. Preheat the oven to 325°F/160°C/Gas Mark 3.
2. Heat the drippings in a frying pan and brown the meat. Remove to a casserole. Sauté the onions in the remaining fat until they just begin to color, then put with the meat.
3. Pour off any excess fat leaving about 1 tablespoon. Stir in the flour; add the wine, bouquet garni, garlic (crushed with a little salt), and 1½ cups [350 ml/12 fl oz] stock. Stir until boiling, and pour over the contents of the casserole. Add the extra stock, if necessary, just to cover the meat. Add a little seasoning. Cover tightly and cook for about 2 hours.
4. Trim the celery and cut into strips crosswise. Heat the butter, add celery, walnut meats, and a pinch of salt. Toss over the heat for a few minutes.
5. When ready to serve, scatter the celery, walnut meats, and orange rind over the meat.

Beef with Dumplings

| | 00:25 | | |
| | 01:40 | Serves 4–5 | Mid Atlantic |

American	Ingredients	Metric/Imperial
2 tbsp	Flour	1½ tbsp
1½ tsp	Salt	1½ tsp
¼ tsp	Pepper	¼ tsp
2 lb	Lean beef chuck [stewing steak]	900 g/2 lb
3 tbsp	Oil	2 tbsp
3	Medium onions, peeled	3
3	Cloves	3
4	Carrots, peeled and cut into strips lengthwise	4
1½ cups	Beef consomme	350 ml/12 fl oz
1 tbsp	Red or white wine vinegar	1 tbsp
3 tbsp	Chopped chives	2 tbsp
1 (1 lb)	Package biscuit mix [dumpling mix]	1 (450 g/1 lb)

1. Preheat the oven to 350°F/180°C/Gas Mark 4.
2. Sift the flour with salt and pepper. Cut the meat into 1-inch cubes and dredge well with the flour.
3. Heat the oil in a casserole; add the meat and onions, each stuck with a clove, and stir until the meat is well browned. Add the carrots, consomme, and vinegar. Bring to a boil, then cover and remove to the oven. Cook for about 1 hour.
4. Make up the dumplings according to the instructions on the package of biscuit mix. Drop them into the casserole in spoonfuls, replace the lid, and continue cooking for 30 minutes. Sprinkle with chives before serving.
5. Spinach, cooked and chopped, with a pinch of nutmeg and a few sautéed mushrooms added, would make a very good accompaniment.

Beef Olives or Boneless Birds

| | 00:35 | | |
| | 02:20 | Serves 8 | New England |

American	Ingredients	Metric/Imperial
2½–3 lb	Chuck or round steak [rolled fillet]	1.25 kg/2½–3 lb
2 cups	Fresh white bread crumbs	100 g/4 oz
5 tbsp	Chopped parsley	4 tbsp
1 tbsp	Mixed chopped thyme and marjoram and lemon rind	1 tbsp
2	Eggs	2
1 tbsp	Butter	15 g/½ oz
8 slices	Streaky bacon	8 rashers
6 tbsp	Oil (or shortening)	5 tbsp
2	Onions	2
2 cups	Chopped mushrooms	225 g/8 oz
1½ cups	Strong beef stock	350 ml/12 fl oz
1	Bay leaf	1
	Cornstarch [cornflour], optional	

1. Preheat the oven to 325°F/160°C/Gas Mark 3.
2. Make the stuffing by mixing the bread crumbs, herbs, and seasoning together. Add the beaten eggs and melted butter.
3. Cut the beef into slices about 3–4 inches square, allowing 2 slices each. Pound the slices of beef and season with a little salt and pepper. Cover the center of each beef slice with half a slice of bacon, then a spoonful of stuffing. Roll each slice up neatly and tie with thread.
4. Brown the beef olives quickly on all sides in hot oil or shortening in a frying pan. Remove and keep warm. Now fry the onions for a few minutes. Add the mushrooms and cook for 5 minutes without browning. Add the beef stock and bring to a boil.
5. Pack the beef olives into an ovenproof casserole, pour the onion sauce over them, and add a bay leaf. Cover tightly and cook slowly in the oven for 1½–2 hours, or until the beef is tender. Remove the threads before serving. Thicken the sauce, if necessary, with a teaspoon of cornstarch mixed to a paste in cold water and boiled in the sauce for 3–5 minutes.

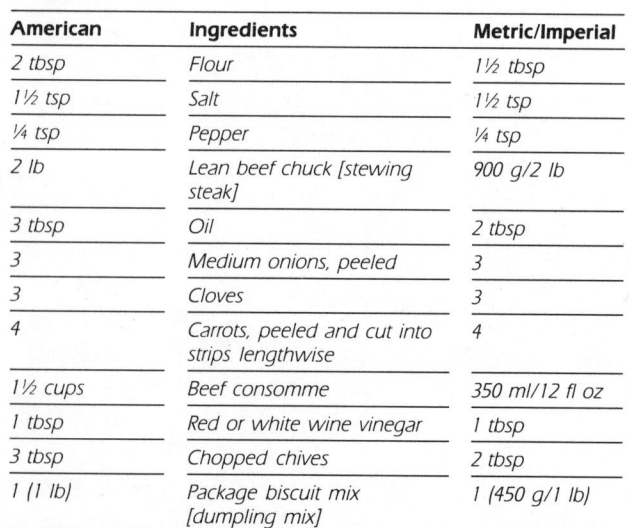

Casserole of Beef with Walnuts

Paprika Goulash

 00:15 02:10   Serves 4   Mid Atlantic

American	Ingredients	Metric/Imperial
1½ lb	Beef chuck or round [skirt of beef or stewing steak]	675 g/1½ lb
3 tbsp	Oil	2 tbsp
3	Medium onions, peeled and sliced	3
2 tbsp	Paprika	1½ tbsp
2 tbsp	Flour	1½ tbsp
2 tsp	Tomato purée	2 tsp
2 cups	Beef stock	450 ml/¾ pint
	Bouquet garni	
1	Clove garlic, crushed	1
1	Red or green pepper	1
2–3	Tomatoes, peeled and sliced	2–3
6 tbsp	Sour cream	5 tbsp

1. Preheat the oven to 325°F/160°C/Gas Mark 3.
2. Cut the meat into cubes. Heat the oil in a frying pan and brown the meat over fairly high heat, then transfer to a casserole.
3. Reduce the heat in the pan. Sauté the onions in the remaining oil; add the paprika, flour, tomato purée, and stock. Stir until boiling, then pour over the meat in the casserole. Add the bouquet garni, seasoning, and garlic. Cover and cook about 1¾ hours.
4. Blanch the pepper, remove the seeds, and cut into strips. Add to the casserole with the tomatoes, and cook for 15 minutes more.
5. Just before serving, stir in the sour cream and adjust the seasoning. Serve with noodles.

Mediterranean Style Beef

 00:20 04:00   Serves 4–6   Midwest

American	Ingredients	Metric/Imperial
1½–2 lb	Cross-cut beef roast [sirloin]	675–900 g/ 1½–2 lb
4 strips	Bacon	4 rashers
6	Tomatoes	6
2	Onions	2
¼ cup	Red wine	60 ml/2 fl oz
2	Cloves garlic	2
¾ tsp	Rosemary	¾ tsp
1	Bay leaf	1
5	Juniper berries	5

1. Preheat the oven to 250°F/130°C/Gas Mark ½.
2. Cut the meat into even-sized pieces. Put the meat in a casserole and cover with the bacon, cut into pieces.
3. Add the peeled and sliced tomatoes, the sliced onion, wine, crushed garlic, chopped rosemary, bay leaf, crushed juniper berries, and seasoning. Cover and cook in the oven for 3–4 hours, or until the meat is tender.

Anchovy Steaks

 02:00 00:10   Serves 4   United States

American	Ingredients	Metric/Imperial
4	Large, tender steaks (sirloin or club [fillet] steaks)	4
	Oil	
1	Clove garlic	1
3 tbsp	Butter	40 g/1½ oz
1–2 tbsp	Anchovy paste	1–1½ tbsp
	A squeeze of lemon juice	

1. Preheat the broiler [grill].
2. Brush the steaks with oil and crushed garlic. Leave for an hour at least, longer if possible, to marinate.
3. Cream the butter until soft. Add the anchovy paste gradually, using more or less paste according to personal taste. Add the lemon juice and ground black pepper. Make into 4 balls or pats. Put in the refrigerator to chill.
4. When the broiler is very hot, put the steaks under and cook for 3–5 minutes on each side, depending on the thickness of the steaks and on personal taste.
5. When ready, put a pat of anchovy butter on each steak and serve at once with broiled tomatoes, French fried potatoes [chips], and a green salad.

Barbecued Herb Steaks

 03:00 00:10   Serves 4   Southwest

American	Ingredients	Metric/Imperial
4 (6–8 oz)	Tender steaks	4 (175–225 g/ 6–8 oz)
	Marinade	
¼ cup	Oil	60 ml/2 fl oz
½ cup	Lemon juice, fresh, frozen or canned	125 ml/4 fl oz
½ cup	Chopped onion	50 g/2 oz
½ tsp	Salt	½ tsp
½ tsp	Celery salt	½ tsp
½ tsp	Pepper	½ tsp
½ tsp	Thyme	½ tsp
½ tsp	Oregano	½ tsp
½ tsp	Rosemary	½ tsp
1	Clove garlic, finely crushed	1

1. Combine all the marinade ingredients.
2. Put the steaks into a shallow pan, pour over the marinade, and leave for 2–3 hours, turning several times.
3. Heat the coals in an outdoor grill until hot, about 30 minutes, or preheat the broiler [grill].
4. Cook on the rack over hot coals, or in the broiler, basting several times with the marinade. Cook as desired—rare, medium rare, or well done. Mushrooms and tomatoes can be cooked on the rack at the same time. Remember to brush the mushrooms frequently with oil or butter.

Filets Mignons Rossini

 00:25

00:55   Serves 8   South

American	Ingredients	Metric/Imperial
2½ lb	Fillet beef (cut into 1–1½ inch thick slices)	1.25 kg/2½ lb
1 tbsp	Shortening (or lard)	1 tbsp
2 tbsp	Chopped onions	1½ tbsp
1 slice	Bacon	1 rasher
½ tbsp	Flour	½ tbsp
1 tsp	Tomato purée	1 tsp
8	Large mushroom caps	8
2 cups	Beef stock (or water and beef cube)	450 ml/¾ pint
¼ cup	Red wine (if available)	60 ml/2 fl oz
1 tsp	Chopped parsley and thyme	1 tsp
1 cup	Butter	225 g/8 oz
1 cup	Cooking oil	250 ml/8 fl oz
8	Slices white bread	8
1 can (8 oz)	Pâté de foie gras	1 tin (225 g/8 oz)

1. Preheat the oven to 350°F/180°C/Gas Mark 4.
2. First make the sauce: Melt the shortening. Add the onion and diced bacon. Cook to golden color slowly. Stir well. Add flour and cook until just turning light brown. Add the tomato purée, chopped mushroom stems, stock, wine, salt, and pepper. Bring to a boil and simmer for 15 minutes. Now add the parsley and thyme and cook a few more minutes. Strain through a fine sieve into a dish ready to serve, and keep warm.
3. Put the mushroom tops in a buttered dish, with a small pat of butter and salt and pepper on each. Cook in the oven for 10 minutes.
4. Cut the bread into slices the same size as the fillets. Heat the oil and add 1 tablespoon [15 g/½ oz] of butter. When foaming, fry the bread until golden brown on both sides. Drain and keep warm.
5. Melt ½ cup [100 g/4 oz] of butter in a large frying pan. When foaming, cook the fillets 4–6 minutes each side, according to taste. (Or brush with melted butter and broil [grill] 5–8 minutes each side.)
6. Place the fillets on the fried bread. Top each with a slice of pâté and a mushroom. Garnish with watercress and serve with French fried potatoes [chips] and a green vegetable.

Filets Mignons Rossini

Shish Kebabs

12:45
00:12

Serves 4

New England

American	Ingredients	Metric/Imperial
2 lb	Lamb, without bone	900 g/2 lb
2	Green peppers, seeded and cut into squares	2
4–6	Small onions	4–6
12	Medium-sized mushroom caps	12
8	Small tomatoes	8
	Marinade	
½ cup	Oil	125 ml/4 fl oz
	Juice of 1 lemon	
1 tsp	Salt	1 tsp
½ tsp	Marjoram	½ tsp
½ tsp	Thyme	½ tsp
½ tsp	Rosemary	½ tsp
¼ tsp	Pepper	¼ tsp
1	Clove garlic, crushed	1
1	Onion, finely chopped	1
1 tbsp	Chopped parsley	1 tbsp

1. Combine all the marinade ingredients.
2. Remove any excess fat from the meat and cut into cubes. Put into a shallow bowl, cover with the marinade, and leave for as long as possible, preferably overnight.
3. Heat the coals in an outdoor grill until hot, about 30 minutes, or preheat the broiler [grill].
4. Thread the skewers with alternate cubes of meat and squares of pepper, onion and mushroom caps, finishing with tomatoes.
5. Brush with melted butter and cook until done, brushing frequently while cooking.

Tenderloin Beef Wellington

00:30
00:45

Serves 4

New England

American	Ingredients	Metric/Imperial
1	Fillet tenderloin beef, 2–2½ lb (900 g–1.25 kg)	1
4–5 tbsp	Oil or shortening	3½–4 tbsp
1	Clove garlic	1
3 tbsp	Butter	40 g/1½ oz
1 tbsp	Mixed herbs	1 tbsp
1	Onion	1
1 cup	Mushrooms	100 g/4 oz
2 tbsp	Brandy	1½ tbsp
1 (1 lb)	Package puff pastry	1 (450 g/1 lb)
1	Egg	1

1. Preheat the oven to 450°F/230°C/Gas Mark 8.
2. Heat the oil or shortening in the oven. Rub the fillet or tenderloin with a cut piece of garlic and season with pepper. Sauté until browned all around. Allow to cool.
3. Melt the butter; cook the finely chopped onion and mushrooms for 5 minutes, until the onion is soft. Add brandy, seasoning, and herbs; allow to cool.
4. Roll out the puff pastry thinly on a floured board to a size that will completely cover the tenderloin. Lay the cooled meat in the center, spoon the mushroom and onion mixture over the top. Brush the edges of the pastry with water. Fold over the top and pinch together to make a pattern. Fold the pastry carefully over the ends to seal. Garnish with leaves made from leftover pastry.
5. Brush the whole surface with beaten egg, to glaze, and bake in the oven for 20–30 minutes or until the pastry is browned. Allow to rest for 15–20 minutes before slicing.
6. Cut in slices to serve.

Sukiyaki

00:25
00:15

Serves 5–6

Pacific Northwest

American	Ingredients	Metric/Imperial
1½ lb	Lean tender steak	675 g/1½ lb
	Oil	
2	Large onions, peeled and sliced very thinly	2
2	Cloves garlic, crushed	2
2	Carrots, peeled and sliced thinly	2
6–8	Leeks, cut into strips	6–8
1 can (8 oz)	Sliced bamboo shoots	1 tin (225 g/8 oz)
1	Small cabbage, very finely shredded	1
1 cup	Sliced mushrooms	100 g/4 oz
	Sauce	
4 tbsp	Soy sauce	3½ tbsp
4 tbsp	Dry sherry	3½ tbsp
2 tsp	Sugar	2 tsp
½ cup	Water	125 ml/4 fl oz

1. Heat all the sauce ingredients together in a small pan.
2. Slice the meat into very thin strips about 1 inch wide and 2 inches long. Heat a little oil in a pan and just sear the meat on both sides.
3. Heat some more oil in a large pan. Add the onions and garlic, then the carrots and leeks, and stir until the vegetables are well coated with the oil and beginning to soften. Add the bamboo shoots, cabbage, and mushrooms; cook for about 2 minutes, stirring all the time.
4. Stir a little of the sauce into the vegetables, arrange the meat on top, and cook until the vegetables are tender, about 8–10 minutes.
5. Serve with hot rice. Put a bowl with a beaten egg in it in front of each guest; dip each mouthful in the beaten egg.

Steak and Pepper Kebabs

| | 12:15 | | |
| 00:15 | Serves 4 | United States | |

American	Ingredients	Metric/Imperial
2 lb	Fillet or tenderloin steak	900 g/2 lb
2	Onions	2
1	Sweet red pepper	1
1	Green pepper	1
4	Mushrooms	4
	Marinade	
3 tbsp	Red wine	2 tbsp
1 tbsp	Oil	1 tbsp
1 tbsp	Lemon juice	1 tbsp
1 tbsp	Soy sauce	1 tbsp
1	Clove garlic, crushed	1
1/8 tsp	Dry mustard	1/8 tsp
	A pinch of ground thyme	
1	Small onion, peeled and chopped	1

1. Combine all the marinade ingredients.
2. Cut the meat into 1½-inch cubes. Pour the marinade over the meat, cover, and refrigerate overnight.
3. Heat the coals in an outdoor grill until hot, about 30 minutes, or preheat the broiler [grill].
4. Peel the onions, cut in halves, and remove the center piece. Cut the peppers in halves, remove the seeds and membrane, and cut into 1½-inch squares.
5. Place the meat and vegetables on 4 skewers and put a mushroom on the end of each.
6. Brush well with the marinade and cook over the hot coals, brushing frequently.
7. Serve with Mustard Dip (see Index) and a salad.

Steak and Kidney Pie

| | 01:00 | | |
| 02:00 | Serves 4–5 | Midwest  | |

American	Ingredients	Metric/Imperial
1½ lb	Round steak [beef skirt]	675 g/1½ lb
6 oz	Ox kidney	175 g/6 oz
¼ cup	Flour	25 g/1 oz
2	Onions, peeled and finely chopped	2
	Beef stock or water	
	Flaky pastry (see Index)	
	Egg or milk for glazing	

1. Preheat the oven to 325°F/160°C/Gas Mark 3.
2. Cut the steak into strips and pound lightly. Put a piece of kidney on each strip and roll up.
3. Mix some salt and pepper with the flour, and dredge the meat rolls.

4. Put the meat into a baking dish with the onion and sprinkle any remaining flour on top. Add enough stock or water to half fill the dish, cover with foil, and cook about 1½ hours. Set aside to get quite cold.
5. Reset the oven to 450°F/230°C/Gas Mark 8. Roll out the pastry thinly and cover the pie, pressing the edges of the pastry well down. Make a hole in the center and garnish as desired with leaves cut from the pastry trimmings. Brush with beaten egg or milk and bake for about 30 minutes.

Beef Stroganoff

Beef Stroganoff

| | 00:20 | | |
| 00:15 | Serves 4 | New England | |

American	Ingredients	Metric/Imperial
1–1½ lb	Beef tenderloin [fillet]	450–675 g/ 1–1½ lb
1–2	Onions	1–2
8–10	Medium-sized mushrooms	8–10
4–5 tbsp	Butter	50–65 g/ 2–2½ oz
1 cup	Sour cream	250 ml/8 fl oz
	A pinch of grated nutmeg	

1. Cut the beef tenderloin into strips about 2½ inches long and ½ inch thick. Slice the onions and mushrooms finely. Melt 2 tablespoons [25 g/1 oz] of butter in a frying pan and cook the onions slowly until they are golden brown. Remove from the pan and keep warm. Add a little more butter. Cook the mushrooms for about 5 minutes and add them to the onions.
2. Melt the remaining butter. When foaming, put in about half the strips of steak and sauté quickly for about 3 minutes, until they are brown on all sides. Remove and repeat with the remaining steak.
3. Place all the meat and vegetables in the pan, shake over heat; add salt, pepper, and nutmeg. Lastly, add the sour cream; heat until it nearly boils and serve immediately with plain boiled rice.

Peppered Steaks

Pepper Steaks

	00:05	Serves 4	New England
	00:15		

American	Ingredients	Metric/Imperial
4	Large sirloin steaks (1 inch thick)	4
2 tbsp	Peppercorns	1½ tbsp
3–4 tbsp	Oil	2–3½ tbsp
¼ cup	Butter	50 g/2 oz
½ cup	White wine	125 ml/4 fl oz
2 tbsp	Brandy (optional)	1½ tbsp
	A little lemon juice	

1. Preheat the broiler [grill].
2. Press the crushed pepper well into the steaks, using a wooden spoon.
3. Heat the oil in a pan and add half the butter. When foaming, sauté the steaks for 4–6 minutes on each side or longer if preferred. Add the remaining butter, if needed. Remove to a heated dish to keep warm.
4. Add the wine and brandy to the juices in the pan; add the lemon juice. Bring to a boil, season with salt and pepper, and pour over the steaks. Serve at once. (The pepper may be scraped off before adding the sauce, if preferred.)

Peppered Steaks

	02:30	Serves 4	South
	00:15		

American	Ingredients	Metric/Imperial
4	Fillet or tenderloin steaks (about 200–225 g/7–8 oz each)	4
3 tbsp	Oil	2 tbsp
1 tbsp	Lemon juice	1 tbsp
4 tbsp	Cracked [crushed] peppercorns	3½ tbsp
	Barbecue Baste (see Index)	

1. Marinate the steaks in the oil and lemon juice for at least 2 hours.
2. Heat the coals in an outdor grill until hot, about 30 minutes, or preheat the broiler [grill].
3. Drain the steaks and press the crushed pepper into both sides.
4. Make several slashes around the steaks to prevent them curling up. Brush with barbecue baste, and put on the rack above the glowing coals. Baste and turn once while cooking.
5. Serve with Barbecue Sauce (see Index), a crisp salad and baked potatoes.

Teriyaki Steak

	03:30	Serves 6	Pacific Northwest
	00:10		

American	Ingredients	Metric/Imperial
2½–3 lb	Sirloin steak, cut about ½ inch thick	1.25 kg/2½–3 lb
1 cup	Soy sauce	250 ml/8 fl oz
5 tbsp	Dry sherry	4 tbsp
4 tbsp	Brown [demerara] sugar	3½ tbsp
1½ tsp	Ground ginger	1½ tsp
2 tsp	Grated onion	2 tsp
1	Clove garlic, crushed	1
18	Chunks canned pineapple	18
18	Small mushroom caps	18
2 tbsp	Pineapple juice	1½ tbsp
1 tbsp	Cornstarch [cornflour]	1 tbsp

1. Cut the steak into 1-inch squares.
2. Mix the soy sauce, sherry, sugar, ginger, onion, and garlic together. Put in the meat and marinate for 3 hours.
3. Heat the coals in an outdoor grill until hot, about 30 minutes, or preheat the broiler [grill].
4. Place the steak, pineapple, and mushrooms on the skewers, starting and finishing with a piece of meat. Cook for about 4–5 minutes or until the meat is cooked to your taste, turning once or twice to brown evenly.
5. Mix the pineapple juice slowly into the cornstarch, add the marinade, and cook, stirring constantly until the sauce thickens. Serve with the kebabs.

Steak and Onions

	00:10	Serves 4	New England 
	00:35		

American	Ingredients	Metric/Imperial
4	Broiling [grilling] steaks about 1½ inches thick	4
6–8	Medium onions	6–8
3–4 tbsp	Oil	2–3½ tbsp
½ tsp	Sugar	½ tsp
3–4 tbsp	Butter	40–50 g/ 1½–2 oz
3–4 tbsp	Chopped parsley	2–3½ tbsp

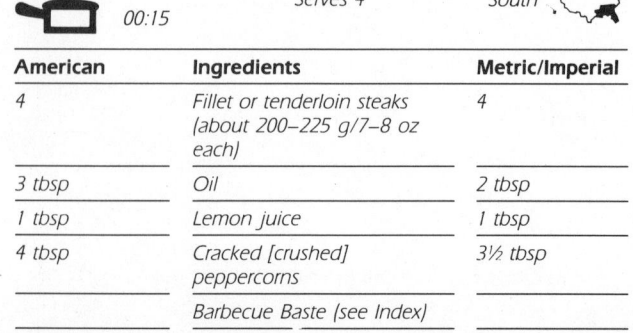

Teriyaki Steak

1. Preheat the broiler [grill].

2. Heat the oil in a pan and add the thinly sliced onions. Cover the pan and cook over moderate heat for 6 minutes; then remove the lid, and add salt, pepper, and sugar. Continue cooking, stirring constantly until the onions are crisp and brown, about 5 minutes. Drain and keep warm.

3. When the broiler is hot and while the onions are cooking, brush the steaks with oil. Put under the broiler, allowing 8–12 minutes on each side if liked rare, or 15–18 minutes if liked medium. Brush frequently with oil. Season when partly cooked.

4. Arrange on a hot serving dish. Surround with onions, put a pat of butter rolled in parsley on each steak, and serve at once.

Steak and Ham Rolls

 00:40 / 00:20   Serves 6   Southwest

American	Ingredients	Metric/Imperial
6	Fillets beef, cut about ¾ inch thick	6
6	Slices cooked ham	6
1	Egg	1
½ cup	Dry bread crumbs	25 g/1 oz
1½ tsp	Salt	1½ tsp
½ tsp	Freshly ground black pepper	½ tsp
3 tbsp	Chopped parsley	2 tbsp
2	Cloves garlic, minced	2
¼ cup	Butter or margarine	50 g/2 oz

1. Heat the coals in an outdoor grill until hot, about 30 minutes, or preheat the broiler [grill].

2. Pound the fillets as thinly as possible. Place a slice of ham over each and roll up. Fasten with toothpicks.

3. Dip in beaten egg, then in a mixture of bread crumbs, salt, pepper, parsley, and garlic.

4. Heat the butter in the pan, put in the meat rolls, and grill, shaking the pan gently to get even browning.

5. Serve with Barbecue Sauce (see Index).

Barbecued Sirloin Steak

 00:35 / 00:20   Serves 4   Southwest

American	Ingredients	Metric/Imperial
2 lb	Sirloin, porterhouse, or T-bone steaks, 1½–2 inches thick	900 g/2 lb
	Parsley Butter	
2 tbsp	Minced parsley	1½ tbsp
2 tsp	Lemon juice	2 tsp
4 tbsp	Butter	50 g/2 oz

1. Heat the coals in an outdoor grill until hot, about 30 minutes, or preheat the broiler [grill]. The rack should be about 6 inches above the top of the coals.

2. Trim some of the fat from the meat and use this fat to rub over the hot rack so that the steaks will not stick. (If you spear the piece of fat with a fork, there is no danger of burned fingers.)

3. Put the steaks on the rack and broil [grill] on one side until well browned; this will probably take about 10–15 minutes. Turn over with tongs and sprinkle the browned side with salt and pepper. (If the fire blazes up from the meat drippings, extinguish the flames with a few drops of water.) Continue broiling until the steaks are cooked as desired, then serve with a pat of butter on each steak.

Monday's Dinner

00:15
00:35   Serves 6–7   Mid Atlantic

American	Ingredients	Metric/Imperial
3–4 tbsp	Butter	40-50 g/1½–2 oz
1 tbsp	Oil	1 tbsp
2	Medium onions, peeled and finely chopped	2
1 cup	Chopped cooked meat	175 g/6 oz
1 small can (6 oz)	Tomato or mushroom soup	1 small tin (175 g/6 oz)
1 tbsp	Finely chopped parsley	1 tbsp
½	Bay leaf	½
1 cup	Cooked vegetables (peas, carrots, potatoes, etc.)	100 g/4 oz
1 cup	Stock (or gravy)	250 ml/8 fl oz
1 package (7–8 oz)	Macaroni	1 package (200-225 g/7–8 oz)
	Grated cheese (optional)	

1. Heat 2 tablespoons [25 g/1 oz] of the butter and the oil in a saucepan, put in the onions, and sauté for a few minutes. Add the meat, and stir for about 5 minutes. Add the soup, parsley, and ½ bay leaf. Cover and simmer for 15 minutes.
2. Add the vegetables and the stock or gravy. Heat through, adjust the seasoning to taste, and remove the bay leaf.
3. Cook the macaroni; drain and toss in 1–2 tablespoons [15–25 g/½–1 oz] of butter. Turn onto a large platter, and pour the meat and vegetable mixture on top.
4. If you wish to sprinkle cheese on top, use a little Parmesan or sharp Cheddar.

Meat Croquettes

01:15
00:15   Serves 4   Midwest

American	Ingredients	Metric/Imperial
2 tbsp	Butter	25 g/1 oz
2 tbsp	Flour	1½ tbsp
¾ cup	Milk	175 ml/6 fl oz
2 tbsp	Grated cheese	1½ tbsp
2–2½ cups	Chopped cooked meat	350–425 g/12–15 oz
1	Egg yolk	1
1 tbsp	Chopped parsley	1 tbsp
½ tsp	Mixed herbs	½ tsp
	Bread crumbs	
	Oil for frying	

1. Make a thick roux with the butter, flour and scalded milk. Add seasoning and grated cheese. Let cool a little.
2. Combine the meat, egg yolk, and herbs with the sauce; add extra seasoning as required, mix well, and chill.
3. Divide into 8 portions, shape into croquettes, and coat well with bread crumbs. Chill again if convenient. Fry in hot oil until brown and crisp.

Steak and Mushroom Kebabs

02:20
00:15   Serves 4   United States

American	Ingredients	Metric/Imperial
1 lb	Tenderloin [fillet] steak	450 g/1 lb
12	Small mushroom caps	12
½ cup	Red wine	125 ml/4 fl oz
½ cup	Corn oil	125 ml/4 fl oz
1 tsp	Worcestershire sauce	1 tsp
1	Clove garlic, crushed	1
2 tbsp	Tomato ketchup	1½ tbsp
1 tsp	Sugar	1 tsp
½ tsp	Salt	½ tsp
1 tbsp	Vinegar	1 tbsp
	A pinch of dried marjoram	
	A pinch of dried rosemary	

1. Heat the coals in an outdoor grill until hot, about 30 minutes, or preheat the broiler [grill].
2. Cut the steak into small cubes.
3. Mix all the other ingredients together in a bowl; add the steak and marinate for at least 2 hours.
4. Alternate the steak and mushrooms on skewers, and cook until the meat is tender, about 15 minutes. Baste frequently with the marinade.

Meat Pie with Biscuit Topping

00:20
00:40   Serves 5–6   South

American	Ingredients	Metric/Imperial
	Biscuit Topping	
1 cup	All-purpose [plain] flour	100 g/4 oz
1½ tsp	Baking powder	1½ tsp
¼ tsp	Salt	¼ tsp
5 tbsp	Milk	4 tbsp
¼ cup	Shortening	50 g/2 oz
	Filling	
2 tbsp	Cooking fat	1½ tbsp
¼ cup	Finely chopped onion	25 g/1 oz
2 tbsp	Chopped green pepper	1½ tbsp
2 cups	Diced cooked meat	350 g/12 oz
2 cups	Diced cooked vegetables (peas, carrots, corn, etc.)	225 g/8 oz
1½–2 cups	Gravy or stock	350–450 ml/12 fl oz–¾ pint
1 tsp	Mixed herbs	1 tsp

1. Preheat the oven to 425°F/220°C/Gas Mark 7.
2. Make the biscuit dough in the usual way, and roll it out about ¼ inch thick, large enough to cover the baking dish.

3. Heat the fat in a small frying pan, and sauté the onion and green pepper for 5 minutes.
4. Put the meat and vegetables into a baking dish; stir in the onion and green pepper. Add seasoning to taste, herbs, and the gravy. Put into the oven for 15 minutes. Then remove and cover with the biscuit dough. Cut 2–3 slits in the top to allow the steam to escape.
5. Return to the oven, and cook for about 20 minutes or until the biscuit topping is golden brown.
6. Serve with a green salad.

Hamburgers 1

 00:35
00:10   Serves 4   Mid Atlantic

American	Ingredients	Metric/Imperial
1 lb	Ground [minced] beef	450 g/1 lb
1 tsp	Salt	1 tsp
¼ tsp	Freshly ground black pepper	¼ tsp
1 tsp	Worcestershire sauce	1 tsp
1 tbsp	Minced or very finely chopped onion	1 tbsp
¼ cup	Water or stock	60 ml/2 fl oz
4–6	Hamburger buns (optional)	4–6

1. Heat the coals on an outdoor grill until hot, about 30 minutes, or preheat the broiler [grill].
2. Combine all the ingredients and shape into patties.
3. Brush with Barbecue Baste (see Index) and cook for about 6 minutes on one side; then turn, baste again, and cook another 4–5 minutes.

Hamburgers 2

 00:45
00:10   Serves 2   Midwest

American	Ingredients	Metric/Imperial
1	Potato	1
1	Small onion	1
1 tbsp	Chopped parsley	1 tbsp
½ lb	Ground [minced] beef	225 g/½ lb
¼ tsp	Dried mixed herbs	¼ tsp
	Dry bread crumbs	

1. Heat the coals in an outdoor grill until hot, about 30 minutes, or preheat the broiler [grill].
2. Peel and grate the potato and onion. Combine with all the other ingredients except the bread crumbs. Mix well and shape into 4 patties.
3. Roll in bread crumbs. Brush with Barbecue Baste (see Index) and cook for 10–15 minutes, turning once.
4. Variation: Cook some diced mushrooms and bacon in a pan while the hamburgers are cooking and pile on top of them before serving.

Steak and Tomato Pudding

Steak and Tomato Pudding

00:30
03:30   Serves 6   Mid Atlantic

American	Ingredients	Metric/Imperial
	Suet Pastry	
2 cups	All-purpose [plain] flour	225 g/8 oz
½ tsp	Salt	½ tsp
1 cup	Shredded suet	225 g/8 oz
½ cup	Cold water	125 ml/4 fl oz
	Filling	
1½ lb	Chuck steak [stewing steak]	675 g/1½ lb
2 tbsp	Flour	1½ tbsp
2	Onions, peeled and sliced thinly	2
1 lb	Tomatoes, peeled, quartered and seeded	450 g/1 lb
½ tsp	Oregano	½ tsp
1 tbsp	Worcestershire sauce	1 tbsp

1. To make the crust: Combine the flour, salt, and suet and mix to an elastic dough with the cold water. Cut off a piece for the top, roll out the remainder, and line a 2½-pint [2-pint] bowl.
2. Cut the meat into 1-inch cubes, and toss in flour to which some salt and pepper has been added. Arrange the meat, onions, and tomatoes in layers in the bowl, sprinkling each layer with seasoning and oregano. Mix the Worcestershire sauce with a little water and pour over the meat.
3. Roll out the remaining pastry into a circle, dampen the edges, and put on top, pressing the edges well together. Cover loosely with foil, and steam for 3–3½ hours.
4. Serve with boiled potatoes and a green vegetable.

Beef Roll

Beef Roll

 00:30 / 00:40   Serves 6   United States

American	Ingredients	Metric/Imperial
	Filling	
1 tbsp	Vegetable oil	1 tbsp
1 lb	Ground [minced] beef	450 g/1 lb
1	Onion, peeled and chopped	1
½ cup	Chopped mushrooms	50 g/2 oz
1 tsp	Salt	1 tsp
¼ tsp	Freshly ground black pepper	¼ tsp
¼ tsp	Dry mustard	¼ tsp
¼ cup	Chopped olives	25 g/1 oz
2 tbsp	Finely chopped parsley	1½ tbsp
1¼ cups	Beef gravy	300 ml/½ pint
	Pastry	
1¾ cups	All-purpose [plain] flour	200 g/7 oz
1 tsp	Salt	1 tsp
2½ tsp	Baking powder	2½ tsp
3 tbsp	Finely chopped parsley	2 tbsp
5 tbsp	Shortening	4 tbsp
⅔ cup	Milk	150 ml/¼ pint

1. Preheat the oven to 400°F/200°C/Gas Mark 6.
2. Heat the oil in a frying pan. Add the meat, onion, and mushrooms; cook, stirring frequently, until the meat and onion are brown. Stir in all the dry ingredients, the olives, parsley, and enough of the gravy to moisten (about ¼ cup/60 ml/2 fl oz). Stir all together over low heat for 5 minutes, then let cool while making the pastry.
3. Sift the flour, salt, and baking powder into a bowl; add the parsley. Cut in the shortening until the mixture looks like bread crumbs. Add enough milk to make a fairly soft dough. Turn onto a floured surface and knead lightly.
4. Roll into an oblong shape about 10 × 14 inches. Spread the meat mixture over the dough to within ½ inch of the edges. Dampen the edges of the pastry and roll up like a jelly roll, pressing the edges well together.
5. Place on a greased baking sheet and bake for about 30 minutes. Serve hot, cut into slices, with the remaining gravy, or cold with salad.

Beef Pie with Potato Crust

00:30 / 00:30   Serves 5–6   Midwest

American	Ingredients	Metric/Imperial
¼ cup	Olive oil	60 ml/2 fl oz
2–3	Onions, peeled and chopped	2–3
1½ lb	Ground [minced] beef	675 g/1½ lb
1 tsp	Salt	1 tsp
⅛ tsp	Tabasco	⅛ tsp
2 tbsp	Finely chopped parsley	1½ tbsp
½ cup	Seedless raisins	50 g/2 oz
¾ cup	Sliced green olives	75 g/3 oz
½ cup	Beef stock	125 ml/4 fl oz
3	Hard-boiled eggs, sliced	3
2 cups	Mashed potatoes	450 g/1 lb
1 tbsp	Butter or margarine	15 g/½ oz
1	Egg	1
	Milk	

1. Preheat the oven to 400°F/200°C/Gas Mark 6.
2. Heat the oil in a frying pan; sauté the onion until transparent. Then add the beef and cook until browned. Add salt, tabasco, parsley, raisins, and olives. Stir in the stock and mix well.
3. Put half the meat mixture into a buttered baking dish, arrange the slices of egg on top, and cover with the rest of the meat.
4. Beat the potatoes, butter, and egg until light and fluffy; spread over the meat. Ridge the top with a fork, brush with milk, and bake 15–20 minutes until the crust is well browned.

Beef Hedgehog

00:35 / 01:45   Serves 4–6   Midwest

American	Ingredients	Metric/Imperial
1 lb	Ground [minced] beef	450 g/1 lb
½ lb	Ham (or bacon)	225 g/8 oz
5–7 tbsp	Oil	4–6 tbsp
1	Small onion	1
2 tbsp	Flour	1½ tbsp
1 cup	Strong beef stock (or water and cube)	250 ml/8 fl oz
¾ cup	Fresh bread crumbs	40 g/1½ oz
1	Egg	1
2 tbsp	Tomato ketchup	1½ tbsp
2 tbsp	Chopped mixed herbs, mainly parsley	1½ tbsp
2 lb	Potatoes	900 g/2 lb
2 tbsp	Butter (or margarine)	25 g/1 oz
½ cup	Milk	125 ml/4 fl oz
12	Small button mushrooms	12
12	Pickling onions	12

1. Preheat the oven to 375°F/190°C/Gas Mark 5.
2. Mix the ground beef and chopped ham in a bowl.
3. Heat 3–4 tablespoons [2–3½ tbsp] of the oil in a fairly large pan. Cook the finely chopped onion with the lid on the pan for 5 minutes. (If using bacon, chop and cook for a few minutes before adding the beef). Add the beef and ham. Mix in the flour and blend well. Add the stock and bring to a boil, stirring all the time. Cook for a minute or two. Then cool slightly. Add the bread crumbs, then the beaten egg and sauce. Mix well, adding the ketchup, herbs, and seasoning to taste.
4. Butter a loaf tin or oval baking dish well and turn the meat mixture into it. Cover with a lid or foil, and bake for about 1 hour.
5. Peel and boil the potatoes; drain and dry before mashing. Beat in the butter and enough milk to make a dryish mixture. Season well and keep warm.
6. Heat 2–3 tablespoons [1½–2 tbsp] of oil and cook the baby onions for about 10 minutes, sprinkling with a little sugar to help browning. Remove and keep warm. Add the button mushrooms to the pan and cook these for 3–4 minutes.
7. When the beef roll is cooked, turn onto an ovenproof dish, reserving any juice to make gravy. Coat the meat roll all over with an even layer of mashed potato, and mark with a fork. Press the onions and mushrooms into the potato in rows to represent the hedgehog's spines. Then return the roll to the oven for 15 minutes or until golden brown. (If in a hurry, this can be done more quickly under the broiler/grill.)

Beef in Batter

 00:45 / 00:35   Serves 5–6   Midwest

American	Ingredients	Metric/Imperial
	Batter	
1 cup	All-purpose [plain] flour	100 g/4 oz
½ tsp	Salt	½ tsp
⅛ tsp	Nutmeg	⅛ tsp
	A pinch of cayenne pepper	
2	Eggs	2
1 cup	Milk	250 ml/8 fl oz
	Filling	
1½ lb	Ground [minced] beef	675 g/1½ lb
1½ tsp	Salt	1½ tsp
½ tsp	Black pepper	½ tsp
3 tbsp	Grated or finely chopped onion	2 tbsp
1 tbsp	Finely chopped parsley	1 tbsp
2 tbsp	Corn oil	1½ tbsp

1. Preheat the oven to 425°F/220°C/Gas Mark 7.
2. Sift the flour, salt, nutmeg, and cayenne into a bowl. Gradually add the beaten eggs and milk and beat until the mixture is smooth. Chill for at least ½ hour, then beat again until frothy.
3. Mix the beef with seasonings, onions, and parsley.
4. Put the oil into a shallow baking pan about 8 × 12 inches and heat in the oven. Pour in half the batter, put in the meat, and pour the remaining batter on top.
5. Bake for 15 minutes. Then reduce the heat to 350°F/180°C/Gas Mark 4 and cook for 20 more minutes, when the batter should be well puffed up and brown. Serve with tomato or mushroom sauce.

Pizza Hamburgers

Pizza Hamburgers

 00:40 / 00:12   Serves 8   United States

American	Ingredients	Metric/Imperial
1½ lb	Ground [minced] beef	675 g/1½ lb
¼ cup	Grated Parmesan cheese	25 g/1 oz
¼ cup	Finely chopped onion	25 g/1 oz
¼ cup	Chopped stuffed olives	25 g/1 oz
1 tsp	Oregano	1 tsp
1 can (8 oz)	Tomato purée	1 small tin (225 g/8 oz)
8	Thin slices Bel Paese cheese (or Mozzarella)	8
4	Tomatoes	4
8	Hamburger buns, split and toasted	8

1. Heat the coals in an outdoor grill until hot, about 30 minutes, or preheat the broiler [grill].
2. Mix the meat, grated cheese, onion, olives, oregano, and tomato purée together. Season with salt and black pepper. Shape into 8 patties.
3. Broil [grill] over medium heat for about 10 minutes. Then turn and place a slice of cheese and half a tomato on each.
4. Cook a few minutes longer until the cheese melts and the hamburgers are cooked.
5. Serve in the hamburger buns.

Bobotee

Bobotee

00:25
00:35
Serves 8
South

American	Ingredients	Metric/Imperial
2 lb	Ground [minced] beef	900 g/2 lb
2	Thick slices white bread	2
1 cup	Milk	250 ml/8 fl oz
3	Onions	3
3 tbsp	Curry powder (or paste)	2 tbsp
½ tbsp	Sugar	½ tbsp
	Juice of a lemon	
10	Almonds	10
3	Eggs	3
1 tbsp	Butter	15 g/½ oz
¼ cup	Strong beef stock	60 ml/2 fl oz
2	Bay leaves	2
½ cup	Chopped parsley	25 g/1 oz

1. Preheat the oven to 350°F/180°C/Gas Mark 4.
2. Grind the meat fairly coarsely. Soak the bread in some of the milk; squeeze until dry but save the milk.
3. Fry the chopped onions in butter. Add curry powder or paste, and fry for another minute. Add the meat, sugar, salt, lemon juice, and slivered almonds. Beat the eggs, and add half to the meat mixture. Whisk the other half into the milk. Now mix the soaked bread into the meat mixture thoroughly. Add the stock.
4. Put the meat mixture into a buttered ovenproof dish and smooth it on top. Pour the egg and milk mixture over the meat and add 2 bay leaves. Cook in the oven for 30 minutes, or until set.
5. Remove from the oven. Garnish the top with chopped parsley and serve with plain boiled rice and chutney.

Deviled Burgers

00:40
00:15
Serves 4
United States

American	Ingredients	Metric/Imperial
1 lb	Ground [minced] beef	450 g/1 lb
1	Egg	1
¼ cup	Chili sauce	60 ml/2 fl oz
1 tsp	Perpared mustard	1 tsp
1 tsp	Horseradish cream	1 tsp
1 tsp	Worcestershire sauce	1 tsp
4	Hamburger buns	4

1. Heat the coals in an outdoor grill until hot, about 30 minutes, or preheat the broiler [grill].
2. Mix all the ingredients for the burgers together, season with salt and just a dash of pepper, and shape into 4 patties.
3. Broil [grill] for 10 minutes. Then turn and cook 5–7 minutes more.
4. Split the buns, and toast them on the hot coals during the last few minutes, while the meat is cooking. Then fill them with the burgers.

Stuffed Squash

00:15
01:00
Serves 4–6
South

American	Ingredients	Metric/Imperial
¾ lb	Chopped cooked meat	350 g/12 oz
1	Summer squash [marrow] about 2 lb [900 g]	1
3 tbsp	Oil	2 tbsp
1	Onion	1
1 cup	Chopped mushrooms	100 g/4 oz
1 tbsp	Flour	1 tbsp
1 cup	Gravy (or tomato sauce)	250 ml/8 fl oz
1 tbsp	Soy or Worcestershire sauce	1 tbsp
1 tbsp	Mixed herbs	1 tbsp
¼ cup	Leftover peas, beans, carrots, corn or rice	25 g/1 oz
3 tbsp	Dried white bread crumbs	2 tbsp
	A little melted butter	
2 tbsp	Chopped parsley	1½ tbsp

1. Preheat the oven to 375°F/190°C/Gas Mark 5.
2. Heat the oil and cook chopped onion until golden brown. Then add the chopped meat and mushrooms; cook for 2 minutes. Sprinkle with flour and mix in. Add enough gravy (or tomato sauce) to moisten, but do not make too soft. Add soy or Worcestershire sauce, mixed herbs, and vegetables or rice.
3. Cut the squash in half lengthwise and remove the seeds, or cut into 1½-inch thick rings and remove seeds. Boil the squash for 5 minutes in salted water, and drain. Put in a buttered ovenproof dish and fill with the meat mixture.
4. Sprinkle with dried white bread crumbs. Pour a little melted butter over the squash. Pour the remaining gravy around the squash. Cook in the oven for about 35–50 minutes, according to the thickness of the squash. Test with a skewer. When tender, sprinkle with chopped parsley.

Cheeseburgers

00:15
00:20   Serves 4   United States

American	Ingredients	Metric/Imperial
1 lb	Ground [minced] round steak	450 g/1 lb
1	Onion	1
2 tbsp	Oil	1½ tbsp
½ cup	Mushrooms	50 g/2 oz
1 tsp	Mixed herbs	1 tsp
2 tsp	Chutney	2 tsp
4	Slices processed cheese, cut in half	4
8	Hamburger buns	8

1. Preheat the broiler [grill].
2. Cook the chopped onion in hot oil until soft for about 4 minutes. Add the chopped mushrooms; cook for another 2–3 minutes. Add the steak, herbs, chutney, and seasoning; mix well.
3. Divide into 8 round cakes, brush with oil, and broil [grill] for 5–6 minutes on each side.
4. Put a slice of cheese on top of each beefburger, and broil for another 2 minutes.
5. Put into slit-open buns and eat at once.

Beef and Macaroni Stew

00:15
00:40   Serves 4   New England

American	Ingredients	Metric/Imperial
1 lb	Ground [minced] beef	450 g/1 lb
1 tbsp	Butter or oil	15 g/½ oz
½ cup	Chopped onion	50 g/2 oz
1	Clove garlic	1
1	Small green pepper	1
1 large can (20 oz)	Tomatoes	1 large tin (575 g/20 oz)
1 cup	Uncooked macaroni	225 g/8 oz
2 tbsp	Chopped parsley and thyme	1½ tbsp
2 tsp	Salt	2 tsp
¼ tsp	Pepper	¼ tsp
½–¾ cup	Stock or water	125–175 ml/ 4–6 fl oz

1. Melt the butter or oil. Add the meat and brown gently all over for about 10 minutes. Add the onion, garlic, chopped pepper, tomatoes, macaroni (broken into small pieces), seasoning, and half the herbs and stock.
2. Mix in well and cook in a covered pan, stirring occasionally, for about 20–30 minutes, until the macaroni is soft.
3. Sprinkle the remaining herbs on top and serve.

Chili Con Carne

Chili Con Carne

00:15
01:30   Serves 4–5   Southwest

American	Ingredients	Metric/Imperial
2 tbsp	Vegetable oil	1½ tbsp
½ cup	Thinly sliced onion	50 g/2 oz
½ cup	Diced green pepper	50 g/2 oz
1	Clove garlic, crushed	1
¾ lb	Ground [minced] beef	350 g/12 oz
¾ cup	Boiling water	175 ml/6 fl oz
1 can (about 20 oz)	Peeled tomatoes	1 tin (about 575 g/20 oz
1–2 tbsp	Chili powder (according to taste)	1–1½ tbsp
⅛ tsp	Paprika	⅛ tsp
2 cups	Canned kidney beans	450 g/1 lb

1. Heat the oil in a saucepan; cook the onion, green pepper, and garlic for about 10 minutes.
2. Add the meat, increase the heat, and stir until the meat has browned.
3. Add the water, tomatoes, chili powder, paprika, and a little salt. Cover and cook over low heat for about 45 minutes.
4. Add the beans, cook for 30 minutes longer, and adjust the seasoning to taste before serving.

Mexican Beef Pie

Mexican Beef Pie

| | 00:45 | Serves 5–6 | Southwest |
| | 01:05 | | |

American	Ingredients	Metric/Imperial
	Pastry for a 9-inch 2-crust Pie (see Index)	
2 tbsp	Vegetable oil	1½ tbsp
½ cup	Chopped onion	50 g/2 oz
½ cup	Chopped green pepper	50 g/2 oz
1 lb	Ground [minced] beef	450 g/1 lb
1 tsp	Salt	1 tsp
¼ tsp	Freshly ground black pepper	¼ tsp
1 tbsp	Chili powder	1 tbsp
1 can (about 8 oz)	Tomato sauce	1 tin (about 225 g/8 oz)
½ cup	Sliced stuffed olives	50 g/2 oz

1. Preheat the oven to 400°F/200°C/Gas Mark 6.
2. Line a 9-inch pie plate with half the pastry.
3. Heat the oil in a frying pan; sauté the onion and green pepper for 5 minutes. Add the beef and cook until browned, stirring frequently.
4. Add the seasonings and tomato sauce and cook over low heat for 15 minutes. Let cool. Add the olives, then turn the mixture into the pastry shell.
5. Roll out the remaining pastry and cut into thin strips. Arrange over the meat in a lattice pattern.
6. Bake for 35–40 minutes, or until the pastry is well browned.

Beef with Eggplant

| | 00:45 | Serves 4–6 | Midwest |
| | 00:50 | | |

American	Ingredients	Metric/Imperial
2	Large eggplants [aubergines], peeled and cut into ¼-inch slices	2
1 tbsp	Oil	1 tbsp
1	Onion, peeled and finely chopped	1
½ lb	Ground [minced] beef	225 g/8 oz
	A pinch of thyme	
1	Large tomato, peeled, seeded and chopped	1
	Cracker crumbs	
1	Egg	1
½ cup	Milk	125 ml/4 fl oz
¼ cup	Grated cheese	25 g/1 oz
	Chopped parsley	

1. Preheat the oven to 350°F/180°C/Gas Mark 4.
2. Put the slices of eggplant into a colander, sprinkle with salt, and let stand for 30 minutes. Drain the liquid from the eggplant.
3. Heat the oil in a frying pan; add the onion and sauté until just beginning to brown. Add the meat and cook together, stirring, until the meat has browned. Season with salt, pepper, and a pinch of thyme. Add the tomato.
4. Rinse and dry the eggplant; sauté it in 4 tablespoons [3½ tbsp] heated oil until golden brown. Cover the bottom of a greased casserole with a thin layer of cracker crumbs, and arrange a layer of eggplant slices on top.
5. Separate the egg. Beat the white until stiff, and fold it into the meat mixture with 2 teaspoons of cracker crumbs. Adjust the seasoning to taste. Arrange a layer of the meat mixture over the eggplant, and repeat the layers, finishing with slices of eggplant.
6. Combine the egg yolk, milk, and cheese, and pour into the casserole. Cook for 30 minutes, and sprinkle with parsley before serving.

Filled Green Peppers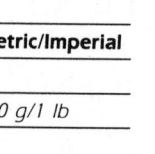

| | 00:20 | Serves 6 | New England |
| | 00:25 | | |

American	Ingredients	Metric/Imperial
6	Green peppers	6
1 lb	Ground [minced] beef	450 g/1 lb
	Margarine or oil for frying	
1	Whole garlic, peeled and chopped	1
	Salt	
	Pepper	
1 can (8 oz)	Crushed tomatoes	1 tin (225 g/8 oz)
2–3 tsp	Mixed herbs (oregano, basil, and chervil)	2–3 tsp

1. Boil the green peppers in salted, boiling water for 10 minutes. Cut a lid off each pepper and let the peppers drain. Remove the seeds.
2. Brown the ground beef and garlic cloves in margarine for about 10 minutes. Season with salt and pepper, and pour the mixture into a pot with the crushed tomatoes. Simmer for 5 minutes. Season by adding oregano, basil, and chervil, according to your taste.
3. Serve with boiled potatoes or rice.

Corn Rolls

Corn Rolls

 00:30
00:45 | Serves 4 | Southwest

American	Ingredients	Metric/Imperial
¾ lb	Ground [minced] chuck steak	350 g/12 oz
1	Large onion, chopped	1
1 (14-oz)	Can crushed tomatoes	1 (400 g/14 oz)
3–4 tbsp	Tomato purée	2–3½ tbsp
6–8	Fresh corn cobs	6–8
1	Green pepper, chopped	1
	Herb salt	
	Black pepper	
2 cups	Beef stock	450 ml/¾ pint

1. Place the ground beef and onion in an ungreased pan; brown. Add the crushed tomatoes and tomato paste and let simmer for 25 minutes, stirring occasionally.
2. Shuck the corn, but save husks. Scrape the corn from the cob and add it to the ground beef mixture. Cut the pepper into small bits and add. Season and let simmer a few minutes.
3. Rinse the corn husks. You'll need several for each roll. Place a spoonful of the ground beef mixture in the center of a husk. Roll into a tight package and fasten with a toothpick. Place the corn rolls together in a shallow pan. Pour boiling stock over the rolls. Cover and simmer for 15 minutes. Turn and baste after 7 minutes.

Beef and Tomato Gratin

 00:15
01:10 | Serves 4–5 | Midwest

American	Ingredients	Metric/Imperial
2 tbsp	Bacon or other fat	1½ tbsp
2	Large onions	2
1 lb	Ground [minced] beef	450 g/1 lb
1 tbsp	Finely chopped parsley	1 tbsp
	A pinch of rosemary	
1½ lb	Tomatoes, peeled, seeded, and chopped	675 g/1½ lb
1 tbsp	Worcestershire sauce	1 tbsp
1 tbsp	Water	1 tbsp
½ cup	Grated cheese	50 g/2 oz
3 tbsp	Dry bread crumbs	2 tbsp
1 tbsp	Butter	15 g/½ oz

1. Preheat the oven to 375°F/190°C/Gas Mark 5.
2. Heat the fat in a frying pan, add the onions, and cook slowly until soft. Add the meat, increase the heat, and stir until the meat has browned.
3. Remove from the heat; add the parsley, rosemary, and seasoning.
4. Put half the tomatoes into a casserole, cover with the meat mixture, and top with the rest of the tomatoes. Add Worcestershire sauce mixed with 1 tablespoon of water.
5. Sprinkle the cheese and bread crumbs on top, dot with butter, and cook for about 1 hour.

Meat Balls in Lemon Sauce

	00:40		
	00:35	Serves 4	Mid Atlantic

American	Ingredients	Metric/Imperial
1 lb	Finely ground [minced] lean beef	450 g/1 lb
1	Onion	1
1	Clove garlic	1
3 tbsp	Ground rice	2 tbsp
2 tbsp	Parsley	1½ tbsp
¼ tsp	Ground coriander seed	¼ tsp
1	Egg	1
3	Egg yolks	3
2	Lemons	2

1. Have the meat ground twice. Mix the meat in a bowl with the finely chopped onion and crushed garlic. if you have an electric blender or liquidizer, these ingredients can be mixed for a few minutes at a high speed. Return to the bowl. Mix in the ground rice, herbs and seasoning, and the well-beaten egg. The mixture should now be beaten to a very smooth paste with a wooden spoon or by hand.
2. Roll the meat paste into balls the size of walnuts and simmer in lightly salted water for about 20 minutes.
3. While meat balls are cooking, prepare the lemon sauce. Beat the egg yolks until light and fluffy, then add the juice of 2 lemons and ⅔ cup [150 ml/¼ pint] of water slowly. This can be done with an electric mixer. Heat the sauce in a double boiler and cook until thickened. Do not let the mixture boil. If not using at once, keep warm with the lid on the double boiler.
4. Drain the meat balls, submerge them in the sauce, and warm through gently. Sprinkle the grated rind of 1 lemon over the top and serve with plain boiled rice or pasta.

Nasi Goreng

	01:00		
	00:45	Serves 6	Pacific Southwest

American	Ingredients	Metric/Imperial
½ lb	Lean beef, ground [minced]	225 g/8 oz
2 tbsp	Bread or cereal crumbs	1½ tbsp
1¼ cups	Finely chopped onion	150 g/5 oz
1	Egg	1
½ cup	Corn oil	125 ml/4 fl oz
1 cup	Diced celery	100 g/4 oz
½ lb	Canned crabmeat	225 g/8 oz
½ lb	Shelled and deveined shrimp [prawns]	225 g/8 oz
2 cups	Chicken stock	450 ml/¾ pint
2 cups	Cooked rice	450 g/1 lb
2 tbsp	Curry powder	1½ tbsp

1. Preheat the oven to 350°F/180°C/Gas Mark 4.
2. Mix the meat, bread crumbs, ¼ cup [25 g/1 oz] of the onion, and salt and pepper and bind with the beaten egg. Shape into small balls the size of a walnut and leave in a cold place for about 40 minutes.
3. Heat 2 tablespoons [1½ tbsp] of the oil in a frying pan and sauté the rest of the onion and the celery. Put into a large casserole.
4. Heat a little more oil in the frying pan and sauté the crabmeat and shrimp for 2–3 minutes. Put into the casserole with the onion and celery.
4. Brown the meat balls and add to the other ingredients in the casserole.
5. Put the chicken stock into the frying pan with the rice, curry powder, and any remaining oil. Bring to the boiling point. Then pour it over the contents of the casserole. Stir to mix the ingredients together, then cover and cook in the oven for about ½ hour.

Spaghetti with Meat Balls

	00:30		
	00:25	Serves 4	New England

American	Ingredients	Metric/Imperial
1 lb	Ground [minced] beef	450 g/1 lb
½ lb	Package of spaghetti	225 g/8 oz
4 tbsp	Butter	50 g/2 oz
2	Small onions	2
3 tbsp	Finely chopped parsley, thyme and marjoram	2 tbsp
2	Cloves garlic	2
1 cup	Fresh white bread crumbs	50 g/2 oz
1 tbsp	Flour	1 tbsp
1 can (8 oz)	Tomatoes	1 tin (225 g/8 oz)
2 tsp	Tomato purée	2 tsp
1 cup	Stock	250 ml/8 fl oz
1 tbsp	Mixed herbs	1 tbsp
½ cup	Grated Parmesan cheese	50 g/2 oz

1. Bring a large pan of water to a boil. Add the salt. Curl in the spaghetti and bring to a boil, stirring constantly. Simmer for 10–15 minutes until done but still firm. Drain and wash with hot water; drain again. Melt 1 tablespoon [15 g/½ oz] butter and toss the spaghetti in this, adding black pepper. Keep warm.
2. Mix the ground beef and 1 chopped onion together. Add the chopped herbs and crushed garlic clove, together with the bread crumbs. Season well with salt and black pepper. Shape the mixture into small meat balls. Melt 1 tablespoon [15 g/½ oz] butter and fry the meat balls until brown. This takes 5–7 minutes.
3. To make the tomato sauce: Melt 2 tablespoons [25 g/1 oz] butter and cook 1 sliced onion and 1 crushed garlic clove for 5 minutes. Mix in the flour. Add the tomatoes and purée, stock, and herbs. Bring to a boil and simmer for 10–15 minutes.
4. Strain the sauce and add the meat balls. Heat through and serve with the spaghetti. Serve the grated Parmesan separately.

Spaghetti with Meat Balls

Roast Rack of Lamb with Anchovies

Barbecued Stuffed Leg of Lamb

  00:40
01:00   Serves 4–6   Mid Atlantic

American	Ingredients	Metric/Imperial
1	Leg of lamb weighing 3 lb [1.25 kg] after removal of bone	1
1	Onion	1
½ cup	Dried apricots	100 g/4 oz
3 tbsp	Raisins	2 tbsp
3 tbsp	Dates	2 tbsp
2 tbsp	Chopped nuts	1½ tbsp
5 tbsp	Cooked rice	4 tbsp
2 tbsp	Chopped parsley	1½ tbsp
1 tsp	Chopped marjoram	1 tsp
	A little lemon rind, and juice	
¼ cup	Strong stock	60 ml/2 fl oz
1	Clove garlic	1
	Oil	

1. Heat the coals in an outdoor grill until hot, about 30 minutes. This can also be cooked in a 375°/190°C/Gas Mark 5 oven.
2. Chop the onion and mix with the chopped, soaked dried apricots, chopped raisins, and dates. Add the chopped nuts, rice, parsley, marjoram, lemon rind and juice, salt and pepper, and enough stock to moisten. Fill this stuffing into the cavity left by the removal of the bones. Sew up the slits.
3. Cut the garlic into slivers and insert these into small shallow slits cut into the surface of the lamb with the point of a sharp knife. Put the lamb onto the rod of the spit, spoon the oil over the surface, and season well with salt, pepper, and barbecue sauce.
4. Cook for about 1 hour, or until the meat is tender and browned, basting with oil and seasoning when necessary.
5. Make a sauce with the liquids from the lamb and some stock and seasoning.

Roast Rack of Lamb with Anchovies

  00:25
00:40   Serves 4   Mid Atlantic

American	Ingredients	Metric/Imperial
1	Rack of lamb	1
1	Clove garlic	1
	Black pepper	
1 can (3 oz)	Anchovy fillets	1 tin (75 g/3 oz)
	A little milk	
2–3 tbsp	Oil	1½–2 tbsp
1 cup	Brown stock	250 ml/8 fl oz

1. Preheat the oven to 400°F/200°C/Gas Mark 6.
2. Trim the rack of lamb by exposing the last inch of the bones and scraping these clean. Score the fat of the lamb in a trellis pattern and rub in the crushed clove of garlic and black pepper.
3. Drain the anchovies of oil, soak in milk for 10 minutes, rinse carefully, and dry.
4. Heat the oil in a roasting pan. When smoking put in the meat. Baste with hot fat and cook in the oven for about 30–40 minutes, according to size and personal preference. Baste every 10 minutes. After 15–25 minutes, place the anchovy fillets in a crisscross design over the fat of the meat and continue cooking.
5. When cooked, remove and keep warm while the roasting liquid is heated with the stock to make gravy. Serve with potatoes and a green salad.

Lamb and Apricot Pilau

 00:15
02:00   Serves 4–6   Pacific Southwest

American	Ingredients	Metric/Imperial
1½–2 lb	Lean lamb	675–900 g/ 1½–2 lb
½ cup	Butter	50 g/2 oz
1	Onion	1
4 tbsp	Seedless raisins	3½ tbsp
1 cup	Dried apricots	225 g/8 oz
½ tsp	Ground cinnamon	½ tsp
½ tsp	Chopped thyme	½ tsp
2 cups	Long-grain rice	450 g/1 lb
2 tbsp	Almonds	1½ tbsp

1. Preheat the oven to 325°F/160°C/Gas Mark 3.
2. Melt half the butter in the pan and cook the onion until soft and golden brown. Add the meat, cut into cubes, and brown all over slowly. Add the raisins and halved apricots. Sprinkle with cinnamon, thyme, salt, and pepper. Pour in enough cold water to barely cover the meat. Cover and cook gently in the oven for about 1½ hours.
3. When the meat is tender, if there seems to be too much liquid, simmer it on the stove to reduce the quantity.
4. Boil the rice in the usual way for 10–12 minutes, or follow the instructions on the package and drain well. Melt the remaining butter and stir into the rice before drying it over gentle heat.
5. Arrange the rice and meat in layers in a casserole. Bake in a moderate oven for 15–20 minutes. Peel, shred, and lightly brown the almonds in the oven. Sprinkle on top of the dish and serve hot.

Barbecued Stuffed Leg of Lamb

Lamb on Brochette

01:40
00:20
Serves 2
Pacific Southwest

American	Ingredients	Metric/Imperial
1–1½ lb	Lean lamb, without bone	450–675 g/ 1–1½ lb
1	Clove garlic	1
	A few sprigs of rosemary	
	Marinade	
4 tbsp	Corn oil	3½ tbsp
3 tbsp	Soy sauce	2 tbsp
¼ tsp	Freshly ground black pepper	¼ tsp
1	Onion, peeled and finely grated	1
2 tbsp	Lemon juice	1½ tbsp

1. Heat the coals in an outside grill until hot, about 30 minutes, or preheat the broiler [grill].
2. Trim the lamb and cut it into cubes.
3. Mix all the ingredients for the marinade, and marinate the lamb for at least 1 hour, turning frequently.
4. Thread onto skewers and cook for about 20 minutes, basting frequently.
5. Toward the end of the cooking, toss a cut clove of garlic, or a couple sprigs of rosemary onto the coals. It will give the lamb a wonderful flavor.

Roast Lamb with Rosemary

00:10
02:00
Serves 6
Mid Atlantic

American	Ingredients	Metric/Imperial
1	Small leg or shoulder of lamb	1
1	Clove garlic	1
	Fat for roasting	
2 tbsp	Dried rosemary leaves	1½ tbsp
½ cup	Stock	125 ml/4 fl oz

1. Preheat the oven to 375°F/190°C/Gas Mark 5.
2. Cut the garlic into small slivers and with a sharp knife push these slivers into the fatty parts of the meat, near the bone. Sprinkle the lamb with seasoning.
3. Heat the fat in a roasting pan. Put in the meat. Sauté with hot fat until lightly browned. Then cook in the oven, allowing 20 minutes per pound.
4. During the last 45 minutes, add the rosemary, allowing it to flavor the meat. When the meat is cooked, put it onto a serving dish. Make the gravy with the juices from the roasting pan adding stock, but strain out the rosemary leaves.

Flamed Crown Roast of Lamb

Flamed Crown Roast of Lamb

	00:30		
	01:10	Serves 8	United States

American	Ingredients	Metric/Imperial
2	Racks of lamb (about 16 ribs)	2
2	Cloves garlic, cut into very thin slivers	
	Rosemary and lemon	
	Salt and black pepper	
1 cup	Bread crumbs	50 g/2 oz
1 tsp	Chopped parsley	1 tsp
1 tsp	Chopped scallions [spring onions]	1 tsp
6 tbsp	Melted butter or margarine	75 g/3 oz
½ cup	Chopped celery	50 g/2 oz
½ cup	Chopped onion	50 g/2 oz
½ cup	Chopped carrot	50 g/2 oz
2 tsp	Flour	2 tsp
2 cups	Chicken stock	450 ml/¾ pint
1	Bay leaf	1
3–4	Crushed peppercorns	3–4
4 tbsp	Cognac	3½ tbsp

1. Preheat the oven to 375°F/190°C/Gas Mark 5.
2. Have your butcher prepare the crown. Make small slits in the meat and insert slivers of garlic. Rub over the outside with rosemary and a cut lemon, and sprinkle with salt and pepper. Mix the bread crumbs, parsley, and scallions. Add 4 tablespoons [50 g/2 oz] of the butter, mix well, and rub this over the meat, coating the outside well. Wrap the tip of each rib bone with foil.
3. Put the vegetables and remaining butter into the bottom of a roasting pan and place the meat on top. Cook for about 1 hour. The meat should not be overcooked. Remove the lamb to an ovenproof serving dish and keep warm.

4. Pour off excess fat from the roasting pan, stir in the flour, and cook for 2 minutes. Add the stock, bay leaf, and peppercorns. Stir until boiling; boil for 5 minutes. Strain, season to taste, and serve separately.
5. Remove the foil from the ribs of the roast and garnish the dish as required with vegetables cooked separately. A small potato or piece of carrot can be impaled on the tip of each rib bone.
6. Warm the cognac, pour it over the outside of the crown at the table, and ignite.
7. If the crown of lamb is served without the cognac, little paper frills can be put onto the rib ends.

Californian Stuffed Breast of Lamb

	00:25		
	01:40	Serves 4	Pacific Southwest

American	Ingredients	Metric/Imperial
3 lb	Breast lamb without bones	1.25 g/3 lb
4–5 tbsp	Butter	50–65 g/ 2–2½ oz
1 cup	Chopped onion	100 g/4 oz
½ cup	Chopped celery	50 g/2 oz
1½ cups	Fresh white bread crumbs	75 g/3 oz
½ cup	Raisins	100 g/4 oz
1 tsp	Sugar	1 tsp
1	Lemon	1
1	Egg	1
	Garlic powder	
2 tbsp	Flour	1½ tbsp
2–3 tbsp	Oil (or shortening)	1½–2 tbsp
1 cup	Stock	250 ml/8 fl oz

1. Preheat the oven to 350°F/180°C/Gas Mark 4.
2. Make the stuffing: Melt the butter and cook the onion and celery slowly until soft without browning. Mix with the bread crumbs, adding raisins, sugar and the grated rind of 2 oranges and 1 lemon. Now add the lemon juice and beaten egg. Season with salt and black pepper. Add sections of 2 oranges. Mix well and stand for a few minutes before using.
3. Flatten out the boneless breast of lamb and dust with garlic powder. Spread the orange stuffing evenly over the meat about ¼ inch thick. (Any leftover can be cooked separately in a buttered dish). Roll the meat up tightly and tie in 3 or 4 places with white string, and roll in seasoned flour.
4. Warm the oil or shortening in a baking pan in the oven. Add the rolled breast of lamb and baste well. Cook for 1½ hours, basting every 15 minutes. For the last 10 minutes, turn up the oven to 400°F/200°C/Gas Mark 6 to brown the outside of the roll.
5. When the meat is tender and cooked through, remove and keep warm on a serving dish. Pour away the excess fat, reserving the juices; add a teaspoon of flour and mix well then add stock and grated rind and juice of 1 orange. Bring to a boil, season and serve.

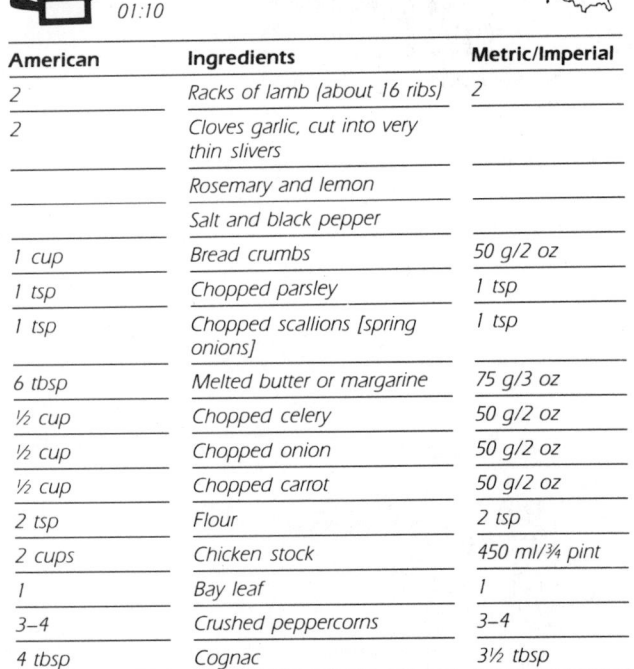

Bittersweet Lamb Casserole

 00:10 / 02:15 — Serves 4–6 — Pacific Southwest

American	Ingredients	Metric/Imperial
2–2½ lb	Rack of lamb	900 g–1.25 kg/ 2–2½ lb
2 tbsp	Oil	1½ tbsp
3 tbsp	Vinegar	2 tbsp
1 can (6–8 oz)	Orange juice	1 tin (175–225 g)
2 tsp	Worcestershire sauce	2 tsp
½ tsp	Salt	½ tsp
⅛ tsp	Freshly ground pepper	⅛ tsp
	A pinch of dry mustard	
	A pinch of paprika	
½ tsp each	Celery seed, basil, oregano	½ tsp each
3–4	Cloves	3–4
2 tsp	Sugar	2 tsp
	Cooked rice or noodles	

1. Preheat the oven to 350°F/180°C/Gas Mark 4.
2. Trim and cut the meat into chops. Brown the lamb in the hot oil and put into a casserole with 1 cup [250 ml/8 fl oz] water and vinegar. Cover and cook for 1 hour.
3. Put the orange juice, Worcestershire sauce, seasonings, and flavorings into a small pan and simmer, uncovered, for 10 minutes.
4. When the meat has cooked for 1 hour, stir in the orange juice mixture and cook for another hour.
5. Serve with rice or noodles.

Deviled Lamb Chops

 00:15 / 01:30 — Serves 4 — Mid Atlantic

American	Ingredients	Metric/Imperial
1½–2 lb	Rack of lamb	675–900 g/ 1½–2 lb
	Butter or margarine	
1	Onion, peeled and chopped	1
¼ cup	Finely chopped celery	25 g/1 oz
1	Clove garlic, crushed	1
1 can (about 10 oz)	Tomato soup	1 tin (about 275 g/10 oz)
1 tbsp	Worcestershire sauce	1 tbsp
1 tbsp	Lemon juice	1 tbsp
2 tbsp	Sherry	1½ tbsp
1 tbsp	Brown sugar	1 tbsp
2 tsp	Prepared mustard	2 tsp

1. Preheat the oven to 350°F/180°C/Gas Mark 4.
2. Trim and cut the meat into chops and arrange in a buttered casserole. Sprinkle with salt, pepper, onion, celery, and garlic. Cover and cook for about 20 minutes. Remove any excess fat.
3. Heat the tomato soup, add all the other ingredients, and mix well. Adjust the seasoning, and pour over the chops.
4. Cover and cook for about 1 hour, basting occasionally.
5. Serve with some chutney or pickled pears.

Casseroled Lamb with Pears

 00:10 / 01:20 — Serves 4 — Pacific Southwest

American	Ingredients	Metric/Imperial
2 lb	Stewing lamb	900 g/2 lb
2 tsp	Ground ginger	2 tsp
6	Medium-sized cooking pears, peeled, quartered, and cored	6
1 (10 oz)	Package frozen string beans	1 (275 g/10 oz)
	White wine	
	Dressing	
½ cup	Sour cream	125 ml/4 fl oz
1 tsp	Lemon juice	1 tsp
½ tsp	Dry mustard	½ tsp
2 tsp	Poppy seeds	2 tsp

1. Preheat the oven to 350°F/180°C/Gas Mark 4.
2. Trim any excess fat from the meat and cut it into pieces.
3. Put the meat into a lightly greased frying pan and brown it in its own fat. Then transfer to a casserole with a tightly fitting lid.
4. Sprinkle the ginger over the meat and add the pears, beans, and a little salt and pepper. Add 2 tablespoons [1½ tbsp] white wine; the juice from the pears should provide sufficient liquid, but if it begins to look dry, add a little more white wine. Cover tightly and cook for 1¼ hours.
5. A plain lettuce salad with a sour cream dressing makes a good accompaniment. For the dressing, mix the sour cream with lemon juice, dry mustard, and poppy seeds.

Casseroled Lamb with Pears

Blue Cheese Lamb Chops

Blue Cheese Lamb Chops 🍖

| | 02:00 | | |
| | 00:10 | Serves 4 | South |

American	Ingredients	Metric/Imperial
8	Loin or rib lamb chops, 1 inch thick	8
	Oil	
½ cup	Blue or Roquefort cheese	100 g/4 oz
2 tbsp	Thick cream	1½ tbsp
1	Clove garlic	1

1. Preheat the broiler [grill].
2. If using rib chops, trim and scrape the rib bones. Brush the chops with oil and sprinkle with black ground pepper (and garlic powder or crushed fresh garlic, if liked). Leave for a couple of hours if possible before broiling.
3. Mix the cheese and the cream and mash well together to form a paste.
4. Broil [grill] the chops 3–5 minutes on each side. Remove from the heat and spread the cheese mixture on one side of each chop. Replace under the heat until the cheese is light brown and bubbling.
5. Serve with mashed or baked potatoes and a salad.

Marinated Lamb Chops 🍖

| | 12:00 | | |
| | 00:20 | Serves 6 | Pacific Southwest |

American	Ingredients	Metric/Imperial
6	Thick lamb chops	6
	Marinade	
½ cup	Salad oil	125 ml/4 fl oz
½ cup	Burgundy or other red wine	125 ml/4 fl oz
2 tbsp	Grated onion	1½ tbsp
1	Clove garlic, crushed	1
1½ tsp	Salt	1½ tsp
3–4 drops	Tabasco sauce	3–4

1. Combine all the ingredients for the marinade.
2. Put the chops into a shallow pan and pour on the marinade. Cover and leave overnight if possible, or for several hours, turning the chops several times.
3. Heat the coals in an outdoor grill until hot, about 30 minutes, or preheat the broiler [grill].
4. When ready to cook, remove the chops from the marinade, put on the grid, and cook for 7–10 minutes each side, basting frequently with the marinade.

Stuffed Crown Roast of Lamb 🍖🍖

| | 00:20 | | |
| | Varies | Serves 6–8 | Mid Atlantic |

American	Ingredients	Metric/Imperial
1	Crown of lamb, allowing at least 2 ribs per person	1
	Oil for roasting	
1–1½ cups	Cooked rice	225–350 g/ 8–12 oz
½ cup	Cooked peas	50 g/2 oz
½ cup	Cooked corn	50 g/2 oz
¼ cup	Chopped cooked red and green sweet peppers	25 g/1 oz
1	Onion	1
2 tbsp	Butter	25 g/1 oz
¼ cup	Almonds skinned, sliced	25 g/1 oz
½ cup	Raisins	50 g/2 oz
2–3 tbsp	Sherry	1½–2 tbsp
	Chopped mixed herbs	

1. Preheat the oven to 450°F/230°C/Gas Mark 8.
2. Have the butcher prepare the crown roast, allowing 16 ribs to make a nice size roast. Cover the tips of the rib bones with foil to prevent burning, and crumple some foil into the center of the crown roast to preserve the shape while roasting.
3. Heat 2–3 tablespoons [1½–2 tbsp] of oil in a roasting pan and, when hot, put the crown roast into the pan. Baste with the hot fat before putting it in the oven. After 10 minutes, reduce the heat to 350°F/180°C/Gas Mark 4 and cook for 25 minutes per pound of meat. Season with salt and pepper, and baste every 15 minutes.
4. Meanwhile, prepare the stuffing. Boil the rice. When cooked and drained, mix in the cooked peas, corn, and red and green peppers. Cook the chopped onion gently in the butter until golden brown. Add to the rice along with the lightly browned almonds and the raisins, which have been soaked in a little sherry. Lastly, add the seasoning and herbs.
5. When the crown roast is cooked, remove from the oven. Put on a serving dish and remove the foil. Fill the center with the rice stuffing. Garnish the chop bones, with paper or foil frills and serve the crown roast with a green vegetable and gravy made with the roasting juices and red current jelly. Carve down between the bones allowing 2 per person.

Lamb Chops Princess

 00:10
00:40   Serves 4   South

American	Ingredients	Metric/Imperial
8	Lamb chops	8
2 tbsp	Flour	1½ tbsp
2	Small eggs	2
1 cup	Fresh white bread crumbs	50 g/2 oz
16–20	Fresh asparagus tips	16–20
5–6 tbsp	Butter	65–75 g/ 2½–3 oz
½ cup	Chopped mushrooms	50 g/2 oz
2 tsp	Flour	2 tsp
1 cup	Brown stock	250 ml/8 fl oz
1 tsp	Chopped parsley	1 tsp
½ cup	Madeira or sherry wine	125 ml/4 fl oz

1. Dip each chop into the flour and beaten egg. Then sprinkle bread crumbs all over the surface. Heat the butter in a frying pan until foaming. Fry the chops for about 4 minutes on each side, until the crumbs are golden brown and crisp, and the chops tender. Keep warm.

2. Cook the asparagus tips in boiling salted water until tender. Then drain and toss in 1 tablespoon [15 g/½ oz] of melted butter. Keep warm.

3. To make the sauce: Melt the butter and cook the chopped mushrooms for 3–4 minutes. Mix in the flour and cook for 1 minute before adding the stock, parsley, and Madeira. Bring to a boil and simmer for 10–15 minutes. Strain through a fine sieve or strainer, and add salt and pepper to taste.

4. Arrange the chops on a hot dish with a bunch of asparagus tips for each. Serve the sauce separately, very hot.

Lamb Chops Princess

Lamb Chops with Herbs

Lamb Chops with Herbs

| | 03:45 | Serves 4 | Mid Atlantic |
| | 00:20 | | |

American	Ingredients	Metric/Imperial
4 large loin or 8 rib	Lamb chops	4 large loin or 8 cutlets
1 tsp	Thyme	1 tsp
1 tsp	Oregano	1 tsp
1 tsp	Rosemary	1 tsp
3	Small bay leaves, crushed	3
6	Coriander seeds, crushed	6
	Grated rind and juice of 1 lemon	
	A pinch of paprika	
6 tbsp	Oil	5 tbsp
	Butter	

1. Trim the chops of excess fat.
2. Mix the herbs, grated lemon rind, and paprika. Rub this mixture well into both sides of the chops.
3. Arrange the chops on a large shallow dish, pour the lemon juice and oil over them, season lightly with salt and pepper, and set aside in a cool place for about 3 hours, turning occasionally.
4. Heat the coals in an outdoor grill until hot, about 30 minutes, or preheat the broiler [grill].
5. When ready to cook, drain the chops well and put on the grid over the hot coals or in the broiler. Turn once or twice while cooking, allowing about 20–30 minutes.
6. If you have any of the dried herbs left over, a good pinch sprinkled over the hot coals just before you remove the chops will give a delicious aroma and improve the flavor.
7. Serve the chops with a pat of butter on each and a plain tossed salad.

Lamb Chops on Vegetables

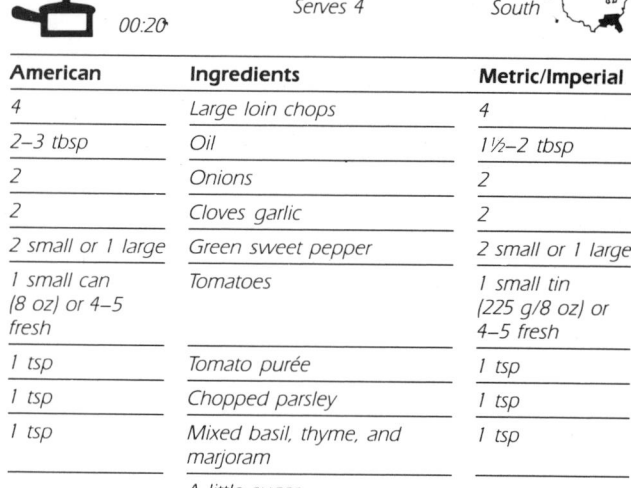

| | 00:10 | Serves 4 | South |
| | 00:20 | | |

American	Ingredients	Metric/Imperial
4	Large loin chops	4
2–3 tbsp	Oil	1½–2 tbsp
2	Onions	2
2	Cloves garlic	2
2 small or 1 large	Green sweet pepper	2 small or 1 large
1 small can (8 oz) or 4–5 fresh	Tomatoes	1 small tin (225 g/8 oz) or 4–5 fresh
1 tsp	Tomato purée	1 tsp
1 tsp	Chopped parsley	1 tsp
1 tsp	Mixed basil, thyme, and marjoram	1 tsp
	A little sugar	

1. Preheat the oven to 350°F/180°C/Gas Mark 4.
2. Heat the oil and cook the chops quickly on each side until light brown. Drain and keep warm.
3. Slice the onions and crush the garlic; cook for 2–3 minutes in the hot oil. Add the seeded and chopped pepper, the canned or fresh peeled and chopped tomatoes, and tomato purée. Stir in the herbs, seasoning, and sugar and cook together until thoroughly heated.
4. Put a layer of the vegetables in the bottom of an ovenproof dish or casserole. Lay the chops on top. Cover the chops with the remaining vegetables and cook in a medium oven for 10 minutes, or until the chops are tender.
5. Serve with potatoes or spaghetti.

Curate's Lamb

| | 00:20 | Serves 4 | Midwest |
| | 00:40 | | |

American	Ingredients	Metric/Imperial
2	Breasts lamb (boned)	2
1	Package sage and onion stuffing (or apple and lemon stuffing)	1
1 can (8 oz)	Mushrooms	1 tin (225 g/8 oz)
1 can (10¾ oz)	Condensed mushroom soup	1 tin (300 g/10¾ oz)
1 tsp	Worcestershire sauce	1 tsp

1. Preheat the oven to 425°F/220°C/Gas Mark 7.
2. Prepare the stuffing from the instructions on the package. Drain and add the mushrooms.
3. Halve the breasts of lamb, and place them in layers with the stuffing mixture, with the 2 thicker pieces of lamb at the bottom and top. Tie with string to hold the meat together during cooking. Place in an ovenproof dish, and cook in the oven for 40 minutes.
4. Add the Worcestershire sauce to the heated soup, and pour over as a sauce.

Lamb Curry

	00:45	Serves 4	South
	01:10		

American	Ingredients	Metric/Imperial
1½ lb	Lean lamb	675 g/1½ lb
3 tbsp	Oil	2 tbsp
1	Large onion	1
2	Stalks celery	2
1½ tbsp	Curry powder	1¼ tbsp
2 tsp	Curry paste	2 tsp
1½ tbsp	Flour	1¼ tbsp
1 cup	Stock	250 ml/8 fl oz
1	Apple	1
2 tbsp	Sultanas	1½ tbsp
2 tbsp	Chutney	1½ tbsp
1	Bay leaf	1
2 tbsp	Shredded coconut	1½ tbsp
	Juice of ½ lemon	
2 tsp	Jam or jelly	2 tsp

1. Cut the meat into cubes and brown quickly all over in oil. Put into a casserole and keep warm. Cook the finely sliced onion and celery in the hot oil for 2–4 minutes. Add curry powder and paste, and cook for 2 minutes. Add the flour and cook for 1 minute. Add the warmed stock and stir until smooth. Bring to a boil and cook for 3 minutes. Add the peeled and diced apple, raisins, chutney, salt, and bay leaf. Pour over the meat, and cook over gentle heat for 1 hour, stirring occasionally. By this time, the meat should be tender.
2. While the meat is cooking, pour ¼ cup [60 ml/2 fl oz] of boiling water over the coconut and let stand for 30 minutes. When the meat has been cooking for 50 minutes, add the strained juice of coconut to the meat with the lemon juice and jam or jelly. Continue cooking for 10 minutes.
3. When cooked, serve with plenty of plain boiled rice, chutney, quartered lemon, shredded coconut, sliced bananas, and grated cucumber in yogurt.

Curried Lamb Casserole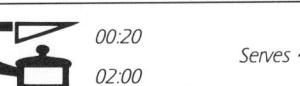

	01:10	Serves 4	South
	01:15		

American	Ingredients	Metric/Imperial
½ cup	Prunes	100 g/4 oz
½ cup	Dried apricots	100 g/4 oz
4	Thick lamb chops	4
1 tbsp	Oil	1 tbsp
¼ cup	Sultanas	50 g/2 oz
1	Lemon, thinly sliced	1
1 cup	Rice	225 g/8 oz
2 tsp	Curry powder	2 tsp

Lamb Hot Pot I

1. Preheat the oven to 350°F/180°C/Gas Mark 4.
2. Soak the prunes and apricots in warm water for at least 1 hour, then drain.
3. Trim the chops and sauté them in the hot oil for a few minutes.
4. Put a layer of fruit in a deep, buttered casserole with a tightly fitting lid. Sprinkle with raisins and add 1 or 2 slices of lemon and some of the rice. Sprinkle with curry powder, salt, and pepper. Continue in alternate layers until all the ingredients are used up.
5. Place the chops on top and pour in 3 cups [700 ml/1¼ pints] water. Cover tightly and cook for 1–1¼ hours, or until most of the liquid has been absorbed. Adjust the seasoning, and serve with a tossed green salad.

Lamb Hot Pot 1

	00:20	Serves 4	Mid Atlantic
	02:00		

American	Ingredients	Metric/Imperial
2½–3 lb	Neck of lamb	1.25 kg/2½–3 lb
2	Onions, peeled and thinly sliced	2
1½ lb	Potatoes	675 g/1½ lb
1 lb	Parsnips, peeled and sliced	450 g/1 lb
	A pinch of mixed herbs	
3 tbsp	Chopped parsley	2 tbsp
2 tbsp	Worcestershire sauce	1½ tbsp
2 tbsp	Water	1½ tbsp

1. Preheat the oven to 300°F/150°C/Gas Mark 2.
2. Cut the meat into pieces. Arrange one third of the onions, potatoes, and parsnips in a casserole. Add the seasoning and a little of the parsley. Add half the meat, a little more seasoning, and the herbs. Repeat the layers, finishing with the vegetables.
3. Pour the Worcestershire sauce mixed with the water over the meat and vegetables. Cook for about 1½ hours.
4. Remove the cover and cook for 30 minutes longer. Sprinkle with the remaining parsley before serving.

Lamb Hot Pot 2

00:15
01:08   Serves 4   Mid Atlantic

American	Ingredients	Metric/Imperial
1–1½ lb	Lean lamb neck or shoulder slices	450–675 g/ 1–1½ lb
2–3 tbsp	Oil	1½–2 tbsp
2	Onions	2
4	Potatoes	4
2	Carrots	2
2	Stalks celery	2
1 can (8 oz)	Tomatoes	1 tin (225 g/8 oz)
1 cup	Mushrooms	100 g/4 oz
2 cups	Stock	450 ml/¾ pint
2 tbsp	Herbs	1½ tbsp
1	Bay leaf	1

1. Preheat the oven to 350°F/180°C/Gas Mark 4.
2. Heat the oil, brown the meat quickly on both sides. Put the meat into a deep casserole and keep warm.
3. Cook the thickly sliced onion, carrot, celery, and potatoes in oil for a few minutes. Add the drained tomatoes, and mushrooms. Pour over the meat. Moisten with 2 cups [450 ml/¾ pint] of water or stock. Sprinkle the herbs over top; add the bay leaf and seasoning, and put in the oven for about 1 hour, or until the meat is tender.

Hungarian Style Lamb Casserole

Lamb with Dill

00:20
01:35   Serves 4   Mid Atlantic

American	Ingredients	Metric/Imperial
2½ lb	Lamb meat with the bone— shoulder, breast, rib	1.25 kg/2½ lb
	Water	
2 tsp	Salt per quart [liter] water	2 tsp
	Dill stalks	
6	White peppercorns	6

American	Ingredients	Metric/Imperial
2	Unpeeled cloves garlic	2
1	Small carrot, cut into small pieces	1
1	Leek or onion, cut into small pieces	1
	Sauce	
1½ tbsp	Butter or margarine	20 g/¾ oz
2½ tbsp	Flour	1¾ tbsp
2 cups	Stock	450 ml/¾ pint
3 tbsp	Snipped dill	2 tbsp
1 tbsp	Lemon juice	1 tbsp
1	Egg yolk	1
¼ cup	Cream	60 ml/2 fl oz

1. Place the meat in a pan. Measure and pour over as much water as needed to cover the meat. Add salt and bring to a boil. Skim well and add dill, pepper, garlic, carrot, and leek or onion. Let the meat simmer over low heat until it feels tender, 1 to 1½ hours.
2. To make the sauce, melt the butter in a pan, stir in the flour, and dilute with the liquid. Let the sauce boil for several minutes. Season with the dill and lemon juice.
3. Remove the pan from the heat and add the yolk, which has been beaten first together with the cream. The sauce should not be allowed to boil again as it can curdle.
4. Cut up the meat and serve it with the sauce, boiled potatoes, and vegetables.

Hungarian Style Lamb Casserole

00:15
02:40   Serves 4–5   Midwest

American	Ingredients	Metric/Imperial
2 lb	Stewing lamb	900 g/2 lb
3 tbsp	Oil	2 tbsp
1	Large onion, peeled and sliced	1
1	Sweet red pepper, seeded and sliced	1
3 tbsp	Flour	2 tbsp
1 tbsp	Paprika	1 tbsp
1	Chicken bouillon [stock] cube	1
5 tbsp	Lima or navy beans, soaked overnight	4 tbsp
3–4	Potatoes, peeled and cut into slices	3–4

1. Preheat the oven to 350°F/180°C/Gas Mark 4.
2. Trim the meat and cut it into small pieces.
3. Heat the oil in a frying pan. Add the meat, onion, and red pepper, and sauté for a few minutes. Then remove to a casserole.
4. Add the flour, paprika, crumbled bouillon cube, and a little salt to the pan drippings. Mix well, add 2 cups [450 ml/¾ pint] water, and stir until boiling. Add the drained beans and simmer for 5 minutes. Pour all into the casserole. Cover and cook for 2 hours.
5. Arrange the potatoes in overlapping slices on top of the casserole and cook for another 25–30 minutes, or until the potatoes are tender.

Lamb Kebabs with Orange

Durham Lamb Cutlets

	00:20		
	00:10	Serves 4	South

American	Ingredients	Metric/Imperial
½ lb	Cold cooked lamb	225 g/8 oz
1	Small onion	1
1 tbsp	Butter	15 g/½ oz
½ lb	Mashed potato	225 g/8 oz
1 tbsp	Chopped parsley	1 tbsp
1 tsp	Tomato purée	1 tsp
2 tbsp	Flour	1½ tsp
1	Egg	1
3–4 tbsp	White bread crumbs	2½–3 tbsp
	Fat for deep frying	

1. Grind [mince] or chop the meat very finely. Chop the onions finely and cook in melted butter, until golden brown. Add the mashed potato and meat to the onion. Then add the chopped parsley and tomato purée, and salt and pepper to taste. Cook all together for a few seconds.

2. Turn the mixture onto a plate to cool. Then divide into 8 equal-sized portions and shape into cutlet shapes. Roll each in flour, then dip into beaten egg until coated all over. Now roll in dried bread crumbs.

3. Heat the fat in a deep frying pan. When smoking slightly, put 3–4 cutlets into a frying basket and lower into the hot fat. Cook until the cutlets are a rich brown. Drain on paper towels [kitchen paper] and keep warm while frying the remaining cutlets.

4. Arrange in an overlapping circle around a hot dish, and serve with vegetables and a brown or tomato sauce.

Lamb Kebabs with Orange

	00:45		
	00:20	Serves 4	Pacific Southwest

American	Ingredients	Metric/Imperial
2 lb	Lamb without bone	900 g/2 lb
2	Small onions, peeled and quartered	2
	Fresh rosemary, if available	
	Baste	
1 cup	Brown sugar	225 g/8 oz
1 can (6 oz)	Frozen concentrated orange juice	1 tin (175 g/6 oz)
4 tbsp	Worcestershire sauce	3½ tbsp
1 tsp	Prepared mustard	1 tsp
	Juice of 1 lemon	
1 tbsp	Cornstarch [cornflour]	1 tbsp

1. Heat the coals in an outdoor grill until hot, about 30 minutes, or preheat the broiler [grill].

2. Trim any excess fat from the meat and cut into pieces.

3. Place the onion quarters on skewers alternately with the pieces of meat, adding a leaf of rosemary here and there.

4. Put the sugar, orange juice, and Worcestershire sauce into a pan, add the mustard, mixed smoothly with the lemon juice, and stir over low heat until the sugar has dissolved.

5. Brush the kebabs liberally with this baste, put on the grid over the hot coals or in the broiler, and cook for about 10–15 minutes, turning and basting frequently.

6. Blend the cornstarch with a little water, add to the remaining baste, and stir until boiling. Check the seasoning and serve as a sauce with the kebabs.

Lamb Kebabs on Saffron Rice

	00:20		
	00:40	Serves 4	Pacific Southwest

American	Ingredients	Metric/Imperial
1–1½ lb	Lamb cut into small chunks	450–675 g/ 1–1½ lb
1 cup	Long-grain rice	225 g/8 oz
	A large pinch of saffron	
5–6 tbsp	Oil	4–5 tbsp
2¾ cups	Boiling stock or water	625 ml/1¼ pints
1 tsp	Salt	1 tsp
¼ tsp	Pepper	¼ tsp
	Onion salt	
1 tsp	Chopped parsley	1 tsp
16	Small onions	16
12	Button mushrooms	12
1	Green or red sweet pepper	1
4	Cherry tomatoes	4
12	Chunks pineapple	12

1. Preheat the broiler [grill].
2. To make the saffron rice, first put a pinch of saffron to soak in 2–3 tablespoons [1½–2 tbsp] of hot water. Cook the rice slowly in 2 tablespoons [1½ tbsp] of oil until slightly brown, stirring all the time. Remove from the heat. Add the boiling stock, saffron water, salt, pepper, and a little onion salt. Cook, covered, over low heat for 20–30 minutes, until the liquid is completely absorbed. Then add the parsley. Turn into a buttered cake pan and press in firmly. Keep warm.
3. Cut the meat into even-sized chunks and soak in 3–4 tablespoons [2–3½ tbsp] of oil. Peel the onions and cook for a few minutes in boiling water. Then drain and cool. Cut the stems off the mushrooms; cut the pepper into squares, removing the seeds, and the tomatoes in half. Drain the pineapple chunks.
4. Thread the various kebab ingredients onto 4 skewers and brush all over with oil. Sprinkle with salt and pepper, and a little garlic powder if liked. Cook under the broiler for 10–15 minutes, until the meat is tender and thoroughly cooked. Brush with oil from time to time while broiling. (This broiling can be done on a barbecue or charcoal grill).
5. When the meat is cooked, turn the rice onto a hot plate and lay the kebabs on top. Serve with tomato, barbecue or brown sauce, and a salad.

Navarin of Lamb or Mutton

	00:20		
	01:50	Serves 4	Midwest

American	Ingredients	Metric/Imperial
1½–2 lb	Breast or shoulder of lamb or mutton	675–900 g/ 1½–2 lb
2 tbsp	Oil	1½ tbsp
1 tbsp	Flour	1 tbsp

3 tbsp	Tomato purée	2 tbsp
1 cup	Water	250 ml/8 fl oz
1	Clove garlic	1
1 tbsp	Mixed herbs	1 tbsp
4	Onions	4
4	Carrots	4
2	Small turnips	2
3–4	Stalks celery	3–4
4–6	Potatoes	4–6

1. Cut the meat into fairly big, even-sized pieces. Heat the oil; brown the meat quickly all over. Add the flour; brown this slightly. Add the tomato purée, water, and crushed garlic and bring to a boil. Sprinkle in the herbs and seasoning. Simmer gently for 45 minutes.
2. Meanwhile, prepare the vegetables. Peel the onions, and cut them in quarters; peel the carrots and slice them. Peel the turnips and quarter them. Slice the celery. Peel the potatoes and cut them into thick slices.
3. Take a little of the fat from the top of the stewing meat and brown the vegetables in this. When the meat has been cooking for 45 minutes, add the vegetables, but reserve the potatoes to add later. When the vegetables have been cooking for about 30 minutes, add the sliced potatoes and cook for another 30 minutes.
4. Skim all fat from the top of the stew, and check the seasoning before serving.

Lamb and Potato Casserole

	00:10		
	02:10	Serves 4	Midwest

American	Ingredients	Metric/Imperial
2 tbsp	Flour	1½ tbsp
4 large loin or 8 rib	Lamb chops	4 large loin or 8 cutlets
4 tbsp	Butter	50 g/2 oz
½ lb	Onions, peeled and sliced	225 g/8 oz
1	Small clove garlic, crushed	1
4	Tomatoes, peeled and sliced	4
1–2 sprigs fresh or ⅛ tsp dried	Rosemary	1–2 sprigs fresh or ⅛ tsp dried
1 lb	Potatoes, peeled and sliced	450 g/1 lb
3–4 tbsp	Stock or water	2–3½ tbsp

1. Mix the flour with a little salt and pepper and dredge the chops well.
2. Heat 3 tablespoons [40 g/1½ oz] of butter in a frying pan. Brown the chops on both sides, then remove from the pan. Add the onion and garlic to the remaining fat and cook until softened.
3. Arrange the meat, onion, tomato, rosemary, and potatoes in layers in a casserole, seasoning each layer lightly and finishing with potato. Add the stock or water, and dot with the remaining butter.
4. Cover and cook for about 2 hours. About 15 minutes before the end of the cooking, remove the lid to allow the potatoes to brown.

Lamb and Potato Pies

Lamb and Potato Pies

	00:30			
	01:05	Serves 4–5	Midwest	

American	Ingredients	Metric/Imperial
	Pastry	
4 cups	All-purpose [plain] flour	450 g/1 lb
2 tsp	Salt	2 tsp
1⅓ cups	Shortening	300 g/11 oz
5 tbsp	Water	4 tbsp
	Filling	
¾ lb	Lean lamb, shoulder cut	350 g/12 oz
2 cups	Peeled, diced potato	225 g/8 oz
⅛ tsp	Dried rosemary	⅛ tsp
	A pinch of dried thyme	
1 tbsp	Finely chopped onion	1 tbsp
	Egg or milk to glaze	

1. Preheat the oven to 450°F/230°C/Gas Mark 8.
2. Combine the pastry ingredients. Roll out thinly and cut into rounds the size of a saucer.
3. Cut the meat into very small pieces; mix with potato, seasoning, herbs, and onion. Add 2–3 tablespoons [1½–2 tbsp] of water.
4. Divide equally among the rounds of pastry, moisten the edge, fold over, and press the edges well together. Flute with the fingers.
5. Stand the pies upright on a baking sheet, glaze with egg or milk, and bake about 20 minutes or until the pastry begins to brown. Reduce the heat to 350°F/180°C/Gas Mark 4 and cook for another 40–45 minutes.

Holiday Stew

	00:20			
	03:30	Serves 4–5	Mid Atlantic	

American	Ingredients	Metric/Imperial
2–2½ lb	Boned shoulder of lamb	900 g–1.25 kg/ 2–2½ lb
6 slices	Bacon	6 rashers
2	Onions, peeled and sliced	2
3	Medium potatoes, peeled and sliced	3
1 can (about 12 oz)	Whole kernel corn	1 tin (about 350 g/12 oz)
2	Tomatoes, peeled and sliced	2
1 tbsp	Worcestershire sauce	1 tbsp
1 tbsp	Chopped parsley	1 tbsp
1 cup	Dry white wine or cider	250 ml/8 fl oz

1. Preheat the oven to 300°F/150°C/Gas Mark 2.
2. Cut the meat into pieces; sprinkle with salt and pepper.
3. Put half the bacon into a deep casserole; cover with half the meat and half the onions. Add remaining bacon and cover with potatoes.
4. Add the rest of the meat, corn, and tomatoes.
5. Mix the Worcestershire sauce and parsley with the wine, and pour over the contents of the casserole. Cover very tightly and cook for about 3½ hours.

Lamb Parcels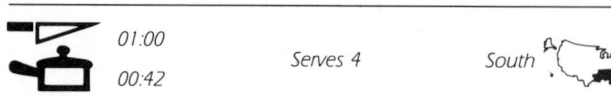

🏳️ 01:00 00:42   Serves 4   South

American	Ingredients	Metric/Imperial
2	Racks of lamb with bones and excess fat removed	2
2 tbsp	Oil	1½ tbsp
1	Onion	1
½	Clove garlic	½
2 tbsp	Butter	25 g/1 oz
1 cup	Chopped mushrooms	100 g/4 oz
½ cup	Chopped ham	75 g/3 oz
1 tbsp	Tomato purée	1 tbsp
1 tbsp	Chopped mixed herbs	1 tbsp
1 tbsp	Sherry or brandy	1 tbsp
1 (8 oz)	Package frozen puff pastry	1 (225 g/8 oz)
1	Beaten egg	1

1. Preheat the oven to 425°F/220°C/Gas Mark 7.
2. Cut each rack into 4 slices, roll each slice neatly, and fix with a toothpick. Brush with oil and season with pepper. Heat the broiler [grill] and broil the lamb until partially cooked, allowing 3–4 minutes on each side depending on the thickness of the lamb. Remove from the broiler and allow to get completely cold.
3. Meanwhile, cook the chopped onion and crushed garlic for 2–3 minutes in butter. Add the chopped mushrooms and ham. Stir in tomato purée and cook for a few seconds before adding the herbs, sherry, and seasoning. Let cool.
4. Roll out the puff pastry until large enough to cut into 8 pieces, each piece large enough to cover a lamb roll completely. Put a small spoonful of mushroom mixture on the center of each piece of pastry. Lay a lamb roll on top, and spread the remaining mushroom mixture on top of the lamb. Fold the pastry over to make a neat parcel of each slice, sealing the edges with beaten egg. Brush the parcels well with beaten egg, and bake in a hot oven for 20–30 minutes, until the pastry is brown and well risen.
5. Serve with spinach and French fried potatoes and a rich brown sauce. (The parcels can be prepared ahead of time and glazed with egg just before baking in the oven).

Braised Lamb Shanks

🏳️ 00:10 01:45   Serves 4   Mid Atlantic

American	Ingredients	Metric/Imperial
4	Lamb shanks [thick slices leg or breast]	4
2 tbsp	Oil	1½ tbsp
2	Large onions	2
1	Clove garlic	1
2 tbsp	Flour	1½ tbsp
1½ cups	Stock or water	350 ml/12 fl oz
1 cup	Ale or beer	250 ml/8 fl oz
2	Carrots	2
2–3	Stalks celery	2–3
1 tbsp	Vinegar	1 tbsp
1 tbsp	Worcestershire sauce	1 tbsp
1	Bay leaf	1
2 tbsp	Chopped parsley and thyme	1½ tbsp
1 tbsp	Chutney	1 tbsp
4	Tomatoes	4

1. Preheat the oven to 325°F/160°C/Gas Mark 3.
2. Heat the oil and brown the lamb shanks all over. Put into a casserole and keep warm.
3. Cook the chopped onion and crushed garlic for a few minutes until light brown. Remove from the heat, add the flour and stir in well. Cook for another minute. Then add the stock or water and ale. (If not using ale or beer, increase the quantity of the stock). Add the sliced carrots and celery, vinegar, Worcestershire sauce, herbs, and bay leaf. Bring to a boil, stirring all the time. Then cover the casserole and cook in the oven for about 1½ hours, or until the lamb is tender.
4. If the lamb is to be served the same day, put the peeled tomatoes, cut in slices, into the pan 15 minutes before the end of cooking, together with chutney. If keeping until next day, add the tomato and chutney just before reheating for half an hour in a moderate oven. Serve with plain boiled rice or mashed potatoes.

Lamb Shanks with Horseradish

🏳️ 00:15 02:15   Serves 4   New England

American	Ingredients	Metric/Imperial
4	Lamb shanks [thick slices leg or breast]	4
2 tbsp	Oil	1½ tbsp
1 tsp	Paprika	1 tsp
1	Large onion, peeled and sliced	1
1 cup	Sliced mushrooms	100 g/4 oz
1 tbsp	Prepared horseradish	1 tbsp
1 tsp	Chopped parsley	1 tsp
¼ tsp each	Dried rosemary, sweet basil, oregano	¼ tsp each
1 cup	Sour cream	250 ml/8 fl oz

1. Preheat the oven to 325°F/160°C/Gas Mark 3.
2. Heat the oil in a heavy frying pan, sprinkle the lamb shanks with paprika, and brown in the oil with the onion. Add the mushrooms and cook all together for a few minutes; then remove all to a casserole.
3. Add 1 cup [250 ml/8 fl oz] of water to the pan drippings, scrape up all the brown particles, and bring to a boil; then pour into the casserole.
4. Add the horseradish, herbs, and seasoning. Cover and cook for 2 hours, or until the meat is quite tender.
5. Remove the shanks from the casserole and cut off all the meat. Stir the sour cream into the casserole and adjust the seasoning. Put the meat back and leave just long enough for it to reheat.

Lamb or Mutton Scallops

Casseroled Shanks of Lamb

	00:15		
	01:40	Serves 4	United States

American	Ingredients	Metric/Imperial
4 tbsp	Oil	3½ tbsp
4	Lamb shanks [thick slices leg or breast]	4
1	Large onion, peeled and chopped	1
1	Clove garlic, crushed	1
2 tbsp	Flour	1½ tbsp
2½ cups	Stock	600 ml/1 pint
2	Carrots, peeled and sliced	2
2	Leeks, washed and sliced	2
2 tbsp	Worcestershire sauce	1½ tbsp
1	Bay leaf	1
1 tbsp	Chopped parsley	1 tbsp
4	Tomatoes, peeled and sliced	4

1. Preheat the oven to 325°F/160°C/Gas Mark 3.
2. Heat the oil in a frying pan, put in the lamb shanks, and brown on all sides. Remove to a deep casserole.
3. Put the onion and garlic into the pan with the remaining oil, and cook until the onion begins to brown. Add the flour and stir for 1 minute. Gradually add the stock and stir until boiling. Add the carrots, leeks, Worcestershire sauce, bay leaf, and parsley, and pour all into the casserole with the lamb shanks. Cover and cook for 1¼ hours.
4. Add the tomatoes and seasoning, and cook for 15 minutes more. Remove the bay leaf, and serve with potatoes and a green vegetable.

Lamb or Mutton Scallops

	00:15		
	00:20	Serves 4	United States

American	Ingredients	Metric/Imperial
1 lb	Cold lamb or mutton	450 g/1 lb
1	Onion	1
4–6 tbsp	Butter	50–75 g/2–3 oz
2 tsp	Chopped parsley	2 tsp
½ tsp	Chopped thyme	½ tsp
1 tsp	Worcestershire sauce	1 tsp
2	Large tomatoes	2
2 tbsp	Dried bread crumbs	1½ tbsp
2 tbsp	Grated Parmesan or strongly flavored cheese	1½ tbsp

1. Preheat the oven to 400°F/200°C/Gas Mark 6.
2. Grind [mince] or chop the lamb or mutton finely. Chop the onion and cook in 2–3 tablespoons [25–40 g/1–1½ oz] of butter, until light golden brown. Add the meat and mix well, adding the chopped herbs and Worcestershire sauce, and salt and pepper to taste.
3. Butter 4 scallop shells or gratin dishes and divide the mixture evenly between them. Smooth down and put 2–3 slices of tomato on top of each. Sprinkle the top with mixed bread crumbs and cheese. Dot the top with the remaining butter.
4. Cook in a hot oven for about 15 minutes. If the top of the scallops are not brown and crisp, finish off under a hot broiler [grill] for a few minutes.

Lamb Stew

Lamb Stew

	00:20		
	01:00	Serves 4	Mid Atlantic

American	Ingredients	Metric/Imperial
1½–2 lb	Lamb meat with bone—back, shoulder, or cracked breast	675–900 g/1½–2 lb
8	Small onions	8
4	Tomatoes, cut into pieces	4
1 tsp	Salt	1 tsp
½ tsp	Black pepper	½ tsp
1–2	Cloves garlic, crushed	1–2
	Slightly less than 1 tsp thyme	
¼ cup	Parsley, chopped	15 g/½ oz
¼ cup	Snipped chives	15 g/½ oz
1¼ cups	Stock	300 ml/½ pint
1 tbsp	Flour	1 tbsp
½ cup	Crème fraîche or sour cream	125 ml/4 fl oz

1. Cut the meat into pieces and brown them in a small amount of butter in a frying pan. Pour into a stewing pan. Peel and brown the onions and mix them with the meat; add the tomatoes. Season and pour in the stock. Cover and simmer until the meat feels tender, about 45 minutes.

2. Stir the flour into a small amount of water, and mix in with the stew together with crème fraîche or sour cream. Simmer for another 5 to 10 minutes. Season to taste. Serve with boiled potatoes.

Irish Style Stew

	00:10		
	02:30	Serves 4	New England

American	Ingredients	Metric/Imperial
1½–2 lb	Ribs [cutlets] or shoulder chops of lamb	675–900 g/1½–2 lb
4	Medium potatoes	4
2–3	Medium onions	2–3
1 tbsp	Chopped parsley	1 tbsp
½ tsp	Chopped thyme	½ tsp
1	Small bay leaf	1

1. Trim excess fat off the chops, and cut the potatoes and onions into quarters or thick slices.

2. Place the meat and vegetables in a thick stew pan in layers, starting and ending with a layer of potatoes, and sprinkling herbs and seasoning on each layer. Add 2 cups [450 ml/¾ pint] of water. Cover tightly.

3. Simmer the stew over gentle heat (or cook in low oven, 250°F/130°C/Gas Mark ½) for 2–2½ hours. Shake the pan from time to time to prevent the stew from sticking. Toward the end of the cooking time, check the liquid in the pan. The consistency should be thick and creamy but not dry, so add a little more liquid if necessary.

Lamb and Vegetable Stew

	00:15		
	01:30	Serves 4	Mid Atlantic

American	Ingredients	Metric/Imperial
2–3 lb	Breast of lamb cut into strips	900 g–1.25 kg/2–3 lb
2	Onions, peeled and sliced	2
3	Carrots, peeled and sliced	3
2–3	Leeks, well washed and sliced	2–3
1	Small turnip, peeled and diced	1
3 cups	Stock or water	700 ml/1¼ pints
¼ tsp	Rosemary	¼ tsp
½ tsp	Grated lemon rind	½ tsp
1 tbsp	Cornstarch [cornflour]	1 tbsp
	Chopped parsley	

1. Trim the excess fat from the lamb. Heat the fat in a saucepan, and fry the lamb for about 1 minute on each side. Add the vegetables and cook for a few minutes, stirring occasionally.

2. Add the stock, rosemary, lemon rind, and seasoning. Bring to a boil, then simmer slowly for 1–1¼ hours, or until the meat and vegetables are tender.

3. Blend the cornstarch to a smooth paste with a little cold water, stir into the stew, and continue to stir until boiling. Cook for 1 minute longer, adjust the seasoning to taste, and serve sprinkled with parsley.

Lamb-and-Tomato Pudding

	00:25		
	00:40	Serves 4–6	South

American	Ingredients	Metric/Imperial
6–8	Slices of roast lamb	6–8
2 cups	Fresh bread crumbs	100 g/4 oz
1	Onion	1
8	Tomatoes	8
2 tsp	Brown [demerara] sugar	2 tsp
	A little Worcestershire sauce	
2 tbsp	Butter	25 g/1 oz

1. Preheat the oven to 375°F/190°C/Gas Mark 5.
2. Butter a baking dish. Sprinkle in a layer of bread crumbs. Add a layer of diced cold lamb, then a sprinkling of finely chopped onion and some salt and pepper. Add another layer of tomatoes with sugar, a dash of Worcestershire sauce, and a little of the butter on top.
3. Repeat this layering again, but reserve ½ cup [25 g/1 oz] of crumbs to sprinkle over the top of the dish. Add the remaining butter in small pieces and bake for about 40 minutes in the oven until the crumbs are brown.

Lamb with Vegetables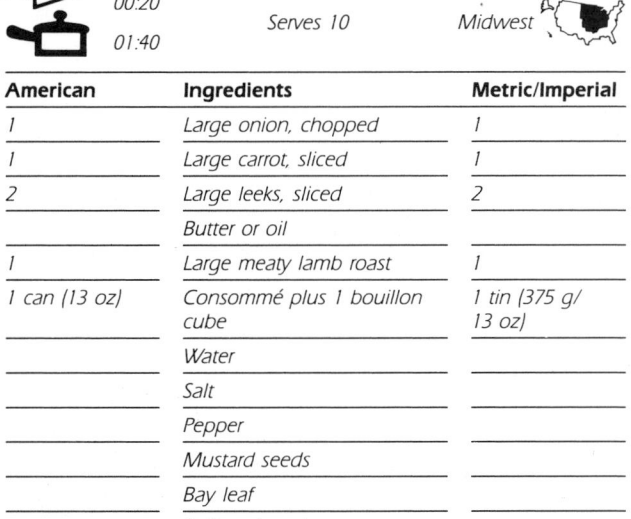

	00:20		
	01:40	Serves 10	Midwest

American	Ingredients	Metric/Imperial
1	Large onion, chopped	1
1	Large carrot, sliced	1
2	Large leeks, sliced	2
	Butter or oil	
1	Large meaty lamb roast	1
1 can (13 oz)	Consommé plus 1 bouillon cube	1 tin (375 g/13 oz)
	Water	
	Salt	
	Pepper	
	Mustard seeds	
	Bay leaf	
	Sprigs of parsley	

1. Brown the onion, carrot, and leeks in butter or oil in a thick-bottomed pot. Insert a cooking thermometer in the well-trimmed lamb roast. Place the roast on the vegetables, cover with the consommé, bouillon cube, and enough water to come more than halfway up the roast. Salt lightly, season with pepper, mustard seeds, bay leaf, and sprigs of parsley. Cover and cook slowly until thermometer shows 160°F/70°C. Remove the roast, wrap it up in aluminum foil, and keep it warm.
2. Strain the roast juice and simmer it so that it becomes a thick gravy. Then mix in more mustard seeds to make a strong sauce.
3. Serve the roast with potato cakes and applesauce.

Lamb with Vegetables

Lamb-Stuffed Cabbage Leaves

	00:25		
	01:00	Serves 4	New England

American	Ingredients	Metric/Imperial
1 lb	Lean ground [minced] lamb	450 g/1 lb
8–12	Medium-sized green cabbage leaves	8–12
2–3 tbsp	Butter	25–40 g/1–1½ oz
1	Onion	1
1 tbsp	Flour	1 tbsp
2 tbsp	Tomato purée	1½ tbsp
1 tbsp	Chopped parsley	1 tbsp
1 cup	Cooked rice	225 g/8 oz
¼ tsp	Mixed spice	¼ tsp
2 cups	Stock	450 ml/¾ pint
2 tbsp	Seasoned flour	1½ tbsp
2 cups	Tomato sauce or brown gravy	450 ml/¾ pint

1. Preheat the oven to 350°F/180°C/Gas Mark 4.
2. Put the cabbage leaves into a pan of boiling salted water and cook for 2–3 minutes. Drain, rinse in cold water, and let dry.
3. Heat the butter and cook lamb and finely chopped onion until the meat is brown. Sprinkle in the flour and stir well. Add the tomato purée, chopped parsley, rice, mixed spice, seasoning, and about ½ cup [125 ml/4 fl oz] of stock. Bring to a boil and cook for 5 minutes. Then cool slightly. Put a spoonful on the center of each cabbage leaf and roll up neatly, tucking in the ends to hold in the stuffing while cooking. Roll in seasoned flour and place in a casserole, packing them tightly together. Pour over 1 cup [250 ml/8 fl oz] of stock to cover half the cabbage leaves.
4. Put a lid on the casserole and cook for 45 minutes until tender, adding more stock if necessary; serve with a tomato sauce or brown gravy.

Lamb Loaf

| | 04:00 | | |
| | 00:55 | Serves 5–6 | Mid Atlantic  |

American	Ingredients	Metric/Imperial
½ cup	Bread crumbs	25 g/1 oz
3 cups	Ground [minced] lean cooked lamb	500 g/18 oz
½ cup	Lean ham or bacon, finely chopped or ground [minced]	75 g/3 oz
1	Medium-sized onion, peeled and finely chopped	1
3–4	Tomatoes, peeled, seeded and chopped	3–4
1 tbsp	Chopped mint	1 tbsp
1–2	Sprigs chopped fresh rosemary	1–2
1	Egg	1
	A little stock or gravy	
3 tbsp	Heavy [double] cream	2 tbsp

1. Preheat the oven to 300°F/150°C/Gas Mark 2.
2. Grease a 9 × 5 × 3-inch loaf pan well, and coat with some of the bread crumbs.
3. Combine the lamb, bacon, onion, tomatoes, herbs, and seasoning. Soak the remaining bread crumbs in cream and add them to the lamb mixture. Mix well and bind with the beaten egg and a little stock or gravy.
4. Pack the mixture into the prepared pan, pressing it well down. Cover with greased paper or foil, and bake for 55 minutes.
5. Let it get quite cold before turning out, and serve with salad.

Summer Casserole

| | 00:20 | | |
| | 01:50 | Serves 4–6 | Mid Atlantic |

American	Ingredients	Metric/Imperial
2–2½ lb	Stewing lamb	900 g–1.25 kg/ 2–2½ lb
2 tbsp	Drippings	1½ tbsp
1	Onion, peeled and chopped	1
½ lb	Young carrots, sliced lengthwise	225 g/8 oz
1	Small turnip, peeled and chopped	1
2 cups	Stock or water	450 ml/¾ pint
1	Sprig mint	1
1	Sprig thyme	1
1 cup	Cooked green peas	100 g/4 oz

1. Preheat the oven to 350°F/180°C/Gas Mark 4.
2. Trim the meat and cut it into pieces. Heat the fat in a frying pan, brown the meat, and place in a casserole.
3. Brown the onion in the remaining fat and add to the casserole. Add the other ingredients, except the peas; cover and cook for 1¼ hours.
4. Add the peas and continue to cook for another 20–30 minutes. Before serving, remove the mint and thyme, and adjust the seasoning to taste.

Stuffed Zucchini

| | 01:00 | | |
| | 01:00 | Serves 4 | Pacific Southwest |

American	Ingredients	Metric/Imperial
1 lb	Ground [minced] lamb	450 g/1 lb
8–12	Small zucchini [courgettes]	8–12
2 tbsp	Oil	1½ tbsp
1	Onion	1
1	Clove garlic	1
8	Tomatoes	8
4–6 tbsp	Cooked rice	3½–5 tbsp
2 tbsp	Chopped parsley	1½ tbsp
1 tsp	Chopped marjoram	1 tsp
2 tbsp	Raisins	1½ tbsp
1	Lemon	1
	A touch of garlic salt	
1 tsp	Chopped basil	1 tsp
2–3 tsp	Chopped parsley	2–3 tsp
6 tbsp	Stock	5 tbsp
1 (1 cup)	Carton yogurt for garnish	1 (250 ml/8 fl oz)

1. Preheat the oven to 350°F/180°C/Gas Mark 4.
2. Cut a small slice off the stalk end of each zucchini and scoop out the inside with an apple corer or spoon. Cook the skins in boiling salted water for 3–4 minutes and drain. Put the chopped pulp into a bowl with a good sprinking of salt and leave for a half hour. Then wash well in cold water and drain.
3. Heat the oil and cook the chopped onion and crushed garlic until soft, about 4 minutes. Add the meat and drained zucchini pulp; cook, stirring frequently, until the meat is slightly browned. Add 2 skinned and chopped tomatoes, cooked rice, parsley, marjoram, and raisins, and season to taste. Put this mixture into zucchini skins but do not fill more than three quarters full to allow for the expansion of the rice.
4. Slice 6 tomatoes and place in a layer on the bottom of the casserole. Place the stuffed zucchini on top in rows. Heat the remaining tomatoes with lemon juice, herbs, and 2–3 tablespoons of stock. Add seasoning and a pinch of sugar. Spoon this sauce over the zucchini. Cover casserole and cook in the oven for about 45 minutes, until the zucchini are tender. If the sauce appears dry, add more stock.
5. Just before serving, mix the yogurt with grated lemon rind, and spoon over the dish. Serve with plain boiled rice or noodles.

Stuffed Eggplant

| | 01:00 | | |
| | 01:20 | Serves 4 | South |

American	Ingredients	Metric/Imperial
1 lb	Lean lamb	450 g/1 lb
4 medium or 8 small	Eggplants [aubergines]	4 medium or 8 small
4 tsp	Salt	4 tsp
2 tbsp	Butter	25 g/1 oz
1	Onion	1
½ cup	Rice	100 g/4 oz

2	Tomatoes	2
2 tbsp	Chopped parsley	1½ tbsp
2 tbsp	Pine nuts (or chopped walnuts)	1½ tbsp
2 tbsp	Raisins	1½ tbsp
	Juice of 1 lemon	
2–3 tbsp	Oil	1½–2 tbsp
1½ cups	Stock	350 ml/12 fl oz
3–4 tbsp	Tomato purée	2–3½ tbsp
2 tbsp	Browned bread crumbs	1½ tbsp

1. Preheat the oven to 425°F/220°C/Gas Mark 7.
2. Cut the eggplants in half lengthwise and score the surface deeply without piercing the skin. Sprinkle with salt and leave for at least 30 minutes.
3. Heat the butter and cook the finely chopped onion for 3–4 minutes. Add the rice and cook for another 3–4 minutes. Add the finely chopped meat and stir for a few minutes over the heat. Stir in the chopped tomatoes, chopped parsley, nuts and raisins, lemon juice, and seasoning.
4. Squeeze the juice from the eggplants and wash them in cold water. Drain well and dry thoroughly. Heat the oil and cook the cut side of the eggplants until they are brown and fairly soft. Scrape the flesh from the skins and add to the meat mixture. Stir in well, adding about ¾ cup [175 ml/6 fl oz] of stock, or as much as will moisten the mixture. Put this mixture into the eggplant skins and lay them in an ovenproof dish.
5. Mix the remaining stock with the tomato purée, and season. Pour this sauce around the edge of the dish, and cook in the oven for 20 minutes. Then turn the oven down to 325°F/160°C/Gas Mark 3, and cook for another 40 minutes. During the last 15 minutes, sprinkle with browned bread crumbs.

Meat Balls in Tomato Sauce

	00:30	Serves 4	Midwest
	00:55		

American	Ingredients	Metric/Imperial
1 lb	Ground [minced] fresh mutton or lamb	450 g/1 lb
½ cup	Cider (or light white wine)	125 ml/4 fl oz
2	Slices stale white bread	2
1	Large onion	1
2 tbsp	Chopped parsley	1½ tbsp
1 tsp	Chopped thyme	1 tsp
1 tsp	Lemon rind	1 tsp
3 tsp	Paprika	3 tsp
2	Eggs	2
2–3 tbsp	Seasoned flour	1½–2 tbsp
8 tbsp	Butter	100 g/4 oz
1	Medium onion	1
1	Clove garlic	1
4–5	Peeled and chopped tomatoes	4–5
1 tsp	Basil	1 tsp
½ pint	Sour cream or plain yogurt	125 ml/4 fl oz

1. Preheat the oven to 350°F/180°C/Gas Mark 4.
2. Pour the cider over the bread; leave for several minutes to soak. Put the ground meat in a large bowl with finely chopped or ground onion, 1 tablespoon chopped parsley, thyme, lemon rind, 2 teaspoons paprika, and salt. Squeeze the cider out of the bread and put the bread into the meat mixture. Beat this mixture by hand, adding the beaten egg gradually. This beating should take 7–10 minutes and gives the meat balls their light texture. Take 1 tablespoon of mixture at a time and roll in either wet or oiled hands to shape into rounds. Then cover with seasoned flour.
3. Melt 5–6 tablespoons [65–75 g/2½–3 oz] of butter in a frying pan. Brown the meat balls in butter, then put into an ovenproof dish. Pour the tomato sauce over the meat balls and bake for 30–40 minutes.
4. To make the sauce: melt 3 tablespoons [40 g/1½ oz] of butter, and cook the sliced onion and crushed garlic for 5–6 minutes. Add the tomatoes, 1 tablespoon chopped parsley, basil, seasoning, 1 teaspoon paprika, and cider from the soaked bread. Heat together to boiling point and pour over the meat balls.
5. Serve with sour cream or yogurt spooned over the meat dish, and a sprinkling of chopped parsley on top.

Baked Stuffed Mushrooms

	00:25	Serves 4	United States
	00:55		

American	Ingredients	Metric/Imperial
½ lb	Ground [minced] lamb	225 g/8 oz
3 tbsp	Butter	40 g/1½ oz
1	Small onion	1
¾ cup	Fresh bread crumbs	25 g/1 oz
½	Clove garlic	½
1 tbsp	Parsley	1 tbsp
½ tbsp	Chopped capers	½ tbsp
	A pinch of mace (or nutmeg)	
1	Egg	1
16	Large flat mushrooms	16
8 slices	Bacon	8 rashers
2–3 tbsp	Mixed brown bread crumbs and grated cheese	1½–2 tbsp

1. Preheat the oven to 350°F/180°C/Gas Mark 4.
2. Heat 2 tablespoons [25 g/1 oz] of butter, and cook the chopped onion and crushed garlic for 4–5 minutes. Add the ground meat and cook for another 7–8 minutes, stirring constantly. Mix in the bread crumbs, parsley and capers, and season well with salt, pepper, and mace. When it has cooled slightly, add enough beaten egg to moisten the mixture without making it at all runny.
3. Remove the stems from the mushrooms level with their base. Chop the stems and add to the stuffing mixture. Divide the stuffing into 8 mushrooms, mold over the mushroom caps, and lay the other 8 mushroom caps on top, pressing firmly together. Wrap each mushroom sandwich in a strip of bacon and place in a buttered ovenproof dish.
4. Spoon 1 tablespoon [15 g/½ oz] of melted butter over the mushrooms, cover with foil, and bake in the oven for 20–30 minutes. After 15 minutes remove the foil and sprinkle the bread crumb and grated cheese mixture over the dish. Cook for another 10–15 minutes and, if necessary, brown under the broiler [grill].

Pork with Artichoke Hearts

		00:15				
		01:00	Serves 4		United States	

American	Ingredients	Metric/Imperial
4	Artichokes	4
4	Boneless loin of pork steaks	4
2 tsp	Salt	2 tsp
	Black pepper	
2 tbsp	Margarine	25 g/1 oz
4	Slices cheese	4
¾ cup	Chili sauce	175 ml/6 fl oz
1–2 tbsp	Grated horseradish	1–1½ tbsp

1. Twist off the stalks of the artichokes and remove the outermost leaves. Place the artichokes in lightly salted, boiling water. Cover and boil for 30–45 minutes. They are ready when the leaves come off easily. Remove the leaves from the artichokes. Place them in a covered pot so that they keep warm. Save the artichoke hearts.
2. Brown the meat on both sides in margarine. Add the salt and pepper. Sauté until the meat is cooked all the way through. Place an artichoke heart on each slice of meat. Cover with a slice of cheese. Place a lid over the frying pan. Allow the cheese to melt.
3. To make the sauce, mix the chili sauce with grated horseradish. Place the meat on plates, putting the artichoke leaves decoratively around each slice. Dip the leaves in the sauce.

Breaded Pork Chops

		00:05				
		00:30	Serves 4		Midwest	

American	Ingredients	Metric/Imperial
4	Loin pork chops, 1 inch thick	4
	Salt and pepper	
1	Large egg	1
2 tbsp	Water	1½ tbsp
	Bread crumbs	
¼ cup	Clarified butter	50 g/2 oz
½ tsp	Dried sage	½ tsp

1. Carefully trim the excess fat from the pork chops. Season with salt and pepper.
2. Beat the egg and water together. Dip the chops in the egg, then coat them with bread crumbs. Press the crumbs firmly onto the chops.
3. In a heavy frying pan, heat the butter over moderate heat. Crumble the sage; add to the butter. Add the chops; cook slowly until well browned and done through, about 30 minutes.

Pork Chops

		01:35				
		00:30	Serves 4		Mid Atlantic	

American	Ingredients	Metric/Imperial
4	Loin pork chops, 1 inch thick	4
	Marinade	
	Tomato sauce	
	A pinch of sugar	
2–3	Cloves garlic, crushed	2–3

1. Season some tomato sauce to taste with salt and pepper, and add a pinch of sugar and 2–3 cloves crushed garlic. Leave the chops in this at least 1 hour.
2. Heat the coals in an outdoor grill until hot, about 30 minutes, or preheat the broiler [grill].
3. When ready to cook, pat the chops dry, brush with oil or Barbecue Baste (see Index) and cook for about 30 minutes, turning once or twice.
4. If there is sufficient marinade, it can be heated with a few drops of Tabasco or Worcestershire sauce and a pat of butter and served with the chops.

Pork Chops in Sour Cream

		00:15				
		01:00	Serves 4		Midwest	

American	Ingredients	Metric/Imperial
4	Thick pork chops	4
	Flour	
½ cup	Sour cream	125 ml/4 fl oz
1 tbsp	Lemon juice	1 tbsp
½ tsp	Grated lemon rind	½ tsp
1 tsp	Sugar	1 tsp
½ tsp	Powdered thyme	½ tsp
	Orange or grapefruit sections	
	Honey	

1. Preheat the oven to 350°F/180°C/Gas Mark 4.
2. Trim the excess fat from the chops and dredge lightly with flour. Put the fat trimmings into a frying pan, and fry to render the fat. Remove the pieces of skin that remain, put the chops in the pan, and brown lightly on both sides. Remove to a casserole.
3. Mix the sour cream with lemon juice, lemon rind, sugar, salt, pepper, and thyme. Add ½ cup [125 ml/4 fl oz] water, and pour over the chops. Cook for 45–50 minutes.
4. Brush some sections of orange or grapefruit (or both) with a little honey and broil [grill] for few minutes.
5. Garnish the chops with the fruit, and serve with string beans, or spinach, and sweet potatoes.

Pork Chops in Sour Cream

Pork Fillets

00:20
01:05   Serves 4   United States

American	Ingredients	Metric/Imperial
2 lb	Pork tenderloin	900 g/2 lb
1	Large apple	1
2 tbsp	Almonds, chopped	1½ tbsp
1 tsp	Sugar	1 tsp
¼ tsp	Cinnamon	¼ tsp
¼ tsp	Garlic powder	¼ tsp
1 tsp	Salt	1 tsp
¼ tsp	Freshly ground pepper	¼ tsp
¼ cup	Olive oil	60 ml/2 fl oz
½ cup	Dry red wine	125 ml/4 fl oz
1 cup	Stock	250 ml/8 fl oz

1. Slice the tenderloin into 6 pieces. Peel, core, and finely chop the apple. Combine the apple, almonds, sugar, and cinnamon; mix well. Make a slash in the center of each tenderloin. Stuff with apple filling. Press the meat together; secure with metal clamps, if necessary.

2. Combine the garlic powder, salt, and pepper. Rub the tenderloins with the mixture. Heat the oil in a deep frying pan. Brown the tenderloins on all sides. Add the wine and stock; bring to a boil. Reduce the heat; simmer 1 hour, turning the meat at 15-minute intervals.

Casserole of Pork

00:15
02:15   Serves 6   Mid Atlantic

American	Ingredients	Metric/Imperial
2 lb	Pork shoulder	900 g/2 lb
12	Small white onions	12
2 tbsp	Flour	1½ tbsp
½ cup	Dry white wine	125 ml/4 fl oz
½ cup	Chicken stock	125 ml/4 fl oz
2–3 sprigs fresh or 1 tsp dried	Rosemary	2–3 sprigs fresh or 1 tsp dried
1 tsp	Dried oregano	1 tsp
1 tsp	Chopped parsley	1 tsp
1 lb	Tart cooking apples, peeled, seeded, and quartered	450 g/1 lb

1. Preheat the oven to 300°F/150°C/Gas Mark 2.

2. Trim the fat from the meat and cut it into slices. Put the fat trimmings into a frying pan and fry until the fat melts. Then remove the pieces of brown skin, and sauté the meat and onions in the fat. Remove to a casserole.

3. Pour off the excess fat from the pan leaving 2 tablespoons [1½ tbsp]. Mix in the flour, add the wine and stock and stir until boiling and the sauce is smooth and thickened. Add the seasoning and herbs, and pour over the meat in the casserole. Cover very tightly, and cook for 1½ hours.

4. Add the apple quarters, cover again, and cook for another ½ hour.

Spicy Pork Casserole

00:20
01:45   Serves 6   Southwest

American	Ingredients	Metric/Imperial
6	Loin pork chops	6
1	Clove garlic	1
2 tbsp	Butter or margarine	25 g/1 oz
2	Cooking apples, peeled, cored, and cut into ½-inch slices	2
2	Onions, peeled and sliced	2
2 tbsp	Flour	1½ tbsp
1 tbsp	Lemon juice	1 tbsp
2 cups	Applesauce	450 ml/¾ pint
¼ tsp	Ground cinnamon	¼ tsp
¼ tsp	Ground nutmeg	¼ tsp
⅛ tsp	Ground cloves	⅛ tsp

1. Preheat the oven to 350°F/180°C/Gas Mark 4.

2. Trim the chops, rub both sides with a cut clove of garlic, and sprinkle with salt and pepper. Put into a lightly buttered frying pan and brown on both sides.

3. Put a layer of apples and onions into a buttered casserole, arrange the chops on top, and cover with the remaining apple and onion slices.

4. Stir the flour into the sediment in the pan, add 2 cups [450 ml/¾ pint] boiling water, and stir until thickened. Add the lemon juice, applesauce, and spices. Mix all well and pour into the casserole. Cook for 1½ hours, removing the lid for the last 20 minutes.

Braised Pork Chops

00:15
00:55   Serves 4   Mid Atlantic

American	Ingredients	Metric/Imperial
4	Pork loin chops	4
2 tbsp	Oil	1½ tbsp
5	Medium carrots	5
2	Celery stalks	2
2	Medium onions	2
1	Clove garlic	1
1 tbsp	Flour	1 tbsp
1 tbsp	Tomato purée	1 tbsp
½ cup	Red wine or cider	125 ml/4 fl oz
1½ cups	Stock	350 ml/12 fl oz
1 tsp	Chopped thyme	1 tsp
1 tbsp	Chopped parsley	1 tbsp
1	Bay leaf	1
3	Medium cooking apples	3
1 tbsp	Brown [demerara] sugar	1 tbsp
1 cup	Quartered mushrooms	100 g/4 oz

Braised Pork Chops

1. Preheat the oven to 350°F/180°C/Gas Mark 4.
2. Brown the chops on both sides in hot oil, about 2 minutes on each side. Place in an ovenproof dish with a lid and keep warm.
3. Fry the chopped onions, crushed garlic, carrots, and celery cut into strips, until golden brown. Stir in the flour; add the tomato purée and stock. Bring gently to a boil, stirring all the time. Add the wine, or cider, and herbs. Pour the vegetable mixture over the chops and replace the lid on the dish. Bake in the oven for 40 minutes.
4. Meanwhile, cut the apples into rings. After 20 minutes, add the mushrooms and stir these well into the sauce. Lay the apple rings in an overlapping layer all over the dish. Sprinkle with brown sugar and finish cooking with the lid off the dish.

Stuffed Pork Chops

 00:40 01:30   Serves 4   Mid Atlantic

American	Ingredients	Metric/Imperial
4	Large pork chops	4
3 tbsp	Butter	40 g/1½ oz
1	Onion	1
1	Stalk celery	1
1	Apple	1
2 cups	Fresh bread crumbs	100 g/4 oz
4 tbsp	Chopped parsley, thyme and a little sage	3½ tbsp
	Grated rind of ½ lemon	
	A few drops lemon juice	
1	Small egg	1
2–3 tbsp	Oil	1½–2 tbsp

	Barbecue Sauce	
1	Onion	1
1	Clove garlic	1
1½ tbsp	Oil	1¼ tbsp
1 tsp	Flour	1 tsp
1 can (8 oz)	Tomatoes	1 tin (225 g/8 oz)
1 cup	Brown stock	250 ml/8 fl oz
2 tbsp	Vinegar	1½ tbsp
2 tbsp	Worcestershire sauce	1½ tbsp
1 tbsp	Tomato chutney	1 tbsp
1 tbsp	Sugar	1 tbsp
1 tsp	Lemon juice	1 tsp
1 tbsp	Chopped parsley and thyme	1 tbsp
¼ tsp	Celery salt	¼ tsp

1. Preheat the oven to 350°F/180°C/Gas Mark 4.
2. Make the barbecue sauce: Heat the oil and cook the chopped onion and crushed garlic for 3–4 minutes to soften. Then remove the lid and brown slightly; add the flour and brown a little. Add the canned tomatoes and stock. Bring to a boil. Add all the other ingredients; cook for 15 minutes. Strain and set aside.
3. Make the stuffing: Cook the chopped onion and celery in butter. Add to the bread crumbs together with the chopped apple, herbs, and grated lemon rind. Bind the mixture with a beaten egg or a dash of lemon juice, and if too dry add a little milk or stock.
4. Make a cut in the center of the side of each pork chop, being careful to make a pocket without piercing the top or bottom surface of the meat. Push the stuffing into the pocket. Sew up the slits in the chops and then dry them. Brown on both sides in a little hot oil, then remove and put into an ovenproof dish.
5. Spoon a little barbecue sauce thinned with a little extra stock over the dish. Cook in the oven for about 1 hour. Take out and remove the threads, and serve with barbecue sauce and boiled potatoes.

Grilled Pork Delight

Hawaiian Pork Chops

01:15
01:05   Serves 4   Pacific Southwest

American	Ingredients	Metric/Imperial
4	Pork chops	4
1	Green pepper	1
1	Medium-sized onion	1
4	Stalks celery	4
1 tbsp	Oil	1 tbsp
1 tbsp	Butter	15 g/½ oz
4	Slices pineapple	4
1 cup	Chicken or veal stock	250 ml/8 fl oz
	A little paprika	
	Marinade	
1	Clove garlic, crushed	1
	Grated rind of half an orange	
1 cup	Soy sauce	250 ml/8 fl oz
¼ cup	Sherry or port	60 ml/2 fl oz
¼ tsp	Grated fresh ginger	¼ tsp
½	Bay leaf, crushed	½

1. Mix the marinade ingredients together with the seasoning and pour over the pork chops. Leave for at least 1 hour.
2. Preheat the oven to 350°F/180°C/Gas Mark 4.
3. Remove the seeds from the pepper and cut 4 rings; chop the rest. Chop the onion and the celery; mix the chopped vegetables together.
4. Remove the chops from the marinade and dry on a paper towel [kitchen paper]. Heat the oil and add the butter; when foaming, put in the chops and brown on both sides (this takes about 2–3 minutes each side). Put them into an ovenproof dish with a lid. Put a slice of pineapple on each chop and a spoonful of the chopped vegetables. Mix the stock with the remaining marinade and pour around the chops in the dish. Replace the cover and bake in a moderate oven for about 1 hour. If the meat looks as if it is becoming dry, add a little more stock.
5. During the last 5 minutes, put the pepper rings on top of the pineapple. Just before serving, dust each pineapple ring with paprika.

Pork Chop Suey

00:20
00:20   Serves 4   New England

American	Ingredients	Metric/Imperial
3 cups	Cooked pork	500 g/18 oz
½ cup	Celery	50 g/2 oz
½ cup	Spring onions	50 g/2 oz
1 cup	Mushrooms	100 g/4 oz
1	Green pepper	1
1 lb can	Bean sprouts	450 g/1 lb tin
2 tbsp	Oil	1½ tbsp
1 cup	Chicken stock	250 ml/8 fl oz
1 tbsp	Cornstarch [cornflour]	1 tbsp
1 tbsp	Soy sauce	1 tbsp

1. Cut the pork into thick strips. Cut the celery into slices and the spring onions into lengths. Slice the mushrooms. Seed and chop the green pepper and blanch for 5 minutes in boiling, salted water. Drain. Rinse the bean sprouts in cold water and drain.
2. Heat the oil and cook the celery and onions for 2–3 minutes. Add the mushrooms and pork, and cook for 2 minutes. Add the chopped pepper and bean sprouts, and cook for 2 minutes, stirring all the time.
3. Add the stock with cornstarch dissolved in it. Bring to a boil and simmer for 5 minutes. Add the soy sauce; season and serve with plain boiled rice or fried noodles.

Pork in Cider Sauce

00:10
00:40   Serves 4   Mid Atlantic

American	Ingredients	Metric/Imperial
2 lb	Pork tenderloin	900 g/2 lb
2 tbsp	Brown [demerara] sugar	1½ tbsp
2 tsp	Dry mustard	2 tsp
2 tbsp	Corn oil	1½ tbsp
1 tbsp	Cornstarch [cornflour]	1 tbsp
1	Orange	1
¾ cup	Cider	175 ml/6 fl oz
1	Clove garlic, crushed	1
6	Stuffed olives, sliced	6
4	Cloves	4
	Pineapple	

1. Preheat the oven to 350°F/180°C/Gas Mark 4.
2. Have the butcher cut the tenderloin into slices and pound them flat.
3. Mix the sugar and mustard and coat both sides of the meat. Heat the oil in a frying pan, brown the meat on both sides, and remove to a casserole.
4. Add the cornstarch to the remaining fat; stir and cook for 1 minute. Add the orange juice, made up to 1¼ cups [300 ml/½ pint], with cider. Stir until boiling, boil for 2 minutes. Add the seasoning, garlic, olives, and cloves. Pour over the meat and cook for 30–35 minutes.
5. Remove the cloves, check the seasoning, and serve with broiled [grilled] slices of pineapple.

Grilled Pork Delight

 00:10
00:15   Serves 4   United States

American	Ingredients	Metric/Imperial
4	Pieces thin belly pork or pork for frying	4
⅔ cup	Cheese, grated	75 g/3 oz
½ tbsp	Prepared mustard	½ tbsp
4 tbsp	Cider or beer	3½ tbsp
1	Tomato, sliced, for garnish	1

1. Preheat the broiler [grill].
2. Grill the pork for 5–7 minutes on each side. Mix the cheese, mustard, and cider or beer together in a bowl.
3. Spread the topping equally over the pork. Grill until brown. Garnish with a slice of tomato.

Roast Stuffed Pork Tenderloin

00:25
01:00   Serves 4   Mid Atlantic

American	Ingredients	Metric/Imperial
2	Pork tenderloins weighing 1–1½ lbs [450–675 g] each	2
2	Cooking apples	2
12	Cooked seeded prunes	12
1 tsp	Grated lemon rind	1 tsp
	A little lemon juice	
2 tbsp	Oil	1½ tbsp
1 tbsp	Butter	15 g/½ oz
1 cup	Stock	250 ml/8 fl oz
1 tbsp	Cream	1 tbsp
2	Apples	2
4 tsp	Red currant or cranberry jelly	4 tsp

1. Preheat the oven to 450°F/230°C/Gas Mark 8.
2. Split the tenderloins lengthwise without cutting completely in half. Beat the meat to flatten and tenderize it. Peel, core, and dice the cooking apples. Mix them with the prunes and lemon rind together with the seasoning, and spread half the mixture on each tenderloin. Sprinkle with a little melted butter and lemon juice. Roll each loin up like a jelly roll, and tie in several places.
3. Preheat the oil in a roasting pan. Put the loins in the oven and baste. Brown the outside of the meat for 10–15 minutes. Reduce the heat to 375°F/190°C and cook for 50 minutes, basting frequently. When cooked and tender, remove the meat for carving. Pour off the excess fat and make gravy with the residue and stock, adding cream at the last minute.
4. Carve the pork into slices for serving, and place on a hot serving dish. Surround the meat with a garnish of apples, peeled, halved, cored, and poached in light syrup, with a teaspoonful of red currant or cranberry jelly in the center of each.

Smoked Pork Loin with Rice

Smoked Pork Loin with Rice

 00:10
00:25   Serves 4   Mid Atlantic

American	Ingredients	Metric/Imperial
1 cup	Long-grain rice	225 g/8 oz
1 tsp	Salt	1 tsp
2 cups	Meat stock (from cubes)	450 ml/¾ pint
1 can (12 oz)	Sweet corn	1 tin (350 g/12 oz)
1½ lb	Smoked pork loin, cut in 6–8 slices	675 g/1½ lb
1 can (8 oz)	Whole, peeled tomatoes	1 tin (225 g/8 oz)
1½ tsp	Sage or basil	1½ tsp
½ tsp	Lemon pepper	½ tsp
½ tsp	Garlic salt (optional)	½ tsp

1. Place the rice, salt, and stock in a wide, shallow pan and bring to a boil. Simmer slowly, covered, for about 15 minutes.
2. Drain the sweet corn and mix with the rice. Place the pork slices in a ring on top of the rice. Finally, place the tomatoes, with some of the liquid, in the center.
3. Mix the sage, lemon pepper, and garlic salt and sprinkle the mixture over all the ingredients in the pan. Cover and simmer slowly for 5–8 minutes more. Serve immediately.

Paprika Pork with Sauerkraut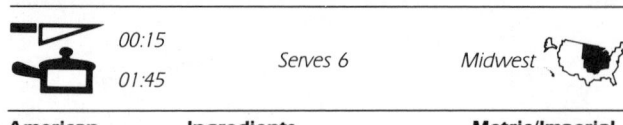

🚩 00:15
01:45
Serves 6   Midwest

American	Ingredients	Metric/Imperial
2½ lb	Pork shoulder meat	1.25 kg/2½ lb
3 tbsp	Flour	2½ tbsp
3 tsp	Salt	3 tsp
¼ tsp	Pepper	¼ tsp
3 tbsp	Oil	2 tbsp
3–4	Onions, peeled and sliced	3–4
2 tbsp	Paprika	1½ tbsp
2 cans (about 15 oz each)	Sauerkraut	2 tins (about 425 g/15 oz each)
1	Green pepper, seeded and chopped	1
1 cup	Sour cream	250 ml/8 fl oz

1. Preheat the oven to 350°F/180°C/Gas Mark 4.
2. Trim the meat and cut into 1½-inch cubes. Mix the flour with 1 teaspoon of salt and half the pepper and dredge the meat thoroughly. Heat the oil in a frying pan and sauté the meat until brown. Remove to a casserole.
3. Brown the onion in the remaining oil; add paprika, 1½ cups [350 ml/12 fl oz] of water and the rest of the pepper. Simmer until all the brown pieces in the pan are loosened. Add the sauerkraut, green pepper, and remaining 2 teaspoons of salt. Mix well and pour over the meat in the casserole.
4. Cover and cook for 1½ hours. Just before serving, adjust the seasoning and stir in the sour cream.

Fried Pork Cutlets

🚩 00:15
00:35
Serves 4   Mid Atlantic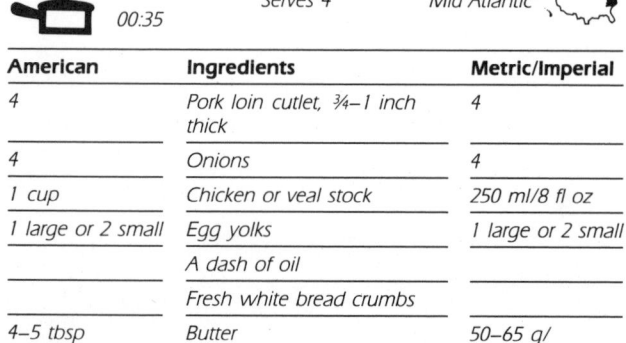

American	Ingredients	Metric/Imperial
4	Pork loin cutlet, ¾–1 inch thick	4
4	Onions	4
1 cup	Chicken or veal stock	250 ml/8 fl oz
1 large or 2 small	Egg yolks	1 large or 2 small
	A dash of oil	
	Fresh white bread crumbs	
4–5 tbsp	Butter	50–65 g/ 2–2½ oz

1. Preheat the oven to 450°F/230°C/Gas Mark 8.
2. Peel and slice the onions and cook until tender in stock. Purée in the electric blender or put through a sieve. Season and keep warm.
3. Coat the cutlets with egg yolks mixed with salt and a dash of oil. Then roll in bread crumbs. Melt the butter and, when foaming, fry the cutlets for about 7–10 minutes until golden brown on each side. Drain on paper towels [kitchen paper] and put into the oven for 10 more minutes.
4. To serve, pile the onion purée in the center of a dish and arrange fried cutlets around the edge.

Pork Kebabs Yucatan

🚩 24:15
00:25
Serves 4   Southwest

American	Ingredients	Metric/Imperial
	Juice of 1 lime	
¼ cup	Salad oil	60 ml/2 fl oz
¼ tsp	Crushed whole coriander	¼ tsp
¼ cup	Onion, chopped	25 g/1 oz
1	Clove garlic, mashed	1
¼ tsp	Pepper	¼ tsp
1¼ lb	Lean pork, cut in 1½-inch cubes	575 g/1¼ lb
1	Medium zucchini [courgettes], sliced	1
2	Red peppers, stemmed, seeded, and cut in chunks	2
½ lb	Mushrooms, cleaned and stems cut off	225 g/8 oz

1. The day before cooking, combine the lime juice, oil, coriander, onion, garlic, and pepper in a glass or pottery bowl or casserole. Add the meat; stir to coat with the marinade. Cover; refrigerate 24 hours, stirring once or twice.
2. Preheat the broiler [grill].
3. To cook, drain the meat, reserving the marinade. Skewer the meat alternately with zucchini, red peppers, and mushrooms. Broil [grill] until done through (20–25 minutes), basting occasionally with marinade. Serve the kebabs with cooked rice.

Pork Spareribs

🚩 01:30
00:40
Serves 4   Southwest

American	Ingredients	Metric/Imperial
4 lb	Spareribs	1.75 kg/4 lb
	Marinade	
1 cup	Pineapple juice	250 ml/8 fl oz
½ cup	White wine vinegar	125 ml/4 fl oz
1 tbsp	Worcestershire sauce	1 tbsp
1 tbsp	Tomato purée	1 tbsp
1 tbsp	Dry mustard	1 tbsp
1 tsp	Chili powder	1 tsp
½ cup	Brown [demerara] sugar	100 g/4 oz
	Pepper and salt	

1. Combine all the marinade ingredients, pour over the meat and leave in a cool place for at least 1 hour.
2. Heat the coals in an outdoor grill until hot, about 30 minutes, or preheat the broiler [grill].
3. When ready to cook, arrange the spareribs on the barbecue and baste frequently with the marinade. Cook slowly until crisp and well done, about 30–40 minutes.
4. The remaining marinade can be heated and poured over the spareribs.

Savory Pork

Savory Pork

	00:20		
	00:40	Serves 4	Southwest

American	Ingredients	Metric/Imperial
1–1½ lb	Lean pork	450–675 g/ 1–1½ lb
2	Large onions	2
1–2 tbsp	Peanut oil	1–1½ tbsp
1	Clove garlic	1
½ tbsp	Lemon juice	½ tbsp
3	Large ripe tomatoes	3
1–2	Chilis (or ¼ tsp tabasco or chili sauce)	1–2
½ tbsp	Sugar	½ tbsp
1½ tbsp	Worcestershire sauce	1¼ tbsp
3 cups	Uncooked noodles	350 g/12 oz
1 cup	Grated Cheddar cheese	100 g/4 oz
½ cup	Salted peanuts	50 g/2 oz

1. Dice the pork. Cook the pork and chopped onions together in oil until golden brown. Add the garlic and lemon juice. Stir well.
2. Skin and chop the tomatoes; seed and chop the chilis. Add them to the mixture, with sugar, Worcestershire sauce, pepper, and a little salt. Simmer gently for 15–20 minutes, or until the pork is tender and thoroughly cooked.
3. Meanwhile, cook the noodles in plenty of boiling salted water for 10–15 minutes until tender. Drain; rinse with hot water. Allow to dry slightly.
4. When the pork is cooked and just before serving, mix in the cheese and peanuts. Check seasoning. Serve the pork mixture and noodles together in one large dish, or serve the noodles separately.

Pork Pie

	00:25		
	01:00	Serves 6	South

American	Ingredients	Metric/Imperial
1	Medium-sized head of cauliflower	1
1 tbsp	Oil	1 tbsp
2	Small onions, peeled and very finely chopped	2
1	Clove garlic, crushed	1
3½ cups	Canned [tinned] tomatoes	900 g/2 lb
	A pinch of thyme	
¼ tsp	Paprika	¼ tsp
3 tbsp	Flour	2 tbsp
3 cups	Diced cooked pork	500 g/18 oz
	Pastry for a 9-inch 1-crust pie (see Index)	

1. Preheat the oven to 450°F/230°C/Gas Mark 8.
2. Cook the cauliflower until just tender in boiling, salted water. Drain and divide into small flowerets.
3. Heat the oil in a frying pan; add the onion and garlic and sauté for a few minutes. Add the tomatoes, thyme, salt, pepper, and paprika. Simmer for 10 minutes, then press through a sieve.
4. Blend the flour with a little cold water; add to the sauce and stir until boiling, cooking 3–5 minutes.
5. Put the pork and cauliflower into a deep dish and pour the sauce over them.
6. Cover with the pastry and bake for about 25 minutes, or until the crust is well browned.

Barbecued Spareribs

Cold Pork Pies

	06:00	Serves 5	Midwest
	00:55		

American	Ingredients	Metric/Imperial
	Hot water pastry (see Index)	
1 lb	Lean pork	450 g/1 lb
½ tsp	Salt	½ tsp
¼ tsp	Pepper	¼ tsp
	A pinch of mixed herbs	
2	Hard-boiled eggs, sliced	2
	Egg or milk for glazing	
2 tsp	Gelatin [gelatine]	2 tsp
½ cup	Stock or water	125 ml/4 fl oz

1. Preheat the oven to 400°F/200°C/Gas Mark 6.

2. Divide the pastry into 5 portions and cut about one third from each portion for the lid of the pie. Keep these pieces warm.

3. Mold the 5 pieces of dough into a pie shape with the hands or mold the dough around a glass jar. Fix a double band of waxed paper around each and secure with string.

4. Cut the pork into small cubes; sprinkle with salt, pepper, and herbs. Put into the pie cases with slices of egg and add 1–2 tablespoons [1–1½ tbsp] water.

5. Roll out the small portions of dough for the lids. Moisten the edges of the pastry and put on the lids. Make a hole in the top and flute around the edges. Decorate as liked.

6. Bake for 30 minutes, then remove the paper and brush the top and sides of the pies with beaten egg or milk. Return to the oven and cook for 20–25 minutes.

7. Dissolve the gelatin in the stock. If water is used, add a little meat extract. When just beginning to set, pour into the cooled pies through the hole in the top. Allow to get quite cold before serving.

Barbecued Spareribs

	00:10	Serves 4	Pacific Southwest
	01:10		

American	Ingredients	Metric/Imperial
3 lb	Spareribs	1.25 kg/3 lb
	Salt and pepper	
1	Onion, finely chopped	1
1 tbsp	Oil	1 tbsp
1	Clove garlic (optional)	1
1 cup	Tomato soup	250 ml/8 fl oz
1 tbsp	Worcestershire sauce	1 tbsp
2 tbsp	Brown [demerara] sugar	1½ tbsp
	Watercress for garnish	

1. Chop the spareribs into separate ribs or ask the butcher to do this for you. Place in a large saucepan with salted water to cover. Bring to a boil, cover pan, and simmer for 20 minutes.

2. Meanwhile, fry the onion in oil in a small saucepan until softened. Add the garlic, tomato soup, Worcestershire sauce, brown sugar, and salt and pepper. Bring to a boil, stirring until the sugar is dissolved. Cover the pan and simmer for 10 minutes. Drain the spareribs well.

3. Brush them with some of the sauce and cook over a moderately hot fire or in a broiler [grill] for 30 minutes, until golden and tender. Baste with the sauce and garnish with sprigs of watercress.

Pork Stroganoff

	00:15	Serves 4	Pacific Northwest 
	00:35		

American	Ingredients	Metric/Imperial
1½ lb	Shoulder of pork	675 g/1½ lb
4	Onions	4
	Butter or margarine for frying	
	Salt	
	Pepper	
1⅔ cups	Strong beef stock	375 ml/13 fl oz
2 tbsp	Tomato purée	1½ tbsp
1½ cups	Crème fraîche or sour cream	350 ml/12 fl oz
1–2 tsp	Soy sauce	1–2 tsp

1. Cut the meat into strips. Peel and slice the onions. Brown the meat in the butter in a stew pan. Add salt and pepper. Add the onions so that they also become brown.

2. Lower the heat and gradually add the beef stock. Add the tomato purée. Simmer the meat and the onions in the gravy for about 25 minutes, or until the meat is tender and thoroughly cooked. Cover the pan when simmering the meat.

3. Remove the pan from the heat and stir in the crème fraîche. Bring to a boil and add the soy sauce. This dish should have a rich and rather strong taste. Serve with rice.

Pork Stroganoff

Sweet and Sour Pork

00:10
00:38

Serves 4   Pacific Southwest

American	Ingredients	Metric/Imperial
1½ lb	Lean pork cut in small cubes	675 g/1½ lb
3 tbsp	Oil	2 tbsp
3	Onions	3
2	Carrots	2
3 tbsp	Sweet pickle chutney	2 tbsp
1 can (8 oz)	Pineapple chunks (drained)	1 tin (225 g/8 oz)
½ cup	Pineapple juice	125 ml/4 fl oz
3 tbsp	Soy sauce	2 tbsp
½ cup	Stock	125 ml/4 fl oz
3 tbsp	Sugar	2 tbsp
3 tbsp	Vinegar	2 tbsp
2 tbsp	Cornstarch [cornflour]	1½ tbsp
2	Eggs	2
2 tsp	Flour	2 tsp
	Oil for deep frying	

1. Make the sauce: Heat the oil and fry the sliced onion and carrots until golden brown, about 10 minutes. Add the chutney, pineapple chunks and juice, soy sauce, stock, sugar, vinegar, and salt. Cover the pan and cook slowly for 15 minutes. Mix 2 teaspoons cornstarch with a little cold water. Add to the sauce and heat again almost to the boiling point, stirring all the time for 5–6 minutes. Season. Keep hot.

2. Heat the oil and fry the meat cubes until golden brown. This should take 3–4 minutes. Drain on paper towels [kitchen paper].

3. Beat the egg; add the flour and remaining cornstarch and mix well. Reheat the fat until it will cook a bread cube in 20 seconds. Coat the pork pieces with the egg mixture and fry until golden brown, 1–2 minutes.

4. Drain and serve with plain boiled rice, pouring sauce over the top.

Ham and Apricot Pie

 12:05
00:48
Serves 4   Mid Atlantic

American	Ingredients	Metric/Imperial
1 slice (about 1½ lb)	Ham, cut 1 inch thick	1 slice (about 675 g/1½ lb)
	Prepared mustard	
1 cup	Dried apricots, soaked overnight	225 g/8 oz
3 tbsp	Seedless raisins	2 tbsp
4 tbsp	Chicken stock	3½ tbsp
6	Medium potatoes, peeled and sliced	6
1 tbsp	Butter or margarine	15 g/½ oz

1. Preheat the oven to 375°F/190°C/Gas Mark 5.
2. Heat a frying pan, put in the ham, and brown lightly on both sides.
3. Put into a deep baking dish, spread very lightly with mustard, and sprinkle with pepper.
4. Arrange the apricots and raisins on top.
5. Add the chicken stock and cover with slices of potato. Dot with butter. Bake for ¾ hour.

Baked Glazed Ham

 00:10
00:30
Serves 4–6   Mid Atlantic

American	Ingredients	Metric/Imperial
2–3 lb	Canned [tinned] ham	900 g–1.25 kg/ 2–3 lb
2 tbsp	Honey	1½ tbsp
	Grated rind of 1 orange	
1 tsp	Dry mustard	1 tsp
4 tbsp	Brown [demerara] sugar	3½ tbsp
½ cup	Cider (or pineapple juice)	125 ml/4 fl oz
1 can (8 oz)	Pineapple rings	1 tin (225 g/8 oz)
1 tbsp	Butter	15 g/½ oz
	A dusting of sugar	
6–8	Canned [tinned] sweet cherries	6–8

1. Preheat the oven to 400°F/200°C/Gas Mark 6.
2. Scrape the jelly off the canned ham and reserve. Place in a baking pan.
3. Melt the honey; spread over the surface of the ham. Mix the orange rind, mustard, and brown sugar together and sprinkle over the surface of the meat. Pour the cider (or pineapple juice) over the ham. Add the jelly from the ham and baste very gently over the ham without disturbing the sugar coating. Bake for 30 minutes, basting after 15 minutes.
4. Melt the butter in a frying pan. Sprinkle the pineapple slices with sugar and brown in butter on both sides. Serve around the ham with cherries in the center of each ring.
5. Use the liquid from the baking pan to make a sauce, adding water and a squeeze of lemon if too sweet.

Scandinavian Style Cabbage

 00:20
02:20
Serves 4   Pacific Southwest

American	Ingredients	Metric/Imperial
2 cups	Chopped ham (or other cold cooked meat)	350 g/12 oz
1	Medium-sized firm head of cabbage	1
4 tbsp	Butter	50 g/2 oz
½ cup	Chopped onion	50 g/2 oz
1 cup	Bread crumbs	50 g/2 oz
2 tbsp	Mixed herbs	1½ tbsp
1 tbsp	Tomato purée	1 tbsp
	A dash of tabasco	
	A little strong stock (or tomato juice)	
2 tbsp	Flour	1½ tbsp
1½ cups	Milk	350 ml/12 fl oz
¼ cup	Strongly flavored grated cheese	25 g/1 oz
½ tsp	Dry mustard	½ tsp

1. Trim the cabbage and cook whole in boiling salted water for about 5–10 minutes. Drain. Plunge in cold water. Remove 3–4 outside leaves and reserve these.
2. Melt 2 tablespoons [25 g/1 oz] of the butter and cook the onion until soft. Mix with the ham, bread crumbs or rice, herbs, tomato purée, seasoning, tabasco, and enough stock (or tomato juice) to make a moist but firm mixture.
3. Cut the stalk out of the cabbage and enough from the center to fill with the stuffing mixture. Cover the hole with the reserved leaves and tie on with string. Wrap in foil and boil for 1–2 hours, until the cabbage is tender. Remove the string and serve with a cheese sauce.
4. Make the sauce: heat the remaining butter. Mix in the flour and blend over the heat. Add the milk gradually. When the sauce is smooth, bring to a boil. Add the cheese, mustard, and seasoning to taste and pour over the cabbage.

Ham with Orange and Raisin Sauce

 00:10
00:20
Serves 4   New England

American	Ingredients	Metric/Imperial
4 large or 8 small	Slices lean cooked ham (cut thick)	4 large or 8 small
4 tbsp	Raisins	3½ tbsp
1	Orange	1
1 tbsp	Cornstarch [cornflour]	1 tbsp
	A dash of lemon juice	
4 tbsp	Brown [demerara] sugar	3½ tbsp
1 tbsp	Butter	15 g/½ oz

1. Preheat the oven to 350°F/180°C/Gas Mark 4.
2. Place the slices of ham overlapping in an ovenproof dish.
3. Put the raisins into the pan, cover with water, and bring to a boil slowly. Simmer for 4–5 minutes.
4. Remove the outer rind from the orange without the white pith. Cut into thin strips and put in a pan of boiling water for 1 minute. Drain and remove. Mix the orange and lemon juice with cornstarch until smooth. Now add the sugar. Pour the mixture into the pan with the raisins and water, and stir over the heat until this thickens and is clear. Stir in the orange rind and butter and pour over the ham slices.
5. Bake in the oven for about 10–15 minutes.

Ham and Pasta Savory

 00:10
00:15   Serves 4   Pacific Southwest

American	Ingredients	Metric/Imperial
2 cups	Shell pasta	450 g/1 lb
1 cup	Cottage cheese, sieved	225 g/8 oz
4 tbsp	Butter	50 g/2 oz
1 cup	Cooked diced ham	175 g/6 oz
	Cayenne pepper	
	Chopped parsley	

1. Cook the pasta for about 12 minutes, or follow the package instructions. Drain well and combine with the cheese.
2. Melt the fat in a pan, add the ham, and heat through. Add the pasta and cheese, and season to taste with salt and cayenne.
3. Put into a hot serving dish, and sprinkle with parsley. Serve with a tossed green salad.

Barbecued Ham with Raisin and Cranberry Sauce

00:35
00:30   Serves 4–5   Southwest

American	Ingredients	Metric/Imperial
1½–2 lb	1-inch thick ham slices	675–900 g/ 1½–2 lb
	A few cloves	
½ cup	Brown [demerara] sugar	100 g/4 oz
2 tbsp	Cornstarch [cornflour]	1½ tbsp
1½ cups	Cranberry juice	350 ml/12 fl oz
½ cup	Orange juice	125 ml/4 fl oz
½ cup	Seedless raisins	50 g/2 oz

1. Heat the coals in an outdoor grill until hot, about 30 minutes, or preheat the broiler [grill].
2. Score the fat edge of the ham at intervals of about 2 inches, and insert 2 or 3 cloves in the fat.
3. Mix the sugar and cornstarch smoothly with the cranberry juice, put into a pan, and add the orange juice and raisins. Bring to a boil, stirring constantly until the mixture thickens.
4. Put the ham on the grid over the hot coals, away from the hottest part. Cook for about 15 minutes, then turn over and brush liberally with the glaze. Cook for 10 more minutes. Then turn and brush the other side.
5. Brush again just before serving, and serve any remaining glaze with the ham.

Ham and Apricot Pie

Ham, Chicken and Mushroom Patties

 00:30 / 00:30   Serves 4   United States

American	Ingredients	Metric/Imperial
3–4	Slices cooked ham	3–4
½ cup	Cooked chicken	75 g/3 oz
1	Package frozen puff pastry, about ½ lb [225 g]	1
1	Egg	1
3 tbsp	Butter	40 g/1½ oz
6–8	Mushrooms	6–8
2 tbsp	Flour	1½ tbsp
1 cup	Milk (or milk and cream)	250 ml/8 fl oz
1 tbsp	Chopped parsley	1 tbsp
	Onion salt	
	A pinch of mace	

1. Preheat the oven to 475°F/240°C/Gas Mark 9.
2. Roll out the pastry until ¼ inch thick. Using a 2½-inch diameter cutter, cut out 8 patties. Now using a smaller cutter, about 1½-inch diameter, make a central cut in each patty, being careful not to cut through to the bottom. Brush the surface of each patty with beaten egg. Do not allow the egg to run over the sides, or this will keep the pastry from rising.
3. Put on a dampened baking sheet and cook for about 15–20 minutes, until the patties are well risen and golden brown. Remove from the oven. Carefully take off the center lid and scoop out the soft pastry inside. Keep warm.
4. Melt the butter and cook the quartered mushrooms for a few minutes. Mix in the flour. Then add the milk. Bring to a boil, stirring all the time. Add the chopped ham, chicken, and parsley. Season with onion salt, pepper, and a pinch of mace. When heated through, spoon the mixture into patty shells. Place the lids on top and serve at once, or keep warm for a short time.

Ham and Potato Cakes

 00:15 / 00:10   Serves 4   Mid Atlantic

American	Ingredients	Metric/Imperial
1 lb	Cooked mashed potato	450 g/1 lb
2 tbsp	Butter	25 g/1 oz
	Milk	
4	Slices ham	4
4	Slices gruyère or processed cheese	4
	Chopped parsley	

1. Preheat the oven to 400°F/200°C/Gas Mark 6.
2. Season the potatoes well with salt and pepper. Add 1 tablespoon [15 g/½ oz] of butter and a little milk if required. Shape into 4 flat cakes. Put onto a greased baking pan, dot with the remaining butter, and brown in the oven.
3. Top with a slice of ham and cheese, and return to the oven until the cheese begins to melt.
4. Sprinkle with parsley before serving.

Ham and Pineapple Toast

 00:05 / 00:07   Serves 4   Pacific Southwest

American	Ingredients	Metric/Imperial
1½ cups	Ground [minced] cooked ham	250 g/9 oz
1 tsp	Prepared mustard	1 tsp
⅛ tsp	Cayenne pepper	⅛ tsp
1–2 tbsp	Mayonnaise	1–1½ tbsp
4	Slices canned pineapple	4
4	Slices hot, lightly buttered toast or hamburger rolls	4

1. Preheat the oven to 400°F/200°C/Gas Mark 6.
2. Season the ham with mustard and pepper and add just enough mayonnaise to bind.
3. Arrange the slices of pineapple in an ovenproof pan, pile the ham mixture in a mound on top, and heat through in a moderately hot oven for about 5–7 minutes.
4. Serve on lightly buttered hot toast on halves of toasted hamburger rolls.

Belgian Ham and Celery Rolls

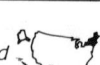 00:20 / 00:25   Serves 4   New England

American	Ingredients	Metric/Imperial
4	Large slices lean ham	4
2 (8-oz) cans	Celery hearts (allowing 1 celery heart per person)	2 (225 g/8 oz) tins
2 tbsp	Butter	25 g/1 oz
1¾ tbsp	Flour	1½ tbsp
1½ cups	Milk	350 ml/12 fl oz
1 cup	Grated Cheddar cheese	100 g/4 oz
½ tsp	French mustard	½ tsp
2 tbsp	Dried bread crumbs	1½ tbsp

1. Preheat the oven to 350°F/180°C/Gas Mark 4.
2. Drain the canned celery hearts. If they are very large, cut in half. Wrap each in a slice of ham, and put the ham and celery rolls in buttered ovenproof dish.
3. Make the cheese sauce: Melt the butter, remove from the heat, stir in the flour, and add the milk. Bring to a boil, stirring all the time. Add ¾ cup [75 g/3 oz] of the grated cheese, mustard, and seasoning; stir over the heat until the cheese has melted.
4. Pour the sauce over the ham and celery rolls. Sprinkle with the remaining cheese and bread crumbs. Bake in the oven for 15–20 minutes. The top should be golden brown and crisp.

Ham Gougere

Ham Gougere

00:50
00:45
Serves 4   Pacific Southwest

American	Ingredients	Metric/Imperial
½–1 cup	Cooked ham	75–175 g/3–6 oz
5 tbsp	Butter	65 g/2½ oz
1	Onion	1
½ cup	Mushrooms	50 g/2 oz
½ tbsp	Flour	½ tbsp
1 tbsp	Tomato purée	1 tbsp
½ cup	Stock	125 ml/4 fl oz
1 tbsp	Sherry	1 tbsp
1 tbsp	Chopped herbs	1 tbsp
½ cup	All-purpose [plain] flour	50 g/2 oz
2	Eggs	2
4 tbsp	Grated Cheddar cheese	3½ tbsp
½ tsp	Dried mustard	½ tsp
2 tbsp	Grated Parmesan cheese	1½ tbsp
2 tbsp	Cornflake crumbs	1½ tbsp
2 tsp	Chopped parsley	2 tsp

1. Preheat the oven to 375°F/190°C/Gas Mark 5.
2. Melt 1 tablespoon [15 g/½ oz] of the butter. Cook sliced onion until soft. Add the mushrooms and cook for 3 minutes. Add the flour and when well mixed add the tomato purée and stock. Stir until it boils and then cook until it has thickened a little. Add the sherry, diced ham, and herbs. Allow to cool slightly before spooning into a dish.
3. Sift the warmed flour. In a pan with sloping sides, heat ½ cup [125 ml/4 fl oz] of water and ¼ cup [50 g/2 oz] of butter. When the butter has melted, bring the mixture to a boil. As soon as it boils, remove from the heat and add all the flour at once. Beat hard with a wooden spoon until the mixture forms a ball in the bottom of the pan. Let it cool. Beat the eggs. When the mixture is cool, add the egg by degrees, beating hard between each addition. The final mixture should be shiny and smooth and hold its shape. A little egg may be left over. Add the cheese and mustard.
4. Butter an ovenproof dish about 3 inches deep. Arrange the pastry in a ring around the outside of the dish. Put the mixture in the center and brush the top with a little beaten egg to give a shine. Sprinkle the top with grated cheese and cornflake crumbs. Bake in the oven for 30–45 minutes for a large dish, or 15–20 minutes for a small one. Sprinkle the top with chopped parsley and serve.

Ham Rolls

 01:15
00:28   Serves 4   Mid Atlantic

American	Ingredients	Metric/Imperial
½ cup	Rice	100 g/4 oz
	Chicken stock or water	
1	Bay leaf	1
1 tbsp	Oil	1 tbsp
2 tbsp	Butter	25 g/1 oz
½	Small onion, peeled and finely chopped	½
1	Small apple, peeled, cored and chopped	1
1½ tsp	Curry powder	1½ tsp
4 tbsp	Light [single] cream	3½ tbsp
	Grated rind of 1 lemon	
2 tbsp	Lemon juice	1½ tbsp
2 tbsp	Chopped cooked ham	1½ tbsp
2 tbsp	Chopped red pepper	1½ tbsp
8	Slices cooked ham	8
	Lettuce	
	Black olives and canned pimento for garnish	

1. Cook the rice in boiling stock with the bay leaf. Drain and, while still hot, stir in the oil, making sure the rice is well coated.
2. Heat the butter in a frying pan, add the onion and, after 3 minutes, add the apple; cook for 5 minutes. Stir in the curry powder; cook for a few minutes. Remove from the heat, add the cream, grated lemon rind and juice, chopped ham, red pepper, and rice. Set aside for about 1 hour to chill.
3. Roll this mixture in the slices of ham and secure with a cocktail stick or toothpick if necessary.
4. Arrange on a bed of lettuce and garnish with black olives and strips of pimento.

Stuffed Ham Rolls

00:20
00:28   Serves 4   Mid Atlantic

American	Ingredients	Metric/Imperial
8	Round slices ham or Canadian style bacon	8
2 tbsp	Butter	25 g/1 oz
1	Large onion	1
1	Clove garlic	1
½ cup	Chopped mushrooms	50 g/2 oz
½ cup	White bread crumbs	25 g/1 oz
½ lb	Ground fat [streaky] bacon	225 g/8 oz
2 tbsp	Parsley and thyme	1½ tbsp
1	Egg	1
2 tbsp	Cranberry jelly (or sauce)	1½ tbsp
1¼ cups	Stock	300 ml/½ pint

1. Heat the oven to 400°F/200°C/Gas Mark 6.
2. Heat the butter and cook the finely chopped onion with a lid on the pan until soft but not brown. Add the garlic and chopped mushrooms and cook for a few more minutes.
3. Mix the bread crumbs, ground bacon, and herbs in a bowl. Add the onion mixture. Mix well. Beat the egg and add to the stuffing with the cranberry jelly (or sauce) and seasoning. Add about ¼ cup [60 ml/2 fl oz] stock, to make a fairly moist stuffing.
4. Divide the stuffing into equal portions. Wrap 1 slice of ham or bacon around each portion, fixing with a toothpick. Put the ham rolls in a buttered baking pan. Pour a little stock around the rolls and cook in the oven for about 20 minutes.

Ham Toasts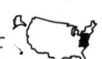

00:15
00:08   Serves 4   Mid Atlantic

American	Ingredients	Metric/Imperial
1–1½ cups	Ground [minced] ham	175–250 g/ 6–8 oz
2 tsp	Chutney (optional)	2 tsp
4–6	Eggs	4–6
2 tbsp	Cream	1½ tbsp
	A pinch of cayenne pepper	
4	Large slices bread	4
2 tsp	Mustard	2 tsp
3 tbsp	Butter	40 g/1½ oz
1 tbsp	Chopped parsley	1 tbsp

1. Mix the ground ham with the chutney. Beat the eggs with the cream, and stir into the ham. Add salt, pepper, and cayenne pepper to taste.
2. Make the bread into toast, remove the crusts, and spread with butter and mustard. Keep warm in an ovenproof dish.
3. Melt the remaining butter and, when foaming pour in the ham and egg mixture. Cook as if making scrambled eggs. When the mixture thickens, spoon onto the toast. Sprinkle the top with chopped parsley and serve at once.

Ham Mousseline

Ham Mousseline

	00:15		
	01:20	Serves 4	Mid Atlantic

American	Ingredients	Metric/Imperial
2 cups	Ground [minced] ham	350 g/12 oz
1 tbsp	Butter	15 g/½ oz
1 tbsp	Flour	1 tbsp
2 cups	Milk	450 ml/¾ pint
3	Eggs	3
	Ground nutmeg or mace	
1 cup	Cream	250 ml/8 fl oz
1 tbsp	Chopped parsley	1 tbsp

1. Pound the ground ham until really fine. Add a white sauce made with the butter, flour, and milk; cook for a few moments. Let cool.
2. Separate the egg yolks from the whites. Mix the yolks with cream and add to the ham, with parsley and salt and pepper. Beat the egg whites until stiff, fold into the meat mixture, and put into a buttered dish large enough to allow it to rise.
3. Place this dish, with a buttered paper tied over the top, into the top of a steamer and simmer gently for 1¼ hours.
4. It can then be served either in the same dish, or after a few moments turned out onto a warmed flat dish, with a cheese sauce and buttered spinach or green peas.

Ham Sandwich Loaf

	04:15		
	00:00	Serves 7-8	United States

American	Ingredients	Metric/Imperial
1	Loaf uncut bread	1
½ lb	Cooked ham, chopped	225 g/8 oz
1 can (about 3½ oz)	Pimentos, drained and chopped	1 (about 3½ oz) tin
	Mayonnaise	
1 cup	Sweet pickle	100 g/4 oz
2	Hard-boiled eggs	2
	Butter	
1–1½ cups	Cream cheese	225-350 g/ 8-12 oz

1. Remove all crusts from the loaf and cut lengthwise into 4 slices of equal thickness.
2. Combine the ham and pimentos, and add enough mayonnaise to make a spreadable paste. Chop the pickle and eggs together and moisten with mayonnaise.
3. Spread one slice of bread with butter, then with half the ham mixture. Butter both sides of the second slice of bread and press over the first slice. Spread with the egg and pickle mixture.
4. Butter both sides of the third slice of bread, press on top of the egg and pickle, and spread with the remaining ham and pimento mixture.
5. Butter the bottom of the top slice and press into position.
6. Place the reshaped loaf onto a serving platter and spread the top and sides with a thick layer of cream cheese. If this does not spread easily, soften it with a little cream or milk. Refrigerate for 3–4 hours; cut into slices when needed.

Sausages with Braised Red Cabbage

00:15
02:10
Serves 4   New England

American	Ingredients	Metric/Imperial
16–20	Pork sausages	16–20
1	Red cabbage, about 2 lb [900 g]	1
2 tbsp	Butter	25 g/1 oz
1	Large onion	1
3 tbsp	Vinegar	2 tbsp
2	Cooking apples	2
1 tbsp	Sugar	1 tbsp

1. Remove and discard the outer leaves from the cabbage. Shred the rest finely. Heat the butter in a casserole. Chop the onion and cook for a few minutes without burning. Add the cabbage. Mix well. Add 1 cup [250 ml/8 fl oz] of water, vinegar, salt, and pepper.
2. Cook for about 1 hour. Add the peeled, chopped apple, and sugar and cook for another hour, stirring from time to time. Remove the lid; boil if necessary to evaporate any extra liquid.
3. Broil [grill] or bake the sausages until brown. Serve with mashed potato and cabbage.

Mock Goose

00:15
01:00
Serves 4   New England

American	Ingredients	Metric/Imperial
1 lb	Sausage meat	450 g/1 lb
3 tbsp	Shortening	40 g/1½ oz
2–3	Medium onions	2–3
1	Egg	1
½ cup	Bread crumbs	25 g/1 oz
½ cup	Cider	125 ml/4 fl oz
2 tsp	Chopped dried sage	2 tsp
5–6	Cooking apples	5–6
	A strip of lemon rind	
1 tbsp	Sugar	1 tbsp

1. Preheat the oven to 375°F/190°C/Gas Mark 5.
2. Melt the shortening; slice and cook the onion until it is a medium brown. Add the sausage meat and cook for 3–5 minutes. Beat the egg, and add it and the bread crumbs, cider, and sage. Mix well and season. Pack into an ovenproof dish and bake in the oven for 40–45 minutes.
3. For the apple sauce: Put the apples, lemon rind, and 2–3 tablespoons [1½–2 tbsp] of water into a saucepan and cook until the apples are soft. Put through a fine strainer or liquidize and add sugar. (The sauce should not be too sweet). Allow to cool and serve with Mock Goose.

Sausage Pie

00:25
00:45
Serves 4–5   Mid Atlantic

American	Ingredients	Metric/Imperial
	Pastry for an 8–9 inch, 1-crust pie (see Index)	
¾ cup	Butter or margarine	175 g/6 oz
1	Small onion, peeled and chopped	1
4 tbsp	Chopped cooked ham	3½ tbsp
1 cup	Sliced mushrooms	100 g/4 oz
1 tbsp	Flour	1 tbsp
1 cup	Milk	250 ml/8 fl oz
⅛ tsp	Grated nutmeg	⅛ tsp
1	Egg yolk	1
2 tbsp	Heavy [double] cream	1½ tbsp
8	Small link sausages	8
2–3 tbsp	Grated cheese	1½–2 tbsp

1. Preheat the oven to 450°F/230°C/Gas Mark 8.
2. Line an 8–9 inch pie plate with the pastry, prick the bottom, and bake for 10–15 minutes. Remove from the oven.
3. Heat ¼ cup [50 g/2 oz] of the butter in a small pan; sauté the onion, ham, and mushrooms until the onion is transparent, then set aside.
4. Make a sauce with another ¼ cup [50 g/2 oz] of the butter, flour, and milk. When smooth and thickened, add the salt, pepper, and nutmeg. Remove from the heat; stir in the egg yolk and cream.
5. Sauté the sausages in the remaining butter until lightly brown.
6. Put the onion and ham mixture into the pie shell. Arrange the sausages in spoke fashion on top. Pour the sauce over, sprinkle with cheese, and bake for about 20 minutes.

Stuffed Sausageburgers

00:10
00:15
Serves 4   New England

American	Ingredients	Metric/Imperial
1 lb	Skinless pork sausages	450 g/1 lb
8	Hamburger rolls	8
2 tbsp	Butter	25 g/1 oz
1 tsp	Mustard	1 tsp
2–3 tbsp	Grated Cheddar cheese	1½–2 tbsp
1 tbsp	Chutney	1 tbsp

1. Preheat the oven to 350°F/180°C/Gas Mark 4.
2. Brush the sausages with a little melted fat and then broil [grill] for about 7–10 minutes until cooked all over. Keep warm.
3. Split the buns or rolls; spread with half the butter and mustard.
4. Mix the cheese with chutney. Split the sausages lengthwise; fill with cheese and chutney mixture. Put 1 sausage in each bun. Put in the oven to warm through.

Bacon and Apple Pie

 00:25
00:40   *Serves 4–5*   *Mid Atlantic*

American	Ingredients	Metric/Imperial
½ lb	Blanched bacon slices, cut into strips	225 g/8 oz
1	Large onion, peeled and chopped very finely	1
1 lb	Cooking apples, peeled, cored and thinly sliced	450 g/1 lb
2 tsp	Dried sage	2 tsp
3 tsp	Sugar	3 tsp
	Pastry for an 8-inch pie	
	Milk	

1. Preheat the oven to 425°F/220°C/Gas Mark 7.
2. Line an 8-inch pie pan with the strips of bacon. Arrange the layers of onion and apple on top, sprinkling each layer with sage, salt, pepper, and sugar. (Use salt with discretion, depending on the saltiness of the bacon).
3. Cover with the pastry, brush with a little milk to glaze, and bake for 25 minutes.
4. Reduce the heat to 350°F/180°C/Gas Mark 4. Cover the pie with foil if it is browning too quickly, and cook for 10–15 minutes longer.

Bacon and Apple Pie

Toad in the Hole

 01:10
00:45   *Serves 4*   *New England*

American	Ingredients	Metric/Imperial
12	Sausages, blanched or precooked	12
7 tbsp	Flour	6 tbsp
½ tsp	Salt	½ tsp
1	Egg	1
1¼ cups	Milk and water mixed	300 ml/½ pint

1. Preheat the oven to 425°F/220°C/Gas Mark 7.
2. Sift the flour and salt into a bowl. Make a well in the center and put in the egg and half of the liquid. Mix together and gradually draw in flour and beat until it is a smooth batter, about 4–5 minutes. Add the remaining liquid. Set aside for at least 1 hour.
3. Grease a baking pan or shallow ovenproof dish. Put in the sausages. Pour the batter over the sausages. Bake for 40–45 minutes, until the batter is well risen and brown and the sausages are cooked.
4. Serve with brown gravy.

Sausage Balls

 00:20
00:22   *Serves 6*   *Mid Atlantic*

American	Ingredients	Metric/Imperial
1	Thick slice of white bread without crusts	1
½ cup	Cold water	125 ml/4 fl oz
½ lb	Sausage meat	225 g/8 oz
1	Small chopped onion	1
1	Clove garlic	1
1–2 tbsp	Butter	15–25 g/½–1 oz
1 tbsp	Chopped parsley	1 tbsp
¼ tsp	Thyme and oregano	¼ tsp
1 tsp	Worcestershire sauce	1 tsp
2 tsp	Tomato sauce	2 tsp
	A dash of tabasco	
1	Beaten egg	1

1. Soak the bread in cold water. Put the sausage meat into a bowl. Squeeze the water from the bread and add to the meat. Mix with a fork.
2. Chop the onion and crush the garlic. Melt the butter and cook onion and garlic gently until golden brown, about 6–7 minutes. Add this to the meat together with the parsley, thyme, oregano, and the sauces. Add seasoning to taste and enough of the beaten egg to hold the mixture together. Mix thoroughly.
3. Take the mixture by large teaspoonful and roll into balls. Cook these in boiling stock or soup for about 15 minutes, or roll in seasoned flour and fry gently in butter or oil for about the same length of time.

Frankfurters with Peaches

Frankfurters with Peaches

00:40
00:10
Serves 6
Mid Atlantic

American	Ingredients	Metric/Imperial
12	Frankfurters	12
40	Mushroom caps	40
1 can (8 oz)	Peach halves	1 tin (225 g/8 oz)
1 small can (3 oz)	Cherries	1 small tin (75 g/3 oz)
1 cup	Butter or margarine	250 g/8 oz

1. Heat the coals in an outdoor grill until hot, about 30 minutes, or preheat the broiler [grill].
2. Cut the frankfurters into 3–4 pieces, and impale on skewers alternately with mushroom caps and peach halves, with a cherry in the center.
3. Brush generously with butter and cook for about 10 minutes, turning once or twice.

Frankfurter Hash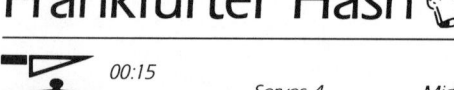

00:15
00:25
Serves 4
Mid Atlantic

American	Ingredients	Metric/Imperial
2 tbsp	Cooking fat	1½ tbsp
1½ cups	Diced potatoes	175 g/6 oz
1 cup	Finely chopped onion	100 g/4 oz
2	Green peppers, seeded and thinly sliced	2
8	Frankfurters, cut in 1-inch slices	8
4 tbsp	Water	3½–5 tbsp

1. Heat the fat in a frying pan. Add the potatoes and onions, and cook over a low heat for about 10 minutes.
2. Add the green pepper and frankfurters, mix well, and cook for 5 minutes.
3. Add the water, salt, and pepper to taste. Cook for 10 minutes longer.

Bacon with Parsley Sauce

00:05
00:20
Serves 4
New England

American	Ingredients	Metric/Imperial
16 slices	Lean bacon	16 rashers
3 tbsp	Butter	40 g/1½ oz
1 tbsp	Finely chopped onion	1 tbsp
1½ tbsp	Flour	1 tbsp
1 cup	Milk	250 ml/8 fl oz
4–6 tbsp	Chopped parsley	3½–5 tbsp
	A pinch of nutmeg	
1 tbsp	Cream (optional)	1 tbsp

1. Make the sauce: Melt the butter and cook the onion for a few minutes with a lid on the pan. Add the flour and mix well. Add the warmed milk and mix until smooth before returning to the stove. Bring slowly to a boil, stirring constantly. Boil for 2 minutes; add parsley, salt, pepper, and a pinch of powdered nutmeg. (If you have a tablespoon of cream, this can be added now.)
2. Remove the rind from the bacon and broil [grill] or fry until crisp.
3. Serve the bacon hot with mashed or boiled potatoes and a good helping of parsley sauce for each serving.

Bacon, Egg, and Corn Pie

00:20
00:50
Serves 4
New England

American	Ingredients	Metric/Imperial
	Pastry for an 8-inch pie	
4–6 slices	Bacon	4–6 rashers
3	Eggs	3
¼ tsp	Dry mustard	¼ tsp
1 cup	Grated Cheddar cheese	100 g/4 oz
4–6 tbsp	Canned sweet corn	3½ tbsp
¼ cup	Milk or heavy [double] cream	60 ml/2 fl oz

1. Preheat the oven to 375°F/190°C/Gas Mark 5.
2. Roll out the pastry and line the pie plate. Prick the bottom and bake filled with foil or waxed paper [greaseproof paper] filled with rice or beans. Cook for 15 minutes. Take out the paper and beans and let the pie shell cool.
3. Fry the bacon for 2–3 minutes on each side, cool, and cut into small pieces and sprinkle over the pie shell.
4. Beat the eggs together with seasoning and mustard. Add the cheese, corn, and milk. Pour into the pie shell. Bake in the oven for about 25–30 minutes, until the mixture is set.

Pigs in Bacon

Spicy Frankfurter Rolls

	00:10		
	00:15	Serves 6	Mid Atlantic

American	Ingredients	Metric/Imperial
12	Frankfurters	12
1 cup	Butter or margarine	250 g/8 oz
1	Small onion, peeled and finely chopped	1
2 tbsp	Finely chopped parsley	1½ tbsp
2 tsp	Prepared mustard	2 tsp
2 tbsp	Tomato ketchup	1½ tbsp
12	Soft rolls	12

1. Heat the coals in an outdoor grill until hot, about 30 minutes, or preheat the broiler [grill].
2. Cook the frankfurters, turning occasionally.
3. Soften the butter; add the onion, parsley, mustard, ketchup, and pepper to taste and mix well.
4. Split the rolls and spread with the butter mixture. Put them on the coolest part of the barbecue to heat through. Then place a frankfurter in each roll.

Pigs in Bacon

	00:40		
	00:10	Serves 8–12	Mid Atlantic

American	Ingredients	Metric/Imperial
12	Frankfurters	12
2 tsp	Prepared mustard (or ketchup)	2 tsp
½ cup	Cheese	50 g/2 oz
12 slices	Bacon	12 rashers

1. Heat the coals in an outdoor grill until hot, about 30 minutes, or preheat the broiler [grill].
2. Cut a slit the length of the frankfurter but not quite through to the bottom. Spread with mustard (or ketchup) and fill the slits with thin strips of cheese.
3. Roll a slice of bacon in a spiral around each frankfurter, and fasten with toothpicks.
4. Cook until the bacon is crisp, turning frequently.

Veal Birds

 00:15 01:30		Serves 6	South

American	Ingredients	Metric/Imperial
6	Thin slices veal breast	6
¼ cup	Soft white bread crumbs	15 g/½ oz
2 tbsp	Fat, chopped	1½ tbsp
1 tbsp	Parsley, chopped	1 tbsp
1 tsp	Dried thyme	1 tsp
½ tsp	Lemon rind, grated	½ tsp
	Salt and pepper	
	Beaten egg	
3 tbsp	Oil	2 tbsp
1	Onion, chopped	1
2 tbsp	Flour	1½ tbsp
1½ cups	Veal stock or water and chicken stock cube	350 ml/12 fl oz
	Chopped parsley for garnish	

1. Trim veal slices. If they are too thick, beat until thinner. Put the bread crumbs into a bowl with fat, parsley, thyme, lemon rind, salt, and pepper. Mix in enough beaten egg to bind. Divide the stuffing between the 6 slices of veal. Roll up each piece and secure with wooden cocktail sticks or thread.
2. Heat the oil in a frying pan and fry the rolls until browned all over. Put them in a casserole. Add the onion to the pan and fry until softened. Stir in the flour and cook, stirring, for 2 minutes. Gradually add the stock and bring to a boil, stirring constantly. Season.
3. Pour the sauce over the veal rolls. Cover and cook in a 325°F/160°C/Gas Mark 3 oven for 1¼ hours. Remove the skewers or thread and serve garnished with chopped parsley.

Veal Chops

00:35 00:10		Serves 4	Mid Atlantic

American	Ingredients	Metric/Imperial
4	Veal chops	4
	Sauce	
½ cup	Sour cream	125 ml/4 fl oz
	A few capers	
1–2	Anchovy fillets	1–2
	A squeeze of lemon juice	

1. Heat the coals in an outdoor grill until hot, about 30 minutes, or preheat the broiler [grill].
2. Brush the veal with oil or Barbecue Baste (see Index) and cook slowly.
3. Heat some sour cream; add a few capers, 1–2 chopped anchovy fillets, pepper, salt, and a squeeze of lemon juice and have this ready to pour over the chops when they are cooked.
4. Serve with wedges of lemon.

Veal Cutlet

00:20 00:40		Serves 4	Midwest

American	Ingredients	Metric/Imperial
4	Thick veal cutlets	4
1 cup	Ground cooked ham	175 g/6 oz
1 cup	Grated gruyère cheese	100 g/4 oz
	Garlic salt	
2 tbsp	Butter	25 g/1 oz
2–3 tbsp	Flour	1½–2 tbsp
2–3 tbsp	Oil	1½–2 tbsp
1 cup	White wine	250 ml/8 fl oz
½ cup	Chicken stock	125 ml/4 fl oz
2 tbsp	Chopped parsley and tarragon	1½ tbsp

1. Preheat the oven to 350°F/180°C/Gas Mark 4.
2. Cut a pocket in each cutlet from the boneless side, being careful not to pierce the outer surface. Mix the ham and cheese together, adding the garlic salt and pepper. Melt 1 tablespoon [15 g/½ oz] of butter and stir in. Stuff the cutlets carefully. Do not overfill. Seal the openings with toothpicks, and roll the cutlets in seasoned flour.
3. Heat the oil. Add the remaining butter and, when foaming, fry the cutlets taking about 3 minutes to brown each side. Place in an ovenproof dish. Add the stock and wine to the liquid in the pan and bring to a boil. Stir in the chopped herbs. Pour the sauce over the cutlets and cook in the oven until the veal is tender, about 20–30 minutes.

Veal Cutlets in Tarragon Cream Sauce

 00:10 00:20		Serves 4	Midwest

American	Ingredients	Metric/Imperial
4	Thin veal cutlets	4
¼ cup	Butter	50 g/2 oz
¼ cup	Madeira (or sherry)	60 ml/2 fl oz
½ cup	Cream	125 ml/4 fl oz
½ tbsp	Fresh tarragon leaves (or teaspoon dried tarragon soaked in water)	½ tbsp

1. Preheat the oven to 350°F/180°C/Gas Mark 4.
2. Beat the cutlets between oiled waxed [greaseproof] paper until very thin. Heat half the butter in a frying pan. When foaming, cook half the cutlets for about 3 minutes on each side until golden brown. Remove and keep warm. Repeat with the remaining cutlets.
3. Add the Madeira or sherry to the liquid in the frying pan and cook for a few minutes to reduce to 3 tablespoons. Add the cream and tarragon leaves. Bring to a boil and season to taste.
4. Pour the sauce over the cutlets and cook in the oven for about 6–8 minutes. Serve immediately.

Veal Birds

Hungarian Style Veal Chops

	00:10	Serves 4	Midwest
	00:30		

American	Ingredients	Metric/Imperial
4	Veal chops	4
3 tbsp	Butter	40 g/1½ oz
1	Small onion or shallot	1
1½ tbsp	Paprika	1¼ tbsp
½ cup	White wine	125 ml/4 fl oz
½ cup	Cream	125 ml/4 fl oz
	Chopped parsley	

1. Preheat the oven to 350°F/180°C/Gas Mark 4.
2. Mix 2 teaspoons of paprika with 1 teaspoon of salt and black pepper. Sprinkle on both sides of the chops and rub in gently.
3. Melt 2 tablespoons [25 g/1 oz] butter in a frying pan and cook the chops for about 2 minutes on each side until well browned. Remove and keep warm. Now add the finely chopped onion. Cook gently until tender. Then add the remaining paprika, put on the lid, and cook for another minute or two. Return the chops to the pan and add a few drops of wine. Bake for about 20 minutes in the oven, then place on a serving dish to keep warm.
4. Pour the white wine into the pan and reduce by cooking for a few minutes; stir in the cream, simmer again; then stir in the remaining butter. Pour over the chops, sprinkle the top with chopped parsley, and serve with plain boiled noodles.

Veal with Cheese

Veal and Ham Casserole

	00:20			
	01:45	Serves 7–8	Midwest	

American	Ingredients	Metric/Imperial
1½ lb	Veal fillet, cut into thin slices	675 g/1½ lb
1½ cups	Bread crumbs	75 g/3 oz
1	Egg	1
½ cup	Milk	125 ml/4 fl oz
2 tbsp	Oil	1½ tbsp
3 tbsp	Butter	40 g/1½ oz
1 lb	Cooked ham, sliced thinly	450 g/1 lb
3 cups	Sliced mushrooms	350 g/12 oz
2 cans (about 8 oz each)	Tomato sauce	2 tins (about 225 g/8 oz each)
¾ cup	Chicken stock	175 ml/6 fl oz
2–3 tbsp	Blanched almonds	1½–2 tbsp
1 tsp	Oregano	1 tsp
¼ tsp	Powdered mace	¼ tsp
¼ tsp	Thyme	¼ tsp
¼ tsp	Rosemary	¼ tsp

1. Preheat the oven to 300°F/150°C/Gas Mark 2.
2. Pound the slices of veal thinly, coat with bread crumbs, dip in egg and milk, and coat again with bread crumbs. Heat the oil and butter in a saucepan, and cook the veal until crisp and golden. Remove to a deep casserole.
3. Crisp the ham in a frying pan and add to the veal.
4. Sauté the mushrooms in the remaining fat for about 5 minutes, adding a little extra butter if necessary. Add the tomato sauce, chicken stock, and almonds, and stir well. Add the seasoning and herbs, simmer for about 10 minutes; then pour into the casserole.
5. Cover and cook for about 1¼ hours. Adjust the seasoning, and serve with noodles or wild rice.

Veal with Cheese

	00:15			
	00:06	Serves 4	Midwest	

American	Ingredients	Metric/Imperial
4 (3 oz)	Veal slices	4 (75 g/3 oz)
2	Slices processed cheese	2
	Salt and pepper	
	Flour	
1	Egg, beaten	1
	Fresh bread crumbs	
	Oil for frying	
	Lemon slices and parsley for garnish	

1. Place the veal between 2 pieces of waxed [greaseproof] paper and beat until very thin. Cut the cheese slices in half. Fold each piece of veal around a piece of cheese to make a neat parcel. Season the flour and coat the veal. Dip the veal in the egg, then coat in bread crumbs. Press the coating on firmly.
2. Heat a little oil in a frying pan and fry the veal parcels until golden, turning once. Garnish with lemon slices and sprigs of parsley. Serve immediately.

Veal Goulash

	00:15			
	01:05	Serves 4	Midwest	

American	Ingredients	Metric/Imperial
1½ lb	Tender boneless leg or shoulder of veal	675 g/1½ lb
1½ tbsp	Butter	20 g/¾ oz
1 lb	Onions	450 g/1 lb
1	Clove garlic	1
1¼ tbsp	Paprika	1 tbsp
1½ tbsp	Tomato purée	1¼ tbsp
1	Red pepper	1
1½ cups	Chicken or veal stock	350 ml/12 fl oz
1 tsp	Chopped thyme	1 tsp
1 tsp	Chopped marjoram	1 tsp
1	Bay leaf	1
1 cup	Sour cream	250 ml/8 fl oz
1 tbsp	Chopped parsley	1 tbsp

1. Preheat the oven to 325°F/160°C/Gas Mark 3.
2. Heat half of the butter and cook the finely sliced onion and crushed garlic in a covered pan until they are soft and transparent but not brown. Make into a purée by using liquidizer or putting through a fine sieve. Then put into the bottom of a casserole, mixing in the paprika, tomato purée, and herbs.
3. Cut the veal into 2-inch squares and cook quickly in the remaining butter without allowing it to color too deeply. Put on top of the onion purée and add the seeded and diced pepper. Add enough stock to cover the meat, adding salt and pepper. Cook in a covered casserole in the oven (or simmer on a gentle heat) for about 1 hour until the meat is tender.
4. Just before serving, spoon sour cream over the meat and sprinkle with chopped parsley. Serve with noodles, macaroni, or potatoes.

Veal Galantine

	12:30		
	02:00	Serves 12	United States 

American	Ingredients	Metric/Imperial
About 3 lb	Breast of veal	About 1.5 kg/3 lb
1 tsp	Chopped mixed herbs	1 tsp
1½ lb	Sausage meat	675 g/1½ lb
¼ cup	Sherry	60 ml/2 fl oz
½ lb	Lean cooked ham or tongue	225 g/8 oz
2	Hard-boiled eggs	2
	A few pistachio nuts	
	Stock	
½ envelope (½ oz)	Gelatin [gelatine]	½ sachet (15 g/½ oz)
¼ cup	Meat stock	60 ml/2 fl oz
¾ cup	Clarified stock	175 ml/6 fl oz

1. Bone the veal or have the butcher do this for you. Sprinkle with salt and pepper and mixed herbs.
2. Add a little seasoning to the sausage meat and moisten with the sherry. Spread over the meat, leaving a margin of about 1 inch all around.
3. Cut the ham into thin strips; arrange on the meat with the whole eggs in the middle. Sprinkle with nuts, and roll up tightly. Secure with thin string. Wrap in foil and then in a cloth. Tie securely, and cook in boiling stock for about 2 hours.
4. Remove the cloth, wrap in a clean dry one, and press the galantine with heavy weights. Leave overnight, then brush several times with an aspic glaze.
5. Make the aspic glaze: Dissolve the gelatin in the hot meat stock. Add clarified stock. Season to taste and chill until thick enough to coat the meat.
6. To serve: Arrange the galantine on lettuce leaves and garnish with lettuce hearts, tomatoes, and cucumber.

Veal Kebabs

	01:40		
	00:15	Serves 4	Mid Atlantic

American	Ingredients	Metric/Imperial
1½ lb	Shoulder veal	675 g/1½ lb
1	Clove garlic, crushed	1
1½ tsp	Curry powder	1½ tsp
	A pinch of paprika	
	A pinch of rosemary	
	A pinch of thyme	
1	Bay leaf, crushed	1
3–4 tbsp	Oil	2–3½ tbsp
4	Firm tomatoes	4
1	Sweet red or green pepper, seeded and cut into strips	1
½ lb	Bacon slices, cut into squares	225 g/8 oz

1. Cut the veal into pieces about 1-inch square, and put into a bowl. Add the garlic, curry powder, herbs, and a little salt and pepper. Pour over the oil, mix well, and let stand for about 1 hour.

Veal Galantine

2. Heat the coals in an outdoor grill until hot, about 30 minutes, or preheat the broiler [grill].
3. When ready to cook, assemble the ingredients on 4 skewers, putting a piece of bacon before and after each piece of meat.
4. Turn frequently while cooking. If the bacon is rather lean, brush the veal occasionally with a little oil.
5. These kebabs are very good served on a bed of rice.

Veal Cutlets in Papillotes

	00:20		
	00:40	Serves 4	Midwest

American	Ingredients	Metric/Imperial
4	Veal cutlets or slices	4
2 tbsp	Butter	25 g/1 oz
½ cup	Mushrooms	50 g/2 oz
2	Shallots (or 1 small onion)	2
	A little lemon juice	
¼ cup	White wine	60 ml/2 fl oz
1 tbsp	Thick [double] cream	1 tbsp
2–3 tbsp	Oil	1½–2 tbsp

1. Preheat the oven to 350°F/180°C/Gas Mark 4.
2. Cut out 4 large heart-shaped pieces of waxed [greaseproof] paper or foil, at least twice the size of the pieces of veal. (These are the papillotes.) Beat out the cutlets on a wet board and season. Brush the paper or foil hearts all over with oil and then lay the cutlets on one half of the heart near the center line.
3. Melt the butter and cook the chopped mushrooms and onion or shallot for 5 minutes. Add the lemon juice and white wine and seasoning. Cook for a few more minutes to reduce the liquid and then add the thick cream. Put a quarter of this mixture on each slice of veal. Fold the empty half of the paper over the top and seal the edges together by folding and pinching to make a tight seal.
4. Put in a well-buttered baking dish and cook in the oven for 25–30 minutes, when the paper should have puffed up. Serve in the papillotes to conserve the flavor.

Veal and Ham Pie

Veal Frikadeller

 00:40   00:25   Serves 4   Midwest

American	Ingredients	Metric/Imperial
1 lb	Finely ground [minced] veal (or veal and pork mixed)	450 g/1 lb
4 tbsp	Veal (or pork) fat	3½ tbsp
1	Onion	1
1½ cups	Crustless bread	75 g/3 oz
2–3 tbsp	Chopped parsley and thyme	1½–2 tbsp
	Grated rind of ½ lemon	
½ tsp	Paprika	½ tsp
	A dash of cayenne pepper	
4–5 tbsp	Flour	3–4 tbsp
¼ cup	Butter	50 g/2 oz
	Tomato sauce	
3–4 tbsp	Yogurt or sour cream	2–3½ tbsp
½ cup	Black olives	50 g/2 oz

1. Preheat the oven to 350°F/180°C/Gas Mark 4.
2. Put the veal with the ground fat and finely chopped onion in a bowl. Put the bread into a dish and cover with milk or water; leave to soak for 10–15 minutes, then squeeze dry and add the bread to the meat. Reserve a cup of liquid. Add the chopped herbs and grated lemon rind. Put the mixture through the fine grinder once again.
3. Beat the meat mixture well by hand, adding the reserved liquid gradually. This beating is important as it affects the final lightness of the Frikadeller. Add salt, pepper, paprika, and cayenne pepper, and mix in well. Spoon the mixture onto a damp board and roll to marble-sized Frikadeller. Roll these in seasoned flour.
4. Heat the butter in a frying pan. Cook the Frikadeller until brown all over, and place in a shallow casserole. Pour tomato sauce over the mixture. There should be enough to cover the Frikadeller completely. Then bake for about 20 minutes in the oven.
5. Just before serving, spoon the yogurt or sour cream over the top of the dish. Add the black olives, and serve with plain boiled rice, noodles or potatoes, and lemon quarters.

Veal and Ham Pie

 04:30   01:15   Serves 6   Midwest

American	Ingredients	Metric/Imperial
1½ lb	Fillet of veal	675 g/1½ lb
½ lb	Cooked ham	225 g/8 oz
2 tbsp	Very finely chopped parsley	1½ tbsp
¼ tsp	Thyme	¼ tsp
¼ tsp	Marjoram	¼ tsp
½ tsp	Grated lemon rind	½ tsp
1¼ tsp	Salt	1¼ tsp
⅛ tsp	Pepper	⅛ tsp
3	Hard-boiled eggs	3
½ cup	Consomme	125 ml/4 fl oz
	Pastry 8–9-inch 1-crust pie (see Index)	
1	Egg	1

1. Preheat the oven to 325°F/160°C/Gas Mark 3.
2. Trim any excess fat from the veal and ham, and cut into cubes.
3. Mix all the herbs together; add salt and pepper. Arrange the veal, ham, herbs, flavorings, and slices of egg alternately in a deep 8-inch pie plate. Add the consomme. Dampen the edge of the pie plate, put on the pastry, press the edge down well, and decorate as desired.
4. Make a hole in the top and decorate with leaves made from the pastry trimmings. Brush with beaten egg and bake for 1–1¼ hours. Chill in the refrigerator for at least 3–4 hours, or leave overnight.

Jellied Veal Loaf

02:10   01:40   Serves 4–6   New England

American	Ingredients	Metric/Imperial
1 lb	Lean veal	450 g/1 lb
¼ lb	Bacon	100 g/4 oz
2	Hard-boiled eggs	2
1 tbsp	Chopped parsley	1 tbsp
2 cups	Well-flavored chicken or veal stock	450 ml/¾ pint
1 tbsp	Gelatin [gelatine]	1 tbsp

1. Preheat the oven to 325°F/160°C/Gas Mark 3.
2. Cut the veal into small strips, dice the bacon, cover with water, and bring to a boil; drain and rinse with cold water.
3. Cut the hard-boiled eggs into slices. Arrange the meat and eggs in layers in a 9 × 5 × 3-inch loaf pan. Sprinkle each layer with parsley, salt, and pepper. Pour 1½ cups [350 ml/12 fl oz] of stock over the meat. Cover with foil, cook in the oven for about 1½ hours, and remove to cool.
4. Soak the gelatin in the remaining stock and melt over gentle heat. Pour this over the meat and put in a cool place to set. When cold, put in the refrigerator for a short time or until needed.
5. Turn out the jellied veal and garnish the dish with green salad, tomatoes, watercress, and cucumber.

Jellied Veal Loaf

Saltimbocca

| 00:20 | Serves 4 | Mid Atlantic |
| 00:25 | | |

American	Ingredients	Metric/Imperial
8	Thin slices tender veal from leg	8
8	Thin slices ham	8
8	Small fresh sage leaves (or pinches of dried sage)	8
2–3 tbsp	Butter	25–40 g/ 1–1½ oz
¾ cup	Marsala or white wine	175 ml/6 fl oz
8	Slices bread	8

1. Preheat the oven to 350°F/180°C/Gas Mark 4.

2. Beat out the veal slices between waxed [greaseproof] paper. Place a thin slice of ham on each veal slice and then a sage leaf (or a small pinch of dried sage). Season with salt and pepper. Roll each slice up tightly and use toothpicks to fasten the rolls securely.

3. Heat the butter and brown the rolls all over for about 5–7 minutes. Add Marsala or other wine and a little salt and pepper. Cover the pan and cook gently in the oven (or on top of the stove) for about 15 minutes, when the meat should be tender.

4. Cut the bread into rounds; fry in oil and butter until golden brown and crisp.

5. Place each roll on a fried bread crouton and serve around a dish of spinach cooked with butter.

Veal Scallops Parmesan

| 00:10 | Serves 4 | New England |
| 00:14 | | |

American	Ingredients	Metric/Imperial
4	Thin veal scallops (or slices cut from leg of veal)	4
1	Large egg	1
½ tbsp	Oil	½ tbsp
3 tbsp	Flour	2 tbsp
½ tsp	Powdered garlic	½ tsp
3–4 tbsp	Grated Parmesan cheese	2–3½ tbsp
3 tbsp	Butter	40 g/1½ oz
	Juice of ½ lemon	
1 tbsp	Finely chopped parsley	1 tbsp

1. Beat out the scallops between waxed [greaseproof] paper. Mix the egg with oil and beat. Add the seasoning and garlic to the flour, and mix with cheese. Brush the scallops with the egg mixture, then press into the cheese and flour until completely coated.

2. Melt the butter and fry the scallops until golden brown, about 5–6 minutes on each side. Place on a warm serving dish and keep hot.

3. Add the lemon juice to the butter in the pan. Reheat and pour over the scallops just before serving. Garnish with parsley.

Osso Bucco

Osso Bucco

	00:20	Serves 4	New England
	02:10		

American	Ingredients	Metric/Imperial
4	Meaty slices of shin of veal, 2–3 inches thick	4
¼ cup	Flour	25 g/1 oz
2½ tbsp	Olive oil	1¾ tbsp
1½ tbsp	Butter	20 g/¾ oz
1	Medium onion	1
3	Stalks celery	3
1–2	Cloves garlic	1–2
2 tbsp	Tomato purée	1½ tbsp
½ cup	Veal or chicken stock	125 ml/4 fl oz
½ cup	Dry white wine	125 ml/4 fl oz
½ tbsp	Chopped basil and lemon thyme	½ tbsp
1½ tbsp	Chopped parsley	1¼ tbsp
½	Lemon	½

1. Preheat the oven to 350°F/180°C/Gas Mark 4.
2. Add the salt and pepper to the flour, and coat the pieces of meat with it. Heat the oil, and add the butter. When foaming, put in the meat and lightly brown all over. Remove and keep warm in a casserole.
3. Slice the onions and celery finely; crush the garlic and brown lightly. Add the tomato purée, stock, and wine to the vegetables; and season to taste.
4. Pour this mixture over the meat and put the casserole with a tightly fitting lid into the oven for 1½–2 hours. After about 1 hour, add half the herbs and a few fine strips of lemon rind. Continue cooking for another hour or so; test the meat and if not completely done, cook until tender.
5. Drain the meat and vegetables onto a serving platter. Boil up the sauce to reduce slightly; add lemon juice to taste and pour over the meat. Sprinkle the top with the remaining chopped parsley and serve with boiled pasta or a plain risotto.

Veal and Pork Pie

	01:00	Serves 4	Midwest
	01:10		

American	Ingredients	Metric/Imperial
2 tbsp	Vegetable oil	1½ tbsp
½ lb	Veal	225 g/8 oz
½ lb	Lean pork	225 g/8 oz
1 tsp	Salt	1 tsp
½ tsp	Paprika	½ tsp
1	Small bay leaf	1
2	Cloves	2
1	Small carrot, peeled and sliced lengthwise	1
3	Stalks celery, cut into diagonal pieces	3
1 cup	Diced potatoes	100 g/4 oz
8	Small white onions	8
2 tbsp	Flour	1½ tbsp
	Pastry for an 8–9 inch, 1-crust pie (see Index)	

1. Preheat the oven to 450°F/230°C/Gas Mark 8.
2. Heat the oil in a frying pan; add the veal and pork cut into 1-inch pieces and stir until lightly browned.
3. Add 3 cups [700 ml/1¼ pints] boiling water, salt, paprika, bay leaf, and cloves. Cover, and simmer for 15 minutes.
4. Remove the bay leaf and cloves. Add the vegetables, cover, and cook over low heat for 20 minutes.
5. Mix the flour to a smooth paste with a little cold water, stir into the meat, cooking 3–5 minutes, and season to taste. Transfer all into a deep baking dish and let get cold.
6. Cover with pastry and bake for 25–30 minutes.

Scallopini of Minced Veal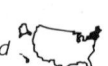

	00:35	Serves 4	New England
	00:30		

American	Ingredients	Metric/Imperial
1 lb	Ground [minced] raw veal	450 g/1 lb
1 tbsp	Finely chopped onion	1 tbsp
	Grated rind of ½ lemon	
1 tbsp	Chopped parsley	1 tbsp
	A pinch of mace or nutmeg	
	A squeeze of lemon juice	
1	Beaten egg	1
	Flour	
3 tbsp	Oil	2 tbsp
3 tbsp	Butter	40 g/1½ oz
¼ cup	Chicken stock	60 ml/2 fl oz
¼ cup	White wine	60 ml/2 fl oz

1. Mix the veal with the onion, lemon rind, and parsley. Mix well, adding the seasoning and a squeeze of lemon juice. Then mix in the beaten egg.

2. Flour a board with seasoned flour and divide the meat into 8 equal portions. Roll each portion into a ball. Roll out with a floured rolling pin into small slices not more than ½ inch thick. Dust each side with seasoned flour.

3. Heat half the oil and butter in a frying pan; cook 4 slices for about 5–7 minutes on each side or until a good brown. Turn onto a serving dish. Repeat the process with the remaining slices.

4. Reheat the remaining oil and butter. Add the stock and white wine, bring to a boil, season and cook for a minute or two. Pour over the scallopini and serve with potatoes and lemon quarters.

Veal and Mushroom Pancakes

01:25
00:15   Serves 4–6   United States

American	Ingredients	Metric/Imperial
1½ cups	Chopped cooked veal	250 g/9 oz
1¼ cups	Flour	150 g/5 oz
2	Eggs	2
1	Egg yolk	1
1½ cups	Milk	350 ml/12 fl oz
3 tbsp	Butter	40 g/1½ oz
1 cup	Mushrooms	100 g/4 oz
½ cup	Corn	50 g/2 oz
1 tbsp	Chopped parsley	1 tbsp
	A little cream	
	A pinch of mace or ground nutmeg	
	A little oil	
3 tbsp	Grated Parmesan cheese	2 tbsp
1½ tbsp	Melted butter	20 g/¾ oz

1. Sift 1 cup [100 g/4 oz] of flour with salt and pepper into a bowl. Make a hollow in the center and drop in the beaten eggs and 3–4 tablespoons [2–3½ tbsp] of milk. Mix the eggs and milk together with a spoon before gradually drawing in the flour. Add 6 tablespoons [5 tbsp] of milk as the mixture thickens and, when it is smooth and like thick cream, beat for about 5 minutes. Then stir in 2 teaspoons of melted butter and another 3 tablespoons [2 tbsp] of milk. Leave the batter in a covered bowl for about 1 hour before using.

2. Melt about 2 tablespoons [25 g/1 oz] of butter and cook the sliced mushrooms in a covered pan for 3–4 minutes. Remove from the stove. Stir in a scant tablespoon of flour and add ½ cup [125 ml/4 fl oz] of milk. Bring slowly to a boil. Add the chopped meat and corn, parsley, mace, seasoning, and cream. Keep warm while cooking the pancakes.

3. Test the thickness of the batter, which should just coat the back of a spoon. If too thick, add the remaining milk and stir well. Grease a 5–6 inch pancake or frying pan with a little oil. When hot, pour in enough batter to coat the pan thinly. When browned on one side, turn and cook on the other side. Pile up and keep warm. Allow 2 to 3 per person.

4. Put a spoonful of filling in the center of each pancake and roll up. Arrange in overlapping rows in an ovenproof dish. Sprinkle with grated cheese and spoon melted butter over it; broil [grill] until golden brown.

Veal and Mushroom Pancakes

Wiener Schnitzel

00:20
00:06
Serves 4
Midwest

American	Ingredients	Metric/Imperial
4	Large thin veal scallops	4
2–3 tbsp	Flour	1½–2 tbsp
1	Egg	1
5–6 tbsp	Dried white bread crumbs	4–5 tbsp
2–3 tbsp	Butter	25–40 g/1–1½oz
1	Hard-boiled egg	1
4	Slices of lemon	4
4	Anchovies	4
2 tsp	Capers	2 tsp
2 tsp	Paprika	2 tsp
4	Olives	4
2 tbsp	Chopped parsley	1½ tbsp

1. Beat out the scallops between pieces of waxed [greaseproof] paper until wafer thin. Toss in seasoned flour until completely coated. Shake to remove excess. Beat the raw egg with a few drips of oil and some salt. Brush each scallop with this, then toss in the dried white crumbs. (A paper bag is a good container for this process.)

2. Melt the butter in a frying pan. After foaming, cook the scallops for 2–3 minutes on each side, until they are golden brown and crisp.

3. Place on a hot dish and garnish the top of each scallop with 1 slice of lemon. In the center of this, place an olive and curl an anchovy fillet around the olive. Surround this with a portion of chopped egg white, chopped capers, and paprika. Sprinkle all over with chopped parsley. Garnish with sieved egg yolk, if desired.

4. Serve at once, with the remaining butter from the frying pan as a sauce. (Extra butter can be added.)

Veal in Sour Cream Sauce

00:20
00:50
Serves 4
Midwest

American	Ingredients	Metric/Imperial
1½ lb	Shoulder of veal without bone	675 g/1½ lb
4–5 tbsp	Flour	3½–4 tbsp
1 tsp	Salt	1 tsp
¼ tsp	Black pepper	¼ tsp
1 tsp	Paprika	1 tsp
2 tbsp	Oil	1½ tbsp
1	Onion	1
1	Clove garlic	1
½ cup	Sour cream	125 ml/4 fl oz
1 tsp	Caraway seeds	1 tsp
1 tbsp	Chopped parsley	1 tbsp

1. Preheat the oven to 350°F/180°C/Gas Mark 4.

2. Cut the veal into squares. Roll in flour mixed with salt, pepper, and paprika. Heat the oil and fry the veal until golden brown all over. Remove to a casserole and keep warm.

3. Cook the chopped onion and crushed garlic in the remaining oil for a couple of minutes, then add 1½ cups [350 ml/12 fl oz] of hot water and bring to a boil. Add the meat and stir in. Return to the casserole and cover with a lid and cook in the oven for 35–40 minutes (or simmer on top of the stove) until the veal is tender.

4. Stir in the sour cream and heat gently without boiling. Sprinkle over the caraway seeds and parsley, and serve with buttered noodles.

Blanquette de Veau

00:25
01:10
Serves 4–6
Mid Atlantic

American	Ingredients	Metric/Imperial
2 lb	Veal from shoulder or breast	900 g/2 lb
4 tbsp	Butter	50 g/2 oz
1	Onion	1
3–4	Medium carrots	3–4
1 tbsp	Flour	1 tbsp
2 cups	Chicken or veal stock	450 ml/¾ pint
	Parsley stems	
1	Bay leaf	1
	A sprig of thyme (or ¼ tsp dried thyme)	
12	Button mushrooms	12
12	Baby or pickling onions	12
1 cup	Cream	250 ml/8 fl oz
1 large or 2 small	Egg yolks	1 large or 2 small
	A squeeze of lemon	

1. Preheat the oven to 350°F/180°C/Gas Mark 4.

2. Cut the veal into cubes about 1¼ inches square. Put into a pan with enough cold water to cover and a little salt. Bring slowly to a boil and cook for 5 minutes. Skim off the scum that rises to the surface. Drain the meat and wash well with cold water. Dry.

3. Melt 3 tablespoons [40 g/1½ oz] of butter and cook the veal cubes slowly together with the quartered onion and carrots, shaking frequently and not allowing them to brown at all. Stir in the flour, and then add the stock, parsley, bay leaf, and thyme. Bring to a boil and place in the oven or simmer on the stove for 1–1½ hours, until the veal is tender.

4. Meanwhile, peel the baby onions and cook in salted water for 10–15 minutes. Drain. Melt the remaining tablespoon of butter and cook the mushrooms for a few minutes. Add to the onions.

5. Remove the veal from the stove and place the meat in a dish, adding the carrots, baby onions, and mushrooms. Strain the cooking liquid and boil to reduce the quantity slightly. Remove from the heat and cool slightly. Beat the egg yolks with cream; add a little hot sauce to this and strain into sauce. Add the lemon juice. Do not boil under any circumstances after this point. Pour over the meat and vegetables and serve at once.

6. Serve with mashed or riced potatoes, or plain boiled rice.

Wiener Schnitzel

Veal Shanks

| | 00:20 | | |
| | 01:10 | Serves 4 | New England |

American	Ingredients	Metric/Imperial
3 lb	Veal shank, sawed into thick slices with marrow intact	1.25 kg/3 lb
	Salt and pepper	
	Flour	
6 tbsp	Butter	75 g/3 oz
1	Medium onion, peeled and chopped	1
1	Clove garlic, peeled and minced	1
2	Carrots, peeled and diced	2
2	Stalks celery, chopped	2
½ cup	White wine	125 ml/4 fl oz
¼ cup	Chicken stock	60 ml/2 fl oz
1	Bay leaf	1
¼ tsp	Thyme	¼ tsp

	Gremolata	
2 tbsp	Parsley, finely chopped	1½ tbsp
1	Clove garlic, peeled and finely minced	1
1 tsp	Lemon peel, finely grated	1 tsp

1. Wipe the veal with a damp cloth. Season with salt and pepper. Dredge in flour; shake off excess. Heat the butter in a deep frying pan or Dutch oven. Add the veal; brown well on all sides. Remove from the pan.

2. Add the onion and garlic to the pan; sauté until tender. Add the vegetables, wine, chicken stock, and seasonings. Add the veal shanks, standing on their sides to prevent the marrow from falling from the bone during cooking. Bring the mixture to a boil. Cover the pan tightly; reduce the heat to simmer. Cook approximately 1 hour, until the veal is tender. If the mixture looks dry at any time, add a little stock.

3. Meanwhile, combine the gremolata ingredients; mix well. Transfer the veal to a heated platter. Pour the sauce over the meat; sprinkle with gremolata. Serve with risotto or plain cooked pasta.

Veal and Pork Roulette

 00:15
01:30   Serves 4   Mid Atlantic

American	Ingredients	Metric/Imperial
½ lb	Raw ground [minced] pork	225 g/8 oz
½ lb	Raw ground [minced] veal	225 g/8 oz
2 slices	Bacon	2 rashers
2 tbsp	Chopped onion	1½ tbsp
2	Slices stale white bread	2
1	Large egg	1
3 tbsp	Dry white bread crumbs	2 tbsp
	Oil	
10–12	Medium-sized mushrooms	10–12
1	Onion	1
2–3 tbsp	Butter	25–40 g/1–1½ oz
1 tsp	Worcestershire sauce	1 tsp
1 tbsp	Flour	1 tbsp
1 cup	Fresh or sour cream	250 ml/8 fl oz

1. Preheat the oven to 450°F/230°C/Gas Mark 8.
2. Mix the ground meat, bacon, and chopped onion together. Remove the bread crusts and soak the bread for a few minutes in cold water. Squeeze dry with the hands and add to the meat, mixing thoroughly. Now add the beaten egg and seasoning.
2. Shape into a loaf or put into a buttered loaf tin. Coat or sprinkle with bread crumbs and bake in the oven for 1–1¼ hours, having sprinkled a little hot oil over the top to prevent the bread crumbs becoming too dry and brown.
4. Make the sauce: Chop the mushrooms and onion and cook in butter for 10–15 minutes without burning. Add the Worcestershire sauce and then the flour. Mix in well. Just before serving, mix in the cream; reheat without boiling and serve.

Veal Schnitzel with Sherry Sauce

00:15
00:25   Serves 2   Midwest

American	Ingredients	Metric/Imperial
1 (10-oz)	Box frozen spinach	1 (275 g/10 oz)
½ lb	Asparagus tips	225 g/8 oz
½ tsp	Salt	½ tsp
⅛ tsp	Pepper	⅛ tsp
⅛ tsp	Garlic powder	⅛ tsp
¼ tsp	Crushed basil	¼ tsp
2	Veal cutlets	2
2 tbsp	Butter	25 g/1 oz
1½ tsp	Soy sauce	1½ tsp
1 tsp	Arrowroot, potato flour, or cornstarch [cornflour]	1 tsp
2 tbsp	Sherry	1½ tbsp

1. Cook the spinach in its own juice over medium heat. When tender, drain and reserve the liquid. Cook the asparagus tips in ½ cup [125 ml/4 fl oz] boiling salted water for 4–5 minutes. Drain and combine the liquid with the spinach broth.
2. Combine the spices; rub half of them into the cutlets and season the spinach with the rest.
3. Heat a frying pan, preferably a nonstick one; add the butter and sauté the cutlets, 1–2 minutes on each side. Place the cutlets on a heated platter along with the asparagus and spinach. Cover with foil and keep warm while making the sauce.
4. Boil the vegetable broth until it measures approximately ⅔ cup [150 ml/¼ pint]. Add the soy sauce. Mix the thickener with sherry and add it to the broth, stirring constantly. Bring to a boil and season with salt and pepper. Pour the sauce around the meat and serve immediately.

Veal Schnitzel with Sherry Sauce

Grilled Oxtail

Grilled Oxtail

	03:20		
	03:30	Serves 4	South

American	Ingredients	Metric/Imperial
1	Large lean oxtail cut into even-sized pieces	1
	Several parsley stalks	
1	Bay leaf	1
1	Sprig of thyme	1
6–7	Peppercorns	6–7
3	Onions	3
2	Carrots	2
6–7 tbsp	Butter	75–90 g/ 3–3½ oz
4–5 tbsp	Dried white bread crumbs	3½–4 tbsp
3 tbsp	Wine vinegar	2 tbsp
1 tbsp	Flour	1 tbsp
1 cup	Brown stock	250 ml/8 fl oz
1 tbsp	Chopped gherkins	1 tbsp
2 tsp	French mustard	2 tsp

1. Soak the pieces of oxtail for at least 3 hours in cold salted water (overnight, if possible). Drain and put into a pan of boiling water with the herbs, peppercorns, 2 onions, and carrots. Cook slowly for 2–3 hours, or until the meat is tender.

2. Drain and reserve the liquid to use as a gravy with the vegetables, if desired. Dry the oxtail. Melt 3–4 tablespoons [40–50 g/1½–2 oz] of butter and roll each piece in this and then in the bread crumbs. Heat the broiler [grill] until red hot. Broil [grill] the pieces of oxtail until brown and crisp, turning frequently.

3. Melt 3 tablespoons [40 g/1½ oz] of butter, and cook 1 chopped onion slowly for 6–8 minutes. Add the vinegar and boil for a few minutes. Add the flour, then the stock; bring to a boil and cook for 10 minutes. Add the gherkins, mustard, salt, and pepper. Reheat and serve with the grilled oxtail.

Spanish Style Kidney

 00:45 / 02:12   Serves 4   Southwest

American	Ingredients	Metric/Imperial
1–1½ lb	Ox kidney	450–675 g/ 1–1½ lb
4 tbsp	Flour	3½ tbsp
¼ cup	Butter or margarine	50 g/2 oz
1 cup	Sliced mushrooms	100 g/4 oz
1	Clove garlic, crushed	1
½ tsp	Dried basil	½ tsp
5–6	Tomatoes, peeled, seeded, and chopped	5–6
4–5 tbsp	Marsala	3½–4 tbsp
	Bacon rolls	
	Cooked spaghetti	

1. Preheat the oven to 325°F/160°C/Gas Mark 3.
2. Remove the core and any fat from the kidney, cut into slices, and let stand in cold water for a half hour. Drain and dry.
3. Coat the kidney with flour to which a little salt and pepper has been added, brown in hot fat, and remove to a casserole.
4. Sauté the mushrooms and garlic in the remaining fat for about 5 minutes. Then add to the kidney. Add basil.
5. Stir any remaining flour into the fat left in the pan; mix well. Add tomatoes and Marsala and a little water if required. Stir until boiling, then pour into the casserole. Cover and cook for 2 hours.
6. Adjust the seasoning, and serve with broiled [grilled] bacon rolls and spaghetti.

Brains with Black Butter

 03:15 / 00:30   Serves 4   South

American	Ingredients	Metric/Imperial
1 lb	Calf or lamb brains	450 g/1 lb
1 tbsp	Vinegar	1 tbsp
½ tsp	Salt	½ tsp
½ cup	Butter	125 g/4 oz
1 tbsp	Wine vinegar	1 tbsp
	Black pepper	
	Chopped parsley	

1. Wash the brains and soak for 2–3 hours in cold water. Remove the skin and then soak again in lukewarm water to remove any blood.
2. Put into a pan of cold water with the vinegar and salt. Bring slowly to just below boiling point. Cook for 15 minutes. Do not boil. Drain. Put in cold water until firm. Then dry carefully.
3. Melt half the butter and, when hot, add the brains. Cook until brown all over. Then put onto a hot dish and keep warm.
4. Heat the rest of the butter until it turns brown. Add the wine vinegar and pour at once over the brains; sprinkle with salt, pepper, and chopped parsley.

Liver Cooked with Rice

 00:15 / 00:40   Serves 4   Pacific Southwest

American	Ingredients	Metric/Imperial
½–¾ lb	Lamb or calf liver	225–350 g/ 8–12 oz
1	Onion	1
1	Clove garlic	1
2–3 tbsp	Butter	25–40 g/ 1–1½ oz
1 cup	Quartered mushrooms	100 g/4 oz
1 cup	Long-grain rice	225 g/8 oz
1 tbsp	Tomato purée	1 tbsp
2½ cups	Stock	600 ml/1 pint
	Salt and pepper	
1 tbsp	Mixed herbs	1 tbsp
1 cup	Grated Parmesan cheese	100 g/4 oz

1. Cut the liver into chunks. Chop the onion finely and crush the garlic. Quarter the mushrooms. melt the butter and sauté the onion and garlic for 3–5 minutes. Add the liver and sauté quickly.
2. Remove from the heat and add the mushrooms, rice, tomato purée, stock, and salt and pepper. Bring to a boil, stirring all the time. Reduce the heat and simmer gently for 25–30 minutes, stirring occasionally and adding extra stock if the rice seems to be getting dry.
3. When cooked, the rice should have absorbed all the moisture. Sprinkle the top with chopped herbs and serve with grated cheese.

Liver and Bacon Burgers

 00:30 / 00:35   Serves 4   Pacific Southwest

American	Ingredients	Metric/Imperial
½ lb	Lamb liver	225 g/8 oz
¼ lb	Bacon	100 g/4 oz
2	Onions	2
6 tbsp	Lard or bacon fat	5 tbsp
¾ cup	Fresh white bread crumbs	20 g/¾ oz
4 tsp	Tomato purée	4 tsp
	Worcestershire sauce	
1	Egg	1
½ cup	Flour	50 g/2 oz
2	Cloves garlic	2
½ cup	Chopped mushroom stems and peelings	50 g/2 oz
4 tbsp	Oil	3½ tbsp
½ cup	Strong beef stock (or water and beef cube)	125 ml/4 fl oz
½ cup	Wine or cider	125 ml/4 fl oz
	Parsley, thyme, and a bay leaf	

1. Prepare the liver and bacon by removing any skin, rind, gristle, or bone; cut into small pieces. Chop the onion coarsely. Melt 2 tablespoons [1½ tbsp] of lard or bacon fat in a pan. Cook the liver, bacon and onion together in this for several minutes, not long enough to cook completely, but enough to set the liver. Remove from the heat and cool slightly.

2. Put the bread crumbs into a large bowl. Grind the liver, bacon, and onion in a food grinder. Do not make too fine. Add the mixture to the bread crumbs. Mix well. Add seasoning, 1 teaspoon tomato purée, a dash of Worcestershire sauce, and half the beaten egg, reserving the second half in case it is needed. (The mixture should not be too soft to hold its shape when divided into small burgers.)

3. Divide the mixture on a floured board and shape with floured hands into small burgers. Coat these with flour, and sauté the burgers for about 5–6 minutes on each side in lard or bacon fat. Drain on paper towels [kitchen paper] and serve with a strong tomato sauce, or piles of fried onions and a Provencale sauce.

4. Make the Provencale sauce: Chop 1 onion finely. Cook the onion, crushed garlic, and mushrooms for a few minutes in oil to soften. Stir in 3 teaspoons flour; add the stock and wine or cider. Bring to a boil. Add the herbs and seasoning. Simmer for 15 minutes. Remove the bay leaf and add 3 teaspoons of tomato purée. Season to taste and serve.

Liver with Orange

 00:25 00:55   Serves 4–6   Pacific Southwest

American	Ingredients	Metric/Imperial
8	Slices veal or lamb liver	8
8 tbsp	Butter	100 g/4 oz
2	Onions	2
¾ cup	Rice	175 g/6 oz
2½ cups	Beef stock	600 ml/1 pint
2 tbsp	Mixed herbs	1½ tbsp
2 tbsp	Flour	1½ tbsp
	Cayenne pepper	
1	Clove garlic	1
¾ cup	Red wine	175 ml/6 fl oz
2	Small oranges cut in slices	2
1–2 tbsp	Sugar	1–1½ tbsp

1. Preheat the oven to 350°F/180°C/Gas Mark 4.

2. Melt 2 tablespoons [25 g/1 oz] of butter and cook 1 onion gently for 2–3 minutes. Add the rice and cook again for a few minutes. Pour on 1½ cups [350 ml/12 fl oz] stock; add 1 tablespoon herbs and seasoning. Cover with foil or a tightly fitting lid, and bake in the oven for 20–25 minutes.

3. Remove the outer skin from the liver. Mix the flour with a little salt, pepper, and cayenne pepper, and roll the liver in this mixture until it is covered. Heat 3 tablespoons [40 g/1½ oz] butter and cook the liver slices quickly until both sides are brown. Put in a dish and keep warm.

4. Add the finely chopped onion and crushed garlic to the pan and cook for 5–6 minutes, until golden brown. Sprinkle in the remaining flour. Add wine and the remaining stock, and bring to a boil. Add the herbs and seasoning. Pour the sauce over the liver and cook in the oven for 5 minutes.

5. Melt 3 tablespoons [40 g/1½ oz] of butter in a clean frying pan. Sprinkle the orange slices with sugar and put them sugar side down in the pan. Fry until brown, then sprinkle the top of the slices with the remaining sugar, and brown the second side. Arrange the orange slices over the liver. Serve hot with the rice.

Liver and Bacon Burgers

Sweetbreads with Garlic

 04:40 00:25   Serves 4   New England

American	Ingredients	Metric/Imperial
1½–2 lb	Sweetbreads	675–900 g/ 1½–2 lb
	Juice of ½ lemon	
	Milk (or chicken stock)	
1 cup	Butter	250 g/8 oz
2	Cloves garlic (more or less according to taste)	2
1 tbsp	Chopped parsley	1 tbsp

1. Soak the sweetbreads for 3–4 hours in several changes of cold salted water until the water no longer has a pinkish tinge.

2. Put in a pan and cover with water and the juice of ½ lemon. Bring to a boil and cook for 2–3 minutes. Drain and soak again in cold water. When cool, remove all the skin and membranes.

3. Melt the butter and add the finely crushed garlic. Cook gently for 10–12 minutes. Add the sliced sweetbreads. Season and turn in hot butter until golden brown. Sprinkle with chopped parsley and serve with boiled rice.

Sweetbread, Bacon, and Prune Kebabs

01:30
01:10
Serves 4–6
New England

American	Ingredients	Metric/Imperial
2	Pairs calf sweetbreads	2
2 tbsp	Vinegar	1½ tbsp
2 tbsp	Butter	25 g/1 oz
1 cup	Chopped onion	100 g/4 oz
1 cup	Rice	225 g/8 oz
3 cups	Chicken stock	700 ml/1¾ pints
½ cup	Sultana raisins	50 g/2 oz
½ cup	Peeled almonds	50 g/2 oz
1 tbsp	Chopped mixed herbs	1 tbsp
8 slices	Bacon, blanched	8 rashers
12	Baby onions	12
12	Large cooked prunes	12
2–3 tbsp	Chutney	1½–2 tbsp

1. Soak the sweetbreads for 3–4 hours in several changes of cold salted water until the water no longer has a pinkish tinge. Then put them in a pan with 4 pints [1.8 l] cold water, vinegar, and some salt. Bring to a boil slowly and simmer for 10–15 minutes. Drain and plunge into cold water. When cool, drain and dry them, and remove the skin and any tough membranes or tubes. Put into the refrigerator between two plates for 30 minutes.
2. Preheat the broiler [grill].
3. Make the rice: Melt the butter and cook the onion for 5 minutes. Add the rice and cook for 2–3 minutes. Add the stock and bring to a boil. Add the raisins, browned sliced almonds, and herbs. Cook the rice in the oven for about 30 minutes, until all the stock has been absorbed. Then put into a buttered mold and turn onto a serving dish.
4. Divide each sweetbread into 4 or 6 pieces. Wrap each piece in ½ slice of bacon. Cook the onions in a little stock for about 10 minutes. Remove the seeds from the prunes and stuff with chutney. Put the sweetbread pieces, onions, and prunes alternately onto the skewers. Brush with melted butter and season. Broil [grill] for 5–7 minutes until the bacon is crisp. Put the cooked kebabs on the rice and serve.

Sweetbread Pie

13:30
02:15
Serves 4–5
South

American	Ingredients	Metric/Imperial
	Pastry	
1½ cups	All-purpose [plain] flour	175 g/6 oz
½ tsp	Salt	½ tsp
¾ cup	Butter or margarine	175 g/6 oz
3–4 tbsp	Sour cream	2–3½ tbsp

American	Ingredients	Metric/Imperial
	Filling	
2 cups	Cooked spaghetti or other pasta	225 g/8 oz
1	Pair blanched and parboiled sweetbreads	1
1 cup	Cooked diced tongue	100 g/4 oz
2	Egg yolks	2
¾ cup	Heavy [double] cream	175 ml/6 fl oz
2–3 tbsp	Dry sherry	1½–2 tbsp

1. Sift the flour and salt into a bowl, cut in the butter until the mixture looks like bread crumbs. Mix lightly with the sour cream, tossing the mixture together until it forms a ball. Wrap in foil and chill overnight, if possible.
2. When ready to use, roll out the pastry and line a deep 8-inch pie plate with it. Reserve the pastry trimmings for decoration. Allow to rest 1 hour.
3. Preheat the oven to 425°F/220°C/Gas Mark 7.
4. Arrange the layers of spaghetti, sweetbreads, and tongue in the pastry shell. Beat the egg yolks, cream, and sherry together; season carefully and pour over the contents of the pie shell.
5. Use the trimmings of pastry to make a lattice design on top or use leaves of pastry.
6. Bake for 15 minutes; then reduce the heat to 375°F/190°C/Gas Mark 5 and cook for 2 minutes, or until the pastry is browned and the custard set.

Bacon and Kidney Stuffed Potatoes

00:40
01:25
Serves 4
Pacific Southwest

American	Ingredients	Metric/Imperial
4	Large potatoes	4
4 slices	Streaky bacon	4 rashers
4	Lambs' kidneys	4
	Salt and pepper	
2 tbsp	Butter	25 g/1 oz
	Watercress for garnish	

1. Preheat the oven to 400°F/200°C/Gas Mark 6.
2. Scrub the potatoes and bake for 1 hour, or until cooked (test with a pointed knife).
3 Place the bacon on a board and remove the rinds and any bones; then flatten each one with a round-bladed knife. Cut the kidneys in half lengthwise and remove the skin. Cut away the white core with a sharp knife or a pair of scissors. Wrap 2 kidney halves in each slice of bacon.
4. Cut off the top of the potatoes and scoop out enough hot potato to make room for the kidney and bacon roll. Sprinkle a little salt and pepper into each one with a pat of butter. Put in the kidneys and pack them in with the scooped-out potato; replace the tops.
5. Return the potatoes to the oven for 20–25 minutes more, or until the kidneys are cooked. After 15 minutes in the oven, remove the potato lids to allow the bacon to crisp. Place each potato in a table napkin, garnish with watercress, and serve hot.

Bacon and Kidney Stuffed Potatoes

Autumn Stew with Tongue

Autumn Stew with Tongue

🏷 00:25 / 01:15   Serves 4   Midwest

American	Ingredients	Metric/Imperial
1½ lb	Tongue	675 g/1½ lb
	Water	
1	Bay leaf	1
10	White peppercorns	10
1 lb	Potatoes	450 g/1 lb
1	Leek	1
¼ lb	Celery root (celeriac)	100 g/4 oz
2	Carrots	2
1 tsp	Mustard seeds	1 tsp
5 tbsp	Snipped green herbs	4 tbsp

1. Place the tongue in a pan and pour over enough water so that it is just covered. Add the bay leaf and the peppercorns. Cover and simmer over low heat for about 1 hour. Test to see if the tongue is done by pricking it with a toothpick. If the toothpick goes easily through, the meat is done.

2. Remove the cooked tongue from the pan and skin it while still warm. Place the meat back in the broth.

3. Peel and prepare the vegetables by cutting them into pieces. Cut the celery root into thinner pieces as it takes longer to cook. Place all the vegetables and spices in a pan and cover with enough broth to cover the vegetables. (Add more broth, if necessary.)

4. Cut the tongue into strips or cubes. Place them in the pan and cover. Cook the stew for about 15 minutes, or until the potatoes and vegetables feel soft. Add the mustard seeds and sprinkle with the snipped herbs (parsley, dill, etc.) just before serving.

Fried Tripe and Onions

🏷 00:25 / 01:45   Serves 4   Midwest

American	Ingredients	Metric/Imperial
1½ lb	Partly cooked and blanched tripe or canned tripe	675 g/1½ lb
1 cup	Milk	250 ml/8 fl oz
3 tbsp	Flour	2 tbsp
2 tbsp	Oil	1½ tbsp
2 tbsp	Butter	25 g/1 oz
3	Onions	3
1	Clove garlic	1
	A little cayenne pepper	
2 tbsp	Chopped parsley	1½ tbsp
2	Lemons	2
	Fat for deep frying	

1. Put the tripe into a pan, cover with milk and 1 cup [250 ml/8 fl oz] of water, and cook gently for 1½ hours. Drain and rinse with cold water. Drain and dry. Then cut the tripe into strips and toss in seasoned flour.

2. While the tripe is cooking, heat the oil. Add the butter and fry the sliced onions and crushed garlic until golden. Add cayenne pepper, salt, parsley, and the juice of 1 lemon, and cook for a few minutes more.

3. Heat the fat and fry the floured tripe until crisp and golden brown. Drain on a paper towel [kitchen paper]. Put the fried tripe on top of the onion mixture, and serve with quartered lemon and crisp French bread.

Brochettes of Lamb Kidneys 🏷🏷

🏷 00:25 / 00:30   Serves 4   New England

American	Ingredients	Metric/Imperial
8	Lamb kidneys	8
8 slices	Bacon, blanched	8 rashers
16–20	Button mushrooms	16–20
8	Baby onions	8
2–3 tbsp	Butter	25–40 g/ 1–1½ oz
1 tbsp	Oil	1 tbsp
1	Slice lean ham	1
½	Small onion	½
¼ cup	White wine	60 ml/2 fl oz
1 cup	Brown stock (or consommé)	250 ml/8 fl oz
1 tbsp	Tomato purée	1 tbsp
	A little chopped parsley	

1. Preheat the broiler [grill].

2. Skin and remove the core from the kidneys and cut each in half. Cut the bacon slices in half and curl each up into a small roll. Remove the stems from the mushrooms and reserve. Peel the baby onions and cook for 5–6 minutes in 1 tablespoon [15 g/½ oz] of butter. Arrange the kidneys, bacon rolls, mushroom caps, and baby onions on skewers to make 4 brochettes.

3. Make the sauce: Cook the chopped mushroom stems for a minute in hot oil. Then add the chopped ham and onion. Cook again for 5 minutes. Pour in the wine and cook, uncovered, for 3–4 minutes on high heat. Then add the stock and tomato purée, herbs, seasoning, and cook together for a few minutes.

4. Brush the brochettes with melted butter, and sprinkle with salt and pepper. Broil [grill] under the hot broiler for 6–10 minutes, turning every 2 minutes. Arrange on a bed of rice.

Kidneys in Sherry Sauce 🦪

	00:15		
	00:30	Serves 4	South

American	Ingredients	Metric/Imperial
8	Lamb kidneys	8
¼ cup	Butter	50 g/2 oz
1	Medium-sized onion, peeled and finely chopped	1
2 tbsp	Flour	1½ tbsp
1	Chicken bouillon [stock] cube dissolved in 1 cup [250 ml/8 fl oz] hot water	1
	Freshly ground black pepper	
2–3 tbsp	Dry sherry	1½–2 tbsp
	Chopped parsley	
	Buttered Rice	
1 cup	Long-grained rice	225 g/8 oz
2 cups	Water	450 ml/¾ pint
1 tsp	Salt	1 tsp
1 tbsp	Butter	15 g/½ oz

1. Skin and remove the core from the kidneys and cut in halves. Heat half the butter in a small frying pan, add the kidney, and sauté for 2–3 minutes; then remove from the pan. Add the remaining butter to the pan; add the onion and cook until soft and lightly browned.

2. Place the kidneys back in the pan; sprinkle with the flour and blend carefully with the fat. Stir in the hot stock and continue stirring until boiling. Simmer for 5 minutes. Add salt and pepper to taste and the sherry.

3. Serve sprinkled with parsley.

4. Make the rice: Butter a pan with a tightly fitting lid and put in the rice, water, and salt. Bring to a boil; stir once, put on the lid, and simmer over a low heat for 12–15 minutes. Do not stir or remove the lid at this stage.

5. When all the liquid has been absorbed, remove from the heat and leave for a few minutes. Then add the butter and toss with a fork.

Marinated Liver with Tomato-Crush

Marinated Liver with Tomato-Crush 🦪

	01:20		
	00:12	Serves 4	United States

American	Ingredients	Metric/Imperial
¾ cup	Red wine	175 ml/6 fl oz
1 tsp	Thyme	1 tsp
4–6	Slices calf liver	4–6
4	Tomatoes	4
1	Small onion	1
1 tbsp	Olive oil	1 tbsp
2 cups	Celery, cut in strips	225 g/8 oz
½ tsp	Basil	½ tsp
1½ tsp	Salt	1½ tsp
5 tbsp	Flour	4 tbsp
¼ tsp	Black pepper	¼ tsp
1 tbsp	Butter or margarine	15 g/½ oz

1. Mix the wine and thyme in a bowl. Place the liver slices in the mixture and marinate for 1 hour in the refrigerator.

2. Dip the tomatoes in boiling water, then peel. Remove the seeds and cut the tomatoes into large pieces. Peel and mince the onion. Heat the oil in a little pot and lightly sauté the onion. Add the tomato pieces, celery, basil, and ½ teaspoon of the salt. Simmer for a few minutes.

3. Dry off the liver. Dredge the slices in flour that has been mixed with the remaining salt and pepper. Brown the butter in a frying pan and sauté the liver slices for about 3 minutes on each side.

4. Divide the tomato mixture over the liver slices and serve immediately.

Kidney Pilaff

Calves Liver with Bean Sprouts

 00:40
00:15   Serves 4   Pacific Southwest

American	Ingredients	Metric/Imperial
3 tbsp	Dry sherry	2 tbsp
1 tsp	Ginger root, grated	1 tsp
1 lb	Calves liver, cubed into bite-sized pieces	450 g/1 lb
2 tbsp	Vegetable oil	1½ tbsp
¼ cup	Blanched, whole almonds	25 g/1 oz
2	Medium onions, finely chopped	2
¼ lb	Mushrooms, cut into cubes	100 g/4 oz
1 cup	Fresh or frozen, defrosted peas	100 g/4 oz
½ cup	Chicken or beef stock	125 ml/4 fl oz
2 tbsp	Soy sauce	1½ tbsp
1 cup	Bean sprouts	100 g/4 oz
1 tbsp	Cornstarch [cornflour]	1 tbsp
2 tbsp	Cold water	1½ tbsp

1. Combine the sherry and grated ginger in a small bowl and add the cubed liver. Marinate for 20–30 minutes.
2. Heat the oil in a frying pan or wok and stir-fry the almonds for 2–3 minutes, until brown. Remove from the pan. Stir-fry the onions with mushrooms 2–3 minutes. More oil may be necessary. Push aside. Stir-fry the peas 1–3 minutes; push aside. Stir-fry the liver 2–3 minutes. Return the vegetables and almonds to the wok.
3. Add the stock, soy sauce, and bean sprouts. Mix the cornstarch with the water. Stir the cornstarch mixture into the wok and heat until the sauce becomes thick and clear and the bean sprouts are heated through. Serve at once with rice.

Stuffed Liver and Bacon

 00:25
00:45   Serves 4   Mid Atlantic

American	Ingredients	Metric/Imperial
8	Large slices lamb or calf liver	8
2 tbsp	Flour	1½ tbsp
2 tbsp	Butter	25 g/1 oz
1	Onion	1
4	Mushrooms	4
2 tbsp	Chopped parsley	1½ tbsp
1 cup	Fresh white bread crumbs	50 g/2 oz
1 tsp	Lemon rind	1 tsp
1 tsp	Lemon juice	1 tsp
8 slices	Bacon, blanched	8 rashers
1 cup	Cider or water	250 ml/8 fl oz

1. Preheat the oven to 350°F/180°C/Gas Mark 4.
2. Skin the liver and remove the gristle. Dip in flour. Heat the butter in a frying pan and brown the liver quickly for 2 minutes. Place in an ovenproof dish.
3. Chop the onion and cook for a few minutes to soften. Chop the mushrooms and add; cook for 2 minutes. Add this mixture to the bread crumbs with the lemon rind and juice, parsley, and seasoning.
4. Put this stuffing on top of the slices of liver and place the bacon slices on top. Pour the cider around the side of the dish, reserving some if there seems to be too much liquid.
5. Bake in the oven until the liver is tender, about 30–40 minutes.

Kidney Pilaff

 00:15
00:17   Serves 4   Pacific Southwest

American	Ingredients	Metric/Imperial
4	Lamb kidneys	4
¼ cup	Butter	50 g/2 oz
4 slices	Bacon, chopped	4 rashers
1	Onion, peeled and finely chopped	1
1 cup	Sliced mushrooms	100 g/4 oz
½ cup	Stock or water	125 ml/4 fl oz
½ cup	Tomato juice	125 ml/4 fl oz
2 tsp	Cornstarch [corn flour]	2 tsp
2 tbsp	Red wine or water	1½ tbsp

1. Skin and core the kidneys and cut into small pieces.
2. Heat the butter in a frying pan; add the kidney, bacon, onion, and mushrooms. Cook until the onion is soft and golden brown.
3. Add the stock or water, tomato juice, and seasoning and simmer over low heat for about 10 minutes.
4. Blend the cornstarch with wine or water. Add to the kidney mixture and stir for 2 minutes. Serve in a border of cooked rice, or on toast.

Lamb Kidneys En Chemise

	00:30		
	02:00	Serves 4	United States

American	Ingredients	Metric/Imperial
4	Lamb kidneys	4
4	Large potatoes	4
4 slices	Streaky bacon, blanched	4 rashers
½	Onion	½
2	Mushrooms	2
2 tbsp	Butter	25 g/1 oz
	Prepared mustard	

1. Preheat the oven to 350°F/180°C/Gas Mark 4.
2. Wash and scrub the potatoes and bake in their skins for just over 1 hour. Remove from the oven and cut a good slice from the top of each one. Take out enough of the potato to make room for a kidney.
3. Skin and core the kidneys. Season with salt and pepper. Roll in a mixture of finely chopped mushrooms and onion, and wrap in half a slice of bacon smeared with mustard. Place the wrapped kidneys into the potatoes. Add ½ tablespoon [10 g/¼ oz] of butter to each potato, replace the potato top, and wrap the whole potato in foil. Return to the oven for another hour to cook the kidneys.

Kidney and Mushroom Sauté

	00:10		
	00:15	Serves 4	New England

American	Ingredients	Metric/Imperial
4 tbsp	Butter	50 g/2 oz
2 tbsp	Finely chopped shallots	1½ tbsp
1 cup	Finely chopped celery	100 g/4 oz
4	Small veal kidneys, skinned and cored	4
1 cup	Sliced mushrooms	100 g/4 oz
2 tbsp	Finely chopped parsley	1½ tbsp
½ cup	Dry red wine	125 ml/4 fl oz
¼ tsp	Dry mustard	¼ tsp
1 cup	Beef gravy	250 ml/8 fl oz

1. Heat the butter in a frying pan and sauté the shallots and celery until the shallots begin to soften.
2. Add the kidneys, cut into small pieces, and cook quickly until browned, about 5 minutes.
3. Add the mushrooms, parsley, the wine mixed with the mustard, seasoning, and gravy. Bring to a boil and cook gently for 3–4 minutes.

Lamb Kidneys En Chemise

Sauté of Lamb Kidneys

	00:20		
	00:45	Serves 4	New England

American	Ingredients	Metric/Imperial
8	Lamb kidneys	8
2 tbsp	Butter	25 g/1 oz
4 slices	Bacon	4 rashers
1	Onion	1
1 cup	Chopped mushrooms	100 g/4 oz
1 tbsp	Flour	1 tbsp
1 cup	Consomme	250 ml/8 fl oz
3–4 tbsp	Sherry or brandy	2–3½ tbsp
1 tbsp	Chopped mixed herbs	1 tbsp
3–4 tbsp	Thick cream	2–3½ tbsp

1. Preheat the oven to 300°F/150°C/Gas Mark 2.
2. Remove the skin and cores from the kidneys and cut each in half. Melt the butter and brown the kidneys quickly all over for about 2–3 minutes, then keep warm. Cut the bacon into small pieces and brown these quickly and add to the kidneys.
3. Add the chopped onion to the pan and cook until just turning brown. Add the chopped mushrooms and cook for 3 minutes. Stir in the flour. Add the consomme. Bring to a boil and cook for 2–3 minutes. Then add the sherry or brandy. Pour over the kidneys. Add the seasoning and herbs. Cook in the oven for 30 minutes. Do not allow to boil as this hardens the kidneys.
4. Remove from the oven, stir in the cream, and serve with mashed potatoes or rice.

Poultry and Game

French Roast Chicken

Traditional Roast Chicken

00:40
02:10

Serves 4–6

United States

American	Ingredients	Metric/Imperial
1 (3–4 lb)	Chicken or capon	1 (1.25–1.75 kg/ 3–4 lb)
¾ cup	Butter	175 g/6 oz
1	Large onion	1
2 cups	Fresh bread crumbs	100 g/4 oz
2 tbsp	Chopped cooked ham	1½ tbsp
1 tbsp	Chopped parsley	1 tbsp
1 tsp	Chopped thyme	1 tsp
	A little grated lemon rind	
1	Beaten egg or 2–3 tbsp [1½–2 tbsp] milk	1
	Salt and pepper	
3–4 tbsp	Bacon fat or oil	2–3½ tbsp
2 cups	Chicken stock made from giblets	450 ml/¾ pint
4–6 slices	Bacon	4–6 rashers
8–12	Chippolata sausages	8–12
	Bread Sauce	
1 cup	Milk	250 ml/8 fl oz
1	Onion	1
2–3	Cloves	2–3
½	Bay leaf	½
3 sprigs or 1 tsp dried	Parsley	3 sprigs or 1 tsp dried
	Pinch of mace or nutmeg	
6	Peppercorns	6
	Salt	
1 cup	Fresh bread crumbs	50 g/2 oz
1 tbsp	Butter	15 g/½ oz
2 tbsp	Cream	1½ tbsp

1. Preheat the oven to 400°F/200°C/Gas Mark 6.
2. First prepare the stuffing: Melt ¼ cup [50 g/2 oz] butter; cook half of the onion, chopped, for 3–4 minutes to soften. Mix with the bread crumbs, chopped ham, herbs, and grated lemon rind. Add the seasoning, beaten egg, or milk to make a fairly moist mixture. Fill into the neck end of the chicken. Fold the skin flap under the wings and skewer or sew to hold in place. Put half of the onion and some seasoning inside the cavity of the bird with a little butter. Rub the remaining butter over the chicken and sprinkle with seasoning.
3. Melt the bacon fat or oil in a roasting pan. When hot, add the chicken, baste thoroughly, then cover with foil and put into the oven. Roast, basting every 15 minutes, turning the chicken from side to side, allowing 20 minutes per pound and a little extra time. During the last 15 minutes, remove the foil to allow the breast to brown. Remove to a hot dish and keep warm while making the gravy. Pour off the fat, pour in the remaining chicken stock, and bring to a boil. To obtain more flavor, reduce the liquid by boiling.
4. Meanwhile, prepare the bread sauce. Stick the cloves into the onion; put in a pan with milk, herbs, and peppercorns. Cook gently for 20–30 minutes without boiling. Strain onto fresh bread crumbs; heat together until creamy, then at the last minute stir in butter and cream. Add seasoning and serve hot.
5. Divide the bacon slices in half and make into rolls; put on skewers and broil [grill] until crisp at the same time as broiling the chippolata sausages. Serve the chicken surrounded by bacon rolls and sausages; serve the gravy and bread sauce separately.

French Roast Chicken

00:20
01:40

Serves 4–6

South

American	Ingredients	Metric/Imperial
1 (3–4 lb)	Chicken	1 (1.25–1.75 kg/ 3–4 lb)
	Chicken giblets	
1	Onion	1
1½ cups	Water	350 ml/12 fl oz
6–7 tbsp	Butter	75–90 g/ 3–3½ oz
3–4	Sprigs fresh parsley	3–4
2–3 slices	Fat bacon	2–3 rashers
1	Bunch watercress	1

1. Preheat the oven to 350°F/180°C/Gas Mark 4.
2. Be sure the chicken is completely thawed out before cooking. Make the stock with giblets, onion, seasoning, and water. Cook slowly for 15 minutes. Put half of the butter inside the bird with herbs, salt, and pepper. Spread the remaining butter over the chicken. Cover with bacon slices, put into a roasting pan, and pour half the stock over the chicken.
3. Cook in the oven, basting with stock every 15 minutes and turning the bird from side to side. Allow 20 minutes per pound weight. For the last 20 minutes, remove the bacon slices and place the bird breast up to brown.
4. Move the bird onto a hot dish and keep hot in the oven. Meanwhile, skim the butter from the top of the pan drippings. Add the remaining stock to the roasting pan and boil until well flavored. Serve as gravy.
5. Serve the chicken either hot or cold, with a green salad and garnished with watercress.

Chicken with Almonds

Deviled Roast Chicken

00:10

00:50

Serves 12

New England

American	Ingredients	Metric/Imperial
2 (3-lb)	Roasting chickens	2 (1.25 kg/3 lb)
¼ lb	Margarine	100 g/4 oz
6 tbsp	Vinegar	5 tbsp
2	Cloves garlic, crushed (optional)	2
3 tsp	Dry mustard	3 tsp
1½ tsp	Salt	1½ tsp
1 tsp	Pepper	1 tsp
¼ tsp	Cayenne pepper	¼ tsp
3 tsp	Worcestershire sauce	3 tsp
3 tsp	Soy sauce	3 tsp
1 tbsp	Sugar	1 tbsp

1. Preheat the oven to 375°F/190°C/Gas Mark 5.
2. Cut each chicken into 6 portions or ask your butcher to do it for you. Place the chicken pieces in a large roasting pan and dot with margarine. Roast in the oven for 45 minutes or until tender and browned.
3. Meanwhile, put all the remaining ingredients in a saucepan and bring to a boil. Arrange the cooked chicken pieces on a serving plate and cover with sauce. Serve as soon as possible.

Chicken with Almonds

00:10

01:10

Serves 4

Mid Atlantic

American	Ingredients	Metric/Imperial
4 tbsp	Oil	3½ tbsp
2 tbsp	Butter or margarine	25 g/1 oz
1 (2–2½ lb)	Jointed broiler chicken	1 (900 g–1.25 kg/ 2–2½ lb)
2	Onions, peeled and thinly sliced	2
3	Tomatoes, peeled, seeded and chopped	3
	A pinch of cinnamon	
1½ cups	Chicken stock	350 ml/12 fl oz
5 tbsp	Blanched almonds	4 tbsp
½ cup	Seedless raisins	50 g/2 oz
¾ cup	Rice, cooked	175 g/6 oz
	Chopped parsley	

1. Preheat the oven to 375°F/190°C/Gas Mark 5.
2. Heat the oil and butter in a frying pan, and brown the chicken pieces on all sides. Add the onions, tomatoes, seasoning, and cinnamon. Cook together for a few minutes. Then remove all to a casserole.
3. Add the chicken stock; cover and cook for 30 minutes. Add the almonds and raisins and cook for 30 minutes more.
4. Line a large oval platter with the hot cooked rice. Pile the chicken pieces in the center, season the sauce to taste, and pour over the chicken.

Barbecued Chicken 2

Boiled Chicken with Mushroom Sauce

 00:15 / 02:10   Serves 6–8   New England

American	Ingredients	Metric/Imperial
3 tbsp	Oil	2 tbsp
2	Onions, peeled and chopped	2
2–3	Stalks celery, chopped	2–3
1 (4–4½ lb)	Boiling fowl, jointed	1 (1.75–2 kg/ 4–4½ lb)
2–3 slices	Bacon	2–3 rashers
4	Peppercorns	4
1	Bay leaf	1
2 cups	Sliced mushrooms	225 g/8 oz
2 tbsp	Butter	25 g/1 oz
1 tsp	Worcestershire sauce	1 tsp
3 tbsp	Flour	2 tbsp

1. Heat the oil in a pan; add the onions and celery, and sauté for a few minutes.

2. Put in the pieces of chicken with the giblets and bacon. Add water to cover, salt, peppercorns, and bay leaf. Cover and simmer until the chicken is tender, about 2 hours.

3. Sauté the mushrooms in the butter for about 3 minutes; stir in the Worcestershire sauce and flour. Remove from the heat, and gradually add 1½ cups [350 ml/12 fl oz] of the strained chicken stock. Return to the heat, stir until boiling, and boil for 2 minutes. Adjust the seasoning and remove the bay leaf.

4. Arrange the chicken pieces on a serving dish, and pour over the sauce. Keep any remaining stock for future use.

Barbecued Chicken 1

 00:30 / 01:20   Serves 4   Southwest

American	Ingredients	Metric/Imperial
4	Large chicken quarters or halves	4
	Barbecue Sauce	
6 tbsp	Oil	5 tbsp
1	Onion	1
1	Clove garlic	1
1 can (225 g/8 oz)	Tomatoes	1 tin (225 g/8 oz)
1 tbsp	Tomato ketchup	1 tbsp
1 tbsp	Chutney	1 tbsp
1 tbsp	Vinegar	1 tbsp
½ cup	Stock (or water)	125 ml/4 fl oz
1 tbsp	Worcestershire sauce	1 tbsp
1 tsp	French mustard	1 tsp
1 tsp	Paprika	1 tsp
	Juice and grated rind of ½ lemon	
2 tsp	Brown [demerara] sugar	2 tsp
1 tbsp	Finely chopped parsley	1 tbsp
1 tsp	Mixed powdered thyme, nutmeg, and bay leaf	1 tsp

1. Prepare the barbecue sauce: Heat the oil and cook the finely chopped onion and crushed garlic for 5 minutes. Add the tomatoes and all the other ingredients. Cook for 20–30 minutes, season to taste, then strain and let cool.

2. With a sharp knife, make small cuts into the chicken pieces. Spoon the cold barbecue sauce over them and let stand for at least a half hour.

3. Heat the charcoal grill or broiler [grill]. Place the chicken pieces on a hot grill and turn every 5–6 minutes, basting frequently with barbecue sauce. Allow 30–45 minutes to barbecue the quarters, depending on the heat of the grill and the thickness of chicken pieces. Test with a skewer: if the juice from the chicken runs clear, the chicken is done.

4. Heat the remaining sauce, and serve the chicken with salad and baked potatoes.

Barbecued Chicken 2

 04:40 / 00:30   Serves 4   Southwest

American	Ingredients	Metric/Imperial
1 (3 lb)	Chicken	1 (1.25 kg/3 lb)
	Marinade	
½ cup	Dry white wine	125 ml/4 fl oz
2 tbsp	Oil	1½ tbsp
	Juice of ½ lemon	
1	Small onion, peeled and chopped	1
½ tsp	Tarragon	½ tsp

	Herb Butter	
½ cup	Butter or margarine	100 g/4 oz
4 tbsp	Chopped parsley	3½ tbsp
2 tsp	Rosemary	2 tsp

1. Combine all the marinade ingredients.
2. Cut the chicken into 8 pieces and leave in the marinade for several hours, turning frequently.
3. Heat the coals in an outdoor grill until hot, about 30 minutes, or preheat the broiler [grill].
4. Drain the chicken, brush with Herb Butter (see below), and cook on the rack over the glowing coals, basting several times. Cook until the chicken is crisp and golden.
5. To make the Herb Butter, put the ingredients into a small pan, and heat just enough to melt the butter. Use half to baste the chicken, and put the rest into the refrigerator to firm. Then cut into pats and serve on the chicken.

Barbecued Chicken 3

	01:45			
	01:00	Serves 6	Southwest	

American	Ingredients	Metric/Imperial
3 (2–2½ lb)	Broiler chickens	3 (900 g–1.25 kg/ 2–2½ lb)
	Marinade	
3 tbsp	Clear honey	2 tbsp
1 tbsp	Dijon mustard	1 tbsp
1 tbsp	Oil	1 tbsp
1 cup	Pineapple juice	250 ml/8 fl oz
½ cup	Orange juice	125 ml/4 fl oz
¼ cup	Tomato ketchup	60 ml/2 fl oz
	Cayenne pepper	
	Ground ginger	

1. Split the chickens in half lengthwise; break the drumstick, thigh, and wing joints so that the birds stay flat during the cooking. Allow half a bird for each person.
2. Put the ingredients, except the pepper and ginger, into a pan, and bring slowly to a boil. Then simmer gently for about 30 minutes or until slightly thickened. Season with salt and pepper, and add a good pinch of cayenne and ground ginger.
3. Brush the chicken generously with the marinade, and leave it in it for an hour or more.
4. Heat the coals in an outdoor grill until hot, about 30 minutes, or preheat the broiler [grill].
5. Drain the chicken well, and cook on the grid over the hot coals in the usual way, brushing occasionally with the marinade.
6. Serve with a salad.

Hawaiian Barbecued Chicken

Hawaiian Barbecued Chicken

	02:45			
	00:20	Serves 4	Pacific Southwest	

American	Ingredients	Metric/Imperial
1 (3 lb)	Chicken	1 (1.25 kg/3 lb)
1	Red pepper	1
1	Green pepper	1
1	Clove garlic, crushed	1
1	Small onion, grated	1
2 tsp	Brown [demerara] sugar	2 tsp
1 tsp	Curry powder	1 tsp
1 cup	Tomato juice	250 ml/8 fl oz
½ tsp	Ground ginger, cayenne, pepper, and salt	½ tsp
1 tbsp	Lemon juice	1 tbsp

1. Cut all the meat from the chicken and cut into bite-sized pieces. Wash the peppers, remove all seeds and membranes, and cut into squares. Thread the chicken and peppers, alternately onto 4 skewers. Place the kebabs in a shallow bowl.
2. Mix all the remaining ingredients in a bowl and whisk thoroughly together. Pour the marinade over the kebabs and leave in a cool place for up to 2 hours, turning occasionally.
3. Heat the coals in an outdoor grill until hot, about 30 minutes, or preheat the broiler [grill].
4. Grill the kebabs for 10–20 minutes, or until the chicken is cooked. Baste occasionally with marinade.

Chicken-Peach Casserole

Chicken-Peach Casserole

	00:25		
	01:05	Serves 6	Mid Atlantic

American	Ingredients	Metric/Imperial
1 (3½-lb)	Frying chicken	1 (1.5 kg/3½ lb)
2 tbsp	Butter or margarine	25 g/1 oz
1 tbsp	Oil	1 tbsp
1	Large onion, peeled and sliced	1
1	Green pepper, seeded and cut into strips	1
1 large can (about 30 oz)	Sliced peaches	1 large tin (about 850 g/30 oz)
1 tbsp	Cornstarch [cornflour]	1 tbsp
1 tbsp	Soy sauce	1 tbsp
3 tbsp	White wine vinegar	2 tbsp
2	Tomatoes, peeled and thickly sliced	2

1. Preheat the oven to 375°F/190°C/Gas Mark 5.
2. Disjoint and skin the chicken. Heat the butter and oil in a frying pan, brown the chicken pieces on all sides; then cover, reduce the heat, and cook for about 10 minutes. Remove the chicken and arrange in a large casserole.
3. Sauté the onion and pepper in the remaining fat until the onion is transparent.
4. Drain the peaches but reserve the syrup. Mix the cornstarch smoothly with the soy sauce and vinegar; add 1 cup [250 ml/8 fl oz] of peach syrup and pour into the pan. Stir until boiling, and boil until clear. Add the peaches and tomatoes. Then pour the contents of the frying pan over the chicken.
5. Cover the casserole, and cook for 30–40 minutes, removing the lid for the last 5 minutes.
6. Adjust the seasoning, and serve with wild rice to which some cooked green peas and a few strips of red pepper have been added.

Chicken Casserole

	00:15		
	01:15	Serves 4	Mid Atlantic

American	Ingredients	Metric/Imperial
½ cup	Butter or margarine	100 g/4 oz
4	Chicken breasts	4
1 can (about 15 oz)	Artichoke hearts	1 tin (about 425 g/15 oz)
1	Onion, peeled and chopped	1
2 tsp	Paprika	2 tsp
3 tbsp	Flour	2 tbsp
½ cup	Water	125 ml/4 fl oz
1	Chicken bouillon [stock] cube	1
½ cup	Sour cream	125 ml/4 fl oz
1 cup	Dry white wine	250 ml/8 fl oz
2–3 slices	Bacon, fried	2–3 rashers
	Almond slivers, toasted	

1. Preheat the oven to 350°F/180°C/Gas Mark 4.
2. Heat the butter in a frying pan; put in the chicken, sprinkle with salt and pepper, and brown on both sides. Put into a casserole with the drained artichokes.
3. Add the onion and paprika to the remaining fat, and sauté until the onion is soft. Remove from the heat, stir in the flour, return to the heat, and cook for 1 minute.
4. Gradually add the water in which the bouillon cube has been dissolved; stir until boiling. Remove from the heat; add the sour cream and wine. Reheat for a few minutes without boiling, then pour over the chicken.
5. Cover and cook for about 1 hour. Before serving, sprinkle with crumbled fried bacon and slivered almonds.

Chicken Casserole with Vegetables

	00:10		
	01:20	Serves 4	New England 

American	Ingredients	Metric/Imperial
2 tbsp	Oil	1½ tbsp
1	Chicken, jointed	1
3–4	Scallions [spring onions] chopped	3–4
1 can (about 15 oz)	Tomatoes	1 tin (about 425 g/15 oz)
1 (10 oz)	Package frozen whole kernel corn	1 (275 g/10 oz)
1 lb	Fresh green beans	450 g/1 lb
1½ cups	Chicken stock	350 ml/12 fl oz
1	Bay leaf	1
½ tsp	Powdered thyme	½ tsp
1 small can (about 8 oz)	New potatoes	1 small tin (about 225 g/8 oz)

1. Preheat the oven to 350°F/180°C/Gas Mark 4.
2. Heat the oil in a frying pan, brown the chicken pieces and onions, and remove to a casserole.
3. Add all the other ingredients except the potatoes.
4. Drain the potatoes, then brown in the oil left in the frying pan; add to the casserole.
5. Cover and cook for 1–1¼ hours. Serve with a tossed salad.

Chicken Chop Suey

Chicken Chop Suey

 01:00
02:20

Serves 4

Pacific Southwest

American	Ingredients	Metric/Imperial
1 (3-lb)	Chicken	1 (1.25 kg/3 lb)
4	Onions	4
2	Carrots	2
1	Bunch herbs	1
6–8	Peppercorns	6–8
1 cup	Rice	250 g/8 oz
3–4	Stalks celery	3–4
6–8	Mushrooms	6–8
	Squeeze of lemon juice	
1 can (8 oz)	Bean sprouts	1 tin (225 g/8 oz)
2 tbsp	Soy sauce	1½ tbsp
1½ tbsp	Cornstarch [cornflour]	1¼ tbsp

1. Boil the chicken with 2 onions, carrots, herbs, and peppercorns until tender. Let cool in water. When cool, remove the skin and bones, and boil the stock with these and a chicken bouillon [stock] cube to make a well-flavored stock.
2. Boil the rice in the usual way: drain well and keep warm in the oven.

3. Cut the chicken into large chunks and reserve. Slice 2 onions and celery, and put these to cook in a little of the stock until just tender, 8–10 minutes. Cook the sliced mushrooms in a little stock and lemon juice for 3–4 minutes; add to the chicken. Mix the chicken with the drained vegetables; add the drained bean sprouts, soy sauce, seasoning, and 1½ cups [350 ml/12 fl oz] of chicken stock.
4. Heat gently. Meanwhile, mix the cornstarch with 1 cup [250 ml/8 fl oz] of stock; add this to the chicken mixture. Heat until the sauce thickens and serve with boiled rice.

Chicken in Cider and Mustard

 00:10
00:40

Serves 4

New England

American	Ingredients	Metric/Imperial
1 (3-lb)	Chicken	1 (1.25/3 lb)
½ tbsp	Margarine	10 g/¼ oz
1	Large onion, peeled and thinly sliced	1
½–1 tsp	Salt	½–1 tsp
½ tsp	Black pepper	½ tsp
⅔ cup	Apple cider	150 ml/¼ pint
1 tbsp	Light French mustard	1 tbsp
½ tsp dried, or 2 sprigs fresh	Thyme	½ tsp dried or 2 sprigs fresh
⅔ cup	Light [single] cream	150 ml/¼ pint

1. Divide the chicken into 6–8 pieces. Brown the chicken on all sides. Add the sliced onion, pepper, and cider. Mix the mustard and thyme with the light cream and pour it into the pot.
2. Mix thoroughly and let the chicken simmer for 30–35 minutes. Serve with chopped parsley, boiled potatoes, and tender boiled carrots.

Chicken in Cider and Mustard

Circassian Chicken

Circassian Chicken

	00:30	Serves 4–6	Pacific Southwest
	01:20		

American	Ingredients	Metric/Imperial
1 (3–4 lb)	Chicken	1 (1.25–1.75 kg/ 3–4 lb)
5	Onions	5
3	Cloves	3
3	Stalks celery	3
	A few sprigs parsley	
1	Bay leaf	1
8	Peppercorns	8
2 cups	Shelled walnuts	225 g/8 oz
½ cup	Dry bread crumbs	25 g/1 oz
2 tbsp	Butter	25 g/1 oz
1	Clove garlic	1
2 tsp	Paprika	2 tsp
	A pinch of cayenne pepper	
3 tbsp	Oil	2 tbsp

1. Put the chicken in deep pan and just cover with cold water. Add 3 onions each stuck with a clove, chopped celery, herbs, peppercorns, and a little salt. Bring to a boil and simmer until tender, about 1 hour. Skim as necessary. Drain and keep warm, reserving the stock for sauce.
2. Grind the walnuts finely in an electric blender and mix with bread crumbs. Melt the butter and cook 2 chopped onions and the crushed garlic until golden brown and soft. Then add to the walnut mixture, blending carefully. When quite smooth, cook until it reaches the boiling point, adding more stock if the sauce becomes too thick. Season with salt and a little pepper.
3. Mix the oil and red pepper together. When the oil is red, strain it. Add enough of this oil to the walnut sauce to make it a delicate pink.
4. Cut the chicken into pieces. Put a layer of sauce in the bottom of an ovenproof dish; lay the chicken pieces on top. Spoon the remaining sauce over the top of the chicken. Reheat thoroughly. Garnish the top with the remaining red oil, sprinkling over the surface of the dish. Serve with plain boiled rice.

Chicken Burgundy

	00:20	Serves 4–6	South
	01:20		

American	Ingredients	Metric/Imperial
1 (3–4 lb)	Capon or chicken	1 (1.25–1.75 kg/ 3–4 lb)
4 slices	Unsmoked bacon	4 rashers
12–16	Small onions	12–16
12–16	Button mushrooms	12–16
1	Clove garlic	1
4 tbsp	Butter	50 g/2 oz
1 cup	Burgundy or red wine	250 ml/8 fl oz
1½ cups	Strong brown stock	350 ml/12 fl oz
2–3 sprigs fresh or 1 tsp dried	Parsley	2–3 sprigs fresh or 1 tsp dried
1	Sprig thyme (or a pinch of dried thyme)	1
1	Bay leaf	1

1. Preheat the oven to 325°F/160°C/Gas Mark 3.
2. Thaw the capon or chicken. Cut it into suitably sized pieces and dry. Chop the bacon into small pieces. Peel the onions and mushrooms. Crush the garlic.
3. Melt 3 tablespoons [40 g/1½ oz] butter and fry the bacon, onions, and garlic until golden brown. Remove to a casserole and keep warm. Fry the chicken pieces in the same butter until golden brown all over. Remove to a casserole.
4. Pour the red wine into a pan and bring to a boil to reduce the quantity to half. Meanwhile, flambé the wine to burn off the alcohol. Add the stock and boil for 5 minutes. Season with salt and black pepper. Pour this sauce over the chicken and vegetables in the casserole. Add the herbs. Bring to a boil; then reduce the heat and cook for 45–60 minutes in the oven.
5. While the chicken is cooking, melt the remaining butter and cook the mushrooms. Add to the casserole for the last 20 minutes of cooking time.

Deviled Chicken

	00:35	Serves 4	Southwest
	00:30		

American	Ingredients	Metric/Imperial
8	Cooked chicken legs	8
6 tbsp	Oil	5 tbsp
1 tsp	Curry powder	1 tsp
2 tsp	Prepared mustard	2 tsp
1 tbsp	Vinegar	1 tbsp
½ tsp	Freshly ground black pepper	½ tsp
	Pinch of cayenne pepper	
1 tbsp	Tomato ketchup	1 tbsp

1. Heat the coals in an outdoor grill until hot, about 30 minutes, or preheat the broiler [grill].
2. Mix the oil and curry powder smoothly, and add all the other ingredients.
3. Brush generously over the chicken legs before and during the cooking. Cook until brown on both sides.

Cinnamon Orange Chicken

Chicken Cordon Bleu

00:45
00:15   Serves 4   Mid Atlantic

American	Ingredients	Metric/Imperial
4	Chicken breasts	4
4 tbsp	Chopped cooked ham	3½ tbsp
4 tbsp	Grated Swiss cheese	3½ tbsp
1	Small clove garlic	1
1–2 tbsp	White wine	1–1½ tbsp
3–4 tbsp	Seasoned flour	2–3½ tbsp
1	Large egg	1
¼ cup	Oil	60 ml/2 fl oz
6–8 tbsp	Dried white bread crumbs	5–7 tbsp
4–5 tbsp	Butter	50–65 g/ 2–2½ oz

1. Place 4 chicken breasts skin side downwards, and with a sharp knife cut a shallow slit down the center of each without cutting through to the skin. Then cut shallow pockets on either side of these slits.
2. Mix the ham and cheese with crushed garlic and a little white wine to moisten. Season well. Fill into the pockets in the chicken breasts and seal the slit with the small finger-shaped fillet that is attached to each breast. Put in the refrigerator to chill for 30 minutes.
3. Coat well in seasoned flour, brush carefully with egg beaten with 1 teaspoon of oil, and roll in bread crumbs. Heat the oil, and add butter. When foaming, fry the chicken breasts until tender, golden brown, and crisp all over. Drain on a paper towel [kitchen paper].

Cinnamon Orange Chicken

00:25
00:25   Serves 4   Pacific Southwest

American	Ingredients	Metric/Imperial
1 (3-lb)	Chicken	1 (1.25 kg/3 lb)
2 tbsp	Flour	1½ tbsp
	Salt and pepper	
1 tsp	Ground cinnamon	1 tsp
4 tbsp	Margarine	50 g/2 oz
½ cup	Chicken stock or water and chicken stock cube	125 ml/4 fl oz
2	Oranges	2
	Freshly boiled rice for serving	

1. Cut the chicken into 4 portions and wipe with a damp cloth. Mix the flour, salt, pepper, and cinnamon together and coat the chicken portions.
2. Heat the margarine in a large frying pan and fry the chicken until tender and golden all over (about 20 minutes). Remove the chicken and drain on paper towels [kitchen paper]. Keep hot.
3. Pour off the fat from the pan. Add the chicken stock and the finely grated rind and juice from 1 orange. Bring to a boil, stirring.
4. Arrange the chicken on a bed of boiled rice and pour the sauce over the top. Carefully peel the remaining orange, removing all skin and pith; slice thinly. Arrange the orange slices on the chicken. Serve with rice.

Chicken Country-Style

Chicken Country-Style

🔪 00:30 / 01:00   Serves 4   South

American	Ingredients	Metric/Imperial
1	Small cooked chicken	1
6 tbsp	Margarine	75 g/3 oz
2	Carrots, diced	2
1	Small turnip, diced	1
1	Leek, sliced	1
1	Onion, chopped	1
2	Sticks celery, sliced	2
	Salt and pepper	
1 tsp	Sugar	1 tsp
½ cup	Chicken stock	125 ml/4 fl oz
2 tbsp	Flour	1½ tbsp
1 cup	Milk	250 ml/8 fl oz
4 tbsp	Cheddar cheese, grated	3½ tbsp
¼ tsp	Dry mustard	¼ tsp
	Parsley for garnish	

1. Cut the chicken into pieces and remove the meat from the bones. Heat 4 tablespoons [50 g/2 oz] of margarine in a saucepan. Add the prepared vegetables, salt, pepper, and sugar. Fry very gently, stirring occasionally, for 10 minutes. Add the chicken stock, cover the pan, and bring to a boil. Then simmer gently for 20 minutes.
2. Preheat the oven to 400°F/200°C/Gas Mark 6.
3. Melt the remaining margarine in a saucepan; stir in the flour. Cook, stirring, for 2 minutes. Add milk gradually, then bring to a boil, stirring until the sauce is thickened and smooth. Stir grated cheese and mustard into the sauce.
4. Put the drained vegetables in an ovenproof dish, arrange the chicken on top, and pour the sauce over top. Bake for 20 minutes. Serve garnished with parsley.

Chicken Florentine 👨‍🍳

🔪 00:10 / 00:55   Serves 4   Midwest

American	Ingredients	Metric/Imperial
4	Pieces frying chicken	4
2–3 tbsp	Seasoned flour	1½–2 tbsp
6 tbsp	Butter	75 g/3 oz
1 lb	Package of frozen spinach	450 g/1 lb
1 tbsp	All-purpose [plain] flour	1 tbsp
3–4 tbsp	Cream	2–3½ tbsp
	Pinch of mace and paprika	
4–5 tbsp	Grated Parmesan cheese	3½–4 tbsp
3 tbsp	Cornflakes or bread crumbs	2 tbsp

1. Preheat the oven to 400°F/200°C/Gas Mark 6.
2. Roll the chicken pieces in seasoned flour; then fry in 3 tablespoons [40 g/1½ oz] hot butter until golden brown, about 10 minutes.
3. Cook a package of frozen spinach, following the instructions on the package. Add 2 tablespoons [25 g/1 oz] of butter. When melted, sprinkle in the flour. Bring to a boil; then add the cream and seasoning, with a dash of paprika. Pour this into a buttered, ovenproof dish. Place the chicken pieces on top.
4. Mix the cheese and cornflake crumbs (or bread crumbs) together, and sprinkle thickly over the top of the chicken. Dribble the remaining butter over the top. Cook in the oven for about 25–30 minutes, or until the topping is crisp and brown.

Creole Chicken 👨‍🍳👨‍🍳

🔪 00:15 / 01:00   Serves 4   South

American	Ingredients	Metric/Imperial
1 (2½-lb)	Chicken	1 (1.25 kg/2½ lb)
6–7 slices	Bacon	6–7 rashers
5 tbsp	Flour	4 tbsp
1 tbsp	Olive oil	1 tbsp
¾ cup	Onion, sliced	75 g/3 oz
1	Clove garlic, chopped	1
2–3	Celery stalks	2–3
1	Green pepper, shredded	1
2 (14-oz) cans	Crushed tomatoes	2 (400 g/14 oz) tins
2 tsp	Thyme	2 tsp
1 tsp	Black pepper	1 tsp
¼ tsp	Cayenne pepper	¼ tsp
1	Bay leaf	1
	Juice from ½ lemon	

1. Divide the chicken into 8 pieces. Fry the bacon slices until brown and crispy in a stew pan. Take them out and let them drain on a paper towel [kitchen paper].
2. Dredge the chicken pieces in flour and fry them in bacon fat so that they become golden brown all over. Take them out of the pan. Pour olive oil into the pan and add the onion and garlic. After about 5 minutes, add the celery and green pepper.

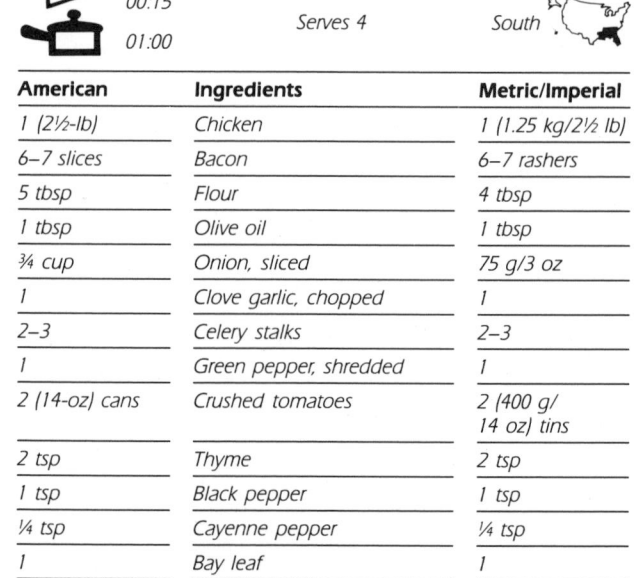

3. After another 3 minutes, add the canned tomatoes and the rest of the spices. Let the mixture come to a boil. Place the chicken pieces on the vegetable mixture, and let simmer for 30 minutes. Add a little water if the mixture becomes too dry.

4. Just before serving, add the lemon juice. Then sprinkle with bacon slices, which also can be slightly crumbled. Serve with rice.

Chicken Curry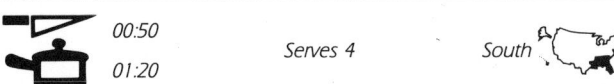

	00:50	Serves 4	South
	01:20		

American	Ingredients	Metric/Imperial
4	Large chicken pieces	4
5 tbsp	Butter	65 g/2½ oz
2	Medium onions	2
1 tbsp	Curry powder (or more according to taste)	1 tbsp
1 tsp	Curry paste	1 tsp
1 tbsp	Flour	1 tbsp
1½ cups	Strong chicken stock	350 ml/12 fl oz
1	Apple	1
2 tbsp	Raisins	1½ tbsp
2 tbsp	Chutney	1½ tbsp
1	Bay leaf	1
2–3 tbsp	Finely shredded coconut	1½–2 tbsp
	Juice of ½ lemon	
2 tsp	Red currant or other sharp jelly	2 tsp
2 cups	Cooked long-grain rice	450 g/1 lb
2–3 tsp	Turmeric powder	2–3 tsp
1	Lemon	1
½ tsp	Paprika	½ tsp

1. Preheat the oven to 350°F/180°C/Gas Mark 4.

2. Heat the butter, and brown the chicken pieces until golden. Remove and put in an ovenproof dish to keep warm.

3. Slice the onions finely and cook until golden brown. Then add the curry powder and paste, and cook for a few minutes. Add the flour and allow to brown slightly. Add the stock, bring to a boil, and simmer for 4–5 minutes. Then add the chopped apple, raisins, chutney, bay leaf, and salt. Cook together for 1 minute. Pour over the chicken pieces, and cook in the oven for 35–40 minutes, by which time the chicken pieces should be nearly tender.

4. Meanwhile, pour ¼ cup [60 ml/2 fl oz] of boiling water over the shredded coconut; let it stand for 30 minutes. Strain the liquid onto the chicken, adding lemon juice and jelly. Cook for 15 minutes.

5. When cooked, remove the chicken pieces and put in the center of a ring of boiled rice, finished with turmeric cooked in the remaining butter. Boil the sauce, sieve or blend it, season it to taste, and spoon over the chicken. Garnish with thin slices of lemon and sprinkle with paprika.

Chicken Curry

Curried Chicken Casserole

	00:20	Serves 4–5	South
	03:10		

American	Ingredients	Metric/Imperial
1	Small stewing fowl	1
2 tbsp	Butter or margarine	25 g/1 oz
2 tbsp	Oil	1½ tbsp
2	Onions, peeled and sliced	2
1	Large apple, peeled, cored and sliced	1
1 tbsp	Curry powder	1 tbsp
1 tbsp	Flour	1 tbsp
½ tsp	Powdered turmeric	½ tsp
¼ tsp	Ground ginger	¼ tsp
2 tsp	Sugar	2 tsp
4 cups	Giblet stock or water	1 1/1¾ pints
1 tsp	Curry paste	1 tsp
2	Stalks celery, chopped	2
2 tbsp	Seedless raisins	1½ tbsp
2 tsp	Chutney	2 tsp
2 tsp	Lemon juice	2 tsp

1. Preheat the oven to 325°F/160°C/Gas Mark 3.

2. Heat the butter and oil in a large frying pan; add the onions and apple, and fry until just soft. Add the curry powder and flour, and cook for 3 minutes, stirring. Add the turmeric, ginger, seasoning, and sugar and mix well. Add the stock or water, and stir until boiling.

3. Add the chicken, cut into neat pieces, and all the other ingredients. Remove to a casserole, cover tightly, and cook for 2½–3 hours.

4. Stir occasionally while cooking to be sure the sauce does not stick, and serve with boiled rice and chutney.

Chicken Maryland

Chicken Maryland

🏁 00:20
00:35
Serves 4
Mid Atlantic

American	Ingredients	Metric/Imperial
1 (2–2½ lb)	Chicken	1 (900 g–1.25 kg/ 2–2½ lb)
2 tbsp	Flour	1½ tbsp
	Salt and pepper	
1	Egg, beaten	1
	Soft white bread crumbs	
	Oil for deep-frying	
2	Bananas	2
4 tbsp	Margarine	50 g/2 oz
¼ cup	Self-rising [self-raising] flour	25 g/1 oz
1	Egg	1
6 tbsp	Water	5 tbsp
1 cup	Sweet corn (canned or frozen)	100 g/4 oz

1. Cut the chicken into 4 serving portions. Mix the flour, salt, and pepper together. Coat the chicken in the flour, then in beaten egg, and finally in bread crumbs. Press the coating on firmly. Heat the oil for deep-frying. Fry the chicken for 20–30 minutes, or until cooked. The temperature may be reduced slightly if the coating becomes overbrowned.
2. Meanwhile, prepare the bananas by cutting them in half and frying them in margarine for 2–3 minutes.
3. Make sweet corn fritters: Sift the flour into a bowl with a pinch of salt. Make a well in the center and add the egg. Mix in with a wooden spoon, then gradually add water. Beat until smooth. Stir in the sweet corn. Fry tablespoonfuls of the mixture in margarine until browned, turning once.
4. Drain the cooked bananas, fritters, and chicken on absorbent paper towels [kitchen paper] and keep hot until needed.

Chicken Maryland with Tomato Sauce

🏁 00:30
00:45
Serves 6
Mid Atlantic

American	Ingredients	Metric/Imperial
6	Pieces frying chicken	6
4 tbsp	Flour mixed with salt, pepper and a pinch of cayenne pepper	3½ tbsp
1	Egg	1
1 tsp	Oil	1 tsp
1–1½ cups	Fresh white bread crumbs	50–75 g/2–3 oz
2 tbsp	Oil	1½ tbsp
7 tbsp	Butter	90 g/3½ oz
3	Bananas	3
6 slices	Bacon	6 rashers
	Fritters	
1 cup	Corn	100 g/4 oz
1	Egg	1
⅔ cup	Flour	70 g/2½ oz
½ tsp	Baking powder	½ tsp
½ tsp	Curry powder	½ tsp
	Fat for deep frying	
	Sauce	
3 tbsp	Butter	40 g/1½ oz
1	Onion	1
1	Clove garlic	1
1 can (8 oz)	Tomatoes	1 tin (225 g/8 oz)
2 tbsp	Mixed herbs	2 tbsp
1 tsp	Sugar	1 tsp
1 tsp	Paprika	1 tsp
½ cup	Cider or stock	125 ml/4 fl oz

1. Roll the chicken pieces in seasoned flour, then brush all over with egg beaten with oil. Coat well with fresh white bread crumbs. Heat the oil and add 4–5 tablespoons [50–65 g/2–2½ oz] butter. When foaming, put in the chicken pieces and fry gently for 20–25 minutes, turning frequently until brown and crisp all over.
2. Meanwhile, prepare the corn fritters: Drain the canned corn and mix with 1 egg yolk and seasoning. Sift the flour, baking powder, and curry powder; stir into the corn mixture. Just before frying, beat the egg white and fold into the corn mixture. Heat the fat until very hot but not smoking. Drop the fritter mixture into the fat by tablespoonfuls and fry until light brown. Drain on a paper towel [kitchen paper]. Keep warm.
3. Fry the halved bananas in 2 tablespoons [25 g/1oz] of butter until golden brown. Keep warm. Cut the bacon slices in half; roll up carefully. Thread onto skewers and broil [grill] until crisp all over. Keep warm.
4. Prepare the tomato sauce: Melt the butter; cook the sliced onion and crushed garlic for 5–6 minutes. Add the tomatoes, herbs, seasoning, sugar, paprika, and cider or stock. Bring to a boil, then strain or blend in an electric blender; serve hot with the chicken.

Cheesy Oven-Fried Chicken

 00:10 / 00:40   Serves 4   Midwest

American	Ingredients	Metric/Imperial
1 (2½-lb)	Chicken	1 (1.25 kg/2½ lb)
1 tbsp	All-purpose [plain] flour	1 tbsp
	Salt and pepper	
½ tsp	Dry mustard	½ tsp
1	Egg, beaten	1
¼ cup	Soft white bread crumbs	15 g/½ oz
¼ cup	Cheddar cheese, grated	25 g/1 oz
4 tbsp	Margarine	50 g/2 oz

1. Preheat the oven to 400°F/200°C/Gas Mark 6.
2. Cut the chicken into 4 portions and wipe with a damp cloth. Season the flour with salt, pepper, and mustard. Coat the chicken in flour, then in beaten egg, and finally in the bread crumbs and cheese, mixed together.
3. Place in a roasting pan and dot with small pieces of margarine. Cook in the oven for about 40 minutes, or until golden and tender.

Oven Fried Chicken

 00:15 / 00:35   Serves 4–5   South

American	Ingredients	Metric/Imperial
1 (3-lb)	Chicken, jointed	1 (1.25 kg/3 lb)
4 tbsp	Flour	3½ tbsp
	Black pepper	
	Paprika	
1	Egg	1
	Fine bread crumbs	
3–4 tbsp	Oil	2–3½ tbsp
Corn Fritters		
¾ cup	Flour	75 g/3 oz
1 tsp	Baking powder	1 tsp
½ tsp	Salt	½ tsp
1	Egg, beaten	1
3 tbsp	Milk	2 tbsp
1 cup	Canned [tinned] corn	100 g/4 oz
	Fat for frying	

1. Preheat the oven to 400°F/200°C/Gas Mark 6.
2. Toss the pieces lightly in flour to which a little salt, black pepper, and paprika has been added. Brush with beaten egg and coat with bread crumbs.
3. Heat 3–4 tablespoons [2–3½ tbsp] of oil in a roasting pan, put in the chicken pieces, brush lightly with the hot oil, and cook for about 30 minutes.
4. To make the corn fritters: Sift the flour with the baking powder and salt. Mix to a smooth batter with the egg and milk. Add the corn and a dash of pepper. Drop by tablespoons into the hot fat and fry until golden brown.

Cheesy Oven-Fried Chicken

Oven Fried Chicken with Tomato Sauce

 00:15 / 01:00   Serves 4   New England

American	Ingredients	Metric/Imperial
4	Chicken parts or quarters	4
2–3 tbsp	Flour	1½–2 tbsp
	A little paprika	
1–2	Eggs	1–2
6–8 tbsp	Cornflake crumbs or bread crumbs	5–7 tbsp
4 tbsp	Butter	50 g/2 oz
Tomato Sauce		
2 tbsp	Butter	25 g/1 oz
1	Onion	1
1	Clove garlic	1
1 tbsp	Flour	1 tbsp
2 tbsp	Tomato purée	1½ tbsp
1 can (8 oz)	Tomatoes	1 tin (225 g/8 oz)
1 cup	Stock	250 ml/8 fl oz
1 tbsp	Chopped mixed herbs	1 tbsp
6	Peppercorns	6
	Strip of lemon peel	
	Pinch of cayenne pepper	
1 tsp	Sugar	1 tsp

1. Preheat the oven to 350°F/180°C/Gas Mark 4.
2. Roll the chicken pieces in flour seasoned with salt, pepper, and paprika. Brush thoroughly with beaten egg and roll in cornflake crumbs or dried bread crumbs. Put the chicken in a well-buttered, ovenproof dish.
3. Pour melted butter over the chicken, put into oven, and cook for 30–35 minutes, or until the pieces are crisp and brown.
4. Meanwhile, make the tomato sauce: Melt the butter and cook the finely chopped onion and crushed garlic until golden. Sprinkle in flour and add tomato purée, canned tomatoes, and stock. Bring to a boil; simmer for 20 minutes, adding the herbs, peppercorns, lemon peel, and a pinch of cayenne pepper. Strain the sauce and add sugar. Season to taste.
5. Serve the chicken very hot with sauce and rice or mashed potatoes.

Chicken Kiev

08:30
00:07

Serves 4

Pacific Southwest

American	Ingredients	Metric/Imperial
4	Whole breasts of chicken	4
6 tbsp	Butter	75 g/3 oz
1	Clove garlic	1
1 tbsp	Mixed parsley, tarragon and lemon thyme	1 tbsp
1 tbsp	Lemon juice	1 tbsp
4 tbsp	Flour	3½ tbsp
2	Eggs	2
1 tsp	Oil	1 tsp
1–2 cups	Dried white bread crumbs	50–100 g/2–4 oz
	Fat (or oil) for deep frying	
1	Lemon	1

1. Mix the butter with finely crushed garlic, chopped herbs, lemon juice, and seasoning; shape into a roll about 3–4 inches long. Wrap in foil and put into the refrigerator.
2. Each chicken breast consists of one large heart-shaped piece and a long thin finger-shaped piece. The smaller pieces flatten out slightly. Place the large pieces skin side down and make a shallow slit down the center of each. Then make a shallow pocket to each side with a sharp knife. Remove the skin. Cut the butter roll into 4 long pieces; place one piece on each chicken breast so that it is in the pocket. Place the flattened smaller pieces of chicken over the butter and then close the slits over them. Turn the ends of the chicken and shape each breast neatly. Wrap each in foil and put into the refrigerator for at least 30 minutes to firm.
3. Just before cooking, roll each breast in seasoned flour, then brush with egg beaten with oil and cover thickly with dried white bread crumbs.
4. Heat the fat (or oil) until a cube of fresh bread takes 60 seconds to brown. Fry the chicken breasts for 5–7 minutes, until golden brown and crisp. Serve at once with boiled rice and lemon quarters. (Warn guests to cut the chicken carefully or hot butter will spurt out.)

Chicken Koulibiaca

00:25
00:40

Serves 4

New England

American	Ingredients	Metric/Imperial
2 cups	Diced chicken	350 g/12 oz
2–3 tbsp	Butter	25–40 g/ 1–1½ oz
1	Small onion	1
1 cup	Chopped mushrooms	100 g/4 oz
1 tbsp	Flour	1 tbsp
¼ cup	Chicken stock	60 ml/2 fl oz
3–4 tbsp	Cooked peas, corn or beans	2–3½ tbsp
1 tbsp	Chopped parsley	1 tbsp
1 tsp	Chopped tarragon	1 tsp
1 (8 oz)	Package frozen puff pastry	1 (225 g/8 oz)
1	Egg	1

1. Preheat the oven to 450°F/230°C/Gas Mark 8.
2. Melt the butter and cook the chopped onion until tender, 3–4 minutes. Add the chopped mushrooms and cook for 1 minute. Stir in the flour, then add the stock and bring to a boil. Mix the diced chicken into the sauce, with herbs, seasoning, and cooked peas, corn, or chopped beans. Let cool completely.
3. Roll out completely thawed puff pastry into a rectangle and place on a baking sheet. Spoon the cooled chicken mixture down the center of one side of the pastry rectangle. Brush the edges of pastry with water, fold the flap of pastry over the top, seal the edges, and crimp to make a pretty edge. With a sharp knife, cut 3–4 slashes diagonally across the pastry to allow the steam to escape. Brush the whole surface with a beaten egg.
4. Bake in the oven for about 30 minutes, until the pastry is brown and done. Remove to a serving dish and serve hot.

Chicken in Lemon Sauce

00:30
01:10

Serves 4

Mid Atlantic

American	Ingredients	Metric/Imperial
4	Chicken quarters seasoned with salt and pepper	4
6 tbsp	Butter	75 g/3 oz
2	Small onions or shallots	2
2	Carrots	2
2	Stalks celery	2
1	Large lemon	1
2 cups	Chicken stock	450 ml/¾ pint
¼ cup	White wine	60 ml/2 fl oz
3–4	Parsley sprigs	3–4
1	Bay leaf	1
	A sprig of lemon thyme	
1½ cups	Baby mushrooms	175 g/6 oz
1 tbsp	Finely chopped parsley	1 tbsp

1. Preheat the oven to 350°F/180°C/Gas Mark 4.
2. Lightly brown the seasoned chicken pieces in 4 tablespoons [50 g/2 oz] of butter in an ovenproof dish or casserole. Remove and keep warm.
3. Chop the onions, quarter the carrots, slice the celery, and cook for 5–10 minutes in the butter to soften, without browning. Put the chicken pieces back into the casserole on top of the vegetables; sprinkle with the grated rind of ½ lemon and all the juice; pour in the stock and wine. Add the parsley sprigs, bay leaf, and lemon thyme if available. Season and cook in the oven for 35–40 minutes, or until the chicken pieces are tender.
4. Remove the chicken to a serving dish and keep warm. Remove the carrots, the bay leaf, and herb stalks. Then sieve or blend the remaining vegetables. Reheat the lemon and vegetable sauce and, if too thick, add enough chicken stock to thin. Check for lemon flavor and add more lemon juice if necessary, to taste.
5. Melt the remaining butter and cook the baby mushrooms for 3–4 minutes until tender, and place on top of the chicken. Spoon the sauce over the chicken and mushrooms. Cut remaining lemon rind into match-like strips, boil for 2 minutes, drain and dip in cold water to revive color. Sprinkle over dish with finely chopped parsley.

Lemon and Garlic-Filled Chicken Breasts

Lemon and Garlic-Filled Chicken Breasts

	00:25		
	00:10	Serves 4	Mid Atlantic

American	Ingredients	Metric/Imperial
8	Chicken breasts	8
	Salt	
	Pepper	
7 tbsp	Butter, at room temperature	90 g/3½ oz
3	Cloves garlic, crushed	3
	Juice of 1 lemon	
2 tbsp	Parsley, finely chopped	1½ tbsp
	Flour	
1	Egg, beaten	1
	Bread crumbs	
	Oil	

1. Remove the bones and pound the breasts until quite thin. Salt and pepper them slightly. Mix the butter with garlic, lemon juice, parsley, salt, and pepper. Spread the butter mixture on the chicken breasts, fold in the edges, and roll them together. Fasten with a toothpick.
2. First roll the breasts in flour, then dip them in a beaten egg. Finally roll in bread crumbs. Fry them rather slowly in hot oil until they are golden brown and cooked through.
3. Serve with peeled, seeded cucumbers, which have simmered slightly in the rest of the butter and rice.

Chicken Kebabs with Peanuts

	00:45		
	00:15	Serves 5–6	Southwest

American	Ingredients	Metric/Imperial
1 lb	Shelled peanuts	450 g/1 lb
	Lemon juice	
	Oil	
1 (4 lb)	Chicken, boned and cut into cubes	1 (1.75 kg/4 lb)
1 can (about 16 oz)	Pineapple cubes	1 tin (about 450 g/1 lb)
½ lb	Mushroom caps	225 g/8 oz
1–2 thick slices	Bacon, cut into cubes or squares	1–2 thick rashers

1. Heat the coals in an outdoor grill until hot, about 30 minutes, or preheat the broiler [grill].
2. Pound half the peanuts or put them through a mill. Season with salt and pepper; add lemon juice and enough oil to make a smooth paste, soft enough to coat the chicken. Roast the rest of the peanuts.
3. Thread the chicken, pineapple, mushroom caps, and bacon on skewers. Roll in the peanut paste until thoroughly coated. Sprinkle with oil and cook, turning frequently.
4. Serve with the roasted peanuts, and sprinkle with lemon juice.

Marsala Chicken

Chicken Hot Pot

| | 00:25 | Serves 4–5 | Mid Atlantic |
| | 01:35 | | |

American	Ingredients	Metric/Imperial
1 (2½–3 lb)	Frying chicken	1 (1.25 g/2½–3 lb)
1 tbsp	Flour	1 tbsp
4 tbsp	Butter or margarine	50 g/2 oz
1	Large onion, peeled and sliced	1
1 can (8 oz)	Tomatoes	1 tin (225 g/8 oz)
2 tsp	Brown [demerara] sugar	2 tsp
2 tsp	Prepared mustard	2 tsp
4	Medium potatoes, peeled and sliced	4
2	Apples, peeled, cored, and sliced	2
	Cream Slaw	
1	Small head firm white cabbage, shredded	1
1	Small green pepper, seeded and shredded	1
2 tsp	Prepared mustard	2 tsp
½ tsp	Paprika	½ tsp
2 tsp	Lemon juice	2 tsp
½ cup	Sour cream	125 ml/4 fl oz

1. Preheat the oven to 350°F/180°C/Gas Mark 4.
2. Joint the chicken, dredge with flour mixed with a little salt and pepper, and brown on all sides in the butter. Remove from the pan.
3. Lightly brown the onion in the remaining butter. Add the tomatoes, sugar, and mustard and heat gently. Arrange the potatoes in the bottom of a buttered casserole. Season lightly, add the apples, and cover with the tomato mixture.
4. Put the chicken pieces on top, cover, and cook for about 1½ hours.
5. Mix the cabbage and green pepper. Add the other ingredients to the sour cream, blend well, and toss the cabbage and pepper lightly in the dressing.

Marsala Chicken

| | 03:10 | Serves 4 | South |
| | 00:35 | | |

American	Ingredients	Metric/Imperial
1 (3-lb)	Chicken, cut into serving pieces	1 (1.25 kg/3 lb)
⅔ cup	Marsala (Port wine or Madeira can be used)	150 ml/¼ pint
1½ tbsp	Butter	20 g/¾ oz
1	Shallot, peeled and chopped	1
1 tsp	Salt	1 tsp
¼ tsp	Black pepper	¼ tsp
5 tbsp	Water	4 tbsp
2 tsp	Flour	2 tsp
5 tbsp	Crème fraîche or heavy [double] cream	4 tbsp
	Chopped walnuts	

1. Place the pieces of chicken in a plastic bag in a bowl. Pour the wine into the bag. Fold up the bag and refrigerate for 2–3 hours. Turn the bag occasionally while it is in the refrigerator. Remove the chicken but save the wine. Dry off the chicken.
2. Brown the pieces of chicken in a deep frying pan in a little butter. Add the shallot and slightly brown. Season with salt and pepper. Add the wine and water. Cover and cook the chicken for about 15–20 minutes, until the chicken is done. Place the pieces of chicken in a warm, deep dish.
3. Prepare the gravy by stirring the flour into the frying pan. Allow the sauce to boil for a few minutes, then add the cream.
4. Season to taste and possibly dilute the sauce slightly more. Pour over the chicken (if you prefer, strain the sauce before pouring it over the chicken). Sprinkle with the chopped nuts.

Paella

| | 00:15 | Serves 4–6 | Southwest |
| | 00:50 | | |

American	Ingredients	Metric/Imperial
4–6	Large chicken pieces seasoned with salt and pepper	4–6
4–5 tbsp	Olive or corn oil	3½–4 tbsp
2	Onions	2
1–2	Cloves garlic	1–2
2 cups	Long-grain rice	450 g/1 lb
4 cups	Chicken stock (or chicken cube and water)	1 l/1¾ pints
	Large pinch of saffron	
2–3 tbsp	Butter	25–40 g/1–1½ oz
3	Tomatoes	3
	Pinch of mace	
1–2 tbsp	Chopped parsley and thyme	1–1½ tbsp
½ cup	Peas	50 g/2 oz
1 cup	Unshelled shrimp [prawns] (or 12 mussels or 4–6 clams)	175 g/6 oz

1. Preheat the oven to 350°F/180°C/Gas Mark 4.
2. Heat the oil in a large flat frying pan and, when hot, cook the chicken pieces for 12–15 minutes until golden brown all over. Remove and keep warm.
3. Add the sliced onions and crushed garlic to the pan, and cook for 5–6 minutes, until golden brown. Add the rice and fry for 1 minute, stirring constantly to prevent sticking.
4. Add the stock, saffron soaked in 2 tablespoons [1½ tbsp] of hot stock, butter, and peeled and chopped tomatoes. Bring to a boil; then add the chicken pieces. Add the seasoning, herbs, peas (or beans) and simmer for 10 minutes.
5. Add the shrimp, mussels, or clams to the pan and heat in the oven for 15 minutes; by this time, the shells of the mussels and clams should have opened. Serve very hot.

Chicken Marengo

Marinated Chicken

| | 00:25 | | |
| | 01:15 | Serves 4 | New England |

American	Ingredients	Metric/Imperial
4	Pieces frying chicken	4
¾ cup	Oil	175 ml/6 fl oz
5 tbsp	Butter	65 g/2½ oz
1 slice	Bacon	1 rasher
1	Onion	1
1	Clove garlic	1
3	Carrots	3
2	Stalks celery	2
2 tbsp	Flour	1½ tbsp
3 tbsp	Tomato purée	2 tbsp
½ cup	White wine or sherry	125 ml/4 fl oz
1 cup	Stock	250 ml/8 fl oz
1	Bay leaf	1
	Several parsley sprigs	
1 cup	Mushrooms	100 g/4 oz
4	Slices bread	4
4	Eggs	4
1 tbsp	Chopped parsley	1 tbsp

1. Preheat the oven to 350°F/180°C/Gas Mark 4.
2. Heat 3 tablespoons [2 tbsp] of oil and add 1 tablespoon [15 g/½ oz] of butter. When foaming, cook the chicken pieces until golden brown. Place in a casserole.
3. Fry the bacon, finely chopped onion, crushed garlic, sliced carrots, and celery for about 5 minutes. Sprinkle in flour and cook for 1 minute. Add tomato purée, wine or sherry, and stock. Bring to a boil; add the seasoning and pour over the chicken pieces. Add the herbs and sliced mushrooms. Cover the casserole and cook in the oven for about 1 hour.
4. After about 50 minutes, fry the bread cut in rounds in oil and butter, and drain on paper towels [kitchen paper]. Fry the eggs in butter and, when cooked, place on fried bread.
5. Serve the chicken pieces on a hot dish. Boil the sauce and strain over the chicken, reserving any excess. Sprinkle the top with chopped parsley. Place the fried eggs around the dish at the last moment, and serve.

Marinated Chicken

| | 08:25 | | |
| | 00:45 | Serves 4 | Pacific Southwest |

American	Ingredients	Metric/Imperial
1 (2½ lb)	Chicken	1 (1.25 kg/2½ lb)
	Marinade	
2 cups	Yogurt	450 ml/¾ pint
1	Onion, peeled and sliced	1
2 tsp	Curry	2 tsp
1 tsp	Ginger	1 tsp
2 tsp	Paprika	2 tsp
1 tsp	Caraway	1 tsp
1–2	Cloves garlic, crushed	1–2
	Cucumber Salad	
2 cups	Yogurt	450 ml/¾ pint
½–¾	Cucumber	½–¾
4 tbsp	Chives, finely snipped	3½ tbsp
1 tsp	Salt	1 tsp
	Black pepper	

1. Divide the chicken in half. Mix all the marinade ingredients together. Place the chicken halves in a deep plate. Cover with the marinade. Refrigerate for 6–8 hours. Turn the chicken several times while it is marinating.
2. Preheat the oven to 350°F/180°C/Gas Mark 4.
3. Place the chicken halves in an ovenproof dish. Pour the marinade over the chicken and brush the chicken well. Bake for about 45 minutes. Brush the chicken occasionally with the marinade while it is baking.
4. When making the cucumber salad, allow the yogurt to drain through a coffee filter for about 15 minutes. Thinly slice the cucumber. It is easiest to do this with a cheese slicer. Mix with the yogurt. Add the chives; season with salt and pepper. Serve with brown rice.

Mexican Style Chicken

 00:15
00:55   Serves 4   Southwest

American	Ingredients	Metric/Imperial
4	Large chicken pieces	4
3–4 tbsp	Flour	2–3½ tbsp
1 tsp	Salt	1 tsp
¼ tsp	Garlic powder	¼ tsp
½ tsp	Pepper	½ tsp
2	Medium onions	2
5 tbsp	Butter	65 g/2½ oz
2	Tomatoes	2
¼ cup	White wine	60 ml/2 fl oz
¾ cup	Chicken stock	175 ml/6 fl oz
¾ cup	Raisins	125 g/4½ oz
½ cup	Pimento-stuffed olives	50 g/2 oz
½ tsp	Cinnamon	½ tsp
3 tbsp	Slivered almonds	2 tbsp

1. Preheat the oven to 350°F/180°C/Gas Mark 4.
2. Roll the chicken pieces in flour seasoned with salt, garlic powder, and pepper; remove and toss the onion slices in the same flour.
3. Melt the butter; when foaming, fry the chicken pieces until golden brown, about 7–10 minutes. Remove; keep warm in an ovenproof casserole. Add the sliced onions and chopped tomatoes to the butter. Cook for 4–5 minutes. Then add the wine, stock, raisins, olives, herbs, and seasoning. Bring to a boil, and pour over the chicken pieces. Put into the oven for 35 minutes, or until the chicken is tender.
4. Sprinkle with cinnamon and stir in. Lastly, sprinkle over the browned almonds and serve at once with plain boiled rice.

Paprika Chicken

 00:15
01:20   Serves 4   New England

American	Ingredients	Metric/Imperial
1 (2½–3 lb)	Chicken	1 (1.25 kg/2½–3 lb)
2 tbsp	Flour seasoned with salt and pepper	1½ tbsp
2 tbsp	Oil	1½ tbsp
4 tbsp	Butter	50 g/2 oz
4	Onions	4
1	Clove garlic	1
2 tsp	Paprika	2 tsp
2 tbsp	Tomato purée	1½ tbsp
1 cup	White wine	250 ml/8 fl oz
1 cup	Strong chicken stock	250 ml/8 fl oz
1 tbsp	Chopped parsley	1 tbsp
1 tsp	Thyme	1 tsp
1 cup	Sour cream	250 ml/8 fl oz

1. Cut the chicken into pieces and roll in seasoned flour. Heat the oil. Add 2 tablespoons [25 g/1 oz] of butter. When foaming,

add the chicken pieces and fry until golden brown. Remove and put into a casserole.
2. Add the remaining butter and sliced onions to the frying pan. Cover and cook until tender but not brown, about 5–6 minutes. Add the crushed garlic; cook for 1 minute. Add paprika and remaining seasoned flour, then the tomato purée. Stir until smooth. Then add the wine and stock. Bring to a boil, stirring constantly.
3. Pour the sauce over the chicken pieces. Add the herbs, salt, and pepper to taste. Cook slowly until tender, for about 1 hour.
4. Spoon sour cream over the top of the casserole, and serve with buttered noodles or rice.

Chicken Pie

00:40
01:10   Serves 4–5   Mid Atlantic

American	Ingredients	Metric/Imperial
1 (2½–3 lb)	Chicken	1 (1.25 kg/2½–3 lb)
1 tsp	Salt	1 tsp
1 tsp	White peppercorns	1 tsp
2	Bay leaves	2
3	Carrots, peeled and sliced	3
2	Onions, peeled and quartered	2
2–3	Sticks celery, diced	2–3
3–4	Sprigs parsley	3–4
2–3	Slices cooked ham	2–3
2	Hard-boiled eggs, sliced	2
2 tbsp	Butter or margarine	25 g/1 oz
2 tbsp	Flour	1½ tbsp
2–3 tbsp	Sherry	1½–2 tbsp
1 tbsp	Lemon juice	1 tbsp
1 tsp	Sugar	1 tsp
	A pinch of ground mace	
1	Egg yolk	1
	Pastry for an 8–9 inch, 1-crust pie (see Index)	
	Egg or milk to glaze	

1. Preheat the oven to 425°F/220°C/Gas Mark 7.
2. Cut the chicken into quarters and put into a large frying pan with the seasoning, vegetables, and enough water to just cover. Put on a lid and simmer for about a half hour. Strain off the stock and set aside.
3. Cut the meat from the chicken in fairly large chunks; cut up the cooked vegetables. Arrange alternate layers of chicken, vegetables, ham, and eggs in an ovenproof baking dish.
4. Make a sauce with the butter, flour, and 1 cup [250 ml/8 fl oz] of the chicken stock. Add the sherry, lemon juice, sugar, and mace. Cook until well mixed and thickened. Stir in the egg yolk; reheat without boiling, check the seasoning.
5. Pour the sauce over the chicken and vegetables and cover with the pastry. Cut a line from the center of the pie toward each of the four corners and fold each pastry triangle back, leaving an open square. Glaze the pastry with beaten egg or milk and bake about a half hour.

Chicken with Biscuit Topping

Chicken with Biscuit Topping 🍞🍞

⏱ 00:30 / 00:25   Serves 4   South

American	Ingredients	Metric/Imperial
	Filling	
2 tbsp	Vegetable oil	1½ tbsp
1	Small onion, peeled and chopped	1
½	Green pepper, finely chopped	½
⅔ cup	Sliced mushrooms	70 g/2½ oz
2 tbsp	Cornstarch [cornflour]	1½ tbsp
1½ cups	Milk	350 ml/12 fl oz
2 cups	Cooked chicken, cut into cubes	350 g/12 oz

	Biscuits	
2 cups	Flour	225 g/8 oz
1 tsp	Salt	1 tsp
2½ tsp	Baking powder	2½ tsp
5 tbsp	Shortening	4 tbsp
⅔ cup	Milk	150 ml/¼ pint

1. Heat the oil in a frying pan; add the onion, green pepper, and mushrooms and sauté for a few minutes. Add the cornstarch and cook for 1 minute, stirring all the time.

2. Add the milk gradually; stir until boiling. Add the chicken and seasoning. Turn into a deep 8–9 inch pie plate.

3. To make the biscuits: Sift the flour, salt, and baking powder. Cut in the shortening with a pastry blender until the mixture looks like coarse bread crumbs. Using a fork, stir in enough milk to make a soft but not sticky dough. Knead lightly on a floured board, roll out about ½ inch thick and cut into 1½-inch rounds with a cookie cutter.

4. Place the rounds on top of the chicken mixture, brush with milk, and bake for 10–15 minutes.

Chicken Stuffed with Mushrooms

00:35
00:45

Serves 4

Mid Atlantic

American	Ingredients	Metric/Imperial
2 (2 lb)	Small spring chickens	2 (900 g/2 lb)
1 cup	Mushrooms	100 g/4 oz
½ cup	Butter	100 g/4 oz
1	Small onion	1
¼ cup	Thin single cream	60 ml/2 fl oz
1 tsp	Cornstarch [cornflour], optional	1 tsp
	Little chopped parsley or paprika	

1. Preheat the oven to 350°F/180°C/Gas Mark 4.
2. Cook the finely chopped onion for about 5 minutes in half the butter with a lid on the pan. Slice or quarter the mushrooms, add to the onions, and cook for 3–4 minutes. Season and let cool.
3. Wipe the prepared spring chickens; stuff them with the cooled mushroom mixture. Melt the remaining butter in an ovenproof dish or iron casserole. Fry the chickens gently until brown all over. Season and pour ¼ cup [60 ml/2 fl oz] of water over the chickens. Cook in the oven for about 20 minutes. When tender, remove from the casserole and split each bird in half. Arrange on a warm serving dish and put into a low oven while making the sauce.
4. Make the sauce: Mix the cream with the gravy in the casserole. Bring slowly to a boil and season to taste. The sauce will be fairly thin. To thicken, if preferred, mix cornstarch with 2–3 tablespoons, [1½–2 tbsp] of cold water until smooth. Add to the hot sauce and boil for ½ minute.
5. Spoon a little of this sauce over each bird and serve the rest separately. Garnish with a little chopped parsley or a sprinkling of paprika.

Chicken with Peanut Sauce

00:15
01:30

Serves 4

Southwest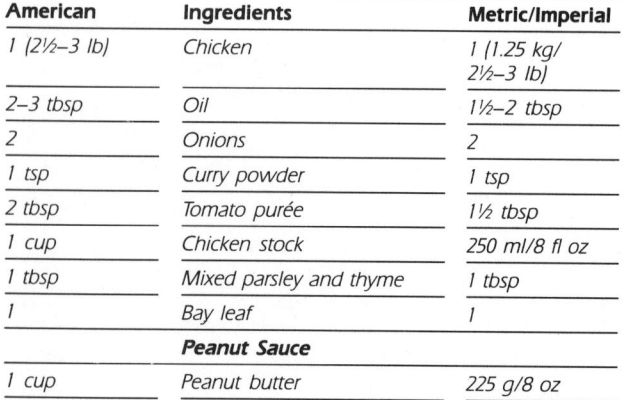

American	Ingredients	Metric/Imperial
1 (2½–3 lb)	Chicken	1 (1.25 kg/ 2½–3 lb)
2–3 tbsp	Oil	1½–2 tbsp
2	Onions	2
1 tsp	Curry powder	1 tsp
2 tbsp	Tomato purée	1½ tbsp
1 cup	Chicken stock	250 ml/8 fl oz
1 tbsp	Mixed parsley and thyme	1 tbsp
1	Bay leaf	1
	Peanut Sauce	
1 cup	Peanut butter	225 g/8 oz
2 cups	Chicken stock	450 ml/¾ pint

1. Cut the chicken into pieces; season with salt and pepper. Heat the oil and brown the chicken pieces all over. Remove and keep warm.
2. Cook the sliced onion until tender. Add the curry powder and tomato puree. Stir until smooth; add the stock and bring to a boil. Add the herbs and seasonings. Pour over the chicken pieces. Simmer until tender, about 1 hour.
3. Make the peanut sauce: Mix the peanut butter with the stock and season. When smooth, pour over the chicken. Heat for 10–15 minutes, and serve with boiled rice.

Chicken in Light Pastry Crust

00:40
02:00

Serves 4–6

Mid Atlantic

American	Ingredients	Metric/Imperial
1 (3 lb)	Chicken	1 (1.25 kg/3 lb)
4	Onions	4
2	Carrots	2
3	Stalks celery	3
	Several parsley sprigs	
1	Bay leaf	1
6	Peppercorns	6
4 tbsp	Butter	50 g/2 oz
1 cup	Mushrooms	100 g/4 oz
2 tbsp	Flour	1½ tbsp
1½ cups	Strong chicken stock	350 ml/12 fl oz
2 tbsp	Mixed chopped parsley, thyme, tarragon	1½ tbsp
	A pinch of mace	
6	Slices ham	6
1 (8 oz)	Package frozen puff pastry	1 (225 g/8 oz)
1	Egg	1

1. Preheat the oven to 450°F/230°C/Gas Mark 8.
2. Cut the meat off the chicken bones in large chunks. Put the carcass and giblets in a pan with 2 onions, carrots, celery, herbs, and peppercorns. Cover with water and cook until well flavored; strain and add salt.
3. Melt 2 tablespoons [25 g/1 oz] of butter; cook 2 thickly sliced onions for 3–4 minutes. Then add the mushrooms; cook for 1 minute, remove, and keep warm. Heat another 2 tablespoons [25 g/1 oz] of butter and fry the chicken pieces in the pan for 4–5 minutes to seal the meat. Sprinkle in the flour, then pour on the stock, and bring to a boil, stirring constantly. Simmer for 1 minute. Then add the onions and mushrooms. Sprinkle in the herbs and seasoning.
4. Chop the ham and make a layer at the bottom of the pie dish. Spoon in half of the chicken mixture, another layer of ham, the remaining chicken mixture, and top with ham. Let cool.
5. Roll out the pastry; place a thin strip around the moistened edge of the pie dish. Brush this strip with water and place the large piece of pastry on top. Crimp the edges together, then cut off the excess with a sharp knife. Make 3–4 holes to allow the steam to escape; decorate with pastry leaves and flowers. Brush the pastry with beaten egg.
6. Bake in a hot oven, 450°F/230°C/Gas Mark 8, for 25 minutes to cook, the pastry. Cover the pastry with damp waxed paper or foil. Reduce the heat to 375°F/190°C/Gas Mark 5 for another 20 minutes to cook the chicken.

Chicken and Ham Pie

Chicken and Ham Pie

00:40
02:15

Serves 4–5

Mid Atlantic

American	Ingredients	Metric/Imperial
	Hot water pastry (see Index)	
½ lb	Ham	225 g/8 oz
1½ lb	Boned uncooked chicken	675 g/1½ lb
1 tsp	Grated lemon rind	1 tsp
½ tsp	Dried rosemary	½ tsp
2	Hard-boiled eggs	2
½ cup	Chicken stock	125 ml/4 fl oz
1	Egg	1
1 envelope	Gelatin [gelatine]	1 sachet

1. Preheat the oven to 375°F/190°C/Gas Mark 5.
2. Make the pastry and keep warm until required.
3. Cut the ham and chicken into 1-inch cubes and sprinkle with salt, pepper, lemon rind, and rosemary.
4. Use about two-thirds of the pastry to line the sides and bottom of a loaf pan, about 9 × 5 × 2 ¾ inches or a 6-inch cake pan. Place half the ham and chicken into the pan. Cut the eggs in halves and arrange on top; then cover with the rest of the meat and add 3–4 tablespoons [2–3½ tbsp] of chicken stock. Turn the top edges of the pastry lining in over the meat and dampen all around. Roll out the remaining pastry to make a lid and press down well, making as secure as possible. Make a hole in the center, decorate the top with pastry leaves, and brush all over with beaten egg.

5. Bake for 2–2¼ hours, then let get cold.
6. Melt the gelatin in the remaining broth and, when beginning to set, pour into the pie through the hole in the top. Let set before serving.

Chicken Cream Pie

00:25
00:40

Serves 4

Mid Atlantic

American	Ingredients	Metric/Imperial
1½ cups	Diced cooked chicken	250 g/9 oz
1	Hard-boiled egg, chopped	1
½ tsp	Grated lemon rind	½ tsp
1 tsp	Finely chopped parsley	1 tsp
3–4 tbsp	Heavy [double] cream	2–3½ tbsp
	Flaky Pastry (see Index)	
	Egg or milk to glaze	

1. Preheat the oven to 450°F/230°C/Gas Mark 8.
2. Mix the chicken and egg with flavorings and seasoning, and blend with the cream.
2. Roll the pastry into a square shape and put the chicken mixture in the center. Moisten the edges of the pastry and fold the four corners up to the center, pressing them well together. Decorate with a rose and leaves cut from the trimmings of the pastry. Glaze with egg or milk.
4. Bake for 15 minutes. Then reduce the heat to 375°F/190°C/Gas Mark 5 and bake for 25 minutes.

Chicken and Celery Pie

 00:25 / 00:40   Serves 4–5   Pacific Southwest

American	Ingredients	Metric/Imperial
	Pastry for an 8-inch, 2-crust pie (see Index)	
1½ cups	Diced cooked chicken	250 g/9 oz
1 cup	Sliced mushrooms	100 g/4 oz
4	Stalks celery, sliced diagonally	4
⅛ cup	Blanched slivered almonds	15 g/½ oz
1 cup	Medium cream sauce (see Index)	250 ml/8 fl oz
	Egg or milk to glaze	

1. Preheat the oven to 450°F/230°C/Gas Mark 8.
2. Line an 8-inch pie plate with half the pastry.
3. Mix all the ingredients for the filling and season carefully. Turn into the pastry shell, moisten the edges of the pastry, and put on the top crust. Press the edges with the back of a knife and decorate the top of the pie with the pastry trimmings.
4. Glaze with egg or milk and bake for 10 minutes. Then reduce the heat to 375°F/190°C/Gas Mark 5 and bake for 20–30 minutes, until the pastry is crisp and brown.

Chicken and Bacon Pie

 00:25 / 01:15   Serves 4   Mid Atlantic

American	Ingredients	Metric/Imperial
1 (2½ lb)	Chicken	1 (1.25 kg/2½ lb)
6 slices	Bacon, chopped	6 rashers
2	Small onions, peeled and chopped	2
3	Tomatoes	3
¼ tsp	Dried rosemary	¼ tsp
	A pinch of thyme	
	Chicken stock	
	Flaky pastry (see Index)	
	Egg or milk to glaze	

1. Preheat the oven to 450°F/230°C/Gas Mark 8.
2. Skin the chicken and cut all the meat from the bones.
3. Arrange the layers of chicken, bacon, onions, and tomatoes in a baking dish. Sprinkle with herbs and a little seasoning, and moisten with the stock. Cover with pastry, crimp and flute the edge, and decorate as desired. Glaze with egg or milk.
4. Bake for 25–30 minutes, then reduce the heat to 375°F/190°C/Gas Mark 5 and cook for 1–1¼ hours. Cover the pastry with a piece of waxed paper toward the end of the cooking if it seems to be getting too brown.

Chicken and Mushroom Pie

 00:25 / 00:35   Serves 4–5   Mid Atlantic

American	Ingredients	Metric/Imperial
¼ cup	Butter or margarine	50 g/2 oz
½ cup	Flour	50 g/2 oz
2 cups	Milk	450 ml/¾ pint
2 cups	Diced cooked chicken	350 g/12 oz
1 cup	Sliced mushrooms	100 g/4 oz
2 tbsp	Chopped green olives	1½ tbsp
2 tbsp	Blanched slivered almonds	1½ tbsp
	Pastry for an 8-inch, 1-crust pie (see Index)	
1	Egg	1
	Milk	

1. Preheat the oven to 450°F/230°C/Gas Mark 8.
2. Make a sauce with the butter, flour, and milk and season carefully. Add the chicken, mushrooms, olives, and almonds and mix well. Turn into a deep 8-inch pie plate.
3. Cover with the pastry; use the trimmings to make pastry leaves to decorate the top.
4. Glaze with beaten egg and milk and bake for 15 minutes, then reduce the heat to 375°F/190°C/Gas Mark 5 and bake for 20 minutes, until the pastry is well browned.
5. Serve hot with vegetables or cold with salad.

Chicken and Oyster Pie

 00:25 / 00:30   Serves 4   Mid Atlantic

American	Ingredients	Metric/Imperial
12	Oysters	12
2 tbsp	Butter or margarine	25 g/1 oz
1	Large breast chicken, cut into strips	1
1 cup	Sliced mushrooms	100 g/4 oz
	Oyster liquid, made up to ¼ cup [60 ml/2 fl oz] with water	
	A pinch each of salt, cayenne pepper, sugar	
½ cup	Light [single] cream	125 ml/4 fl oz
1 tsp	Cornstarch [cornflour]	1 tsp
	Milk	
1	Egg yolk	1
1 (7–8 inch)	Baked pastry shell	1 (7–8 inch)
	Chopped parsley	
1–2	Pimentos	1–2

1. Open the oysters and retain their liquid.
2. Heat the butter in a frying pan; add the strips of chicken and mushrooms and cook quickly for a few minutes.
3. Heat the oyster liquid and water; put in the oysters and leave for 7–8 minutes off the heat. Lift out into a bowl. Add the chicken, mushrooms, salt, pepper and sugar.
4. Stir the cream, except 1 tablespoon, into the oyster liquid; add the cornstarch, mix smoothly with a little milk, stir until boiling, and boil for 1 minute.
5. Mix the remaining 1 tablespoon cream with the egg yolk; stir a little of the hot sauce into it, then return to the pan. Add all the other ingredients, check the seasoning, and heat through. Pour into the warm pastry shell, sprinkle with parsley, and garnish with strips of pimento.

Soufflé Pie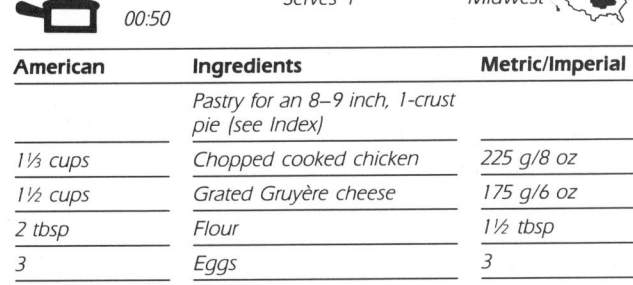

00:15		
00:40	Serves 4	South 

American	Ingredients	Metric/Imperial
3 tbsp	Butter or margarine	40 g/1½ oz
1 cup	Sliced mushrooms	100 g/4 oz
2 tbsp	Cornstarch [cornflour]	1½ tbsp
1	Chicken bouillon [stock] cube	1
1 cup	Milk	250 ml/8 fl oz
1	Egg	1
1 cup	Finely chopped cooked chicken	175 g/6 oz
4 slices	Bacon, cooked and chopped	4 rashers
1 (8-inch)	Baked pastry shell	1 (8-inch)

1. Preheat the oven to 400°F/200°C/Gas Mark 6.
2. Heat the butter in a sauté pan; add the mushrooms and sauté until tender. Add the cornstarch and crumbled bouillon cube, and cook for 1 minute. Gradually add the milk and stir until boiling.
3. Remove from the heat; add the egg yolk, chicken, and bacon.
4. Beat the egg white stiffly and fold into the mixture. Turn into the baked pastry shell and cook for 25–30 minutes.

Swiss Cheese and Chicken Pie

00:25		
00:50	Serves 4	Midwest

American	Ingredients	Metric/Imperial
	Pastry for an 8–9 inch, 1-crust pie (see Index)	
1⅓ cups	Chopped cooked chicken	225 g/8 oz
1½ cups	Grated Gruyère cheese	175 g/6 oz
2 tbsp	Flour	1½ tbsp
3	Eggs	3
1 cup	Light [single] cream or milk	250 ml/8 fl oz

1. Preheat the oven to 425°F/220°C/Gas Mark 7.
2. Line an 8-inch pie plate with the pastry and decorate the edge.

Soufflé Pie

3. Mix the chicken and cheese together, sprinkle with the flour, then put into the pastry shell.
4. Beat the eggs; add the cream and seasoning and pour over the chicken and cheese.
5. Bake for 10 minutes, then reduce the heat to 325°F/160°C/Gas Mark 3 and bake for 35–40 minutes, or until the pastry is brown and the custard set.

Chicken and Raisin Pie

00:30		
00:40	Serves 4–5	Pacific Southwest

American	Ingredients	Metric/Imperial
	Pastry for an 8–9 inch 1-crust pie (see Index)	
2 tbsp	Butter or margarine	25 g/1 oz
2 tbsp	Flour	1½ tbsp
1 cup	Milk	250 ml/8 fl oz
¼ cup	Heavy [double] cream	60 ml/2 fl oz
1 cup	Grated cheese	100 g/4 oz
1	Egg	1
1½ cups	Chopped cooked chicken	250 g/9 oz
⅔ cup	Seedless raisins	70 g/2½ oz
	Egg or milk to glaze	

1. Preheat the oven to 400°F/200°C/Gas Mark 6.
2. Line a deep 8–9 inch [20–22.5 cm] pie plate with half the pastry.
3. Make a sauce with the butter, flour, and milk; add the cream, cheese, and seasoning. Remove from the heat; stir in the beaten egg.
4. Put alternate layers of chicken and raisins into the pastry shell and pour the sauce over all.
5. Cover the pie with the remaining pastry, pressing the edges together well. Decorate the edge as liked; make 2–3 cuts in the top and bake for about 30 minutes.

Chicken Sorrento

Chicken Sorrento

| | 00:25 | Serves 5–6 | Pacific Southwest |
| 01:25 | | | |

American	Ingredients	Metric/Imperial
1 (3–3½ lb)	Chicken	1 (1.25–1.5 kg/ 3–3½ lb)
	Flour	
3 tbsp	Oil	2 tbsp
5 tbsp	Rice	4 tbsp
1	Large onion, peeled	1
1	Orange, cut in half and seeded but not peeled	1
½ cup	Milk	125 ml/4 fl oz
1 cup	Water	250 ml/8 fl oz
3 tbsp	Chopped pimento	2 tbsp
¼ tsp	Thyme	¼ tsp
	A pinch of sugar	
	A pinch of cayenne pepper	

1. Preheat the oven to 350°F/180°C/Gas Mark 4.
2. Cut the chicken into pieces, and coat with flour to which a little salt and pepper has been added.
3. Heat the oil in a frying pan, and brown the chicken on all sides. Then remove. Put the rice into the pan, and stir over low heat until the rice is brown.
4. Put the onion and unpeeled orange through a food grinder, using the coarse blade. Mix in the rice. Put the onion, orange, and rice mixture into a casserole, and arrange the chicken on top. Add milk, water, a little seasoning, and all the other ingredients.
5. Cover and cook in the oven for 1–1¼ hours. Adjust the seasoning to taste before serving.

Chicken on a Spit

| | 00:40 | Serves 4–5 | Southwest  |
| 01:20 | | | |

American	Ingredients	Metric/Imperial
2 (2–2½ lb)	Small broiler chickens	2 (900 g–1.25 kg/ 2–2½ lb)
2 tbsp	Butter or margarine	25 g/1 oz
	Juice of 1 lemon	

1. Heat the coals in an outdoor grill until hot, about 30 minutes.
2. Blend the butter or margarine with the lemon juice, and pour some of the mixture inside the chickens. Truss the legs and wings tightly, and place the birds on the spit.
3. Baste liberally with Tangy Barbecue Sauce (see Index). Baste frequently while the chickens are cooking.
4. Cook until tender. These can also be roasted in the oven.

Chicken Pilau

| | 00:35 | Serves 4–6 | Mid Atlantic |
| 00:50 | | | |

American	Ingredients	Metric/Imperial
4–6	Chicken pieces	4–6
2 tbsp	Oil	1½ tbsp
7–8 tbsp	Butter	90–100 g/ 3½–4 oz
1	Large onion	1
1 cup	Dried apricots	100 g/4 oz
½ tsp	Cinnamon	½ tsp
	Grated rind of 1 lemon	
1 cup	Yogurt	250 ml/8 fl oz
1½ cups	Long-grain rice	350 g/12 oz
2 tbsp	Almonds	1½ tbsp

1. Preheat the oven to 350°F/180°C/Gas Mark 4.
2. Heat the oil and 2 tablespoons [25 g/1 oz] of butter. When foaming, fry the chicken pieces until golden brown. Remove and let cool. Cook the sliced onions until golden in the same oil and butter. Add the chopped apricots; sprinkle with cinnamon, orange rind, salt, and ground pepper. Remove the bones from the chicken pieces and shred the meat. Mix the yogurt with the onion mixture and soak the chicken in this while the rice is cooking.
3. Cook the rice in boiling salted water for 10–12 minutes. Drain and rinse with boiling water. Dry for a few minutes. Heat 3 tablespoons [40 g/1½ oz] butter in a thick pan or casserole; put half the rice into the pan and mix well with butter and seasoning. Spoon the chicken mixture over the rice, and put the remaining rice on top. Sprinkle with salt and pepper.
4. Melt the remaining butter and spoon over the rice. Cover the pan and cook gently for 15–20 minutes, until all the flavors are blended.
5. Brown the slivers of almonds, sprinkle on top of the rice, and serve at once.

Brunswick Stew

| | 00:20 | | |
| | 01:40 | Serves 4–6 | New England |

American	Ingredients	Metric/Imperial
1 (3–4 lb)	Stewing or roasting chicken	1 (1.25–1.75 kg/3–4 lb)
1 tsp	Salt	1 tsp
3	Potatoes	3
1	Large onion	1
1 cup	Green lima beans	100 g/4 oz
5–6	Sliced fresh tomatoes	5–6
1 tbsp	Sugar	1 tbsp
1 cup	Sweet corn	100 g/4 oz
1 tbsp	Tomato ketchup or Worcestershire sauce	1 tbsp
4 tbsp	Butter	50 g/2 oz

1. Cut the chicken into pieces and put in a casserole with enough boiling water to cover; add a little salt. Simmer for about 45 minutes.
2. Add the sliced potatoes, sliced onion, lima beans, tomatoes and sugar to casserole. Cook for 45 minutes, when the beans and potatoes should be tender.
3. Remove as many bones as possible from the chicken; add corn. Cook for 10 minutes. Then season to taste and add ketchup or Worcestershire sauce, if desired. Add the butter and stir well.

Provencale Style Chicken

| | 00:20 | | |
| | 02:15 | Serves 4–5 | New England |

American	Ingredients	Metric/Imperial
1 (5-lb)	Small stewing chicken	1 (2.25 kg/5 lb)
1 tbsp	Cornstarch [cornflour]	1 tbsp
¼ cup	Butter	50 g/2 oz
3	Small onions, peeled and halved	3
4	Small carrots, peeled and quartered	4
1	Clove garlic, crushed	1
4 tbsp	Red wine	3½ tbsp
1 cup	Chicken stock	250 ml/8 fl oz
	A few black olives	

1. Preheat the oven to 325°F/160°C/Gas Mark 3.
2. Cut the fowl into pieces. Mix the salt and pepper with the cornstarch, and dredge the pieces of chicken well. Heat the butter in a frying pan. Brown the chicken; then remove to a casserole.
3. Add the vegetables and garlic to the remaining fat with any remaining cornstarch. Cook for 3–5 minutes. Then add the wine and stock. Stir until boiling. Then pour over the chicken.
4. Cover tightly and cook for 2 hours. Just before serving, adjust the seasoning, and add the olives.

Brunswick Stew

Chicken Supreme with Mushrooms

| | 00:20 | | |
| | 00:40 | Serves 4 | Mid Atlantic |

American	Ingredients	Metric/Imperial
4	Chicken breasts	4
7–8 tbsp	Butter	90–100 g/3½–4 oz
10–12	Large mushrooms	10–12
2 tsp	Lemon juice	2 tsp
1 tbsp	Chopped parsley	1 tbsp
3 tbsp	Flour	2 tbsp
1¼ cups	Chicken stock	300 ml/½ pint
	Salt and white pepper	
¼ tsp	Mace	¼ tsp
½ cup	Cream	125 ml/4 fl oz
2	Egg yolks	2
1–2 tbsp	White wine (or a little lemon juice)	1–1½ tbsp

1. Preheat the oven to 375°F/190°C/Gas Mark 5.
2. Remove 4 complete chicken breasts from 2 chickens (use remaining chicken parts for another meal). Melt 4–5 tablespoons [50–65 g/2–2½ oz] butter in a pan large enough to hold all 4 chicken breasts. Cook them in butter very gently, without browning, for 4–5 minutes on each side. Remove from the pan and put into a buttered dish, cover with foil, and bake in the oven for about 10–15 minutes, or until tender and done.
3. Meanwhile, cook the sliced mushrooms in the butter left from the chicken and 1 teaspoon lemon juice for 5–6 minutes. Season; add chopped parsley. Place in the bottom of a serving dish and, when the chicken is cooked, place the chicken on top. Reduce the oven to 250°F/120°C/Gas Mark ½ and keep warm while making the sauce.
4. Melt 3 tablespoons [40 g/1½ oz] of butter and stir in the flour. When smooth, add the stock and bring slowly to a boil, stirring constantly. Cook for 2 minutes. Add the salt, white pepper, and mace. Mix the cream with the egg yolks. Mix 3–4 tablespoons [2–3½ tbsp] hot sauce with cream and eggs; strain carefully into the sauce, stirring constantly. Reheat very gently over a pan of hot water. Do not allow the sauce to reach the boiling point or the eggs will curdle and the sauce will be ruined. Season to taste and add a little white wine or lemon juice, if desired. Spoon over the chicken and serve with boiled rice.

Chicken and Cheesy Rice Ring

Chicken Stewed with Apples

	00:15		
	01:30	Serves 6–7	Mid Atlantic

American	Ingredients	Metric/Imperial
1 (3½-lb)	Chicken	1 (1.5 kg/3½ lb)
4 tbsp	Oil	3 tbsp
1	Onion, peeled and sliced	1
2	Stalks celery, sliced	2
2	Large apples, peeled, cored and sliced	2
2 tbsp	Flour	1½ tbsp
1½ cups	Chicken stock or water	350 ml/12 fl oz
	A pinch of thyme	
	A pinch of marjoram	
2 tbsp	Grated cheese	1½ tbsp
	Boiled rice	

1. Cut the chicken into small pieces, and season with salt and pepper.

2. Heat 3 tablespoons [2 tbsp] of the oil in a pan, add the pieces of chicken (a few at a time), and brown well. Remove the pieces as they are browned. Put the onion, celery, and apple into the remaining oil, and cook until the onion is tender.

3. Add the remaining 1 tablespoon of oil, stir in the flour, and mix well. Gradually add the stock or water, and stir until boiling.

4. Return the chicken to the sauce. Add the thyme, marjoram, and a little seasoning. Cover and simmer until the chicken is tender.

5. Adjust the seasoning to taste, and stir in the cheese. To serve: put some hot cooked rice onto a large platter, arrange the pieces of chicken on top, and pour on the sauce. Serve any excess sauce separately.

Chicken and Cheesy Rice Ring

	00:25		
	00:40	Serves 4–6	Mid Atlantic

American	Ingredients	Metric/Imperial
3 cups	Cooked chicken (or chicken and ham)	500 g/18 oz
6 tbsp	Butter	75 g/3 oz
2	Onions	2
2 cups	Cooked rice	450 g/1 lb
1	Egg	1
1 cup	Milk	250 ml/8 fl oz
1 cup	Grated Cheddar cheese	100 g/4 oz
2 tbsp	Chopped mixed herbs	1½ tbsp
½ tsp	Dry mustard	½ tsp
1 tsp	Paprika	1 tsp
4–6	Large mushrooms	4–6
2 tbsp	Flour	1½ tbsp
1 cup	Stock (or can condensed chicken or mushroom soup)	250 ml/8 fl oz
	A pinch of nutmeg	
1	Green or red pimento	1
3–4 tbsp	Bread or cornflake crumbs	2–3½ tbsp

1. Melt 5 tablespoons [65 g/2½ oz] of butter and cook the finely chopped onions for 4–5 minutes to soften, without browning. Remove half and put into a bowl. Add the rice to the onion in the bowl. Add the beaten egg mixed with milk, ¾ cup [75 g/3 oz] grated cheese, and 1 tablespoon herbs. Season with salt, pepper, dry mustard, and half the paprika.

2. Butter a 7-inch ring mold and fill with the rice mixture, packing it in well. Bake for about 20 minutes. When firm and cooked, remove from the oven and turn out on a platter.

3. Meanwhile, prepare the chicken sauce: Add the sliced mushrooms to the onion in the pan and cook for 2 minutes. Remove from the heat, add flour, and mix well; then add the stock (or condensed soup). Blend well. Bring to a boil, then cook for a few minutes; add the diced chicken, remaining herbs, and seasoning. Flavor with nutmeg.

4. Boil the chopped pimento for 5 minutes, drain, and add to the sauce. Keep the sauce warm to allow the flavors to blend. Spoon the hot sauce into the center of the rice ring. Any excess can be reheated and served separately.

5. Sprinkle the top with the remaining cheese and crumbs mixed, dot with the remaining butter, and brown under the broiler [grill] for a few minutes. Sprinkle with paprika and serve hot.

Chicken Stew

00:20
02:40 · Serves 6–8 · Mid Atlantic

American	Ingredients	Metric/Imperial
8 tbsp	Pork dripping or other cooking fat	7 tbsp
1 (5-lb)	Stewing chicken, jointed	1 (2.25 kg/5 lb)
	Flour	
2	Large onions, peeled and sliced	2
2–3	Tomatoes, peeled and quartered	2–3
6–8	Green olives (optional)	6–8
2	Bay leaves	2
¼ tsp	Mixed herbs	¼ tsp
1 cup	Sliced mushrooms	100 g/4 oz

1. Heat the fat in a pan. Coat the chicken pieces with flour to which some salt and pepper has been added, and brown them on all sides.
2. Remove the chicken from the pan; add the onions and tomatoes, and fry for about 5 minutes. Add the olives, bay leaves and herbs; sprinkle with 2 tablespoons flour and a little salt and pepper. Mix well.
3. Replace the chicken pieces, and add enough stock or water to cover. Put the lid on the pan, and simmer very slowly for 2–2½ hours or until the chicken is tender. When the chicken is nearly done, add the mushrooms and remove the bay leaves.
4. To serve: put the pieces on a large dish, and arrange the vegetables around. Thicken the stock with a little extra flour, adjust the seasoning, and pour some of it over the chicken. Serve the rest separately.

Chicken à la King

00:10
00:15 · Serves 5—6 · Mid Atlantic

American	Ingredients	Metric/Imperial
4 tbsp	Butter	50 g/2 oz
2 tbsp	Finely chopped onion	1½ tbsp
1 cup	Sliced mushrooms	100 g/4 oz
½ cup	Diced green pepper	50 g/2 oz
4 tbsp	Flour	3½ tbsp
2 cups	Chicken stock	450 ml/¾ pint
3 cups	Diced cooked chicken	500 g/18 oz
2	Pimentos, drained and cut into thin strips	2
3 tbsp	Dry sherry	2 tbsp

1. Heat the butter in a frying pan; add the onion, mushrooms, and green pepper. Cook for 5 minutes.
2. Stir in the flour and mix well with the vegetables. Gradually add the chicken stock and stir until boiling. Add the seasoning and stir over low heat for 5 minutes.
3. Add the chicken, pimentos, and sherry and heat through.

Chicken à la King

Chicken Veronique

00:30
01:10 · Serves 4 · Pacific Southwest

American	Ingredients	Metric/Imperial
1 (3 lb)	Roasting chicken	1 (1.25 kg/3 lb)
6–7 tbsp	Butter	75–90 g/ 3–3½ oz
	Few sprigs tarragon (or dried tarragon)	
3 cups	Stock made with chicken giblets	700 ml/1¼ pints
2 slices	Fat bacon	2 rashers
2 cups	White grapes	175 g/6 oz
	A little lemon juice	
2 cups	Plain boiled rice	450 g/1 lb
	Sauce	
5 tbsp	Flour	4 tbsp
2 cups	Strong chicken stock	450 ml/¾ pint
½ cup	White wine	125 ml/4 fl oz
2–3 tbsp	Heavy [double] cream	1½–2 tbsp

1. Preheat the oven to 375°F/190°C/Gas Mark 5.
2. Roast chicken as in *French Roast Chicken* (see Index), using tarragon as flavoring inside the bird.
3. Meanwhile, dip the grapes in boiling water for 10 seconds and then cold water. Peel (and remove the seeds if necessary). Put the grapes in a small bowl and sprinkle with lemon juice to prevent browning.
4. Remove the chicken from the roasting pan when cooked, and carve. Place the chicken pieces on the rice, cover, and keep warm.
5. Skim off 6 tablespoons [75 g/3 oz] butter into a saucepan. Heat gently. Sprinkle in flour and blend carefully. Pour on the stock and wine and bring to a boil, stirring constantly. Boil for a few minutes, remove from the heat, and let cool slightly. Add the cream and grapes. Allow the grapes to warm through. Then spoon the sauce over the chicken, and serve at once.

Chicken Tetrazzini

Chicken Tetrazzini

 12:25 / 01:45   Serves 4–6   New England

American	Ingredients	Metric/Imperial
1 (3–4 lb)	Stewing chicken	1 (1.25–1.75 kg/ 3–4 lb)
2	Onions	2
2	Carrots	2
	Parsley, thyme, and a bay leaf	
½ lb	Spaghetti	225 g/8 oz
6 tbsp	Butter	75 g/3 oz
	Dash of garlic powder	
4 tbsp	Flour	3½ tbsp
½ cup	White wine	125 ml/4 fl oz
6–8	Mushrooms	6–8
3–4 tbsp	Heavy [double] cream	2–3½ tbsp
¼ cup	Grated Parmesan cheese	25 g/1 oz
2 tbsp	Dried bread crumbs	1½ tbsp
2 tbsp	Sliced almonds	1½ tbsp

1. Preheat the oven to 400°F/200°C/Gas Mark 6.
2. Cook the chicken slowly in water with the onions, carrots, and herbs until tender. Let cool in the stock, overnight if possible. Then remove the skin and bones, and cook these in stock until it is well flavored and reduced to 2–3 cups [450–700 ml/¾–1¼ pints].
3. Boil the spaghetti in the usual way and finish off in 1 tablespoon [15 g/½ oz] of butter flavored with a little garlic powder. Place in an ovenproof dish and keep warm.
4. Make the sauce. Melt 4 tablespoons [50 g/2 oz] butter, add the flour and, when blended add 1½ cups [350 ml/12 fl oz] chicken stock. Bring to a boil and cook for 2 minutes. Then add the wine and simmer for a few minutes.
5. Meanwhile, cut the cold chicken into long strips, place in a mound on top of the spaghetti, and sprinkle with salt and pepper. Cook the sliced mushrooms in 1 tablespoon [15 g/½ oz] butter for 2–3 minutes; then put on top of the chicken.
6. Add the cream to the sauce; check the seasoning. Spoon the sauce over the dish; then sprinkle the top with cheese and crumbs. Bake in the oven for 10–15 minutes, until the dish is well heated, and the top brown and crisp. Lastly, sprinkle browned almonds over the top and serve at once.

Leftover Chicken with Vegetables

 00:15 / 00:40   Serves 4   Mid Atlantic

American	Ingredients	Metric/Imperial
1 cup	Cold cooked chicken	175 g/6 oz
6 tbsp	Margarine	75 g/3 oz
1	Onion, finely chopped	1
½ cup	Mushrooms, chopped	50 g/2 oz
1	Green pepper, chopped	1
1 (10½-oz) can	Condensed chicken or mushroom soup	1 (260 g/10½-oz) tin
1 cup	Long-grain rice	250 g/8 oz
	Salt	
1 tbsp	Chopped parsley, and extra for garnish	1 tbsp

1. Cut the chicken into bite-sized pieces. Melt 4 tablespoons [50 g/2 oz] of margarine in a frying pan and fry the onion until softened. Add the mushrooms and pepper and cook, stirring, for 2–3 minutes. Stir in the soup and chicken. Bring to a boil; simmer very gently for 10–15 minutes.
2. Meanwhile, cook the rice in a large saucepan with plenty of boiling salted water for 10–15 minutes. Drain well, then stir in the parsley and remaining margarine. Arrange the rice on a serving plate and pile the chicken mixture on top. Garnish with chopped parsley.

Giblet Pie

 00:30 / 00:55   Serves 4–5   Midwest

American	Ingredients	Metric/Imperial
	Giblets, as available	
	Flour	
	Pastry for 8-inch, 2-crust pie (see Index)	
2	Hard-boiled eggs	2
1 cup	Sliced mushrooms	100 g/4 oz
6 slices	Lean bacon	6 rashers
	Egg and milk to glaze	

1. Preheat the oven to 450°F/230°C/Gas Mark 8.
2. Wash the giblets and simmer in salted water until tender. Drain and retain some of the stock.
3. Remove the meat from the neck of the chicken and chop the liver, heart, and kidney. Coat with flour to which salt and pepper have been added.
4. Line a deep 8–9 inch pie plate with half the pastry. Put in half the giblet meat, sliced eggs, mushrooms, and bacon. Add 2–3 tablespoons [1½–2 tbsp] giblet stock and cover with the rest of the meat.
5. Cover with the remaining pastry, press the edges well together, and use the trimmings to make a decoration for the top of the pie. Glaze with egg and milk, and bake for 20 minutes. Reduce the heat to 375°F/190°C/Gas Mark 5, and bake for 20–25 minutes.

Leftover Chicken with Vegetables

Chicken in Potato Nest

 00:15
00:35   Serves 4   Mid Atlantic

American	Ingredients	Metric/Imperial
2 cups	Cooked mashed potatoes	450 g/1 lb
2 tbsp	Butter or margarine	25 g/1 oz
2 tbsp	Flour	1½ tbsp
½ tsp	Pepper	½ tsp
1 cup	Chicken stock	250 ml/8 fl oz
¼ cup	Heavy [double] cream	60 ml/2 fl oz
1 small can (about 3 oz)	Sliced mushrooms	1 small tin (about 75 g/3 oz)
2 cups	Cooked chicken, diced	350 g/12 oz
2 tbsp	Grated Parmesan cheese	1½ tbsp

1. Preheat the oven to 400°F/200°C/Gas Mark 6.
2. Line a buttered 8–9-inch pie plate with the potatoes.
3. Melt the butter in a pan; stir in the flour and seasonings. Add the broth gradually and stir until boiling. Add the cream and mushrooms and cook for a few minutes.
4. Put the chicken into the prepared pie plate, pour the sauce over the chicken and sprinkle with the cheese. Bake for 25–30 minutes.

Chicken and Vegetable Casserole

 00:25
01:30   Serves 5–6   Mid Atlantic

American	Ingredients	Metric/Imperial
1 (3–3½ lb)	Chicken	1 (1.25–1.5 kg/ 3–3½ lb)
	Flour	
¼ lb	Salt pork	100 g/4 oz
¼ tsp	Thyme	¼ tsp
	A pinch of marjoram	
1½ cups	Sliced carrot	175 g/6 oz
1 cup	Small white onions	100 g/4 oz
1½ cups	Diced potatoes	175 g/6 oz
1 cup	Sliced mushrooms	100 g/4 oz
½	Bay leaf	½
	A sprig of parsley	
1	Clove garlic, crushed	1

1. Preheat the oven to 350°F/180°C/Gas Mark 4.
2. Cut the chicken into pieces, and coat with flour to which a little salt and pepper has been added.
3. Cut the salt pork into small pieces, put into a frying pan, and fry until crisp. Then remove the pieces of crackling.
4. Brown the chicken on all sides in the pork fat, putting in only a few pieces at a time. Then place in a casserole.
5. Add all the other ingredients and the crisp pieces of pork. Pour over 1½ cups [350 ml/1½ cups] boiling water. Cover and cook for about 1¼ hours. Adjust the seasoning to taste and remove the bay leaf before serving.

Chicken in White Wine Sauce

 00:15
00:50   Serves 4   Mid Atlantic

American	Ingredients	Metric/Imperial
1 (2½–3 lb)	Chicken	1 (1.25 kg/ 2½–3 lb)
2–3	Slices onion	2–3
3–4 sprigs or 1 tsp dried	Parsley	3–4 sprigs or 1 tsp dried
	A pinch of mace or nutmeg	
6	White peppercorns	6
1	Bay leaf	1
2 cups	White wine	450 ml/¾ pint
½ cup	Chicken stock	125 ml/4 fl oz
4 tbsp	Butter	50 g/2 oz
3 tbsp	Flour	2 tbsp
2 tsp	Tarragon leaves	2 tsp
¼ cup	Heavy [double] cream	60 ml/2 fl oz

1. Preheat the oven to 350°F/180°C/Gas Mark 4.
2. Cut the chicken into pieces and put into a casserole with the onion, parsley sprigs, mace, peppercorns, and bay leaf. Add the wine and stock and cook in the oven for 35–45 minutes, until tender. Remove the chicken pieces, put into a serving dish, and keep warm.
3. Boil the liquid left in the casserole for a few minutes to strengthen the flavor, and reduce the quantity. Melt the butter, stir in the flour and, when smooth, strain in 2 cups [450 ml/¾ pint] of the liquid. Season and add 1 teaspoon tarragon leaves and cream.
4. Spoon the sauce over the chicken and sprinkle the top with the remaining tarragon leaves. Serve at once, with rice or mashed potatoes.

Chicken and Corn Croquettes

 01:10
00:20   Serves 4   Midwest

American	Ingredients	Metric/Imperial
2 cups	Finely chopped chicken	350 g/12 oz
5 tbsp	Butter	65 g/2½ oz
10 tbsp	Flour	9 tbsp
1 cup	Milk	250 ml/8 fl oz
1 tsp	Finely chopped onion	1 tsp
½ cup	Canned corn	50 g/2 oz
2 tsp	Parsley	2 tsp
1 tsp	Lemon juice	1 tsp
	A pinch of mace	
3	Eggs	3
1 tsp	Oil	1 tsp
1½ cups	Dried white bread crumbs	75 g/3 oz
	Fat for deep frying	

1. Make a thick cream sauce. Melt 3 tablespoons [40 g/1½ oz] of butter and stir in 4 tablespoons [3½ tbsp] flour. Add the milk and blend smoothly. Bring to a boil and cook for several minutes to reduce the quantity slightly.
2. Melt 1 tablespoon [15 g/½ oz] butter, and cook the onion and corn for 3–4 minutes. Add the chicken meat, chopped parsley, lemon juice, mace, and mix well. Add ¾ cup [175 ml/6 fl oz] of sauce; season well. Let it cool; then add 1 egg yolk. Spread the mixture out on a plate to cool and thicken.
3. Divide into 8 equal portions and form into rolls. Turn in 6 tablespoons [5 tbsp] flour seasoned with salt and pepper until completely covered. Brush all over with egg beaten with oil. Then coat completely with bread crumbs. (They can be left for up to 1 hour at this stage before cooking.)
4. Heat the oil or fat until gently smoking, then lower 3–4 croquettes at a time into the hot fat and cook until golden brown and crisp. Drain on paper towels [kitchen paper] and serve at once with lemon quarters and a salad or green vegetables.

Chicken Cream

| | 00:25 | | |
| | 00:40 | Serves 4–6 | Mid Atlantic |

American	Ingredients	Metric/Imperial
4 cups	Cooked chicken	675 g/1½ lb
2 cups	Fresh bread crumbs	100 g/4 oz
4 tbsp	Butter	50 g/2 oz
2 tbsp	Flour	1½ tbsp
1 cup	Milk	250 ml/8 fl oz
¼ tsp	Ground mace or nutmeg	¼ tsp
1 tbsp	Chopped parsley	1 tbsp
1	Egg	1

1. Preheat the oven to 350°F/180°C/Gas Mark 4.
2. Grind the chicken and mix with fresh bread crumbs.
3. Make the cream sauce: Melt 2 tablespoons [25 g/1 oz] butter and blend in the flour. Add the milk gradually. When smooth, bring to a boil, stirring constantly. Boil 2–3 minutes; add the mace or nutmeg and herbs. Let cool slightly.
4. Add the sauce to the chicken mixture; stir well, adding the remaining butter and beaten egg. Season well. Put in a buttered ovenproof dish, allowing room for the chicken cream to rise slightly; cook in the oven for 30–35 minutes.

Chicken Contadine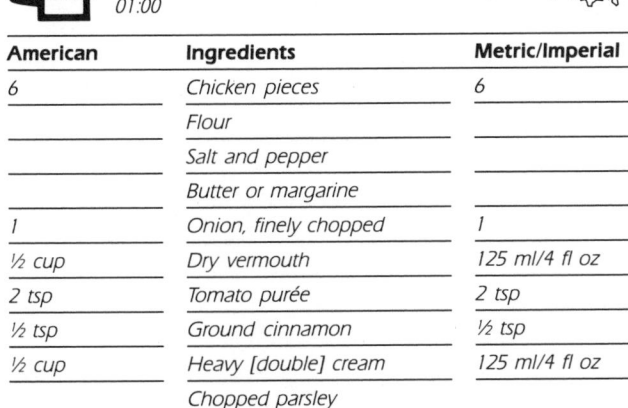

| | 00:10 | | |
| | 01:00 | Serves 6 | New England |

American	Ingredients	Metric/Imperial
6	Chicken pieces	6
	Flour	
	Salt and pepper	
	Butter or margarine	
1	Onion, finely chopped	1
½ cup	Dry vermouth	125 ml/4 fl oz
2 tsp	Tomato purée	2 tsp
½ tsp	Ground cinnamon	½ tsp
½ cup	Heavy [double] cream	125 ml/4 fl oz
	Chopped parsley	

Chicken Contadine

1. Preheat the oven to 375°F/190°C/Gas Mark 5.
2. Skin the chicken pieces and coat with seasoned flour.
3. Melt the butter in a frying pan and sauté the onion until soft and transparent.
4. Put in the chicken joints and brown on all sides. Remove to a casserole.
5. Put the vermouth in the pan and ignite. When the flames have died down, stir in the tomato purée and cinnamon. Mix well and pour over the chicken. Cook for ¾–1 hour, or until the chicken is tender; then stir in the cream.
6. Sprinkle with parsley before serving.

Chicken and Ham Risotto

| | 00:15 | | |
| | 00:30 | Serves 4 | South |

American	Ingredients	Metric/Imperial
1	Onion, peeled and finely chopped	1
3 tbsp	Oil	2 tbsp
1 cup	Long-grain rice	225 g/8 oz
2 cups	Chicken stock	450 ml/¾ pint
¼ tsp	Black pepper	¼ tsp
½ tsp	Mixed herbs	½ tsp
¼ cup	Seedless raisins	25 g/1 oz
1	Stalk celery, chopped	1
1 cup	Diced cooked chicken	175 g/6 oz
½ cup	Diced cooked ham	175 g/6 oz
1	Canned [tinned] pimento for garnish (if desired)	1

1. Sauté the onion in the oil until it is transparent. Add the rice and cook over low heat for 5 minutes, stirring all the time.
2. Add the hot stock, pepper, herbs, raisins, and celery. Stir until boiling. Then cover and simmer until the rice is tender and most of the liquid absorbed.
3. Stir in the chicken and ham, adjust the seasoning, and heat through.
4. Serve on a hot platter, garnished with strips of pimento and a tossed greed salad.

Chicken Liver Risotto

Chicken Crisps 👨‍🍳

00:20		
00:20	Serves 4	Midwest

American	Ingredients	Metric/Imperial
2 cups	Chopped or diced cooked chicken	350 g/12 oz
2 tbsp	Butter	25 g/1 oz
2 tbsp	Flour	1½ tbsp
1 cup	Milk	250 ml/8 fl oz
8	Mushrooms, sliced	8
4 tbsp	Stock	3½ tbsp
½ cup	Cooked peas or corn	50 g/2 oz
5	Thick slices of white bread	5
1 cup	Oil	250 ml/8 fl oz
1 tbsp	Butter	15 g/½ oz
1 tbsp	Chopped parsley	1 tbsp

1. Make the cream sauce: Melt the butter and blend in the flour. Gradually add the milk; when smooth, bring to a boil, stirring constantly. Boil for 3 minutes, then cool slightly.
2. Slice the mushrooms and cook in the stock for 3–4 minutes. Chop or dice the chicken, and mix with the mushrooms and cooked vegetables. Add the mixture to the cream sauce, season well, heat thoroughly, and keep warm.
3. Remove the crusts from the slices of bread and, with a small cutter, cut 4 crescent-shaped pieces from the fifth slice. Heat the oil and add butter. When foaming, fry the bread slices until golden brown on both sides. Also fry the 4 small crescents. Drain on paper towels [kitchen paper].
4. Arrange the fried squares on a serving dish, spoon the hot chicken mixture onto the squares, and garnish with the crescents and chopped parsley.

Chicken Sandwich 👨‍🍳

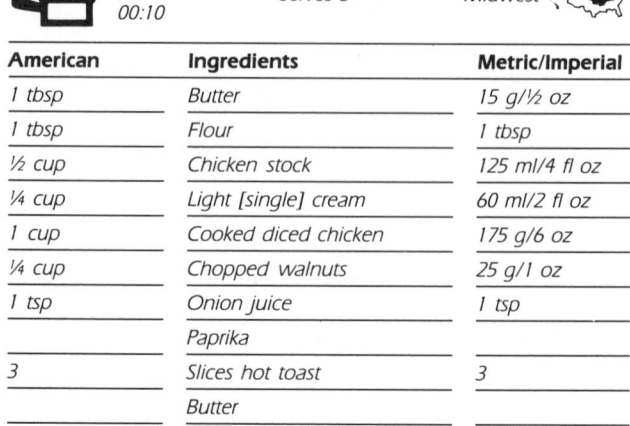

00:05		
00:10	Serves 3	Midwest

American	Ingredients	Metric/Imperial
1 tbsp	Butter	15 g/½ oz
1 tbsp	Flour	1 tbsp
½ cup	Chicken stock	125 ml/4 fl oz
¼ cup	Light [single] cream	60 ml/2 fl oz
1 cup	Cooked diced chicken	175 g/6 oz
¼ cup	Chopped walnuts	25 g/1 oz
1 tsp	Onion juice	1 tsp
	Paprika	
3	Slices hot toast	3
	Butter	
	Stuffed olives for garnish	

1. Make a sauce with the butter, flour, and stock. Add the cream, chicken, and nuts; season carefully with the onion juice, salt, pepper, and paprika.
2. Heat and then pile onto the slices of toast. Brush with a little melted butter and garnish with rings of stuffed olives. Serve at once.

Chicken Club Sandwich 👨‍🍳

00:05		
00:10	Serves 1	United States

American	Ingredients	Metric/Imperial
3	Slices bread	3
	Butter	
	Mayonnaise	
	Lettuce	
	Slices of chicken breast	
	Prepared mustard	
2 slices	Bacon, fried until crisp	2 rashers
1–2	Slices tomato or onion	1–2
	Gherkins or stuffed olives for garnish	

1. Remove the crusts from the bread; toast and spread with butter.
2. Spread the first slice with a little mayonnaise, cover with 1–2 leaves of lettuce, and slices of chicken. Spread a little more mayonnaise on the chicken and cover with the second slice of toast.
3. Spread a very little mustard on the toast and then a little mayonnaise. Cover with the slices of bacon and slices of tomato or onion.
4. Place the third slice of toast on top and press down firmly. Serve at once, garnished with slices of gherkin or stuffed olives.

Chicken Liver Risotto

00:15
00:35
Serves 4
Mid Atlantic

American	Ingredients	Metric/Imperial
2 tbsp	Oil	1½ tbsp
1	Onion, peeled and chopped	1
2 slices	Lean bacon, chopped	2 rashers
1¼ cups	Long-grain rice	275 g/10 oz
2 cups	Chicken stock or water and chicken stock cube	450 ml/¾ pint
2 tbsp	Margarine	25 g/1 oz
¼ lb	Mushrooms, sliced	100 g/4 oz
½ lb	Chicken livers	225 g/8 oz
	Chopped parsley for garnish	
	Grated cheese for serving	

1. Heat the oil in a large saucepan. Fry the onion and bacon until softened; add the rice and cook, stirring, until lightly browned. Add the chicken stock and bring to a boil. Cover the pan tightly and simmer for 15 minutes. Do not lift the lid until the end of the cooking time, when all the liquid is absorbed and the rice is tender.

2. Meanwhile, heat the margarine in a frying pan and cook the mushrooms and chicken livers until the livers are browned all over. Add the mushrooms and livers to the cooked rice and reheat if necessary. Serve in a hot dish; garnished with chopped parsley. Serve a bowl of grated cheese separately.

Italian Style Roast Turkey

00:35
04:20
Serves 8–10
New England

American	Ingredients	Metric/Imperial
1 (8–9 lb)	Turkey (if frozen allow ample time to defrost)	1 (3.5–4 kg/ 8–9 lb)
	Stuffing	
1 cup	Raw prunes	225 g/8 oz
2 cups	Peeled chestnuts	450 g/1 lb
2 cups	Sausage meat	225 g/8 oz
1	Large onion	1
2–3 tbsp	Butter	25–40 g/ 1–1½ oz
1	Turkey liver	1
2–3	Pears	2–3
¼ cup	White wine	60 ml/2 fl oz
	For Braising	
3–4 tbsp	Butter	40–50 g/ 1½–2 oz
2	Onions	2
2	Carrots	2
4–6	Celery stalks	4–6
3 slices	Bacon	3 rashers
2	Cloves garlic	2
1 sprig fresh or 2 tsp dried	Rosemary	1 sprig fresh or 2 tsp dried
8	Peppercorns	8
	Parsley, thyme, and 2 bay leaves	
½	Bottle red wine	½
1–2 cups	Stock	250–450 ml/ 8 fl oz–¾ pint
	For Roasting	
3–4 tbsp	Oil	2–3 tbsp
1 tbsp	Butter	15 g/½ oz

1. Preheat the oven to 325°F/160°C/Gas Mark 3.

2. Prepare the stuffing: Soak and cook the prunes in tea. Remove the seeds when tender; chop roughly. If using fresh chestnuts, cook in boiling water for 5 minutes, then remove the outer and inner skins. Cook for 30 minutes in stock; drain and chop roughly. Mix these ingredients with the sausage meat. Melt the butter and fry the turkey liver and onion for 3–4 minutes. Let cool and chop. Peel and core the pears; chop roughly and add to the liver with the other ingredients. Add the seasoning and wine. Stir the whole mixture over the heat for a few minutes until thoroughly blended and hot. Let cool before stuffing the turkey.

3. When the turkey is stuffed and sewn up, melt the butter in an ovenproof casserole and cook the sliced onion, sliced carrot, chopped celery, and diced bacon for a few minutes. Add the garlic, rosemary, peppercorns, and other seasoning and herbs. Place turkey on top of this, pour over ½ bottle red wine and enough stock to come halfway up the bird. Cover the casserole with a lid and braise the turkey for 3½ hours, turning from side to side every half hour to allow all sides to cook equally.

4. Remove from the casserole and drain from the sauce. Heat some oil and 1 tablespoon [15 g/½ oz] butter in a roasting pan, put in the turkey, and baste. Roast in the oven for a half hour, until the bird has browned and is well done, basting every 10 minutes.

5. Remove the garlic cloves. Boil up the pan drippings and vegetables to reduce slightly. Strain and serve as sauce.

Turkey Casserole

00:10
00:40
Serves 4
Southwest

American	Ingredients	Metric/Imperial
1 tbsp	Cooking fat or oil	1 tbsp
2 tbsp	Finely chopped onion	1½ tbsp
1 can (10¾ oz)	Condensed mushroom soup	1 tin (300 g/ 10¾ oz)
1 canned	Pimento, chopped	1 tinned
1 tsp	Pickled hot green chili pepper, deseeded and finely chopped	1 tsp
2½ cups	Cooked noodles	350 g/12 oz
1 cup	Cooked diced turkey	175 g/6 oz
½ cup	Grated sharp cheese	50 g/2 oz

1. Preheat the oven to 350°F/180°C/Gas Mark 4.

2. Heat the fat in a pan and sauté the onion until it begins to color. Add the soup, pimento, and chili pepper.

3. Arrange a layer of turkey, noodles, and the soup mixture in a casserole. Sprinkle lightly with salt, pepper, and cheese.

4. Repeat the layers, sprinkle the remaining cheese on top, and bake for 30–40 minutes.

5. Serve with a green vegetable or a salad.

Traditional Quick Roast Turkey

 00:20
02:45   Serves 8–10   New England

American	Ingredients	Metric/Imperial
1 (8–9 lb)	Fresh turkey unfrozen	1 (3.5–4 kg/ 8–9 lb)
8 cups	Stuffing	900 g/2 lb
1	Onion	1
6–8 tbsp	Butter	75–100 g/3–4 oz
	Salt, pepper, and poultry seasoning	
8–10 slices	Fat bacon	8–10 rashers
8 tbsp	Oil	7 tbsp
10–20	Potatoes according to size	10–20
1–2 cups	Stock	250–450 ml/ 8 fl oz–¾ pint

1. Preheat the oven to 450°F/230°C/Gas Mark 8.
2. Wash the turkey inside and out with cold water. Dry thoroughly with a paper towel [kitchen paper]. Rub the surface all over with a cut lemon to keep the flesh white. Fill the body cavity with sausage meat stuffing and the neck with chestnut stuffing or, if using other stuffings, fill the neck first not too tightly and put the remaining stuffing inside the body.
3. Use wing tips to help hold the neck skin in place under the bird and sew down the neck skin to keep the stuffing in place. Close the cavity as well as possible and put an onion at the entrance; tie or sew the leg bones together to keep it closed as much as possible. Rub the breast and legs thickly with butter and seasoning, cover with strips of fat bacon, and tie these in place.
4. Heat the oil in a roasting pan. When hot, put in the bird and baste thoroughly. Place a large piece of foil over the top and roast for 2½–2¾ hours, basting every 20 minutes and turning the bird from one side to the other every 20 minutes to allow the legs to cook without overcooking the breast. For the last 30 minutes, place the bird breast up and remove the foil covering to brown the breast.
5. Test if the bird is done by running a skewer into the thickest part of the leg. If the juice is pink, cook longer; if clear, the bird is done. Another indication is when the meat on the legs shrinks back on the bones.
6. Parboiled potatoes can be roasted around the turkey during the last hour of cooking or in a separate pan in the same oven.
7. Remove from the roasting pan and put on a large serving dish. Keep warm. Pour off the fat from the pan. Add ½ tablespoon flour to the juices in the pan. Pour on the stock. Bring to a boil, stirring constantly. When well-flavored, skim off any fat that has risen to surface and pour the gravy into a sauceboat to serve with the turkey.

Boiled Turkey

 00:35
03:25   Serves 6–8   New England

American	Ingredients	Metric/Imperial
1 (6-lb)	Turkey	1 (3 kg/6 lb)
1½ cups	Lean ground [minced] veal	250 g/8 oz
¾ cup	Lean ground [minced] ham	150 g/5 oz
6 tbsp	Butter	75 g/3 oz
½ cup	Mushrooms	50 g/2 oz·
¾ cup	White bread crumbs	40 g/1½ oz
	A little milk	
2 tbsp	Chopped parsley and thyme	1½ tbsp
1 tsp	Onion powder	1 tsp
1	Egg	1
4–5	Onions	4–5
3–4	Carrots, sliced	3–4
3–4	Stalks celery	3–4
8–9	Peppercorns	8–9
2–3	Bouillon [stock] cubes	2–3
3 tbsp	Flour	2 tbsp
½ cup	White wine	125 ml/4 fl oz
1 envelope	Gelatin [gelatine]	1 sachet

1. First prepare the stuffing: Grind the lean veal and ham finely. Melt 1 tablespoon [15 g/½ oz] of butter and cook the mushrooms for 5–6 minutes. Allow to cool before adding to the meat. Soak the bread crumbs in milk for 15 minutes, then squeeze out as much milk as possible. Add this to the meats with the chopped mushrooms, herbs and seasoning, and onion powder. Beat together until very smooth.
2. Stuff the cleaned turkey with the mixture. Sew up the opening carefully to prevent the stuffing from escaping during boiling. If a large piece of muslin is available, wrap the bird in this and tie securely.
3. Put into a pan of cold water which just covers the bird; add the onions, sliced carrots, sliced celery, peppercorns, and bouillon cubes. Bring the water slowly to a boil, then cook slowly, allowing 30 minutes per pound.
4. Remove from the cooking liquid and test for tenderness. Strain the stock and boil to reduce quantity. melt 3 tablespoons [40 g/1½ oz] of butter and add 3 tablespoons [2 tbsp] flour. Pour on 2½ cups [600 ml/1 pint] of the stock and white wine. Blend carefully. Bring to a boil and, when smooth and cooked, spoon over the turkey and serve hot.
5. If serving cold, add 1 package gelatin to the sauce and dissolve before allowing to cool. When cool, spoon over the turkey and let set.

Traditonal Quick Roast Turkey

Roast Turkey with Fruit Stuffing

Roast Turkey with Fruit Stuffing 👨‍🍳👨‍🍳

 00:30 04:00   Serves 18–20   Pacific Southwest

American	Ingredients	Metric/Imperial
1 (14-pound)	Turkey	1 (6.25 kg/14-lb)
	Salt and pepper	
3 lb	Cooking apples	1.25 kg/3 lb
⅔ cup	Prunes	200 g/7 oz
¼ lb	Margarine	100 g/4 oz
	Sugar to taste	
6 strips	Bacon	6 rashers
1 lb	Sausages	450 g/1 lb
	Watercress for garnish	

1. Prepare the turkey. Wipe the inside with a damp cloth and season with salt and pepper. Peel, core, and slice the apples.
2. Chop the prunes coarsely; remove the stones. Melt half of the margarine in a saucepan; add the apple, cover the pan, and cook gently until the apple is tender. Occasionally shake the pan gently to prevent the apple from sticking. Stir in the prunes and sugar to taste. Cool, then spoon the stuffing into the turkey.
3. Preheat the oven to 375°F/190°C/Gas Mark 5.
4. Truss the turkey, then rub the outside with the remaining margarine. Roast in the oven for 15 minutes per pound plus 15 minutes over. If the bird becomes over-brown, place a piece of foil over the breast. Stretch the bacon with the back of a knife until doubled in length. Cut into 2 or 3 pieces, roll up, and put on a skewer. Place the bacon rolls and sausages in the roasting pan and cook beside the turkey for the last 30 minutes, or until brown.
5. Serve the turkey on a large dish surrounded with bacon and sausages and garnished with watercress.

French Style Roast Turkey 👨‍🍳👨‍🍳

 00:30 03:30   Serves 8–10   South

American	Ingredients	Metric/Imperial
1 (8–9 lb)	Turkey	1 (3.5–4 kg/ 8–9 lb)
½	Lemon	½
1 cup	Butter	225 g/8 oz
	Salt, ground pepper, and poultry seasoning	
	A few sprigs parsley	
	Giblets	
	A little mixed herbs	
½ tbsp	Flour	½ tbsp
	Turkey liver	

1. Preheat the oven to 350°F/180°C/Gas Mark 4.
2. Wash and dry the turkey thoroughly. Rub the surface with cut lemon to keep the flesh white. Put half the butter inside with 2 peeled onions and several sprigs of parsley and some seasoning, or stuff the turkey and sew in carefully.
3. Rub the remaining butter all over the breast and legs, season, and cover with foil. Put in a roasting pan and cover with 1¼ cups [300 ml/½ pint] stock made with giblets, 1 onion, and herbs.
4. Put into the oven and roast for 2¾–3½ hours, removing the foil every 20 minutes and turning bird from side to side to cook the legs. Baste each time with stock, adding more if it seems to be evaporating too quickly. During the last half hour, place the bird breast up and allow to brown. It may be necessary to put the oven up to 400°F/200°C/Gas Mark 6 for the last 10 minutes. Test to see if the bird is cooked thoroughly by sticking a skewer into the thickest part of the leg. If the juice runs pink, further cooking is required; if clear, it is done.
5. Remove the turkey to a serving dish and make the gravy. Skim some of the butter from the roasting pan and put into a small pan. Fry the turkey liver until tender. Sprinkle in the flour; then add the skimmed pan drippings, plus the remaining stock. Bring to a boil and simmer. Add seasoning to taste, and serve.

Hunter's Turkey

Hunter's Turkey

American	Ingredients	Metric/Imperial
2	Turkey legs cut into 4 joints or 8 slices turkey	2
3 tbsp	Oil	2 tbsp
1	Onion	1
1	Clove garlic	1
2 tbsp	Flour	1½ tbsp
3–4 tbsp	Tomato purée	2–3½ tbsp
¼ cup	White wine	60 ml/2 fl oz
1 cup	Brown stock	250 ml/8 fl oz
6–8	Mushrooms	6–8
2 tbsp	Butter	25 g/1 oz
1 tbsp	Chopped parsley	1 tbsp
½ tsp	Oregano	½ tsp
3–4 tbsp	Grated Cheddar cheese	2–3½ tbsp
2 tbsp	Bread crumbs	1½ tbsp

00:15 / 00:30 — Serves 4–6 — New England

1. Preheat the oven to 350°F/180°C/Gas Mark 4.
2. Make the hunter's sauce: Heat the oil and cook the chopped onion and crushed garlic until golden brown. Sprinkle in flour; cook for 1 minute to brown lightly. Add the tomato purée, wine, and stock. Bring to a boil, stirring frequently. Add the sliced mushrooms, cooked for a few minutes in butter. Add the herbs and seasoning, and simmer for a few minutes.
3. Cut the turkey legs at the joint or the breast pieces into slices, and place in an ovenproof dish. Spoon sauce over the turkey.
4. Put in the oven for 15 minutes. Then sprinkle the top with cheese and bread crumbs, and put under the broiler [grill] to brown.

Turkey Gratin

00:10 / 00:15 — Serves 4 — South

American	Ingredients	Metric/Imperial
1½ tbsp	Butter	20 g/¾ oz
1½ tbsp	Flour	1¼ tbsp
¼ tsp	Dry mustard	¼ tsp
1 cup	Milk	250 ml/8 fl oz
3 cups	Grated cheese	350 g/12 oz
1 tsp	Worcestershire sauce	1 tsp
4	Slices toast	4
8	Fairly thick slices turkey	8
	Paprika	

1. Heat the butter; stir in the flour and mustard. Cook for 2 minutes. Then add the milk gradually and stir until boiling. Add salt and pepper to taste.
2. Add the cheese and Worcestershire sauce, and stir over low heat until the cheese has melted.
3. Arrange the toast in a shallow baking pan. Put the slices of turkey on top and cover with the cheese sauce.
4. Brown under a hot broiler [grill] and sprinkle with paprika before serving.

Curried Turkey

Curried Turkey

00:15 / 00:35 — Serves 4 — South

American	Ingredients	Metric/Imperial
1½ cups	Cooked turkey	250 g/9 oz
	Juice of ½ lemon	
4 tbsp	Margarine	50 g/2 oz
1	Clove garlic, crushed	1
½ tsp	Ground ginger	½ tsp
1	Onion, chopped	1
1 tbsp	All-purpose [plain] flour	1 tbsp
1 tbsp	Curry powder, or to taste	1 tbsp
1 cup	Chicken stock	250 ml/8 fl oz
1 tbsp	Tomato purée	1 tbsp
1	Small dessert apple, peeled, cored, and chopped	1
1 tbsp	Raisins	1 tbsp
	Pinch of sugar	
	Salt and pepper	

1. Cut the turkey into bite-sized pieces and mix with lemon juice in a bowl.
2. Heat the margarine in a saucepan; add the garlic, ginger, onion, flour, and curry powder. Fry gently, stirring, for 3–4 minutes. Stir in the chicken stock; bring to a boil. Add the tomato purée, apple, raisins, sugar, and salt and pepper to taste. Cover the pan and simmer for 15 minutes. Stir in the turkey and cook for a further 10 minutes.

Turkey Loaf

Turkey-Breast Cutlets with Lemon and Wine Sauce

⏲ 00:15 / 00:10   Serves 4   United States

American	Ingredients	Metric/Imperial
2 tbsp	Flour	1½ tbsp
3 tbsp	Parmesan cheese, freshly grated	2 tbsp
½ tsp	Salt	½ tsp
¼ tsp	White pepper	¼ tsp
¼ tsp	Nutmeg	¼ tsp
1	Egg, well beaten	1
½ cup	Milk	125 ml/4 fl oz
1 lb	Raw boneless turkey breast	450 g/1 lb
	Flour	
4 tbsp	Sweet butter	50 g/2 oz
5 tbsp	Dry white wine	4 tbsp
	Juice of ½ lemon	
	Chopped fresh parsley	
	Lemon wedges	

1. In a shallow bowl, combine the flour, cheese, salt, pepper, and nutmeg. Add the egg and milk; beat until well blended.
2. Skin the turkey breast; cut crosswise into 6 slices. Pound with a meat mallet or side of a plate until thin. Dredge lightly in flour; shake off excess. Heat the butter in a large, heavy frying pan over moderate heat until the foam subsides. Dip the turkey in the batter and fry until golden. Remove from the pan; keep warm.
3. When all the turkey is cooked, add wine to the pan. Cook over low heat 2 minutes, stirring to loosen browned bits from the pan. Add lemon juice; mix well. Pour the sauce over the turkey cutlets; sprinkle with chopped parsley. Serve immediately with lemon wedges.

Turkey Loaf

⏲ 01:20 / 01:15   Serves 4   New England

American	Ingredients	Metric/Imperial
2	Eggs	2
1 cup	Cooked turkey, ham, and stuffing (as available)	170 g/6 oz
½ lb	Bacon	225 g/8 oz
2 tbsp	Margarine	25 g/1 oz
2 tbsp	Flour	1½ tbsp
1 cup	Milk	250 ml/8 fl oz
	Salt and pepper to taste	
	Watercress and tomatoes for garnish	

1. Cook the eggs in boiling water to cover for 10 minutes. Cool in cold water; crack the shells.
2. Cut the turkey, ham, and stuffing into small pieces. Remove any small bones. Using the back of a knife, stretch the bacon strips until they are doubled in length. Arrange the bacon over the base and sides of a loaf tin. Reserve some bacon strips for the top.
3. Preheat the oven to 350°F/180°C/Gas Mark 4.
4. Melt the margarine in a saucepan; add the flour and cook gently, stirring, for 2–3 minutes. Blend in the milk. Bring to a boil, stirring constantly; then add salt and pepper. Stir in the prepared turkey, ham, and stuffing.
5. Put half of the mixture into the loaf pan, place the eggs on top, and cover with the remaining mixture. Press down firmly. Cover with the reserved bacon. Cover the pan with foil and place it in a larger tin with enough water to come halfway up the sides. Bake in the oven for 1 hour. Leave the loaf in the pan to cool, then chill in the refrigerator. Turn the loaf out onto a serving plate and garnish with watercress and tomatoes.

Quick Turkey Hash

⏲ 00:05 / 00:10   Serves 4   Mid Atlantic

American	Ingredients	Metric/Imperial
2–3 cups	Chopped cooked turkey meat	350–500 g/ 12–18 oz
1 can (10¾ oz)	Condensed mushroom or asparagus soup	1 tin (300 g/ 10¾ oz)
1 can (12 fl oz)	Evaporated milk	1 tin (350 ml/ 12 fl oz)
3–4	Sliced mushrooms if available	3–4
½ cup	Cooked peas, beans, corn, tomato etc.	50 g/2 oz
1 tbsp	Chopped herbs or 2–3 tbsp [1½–2 tbsp] grated cheese	1 tbsp

1. Empty the can of condensed soup into a pan and heat with enough milk to make it the consistency of sauce. Add sliced mushrooms, if available, and cook gently for 4–5 minutes. Then add the chopped turkey meat and any available cooked vegetables.
2. Heat the hash gently until completely hot; then add the herbs or grated cheese. Serve hot with rice or mashed potatoes.

Fried Turkey Crisps

02:20
00:20 — Serves 4–6 — Midwest

American	Ingredients	Metric/Imperial
1 cup	Chopped cold turkey	175 g/6 oz
3 tbsp	Butter	40 g/1½ oz
1 tbsp	Chopped onion	1 tbsp
3 slices	Bacon	4 rashers
½ cup	Chopped mushrooms	50 g/2 oz
3 tbsp	Flour	2 tbsp
1 cup	Stock	250 ml/8 fl oz
3	Egg yolks	3
2 tbsp	Grated Parmesan cheese	1½ tbsp
2 tbsp	Bread crumbs	1½ tbsp
5–6 tbsp	Flour seasoned with salt, pepper, and paprika	4–5 tbsp
2	Eggs	2
1–1½ cups	Dry white bread crumbs	50–75 g/2–3 oz

1. Melt the butter; cook the chopped onion and diced bacon for 3–4 minutes. Then add the finely chopped mushrooms; cook again for 2 minutes, sprinkle in the flour, and blend smoothly. Add the stock and, when thoroughly mixed, bring the mixture to a boil, stirring constantly. Cook for 2 minutes and let cool slightly. Add the beaten egg yolks and seasoning, cheese, and bread crumbs. Let it cool completely in the refrigerator.
2. Form tablespoonfuls of the mixture into balls. Roll in seasoned flour. Brush thoroughly with beaten egg all over. Then shake in a bag of dry white bread crumbs until completely coated.
3. Heat the fat to 350°F/180°C/Gas Mark 4 (until a cube of bread turns brown in 1 minute). Cook the crisps until brown all over, remove, and drain on paper towels [kitchen paper]. Serve at once, very hot, with a sharp tomato sauce.

Smothered Turkey

00:10
00:50 — Serves 4 — South

American	Ingredients	Metric/Imperial
8	Large slices of cold turkey	8
1½ cups	Rice	350 g/12 oz
3 tbsp	Butter	40 g/1½ oz
1	Onion	1
1½ cups	Sour cream	350 ml/12 fl oz
	A pinch of nutmeg	
2 tbsp	Chopped chives	1½ tbsp

1. Preheat the oven to 350°F/180°C/Gas Mark 4.
2. Cook the rice in boiling, salted water. Drain and rinse with hot water. Dry and put in the bottom of a serving dish.
3. Cut the cold turkey into slices and place over the rice. Cover with buttered parchment paper and heat in the oven for 15–20 minutes.
4. Melt the butter and cook the finely chopped onion until tender but not brown, 6–8 minutes. Add the sour cream. Blend well. Add salt, pepper, and a little nutmeg.
5. Spoon the sour cream sauce over the turkey and rice, and sprinkle with chopped chives. Serve at once.

Turkey and Mushroom Croquettes

Turkey and Mushroom Croquettes

01:30
00:25 — Serves 4–6 — Midwest

American	Ingredients	Metric/Imperial
2 cups	Chopped cooked turkey	350 g/12 oz
5 tbsp	Butter	65 g/2½ oz
4 tbsp	Flour for sauce	3½ tbsp
½ cup	Strong turkey or chicken stock	125 ml/4 fl oz
½ cup	Milk	125 ml/4 fl oz
	Salt and pepper	
	A pinch of mace	
	A small pinch of cayenne pepper	
1 tbsp	Chopped parsley	1 tbsp
3–4 tbsp	Chopped mushrooms	2–3½ tbsp
	A little lemon juice	
1	Egg yolk	1
½ cup	Seasoned flour	50 g/2 oz
2	Eggs, beaten with 1 teaspoon oil	2
1–1½ cups	Dried white bread crumbs	50–75 g/2–3 oz
	Fat for deep frying	

1. Make a thick sauce: Melt 4 tablespoons [50g/2 oz] of butter and add flour. Add the stock and milk, and bring to a boil. Cook until thick and smooth. Add the seasonings and parsley and let cool.
2. Meanwhile, chop the turkey into small pieces. Chop the mushrooms and cook in 1 tablespoon [15 g/½ oz] of butter. Sprinkle with lemon juice. Add the chopped turkey; then add the sauce. Stir well. When almost cold, add the beaten egg yolk, put the mixture into the refrigerator to chill and set.
3. Divide the mixture into 12 equal portions. Shape each into a small roll with floured fingers. Roll in seasoned flour, coating the ends carefully. Brush all over with beaten egg and then cover thickly with dried white bread crumbs.
4. Heat the fat to 400°F/200°C/Gas Mark 6 or smoking hot. Fry 4 croquettes at a time until well browned. Then drain well and serve at once with a piquant brown or tomato sauce.

Turkey and Tomato Pancakes

Turkey Cottage Pie

00:30
00:55

Serves 4

Mid Atlantic

American	Ingredients	Metric/Imperial
3 cups	Chopped or diced cooked turkey	500 g/18 oz
1 lb	Potatoes	450 g/1 lb
3	Onions	3
6 tbsp	Butter	75 g/3 oz
¼–½ cup	Milk	60–125 ml/ 2–4 fl oz
2–3 slices	Bacon	2–3 rashers
½ cup	Chopped mushrooms	50 g/2 oz
1 tbsp	Chopped parsley and tarragon	1 tbsp
1 tbsp	Flour	1 tbsp
	A pinch of mace, salt, pepper	
1–1½ cups	Turkey or chicken stock	250–375 ml/ 8–12 fl oz
2–3 tbsp	Milk	1½–2 tbsp

1. Preheat the oven to 400°F/200°C/Gas Mark 6.
2. Peel the potatoes and boil in salted water with 1 peeled onion to flavor. When tender, in 15–20 minutes, remove the onion and drain the potatoes. Mash thoroughly. Beat in 2 tablespoons [25 g/1 oz] of butter and some warmed milk, enough to make a soft mixture without being at all runny. Heat carefully, adding salt, pepper, and mace.
3. While the potatoes boil, cook the chopped onions gently to soften in 2–3 tablespoons [25–40 g/1–1½ oz] of butter. After 3 minutes, add the chopped bacon and after another 3 minutes, add the sliced mushrooms. Cook for 1 minute. Sprinkle in the flour; when blended, stir in the stock and add the herbs and seasoning. Bring the mixture to a boil, simmer for a few minutes, and add the diced or chopped turkey meat. Add a little milk. Then turn into an ovenproof dish.
4. Spread the mashed potato carefully all over the top of the dish and smooth. Score the potato with a fork and dot with tiny flakes of butter. Bake in the oven for 20–30 minutes, or until the surface of the potato is golden brown and crisp.

Leftover Turkey and Vegetables

00:10
00:15

Serves 4–6

Mid Atlantic

American	Ingredients	Metric/Imperial
2–3 cups	Chopped cooked turkey (or other poultry or game)	350–500 g/ 12–18 oz
3 tbsp	Butter	40 g/1½ oz
1	Onion	1
2–3	Large mushrooms	2–3
2½ tbsp	Flour	1¾ tbsp
1½ cups	Stock	350 ml/12 fl oz
1–2 cups	Cooked vegetables, (peas, beans, corn, chopped carrots, pimento, etc)	100–225 g/ 4–8 oz
3–4 tbsp	Thick cream	2–3½ tbsp
1 tbsp	Chopped parsley and thyme	1 tbsp
4–5 tbsp	Grated Cheddar cheese	3–4½ tbsp

1. Preheat the broiler [grill]
2. Melt the butter and cook the chopped onion until tender. Add the chopped mushrooms and cook for 1 minute. Sprinkle in the flour and blend well. Add the stock and bring to a boil, stirring constantly. Add the chopped turkey and any available cooked vegetables. Stir well into the sauce. Add herbs and cream.
3. Turn into a buttered baking dish and sprinkle thickly with grated cheese and a little paprika. Broil [grill] until crisp and brown all over. Serve with cooked noodles, rice, or potatoes.

Turkey and Tomato Pancakes

00:45
00:30

Serves 6

South

American	Ingredients	Metric/Imperial
	Pancakes	
1 cup	Flour	100 g/4 oz
2	Eggs	2
1 cup	Milk	250 ml/8 fl oz
1 tbsp	Butter, melted	15 g/½ oz
	Oil for frying	
	Filling	
2 cups	Ground turkey	175 g/6 oz
1 can (10¾ oz)	Condensed tomato soup (or equivalent sauce)	1 tin (300 g/ 10¾ oz)
½ cup	Cooked vegetables (as available)	50 g/2 oz
1–2 tsp	Tomato purée (if necessary)	1–2 tsp
¼ tsp	Onion powder	¼ tsp
	A pinch of garlic powder	
2 tbsp	Butter	25 g/1 oz
2 tbsp	Grated Cheddar cheese	1½ tbsp

1. Preheat the broiler [grill].

2. Sift the flour with salt and pepper into a bowl. Make a hollow in the center, and add the beaten eggs and 3–4 tablespoons [2–3½ tbsp] of milk. Mix the eggs and milk together with a spoon before gradually drawing in the flour. Add a ¼ cup [60 ml/2 fl oz] of milk as the mixture thickens. When it is smooth and like thick cream, beat for 5 minutes by hand or in a mixer. Stir in the melted butter and another ¼ cup [60 ml/2 fl oz] of milk. Leave batter in a covered bowl for 30 minutes before cooking.

3. Test the thickness of the batter, which should just coat the back of a spoon. If too thick, add the remaining milk and stir well. Grease a 5–6 inch griddle or frying pan with a little oil. When hot, pour in enough batter to coat the pan thinly. Cook until golden brown on one side, turn and cook on the other side. Pile up and keep warm. Allow 2–3 per person. (After frying, pancakes can be frozen. If using frozen pancakes, allow to defrost before filling.)

4. Grind the turkey and mix with a can of condensed tomato soup. Add any cooked vegetables such as peas or corn, and herbs if available. Heat the mixture and add a little tomato puree to taste, if desired. Sprinkle in a little onion and garlic powder, salt, and pepper to taste.

5. Put the filling into the pancakes, roll up, and place in the center of an ovenproof dish. Sprinkle with butter and cheese. Boil until the cheese is golden brown and crisp. Serve at once.

Sliced Turkey in Chestnut Sauce

 00:20
00:40   Serves 4   Pacific Southwest

American	Ingredients	Metric/Imperial
8	Large slices cooked turkey	8
3 tbsp	Butter	40 g/1½ oz
2	Onions	2
1	Carrot	1
1½ tbsp	Flour	1¼ tbsp
2 tsp	Tomato purée	2 tsp
3 cups	Brown stock	700 ml/1¼ pints
¼ cup	Sherry or wine (optional)	60 ml/2 fl oz
1	Bay leaf	1
	A few sprigs of parsley	
1	Sprig thyme	1
4–5 tbsp	Chestnut purée	3¼–4 tbsp
3–4	Roughly chopped cooked chestnuts	3–4
2	Tomatoes (optional)	2

1. Preheat the oven to 350°F/180°C/Gas Mark 4.

2. Make the sauce: Chop the onions and carrots. Cook in melted butter until tender, about 10 minutes. Then brown gently. Add the flour. When blended, add the tomato purée and stock. A little sherry or wine can be added in place of some of the stock. Bring to a boil; cook for 10–15 minutes, adding herbs and seasoning. Strain throught a sieve. Add 4–5 tablespoons [3½–4 tbsp] of chestnut purée. Reheat and stir until smooth. Add a few pieces of cooked whole chestnuts to the sauce if available.

3. Cut the turkey into thin slices and place in an ovenproof dish. Garnish with sliced tomatoes, if desired. Then cover with sauce and reheat in the oven for a few minutes. Serve with crisp fried potatoes and green vegetables.

Turkey Noodle Ring

Turkey Noodle Ring

 00:20
01:15   Serves 4   Midwest

American	Ingredients	Metric/Imperial
2 cups	Cooked turkey	350 g/12 oz
½ lb	Noodles	225 g/8 oz
5–7 tbsp	Butter	65–90 g/ 2½–3½ oz
3	Onions	3
1	Clove garlic	1
1 cup	Heavy [double] cream	250 ml/8 fl oz
1	Egg	1
3–4 tbsp	Grated Cheddar cheese	2–3½ tbsp
1 tbsp	Chopped herbs	1 tbsp
1 cup	Mushrooms	100 g/4 oz
2 tbsp	Flour	1½ tbsp
½ cup	Stock	125 ml/4 fl oz
¾ cup	Milk	175 ml/6 fl oz
¼ cup	Cooked peas and corn	25 g/1 oz
2 tbsp	Chopped cooked pimento	1½ tbsp
2	Hard-boiled eggs	2
	A pinch of paprika	

1. Preheat the oven to 350°F/180°C/Gas Mark 4.

2. Boil the noodles in plenty of salted water until they are almost cooked. Drain. Heat 3–4 tablespoons [40–50 g/1½–2 oz] of butter in a pan and cook 1 chopped onion and garlic for a few minutes to soften. Stir the noodles into this. Then add the cream beaten with an egg, the grated cheese, and chopped herbs. Sprinkle liberally with salt and pepper, and mix thoroughly. Turn into a buttered, 7-inch ring mold and press in well. Cover with buttered parchment paper and put in the oven for 45 minutes to set and to finish cooking the noodles. Remove when done, and turn out on a hot dish. Fill with turkey filling.

3. Melt 2–3 tablespoons [25–40 g/1–2 oz] ;of butter and cook 2 finely sliced onions to soften for 5–6 minutes. Add the mushrooms, stir well, then sprinkle in the flour. Blend well. Then add the stock and milk. Bring to a boil and simmer for 4–5 minutes. Then remove from the heat. Add the chopped turkey meat, cooked peas, corn, pimento, and 2 hard-boiled eggs (quartered). Season well and allow to stand in a warm place until the noodle ring is ready. Spoon the turkey mixture into the center of the noodle ring, and sprinkle with paprika.

Turkey and Ham Patties

	00:30		
	00:30	Serves 4	Mid Atlantic

American	Ingredients	Metric/Imperial
½–¾ cup	Chopped turkey	75–100 g/3–4 oz
½ cup	Chopped ham	75 g/3 oz
1	Package of frozen puff pastry, about 1 lb [450 g]	1
1	Egg	1
3 tbsp	Butter	40 g/1½ oz
1	Onion	1
3 tbsp	Flour	2 tbsp
1 cup	Milk	250 ml/8 fl oz
1 tbsp	Parsley	1 tbsp
	Salt, pepper, pinch of mace	

1. Preheat the oven to 475°F/240°C/Gas Mark 9.
2. Roll out pastry until ¼ inch thick. Using a 2½–inch diameter cutter, cut out 8 patties. Now using a smaller cutter, 1½ inches in diameter, make a central cut in each patty, being careful not to cut through to the bottom. Brush the surface of each patty with beaten egg. Do not allow the egg to run over the sides, or this will prevent the pastry rising.
3. Put on a dampened baking sheet and bake for about 15–20 minutes, until the patties have risen and are golden brown. Remove from the oven, take off the center lids carefully, and reserve. Scoop out the soft pastry inside and throw away. Keep warm.
4. Meanwhile make the filling: Melt the butter and cook the finely chopped onion for 5–6 minutes to soften. Mix in the flour. Add the milk. Blend well before bringing to a boil, stirring all the time. Add the chopped turkey and ham, parsley, and seasoning. heat together and spoon into patty shells. Place the lids on top and serve at once, or keep warm for a short time.

Turkey with Lemon Mayonnaise

	00:40		
	00:20	Serves 6–8	New England

American	Ingredients	Metric/Imperial
1½–2 lb	Cooked turkey meat	675–900 g/1½–2 lb
2 cups	Rice	450 g/1 lb
½ cup	Peas	50 g/2 oz
½ cup	Chopped beans	50 g/2 oz
½ cup	Corn	50 g/2 oz
4	Tomatoes	4
1	Medium cucumber	1
2½ cups	Mayonnaise (approx.)	600 ml/1 pint
	Grated rind of 2 lemons	
1 tbsp	Chopped parsley	1 tbsp
6–8	Thin slices lemon	6–8

	French Dressing	
½ tsp	French mustard	½ tsp
1½ cups	Oil	350 ml/12 fl oz
½ cup	Wine vinegar	125 ml/4 fl oz
1–2 tbsp	Fresh chopped mixed herbs	1–1½ tbsp

1. Boil the rice in plenty of salt water for 10–12 minutes, or according to the instructions on the package. Drain and wash well with cold water. Drain and dry. Boil the peas, beans, and corn in salted water. Drain and let cool. Peel and slice the tomatoes, reserving the juice. Peel the cucumber, dice it, and sprinkle it with salt. Leave for 20 minutes; then wash well and drain.
2. Make the French dressing: Mix the salt, pepper, and sugar to taste with French mustard and oil. Add the vinegar. Beat well. Add the chopped herbs.
3. Make the mayonnaise as described in Smoked Turkey Salad (see Index), using double quantities and lemon instead of vinegar. Add 2–3 teaspoons grated lemon rind for flavor. Cut the turkey into cubes or strips, mix with half the mayonnaise. Thin the remaining mayonnaise slightly with the strained juice of the tomatoes.
4. Add all the vegetables to the cold cooked rice and moisten with French dressing. Arrange this mixture down the sides of a dish. Spoon the turkey mayonnaise down the center. Spoon a little extra mayonnaise over the top. Sprinkle with chopped parsley mixed with the remaining lemon rind, and garnish with slices of lemon made into twists.

Deviled Turkey Legs

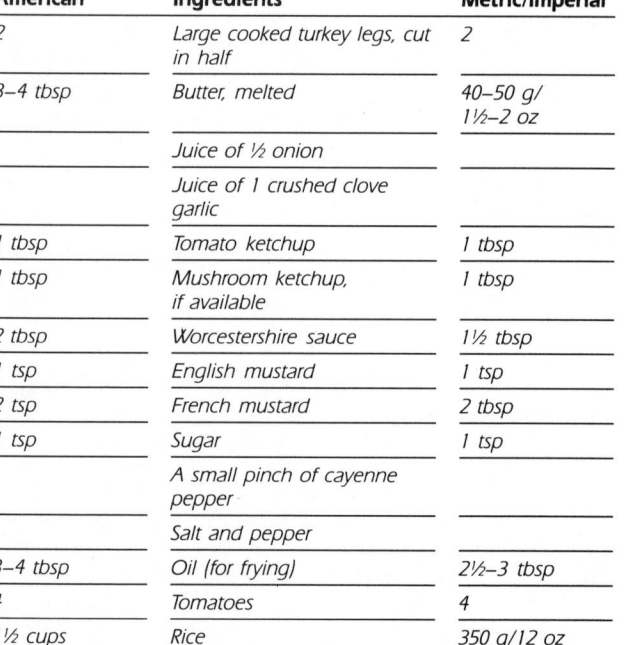

	01:15		
	00:25	Serves 4	New England

American	Ingredients	Metric/Imperial
2	Large cooked turkey legs, cut in half	2
3–4 tbsp	Butter, melted	40–50 g/1½–2 oz
	Juice of ½ onion	
	Juice of 1 crushed clove garlic	
1 tbsp	Tomato ketchup	1 tbsp
1 tbsp	Mushroom ketchup, if available	1 tbsp
2 tbsp	Worcestershire sauce	1½ tbsp
1 tsp	English mustard	1 tsp
2 tsp	French mustard	2 tbsp
1 tsp	Sugar	1 tsp
	A small pinch of cayenne pepper	
	Salt and pepper	
3–4 tbsp	Oil (for frying)	2½–3 tbsp
4	Tomatoes	4
1½ cups	Rice	350 g/12 oz
½ cup	Tomatoes	100 g/4 oz
½ cup	Turkey stock	125 ml/4 fl oz

1. Preheat the broiler [grill].
2. Make the devil mixture: Mix the melted butter with onion and crushed garlic juices, tomato and mushroom ketchup, Worcestershire sauce, mustards, sugar, cayenne pepper, salt, and black pepper.
3. Joint each turkey leg. With a sharp knife, cut shallow gashes into the meat. Put the joints into a dish with the devil mixture and spoon the devil sauce all over them. Marinate for at least 1 hour, longer if possible, turning frequently.
4. Heat the oil in a frying pan. Fry the joints until brown all over, turning frequently. Broil [grill] 4 tomatoes at the same time. Serve with plain boiled rice and sauce made by adding the tomatoes and stock to the remaining devil sauce. Heat the sauce and strain. Serve with a green salad.

Turkey Timbale

	00:25		
	00:45	Serves 4	Mid Atlantic

American	Ingredients	Metric/Imperial
2–3 cups	Finely chopped turkey meat	350–500 g/ 12–18 oz
6 tbsp	Butter	75 g/3 oz
4 tbsp	Flour	3½ tbsp
1 cup	Milk flavored with onion and herbs	250 ml/8 fl oz
2	Eggs	2
3–4 tbsp	Thick cream	2–3½ tbsp
16–20	Mushrooms	16–20
1½ cups	Well-flavored brown stock	350 ml/12 fl oz
1 tbsp	Chopped herbs	1 tbsp
2 tsp	Worcestershire sauce	2 tsp
2–3 tbsp	Madeira or sherry	1½–2 tbsp

1. Preheat the oven to 350°F/180°C/Gas Mark 4.
2. First make a thick cream sauce: Melt 2 tablespoons [25 g/1 oz] of butter; stir in 2 tablespoons [1½ tbsp] of flour until blended. Pour in the hot milk and bring to a boil, stirring constantly. Cook for a few minutes, add the seasoning, and let cool.
3. Grind the turkey finely and mix with eggs beaten in cream. Add the cooled sauce. Mix everything well together and turn into a thoroughly buttered, 7-inch ring mold, alowing a little space at the top for expansion while cooking. Cover with buttered parchment paper. Put in a roasting pan of hot water and bake for 25–35 minutes, or until a skewer can be inserted into the center and come out clean. Run a knife around the outside and inner ring of the mold, and turn out onto a large round plate. Pour the mushroom sauce into the center and serve at once.
4. While the timbale cooks, make the mushroom sauce: Melt 3 tablespoons [40 g/1½ oz] of butter and cook the quartered mushrooms for 2–3 minutes. Then sprinkle in 2 tablespoons [1½ tbsp] of flour. Cook for 1 minute; remove from the heat, add the brown, well-flavored stock, and blend thoroughly. Bring to a boil and simmer for a few minutes. Add seasoning, herbs, Worcestershire sauce, and Madeira or sherry. Allow the flavors to blend well before pouring into the center of the mold.

Boned Duck with Orange Stuffing

Boned Duck with Orange Stuffing

	00:20		
	02:05	Serves 8–10	United States

American	Ingredients	Metric/Imperial
1 (5-lb)	Duck	1 (2.25 kg/5-lb)
	Salt and pepper	
4 tbsp	Margarine	50 g/2 oz
1	Large onion, chopped	1
4 sticks	Celery, finely chopped	4
¾ lb	Sausage	350 g/12 oz
¼ tsp	Ground nutmeg	¼ tsp
½ cup	Soft white bread crumbs	25 g/1 oz
1	Orange	1
1 tsp	Orange rind	1 tsp
	Beaten egg to mix	
	Watercress for garnish	

1. Preheat the oven to 375°F/190°C/Gas Mark 5.
2. Bone the duck or ask your butcher to do this for you. Season the inside with salt and pepper. Melt the margarine in a suacepan and fry the onion and celery until soft and golden. Stir in the sausage, nutmeg, bread crumbs, 1 teaspoon finely grated orange rind, and enough egg to bind.
3. Peel the orange and cut into quarters. Place one third of the stuffing in the duck. Arrange the orange quarters evenly on top, then cover with the remaining stuffing. Make the duck into a neat parcel and sew the opening together with fine string.
4. Place the duck on a rack in a roasting pan and cook in the oven for 2 hours. Cover the duck with foil if it becomes too brown. Serve hot or cold, garnished with watercress.

Roast Duck with Celery Stuffing

Roast Duck with Celery Stuffing

	00:25	Serves 4	United States
	01:35		

American	Ingredients	Metric/Imperial
1 (4-lb)	Duck	1 (1.75 kg/4 lb)
	Salt and pepper	
¼ lb	Streaky bacon, chopped	100 g/4 oz
	Liver from the duck	
2	Onions, chopped	2
2	Sticks celery, chopped	2
1 cup	Soft white bread crumbs	50 g/2 oz
½ cup	Milk	125 ml/4 fl oz
2 tbsp	Parsley, chopped	1½ tbsp
¼ tsp each	Dried sage and thyme	¼ tsp each
	Beaten egg to bind	
	Extra celery, canned cherries, and watercress for garnish	

1. Preheat the oven to 375°F/190°C/Gas Mark 5.
2. Prepare the duck; wipe the inside with a clean damp cloth. Sprinkle with salt and pepper. Fry the bacon in a saucepan; add the liver, then chop when cooked. Fry the onions and celery until soft; then stir in the bread crumbs, milk, herbs, salt and pepper, and enough beaten egg to bind. Pile the stuffing into the duck and truss. Roast the duck in the oven for 15 minutes per pound plus 15 minutes over.
3. To prepare the garnish, cut some celery into 1-inch lengths; cook in boiling salted water until tender. Heat the cherries in their own syrup. Place the duck on a large serving dish and arrange the garnish around it. Add watercress to complete the garnish.

Danish Christmas Duck

	00:25	Serves 6	Midwest 
	01:35		

American	Ingredients	Metric/Imperial
1 (5-lb)	Duck	1 (2.25 kg/5 lb)
1 tbsp	Butter	15 g/½ oz
1 lb	Apples	450 g/1 lb
1½ cups	Seeded [stoned] prunes	175 g/6 oz
	Grated rind of ½ orange	
	Salt, pepper, and sugar	
2 tbsp	Oil	1½ tbsp
2 cups	Brown stock	450 ml/¾ pint
¼ cup	Port or red wine (optional)	60 ml/2 fl oz
1 tbsp	Cornstarch [cornflour]	1 tbsp
¼ cup	Heavy [double] cream	60 ml/2 fl oz

1. Preheat the oven to 350°F/180°C/Gas Mark 4.
2. Rinse the duck out with cold water and dry thoroughly. Prick the breast with a fork and rub over with butter and seasoning.
3. For the stuffing, peel and thickly slice the apples. Seed the soaked prunes. Mix both with some grated orange rind and a little salt and sugar. Stuff the inside of the duck and sew up the opening.
4. Heat the oil in the oven. When hot, add the duck and baste thoroughly. Roast for 1¼–1½ hours, basting frequently, adding a little stock halfway through the cooking. Just before the duck is done, pour off the pan drippings and brown the bird in a slightly hotter oven.
5. Put the duck onto a serving dish and keep hot while making the sauce. Skim the fat off the roasting juices and add the remaining stock. Cook for a few minutes; add the port or red wine (if available). Mix the cornstarch with a little cold water. Spoon a little hot sauce into the cornstarch, then return to the pan, and bring to a boil. Lastly, add the cream and seasoning. Serve with red cabbage and browned potatoes.

Peking Duck

	00:10	Serves 4	Pacific Southwest
	01:20		

American	Ingredients	Metric/Imperial
1 (3–4 lb)	Tender roasting duck	1 (1.25–1.75 kg)
5–6 tbsp	Honey	4–5 tbsp
1 tbsp	Wine vinegar	1 tbsp
2 tbsp	Soy sauce	1½ tbsp
2–3 tsp	Sherry	2–3 tsp
1	Orange	1
1	Onion	1

1. Preheat the broiler [grill] or barbecue charcoal grill.
2. Prepare the special basting sauce: In a pan, put the honey, vinegar, soy sauce, sherry, juice of ½ orange, and 3 tablespoons [2 tbsp] of water. Heat all these ingredients together and bring to a boil. Let cool.

3. Prick the skin of the duck lightly with a sharp fork; cover with several pints of boiling water to soften the skin. Let dry. Put the onion and ½ orange inside the duck and season. Put the bird on a spit and when the broiler or barbecue is very hot, cook the bird, basting frequently with the special sauce. Allow 20 minutes per pound. Lower the heat after the first half hour. Test if the duck is done by sticking a skewer deeply into the leg meat. If the juice is clear, the duck is done.

4. Remove from the heat, and serve with rice and bean sprouts.

Cold Duck Soufflé

04:35
00:30   Serves 4–6   South

American	Ingredients	Metric/Imperial
3 cups	Ground [minced] cold duck	500 g/18 oz
1 cup	Milk	250 ml/8 fl oz
1	Onion	1
1	Carrot	1
6	Peppercorns	6
	A pinch of mace	
4 sprigs or 2 tsp dried	Parsley	4 sprigs or 2 tsp dried
1 sprig or ½ tsp dried	Thyme	1 sprig or ½ tsp dried
1	Bay leaf	1
3	Cloves	3
2 tbsp	Butter	25 g/1 oz
2 tbsp	Flour	1½ tbsp
1½ cans (20 fl oz)	Beef consomme	1½ tins (600 ml/ 1 pint)
2 tbsp	Gelatin [gelatine]	1½ tbsp
3 tbsp	Sherry	2 tbsp
½ cup	Heavy [double] cream, whipped	125 ml/4 fl oz
2	Eggs	2
2	Oranges	2

1. Make a cream sauce: Put the milk into a small pan with the sliced onion and carrot, peppercorns, mace, herbs, and cloves. Heat slowly for 20 minutes. Melt the butter and stir in the flour; add the strained milk and bring to a boil, stirring constantly. Simmer for 3–4 minutes. Let cool.

2. Meanwhile, dissolve 4 teaspoons gelatin in half the can of consomme. Add 1 tablespoon sherry and the finely ground duck. Mix well.

3. When the sauce is cool, beat and mix it into the duck and jelly mixture. Season well, as the flavor dulls when cold. Put the bowl into a large bowl containing iced water and ice. Stir from time to time. When on the point of setting, stir in whipped cream and whipped egg whites. Put into a soufflé dish large enough to leave a little space for the orange garnish and jelly. Put in the refrigerator to set.

4. Meanwhile, prepare the garnish: With a sharp serrated knife, remove the peel, pith, and skin from the oranges. Cut into wafer-thin slices. In the remaining consomme, dissolve 2 tablespoons [1½ tbsp] gelatin. When cool, add 2 tablespoons [1½ tbsp] sherry.

5. When the soufflé has set, arrange the orange slices in over-lapping layers on top and spoon over the setting consomme. Return to the refrigerator to set the jelly and serve with a green salad and potato with mayonnaise.

Cold Duck Soufflé

Wild Duck with Red Cabbage

00:25
02:00   Serves 4   Pacific Southwest

American	Ingredients	Metric/Imperial
1 (2–3 lb)	Wild duck	1 (900 g–1.25 kg/ 2–3 lb)
1 (1–1½ lb)	Cabbage	1 (450–675 g/ 1–1½ lb)
3	Onions	3
2–3 tbsp	Vinegar	1½–2 tbsp
2–3 tbsp	Water	1½–2 tbsp
4	Sour apples	4
1 tsp	Sugar	1 tsp
3 tbsp	Oil	2 tbsp
1 tsp	Caraway seeds	1 tsp
½ cup	Stock	125 ml/4 fl oz
1 tbsp	Chopped parsley	1 tbsp

1. Preheat the oven to 350°F/180°C/Gas Mark 4.

2. First braise the red cabbage: Shred the cabbage very finely, discarding any hard stem. Chop the onion and mix with the cabbage. Put in a well-buttered casserole. Add the vinegar, water, and seasoning. Cook in the oven for 1 hour. Add the sliced apples and a little sugar. Cook for 15 minutes more.

3. Cut the duck into 4 pieces. Heat 2–3 tablespoons [1½–2 tbsp] of oil and, when hot, brown the pieces of duck all over. Remove and place on top of the cabbage in the casserole. Cook the sliced onions in the remaining oil until soft without browning. Sprinkle in the caraway seeds and add a little stock. Add the seasoning and pour over the pieces of duck. Return to the oven for 30–40 minutes, until tender.

4. Scrape the onion mixture off the duck and mix it well into the red cabbage. Arrange the duck pieces on top of the cabbage and sprinkle with chopped parsley. Serve hot, with mashed potatoes and red currant jelly.

Duck Stuffed with Apricots

	00:20	Serves 4–6	Pacific Southwest
	01:25		

American	Ingredients	Metric/Imperial
1 (4–5 lb)	Roasting duck	1 (1.75–2.25 kg/ 4–5 lb)
1 lb	Fresh apricots	450 g/1 lb
1	Orange	1
1	Onion	1
	Salt and pepper	
2–3 tbsp	Oil	1½–2 tbsp
3 tbsp	Honey	2 tbsp
1–1½ cups	Stock made with duck giblets	250–350 ml/ 8–12 fl oz
3–4 tbsp	Apricot brandy	2–3½ tbsp

1. Preheat the oven to 400°F/200°C/Gas Mark 6.
2. Stuff the duck with half the seeded apricots, 3 strips of orange zest (the thin outer skin of the orange), the finely chopped onion, and seasoning. Prick the skin of the duck with fork to allow the fat to run out while cooking. Season with pepper and salt.
3. Heat the oil in a baking pan. When very hot, add the duck and baste all over with oil. Roast in the oven, allowing 20 minutes per pound. Half an hour before the cooking is completed, cover with the melted honey and the juice of the orange, which will give the skin a shiny crispness. Ten minutes before the end of cooking, add the rest of the apricots to the pan to heat through and brown slightly. Remove the duck to a warm dish, and remove the stuffing to a bowl. Arrange the roasted apricots around the duck.
4. Pour off the fat from the roasting pan; add stuffing to it with the stock and bring to a boil, stirring all the time. When the sauce has a pleasant flavor, strain or blend in a liquidizer or blender. Return to the heat and add apricot brandy. Serve at once with the duck and apricots.

Roast Wild Duck with Baked Oranges

	00:20	Serves 4	Pacific Southwest
	00:35		

American	Ingredients	Metric/Imperial
2 (1½ lb)	Wild ducks	2 (675 g/1½ lb)
2	Onions	2
4	Stalks celery	4
2 tbsp	Lemon juice	1½ tbsp
6 tbsp	Butter	75 g/3 oz
2 tbsp	Oil	1½ tbsp
4	Small oranges or mandarins	4
4 tsp	Sugar	4 tsp
½ cup	Clear stock	125 ml/4 fl oz

1. Preheat the oven to 400°F/200°C/Gas Mark 6.

2. Put a quartered onion and some celery into each duck with a little lemon juice and seasoning. Rub the breast all over with 2 tablespoons [25 g/1 oz] of butter; sprinkle with salt. Heat the oil and 2 tablespoons [25 g/1 oz] of butter in roasting pan. When hot, put in the birds, basting well. Roast in the oven for 25–30 minutes, depending on the size of the birds, basting every 15 minutes.
3. Wipe the small oranges or mandarins, and rub the skins with butter. Put them around the ducks for the last 15 minutes of cooking time. The oranges should swell and burst.
4. Remove the ducks, put on a serving dish, and keep warm. make a hole in each orange, fill with a little sugar, and arrange around the ducks. Skim the fat from the pan drippings and add the stock. Boil for several minutes to reduce the quantity and season to taste. Serve with a salad and crisp potatoes.

Duck and Green Pea Pancakes

	00:45	Serves 4–6	Midwest
	00:20		

American	Ingredients	Metric/Imperial
	Pancakes	
1 cup	Flour	100 g/4 oz
2	Eggs	2
1 cup	Milk	250 ml/8 fl oz
1 tbsp	Butter	15 g/½ oz
	Oil for frying	
	Filling	
1–1½ cups	Diced cooked duck	175–250 g/ 6–9 oz
4 tbsp	Butter	50 g/2 oz
1	Onion	1
6–8	Mushrooms	6–8
1½ tbsp	Flour	1¼ tbsp
¾ cup	Strong stock	175 ml/6 fl oz
¾ cup	Peas	75 g/3 oz
1 tbsp	Chopped parsley and thyme	1 tbsp
2–3 tbsp	Cream	1½–2 tbsp
2 tbsp	Browned bread crumbs	1½ tbsp
	Grated rind of 1 orange	

1. Preheat the oven to 350°F/180°C/Gas Mark 4.
2. Make the pancakes as in Turkey and Tomato Pancakes (see Index).
3. Melt 2 tablespoons [25 g/1 oz] of butter, and cook the chopped onion and mushrooms in a covered pan for 3–5 minutes to soften. Stir in the flour; blend well. Then add the stock. When smooth, bring slowly to a boil and cook for a few minutes. Add the diced duck meat, peas, and herbs. Heat for a few minutes. Add the cream last. Keep warm while cooking the pancakes.
4. Put a spoonful of filling in the center of each pancake and roll up. Arrange in an overlapping row in an ovenproof dish. Cover with the remaining melted butter and some bread crumbs, mixed with a little grated orange rind. Heat for a few minutes in the oven and serve.

Duck Stuffed with Apricots

Barbecued Duck

00:45
01:25

Serves 4–6

Mid Atlantic

American	Ingredients	Metric/Imperial
1 (3–4 lb)	Duck	1 (1.25–1.75 kg/ 3–4 lb)
6–7 tbsp	Oil	5–6 tbsp
½ tsp	Dry mustard powder	½ tsp
1	Clove garlic	1
¼ tsp	Seasoning salt	¼ tsp
1 tsp	Sugar	1 tsp
	A pinch cayenne pepper	
	Black pepper	
1	Onion	1
1 tbsp	Worcestershire sauce	1 tbsp
4 tbsp	Bitter marmalade	3¼ tbsp
2 tbsp	Tomato ketchup	1½ tbsp
1 tbsp	Honey	1 tbsp
1 tbsp	Vinegar	1 tbsp
1	Orange	1
3–4 tbsp	Stock	2–3½ tbsp
2 tbsp	Butter	25 g/1 oz

1. Heat the coals in an outdoor grill until hot, about 30 minutes, or preheat the broiler [grill].
2. Mix 3 tablespoons [2 tbsp] oil with mustard, crushed garlic, seasoning salt, sugar, cayenne, and black pepper. Prick the breast of the duck and rub this paste all over. Fix the duck on a spit. Put an onion and lump of butter and some seasoning inside.
3. Cook the duck, turning frequently. Allow 20 minutes per pound, basting with oil for the first 45 minutes, then frequently with sauce.
4. Mix 2 tablespoons [1½ tbsp] oil with Worcestershire sauce, bitter marmalade (sieved), ketchup, honey, vinegar, the grated rind and juice of an orange, ground pepper, and 3–4 tablespoons [2–3½ tbsp] stock. Heat thoroughly and baste the duck.
5. When the duck is tender and brown all over, remove from the spit. Serve hot with watercress and orange salad.

Duck with Cherries

00:30
02:30

Serves 4–6

Pacific Southwest

American	Ingredients	Metric/Imperial
1 (4–5 lb)	Duck	1 (1.75–2.25 kg/ 4–5 lb)
2	Onions	2
4	Stalks celery	4
3 tbsp	Butter	40 g/1½ oz
2 tbsp	Oil	1½ tbsp
2	Small carrots	2
4–5	Mushrooms	4–5
1½ tbsp	Flour	1¼ tbsp
2 tsp	Tomato purée	2 tsp
2 cups	Stock made with giblets or a chicken bouillon [stock] cube	450 ml/¾ pint
	A few parsley stalks	
	A bay leaf	
1 cup	Red wine (or Madeira or port)	250 ml/8 fl oz
1 lb	Fresh red cherries	450 g/1 lb
1	Orange	1
½ tsp	Sugar	½ tsp

1. Preheat the oven to 400°F/200°C/Gas Mark 6.
2. Put 1 onion and 2 stalks of celery inside the duck. Rub the breast with 1 tablespoon [15 g/½ oz] of butter and sprinkle with salt and pepper. Heat 2 tablespoons [25 g/1 oz] of butter. When hot, put the duck into a roasting pan and baste well. Put into the oven and roast for 15 minutes per pound, basting every 15 minutes. This will not cook the bird completely, allowing 20 minutes for it to be cooked in the sauce.
3. Meanwhile, prepare the sauce: Melt 2 tablespoons [1½ tbsp] of oil, add 1 finely chopped onion, 2 carrots, 2 stalks of celery, and the mushrooms. Cook for 7–10 minutes, allowing the vegetables to brown lightly. Stir in the flour, brown for 1 minute. Add the tomato purée, the stock made from the duck giblets, and the herbs. Bring to a boil, then simmer for 30 minutes. Strain, add seasoning, bring to a boil again, and skim off any impurities that rise to the surface. Add ½ cup [125 ml/4 fl oz] of wine (or Madeira or port) and heat again.
4. Carve the duck and arrange the pieces in a covered casserole. Pour the sauce over and cook in the oven for 20 minutes.
5. Meanwhile, prepare the cherries. If fresh, remove the seeds. If canned, drain off the juice and remove the seeds. Put into a small pan with the juice and the grated rind of an orange, ½ cup [125 ml/4 fl oz] red wine, and a little sugar. Heat gently for 6–7 minutes.
6. When the duck is cooked, arrange the pieces on a serving dish, spoon the sauce over the top, and arrange the cherries around the edge of the dish. Serve hot.

Duck with Turnips

00:10
01:45

Serves 4–6

Mid Atlantic

American	Ingredients	Metric/Imperial
1 (3½–4 lb)	Duck	1 (1.5–1.75 kg/ 3½–4 lb)
2 tbsp	Oil	1½ tbsp
3 tbsp	Butter	40 g/1½ oz
3	Onions	3
12 small or 6 medium	White turnips	12 small or 6 medium
1½ cups	Stock	350 ml/12 fl oz
	Salt, pepper, and a pinch of mace	
3–4	Parsley stalks	3–4
1	Sprig of thyme	1
1	Bay leaf	1
1 tbsp	Chopped parsley	1 tbsp

1. Preheat the oven to 325°F/160°C/Gas Mark 3.
2. Prick the breast of the duck with a fork; then rub with salt and pepper. Heat the oil and butter and, when foaming, brown the duck all over. Keep warm while cooking the sliced onions to a golden brown and the peeled turnips to color their outsides

Salmi of Duck

slightly. Pour in the stock, add seasoning and herbs, and bring to a boil. Then return the duck to a casserole and spoon the sauce over it. Cook in the oven for 1–1½ hours.

3. When tender, remove the duck and turnips to a serving dish, skim off the fat from the sauce. Boil this for a minute or two and season to taste. Add the chopped parsley and spoon around the bird. Serve at once.

Salmi of Duck 🍞🍞🍞

00:50		Serves 6	South
02:00			

American	Ingredients	Metric/Imperial
1 (4–5 lb)	Duck	1 (1.72–2.25 kg/ 4–5 lb)
1 cup	Oil	250 ml/8 fl oz
5 tbsp	Butter	65 g/2½ oz
1	Onion, chopped	1
1½ tbsp	Flour	1¼ tbsp
1 tbsp	Tomato purée	1 tbsp
2 cups	Stock	450 ml/¾ pint
	A few parsley stalks, a sprig of thyme and a bay leaf	
½ cup	Port or red wine	125 ml/4 fl oz
12	Button mushrooms	12
6	Slices white bread	6
1 tbsp	Chopped parsley	1 tbsp

1. Preheat the oven to 400°F/200°C/Gas Mark 6.

2. Heat 2 tablespoons [1½ tbsp] oil and roast the duck for 35 minutes with its giblets, but not the liver. Let cool. When cool enough to handle, carve the breast off in 2 pieces. Remove the legs and any other meat carefully, reserving any blood that runs out while carving. Break up the carcass bones and remove the skin from the carved joints. Put the bones and skin in a pan with the giblets and any blood or juice from the duck. Place the meat in a covered dish and keep warm.

3. Make the sauce: Heat 2 tablespoons [25 g/1 oz] of butter and cook the onion until tender. Then brown slightly, add the flour, stir well, and allow to brown a little. Cool slightly. Add the tomato purée and stock, bring to a boil, and then add the duck bones, skin etc., herbs, and seasoning. Cover the pan and cook for 30 minutes. Then strain and add ½ cup [125 ml/4 fl oz] port or red wine. Cook again for a few minutes, season to taste.

4. Cook the mushrooms in 1 tablespoon [15 g/½ oz] of butter, then add to sauce. Melt another tablespoon butter in the same pan and sauté the duck liver until tender; then season and chop or pound as fine as possible.

5. Carve the duck's legs into 2 pieces and the breast into slices, and arrange these on an ovenproof serving dish. Spoon the sauce over the meat and cover the dish with a lid or foil. Bake in the oven until the legs are tender, 20–30 minutes.

6. Meanwhile, cut the bread slices into heart-shaped croutons. Heat the oil and add 1 tablespoon [15 g/½ oz] of butter. When foaming, fry the croutons until golden brown all over. Drain and spread with duck liver paste.

7. When the salmi is cooked, remove the lid, sprinkle with chopped parsley and arrange croutons around the edge of the dish.

Braised Duck

00:15
02:15
Serves 4
Mid Atlantic

American	Ingredients	Metric/Imperial
1 (3½–4 lb)	Duck	1 (1.5–1.75 kg/ 3½–4 lb)
3	Onions	3
	Thinly pared rind of 1 orange	
	Thinly pared rind of 1 lemon	
3–4 tbsp	Oil	2–3½ tbsp
3–4	Carrots	3–4
3–4	Stalks celery	3–4
1	Small white turnip	1
3 tbsp	Flour	2 tbsp
1 tsp	Tomato purée	1 tsp
2 cups	Brown stock	450 ml/¾ pint
1 cup	Cider or red wine	250 ml/8 fl oz
	Several parsley stalks	
1	Sprig thyme	1
1	Small sage leaf	1
1	Bay leaf	1

1. Preheat the oven to 350°F/180°C/Gas Mark 4.
2. Prick the breast of the bird all over with a fork. Rub the skin with salt and pepper. Put an onion inside the bird with a few pieces of orange and lemon rind. Heat the oil and brown the duck all over for 6–8 minutes. Remove and keep warm.
3. Now add 2 sliced onions, carrots, celery, and a turnip to the pan and brown slowly but thoroughly. Cool slightly, add the flour, and cook for 2–3 minutes. Add the tomato purée, stock, and cider or wine. Boil for 1 minute. Add the parsley, thyme, sage leaf, bay leaf, and remaining orange and lemon rind.
4. Place the duck in a casserole, cover with sauce, and braise slowly in the oven for 2 hours, until duck is tender.
5. Remove the duck and carve. Place the pieces on a hot dish. Strain the sauce and boil to reduce slightly, skimming off the fat that rises to the top. Season to taste, spoon a little sauce over the duck, and serve the rest separately.

Roast Duck with Orange Salad

01:15
01:30
Serves 4
Pacific Southwest

American	Ingredients	Metric/Imperial
1 (3–4 lb)	Duck	1 (1.25–1.75 kg/ 3–4 lb)
2	Onions	2
4	Stalks celery	4
2 tbsp	Butter	25 g/1 oz
1 tbsp	Chopped parsley and thyme	1 tbsp
1	Orange	1
4–5 tbsp	Oil	3½–4 tbsp
2–3 tbsp	Melted honey	1½–2 tbsp
4	Oranges	4
½ tsp	Salt	½ tsp
½ tsp	Sugar	½ tsp
½ tsp	Freshly ground black pepper	½ tsp
3 tbsp	Salad oil	2 tbsp
2 tbsp	Lemon juice	1½ tbsp
1 cup	Red wine	250 ml/8 fl oz
1 cup	Chicken stock	250 ml/8 fl oz

1. Preheat the oven to 400°F/200°C/Gas Mark 6.
2. Slice the onions and celery, cook for a few minutes in a little butter, and mix in the herbs and seasoning, including the grated rind of half an orange and the juice of a whole. Rub the skin of the duck with butter and season.
3. Heat the oil in a roasting pan. When hot, add the duck and baste with hot oil. Roast for 20 minutes per pound, basting every 15 minutes. During the last half hour, baste with melted honey. The honey produces shiny brown skin.
4. Meanwhile, prepare the orange salad: Remove the thin orange skin from 1 orange with a peeler, and cut into match-like shreds. Boil for 3 minutes in water; drain, refresh under the cold tap to restore the color, leave to dry. With a sharp serrated knife, remove the pith and skin from the oranges and cut into thin slices. Place in overlapping circles in a glass dish. Mix the salt, sugar, and pepper with oil, then add lemon juice. Spoon the dressing over the oranges and sprinkle orange shreds over the top. Chill in the refrigerator.
5. When the duck is done, remove from the oven and keep warm on a serving dish. Pour off the excess fat, and pour red wine and stock into the roasting pan. Bring to a boil, and cook until well flavored; add seasoning. The gravy may be too sweet because of the honey, so a little lemon juice may be added.

Hot Game Pie

05:30
02:25
Serves 5–6
Midwest

American	Ingredients	Metric/Imperial
	Flaky pastry for an 8–9 inch, 1-crust pie (see Index)	
2	Partridge, pigeons, or pheasant as available	2
6 tbsp	Red wine	5 tbsp
6 tbsp	Cognac	5 tbsp
1 tbsp	Finely chopped parsley	1 tbsp
2 tbsp	Finely chopped onion	1½ tbsp
3 tbsp	Oil	2 tbsp
4 tbsp	Butter or margarine	50 g/2 oz
¾ lb	Veal, cut into strips	350 g/12 oz
½ lb	Cooked ham, cut into strips	225 g/8 oz
1 cup	Sliced mushrooms	100 g/4 oz
¼ tsp	Oregano	¼ tsp
¼ tsp	Marjoram	¼ tsp
1	Bay leaf	1
1 cup	Game stock or consomme	250 ml/8 fl oz
	Egg for glazing	

1. Cut the game into serving pieces, removing as much bone as possible.
2. Put the wine, cognac, parsley, onion, and seasoning into a bowl; put in the pieces of game and marinate for 3–4 hours; then remove and drain well.

3. Preheat the oven to 450°F/230°C/Gas Mark 8.

4. Heat the oil and 3 tablespoons [40 g/1½ oz] of the butter in a frying pan. Sauté the game until golden brown.

5. Put the veal and ham into a deep oval baking dish, arrange the pieces of game on top, add the mushrooms and herbs. Cover with the marinade and stock, and dot with a few pieces of butter.

6. Roll out the pastry into an oval shape. Dampen the edge of the dish and line with a strip of pastry; dampen the strip, put on the pastry, and press the edges well together. Press and flute the edge of the pastry. Make a hole in the center and decorate with pastry leaves made from the trimmings. Glaze with beaten egg and bake for 20 minutes. Reduce the heat to 375°F/190°C/Gas Mark 5, and bake for 1½–2 hours.

Cold Game Pie

	12:25		
	02:00	Serves 4–5	Midwest

American	Ingredients	Metric/Imperial
	Hot water pastry (see Index)	
¾ lb	Sausage meat	350 g/12 oz
½ cup	Diced lean ham	75 g/3 oz
¾ cup	Cubed lean steak	150 g/5 oz
	Meat from 1 cooked pheasant or 2 pigeons or partridge	
1	Egg	1
1 envelope	Gelatin [gelatine]	1 sachet
1 cup	Meat stock	250 ml/8 fl oz

1. Preheat the oven to 425°F/220°C/Gas Mark 7.

2. Make the pastry and keep it warm while preparing the ingredients for the filling. Cut off a quarter of the dough, and keep it warm for the top.

3. Butter a 7-inch loose-bottomed cake pan and line it with the dough rolled about ¼ inch thick.

4. Line the base and sides of the pie with sausage meat. Mix the ham, steak, and game; season well and fill the pie with the mixture.

5. Dampen the edge of the pie, roll out the dough for the lid, and press it on tightly, fluting the edge. Make a small hole in the center and decorate the top of the pie with pastry leaves made from the pastry trimmings.

6. Bake for 1½ hours. Then remove the pie from the cake pan and put it onto a baking sheet. Brush the top and sides with beaten egg, return to the oven, and bake for ½ hour.

7. Dissolve the gelatin in the meat stock and pour into the pie through the hole in the top. Let it get quite cold—preferably overnight—before cutting. Serve with salad.

Cold Game Soufflé

	12:00		
	00:00	Serves 4	South

American	Ingredients	Metric/Imperial
2 cups	Ground [minced] cold game or turkey	350 g/12 oz
1¾ cups	Stock	425 ml/15 fl oz
1 tbsp	Gelatin [gelatine]	1 tbsp

Hot Game Cutlets

American	Ingredients	Metric/Imperial
3–4 tbsp	Dry sherry or port	2–3½ tbsp
2	Eggs	2
3–4 tbsp	Heavy [double] cream, whipped	2–3½ tbsp
	Cucumber and watercress for garnish	
	Seasoning	

1. Grind the game. Dissolve the gelatin in hot stock. Add to the game with sherry or port. Beat the egg yolks thoroughly and stir into the mixture. Add seasoning.

2. When cold and almost set, add the whipped cream and fold in the beaten egg whites. Turn into a soufflé dish and let set. Keep cold in the refrigerator.

3. Garnish with cucumber and watercress, and serve with a salad.

Hot Game Cutlets

	00:20		
	00:05	Serves 4	Midwest

American	Ingredients	Metric/Imperial
1 cup	Chopped game	175 g/6 oz
2 tbsp	Butter	25 g/1 oz
1	Onion, chopped	1
1 cup	Mashed potato	225 g/8 oz
1 tbsp	Chopped herbs	1 tbsp
2 tbsp	Chutney	1½ tbsp
1	Egg	1
3–4 tbsp	Flour	2–3½ tbsp
1–2	Beaten eggs with 1 teaspoon oil	1–2
1 cup	Dry white bread crumbs	50 g/2 oz
	Fat for deep frying	
1 can (8 oz)	Tomato sauce	1 tin (225 g/8 oz)

1. Chop the cold game. Heat the butter and cook the chopped onion until tender. Add to the game with enough mashed potato to make a firm mixture. Add herbs, chutney, beaten egg, and seasoning.

2. Mold into cutlet shapes and, when firm, roll in seasoned flour. Then brush with eggs beaten with oil and cover completely with dry white bread crumbs.

3. Heat the fat and fry the cutlets for a few minutes until golden brown; drain and serve with tomato sauce.

Continental Roast Goose with Chestnut and Liver Stuffing

Continental Roast Goose with Chestnut and Liver Stuffing 🍗🍗🍗

01:00
04:00
Serves 6–8
Midwest

American	Ingredients	Metric/Imperial
1 (8–10 lb)	Goose	1 (3.5–4.5 kg/ 8–10 lb)
2 lb	Chestnuts	900 g/2 lb
2 cups	Stock	450 ml/¾ pint
6	Apples	6
2	Onions	2
1	Goose liver	1
1 tbsp	Butter	15 g/½ oz
2 cups	Bread crumbs	100 g/4 oz
2 tbsp	Chopped parsley	1½ tbsp
1 tbsp	Mixed thyme and marjoram	1 tbsp
	Grated rind of ½ lemon	
2 tbsp	Flour	1½ tbsp
4–6 tbsp	Oil	3½–5 tbsp
2 tbsp	Red currant jelly	1½ tbsp
	Juice of ½ lemon	
1½ cups	Cider or stock	350 ml/12 fl oz

1. Preheat the oven to 400°F/200°C/Gas Mark 6.
2. Prepare the stuffing: Put the chestnuts in boiling water for 5–6 minutes, or until the skins will remove completely. Then cover the peeled nuts with stock and simmer until tender. Drain and let cool. Reserve the stock for moistening the stuffing. Peel and chop the apples, chop the onions, and cook for 3–4 minutes; then mix in the chestnuts. Cook the goose liver in butter and, when firm, chop and add to the stuffing with the bread crumbs. Add the chopped parsley, thyme, marjoram, lemon rind, salt, and pepper. Mix together, adding enough stock to make a moist but firm mixture.
3. Stuff the goose and sew up the opening. Prick the goose all over lightly with a sharp fork; sprinkle with 1 tablespoon of flour and seasoning. Heat the oil or fat in a roasting pan. Put the

goose into the pan, on a rack if possible to allow the fat to drain. Cook for 20–25 minutes per pound, basting every 20 minutes, turning from side to side. Reduce the heat slightly after the first 20 minutes. For the last 30 minutes, pour off most of the fat, place the bird breast up, and allow to brown, raising the heat again if the breast is not becoming crisp and brown. Test with a skewer in the thick part of the leg to see whether it is cooked. When done, remove to a serving dish and keep warm while making the gravy.
4. Skim off any remaining fat from the roasting pan, sprinkle in 1 tablespoon of flour, and blend with the roasting juices in the pan. Add the red currant jelly and lemon juice; stir in well. Add the cider or stock and bring to a boil. Cook for 2–3 minutes. Strain, season to taste, and serve hot with the goose.

Cassoulet of Goose 🍗🍗🍗

12:15
04:15
Serves 4–6
South

American	Ingredients	Metric/Imperial
2–3 lb	Cooked goose joints	900 g/1.5 kg/ 2–3 lb
2–3 cups	Dried lima beans (medium sized or they will need longer cooking)	225–350 g/ 8–12 oz
3–4 cups	Strong brown meat stock (or water and beef bouillon cubes)	700 ml–1 l/ 1¼–1¾ pints
5–6 tbsp	Goose fat (or butter)	4–5 tbsp
2	Medium onions	2
2–3	Cloves garlic	2–3
4–5 slices	Fat smoked bacon	4–5 rashers
4–5 tbsp	Tomato purée	3½–4 tbsp
2 tbsp	Chopped parsley and thyme	1½ tbsp
	A pinch of sage	
1	Bay leaf	1
6–8	Slices garlic sausage	6–8
1½–2 cups	Dried white bread crumbs	75–100 g/3–4 oz

1. The day before you cook the cassoulet, put the beans to soak. The next day, put them in a pan with water and bring slowly to a boil; lower the heat and simmer for 2½ hours. Drain.
2. While the beans cook, prepare the stock: Cut the goose into portions, add the carcass to the cooking stock to add flavor, and simmer until required. Melt 2–3 [1½–2] tablespoons of fat in which the goose was roasted. Add the sliced onions, crushed garlic, and chopped bacon; cook for 5–6 minutes. Add the tomato purée, herbs, and seasoning. Add the drained stock. Bring to a boil and simmer for 30 minutes.
3. Preheat the oven to 300°F/150°C/Gas Mark 2.
4. Add the drained beans to the stock ingredients and stir well. Then pour half this mixture into the bottom of a thick casserole. Put in pieces of goose; then pour the remaining bean mixture on top. Add the sliced garlic sausage and submerge under the liquid. Bring to a boil, add more seasoning if necessary, then sprinkle a thick layer of bread crumbs all over the surface. Dot the surface with 2 tablespoons [25 g/1 oz] of butter or goose fat. Put into the oven and cook for about 1 hour, until the beans have cooked and the top is crusty and brown.

Fried Goose with Apple Rings

Potted Goose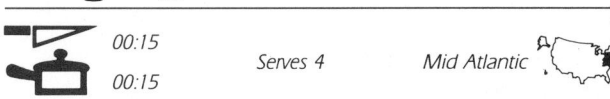

	00:20		
	00:35	Serves 6–8	Midwest

American	Ingredients	Metric/Imperial
1	Goose liver	1
1–1½ lb	Chopped cold goose	450–675 g/ 1–1½ lb
1½–2½ cups	Butter	350–575 g/ ¾–1¼ lb
1	Onion	1
1	Clove garlic	1
2–3 tbsp	Brandy or sherry	1½–2 tbsp
1 tbsp	Chopped parsley and thyme	1 tbsp
½ tsp	Powdered mace (or slightly less nutmeg)	½ tsp

1. Preheat the oven to 300°F/150°C/Gas Mark 2.
2. Melt 2 tablespoons [25 g/1 oz] of butter and cook the chopped goose liver until it has changed color and stiffened. Remove and cool. Add 2 more tablespoons [25 g/1 oz] of butter and soften the chopped onion and crushed garlic for 6–8 minutes without browning. Mix in herbs; add to the liver.
3. Chop the cold goose meat finely and mix with the liver mixture. Pound together until smooth or put into a liquidizer to grind finely, adding a little brandy or sherry if the mixture seems to stick.
4. Weigh the resulting pâté and for each pound add 1 cup [225 g/8 oz] of softened butter. Season with powdered mace or nutmeg, salt, and pepper. Beat together to mix thoroughly. Pack into a thick ovenproof mold. Cover with a lid; heat through in the oven for 15–20 minutes. Remove and cover with a layer of unsalted butter. This helps the potted goose to keep longer.
5. Serve with lots of toast or hot French bread and butter.

Fried Goose with Apple Rings 🍲

	00:15		
	00:15	Serves 4	Mid Atlantic

American	Ingredients	Metric/Imperial
8	Slices cooked breast of goose	8
4–5 tbsp	Flour	3½–4 tbsp
1–2	Eggs	1–2
½ cup	Oil	125 ml/4 fl oz
1–1½ cups	Fresh white bread crumbs	75 g/3 oz
4–5 tbsp	Butter	50–65 g/ 2–2½ oz
2	Cooking apples	2
1 tbsp	Sugar	1 tbsp
1 cup	Brown gravy or sauce	250 ml/8 fl oz
1 tbsp	White vinegar	1 tbsp
2 tsp	Worcestershire sauce	2 tsp

1. Cut 8 thin slices of goose from the breast of the cooked bird. Season well. Cover well with flour, then dip in egg beaten with a little oil until completely coated. Then cover with dried white bread crumbs.
2. Heat the remaining oil and, when hot, add the butter. When foaming, cook the slices of goose until golden brown and crisp all over. Remove, drain, and keep warm.
3. Peel, core, and slice the apples into 8 rings. Reheat the fat in which the goose was fried, having removed any loose crumbs which may burn. Fry the apple rings until golden brown, sprinkling each side with sugar to brown.
4. Make the sauce by adding 1 tablespoon of wine vinegar and 2 tablespoons [1½ tbsp] Worcestershire sauce to brown the gravy. Heat and season to taste.

Guinea Fowl in White Sauce

Guinea Fowl in White Wine Sauce

| | 00:15 | Serves 4 | Midwest |
| | 01:10 | | |

American	Ingredients	Metric/Imperial
1	Guinea fowl large enough to feed 4, or 2 smaller birds	1
1 cup	Mixed chopped onion, carrot and celery	100 g/4 oz
3	Parsley stalks	3
1	Bay leaf	1
6	Peppercorns	6
2	Chicken bouillon [stock] cubes	2
1 cup	Mushrooms	100 g/4 oz
3–4 tbsp	Butter	40–50 g/ 1½–2 oz
1 tsp	Lemon juice	1 tsp
3 tbsp	Flour	2 tbsp
½ cup	White wine	125 ml/4 fl oz
¾ cup	Stock	175 ml/6 fl oz
4–5 tbsp	Cream	3½–4 tbsp
	A pinch of mace	

1. Put the cleaned guinea fowl in a large pan with the mixed chopped vegetables, parsley stalks, bay leaf, peppercorns, and 2 chicken bouillon cubes. Bring to a boil and cook gently until tender. Drain and carve, placing the pieces in a serving dish.
2. Cook the quartered mushrooms in butter and lemon juice. Add the flour and, when blended, the white wine and stock. Bring to a boil slowly. Simmer for 2–3 minutes. Add the cream and seasoning. Spoon over the guinea fowl, and serve hot with rice or fried potatoes and a green vegetable.

Roast Goose with Sage and Onion Stuffing 🍴🍴🍴

| | 00:30 | Serves 6–8 | Midwest |
| | 04:25 | | |

American	Ingredients	Metric/Imperial
1 (8–10 lb)	Young goose	1 (3.5–4.5 kg/ 8–10 lb)
6–8 tbsp	Butter	75–100 g/3–4 oz
2 lb	Onions	900 g/2 lb
8–9	Fresh sage leaves (or 2–3 tbsp powdered dried sage)	8–9
2	Large cooking apples	2
3 cups	Fresh white bread crumbs	175 g/6 oz
	Grated rind of 1 lemon	
1	Egg	1
2 cups	Strong stock made from giblets of goose (or chicken bouillon [stock] cube)	450 ml/¾ pint
4–5 tbsp	Oil	3½–4 tbsp
2 tsp	Flour	2 tsp
	A little cider	
1 (25 oz) jar	Apple sauce	1 (700 g/25 oz) jar

1. Preheat the oven to 400°F/200°C/Gas Mark 6.
2. Prepare the stuffing: Melt the butter and cook the sliced onions slowly for 10–15 minutes without browning, stirring frequently. If using fresh sage leaves, dip these into boiling water for 1–2 minutes, drain, and chop. Peel and chop 1 apple and mix with the bread crumbs; add the chopped (or dried) sage and lemon rind. Mix in the softened onions, beaten egg, and a few spoonfuls of stock. Season well with salt and pepper.
3. Wipe the goose thoroughly inside and out. Fill the cavity inside with stuffing, allowing roughly 1 cup [100 g/4 oz] per pound weight of bird. Sew up the opening. Prick the breast lightly with a sharp fork to allow the fat to run while cooking. Heat the oil in the oven and, when hot, put the goose into a roasting pan, on a rack if possible. Baste well with hot oil. Season with salt and pepper. Put into the oven and cook for 20–25 minutes per pound, basting every 20 minutes. Reduce the heat to 350°F/180°C/Gas Mark 4. During the last half hour, put a cooking apple into the roasting pan, as this gives the gravy a pleasant tang. If the goose does not have a nice brown crisp skin at the last basting, increase the heat to 400°F/200°C/Gas Mark 6 for the last 20 minutes. Remove the bird when done and keep hot while making the gravy.
5. Pour off all fat from the roasting pan and sprinkle in the flour. Add the stock and bring to a boil; mash the roasted apple into the sauce; a little cider may be added in place of some stock. Strain gravy into a sauceboat, and serve the apple sauce separately.

Grouse, Partridge or Pheasant Pâté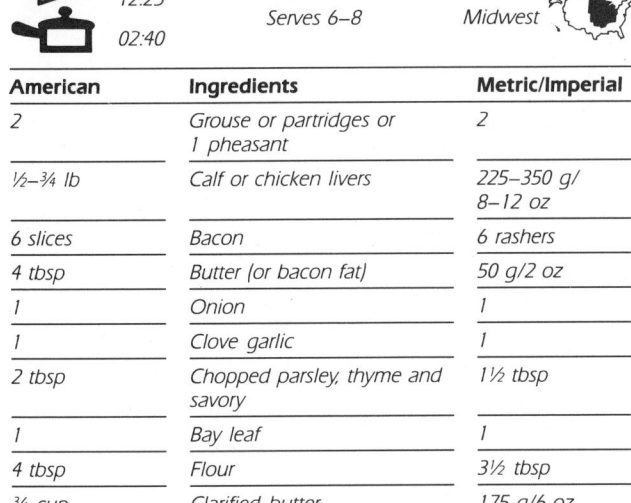

| | 12:25 | Serves 6–8 | Midwest |
| | 02:40 | | |

American	Ingredients	Metric/Imperial
2	Grouse or partridges or 1 pheasant	2
½–¾ lb	Calf or chicken livers	225–350 g/ 8–12 oz
6 slices	Bacon	6 rashers
4 tbsp	Butter (or bacon fat)	50 g/2 oz
1	Onion	1
1	Clove garlic	1
2 tbsp	Chopped parsley, thyme and savory	1½ tbsp
1	Bay leaf	1
4 tbsp	Flour	3½ tbsp
¾ cup	Clarified butter	175 g/6 oz

1. Preheat the oven to 325°F/160°C/Gas Mark 3.
2. Cut the meat off the birds and cut it in slices; chop the liver and bacon. Melt 2 tablespoons [25 g/1 oz] of butter (or bacon fat) and cook the chopped onion and crushed garlic until tender. Add the chopped bacon and liver; cook for a few minutes. Let cool slightly; then grind in a liquidizer or pound in a bowl. Add seasoning and chopped herbs.
3. Cook the game pieces gently in 2 tablespoons [25 g/1 oz] of butter for 2–3 minutes. Then let them cool. Arrange the game and liver paste in layers in a thick casserole with a lid, making sure the top layer is liver. Put a bay leaf on top. Cover, and seal with a flour and water paste.
4. Put into a deep baking pan of hot water, and cook in the oven for 2½ hours. When cooked, remove the lid and put several layers of waxed paper on top. Press down with a weight and leave overnight. Either turn out and eat at once or pour a layer of clarified butter over the top and keep in the refrigerator.

Salmi of Grouse or Partridge

| | 00:10 | Serves 4–6 | South |
| | 01:00 | | |

American	Ingredients	Metric/Imperial
2	Grouse or partridges or small guinea fowl	2
3 tbsp	Oil	2 tbsp
3–4 slices	Bacon	3–4 rashers
2 cups	Strong stock	450 ml/¾ pint
½ cup	Red wine (or port)	125 ml/4 fl oz
1 tbsp	Flour	1 tbsp
1 tbsp	Butter	15 g/½ oz
1 tbsp	Chopped parsley	1 tbsp

1. Preheat the oven 300°F/150°C/Gas Mark 2.
2. Heat the oil in a roasting pan, cover the birds with bacon, and roast in hot fat for 20 minutes. Remove from the oven and let cool slightly. Carve the birds into pieces and put into a casserole. Cover with strong stock, add herbs and seasoning, and cook gently in the oven for 30 minutes, or until tender.
3. Remove the birds to a serving dish and keep warm in the oven. Bring the pan drippings to a boil and reduce the quantity slightly. Add the wine (or port) and cook for a few minutes. Thicken the sauce with small pieces of butter and flour paste, and continue heating until the sauce thickens. Spoon over pieces of game, sprinkle with chopped parsley, and serve.

Grouse, Partridge or Pheasant Pâté

American Braised Guinea Fowl

| | 00:15 | Serves 4 | United States |
| | 01:00 | | |

American	Ingredients	Metric/Imperial
1	Guinea fowl	1
3 tbsp	Butter	40 g/1½ oz
1	Onion	1
1	Clove garlic	1
½ tsp	Dry mustard	½ tsp
2 tsp	Wine vinegar	2 tsp
¾ cup	Chicken stock	175 ml/6 fl oz
1 tbsp	Chopped parsley and tarragon	1 tbsp
2 cups	Cooked rice	450 g/1 lb
1 tsp	Paprika	1 tsp

1. Preheat the oven to 350°F/180°C/Gas Mark 4.
2. Cut the guinea fowl into quarters and brown all over in butter. Add the sliced onion, crushed garlic, mustard, vinegar, stock, chopped herbs, and seasoning. Simmer until the liquid is much reduced, and the bird is done.
3. Boil the rice and arrange in a ring around the dish, spoon the guinea fowl into the center, and sprinkle with paprika as garnish.

Gougere of Grouse, Partridge, and Mushrooms

Roast Guinea Fowl

 00:20
02:05   Serves 4   United States

American	Ingredients	Metric/Imperial
2	Guinea fowl	2
1 cup	Dry white bread crumbs	50 g/2 oz
1 cup	Butter	225 g/8 oz
1	Onion	1
½ cup	Chopped mushrooms	50 g/2 oz
4 tbsp	Chopped parsley	3½ tbsp
2 tbsp	Chopped thyme and basil	1½ tbsp
	A pinch of mace	
1	Egg	1
	A little milk	
1 cup	Stock	250 ml/8 fl oz
	A little white wine (optional)	

1. Preheat the oven to 350°F/180°C/Gas Mark 4.
2. Prepare the mushroom and herb stuffing. Put the bread crumbs in a bowl. Melt ½ cup [100 g/4 oz] of butter and cook the finely chopped onion gently for 5 minutes without browning. Add the mushrooms and cook for 2 minutes. Stir into the bread crumbs. Add parsley, thyme, and basil. Season with salt, pepper, and mace. Add the beaten egg and enough milk to moisten without becoming runny. Let stand for a few minutes before stuffing into the guinea fowl. Sew up the openings.
3. Rub the breast and legs of guinea fowl over with 2 tablespoons [25 g/1 oz] of butter. Sprinkle with seasoning. Melt 4–5 tablespoons [50–65 g/2–2½ oz] of butter in a roasting pan. When hot, put the bird into the pan and baste. Pour in ½ cup [125 ml/4 fl oz] of stock. Roast slowly in the oven, allowing 25 minutes per pound unstuffed weight, basting frequently and turning the birds from side to side. Stand them breast side up for last 30 minutes and turn up the heat slightly to brown. When done, remove from the pan and place on a hot dish; keep warm. Pour off the fat from the roasting pan, add ½ cup [125 ml/4 fl oz] of stock, and stir into the pan drippings to make a delicious gravy. (A little white wine can be added to the gravy, if desired.)

Gougere of Grouse, Partridge and Mushrooms

 00:45
01:05   Serves 4   Midwest

American	Ingredients	Metric/Imperial
1 cup	Flour	100 g/4 oz
½ cup	Butter	100 g/4 oz
2	Eggs	2
4 tbsp	Grated Cheddar cheese	3½ tbsp
½ tsp	Dried mustard	½ tsp
	Filling	
1 cup	Cold cooked grouse and partridge (or other game)	175 g/6 oz
2 tbsp	Butter	25 g/1 oz
1	Onion, chopped	1
6–8	Mushrooms, sliced	6–8
1 tbsp	Flour	1 tbsp
1 tsp	Tomato purée	1 tsp
½ cup	Stock	125 ml/4 fl oz
2 tbsp	Sherry	1½ tbsp
1 tbsp	Chopped herbs	1 tbsp
½ cup	Cooked vegetables, as available	50 g/2 oz
1 tsp	Worcestershire sauce	1 tsp
2–3 tbsp	Grated Parmesan cheese	1½–2 tbsp
2 tbsp	Bread crumbs	1½ tbsp
1 tbsp	Chopped parsley	1 tbsp

1. Preheat the oven to 375°F/190°C/Gas Mark 5.
2. Sift the flour with a large pinch of salt and put in the oven to keep warm. In a sloping sided pan, heat ½ cup [125 ml/4 fl oz] of water and ¼ cup [50 g/2 oz] of butter. When the butter has melted, bring to a boil. As soon as it boils, remove from the heat and add flour all at once. Beat hard with a wooden spoon until the mixture forms a ball in the bottom of the pan. Spread out on a plate to cool. Beat the eggs. When the mixture is cool, add the egg by degrees, beating hard between each addition. The final mixture should be shiny and smooth, and will hold its shape. A little egg may be left over. Add the cheese with mustard and seasoning.
3. Make the filling: Melt the butter and cook the chopped onion for 5–6 minutes until soft. Add the mushrooms, cook for 1 minute. Sprinkle in the flour. When mixed in, add the tomato purée and stock. Bring to a boil; cook for a few minutes to thicken. Add the sherry, diced game, herbs, and any cooked vegetables, such as peas, beans, corn, or pimento, that are available. Add Worcestershire sauce. Let cool slightly.
4. Butter an ovenproof dish about 3 inches deep. Arrange the pastry in a ring around the outside of the dish. Brush over with any remaining egg to give a shiny finish. Spoon the filling into the center of the pastry ring. Sprinkle the top with grated cheese and bread crumbs. Bake in the oven for 30–45 minutes. Sprinkle the top with chopped parsley, and serve.

Turkish Guinea Fowl

Turkish Guinea Fowl

	00:15	Serves 4–6	Midwest
	02:10		

American	Ingredients	Metric/Imperial
1	Guinea fowl	1
2–3 tbsp	Oil	1½–2 tbsp
3	Onions	3
	Several parsley stalks	
1	Bay leaf	1
8	Peppercorns	8
3–4 tbsp	Butter	40–50 g/ 1½–2 oz
1	Clove garlic	1
1 cup	Rice	225 g/8 oz
3 cups	Stock	700 ml/1¼ pints
4 tbsp	Raisins	3½ tbsp
1 tsp	Ground cinnamon	1 tsp
1 tbsp	Chopped herbs	1 tbsp
3 tbsp	Halved almonds	2 tbsp
1 tbsp	Chopped parsley	1 tbsp

1. Preheat the oven to 325°F/160°C/Gas Mark 3.

2. Brown the guinea fowl all over in oil. Then put into a large pan or casserole and barely cover with water; add 2 sliced onions, parsley stalks, bay leaf, peppercorns, and salt. Cook gently until tender, about 1½ hours. Drain and let cool, reserving the stock for cooking the rice.

3. Heat 3–4 tablespoons [40–50 g/1½–2 oz] of butter in a pan; cook 1 chopped onion and the crushed garlic until golden. Add the rice and cook for a few minutes. Pour in the stock and bring to a boil; add the raisins and herbs, cinnamon, and seasoning. Cut the guinea fowl meat into good-sized chunks and add to the rice mixture. Cover the dish and cook in the oven for 20–30 minutes, until all the liquid has been absorbed and the guinea fowl is tender. Sprinkle the top with browned almonds and chopped parsley, and serve hot.

Guinea Fowl Chasseur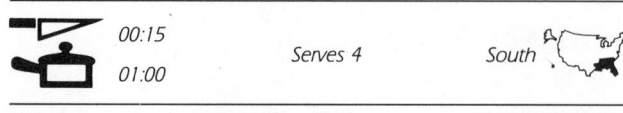

00:15
01:00   Serves 4   South

American	Ingredients	Metric/Imperial
1 large or 2 small	Guinea fowl	1 large or 2 small
5 tbsp	Butter	65 g/2½ oz
½ cup	Chopped mushrooms	50 g/2 oz
3	Shallots (or 1 mild onion)	3
½ cup	White wine	125 g/4 fl oz
3 tsp	Tomato purée	3 tsp
1 cup	Brown sauce (or strong stock)	250 ml/8 fl oz
1 tsp	Chopped tarragon	1 tsp
	Garnish	
4 slices	Bacon	4 rashers
2	Large slices white bread	2
4–6 tbsp	Oil	3½–5 tbsp
3–4 tbsp	Butter	40–50 g/1½–2 oz
1	Guinea fowl liver	1
1 tsp	Chopped onion (or a little onion powder)	1 tsp
1 tsp	Sherry	1 tsp
1 tbsp	Chopped parsley	1 tbsp

1. Preheat the oven to 350°F/180°C/Gas Mark 4.
2. Cook the bird as in Pheasant Chasseur (see Index) except for the garnish.
3. Make the garnish: Cut the bacon slices in half, roll up, and put on a skewer. Broil [grill] or bake in the oven until crisp. Cut the bread into triangles. Dry these until golden brown in oil and butter. Drain; keep hot.
4. Cook the liver in 2 tablespoons [25 g/1 oz] of butter with a little onion and a teaspoon sherry. When cooked, spread the mashed liver onto the croutons and arrange around the dish alternately with the bacon rolls. Sprinkle with chopped parsley.

Braised Partridges with Cabbage

00:20
01:50   Serves 4   Midwest

American	Ingredients	Metric/Imperial
2	Partridges	2
2–3 tbsp	Butter	25–40 g/1–1½ oz
2	Onions	2
1	Carrot	1
1 tbsp	Flour	1 tbsp
1 cup	Stock	250 ml/8 fl oz
2 tbsp	Chopped parsley	1½ tbsp
1	Firm cabbage	1
8–10 slices	Bacon	8–10 rashers
1	Bay leaf	1

1. Preheat the oven to 325°F/160°C/Gas Mark 3.
2. Cut each partridge in half, and brown all over in the butter. Remove and keep warm. Add the sliced onions and carrot and cook until golden brown. Stir in the flour, brown slightly, and add the stock and chopped parsley.
3. Cut the cabbage into quarters and remove the hard core. Boil in salted water for 5–7 minutes; drain and let dry slightly.
4. Line the casserole with bacon slices and place half the cabbage on top with half the sauce. Then put the partridges on top. Place the remaining cabbage on top, and cover with the rest of the sauce. Put a bay leaf on top. Put on a lid, and cook in the oven for 1–1½ hours, until the partridges and cabbage are tender.
5. Remove from the oven and place the partridges on top of the cabbage to serve. Remove the bay leaf.

Pheasant Chasseur

00:20
01:00   Serves 4   Midwest

American	Ingredients	Metric/Imperial
1	Pheasant	1
5 tbsp	Butter	65 g/2½ oz
½ cup	Chopped mushrooms	50 g/2 oz
3	Shallots or 1 mild onion	3
½ cup	White wine	125 ml/4 fl oz
3 tsp	Tomato purée	3 tsp
1 cup	Brown sauce (or strong stock)	250 ml/8 fl oz
1 tsp	Chopped tarragon	1 tsp
2 tbsp	Chopped parsley	1½ tbsp

1. Preheat the oven to 350°F/180°C/Gas Mark 4.
2. Make the sauce: Heat 2 tablespoons [25 g/1 oz] butter or oil, and brown the chopped mushrooms for a few minutes. Add the chopped shallots or onions, cook for another minute. Add the white wine and reduce the liquid by half. Add the tomato purée and brown sauce. Cook together for a minute or two, then add chopped tarragon and 1 tablespoon chopped parsley.
3. Joint the pheasant and brown each piece in 2–3 tablespoons [25–40 g/1–1½ oz] of butter. Put into a casserole and pour the sauce over. Cook in the oven for 40–50 minutes until tender. Just before serving, add ½ teaspoon butter to the sauce. Sprinkle the top with the remaining parsley and serve hot.

Normandy Style Pheasant

00:10
01:05   Serves 4   South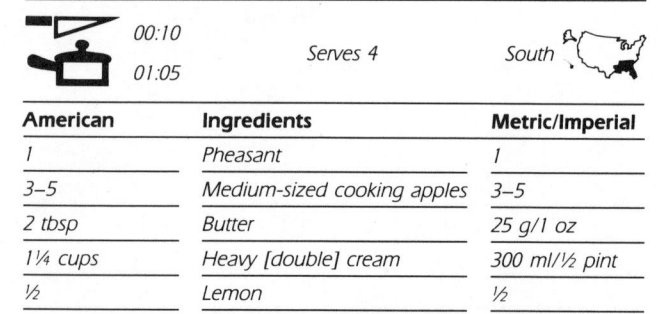

American	Ingredients	Metric/Imperial
1	Pheasant	1
3–5	Medium-sized cooking apples	3–5
2 tbsp	Butter	25 g/1 oz
1¼ cups	Heavy [double] cream	300 ml/½ pint
½	Lemon	½
4–5 tbsp	Calvados [optional]	3½–4 tbsp

1. Preheat the oven to 425°F/220°C/Gas Mark 7.
2. Put the pheasant onto a rotary spit if available or into a hot oven in a little butter, and brown all over for 10–15 minutes. Remove and put into a casserole, which is lined with half the peeled, sliced cooking apples. Pour over any fat or juice from the spit pan or roasting pan, and put the remaining apples on top.
3. Put into the oven at 350°F/180°C/Gas Mark 4, and cook for about 30–35 minutes. Then add cream and lemon juice, and Calvados if available. Return to the oven and cook for 10–15 minutes, until the pheasant is tender.
4. Serve with the apple cream mixture as a thick sauce.

Braised Pheasant with Chestnut Puree and Orange

 00:25 / 01:20   Serves 4–6   Mid Atlantic

American	Ingredients	Metric/Imperial
1	Large pheasant	1
4–5 tbsp	Butter	50–60 g/2–2½ oz
2	Onions	2
2	Small carrots	2
2–3	Stalks celery	2–3
2 tbsp	Flour	1½ tbsp
1½ cups	Stock	350 ml/12 fl oz
¼ cup	Cider (or white wine)	60 ml/2 fl oz
3	Oranges	3
1 tbsp	Mixed herbs	1 tbsp
1 can (1 lb)	Chestnut purée	1 tin (450 g/1 lb

1. Preheat the oven to 350°F/180°C/Gas Mark 4.
2. Melt 2–3 tablespoons [25–40 g/1–1½ oz] of butter in a casserole. Brown the bird slowly all over. Remove the bird and keep warm. Now add the sliced onions, carrots, and celery. Cook until they are beginning to brown slightly; add the flour and cook for a few minutes. Add the stock and cider or wine. Stir well and bring to a boil. Simmer for a few minutes. Add 3 strips of orange zest, herbs, and seasoning. Put the pheasant back into the casserole and spoon the sauce over it. Cover the casserole and put it into the oven for about 50 minutes, until the pheasant is tender. When the pheasant is removed from the casserole, boil the cooking juices and put into a liquidizer or blender. When smooth, return to the pan and, if too thick, add a little extra stock. Season to taste and reheat.
3. Meanwhile, melt 2 tablespoons [25 g/1 oz] of butter in a pan and add the chestnut purée. Heat, to soften the purée, adding 2–3 tablespoons [1½–2 tbsp] strong stock and seasoning. Keep warm until the pheasant is tender; then place it down the center of a serving dish. Place the carved slices and joints on top. Spoon the sauce over all.
4. Remove the zest of orange carefully and cut into thin shreds. Cook in boiling water for a few minutes; drain and put in cold water to restore the color. Remove the white pith and skin from the oranges with a sharp knife and divide into segments. Arrange the orange segments around the edge of the dish and the orange strips down the center. Serve hot with fried or croquette potatoes, and a green vegetable.

Pheasant Casserole

 00:15 / 01:40   Serves 4   Midwest

American	Ingredients	Metric/Imperial
1	Pheasant	1
2 slices	Bacon	2 rashers
½ cup	Butter or margarine	100 g/4 oz
2–3	Shallots, peeled and chopped	2–3
1 can (8 oz)	Button mushrooms	1 tin (225 g/8 oz)
	Chicken stock	
	Lemon juice	
Stuffing		
½ cup	Chopped cooked ham	75 g/3 oz
6 tbsp	Cooked rice	5 tbsp
3 tbsp	Sherry	2 tbsp
	Salt and pepper	
	Pinch marjoram	
	Pinch powdered thyme	
1	Egg	1

1. Preheat the oven to 325°F/160°C/Gas Mark 3.
2. Mix all the ingredients for the stuffing and bind with a beaten egg. Stuff the pheasant, truss, and wrap the bacon slices over the breast.
3. Heat the butter in a frying pan and brown the pheasant all over. Then put into a casserole.
4. Sauté the shallots and drained mushrooms in the remaining butter, and add to the casserole. Moisten with a little stock, cover, and cook for about 1½ hours.
5. Just before serving, adjust the seasoning and sprinkle with lemon juice.

Pheasant Normandy

02:00 / 01:20   Serves 4   South

American	Ingredients	Metric/Imperial
1	Pheasant	1
½ cup	Butter or margarine	100 g/4 oz
1½ lb	Cooking apples, peeled, cored, and sliced	675 g/1½ lb
½ cup	Light [single] cream	125 ml/4 fl oz
1 tbsp	Calvados (or cider)	1 tbsp

1. Preheat the oven to 350°F/180°C/Gas Mark 4.
2. Truss the pheasant as for roasting. Heat the butter in a frying pan, and brown the pheasant on all sides.
3. Put half the apple slices in a deep casserole, pour on a little of the butter, and place the pheasant on top. Surround with the remaining apple slices.
4. Pour the remaining butter and cream on top and sprinkle with salt and pepper. Cover tightly and cook for 1–1¼ hours.
5. When ready to serve, remove the trussing string and place the pheasant on a serving dish. Add the calvados to the contents of the casserole, adjust the seasoning (a little sugar may also be necessary), and serve the sauce separately.

Pheasant à la Creme

 00:10
01:05
Serves 4–6   Mid Atlantic

American	Ingredients	Metric/Imperial
1	Large pheasant	1
8 tbsp	Butter	100 g/4 oz
1	Onion	1
1 tbsp	Chopped parsley	1 tbsp
1 cup	Heavy [double] cream	250 ml/8 fl oz
1	Pheasant liver	1
1	Large slice toast	1
1 tsp	Brandy (optional)	1 tsp
1 tsp	Cornstarch [cornflour] optional	1 tsp

1. Heat 6 tablespoons [75 g/3 oz] of butter. When foaming, brown the pheasant on all sides. Add a little finely chopped onion and herbs. Cover the casserole with a lid or foil, and simmer for 40 minutes, until the pheasant is nearly cooked. Add the cream and cook for 5–10 minutes.

2. Meanwhile, melt 2 tablespoons [25 g/1 oz] of butter and sauté the pheasant liver until it has changed color and stiffened. Remove from the stove and mash with seasoning and a teaspoon of brandy, if available. Spread on toast. When the pheasant is done, place on the toast and keep warm.

3. If the sauce seems rather thin and buttery, mix the cornstarch with 1 tablespoon of cold water and add to the sauce; heat gently until it thickens, season to taste, and pour over the pheasant. Serve at once.

American Pheasant

 00:10
00:20
Serves 4   Midwest

American	Ingredients	Metric/Imperial
1	Pheasant	1
1 cup	Butter	225 g/8 oz
1½–2 cups	Fresh white bread crumbs	75–100 g/3–4 oz
	Salt, pepper, and a pinch of cayenne pepper	
4	Tomatoes	4
4 slices	Bacon	4 rashers
8	Flat mushrooms	8

1. Preheat the broiler [grill].

2. Cut the pheasant open along the back with a sharp knife. Open it out and flatten with a heavy rolling pin. Season with salt and pepper. Melt the butter in a large pan and, when hot, sauté the pheasant on both sides. Remove from the heat.

3. Make plenty of fresh white bread crumbs and cover the surface of the pheasant with these; sprinkle with a little cayenne pepper. Broil [grill] the pheasant slowly so that the crumbs do not become too brown before the bird is cooked. Test with a skewer in the thickest part of the leg.

4. At the same time, broil the halved and seasoned tomatoes. Also broil the bacon and mushrooms filled with butter.

5. When the pheasant is done, serve on a platter surrounded by the broiled accompaniments and some butter balls rolled in parsley. Serve a salad with French dressing, separately.

Roast Pheasant

 00:20
01:10
Serves 4   Midwest

American	Ingredients	Metric/Imperial
1	Young pheasant cleaned and drained	1
2–3 slices	Fat bacon	2–3 rashers
1	Onion	1
6 tbsp	Butter	75 g/3 oz
2–3	Parsley stalks	2–3
1 cup	Chicken stock	250 ml/8 fl oz
1 cup	Red wine	250 ml/8 fl oz
1 lb	Potatoes	450 g/1 lb
	Fat for deep frying	

1. Tie the slices of fat bacon over the breast of pheasant; put the onion and 2 tablespoons [25 g/1 oz] of butter with some seasoning and parsley stalks inside it.

2. Melt 3–4 tablespoons [40–50 g/1½–2 oz] of butter in a roasting pan without burning. Place the pheasant in a roasting pan on a rack and baste well. Pour on ½ cup [125 ml/4 fl oz] of stock and ½ cup [125 ml/4 fl oz] of red wine. Put the bird in the oven and cook for 40–60 minutes, depending on the size, basting every 15 minutes, and turning the bird from side to side. For the last 15 minutes, remove the bacon and string, and allow the breast to brown.

3. Remove the bird and keep warm while making the gravy. Pour off the butter from the roasting juices and add ½ cup [125 ml/4 fl oz] of stock and ½ cup [125 ml/4 fl oz] of red wine. Bring to a boil, stirring constantly. Season to taste and, after 3–4 minutes, strain into a sauceboat.

4. Game chips are made from very thinly sliced potatoes, washed and dried carefully and fried in very hot, deep fat, a few at a time, until brown and crisp.

Pheasant with Grapes and White Wine Sauce

 00:20
01:00
Serves 4   Pacific Southwest

American	Ingredients	Metric/Imperial
1	Pheasant	1
4 tbsp	Butter	50 g/2 oz
2 tbsp	Flour	1½ tbsp
½ cup	Clear stock	125 ml/4 fl oz
½ cup	White wine	125 ml/4 fl oz
1½ cups	White grapes, seedless if available	175 g/6 oz
3 tbsp	Lemon juice	2 tbsp

1. Preheat the oven to 350°F/180°C/Gas Mark 4.

2. Melt the butter in a casserole; when hot, fry the pheasant gently all over until golden brown. Remove the bird. Add the flour, stock, and wine. Blend smoothly, then bring to a boil. Add the seasoning. Return the bird to the casserole. Cover and cook in the oven for 35–45 minutes, until the pheasant is tender; turn the pheasant over during cooking.

3. Peel the grapes by dipping them in boiling water for a few seconds and then in cold. Strip the skins and, if not seedless, remove the seeds. Cover with a little lemon juice to prevent browning.

4. When the bird is tender, remove and carve. Place the meat on a serving dish and keep warm. Add the grapes to the sauce and cook for a couple of minutes. Season to taste and then spoon over the pheasant. Serve with mashed potatoes and peas or spinach.

Pheasant and Mushroom Pancakes

 00:30
00:25   Serves 4–6   Midwest

American	Ingredients	Metric/Imperial
	Pancakes	
1 cup	Flour	100 g/4 oz
2	Eggs	2
1 cup	Milk	250 ml/8 fl oz
2 tsp	Butter	2 tsp
	Oil for frying	
	Filling	
1–1½ cups	Cold cooked pheasant meat	175–250 g/ 6–9 oz
6–7 tbsp	Butter	75–90 g/ 3–3½ oz
2	Medium onions	2
8	Mushrooms	8
2 tbsp	Flour	1½ tbsp
1 tsp	Tomato purée	1 tsp
	A dash of Worcestershire sauce	
¾ cup	Strong stock	175 ml/6 fl oz
2 tbsp	Sherry	1½ tbsp
1 tbsp	Chopped parsley, thyme, and marjoram	1 tbsp
	A pinch of nutmeg	
2–3 tbsp	Dry white bread crumbs	1½–2 tbsp
2 tbsp	Grated Parmesan cheese	1½ tbsp
1 tbsp	Finely chopped parsley or ¾ tsp paprika	1 tbsp

1. Preheat the broiler [grill].

2. Make the pancakes as in Turkey and Tomato Pancakes (see Index).

3. Melt 4–5 tablespoons [50–65 g/2–2½ oz] of butter and cook the finely chopped onions until tender without browning. Add the chopped mushrooms and cook for a few minutes. Sprinkle in the flour, stir well, and add the tomato purée, Worcestershire sauce, and stock. Bring to a boil and simmer 3–4 minutes. Add the sherry and herbs, seasoning, and nutmeg. Lastly, add the pheasant meat cut into shreds. Allow to heat thoroughly without boiling. Keep warm while making pancakes.

4. Put a large spoonful of filling on each pancake and fold into a triangle shape over the filling or roll up. Place in an overlapping row down the center of an ovenproof dish. Sprinkle with 2 tablespoons [25 g/1 oz] of melted butter, then with bread crumbs mixed with cheese. Broil [grill] until golden brown. Garnish with chopped parsley, or a sprinkling of paprika.

Pheasant and Mushroom Pancakes

Pheasant, Celery and Apple Casserole

00:15
01:15   Serves 4   Mid Atlantic

American	Ingredients	Metric/Imperial
1	Pheasant	1
4–5 tbsp	Butter	50–65 g/ 2–2½ oz
2	Onions	2
3–4	Stalks celery	3–4
2	Medium-sized apples	2
2 pints	Chicken stock	1 l/1¾ pints
½ cup	White wine	125 ml/4 fl oz
1 tbsp	Mixed herbs	1 tbsp
1	Bay leaf	1
2 tsp	Sugar	2 tsp
1 tbsp	Chopped parsley	1 tbsp

1. Preheat the oven to 350°F/180°C/Gas Mark 4.

2. Melt 2–3 tablespoons [25–40 g/1–1½ oz] of butter in a casserole; add the pheasant and brown slowly all over. Remove the bird and keep warm. Slice the onions, add to the butter, and soften for 5 minutes. Then add the sliced celery; cook again for 2–3 minutes and add 1 sliced apple. Return the pheasant and cover with stock and white wine. Sprinkle with salt and pepper; add the herbs, and bay leaf. Cover the casserole and cook in the oven for 50 minutes, until the bird is tender.

3. Remove the pheasant to a serving dish and carve into portions. Remove the bay leaf, then put the pan drippings and vegetables into a liquidizer or blender and blend until smooth. Reheat, skim off any surplus butter that rises to surface. Season to taste and pour over the pheasant.

4. Cut the remaining peeled and cored apple into rings, sprinkle with sugar. Melt 2 tablespoons [25 g/1 oz] of butter and fry the rings until golden brown. Place on top of the dish, and sprinkle with chopped parsley.

Roast Pheasant with Red Currant Sauce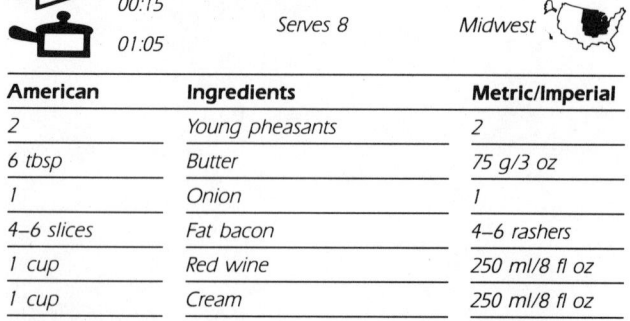

 00:15 01:05   Serves 8   Midwest

American	Ingredients	Metric/Imperial
2	Young pheasants	2
6 tbsp	Butter	75 g/3 oz
1	Onion	1
4–6 slices	Fat bacon	4–6 rashers
1 cup	Red wine	250 ml/8 fl oz
1 cup	Cream	250 ml/8 fl oz
2 tbsp	Red currant jelly	1½ tbsp

1. Preheat the oven to 400°F/200°C/Gas Mark 6.
2. Put 2 tablespoons [25 g/1 oz] of butter and half an onion inside each bird and rub 1 tablespoon [15 g/½ oz] of butter over the skin of each. Sprinkle with pepper and salt and cover with slices of fat bacon. Tie these on securely. Melt 3 tablespoons [40 g/1½ oz] of butter in a roasting pan. When hot, put in the birds and baste well with hot fat. Put into the oven and roast for 45–60 minutes, depending on the size, basting every 15 minutes. After the first half hour, pour the wine over and baste. For the last 15 minutes, remove the bacon and brown the breasts well. When cooked, remove the birds and make the sauce.
3. Pour off all fat. Pour the cream into the sauce left in the pan and stir well. Then bring slowly to a boil, add the softened red currant jelly and seasoning to the sauce, strain into a sauceboat, and serve with the pheasant.

Hot Pheasant Soufflé

00:15 00:45   Serves 4   Midwest

American	Ingredients	Metric/Imperial
1 cup	Cooked pheasant	175 g/6 oz
2 tbsp	Butter	25 g/1 oz
1½–2 tbsp	Flour	1¼–1½ tbsp
1 cup	Milk seasoned with onion, peppercorns, mace, parsley and bay leaf	250 ml/8 fl oz
¼ tsp	Onion powder	¼ tsp
1 tbsp	Mixed herbs	1 tbsp
	A pinch of mace (or nutmeg)	
3	Eggs	3

1. Preheat the oven to 325°F/160°C/Gas Mark 3.
2. Melt the butter, sift in the flour, and blend smoothly; heat for a minute or two, then add the seasoned milk. Blend thoroughly and bring to a boil, stirring constantly. When boiling, cook for 1 minute, then remove from the heat and let cool.
3. Chop or mince the pheasant meat. Add to the sauce, with onion powder and mixed herbs. Season highly, adding mace or nutmeg. Stir in the beaten egg yolks. Let the mixture get quite cool.
4. About 35–40 minutes before you expect to eat the soufflé, beat up the egg whites with a pinch of salt. When very stiff, fold in 1 tablespoon thoroughly, and then fold in the remainder quickly and lightly. Put into a 7-inch soufflé dish and bake for 35–40 minutes, until well risen. Serve at once.

Casserole of Pigeons

00:15 02:10   Serves 4   Pacific Southwest

American	Ingredients	Metric/Imperial
2–4	Young pigeons or squabs	2–4
3 tbsp	Flour	2 tbsp
¼ cup	Butter or margarine	50 g/2 oz
1	Onion, peeled and chopped	1
½ lb	Carrots, peeled and sliced	225 g/8 oz
1	Chicken bouillon [stock] cube	1
1¼ cups	Water	300 ml/½ pint
3–4	Tomatoes, peeled and sliced	3–4
1	Bay leaf	1

1. Preheat the oven to 325°F/160°C/Gas Mark 3.
2. Split the pigeons in halves and dredge with flour mixed with a little salt and pepper. Heat the butter in a sauté pan, brown the pigeons on all sides, and remove to a casserole. Add the onion and carrots sautéed in the remaining fat.
3. Put any remaining flour and a crumbled bouillon cube into the pan, add water, and stir until boiling. Then pour over the contents of the casserole. Add the tomatoes and bay leaf, cover, and cook for about 2 hours.
4. Remove the bay leaf and adjust the seasoning before serving.

Braised Pigeons

00:20 01:45   Serves 4   South

American	Ingredients	Metric/Imperial
4	Young pigeons or squabs	4
2	Small oranges, peeled and halved	2
4 slices	Bacon	4 rashers
¼ cup	Butter or margarine	50 g/2 oz
3–4	Mushrooms, chopped	3–4
1	Small onion, peeled and sliced	1
2 tsp	Cornstarch [cornflour]	2 tsp
½ cup	Sweet sherry (or Marsala)	125 ml/4 fl oz
1 cup	Chicken stock	250 ml/8 fl oz
	Bouquet garni	
	Chopped parsley	

1. Preheat the oven to 350°F/180°C/Gas Mark 4.
2. Prepare the pigeons and put half an orange in each one. Tie a slice of bacon over each breast. Heat the butter in a frying pan, brown the pigeons on all sides and remove to a casserole.
3. Add the mushrooms and onion to the remaining fat and sauté until the onion is transparent. Stir in cornstarch, add sherry and chicken stock, and stir until boiling. Then pour over the pigeons.
4. Add the bouquet garni, sprinkle with parsley, cover, and cook for about 1½ hours.
5. Put the birds onto a serving dish, adjust the seasoning in the sauce, and strain over the birds. Serve with artichoke hearts, marinated in a little French dressing, and a green salad.

Hot Pheasant Soufflé

Braised Quails with Risotto

Braised Quails with Risotto

00:25
01:00   Serves 4   New England

American	Ingredients	Metric/Imperial
4	Quails	4
4	Large vine leaves	4
3 tbsp	Butter	40 g/1½ oz
2	Onions	2
1	Carrot	1
2	Stalks celery	2
½ cup	Mushrooms	50 g/2 oz
½ cup	Stock	125 ml/4 fl oz
2–3 tbsp	Sherry	1½–2 tbsp
1 tbsp	Chopped herbs	1 tbsp
	Risotto	
2 tbsp	Butter	25 g/1 oz
1	Onion	1
1 cup	Rice	225 g/8 oz
4 cups	Stock	1 l/1¾ pints
2 tbsp	Raisins	1½ tbsp
1	Pimento	1
1 tbsp	Chopped herbs	1 tbsp
8–10	Olives	8–10
2 tbsp	Almonds	1½ tbsp

1. Preheat the oven to 350°F/180°C/Gas Mark 4.
2. Wrap the quails in vine leaves and put a small piece of butter inside each one. Melt 2 tablespoons [25 g/1 oz] of butter, and cook the sliced onions, carrot and celery, and chopped mushrooms until golden brown. Place the quails on top of the vegetables in an ovenproof dish and add a little sherry, 3–4 tablespoons [2–3½ tbsp] of stock, a sprinkling of herbs, and seasoning. Put into the oven and braise for 25 minutes, or until tender.
3. Make the risotto: Heat the butter and cook the chopped onion until golden brown. Add the rice and cook for 1 minute. Pour on the stock and add the raisins, chopped pimento, and herbs. Put in a moderate oven for 20–30 minutes, or until the rice has absorbed all the liquid. Mix in the olives and browned almonds, and serve on a dish with the quail on top, and with a sauce made from the pan gravy and the remaining stock and sherry.

Braised Squabs with Red Cabbage

00:15
01:30   Serves 4–6   Pacific Southwest

American	Ingredients	Metric/Imperial
2–3	Large plump squabs	2–3
8 tbsp	Butter	100 g/4 oz
8 slices	Bacon	8 rashers
3	Onions	3
1 small or ½ large	Red cabbage	1 small or ½ large
1½ cups	Strong stock	350 ml/12 fl oz
2 tsp	Sugar	2 tsp
1 tbsp	Vinegar	1 tbsp
4	Cooking apples	4
¼ cup	Red wine	60 ml/2 fl oz

1. Preheat the oven to 350°F/180°C/Gas Mark 4.
2. Melt 6 tablespoons [75 g/3 oz] of butter in a casserole and brown the squabs all over; remove and keep warm. Cook the diced bacon, add the sliced onions, and brown. Then add the thinly sliced red cabbage. Cook for 1 minute; then return the squabs to the pan. Pour over the stock. Add salt, pepper, 1 teaspoon sugar, and vinegar. Cover the casserole, and cook in the oven for 45 minutes.
3. Then remove from the oven, and add 2 sliced apples and wine. Cook again for 30 minutes; then remove the squabs and, if the cabbage is not quite cooked, simmer again until tender, keeping the squabs warm.
4. Cut the squabs in half, and lay on top of the red cabbage. Fry the remaining apples cut in rings in 2 tablespoons [25 g/1 oz] of butter and a sprinkling of sugar, and put 1 ring on top of each squab. Serve with a brown gravy.

Roast Quail in Vine Leaves

00:20
00:20   Serves 4   Pacific Southwest

American	Ingredients	Metric/Imperial
4	Quail	4
5 tbsp	Butter	65 g/2½ oz
	A squeeze of lemon juice	
4	Tender large vine leaves	4
4 slices	Fat bacon	4 rashers
4	Slices white bread	4
	Fried bread crumbs	

1. Preheat the oven to 450°F/230°C/Gas Mark 8.
2. Clean and truss the quail neatly. Put ½ tbsp [10 g/¼ oz] of butter inside each with lemon juice and salt and pepper. Wrap each one in a vine leaf; then tie a slice of fat bacon around each bird.
3. Heat the butter, put the quail into a roasting pan, and baste. Roast in the oven for 15 minutes, or broil [grill] on a spit.
4. Make 4 slices of toast and butter lightly. When the birds are done, spread the toast with the pan drippings and serve.

Braised Squabs with Mushroom Stuffing

	00:15		
	01:30	Serves 4	New England

American	Ingredients	Metric/Imperial
4	Squabs	4
3	Onions	3
2–3 tbsp	Butter	25–40 g/ 1–1½ oz
½ cup	Sliced mushrooms	50 g/2 oz
½ cup	Fresh white bread crumbs	25 g/1 oz
2 tbsp	Oil	1½ tbsp
4 slices	Bacon	4 rashers
1 cup	Stock	250 ml/8 fl oz
½ cup	Red wine	125 ml/4 fl oz
1 tbsp	Parsley and thyme	1 tbsp
1	Bay leaf	1
2 tbsp	Chopped parsley	1½ tbsp

1. Preheat the oven to 350°F/180°C/Gas Mark 4.
2. Chop 1 small onion and cook for 3–4 minutes in butter; slice the mushrooms and cook until tender. Add the bread crumbs, salt, and pepper. Fill the squabs with this mixture.
3. Heat the oil in a casserole and cook the chopped bacon until golden; remove and keep warm. Now brown the squabs all over in the hot oil. Remove and keep warm while cooking the remaining chopped onion for a few minutes until golden brown. Add the bacon; put back the squabs. Cover with the stock and red wine. Add the herbs and pepper, cover, and cook in the oven for about 1 hour, until tender.
4. When done, remove the birds and keep warm; skim the fat from the casserole. Boil the sauce and season to taste. Serve the birds in the sauce, sprinkled with chopped parsley.

Squabs Stuffed with Orange Rice

	00:30		
	01:00	Serves 4	Pacific Southwest

American	Ingredients	Metric/Imperial
4	Squabs	4
1 cup	Rice	225 g/8 oz
3	Oranges	3
½ cup	Seedless grapes	50 g/2 oz
	A little powdered onion	
2–3 tbsp	Oil	1½–2 tbsp
1–2 tsp	Flour	1–2 tsp
½ cup	White wine	125 ml/4 fl oz

1. Preheat the oven to 400°F/200°C/Gas Mark 6.
2. Prepare the stuffing: Cook the rice and let cool. Grate the rind of 1 large orange, mix with 8–9 tablespoons [7–8 tbsp] of cooked rice. Remove the pith and skin from 2 oranges with a serrated knife and cut out segments; add these to the rice. Dip the grapes into boiling water for a few seconds, then into cold, peel and add to the stuffing with salt, pepper, and little powdered onion. Stuff the mixture into the squabs.

Squabs Stuffed with Orange Rice

3. Roast the birds as in Squabs Stuffed with Almonds and Raisins (see Index).
4. Pour away the oil and sprinkle in flour; blend with the pan drippings and add wine and a little stock. Bring to a boil and simmer for 1 minute. Add the juice of 1 orange and a few strips of peel, and serve with the squabs.

Squabs in Parcels

	00:25		
	01:00	Serves 4	South

American	Ingredients	Metric/Imperial
2	Large squabs	2
7 tbsp	Butter	90 g/3½ oz
2 slices	Bacon	2 rashers
1 can (3 oz)	Goose or duck liver pâté	1 tin (75 g/3 oz)
1 cup	Mushrooms	100 g/4 oz
2 tbsp	Chopped parsley, marjoram and tarragon	1½ tbsp
	A pinch of mace	
1 tbsp	Sherry	1 tbsp

1. Preheat the oven to 350°F/180°C/Gas Mark 4.
2. Cut each squab in half and brown all over in 3 tablespoons [40 g/1½ oz] of butter with the bacon. Cover the dish and roast in the oven for 20 minutes. Remove squabs and let cool.
3. Mix the paté with the chopped mushrooms, 4 tablespoons [50 g/2 oz] of butter, chopped mixed herbs, seasoning, and a dash of sherry. Cut 4 large squares of foil, butter these, place one eighth of the stuffing in the center of each square. Place the halved squabs on top; then spread another one eighth of the mixture over each squab. Fold the foil over the birds and seal the edges by turning over several times.
4. Turn the oven up to 400°F/200°C/Gas Mark 6 and bake the parcels for 35 minutes. Serve a parcel per person, and open them at the table to get the full effect of the aroma.

Squab and Steak Pie

Squab and Bacon Brochettes

🍳 04:30 00:55   Serves 4   South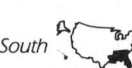

American	Ingredients	Metric/Imperial
2–3	Squabs	2–3
½ cup	Red wine	125 ml/4 fl oz
2	Onions	2
1 tbsp	Chopped herbs	1 tbsp
6 slices	Bacon	6 rashers
8–12	Baby onions	8–12
1½ cups	Stock	350 ml/12 fl oz
8–12	Baby mushrooms (use stems for sauce)	8–12
3 tbsp	Oil	2 tbsp
1	Clove garlic, crushed	1
2	Carrots, chopped	2
2	Stalks celery	2
2 tbsp	Flour	1½ tbsp

1. Remove the breasts from the squabs and cut each into 2 pieces. Put into a bowl and cover with wine, 1 chopped onion, herbs, and pepper. Leave to marinate for a few hours.
2. Cut 4 bacon slices in half and make each into a roll. Cook the peeled baby onions in ½ cup [125 ml/4 fl oz] of stock for 5 minutes; drain and reserve the stock for sauce. Peel the mushrooms, remove the stems, and reserve for the sauce. Remove the pieces of squab from the marinade and dry. Thread these ingredients alternately onto skewers.
3. Make a brown sauce: Heat the oil and cook 2 chopped slices of bacon, 1 chopped onion, crushed garlic, chopped carrots, chopped celery stalks, and mushroom stems until they are golden brown. Sprinkle in 2 tablespoons [1½ tbsp] of flour, blend well, and add the stock and ½ cup [125 ml/4 fl oz] strained marinade. Bring to a boil and simmer for a half hour. Strain and add seasoning.
4. Heat the broiler [grill] or barbecue grill and cook the brochettes, brushing with butter or oil, for about 8 minutes. The squab must not be overcooked, as it becomes tough and tasteless if allowed to do so.
5. Serve with boiled rice, brown sauce, and a salad.

Squab and Steak Pie

🍳 12:30 02:10   Serves 4–6   Mid Atlantic

American	Ingredients	Metric/Imperial
1 lb	Lean round steak	450 g/1 lb
2	Squabs	2
1	Onion	1
12	Baby onions	12
1 cup	Mushrooms	100 g/4 oz
3–4 tbsp	Oil	2–3½ tbsp
2 tbsp	Flour	1½ tbsp
1 cup	Stock	250 ml/8 fl oz
½ cup	Cider or beer	125 ml/4 fl oz
2 tbsp	Mixed chopped parsley and thyme	1½ tbsp
1	Bay leaf	1
1 tbsp	Worcestershire sauce	1 tbsp
1 (8 oz)	Package of frozen puff pastry	1 (225 g/8 oz)
1	Egg	1

1. Preheat the oven to 325°F/160°C/Gas Mark 3.
2. Cut the lean steak into cubes. Cut the squabs into quarters. Chop the onion and peel baby onions. Quarter the mushrooms.
3. Heat the oil; brown the meat cubes and squabs until brown all over, and remove to a pie dish or casserole. Brown the chopped onion and baby onions until golden brown, adding the mushrooms after a few minutes. Stir in the flour off the heat and blend, and add the stock (or water) and cider or beer. Bring to a boil; then add the herbs, bay leaf, meat, and squabs. Cover with a lid or foil, and cook in the oven for 1–1½ hours, until the meat is tender.
4. Let cool, if possible overnight. Skim off any surplus fat. Add more seasoning if needed and a little Worcestershire sauce to give a lively flavor.
5. Roll out the pastry thinly and cut a strip to go around the edge of the dish. Stick this to the dish with water. Moisten the top of the pastry strip with water; then place a large sheet of pastry over the whole dish. Press the edges together and cut off the excess with a sharp knife. Crimp the edges and cut air vents in the pastry crust. Decorate with pastry leaves. Brush the whole top with beaten egg.
6. Preheat the oven to 425°F/220°C/Gas Mark 7. Bake the pie for 20–30 minutes, until the pastry is crisp and brown.

Squabs Stuffed with Almonds and Raisins

🍳 00:25 01:10   Serves 4   South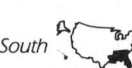

American	Ingredients	Metric/Imperial
4	Squabs	4
1 cup	Cooked rice	225 g/8 oz
2	Onions	2
3 tbsp	Butter	40 g/1½ oz
3–4 tbsp	Peeled flaked almonds	2–3½ tbsp

Squabs with Water Chestnuts

1 tbsp	Chopped herbs	1 tbsp
4 tbsp	Raisins	3½ tbsp
2–3 tbsp	Sherry	1–2 tbsp
4 slices	Fat bacon	4 rashers
2–3 tbsp	Oil	1–2½ tbsp
1–2 tsp	Flour	1–2 tsp
½ cup	Red wine	125 ml/4 fl oz
½ cup	Stock	125 ml/4 fl oz

1. Preheat the oven to 400°F/200°C/Gas Mark 6.

2. Prepare the stuffing: Boil the rice until tender. Drain and let cool. Chop 2 onions and cook until soft in butter. Add the skinned, sliced onions and cook until all are golden brown. Add 8 tablespoons [7 tbsp] rice to the pan, cook for 1 minute; then remove. Add the chopped herbs and raisins which have been soaking in sherry and seasoning. Stuff the mixture into the squabs.

3. Tie a slice of fat bacon around the breast of each bird. Heat the oil in the oven, add the squabs, and baste thoroughly. Roast in the oven for about 35–40 minutes, basting and turning every 10 minutes. Remove the bacon for the last 15 minutes to brown the breast. Remove to a serving dish and keep warm.

4. Pour away the oil and sprinkle in the flour, blend into the pan drippings, and add wine and stock. Stir until smooth and boiling; add seasoning and pour into a sauceboat.

Squabs with Water Chestnuts

00:10
01:20   Serves 4   New England

American	Ingredients	Metric/Imperial
2–4	Squabs or young pigeons	2–3
3 tbsp	Flour	2 tbsp
3 tbsp	Butter or margarine	40 g/1½ oz
1	Chicken bouillon [stock] cube	1
1½ cups	Water	350 ml/12 fl oz
1 tsp	Sugar	1 tsp
1 tbsp	Soy sauce	1 tbsp
1 tbsp	Sherry	1 tbsp
2	Scallions [spring onions], chopped	2
10	Water chestnuts, sliced	10

1. Preheat the oven to 350°F/180°C/Gas Mark 4.

2. Split the squabs in halves, and dredge with flour. Heat the butter in a frying pan, brown the squabs on all sides, and remove to a casserole.

3. Put the remaining flour into the pan with the crumbled bouillon cube and water. Stir until boiling; add sugar, seasoning, soy sauce, sherry, onion, and water chestnuts, and pour all over the squabs.

4. Cover and cook for 1–1¼ hours.

Vegetables, Rice, and Pasta

Oven-Baked Root Vegetables

Fresh Vegetable Feast

	00:20		
	01:35	Serves 12–14	Pacific Southwest

American	Ingredients	Metric/Imperial
1 cup	Butter	225 g/8 oz
1 cup	Onions, sliced thinly	100 g/4 oz
1	Lettuce heart, cut in small cubes	1
2 cups	Potatoes, diced	225 g/8 oz
2 cups	Fresh carrots, cut into 1-inch pieces	225 g/8 oz
1 cup	Celery, cut into 1-inch pieces	100 g/4 oz
1 cup	Green beans, cut into 1-inch pieces	100 g/4 oz
1 cup	Fresh peas or lima beans	100 g/4 oz
2 tbsp	Parsley, finely chopped	1½ tbsp
2 tbsp	Chives, finely chopped	1½ tbsp
2 tbsp	Other fresh herbs, tarragon, chervil, etc., finely chopped	1½ tbsp

1. Preheat the oven to 350°F/180°C/Gas Mark 4.
2. Melt 1 tablespoon [15 g/½ oz] of the butter and brown the onions in it. Put them in a casserole, then add a layer of lettuce, and dot with butter. Then add the other vegetables in layers, dotting each layer with butter.
3. Cover very tightly and cook for 1½ hours in the oven. Check after it has cooked for half an hour and .give the vegetables a light stir so that the juice from the bottom can moisten the top.
4. Mix the chopped herbs and sprinkle them on top before serving.

Oven-Baked Root Vegetables

	00:15		
	00:30	Serves 4	Mid Atlantic

American	Ingredients	Metric/Imperial
1 lb	Carrots	450 g/1 lb
1 lb	Beets [beetroot]	450 g/1 lb
⅔ lb	Parsnips	300 g/11 oz
¼ lb	Celery stalks	100 g/4 oz
3 tbsp	Oil	2 tbsp
½ tsp	Salt	½ tsp

1. Preheat the oven to 425°F/220°C/Gas Mark 7.
2. Peel the carrots, beets, parsnips, and celery. Cut them into ¼-inch wide strips.
3. Place the vegetables in a baking pan. Pour oil over them and sprinkle with a little salt. Bake in the oven for 25–30 minutes, until done as desired. Turn them over several times while baking.

Vegetable Pie

	00:25		
	00:50	Serves 4–5	Mid Atlantic

American	Ingredients	Metric/Imperial
	Pie Shell	
2 tbsp	Butter	25 g/1 oz
1	Small onion, peeled and finely chopped	1
2 cups	Cooked rice	450 g/1·lb
1	Egg	1
	Filling	
2 tbsp	Butter	25 g/1 oz
3–4	Zucchini [courgettes], sliced	3–4
2	Small onions, peeled and chopped	2
2	Stalks celery, chopped	2
1 cup	Sliced mushrooms	100 g/4 oz
1 tsp	Curry powder	1 tsp
	Sauce	
3 tbsp	Butter	40 g/1½ oz
3 tbsp	Flour	2 tbsp
½ tsp	Dry mustard	½ tsp
1 cup	Milk	250 ml/8 fl oz
½ cup	Grated cheese	50 g/2 oz
1 tbsp	Dry bread crumbs	1 tbsp
2 tsp	Chopped parsley	2 tsp

1. Preheat the oven to 400°F/200°C/Gas Mark 6.
2. To make the pie shell: Melt the fat in a pan and sauté the onion until transparent. Add the rice and stir in the beaten egg. Mix well, and press into the bottom and sides of an 8-inch pie pan.

3. To make the filling: Melt the fat in a pan; add the zucchini, onion, celery, and mushrooms, and sauté for 3 minutes. Add salt, pepper, and curry powder. Mix well and place in the rice shell.
4. To make the sauce: Melt the fat in a pan, add the flour and mustard, and stir for 1 minute. Remove from the heat, add milk gradually, return to the heat, and stir until boiling. Add salt, pepper, and most of the cheese.
5. Pour the sauce over the filling, sprinkle with the remaining cheese and bread crumbs mixed together, and cook for 35–40 minutes. Sprinkle with chopped parsley before serving.

Colcannon Casserole

 00:20 / 00:45 — Serves 4–5 — New England

American	Ingredients	Metric/Imperial
4	Large potatoes, peeled and roughly chopped	4
2	Parsnips or small turnips, peeled and roughly chopped	2
1 cup	Cooked, well-drained cabbage or kale	100 g/4 oz
2	Small onions, peeled and finely chopped	2
⅔ cup	Milk	150 ml/¼ pint
2 tbsp	Butter	25 g/1 oz
2	Egg whites	2
½ cup	Grated cheese	50 g/2 oz

1. Preheat the oven to 350°F/180°C/Gas Mark 4.
2. Cook the potatoes and parsnips together in boiling salted water until tender. Then drain well. Mash and mix with the cabbage.
3. While the potatoes are cooking, cook the onion in the milk until it is soft. Then mix with the other vegetables, season with salt and pepper, and add the butter. Pour into a greased casserole.
4. Beat the egg whites until stiff, fold in the grated cheese, and pile on top of the vegetables. Bake for 20–25 minutes, or until well browned.

Jagasee

 00:15 / 03:00 — Serves 6–8 — New England

American	Ingredients	Metric/Imperial
2 tbsp	Bacon fat	1½ tbsp
2	Large onions, peeled and sliced thinly	2
2⅓ cups	Lima beans, cooked, or 2 large cans [tins]	275 g/10 oz
½ lb	Salt pork	225 g/8 oz
1 large can (about 30 oz)	Tomatoes	1 large tin (about 850 g/30 oz)
¾ cup	Diced green or red pepper	75 g/3 oz
¾ cup	Diced celery	75 g/3 oz
2 cups	Rice	450 g/1 lb

Jagasee

1. Preheat the oven to 325°F/160°C/Gas Mark 3.
2. Heat the fat. Sauté the onions until they begin to color, then put them into a large casserole with a tightly fitting lid. Add the cooked beans.
3. Dice the pork and scald with boiling water. Put into the casserole with the tomatoes, green pepper, celery, rice, and seasoning. Add 2½ cups [600 ml/1 pint] of water.
4. Cover tightly, and cook for 2½–3 hours, adding more water from time to time as necessary.

Honeyed Beans with Bacon

12:15 / 03:00 — Serves 4–5 — New England

American	Ingredients	Metric/Imperial
2½ cups	Lima or navy beans, soaked overnight	275 g/10 oz
6 slices	Bacon	6 rashers
1	Onion, peeled and chopped	1
1 tsp	Dry mustard	1 tsp
1 tbsp	Chopped candied ginger	1 tbsp
2 tbsp	Chutney	1½ tbsp
¾ cup	Honey	175 ml/6 fl oz
	Dressing	
½ cup	Sour cream	125 ml/4 fl oz
	A dash of lemon juice	
1 tsp	Caraway seeds	1 tsp

1. Preheat the oven to 325°F/160°C/Gas Mark 3.
2. Drain the beans from the water in which they were soaked and simmer in boiling, salted water until tender (about 1–1½ hours).
3. Dice the bacon. Put the bacon into a frying pan with the onion, stir until the fat begins to melt, and sauté until the onion is transparent.
4. When the beans are cooked, drain and put into a deep casserole. Add the bacon and onion, seasoning, mustard, ginger, and chutney and mix well. Stir in the honey. Cook for about 1–1½ hours.
5. Cole slaw with a sour cream dressing is an excellent accompaniment. For the dressing, mix the sour cream with lemon juice and caraway seeds.

Vegetable Jambalaya

Vegetable Jambalaya

 00:10 / 01:00   Serves 4   South

American	Ingredients	Metric/Imperial
2 tbsp	Oil	1½ tbsp
6–8 oz	Small mushrooms	175–225 g/ 6–8 oz
1 cup	Cooked rice	225 g/8 oz
1	Green pepper, seeded and chopped	1
1	Small onion, peeled and chopped	1
1	Stalk celery, chopped	1
1	Canned [tinned] pimento, chopped	1
½ cup	Canned [tinned] or stewed tomatoes	50 g/2 oz
	Cayenne pepper	
¼ tsp	Paprika	¼ tsp
¼ cup	Melted butter or margarine	50 g/2 oz
	Watercress or parsley for garnish	

1. Preheat the oven to 300°F/150°C/Gas Mark 2.
2. Heat the oil in a pan, add the mushrooms, and sauté for a few minutes. (If small mushrooms are used, leave them whole; if large ones are used, cut into halves or quarters.)
3. Combine the rice, mushrooms, green pepper, onion, celery, pimento, and tomatoes. Add salt to taste, a few grains of cayenne pepper, and paprika. Add the melted butter, and mix well.
4. Put into a greased casserole, cover tightly, and cook for about 1 hour. Serve garnished with a small bunch of watercress or parsley.

Vegetable Roll

 00:35 / 01:00   Serves 4–5   New England

American	Ingredients	Metric/Imperial
	Suet Pastry	
2 cups	All-purpose [plain] flour	225 g/8 oz
½ tsp	Salt	½ tsp
¾ cup	Shredded suet	175 g/6 oz
	Filling	
3	Medium-sized carrots, peeled and grated	3
3	Small parsnips, peeled and grated	3
1	Small young turnip, peeled and grated	1
3	Potatoes, peeled and thinly sliced	3
3–4	Tomaotes, peeled, seeded and chopped	3–4
1 tbsp	Finely chopped herbs (parsley, tarragon, chives, chervil, as available)	1 tsp
	A little meat extract	

1. Preheat the oven to 400°F/200°C/Gas Mark 6.
2. To make the pastry: Combine the flour, salt, and suet; and mix to an elastic dough with cold water. Roll out into an oblong shape.
3. To make the roll: Combine all the vegetables and herbs, and spread over the pastry to within 1-inch all around. Spread a little meat extract over the top and sprinkle with pepper. (When using meat extract, it may not be necessary to add salt.) Dampen the edges of the pastry and roll up like a jelly roll. Press together the ends and the top edge of the roll.
4. Prick the top lightly in several places, place the roll on a baking pan lined with greased paper, and bake for about 1 hour. (If the top of the roll browns too quickly, cover with a piece of paper.) Serve hot with gravy.

Asparagus Delight

 00:05 / 00:10   Serves 4   Pacific Southwest

American	Ingredients	Metric/Imperial
1 (9-oz) can or 20 fresh	Asparagus spears, cooked and cooled	1 (250 g/9 oz) tin or 20 fresh
¾ cup	Crème fraîche or sour cream	175 ml/6 fl oz
1 (2-oz)	Jar red caviar	1 (50 g/2 oz)

1. Place a pile of 5 or 6 asparagus on each plate.
2. Mix together the crème fraîche and red caviar. Dab over asparagus.

Asparagus Delight

Avocado Cream

Asparagus Pie

| | 01:30 | Serves 5–6 | Pacific Southwest |
| | 00:45 | | |

American	Ingredients	Metric/Imperial
	Pastry	
2 cups	All-purpose [plain] flour	225 g/8 oz
½ tsp	Salt	½ tsp
½ cup	Shortening	100 g/4 oz
3–4 tbsp	Milk	2–3½ tbsp
	Filling	
2 cans (about 8 oz each)	Asparagus spears	2 tins (about 225 g/8 oz each)
2 tbsp	Butter or margarine	25 g/1 oz
3 tbsp	Flour	2 tbsp
1 cup	Milk	250 ml/8 fl oz
	A pinch of cayenne pepper	
1 cup	Grated cheese	100 g/4 oz
3–4 tbsp	Heavy [double] cream	2–3½ tbsp
2	Eggs	2

1. Preheat the oven to 400°F/200°C/Gas Mark 6.
2. Make the pastry in the usual way but use milk instead of water for mixing. Chill as long as possible, then roll out and line a 9-inch pie plate.
3. Drain the asparagus and arrange the spears in a wheel shape in the pastry shell. Set aside in a cool place while making the sauce.
4. Melt the butter in a pan, stir in the flour, and cook for 2 minutes, stirring constantly. Add the milk gradually, and stir until boiling. Add seasoning, grated cheese, cream, and beaten egg yolks. Fold in stiffly beaten egg whites.
5. Pour the milk mixture over the asparagus, bake for 30–40 minutes, and serve with broiled [grilled] tomatoes and a green salad.

Avocado Cream

| | 00:20 | Serves 8 | Pacific Southwest |
| | 00:00 | | |

American	Ingredients	Metric/Imperial
4	Avocados	4
2 tbsp	White wine vinegar	1½ tbsp
7–8	Anchovies, very finely chopped	7–8
1 tbsp	Very finely chopped onion	1 tbsp
1 tbsp	Sugar	1 tbsp
	Cayenne pepper	
2 tsp	Paprika	2 tsp
½–1 cup	Heavy [double] cream, whipped	125–250 ml/ 4–8 fl oz
	Black olives	
	Lemon for garnish	

1. Cut the avocados in half, discard the stones, and remove all the flesh. Mash it up and beat until creamy.
2. Add vinegar, anchovies, onion, and sugar. Mix well; add a dash of cayenne and paprika. Check the seasoning—salt may not be required. Fold in the whipped cream and pile into the avocado skins.
3. Garnish with olives and lemon slices.

Puffed Cauliflower Cheese

| | 00:20 | Serves 4 | Midwest |
| | 00:50 | | |

American	Ingredients	Metric/Imperial
1	Medium-sized head of cauliflower	1
¼ cup	Butter	50 g/2 oz
2 tbsp	Flour	1½ tbsp
1 cup	Milk, or milk and water in which the cauliflower has been cooked	250 ml/8 fl oz
¼ cup	Fine white bread crumbs	15 g/½ oz
3	Eggs (separated)	3
1 cup	Grated cheese	100 g/4 oz

1. Preheat the oven to 400°F/200°C/Gas Mark 6.
2. Wash the cauliflower, remove the stalk end, cut into quarters, and remove the hard stalk. Divide into flowerets, and cook in boiling salted water until tender. Then drain.
3. Heat the butter in a pan, add the flour, and stir over low heat for 2 minutes. Remove from the heat, add milk gradually, and stir until smooth. Return to the heat, and stir until boiling. Add salt and pepper and most of the bread crumbs.
4. Stir in the egg yolks, grated cheese, and the cauliflower. Adjust the seasoning to taste.
5. Beat the egg whites until stiff, and fold into the mixture. Put into a greased ovenproof dish, sprinkle with the remaining bread crumbs, and bake for about 30 minutes until well risen and brown.

Grilled Onions 1

	00:40	Serves 8	United States
	00:20		

American	Ingredients	Metric/Imperial
4	Large Bermuda [Spanish] onions	4
2 tbsp	Melted butter	25 g/1 oz

1. Heat the coals in an outdoor grill until hot, about 30 minutes, or preheat the broiler [grill].
2. Cut off the tops and bottoms of the onions, and peel off only the dry outer skin. Cut in ¼-inch slices.
3. Grease the grill, arrange the onion slices on it, pour melted butter over them, and season with salt and pepper.
4. Cook until slightly brown but not soft, about 20 minutes, but the time can vary depending on the onions and your taste.

Grilled Onions 2

	00:35	Serves 4	United States
	01:00		

American	Ingredients	Metric/Imperial
4	Bermuda [Spanish] onions	4
	Butter	

1. Heat the coals in an outdoor grill until hot, about 30 minutes, or preheat the broiler [grill].
2. Wipe the onions, but do not peel them. Place them on a greased grill and let them cook for 45 minutes to an hour. By the time they are done, they should be brown or even charred black on the outside, but soft and creamy inside.
3. If you wish, you can then take out the center and plug it with butter, salt, and pepper.

Puffed Cauliflower Cheese

Barbecued Corn

Barbecued Corn

	00:40	Serves 4	Mid Atlantic
	00:30		

American	Ingredients	Metric/Imperial
4–6 ears	Fresh corn	4–6 cobs
	Softened butter	
	Salt and pepper	

1. Heat the coals in an outdoor grill until hot, about 30 minutes, or preheat the broiler [grill].
2. Remove the husks and silk from the corn and spread generously with softened butter.
3. Sprinkle with salt and pepper and wrap each cob in a double thickness of foil, or use heavy duty foil. Twist the ends to seal it.
4. Place on the grid of the barbecue, close the cover, and cook for about 30 minutes, turning the corn frequently.

Corn Alabama Style

	00:15	Serves 4	South
	00:12		

American	Ingredients	Metric/Imperial
6 ears	Fresh corn	6 cobs
	Water	
	Salt	
	Butter, softened	
	Dill	
	Parsley	
	Chives	
	Leek	
	Tarragon	

1. Rinse and shuck the corn. Save the best pieces of husk. Rinse the corn and husks again. Place the husks in the bottom of a shallow pan. Save a few husks to cover the corn.
2. Add the corn. Cover with the husks and boil in lightly salted water for 10–12 minutes. Serve with herb butter and salt.
3. To make the herb butter, season soft butter with dill, parsley, chives, leek, tarragon, or the spices of your choice.

Corn Casserole with Ham and Cheese

Corn Casserole with Ham and Cheese

⚑ 00:05
🍲 00:25   Serves 3–4   Southwest

American	Ingredients	Metric/Imperial
6	Ears of corn (cut the corn off the cob)	6
3–4	Slices ham	3–4
1¼ cups	Milk	300 ml/½ pint
3	Eggs	3
2 cups	Sharp cheese, grated	225 g/8 oz
	Pinch of nutmeg	

1. Preheat the oven to 400°F/200°C/Gas Mark 6.
2. Place the corn and ham in a greased, ovenproof pan.
3. Beat the eggs and milk together. Add cheese and nutmeg. Pour this mixture over the corn and ham. Bake for 25 minutes.

Ranchero Corn

⚑ 00:10
🍲 00:15   Serves 6   Southwest

American	Ingredients	Metric/Imperial
6 slices	Bacon, diced	6 rashers
1 (4½-ounce)	Jar sliced mushrooms, drained	1 (125 g/4½ oz)
2 tbsp	Onion, finely chopped	1½ tbsp
2 (12-ounce) cans	Vacuum-packed golden whole-kernel corn with sweet peppers, drained	2 (350 g/ 12 oz) tins
¾ cup	Cheddar chese, grated	75 g/3 oz

1. Fry the bacon in a frying pan over medium heat until cooked but not brown; drain off excess fat. Stir in the mushrooms and onion; sauté until the onion is tender.
2. Blend in corn; heat through. Sprinkle with cheese; heat, without stirring, until the cheese is melted.

Sour Pickled Cucumbers

⚑ 00:45
🍲 00:05   6 pints [3 1/5 pints]   Midwest

American	Ingredients	Metric/Imperial
4½ lb	Small green cucumbers	2 kg/4½ lb
	Dill sprigs	
	Several bay leaves	
2 tbsp	Yellow mustard seeds	1½ tbsp
1	Piece horseradish, cut into small cubes	1
	Pickle Juice	
3¼ cups	Water	750 ml/1¼ pints
1½ tbsp	White vinegar	1¼ tbsp
1⅔ lb	Sugar	750 g/1⅔ lb
5 tbsp	Fine salt	4 tbsp

1. Brush the cucumbers extremely well in warm water, then cut them into rather thick slices. In jars, alternate the cucumber slices with sprigs of dill, bay leaves, mustard seeds, and horseradish cubes.
2. Bring all pickle-juice ingredients to a boil. Pour juice over the cucumbers. Let the mixture become cold. Seal the jars and store in a cold place. After 2 weeks, they will have obtained their full taste.

Leeks au Gratin

⚑ 00:15
🍲 00:40   Serves 4   Mid Atlantic

American	Ingredients	Metric/Imperial
8–12	Leeks, according to the size	8–12
3 tbsp	Butter or margarine	40 g/1½ oz
2 tbsp	Flour	1½ tbsp
1 cup	Milk	250 ml/8 fl oz
1 cup	Grated Cheddar cheese	100 g/4 oz
½ tsp	Prepared mustard	½ tsp
	Lemon juice	
4 tbsp	Bread crumbs	3½ tbsp

1. Preheat the oven to 375°F/190°C/Gas Mark 5.
2. Wash the leeks thoroughly and trim off the coarse green tops. Cook until only just tender in boiling salted water, then drain well and put into a buttered casserole.
3. Make a sauce with 2 tablespoons [25 g/1 oz] of the butter, the flour, and milk. Add the cheese and stir until it has melted. Add salt, pepper, mustard, and a squeeze of lemon juice.
4. Pour the sauce over the leeks, sprinkle with bread crumbs, and dot with the remaining 1 tablespoon [15 g/1 oz] of butter.
5. Cook for about 25 minutes, until the top is crisp and brown.

Sour Pickled Cucumbers

Grandfather's Eggplant

	00:15	Serves 4	Mid Atlantic
	00:45		

American	Ingredients	Metric/Imperial
1	Medium-large eggplant [aubergine], chopped	1
1	Small onion, finely chopped	1
1 tbsp	Butter	15 g/½ oz
1 (4-oz) can	Skinless and boneless herrings or anchovies	1 (100 g/4 oz) tin
1 tsp	Flour	1 tsp
1 cup	Crème fraîche or sour cream	250 ml/8 fl oz
4 tbsp	Finely chopped parsley	3½ tbsp
¾ cup	Finely grated cheese, preferably aged Gruyère	75 g/3 oz

1. Preheat the oven to 400°F/200°C/Gas Mark 6.
2. Divide the eggplant lengthwise. Dig out the flesh from the skin, and finely chop the inside flesh.
3. Sauté the onion in the butter until soft but not brown. Drain and mash the herrings. Add to the onion.
4. Save the herring liquid. Whip it together with the flour. Add to the herring mixture. Let simmer a few minutes. Add the crème fraîche. Let simmer until it thickens. Blend in the eggplant and parsley. Remove from the heat.
5. Fill the eggplant skins with the mixture. Place them on an ovenproof plate. Sprinkle the grated cheese over the eggplants. Bake in the oven for 30–35 minutes, or until the top has browned.
6. Let the dish cool before serving. If served warm, it is rather gooey. When served cooled or cold, it is delicious.

Wilted Lettuce

	00:10	Serves 6–8	Midwest 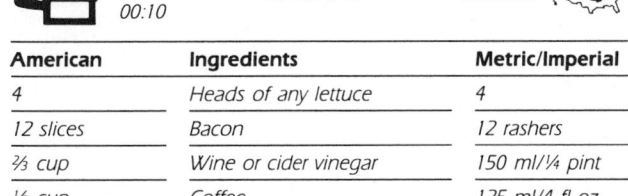
	00:10		

American	Ingredients	Metric/Imperial
4	Heads of any lettuce	4
12 slices	Bacon	12 rashers
⅔ cup	Wine or cider vinegar	150 ml/¼ pint
½ cup	Coffee	125 ml/4 fl oz
	Cream (optional)	

1. Pick over and wash the greens thoroughly and break—not cut—them into small pieces.
2. Fry the bacon, drain and crumble it into bits.
3. Then add the vinegar, coffee, and seasoning to the hot bacon fat and bring to a boil. (This is the time to add the cream if you want to, but turn the heat down so that it does not boil.)
4. Then very quickly, toss the lettuce in the sauce so that it is covered with it and warms through. Serve immediately.

Glazed Mushrooms and Ham

	00:15	Serves 4	Mid Atlantic
	00:10		

American	Ingredients	Metric/Imperial
¼ cup	Butter	50 g/2 oz
⅓ cup	Brown [demerara] sugar	75 g/3 oz
1 tsp	Flour	1 tsp
4 cups	Thickly sliced mushrooms	450 g/1 lb
¼ tsp	Grated nutmeg	¼ tsp
¼ tsp	Ground mace	¼ tsp
4–6	Slices cooked ham	4–6
3 tbsp	Sherry	2 tbsp

1. Melt the butter in a pan, add the sugar and flour mixed together, and stir over a low heat until the sugar has melted. Add the mushrooms, nutmeg, and mace. Cover and cook very slowly for 5 minutes.
2. Uncover, arrange the ham over the mushrooms, and increase the heat just long enough for the ham to heat through.
3. Add the sherry and turn upside down onto a hot serving dish.

Mushroom and Onion Quiche

Mushroom and Onion Quiche

| | 01:25 | | |
| | 00:40 | Serves 4–5 | South |

American	Ingredients	Metric/Imperial
	Pâté Brisée (see Index)	
3 tbsp	Butter or margarine	40 g/1½ oz
2	Onions, peeled and chopped	2
1 can (8 oz)	Button mushrooms	1 tin (225 g/8 oz)
2	Eggs	2
½ can (about 1 cup)	Evaporated milk	½ tin (about 250 ml/8 fl oz)
½ cup	Grated cheese	50 g/2 oz
	A pinch of dry mustard	

1. Preheat the oven to 400°F/200°C/Gas Mark 4.
2. Line a deep 8-inch pie plate with the Pâté Brisée.
3. Heat 2 tablespoons [25 g/1 oz] of the butter in a frying pan and cook the onion until transparent. Drain well and put into the pastry shell with most of the mushrooms, cut in halves. Leave a few uncut for garnishing.
4. Beat the eggs; stir in the evaporated milk, grated cheese, and seasoning. Pour over the mushrooms. Bake for about 35 minutes.
5. Sauté the remaining mushrooms for a few minutes in the remaining 1 tablespoon [15 g/½ oz] of butter. Drain and cut into thin slices.
6. When the pie is cooked, garnish with the sliced mushrooms.

Onion Charlotte

| | 00:15 | | |
| | 00:30 | Serves 4 | South |

American	Ingredients	Metric/Imperial
4	Bermuda [Spanish] onions, peeled and thickly sliced	4
1 cup	Milk	250 ml/8 fl oz
2 tbsp	Cornstarch [cornflour]	1½ tbsp
3 tbsp	Margarine	40 g/1½ oz
⅛ tsp	Grated nutmeg	⅛ tsp
⅛ tsp	Ground cinnamon	⅛ tsp
4–5	Slices stale bread	4–5
¼ cup	Oil or cooking fat	60 ml/2 fl oz
3 tbsp	Grated cheese	2 tbsp
2 tbsp	Fine bread crumbs	1½ tbsp

1. Preheat the oven to 400°F/200°C/Gas Mark 6.
2. Put the onions into a pan, just cover with cold water, cover the pan and boil for 2–3 minutes. Then drain off the water. Return the onions to the pan; add milk and 4 tablespoons [3½ tbsp] of water. Cover and simmer until the onions are tender, 10–15 minutes.
3. Mix the cornstarch to a smooth paste with a little extra milk, add to the onions, and stir until boiling. Add 2 tablespoons [25 g/1 oz] of the margarine, salt, pepper, nutmeg, and cinnamon.
4. Remove the crusts from the bread, and fry in the oil until brown on both sides. Arrange the fried bread in the bottom and around the sides of the baking dish. Pour in the onion mixture.
5. Sprinkle with cheese and bread crumbs mixed together. Melt the remaining tablespoon [15 g/½ oz] of margarine and dribble over the top. Bake until well browned.

Lyonnaise Pie

| | 01:20 | | |
| | 00:50 | Serves 6 | South |

American	Ingredients	Metric/Imperial
	Pastry for an 8–9 inch 1-crust pie (see Index)	
1	Onion, peeled and chopped	1
1 tbsp	Butter or margarine	15 g/½ oz
1½ cups	Milk	350 ml/12 fl oz
⅔ cup	Soft bread crumbs	40 g/1½ oz
3	Eggs	3
½ tsp	Worcestershire sauce	½ tsp
	Bacon rolls	
	Watercress	

1. Preheat the oven to 375°F/190°C/Gas Mark 5.
2. Line an 8–9 inch pie plate with the pastry. Trim and crimp the edge.
2. Sauté the onion in the butter until soft and golden brown; then spread over the bottom of the pastry.
3. Heat the milk. Pour the milk onto the bread crumbs; add the beaten eggs and mix well. Add Worcestershire sauce and seasonings.
4. Pour into the pastry shell, and bake for about 45 minutes, or until the pastry is brown and the custard set. Garnish with broiled [grilled] bacon rolls and watercress.

Onion Charlotte

Pissaladière

Pissaladière

01:25
01:20
Serves 6
South

American	Ingredients	Metric/Imperial
	Pastry for a 9-inch, 1-crust pie (see Index)	
1	Egg yolk	1
6 tbsp	Oil	5 tbsp
6	Large tomatoes, peeled, seeded, and chopped	6
2 tbsp	Tomato purée	1½ tbsp
⅛ tsp	Black pepper	⅛ tsp
2 tbsp	Grated Parmesan cheese	1½ tbsp
3	Large onions, peeled and sliced	3
2	Sprigs fresh rosemary or tarragon, or ¼ tsp dried rosemary	2
1 can (3 oz)	Anchovy fillets*	1 tin (75 g/3 oz)
	Black olives	

1. Preheat the oven to 450°F/230°C/Gas Mark 8.
2. Line a 9-inch pie plate with the pastry and set aside to chill. When required, brush the bottom with a beaten egg yolk and bake just long enough to set the crust, about 15 minutes. Remove from the oven and reduce the heat to 375°F/190°C/Gas Mark 5.
3. Heat 4 tablespoons [3½ tbsp] of the oil in a frying pan; add the tomatoes and tomato purée and cook over low heat, stirring occasionally, until the excess moisture has evaporated. Add pepper, a pinch of salt, and a pinch of sugar.
4. In another pan, sauté the onions in the remaining oil until golden brown.
5. Sprinkle the bottom of the pie shell with the cheese; add the onion and rosemary, and cover with the tomato mixture. Arrange anchovies in a lattice pattern on top and place an olive in the center of each square. Brush lightly wth oil and bake for about 30 minutes.

* If the anchovies are a little salty for your taste, soak them in milk for about 20 minutes and dab dry before using.

Onion Pie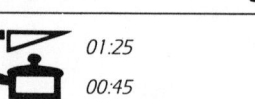

01:25
00:45
Serves 6
South

American	Ingredients	Metric/Imperial
	Pastry for a 8–9 inch, 1-crust pie (see Index)	
3 tbsp	Butter or margarine	40 g/1½ oz
2½ lb	Bermuda [Spanish] onions, peeled and sliced	1.25 kg/2½ lb
3	Eggs	3
1 cup	Sour cream	250 ml/8 fl oz
¼ cup	Dry sherry	60 ml/2 fl oz
1 tsp	Celery salt	1 tsp
1	Egg white	1
4 slices	Bacon	4 rashers

1. Preheat the oven to 450°F/230°C/Gas Mark 8.
2. Line a 9-inch pie plate with the pastry, prick the bottom, and let chill while preparing the filling.
3. Heat the butter in a heavy frying pan, and sauté the onion until transparent. Remove from the heat.
4. Beat the eggs; add the sour cream, sherry, celery salt, and seasoning. Heat just long enough to blend the ingredients together. Stir into the onions.
5. Brush the bottom of the pie shell with lightly beaten egg white, and pour in the filling. Arrange strips of bacon on top. Bake for 10 minutes, then reduce the heat to 300°F/150°C/Gas Mark 2 and bake for a half hour, or until the pastry is cooked.

Red and Green Pepper Pot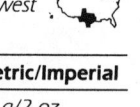

00:15
00:20
Serves 6
Southwest

American	Ingredients	Metric/Imperial
¼ cup	Butter	50 g/2 oz
3	Red peppers, cut into rings	3
3	Green peppers, cut into rings	3
6	Yellow onions, peeled and cut into wedges	6
12	Tomatoes, stem ends cut off, cut into wedges	12
	Salt to taste	
	Freshly ground black pepper to taste	

1. Melt the butter in a frying pan. Add the peppers and onions; sauté over low heat for 10 minutes, stirring frequently.
2. Add the tomato wedges. Season with salt and pepper. Cook 10 minutes, stirring frequently.

Casserole of Stuffed Peppers

Casserole of Stuffed Peppers

| | 00:20 | Serves 4 | New England |
| | 00:35 | | |

American	Ingredients	Metric/Imperial
4	Large red or green peppers	4
2 tbsp	Butter or margarine	25 g/1 oz
1	Small onion, peeled and chopped	1
1 cup	Cooked rice	225 g/8 oz
½ lb	Shrimp [prawns]	225 g/8 oz
	Lemon juice	
1 cup	Consommé	250 ml/8 fl oz

1. Preheat the oven to 350°F/180°C/Gas Mark 4.
2. Cut a slice from the stem end of the peppers and remove all seeds and pith.
3. Heat the butter in a frying pan, add the onion, and sauté until soft. Add the rice and shrimp, season carefully, and add lemon juice to taste.
4. Fill the peppers with this mixture and arrange in a buttered casserole. Add the consommé, cover, and cook for about 30 minutes, or until tender.

Surprise Potatoes

| | 00:20 | Serves 4 | Mid Atlantic |
| | 01:15 | | |

American	Ingredients	Metric/Imperial
4	Large potatoes	4
	Butter	
	Nutmeg	
2–3	Chives, chopped	2–3
4 tbsp	Cooked green peas	3½ tbsp
4	Eggs	4

1. Preheat the oven to 350°F/180°C/Gas Mark 4.
2. Scrub the potatoes, wash, and dry well. Rub all over with butter or brush with oil, prick with a fork, and bake until tender (about 1–1¼ hours).
3. Cut a slice from the top of each potato lengthwise, scoop out the inside carefully, and mash with some butter, salt, pepper, and nutmeg. Add the chives.
4. Put 1 tablespoon of the peas into each potato case. Then replace the potato mixture until about three quarters full.
5. Break an egg into each potato, sprinkle with a little salt and pepper, and dot with butter. Replace the top slice of potato.
6. Reduce the heat of the oven to 325°F/160°C/Gas Mark 3, replace the potatoes, and cook until the eggs are set, about 10 minutes.

Mushroom Pie

	01:30	Serves 4	South
	00:45		

American	Ingredients	Metric/Imperial
	Pastry for an 8-inch 2-crust pie (see Index)	
1 cup	Milk	250 ml/8 fl oz
1	Blade mace	1
1	Bay leaf	1
6	Peppercorns	6
3 tbsp	Butter or margarine	40 g/1½ oz
1	Small onion, peeled and sliced thinly	1
2 cups	Sliced mushrooms	225 g/8 oz
3 tbsp	Flour	2½ tbsp
2 tbsp	Heavy [double] cream	1½ tbsp
1	Egg yolk	1
1	Egg	1

1. Preheat the oven to 400°F/200°C/Gas Mark 6.
2. Line an 8-inch pie plate with about two-thirds of the pastry.
3. Put the milk into a pan; add the mace, bay leaf, and peppercorns, and place over a very low heat to infuse. Strain off the milk and discard the flavorings.
4. Heat half the butter in a pan; add the onion and sauté until soft but not colored. Add the mushrooms, increase the heat a little, and cook for 2–3 minutes, stirring occasionally. Add the remaining butter, and stir in the flour. Add the milk gradually. Stir until boiling, then remove from the heat. Add the cream, egg yolk, and seasoning. Let cool a little; then put into the pastry shell.
5. Roll out the remaining pastry and cut it into thin strips. Arrange in a lattice pattern over the pie, pressing the ends of the strips well down onto the edge of the pastry. Brush with beaten egg. Bake for about 30–35 minutes.

Foil Baked Potatoes

	00:35	Serves 4	Mid Atlantic
	01:00		

American	Ingredients	Metric/Imperial
4	Baking potatoes	4
	Oil	
	Salt	
	Butter or sour cream mixed with chopped chives	

1. Heat the coals in an outdoor grill until hot, about 30 minutes.
2. Scrub the potatoes well. Prick them all over, brush them with oil, and sprinkle with salt.
3. Wrap in foil, and roast directly on the hot coals or place on the barbecue grid. If cooked directly on the coals, they will take about 35 minutes. If put on the grid, allow about 1 hour.
4. To serve, split the potatoes, and top with plenty of butter or sour cream mixed with chopped chives. These can also be baked in a 400°/200°C/Gas Mark 6 oven for 1 hour.

Fidget Pie

	01:35	Serves 4–5	New England 
	01:30		

American	Ingredients	Metric/Imperial
1 lb	Potatoes, peeled and sliced	450 g/1 lb
1 lb	Cooking apples, peeled, cored, and sliced	450 g/1 lb
2–3	Onions, peeled and sliced	2–3
¾ lb	Bacon or ham, cut into dice	350 g/12 oz
1 cup	Consomme	250 ml/8 fl oz
	Pastry for an 8–9 inch 1-crust pie (see Index)	

1. Preheat the oven to 425°F/220°C/Gas Mark 7.
2. Arrange the potatoes, apples, onions, and bacon in layers in a fairly deep baking dish, sprinkling each layer with pepper and a very little salt.
3. Add the consomme; then cover with the pastry. Make a slit in the top, and decorate as desired.
4. Bake for a half hour; then reduce the heat to 375°F/190°C/Gas Mark 5 and bake for 1 hour.

Ratatouille

	00:15	Serves 4	New England 
	01:40		

American	Ingredients	Metric/Imperial
	Olive oil	
2	Onions, peeled and finely chopped	2
2	Peppers, seeded and chopped	2
3–4	Zucchini [courgettes], sliced thinly	3–4
1	Small eggplant [aubergine]	1
4	Tomatoes, peeled, seeded and chopped	4
½ cup	Chopped parsley	15 g/½ oz
1	Clove garlic, crushed	1
	Grated Parmesan cheese	

1. Preheat the oven to 250°F/120°C/Gas Mark ½.
2. Heat some oil in a heavy frying pan; sauté the onions until they begin to color. Add the peppers, sauté a few more minutes.
3. Add the zucchini and eggplant. Adding a little more oil if necessary, cook for about 5 minutes. Then turn all the vegetables into a large casserole and add the tomatoes. Cover and cook in the oven for 1¼ hours.
4. Add the parsley, garlic, and seasoning; cook 20 minutes longer. Sprinkle generously with cheese before serving.

Spinach and Ricotta Pie

 01:20 / 00:50   Serves 5–6   Southwest

American	Ingredients	Metric/Imperial
	Cheese pastry for an 8–9 inch, 1-crust pie (see Index)	
1–2	Packages frozen spinach (about 350 g/¾ lb)	1–2
2 tbsp	Butter	25 g/1 oz
	Salt and pepper	
½ lb	Ricotta or cottage cheese	225 g/8 oz
3	Eggs	3
½ cup	Grated Parmesan cheese	50 g/2 oz
6 tbsp	Heavy [double] cream	5 tbsp
	Nutmeg	

1. Preheat the oven to 450°F/230°C/Gas Mark 8.
2. Line a deep 8-inch pie plate with the pastry, flute the edges, prick the bottom, and chill.
3. When required, bake for about 15 minutes, just long enough to set the pastry; then let cool.
4. Reduce oven heat to 375°F/190°C/Gas Mark 5.
5. Cook the spinach in the butter; drain well and add salt, pepper, ricotta cheese, beaten eggs, half the grated cheese, cream, and a good pinch of nutmeg.
6. Spread in the pastry shell, sprinkle with the remaining cheese, and bake for about 30 minutes, or until the mixture is firm and pastry browned.

Squash and Cheese Pie

 00:15 / 00:15   Serves 4   New England

American	Ingredients	Metric/Imperial
3 cups	Cooked, drained squash [marrow]	350 g/12 oz
1 (8-inch)	Baked pie shell	1 (8-inch)
	Nutmeg	
1 cup	Medium cream sauce (see Index)	250 ml/8 fl oz
1 cup	Grated cheese	100 g/4 oz
1	Egg	1
2	Tomatoes, peeled and sliced	2
	Bacon rolls	

1. Preheat the oven to 400°F/200°C/Gas Mark 6.
2. Cut the well-drained squash into cubes and arrange in the pastry shell. Sprinkle with salt, pepper, and nutmeg.
3. Make the sauce; add most of the cheese and the egg yolk, and fold in the stiffly beaten egg white. Pour the sauce over the squash.
4. Arrange the slices of tomato around the edge and sprinkle the remaining cheese in the middle. Bake for about 15 minutes in a moderately hot oven.
5. Garnish with broiled [grilled] bacon rolls.

Cheese and Spinach Pie

00:25 / 00:45   Serves 5–6   Midwest

American	Ingredients	Metric/Imperial
	Pie Pastry	
1 cup	All-purpose [plain] flour	100 g/4 oz
½ tsp	Salt	½ tsp
5 tbsp	Shortening [vegetable fat]	4 tbsp
2 tbsp	Cold water	1½ tbsp
	Filling	
¾ lb	Well-drained cooked spinach, (or 1 pkg frozen spinach)	350 g/12 oz
	Nutmeg	
1 cup	Cottage cheese	225 g/8 oz
3	Eggs	3
½ cup	Grated cheese	50 g/2 oz
	Milk (if required)	

1. Preheat the oven to 450°F/230°C/Gas Mark 8.
2. Make the pie pastry in the usual way; roll out and line an 8-inch pie pan. Flute the edges and prick the bottom. Chill if possible. Then bake for about 15 minutes and set aside to cool.
3. Chop the spinach, and season well with salt, pepper, and nutmeg to taste. Add the cottage cheese, beaten eggs, and half the grated cheese. If the mixture is a little stiff, add 2–3 tablespoons [1½–2 tbsp] milk.
4. Spread the mixture in the pastry shell, sprinkle the remaining cheese on top, and bake for about 30 minutes, or until the mixture is firm and the pastry well cooked.

Rice Coleslaw

 00:15 / 00:00   Serves 6   Midwest

American	Ingredients	Metric/Imperial
½	Medium head of cabbage, finely shredded	½
1½ cups	Cooked rice	350 g/12 oz
½ cup	Red or green pepper, chopped	50 g/2 oz
1 cup	Sliced radishes	100 g/4 oz
1	Small onion, peeled and finely chopped	1
1 can (8 oz)	Whole kernel corn	1 (225 g/8 oz) tin
½ cup	French dressing (see Index)	125 ml/4 fl oz
½ tsp	Dry mustard	½ tsp
	A pinch of pepper	
2 tsp	Sugar	2 tsp
1	Clove garlic, crushed	1

1. Combine the cabbage, rice, red pepper, radishes, onion, and drained corn in a large bowl. Sprinkle with a little salt.
2. Put the remaining ingredients into a screw-top jar and shake well. Then pour over the cabbage mixture, and toss thoroughly.

Tomato Quiche

 01:25 00:45   Serves 4   New England

American	Ingredients	Metric/Imperial
	Pastry	
1 cup	All-purpose [plain] flour	100 g/4 oz
	Salt and cayenne pepper	
⅛ tsp	Dry mustard	⅛ tsp
¼ cup plus 1 tbsp	Shortening [vegetable fat]	50 g/2 oz plus 1 tbsp
5 tbsp	Grated Cheddar cheese	4 tbsp
1	Egg yolk	1
	Filling	
4–5	Tomatoes, peeled and sliced	4–5
1	Small onion, finely chopped	1
¼ cup	Butter or margarine	50 g/2 oz
2	Eggs	2
¼ cup plus 2 tbsp	Milk	60 ml/2 fl oz plus 2 tbsp
½ cup	Grated cheese	50 g/2 oz
	Chopped parsley	

1. Preheat the oven to 375°F/190°C/Gas Mark 5.
2. Sift the flour and mustard with salt and pepper. Cut in the shortening; add the cheese and bind with the beaten egg. If required, add a little water by teaspoons. Chill if possible, then roll out and line a deep, 7-inch pie plate.
3. Arrange the tomatoes in the bottom, leaving 1 or 2 slices for garnish. Sauté the onion in butter until soft and place on top of the tomatoes.
4. Beat the eggs; add the milk, half the cheese, and seasoning. Pour carefully over the tomatoes, sprinkle with the remaining cheese, and bake for about 40 minutes or until the custard is firm.
5. Garnish with the remaining slices of tomato, return to the oven, just to heat through, and sprinkle with parsley before serving.

Cheese and Tomato Quiche

 01:20 00:42   Serves 4–5   Mid Atlantic

American	Ingredients	Metric/Imperial
	Savory Pie Crust	
1 cup	All-purpose [plain] flour	225 g/8 oz
⅛ tsp	Dry mustard	⅛ tsp
	A pinch of cayenne pepper	
½ tsp	Salt	½ tsp
5 tbsp	Shortening [vegetable fat]	65 g/2½ oz
1–2 tbsp	Grated cheese	1–1½ tbsp
2–3 tbsp	Water	1½–2 tbsp

American	Ingredients	Metric/Imperial
	Filling	
4–5	Tomatoes, peeled and sliced	4–5
1	Small onion, peeled and chopped	1
3–4 tbsp	Butter	40–50 g/1½–2 oz
2	Eggs	2
6 tbsp	Milk	5 tbsp
½ cup	Grated cheese	50 g/2 oz
	Chopped parsley	

1. Preheat the oven to 375°F/190°C/Gas Mark 5.
2. To make the pastry: Sift the flour, mustard, cayenne, and salt together. Cut in the shortening, add the cheese, and mix with water, adding a spoonful at a time. Chill if possible. Then roll out, and line a deep, 7-inch pie pan.
3. Set aside a few slices of tomato for garnish and arrange the rest over the bottom of the pastry. Sauté the onion in the butter until soft, but not browned. Then sprinkle over the tomatoes.
4. Beat the eggs, add the milk, most of the cheese, and seasoning. Pour over the tomatoes, sprinkle the remaining cheese on top, and bake for about 40 minutes.
5. Garnish with the remaining slices of tomato and a little parsley, and serve with a green salad.

Bacon Crust Pie

00:20 00:25   Serves 4–5   United States

American	Ingredients	Metric/Imperial
	Bacon Crust	
2 cups	Ground [minced] lean bacon	350 g/12 oz
1 can (8 oz)	Tomato purée	1 tin (225 g/8 oz)
½ cup	Bread crumbs	25 g/1 oz
1	Small onion, very finely chopped	1
¼ cup	Chopped green pepper	25 g/1 oz
	Filling	
1 cup	Cooked rice	225 g/8 oz
1 can (8 oz)	Tomato purée	1 tin (225 g/8 oz)
⅛ tsp	Oregano	⅛ tsp
1¼ cups	Grated Gruyère cheese	150 g/5 oz

1. Preheat the oven to 375°F/190°C/Gas Mark 5.
2. Mix all of the ingredients for the crust together, knead well, and press into the bottom of an 8–9 inch pie plate. Flute around the edge.
3. Mix the rice, tomato purée, oregano, salt, pepper, and 1 cup [100 g/4 oz] of the cheese; spoon into the pie shell. Cover with waxed [greaseproof] paper and bake for 15–20 minutes.
4. Remove the paper, sprinkle with the remaining cheese, and brown lightly under a hot broiler [grill].

Risotto with Liver and Peas

Rice and Vegetable Ring 👨‍🍳👨‍🍳

	00:15			
	00:40	Serves 6	Midwest	

American	Ingredients	Metric/Imperial
1 cup	Rice	225 g/8 oz
1 cup	Stock	250 ml/8 fl oz
½ lb	Mushrooms	225 g/8 oz
4 tbsp	Butter	50 g/2 oz
	Paprika	
1 lb	Green beans or 1 head of cauliflower	450 g/1 lb

1. Cook the rice in the stock.
2. Chop the mushrooms and sauté for 2–3 minutes in 2 table-spoons [25 g/1 oz] of the butter. Add the stock and rice. Season to taste with salt and paprika.
3. Press the rice mixture firmly into a greased, 7-inch ring mold. Let stand for about 5 minutes. Then turn out onto a platter and keep warm.
4. Cook the vegetable while the rice is cooking. If cauliflower is used, divide into flowerets. Pile the vegetable into the center of the mold, and dot with the remaining butter.

Risotto with Liver and Peas 👨‍🍳

	00:10			
	00:25	Serves 4–5	Mid Atlantic	

American	Ingredients	Metric/Imperial
4 tbsp	Oil	3½ tbsp
1	Onion, peeled and chopped	1
1½ cups	Long-grain rice	350 g/12 oz
2½ pints	Chicken stock	1.5 l/2½ pints
	A pinch of saffron (optional)	
1	Small red pepper, seeded and chopped	1
2 cups	Cooked green peas	225 g/8 oz
½ cup	Cooked diced liver	75 g/3 oz
	Grated cheese	

1. Heat the oil in a pan; add the onion, and sauté until it begins to soften. Add the rice, and stir over low heat until it is almost translucent, but do not allow it to brown.
2. Remove from the heat; stir in half the hot stock, saffron, and red pepper. Return to the heat, and cook until most of the stock has evaporated.
3. Add the remaining stock, and continue to cook until the rice is almost ready.
4. Add the liver and peas, season as desired, and leave just long enough for the liver and peas to heat through. Serve with grated cheese.

Rice and Apricot Bake

	00:40		
	00:55	Serves 4–5	Pacific Northwest

American	Ingredients	Metric/Imperial
1 cup	Dried apricots	225 g/8 oz
½ cup	Raisins	75 g/3 oz
1 cup	Rice	225 g/8 oz
¼ cup	Butter	50 g/2 oz
½ cup	Finely chopped onion	50 g/2 oz
¼ cup	Chopped green pepper	25 g/1 oz
¼ tsp	Curry powder	¼ tsp
	A few toasted almonds (optional)	

1. Preheat the oven to 375°F/190°C/Gas Mark 5.
2. Cover the apricots and raisins with hot water, and let stand for a half hour. Then drain and chop.
3. Cook the rice in boiling, salted water and drain.
4. Heat the fat in a frying pan; add the onion, green pepper, and curry powder, and sauté for about 5 minutes, stirring occasionally. Add the fruit, rice, almonds, and seasoning as required.
5. Put into a greased baking dish, and cook for about 30 minutes.

Curried Rice with Vegetables

	00:50		
	01:30	Serves 4	South 

American	Ingredients	Metric/Imperial
½ cup	Long-grain rice	100 g/4 oz
2 cups	Hot water	450 ml/¾ pint
2 tbsp	Melted margarine	25 g/1 oz
1 tsp	Curry powder	1 tsp
1 can (8 oz)	Tomatoes	1 tin (225 g/8 oz)
¼ cup	Finely chopped onion	25 g/1 oz
½ cup	Thinly sliced red pepper, or use a mixture of red and green peppers	50 g/2 oz

1. Preheat the oven to 350°F/180°C/Gas Mark 4.
2. Put the rice into a casserole with a tight-fitting lid. Add the water, and let stand for ½–¾ hour.
3. Add all the other ingredients and mix well. Cover tightly, and cook for about 1½ hours. (Although most of the liquid should be absorbed, the rice should be served while it is still moist.)

Curried Rice

	00:45		
	01:30	Serves 4	South

American	Ingredients	Metric/Imperial
½ cup	Rice	100 g/4 oz
2 cups	Hot water	450 ml/¾ pint
½ cup	Canned [tinned] tomatoes	100 g/4 oz
¼ cup	Finely sliced onion	25 g/1 oz
¼ cup	Thinly sliced red or green pepper	25 g/1 oz
2 tbsp	Melted butter or margarine	25 g/1 oz
¾ tsp	Curry powder	¾ tsp

1. Preheat the oven to 350°F/180°C/Gas Mark 4.
2. Put the rice into a casserole, add the water, and leave to stand about 45 minutes.
3. Add all the other ingredients and mix well. Cover and cook for about 1½ hours, stirring occasionally.
4. Most of the liquid should now be absorbed, but serve the rice while it is still moist.

Deviled Rice

	00:05		
	00:15	Serves 5–6	Mid Atlantic 

American	Ingredients	Metric/Imperial
1 cup	Rice	225 g/8 oz
	Butter or margarine	
2 tsp	Curry powder	2 tsp
1 tsp	Black pepper	1 tsp
¼ tsp	Cayenne pepper	¼ tsp

1. Cook the rice for 15 minutes in plenty of boiling salted water with 1 teaspoon butter. (This prevents it frothing up and boiling over.)
2. Drain, rinse, and add 1 tablespoon [15 g/½ oz] of butter, curry powder, black and cayenne pepper.

Rice and Peas

	00:10		
	00:30	Serves 4–6	New England 

American	Ingredients	Metric/Imperial
3 tbsp	Butter or margarine	40 g/1½ oz
¼ cup	Onion, chopped	25 g/1 oz
2 cups	Chicken stock	450 ml/¾ pint
1 cup	Raw long-grain rice	225 g/8 oz
1 (10-oz)	Package frozen green peas	1 (275 g/10 oz)
½ cup	Cooked ham, diced	75 g/3 oz
	Salt and pepper	
	Grated Parmesan cheese	

1. In a large saucepan, melt the butter and sauté the onion until transparent. Meanwhile, heat the chicken stock to boiling. Add the rice to the onions and stir to coat with butter. Add the peas, ham, and chicken stock and stir well.
2. Cover and cook over low heat approximately 20 minutes, or until all of the liquid is absorbed.
3. Sprinkle with Parmesan cheese and serve.

Cheese Pilaf

 00:10 00:35　　Serves 4　　Midwest

American	Ingredients	Metric/Imperial
2 tbsp	Butter or margarine	25 g/1 oz
1 tbsp	Oil	1 tbsp
1	Clove garlic	1
1 cup	Long-grain uncooked rice	225 g/8 oz
2 cups	Chicken stock	450 ml/¾ pint
¼ cup	Grated Parmesan cheese	25 g/1 oz

1. Preheat the oven to 350°F/180°C/Gas Mark 4.
2. Heat the butter and oil in a frying pan. Add the garlic, crushed finely with a little salt, and the rice. Sauté until the rice begins to color.
3. Pour the contents of the pan into a casserole. Add the stock, cover, and cook for about 25–30 minutes, or until the liquid has been absorbed.
4. Remove from the oven, add the cheese, and stir with a fork until it has melted and is well mixed with the rice.
5. For variety, some seedless raisins, seeded black or white grapes, or strips of blanched red or green pepper can be stirred into the rice with the cheese.

Pilaf Rice

 00:05 00:25　　Serves 5–6　　Pacific Southwest

American	Ingredients	Metric/Imperial
4 tbsp	Butter	50 g/2 oz
1	Medium onion, finely chopped	1
1	Clove garlic, crushed	1
1 cup	Rice	225 g/8 oz
6	Coriander seeds	6
1 stick or 1½ tsp powdered	Cinnamon	1 stick or 1½ tsp powdered
6 whole or ½ tsp ground	Cloves	6 whole or ½ tsp ground
	Water or stock	

1. Melt the butter in a frying pan; cook the onion and garlic until soft. Add the rice and cook until the rice begins to take on color. Add the coriander, cinnamon, and cloves.
2. Then cover with water or stock, with about ¼ inch of liquid above the rice. Simmer gently, covered, until done. You may have to add a bit of water from time to time to keep it from sticking.

Noodles Romanoff

Noodles Romanoff

 00:05 00:46　　Serves 4–5　　Midwest

American	Ingredients	Metric/Imperial
6 oz	Fine noodles	175 g/6 oz
1 cup	Cottage cheese	225 g/8 oz
1 cup	Sour cream	250 ml/8 fl oz
1	Small onion, peeled and chopped	1
1 tsp	Worcestershire sauce	1 tsp
	A dash of Tabasco	
	Paprika	
½ cup	Grated sharp cheese	50 g/2 oz

1. Preheat the oven to 350°F/180°C/Gas Mark 4.
2. Cook the noodles in boiling, salted water for about 6 minutes; drain well.
3. Mix all the ingredients except the cheese, and put into a greased casserole. Sprinkle with cheese, and bake for about 40 minutes.

Coleslaw with Pasta

 00:20 00:00　　Serves 4–5　　Midwest

American	Ingredients	Metric/Imperial
1 cup	Finely shredded white cabbage	100 g/4 oz
1 cup	Cooked pasta	100 g/4 oz
3 tbsp	Chopped green pepper	2 tbsp
3 tbsp	Grated carrot	2 tbsp
	Salt	
½ cup	Mayonnaise	125 ml/4 fl oz
2 tbsp	Vinegar	1½ tbsp
2 tsp	Sugar	2 tsp

1. Combine the cabbage, pasta, green pepper, and carrot. Add salt to taste.
2. Mix the mayonnaise with vinegar and sugar, pour over the cabbage mixture, and toss until all the ingredients are well coated with the dressing.

Pasta Medley

00:10
00:20
Serves 5–6   United States

American	Ingredients	Metric/Imperial
1½ cups	Shell pasta	175 g/6 oz
1	Small onion, peeled and chopped	1
4 tbsp	Butter	50 g/2 oz
2 tbsp	Flour	1½ tbsp
2	Chicken bouillon [stock] cubes	2
2 cups	Hot water	450 ml/¾ pint
1 cup	Diced cooked turkey or chicken	175 g/6 oz
½ cup	Chopped cooked bacon	50 g/2 oz
1 cup	Cooked mixed vegetables	100 g/4 oz

1. Cook the pasta in boiling, salted water for about 10 minutes, or follow the package instructions. Drain well.
2. Sauté the onion in 2 tablespoons [25 g/1 oz] of the butter until soft.
3. Make a sauce with the remaining 2 tablespoons [25 g/1 oz] of butter, flour, and hot water in which the bouillon cubes have been dissolved. Cook for 2 minutes. Then add the pasta and all other ingredients. Add seasoning as required, and heat through for about 5 minutes.

Macaroni Mousse

00:15
00:45
Serves 6   Midwest

American	Ingredients	Metric/Imperial
1 cup	Macaroni	100 g/4 oz
1½ cups	Milk	350 ml/12 fl oz
1½ cups	Soft bread crumbs	75 g/3 oz
4 tbsp	Melted butter	50 g/2 oz
1 tbsp	Grated onion	1 tbsp
½ cup	Sliced mushrooms	50 g/2 oz
1 tsp	Worcestershire sauce	1 tsp
¼ tsp	Mustard	¼ tsp
1 cup	Grated Swiss cheese	100 g/4 oz
3	Eggs, separated	3

1. Preheat the oven to 350°F/180°C/Gas Mark 4.
2. Cook the macaroni according to directions. Mix the milk, bread crumbs, butter, onion, mushrooms, seasonings, cheese, and slightly beaten egg yolks. Then mix in the macaroni. Add salt and pepper to taste.
3. Beat the egg whites until stiff and fold into the mixture. Pour into a greased casserole, cover, and bake in the oven for half an hour. Then remove the cover to let the top brown.

Noodles with Cold Sauce

00:10
00:10
Serves 4–6   Pacific Southwest

American	Ingredients	Metric/Imperial
⅔ lb	Farfel or tagliatelle	300 g/11 oz
2 tbsp	Chopped parsley	1½ tbsp
½ oz	Grated Parmesan cheese	15 g/½ oz
1	Clove garlic	1
⅔ cup	Olive oil	150 ml/¼ pint
1 tbsp	Dried basil	1 tbsp
3 tbsp	Finely chopped blanched almonds	2 tbsp
	Salt	
	Pepper	

1. Boil the pasta according to the directions on the package.
2. Grind the parsley, cheese, and garlic in a mortar with a little olive oil. Add basil, almonds, salt, and pepper. Add the remaining olive oil in a fine thin trickle.
3. Serve the cold sauce with noodles, preferably prepared "al dente," so that the elasticity is retained.

Noodle Ring with Meat Sauce

00:15
00:45
Serves 4   United States

American	Ingredients	Metric/Imperial
2 tbsp	Oil	1½ tbsp
1	Onion, peeled and chopped	1
1	Clove garlic, crushed	1
1 cup	Ground [minced] beef	175 g/6 oz
1 tbsp	Tomato purée	1 tbsp
1	Cooking apple, peeled, cored and chopped	1
¼ tsp	Sugar	¼ tsp
¼ tsp	Dried basil	¼ tsp
1 (8-oz) can	Peeled tomatoes	1 (225 g/8 oz) tin
12 oz	Noodles	350 g/12 oz
	Chopped parsley	

1. Heat the oil in a pan, add the onion and garlic, and cook until the onion begins to brown. Add the meat and stir over medium heat for 5 minutes.
2. Add the tomato purée, apple, salt, pepper, sugar, basil, and tomatoes. Cover and simmer for about 40 minutes.
3. While the sauce is cooking, cook the noodles in boiling salted water, drain, and pack into a well-greased 7-inch ring mold. Keep hot.
4. When ready to serve, turn the noodle ring out onto a hot dish, pile the meat sauce in the middle, and sprinkle with chopped parsley.

Noodles with Cold Sauce

Gratin Vegetables and Noodles

Gratin Vegetables and Noodles

00:20
00:55
Serves 4–6
Midwest

American	Ingredients	Metric/Imperial
2	Onions	2
2	Green peppers	2
1 lb	Eggplant [aubergine] or squash [marrow]	450 g/1 lb
5–6	Tomatoes	5–6
2 tbsp	Margarine	25 g/1 oz
2	Cloves garlic, crushed	2
2–3 tbsp	Chili sauce	1½–2 tbsp
1 tsp	Salt	1 tsp
1–2 tsp	Thyme or oregano	1–2 tsp
7–8 oz	Noodles	200–225 g/ 7–8 oz
¾–1¼ cups	Coarsely grated cheese	75–150 g/3–5 oz

1. Slice the onions. Remove seeds and membranes from the peppers, and dice. Slice the eggplant or squash. Dip the tomatoes in hot water. Peel off the skins. Cut the tomatoes into pieces.
2. Heat the margarine in a large pot. Sauté the onion. It should not become brown, only a golden yellow. Add the vegetables. Stir, and season with garlic, chili sauce, salt, and thyme or oregano. Cover and simmer over low heat for 10–15 minutes. Uncover and simmer 15 minutes, until the mixture thickens. Should it become too thick, thin with water.
3. Meanwhile boil the noodles according to the package directions.
4. Grease a baking dish. Place half of the noodles in the bottom of the dish. Cover with the vegetable mixture. End with the noodles and a large amount of grated cheese on top. Bake in a preheated 425°F/220°C/Gas Mark 7 oven about 10 minutes.
5. This is ideal for freezing.

Spaghetti with Ham

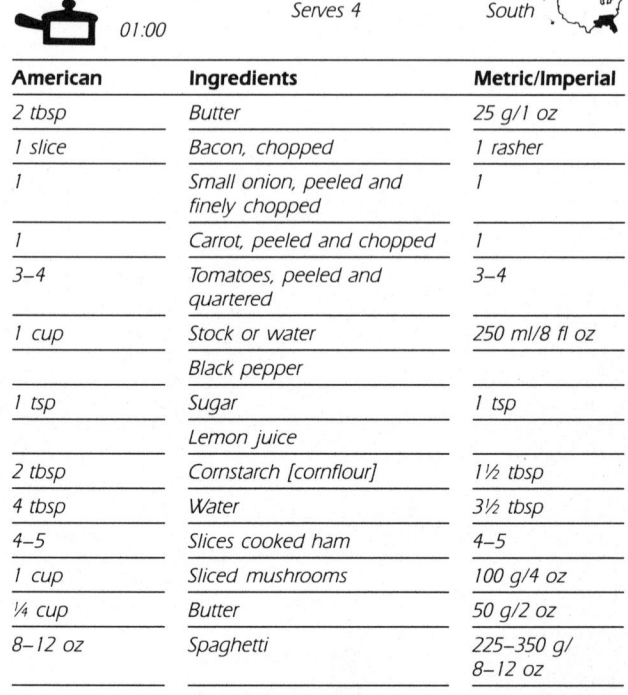

00:20
01:00
Serves 4
South

American	Ingredients	Metric/Imperial
2 tbsp	Butter	25 g/1 oz
1 slice	Bacon, chopped	1 rasher
1	Small onion, peeled and finely chopped	1
1	Carrot, peeled and chopped	1
3–4	Tomatoes, peeled and quartered	3–4
1 cup	Stock or water	250 ml/8 fl oz
	Black pepper	
1 tsp	Sugar	1 tsp
	Lemon juice	
2 tbsp	Cornstarch [cornflour]	1½ tbsp
4 tbsp	Water	3½ tbsp
4–5	Slices cooked ham	4–5
1 cup	Sliced mushrooms	100 g/4 oz
¼ cup	Butter	50 g/2 oz
8–12 oz	Spaghetti	225–350 g/ 8–12 oz
	Grated cheese	

1. Heat the butter in a pan, add the bacon, and cook until the fat begins to melt. Add the onion and carrot, and cook for about 5 minutes. Add the tomatoes; cover and cook gently for 5 minutes. Add the stock, seasoning, sugar, and squeeze of lemon juice. Cover and simmer gently for about 30 minutes. Then rub through a sieve.
2. Return the sauce to the pan; add the cornstarch, blended to a smooth paste with 4 tablespoons [3½ tbsp] of cold water. Stir until boiling, cook for 2 minutes, and adjust the seasoning.
3. Cut the ham into thin strips. Sauté the mushrooms in half of the butter.
4. Cook the spaghetti in boiling salted water for 10 minutes, and drain well. Add the remaining butter, and toss until the spaghetti is evenly coated with the fat. Add the ham and mushrooms.
5. Turn the spaghetti mixture onto a hot dish, pour the hot tomato sauce on top, and sprinkle with grated cheese.

Spaghetti Palermo

00:10
01:00
Serves 6
New England

American	Ingredients	Metric/Imperial
½ lb	Ground [minced] beef	225 g/8 oz
½ lb	Ground [minced] pork	225 g/8 oz
1	Small onion, peeled and chopped	1
1	Green pepper, seeded and sliced thinly	1
½ cup	Sliced green olives	50 g/2 oz
1 small can (2 oz) or ½ cup sliced fresh	Mushrooms	1 small tin (50 g/2 oz) or 50 g/ 2 oz sliced fresh

1 cup	Tomato sauce	250 ml/8 fl oz
1 can (1 lb)	Tomatoes	1 tin (450 g/1 lb)
2 cups	Water	450 ml/¾ pint
1 tsp	Worcestershire sauce	1 tsp
6	Drops Tabasco	6
4 oz	Spaghetti	100 g/4 oz

1. Put the meat into a saucepan, and cook slowly until it begins to brown, stirring constantly. Add the onion and green pepper, and cook for 5 more minutes over low heat. Add the olives, mushrooms, and tomato sauce, and mix in lightly. Mix the tomatoes, water, Worcestershire sauce, and Tabasco, and stir into the meat mixture.
2. Add the spaghetti, placing the ends in first, and coiling them around as they begin to soften. Bring to a boil, cover tightly, and simmer for about 35 minutes, stirring occasionally.
3. Add seasoning to taste, and simmer uncovered for 10–15 minutes more.

Yankee Doodle Macaroni

Spaghetti Bolognese Style

 00:15 / 01:00   Serves 4   New England

American	Ingredients	Metric/Imperial
2 tbsp	Oil	1½ tbsp
1	Onion, peeled and chopped	1
1	Clove garlic, crushed	1
¾–1 lb	Ground [minced] beef	350–450 g/¾–1 lb
2–3	Tomatoes, peeled and halved	2–3
2 tbsp	Flour	1½ tbsp
1–2 tbsp	Tomato purée	1–1½ tbsp
	A pinch of mixed herbs	
1½ cups	Water	350 ml/12 fl oz
1	Beef bouillon [stock] cube	1
8–12 oz	Spaghetti	225–350 g/8–12 oz
2 tbsp	Butter	25 g/1 oz
	Grated cheese	

1. Heat the oil in a pan, and sauté the onion until soft but not browned. Add the garlic, stir in the meat, increase the heat a little, and stir until the meat has browned.
2. Add the tomatoes, flour, seasoning, tomato purée, and herbs. Mix well, add the water in which a bouillon cube has been dissolved, and bring to a boil. Reduce the heat, cover, and simmer for about 40 minutes. Stir occasionally, and add a little extra stock or water if necessary. The sauce should not be too thick.
3. Cook the spaghetti in boiling, salted water for about 10 minutes. Drain well, add the butter, and toss the spaghetti until it is evenly coated with the fat.
4. Turn the spaghetti onto a hot serving dish, pour the sauce over, and sprinkle liberally with grated cheese.

Yankee Doodle Macaroni

 00:15 / 01:00   Serves 6–7   New England

American	Ingredients	Metric/Imperial
3 tbsp	Cooking fat	2 tbsp
2 cups	Finely chopped onion	225 g/8 oz
2	Cloves garlic, crushed	2
½ cup	Sliced mushrooms	50 g/2 oz
1 lb	Ground [minced] beef	450 g/1 lb
1 large can (20 oz)	Peeled tomatoes	1 large tin (575 g/20 oz)
1 tbsp	Chopped parsley	1 tbsp
1 package (7–8 oz)	Macaroni	1 package (200–225 g/7–8 oz)
1–2 tbsp	Butter	15–25 g/½–1 oz
	Grated Parmesan or sharp Cheddar cheese	

1. Heat the fat in a pan; add the onion, garlic, and mushrooms. Sauté until the onion becomes pale yellow in color. Add the meat, and stir until it browns.
2. Add the tomatoes, parsley, and seasoning. Cover and simmer for about 45 minutes.
3. While the meat is cooking, cook the macaroni in boiling salted water for 7–10 minutes (or according to the package instructions). Drain well, and toss in the butter.
4. Turn the macaroni onto a hot platter, pour the meat sauce over it, and sprinkle with grated cheese.

Lasagne

| | 00:25 | | |
| | 01:50 | Serves 6 | Mid Atlantic |

American	Ingredients	Metric/Imperial
2 tbsp	Oil	1½ tbsp
1	Large onion, peeled and finely chopped	1
1	Clove garlic, crushed	1
1 lb	Ground [minced] beef	450 g/1 lb
	Black pepper	
1 can (16 oz)	Tomatoes	1 tin (450 g/1 lb)
1 tbsp	Tomato purée	1 tbsp
4–5 tbsp	Stock or water	4–5 tbsp
½ lb	Lasagne noodles	225 g/8 oz
1 cup	Cottage cheese or ricotta	225 g/8 oz
1	Egg	1
	Grated cheese (preferably Parmesan)	

1. Preheat the oven to 375°F/190°C/Gas Mark 5.
2. Heat the oil in a pan. Add the onion and garlic, cover, and cook slowly until the onion is soft, about 5 minutes. Add the meat and stir until it browns. Add salt, pepper, tomatoes, tomato purée, and stock. Stir until boiling. Then reduce the heat, cover, and simmer very gently for about 1 hour.
3. Cook the lasagne noodles in boiling salted water until tender, 8–10 minutes. Then drain well.
4. Mix the cottage cheese with the beaten egg.
5. When the meat sauce is ready (it should be fairly thick), spoon a little into a shallow baking dish, cover with a layer of noodles, add a little of the cottage cheese mixture, and sprinkle with grated cheese. Repeat the layers, ending with sauce, and sprinkle with the remaining cheese.
6. Cook for about 30 minutes, or until well browned, and serve with a tossed green salad.

Lasagne al Forno

| | 00:25 | | |
| | 01:50 | Serves 4 | Mid Atlantic |

American	Ingredients	Metric/Imperial
½ lb	Lasagne	225 g/8 oz
1 lb	Raw ground [minced] beef	450 g/1 lb
4 tbsp	Oil	3½ tbsp
2	Onions	2
4 tbsp	Flour	3½ tbsp
4 tbsp	Tomato purée	3½ tbsp
1 cup	Beef stock	250 ml/8 fl oz
1 tsp	Oregano	1 tsp
1 cup	Ricotta or cream cheese	225 g/8 oz
½ lb	Mozzarella cheese	225 g/8 oz
4 tbsp	Parmesan cheese	3½ tbsp

1. Preheat the oven to 375°F/190°C/Gas Mark 5.

2. Buy green lasagne noodles preferably and cook them in boiling, salted water for 15 minutes or according to the instructions on the package. Drain well and rinse in cold water to prevent sticking.
3. Prepare the meat sauce: Heat the oil and cook the sliced onion until golden brown. Add the ground meat and sauté for 5–6 minutes, stirring all the time. Add the flour; mix well. Then add the tomato purée and stock. Add pepper, salt, and oregano. Bring to a boil; simmer for 45 minutes.
4. Butter an ovenproof dish. Put a layer of noodles at the bottom. Then put a layer of meat sauce and another layer of noodles. Then a layer of cheese using one half Mozzarella and one half Ricotta. Then noodles, sauce, more noodles, then cheese, etc., finishing with a layer of sauce.
5. Sprinkle the top thickly with grated Parmesan. Bake for 20–30 minutes, until golden brown on top.

Lasagne and Cheese Casserole

| | 00:15 | | |
| | 00:35 | Serves 4 | Midwest |

American	Ingredients	Metric/Imperial
8 oz	Lasagne	225 g/8 oz
½ cup	Seedless raisins	50 g/2 oz
1–2 tbsp	Rum	1–1½ tbsp
1 cup	Sour cream	250 ml/8 fl oz
1 cup	Cottage cheese	225 g/8 oz
2–3 tbsp	Blanched, slivered almonds	1½–2 tbsp

1. Preheat the oven to 350°F/180°C/Gas Mark 4.
2. Soak the raisins in the rum.
3. Cook the lasagne in boiling, salted water until just tender. Drain, rinse with cold water, drain again, and put into a deep buttered casserole. Sprinkle with a little salt and pepper.
4. Mix the sour cream with the cottage cheese and raisins, pour over the lasagne, and toss together lightly. Sprinkle with the almonds, and cook for about 20 minutes.
5. Serve with a salad of watercress, sliced radishes, and cucumber with a little French dressing.

Lasagne and Cheese Casserole

Breads and
Stuffings

Chestnut Stuffing

 00:15
00:30 | Stuffs 1 turkey | South

American	Ingredients	Metric/Imperial
1½ lb	Raw chestnuts in shells	675 g/1½ lb
1–2 cups	Milk or well-flavored stock	250–450 ml/ 8 fl oz–¾ pint
2–3 tbsp	Butter	25–40 g/ 1–1½ oz
1	Large onion	1
2–3 slices	Bacon	2–3 rashers

1. If using raw chestnuts, bake in the oven in dish of salt until the skins come off cleanly, about 20 minutes, or bring to a boil and cook for 5 minutes until the skins are loose. Then remove all outer and inner skins, and cook the chestnuts in milk or stock until tender. Drain and crush in a liquidizer, reserving a few to chop roughly.

2. Melt the butter and cook the onion until tender. After a few minutes, add the chopped bacon and cook. Stir into the chestnut pureé, add salt and pepper and as much milk or stock as is needed to make an easily molded stuffing. Do not make too wet. Add the roughly chopped chestnuts last. Fill this mixture into the neck of the bird and sew up the skin under the back of the bird or skewer securely using wing tips to help hold in the stuffing.

Sausage Meat Stuffing

 00:10
00:03 | Stuffs 1 large turkey | Mid Atlantic

American	Ingredients	Metric/Imperial
1 lb	Pork sausage meat	450 g/1 lb
1 cup	Chopped celery	100 g/4 oz
1 large or 2 medium	Onions	1 large or 2 medium
4 tbsp	Butter	50 g/2 oz
1	Turkey liver	1
2 cups	Bread crumbs	100 g/4 oz
2–3 tbsp	Chopped parsley and thyme	1½–2 tbsp
1	Egg	1
	Juice of ½ lemon	

1. Put the sausage meat in a bowl with the chopped celery. Melt the butter and fry the finely chopped onion and turkey liver for 2–3 minutes. Remove, let cool slightly.

2. Then cut the liver into small pieces and mix into the sausage meat. Add the chopped herbs and bread crumbs. Add a beaten egg to moisten and a little lemon juice. Stuff inside the turkey. Sew up the opening carefully.

Cornbread, Corn, and Mushroom Stuffing

 00:10
00:05 | Stuffs 1 large turkey | Mid Atlantic

American	Ingredients	Metric/Imperial
2 cups	Cornbread [see Index]	225 g/8 oz
2 cups	Fresh white bread crumbs	100 g/4 oz
1½ cups	Whole corn kernels	175 g/6 oz
1½ cups	Mushrooms	175 g/6 oz
6–8 tbsp	Butter	75–100 g/3–4 oz
	Salt, pepper and a pinch of cayenne pepper	
2 tbsp	Chopped mixed herbs	1½ tbsp
2	Beaten eggs	2
6–8 tbsp	Stock	5–7 tbsp

1. Crumble cornbread; add the bread crumbs, corn, and mushrooms, cooked for a few minutes in butter.

2. Add plenty of seasoning, the chopped herbs, beaten eggs, and enough stock to make a moist but not runny mixture. Fill this mixture into the cavity of the bird and sew up the opening.

Oyster Stuffing

 00:10
00:05 | Stuffs 1 large turkey | Mid Atlantic

American	Ingredients	Metric/Imperial
1 pint	Oysters in own liquid	450 ml/¾ pint
5 cups	Fresh bread crumbs	275 g/10 oz
1 cup	Butter	225 g/8 oz
1 cup	Chopped mild onions	100 g/4 oz
½ cup	Sliced celery	50 g/2 oz
4 tbsp	Chopped parsley	3½ tbsp
	Juice of ½ lemon	
	A little white wine or stock	

1. Prepare (or buy ready prepared) oysters in their own salty juice. Prepare the bread crumbs made with 2-day-old loaf. Melt the butter and cook the onions and celery until soft and light golden brown.

2. Add to the bread crumbs, with chopped herbs and seasoning, lemon juice, and the oysters cut in half if large. If too dry, a little white wine or stock may be added, but it must not be too soft. Fill the turkey cavity and sew up carefully.

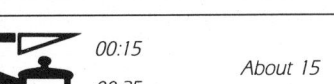

Oyster Stuffing

Banana Bread

00:25		1 loaf	Mid Atlantic
01:00			

American	Ingredients	Metric/Imperial
1¾ cups	Unsifted flour	200 g/7 oz
1 tbsp	Baking powder	1 tbsp
½ tsp	Salt	½ tsp
¾ cup	Sugar	175 g/6 oz
½ cup	Butter	100 g/4 oz
2	Eggs	2
3	Bananas, mashed (ripe)	3
½ cup	Walnuts, chopped (optional)	50 g/2 oz

1. Preheat the oven to 350°F/180°C/Gas Mark 4.
2. Grease a 9 × 5-inch pan.
3. Mix the flour, baking powder, and salt thoroughly. Beat the sugar, shortening, and eggs together until light and fluffy. Mix in the bananas. Add the dry ingredients; stir just until smooth. Pour into the prepared pan.
4. Bake until firmly set when lightly touched in the center, 50–60 minutes. (Bread may crack across the top.) Cool on a rack. Remove from the pan after 10 minutes.

Sour Milk Biscuits

00:15		About 15	Southwest
00:25			

American	Ingredients	Metric/Imperial
2 cups	All-purpose [plain] flour	225 g/8 oz
2 tsp	Baking powder	2 tsp
½ tsp	Salt	½ tsp
2 tsp	Light molasses or corn syrup	2 tsp
½ cup	Sour milk	125 ml/4 fl oz

1. Sift the flour, baking powder, and salt together.
2. Mix the molasses with one half the sour milk, and stir into the flour. Add sufficient extra sour milk to make a pliable dough—it should not be sticky. Roll out on a floured surface to about ¼ inch thick, and cut into rounds with a 2-inch cookie cutter.
3. Bake on a hot griddle, turning once, until well risen and brown on both sides.
4. Keep the first batch warm in a towel while the rest are being cooked.

Sweet Cream Biscuits

 00:20
00:12   36 small biscuits   Midwest

American	Ingredients	Metric/Imperial
4 cups	Flour, sifted	450 g/1 lb
1 tsp	Salt	1 tsp
2 tbsp	Baking powder	1½ tbsp
1½ cups	Heavy [double] cream	350 ml/12 fl oz
4 tbsp	Water (optional)	3½ tbsp

1. Preheat the oven to 450°F/230°C/Gas Mark 8.
2. Sift the flour, salt, and baking powder together. Stir in the heavy cream with a fork, just until all the flour is moistened; add water if necessary to get the proper consistency.
3. Knead on a lightly floured surface, about 10 times. Roll ¾ inch thick; cut with a small floured cutter. Bake on an ungreased baking sheet for 12 minutes, or until golden brown.

Cheddar Cheese Bread

 02:15
00:35   2 loaves   Midwest

American	Ingredients	Metric/Imperial
½ cup	Warm water	125 ml/4 fl oz
2 packages	Dry [dried] yeast	15 g/½ oz
2 tbsp	Sugar	1½ tbsp
1 cup	Milk, scalded	250 ml/8 fl oz
2 tbsp	Butter	25 g/1 oz
2 tsp	Salt	2 tsp
5 cups	Unbleached flour, divided	575 g/1¼ lb
2 cups	Natural sharp Cheddar cheese spread	450 g/1 lb
	Melted butter	

1. Dissolve the yeast and 1 teaspoon of sugar in water in a small bowl. Let stand for 5–10 minutes, or until the mixture expands and becomes bubbly. Set it aside.
2. Combine the shortening, remaining sugar, and salt with milk in a large bowl. Stir until the shortening melts.
3. Stir in 1 cup [100 g/4 oz] of flour. Add the cheese. Add the reserved yeast mixture. Gradually stir in enough of the remaining flour to make a stiff dough.
4. Turn out onto a lightly floured board. Knead 8–10 minutes, or until the dough is smooth and elastic. Dust the board and dough with more flour if necessary to prevent sticking.
5. Shape into a ball. Place in a large, greased bowl. Turn to grease the ball on all sides. Cover and let it rise in a warm draft-free place for 1 hour, or until doubled in bulk.
6. Punch down the dough. Turn out on a lightly floured board. Cover and let it rise for 10 minutes. Cut the dough in half and shape into 2 loaves. Grease 2, 9 × 5 × 3-inch loaf pans.
7. Place the dough in the pans. Cover and let rise in a warm, draft-free place for 30 minutes, or until the dough has risen to the rim of the pans.
8. Bake at 375°F/190°C/Gas Mark 5, for 35 minutes, or until the crust is brown and the top sounds hollow when tapped. Remove from the pans. Cool on racks. Brush the tops lightly with melted butter.

8. Bake at 375°F/190°C/Gas Mark 5, for 35 minutes, or until the crust is brown and the top sounds hollow when tapped. Remove from the pans. Cool on racks. Brush the tops lightly with melted butter.

Blueberry Buckle

 00:15
00:50   Serves 8–10   New England

American	Ingredients	Metric/Imperial
½ cup	Butter	100 g/4 oz
1 cup	Sugar	225 g/8 oz
2½ cups	Flour	275 g/10 oz
2½ tsp	Baking powder	2½ tsp
¼ tsp	Salt	¼ tsp
½ cup	Milk	125 ml/4 fl oz
2 cups	Fresh blueberries	225 g/8 oz
½ tsp	Ground cinnamon	½ tsp
¼ cup	Butter	50 g/2 oz

1. Preheat the oven to 350°F/180°C/Gas Mark 4.
2. Beat the butter with ½ cup [100 g/4 oz] of sugar until creamy. Add the beaten egg and mix well.
3. Sift 2 cups [225 g/8 oz] of the flour with baking powder and salt, and add to the creamed mixture alternately with milk.
4. Pour into a well-greased pan, about 11 × 7 × 1½ inches. Sprinkle blueberries over the batter.
5. Sift the remaining sugar and flour with the cinnamon, blend in the butter, and sprinkle the mixture over the blueberries.
6. Bake for 45–50 minutes. Then cut into squares and serve warm.

Cherry Nut Bread

 00:20
01:00   1 loaf   New England

American	Ingredients	Metric/Imperial
¼ cup	Butter	50 g/2 oz
1 cup	Sugar	225 g/8 oz
1 tsp	Salt	1 tsp
2	Eggs	2
1½ cups	Flour	175 g/6 oz
1½ tsp	Baking powder	1½ tsp
1 (8-oz) can	Pitted [stoned] cherries	1 (225 g/8 oz) tin
½ cup	Pecans, chopped	50 g/2 oz

1. Preheat the oven to 350°F/180°C/Gas Mark 4.
2. Combine the shortening, sugar, salt, and eggs in a medium-sized mixing bowl. Beat well, set it aside. Combine the flour and baking powder; mix well. Drain the cherries, reserving the liquid. Add the flour mixture to the egg mixture alternately with the reserved cherry liquid, mixing after each addition. Stir in the cherries and pecans.
3. Spoon the batter into a floured, greased 9 × 5 × 3-inch loaf pan. Bake for 1 hour. Cool in the pan 10 minutes. Remove to a rack and cool completely.

Coffee Walnut Buns

01:40
00:30   10 buns   United States

American	Ingredients	Metric/Imperial
1 cup	Milk	250 ml/8 fl oz
⅛ cup	Sugar	25 g/1 oz
2 tbsp	Butter	25 g/1 oz
1 cake	Compressed [fresh] yeast	20 g/⅔ oz
4 cups	Flour	450 g/1 lb
	A pinch of salt	
1	Egg	1
¼ cup	Raisins	25 g/1 oz
	Chopped walnuts	
	Sugar Glaze	
1 tbsp	Gelatin [gelatine]	1 tbsp
1 tbsp	Sugar	1 tbsp
½ cup	Water	125 ml/4 fl oz
	Frosting	
1 cup	Confectioners' [icing] sugar	150 g/5¼ oz
1 tsp	Instant coffee powder	1 tsp
1 tsp	Butter	1 tsp
	Milk	

1. Place the milk, sugar, and butter in a small pan and heat until lukewarm and the butter melted. Dissolve the yeast in this mixture.

2. Sift the flour and salt. Make a well in the center, add the egg and lukewarm milk mixture, and beat until thoroughly combined. Stir in the raisins. Cover, and leave in a warm place to rise for about a half hour.

3. Turn onto a lightly floured board, knead for 2 minutes, then place in a lightly greased bowl and leave in a warm place for another 15 minutes.

4. Preheat the oven to 400°F/200°C/Gas Mark 6.

5. Turn onto a floured board, knead lightly, and break off small pieces of dough about the size of a large egg. Roll between the palms of the hands to make a long roll, then twist this into a knot.

6. Put the buns on a well-greased baking sheet about 1–1½ inches apart and leave in a warm place to rise for 20–30 minutes, or until nearly doubled in size. Bake for 20–25 minutes, or until golden brown.

7. While still hot, brush with sugar glaze, drizzle with warm coffee frosting, and sprinkle with chopped walnut meats.

8. To make the sugar glaze, stir the gelatin, sugar, and water over low heat until the sugar dissolves.

9. To make the coffee frosting, sift the confectioners' sugar and instant coffee powder into a bowl. Add the butter and enough milk to make a fairly thin consistency. Heat over a pan of warm water until the butter melts and the frosting is glossy. Keep warm while using.

Coffee Walnut Buns

Garlic Bread

 00:10
00:12 Serves 6–8 United States

American	Ingredients	Metric/Imperial
1	Long French loaf	1
3–4 tbsp	Butter	40–50 g/1½–2 oz
1–2	Cloves garlic	1–2
	Salt and pepper to taste	
1 tsp	Oregano (optional)	1 tsp

1. Cut a long French loaf into slanting slices without quite cutting through the bottom of the loaf. Soften the butter and mix in the crushed garlic and seasonings. Spread this mixture between the slices. Close the loaf and wrap in foil.
2. Heat through at 400°F/200°C/Gas Mark 6 for about 10 minutes, then open the foil and allow the bread to crisp.

Hot Cross Buns

 01:30
00:20 About 16 buns New England

American	Ingredients	Metric/Imperial
2 packages	Dry [dried] yeast	15 g/½ oz
4 cups	Flour	450 g/1 lb
¼ cup	Sugar	50 g/2 oz
1 cup	Lukewarm water	250 ml/8 fl oz
1 tsp	Salt	1 tsp
½ tsp	Ground mixed spices	½ tsp
½ tsp	Ground cinnamon	½ tsp
¼ cup	Butter	50 g/2 oz
3 tbsp	Raisins	2 tbsp
3 tbsp	Currants	2 tbsp
1	Egg	1
	Glaze	
1 tbsp	Sugar	1 tbsp
1 tsp	Gelatin [gelatine]	1 tsp
1 tbsp	Hot water	1 tbsp

1. Preheat the oven to 400°F/200°C/Gas Mark 6.
2. Crumble the yeast into a basin with 1 teaspoon of measured flour and sugar. Stir in lukewarm milk and leave in a warm place for 15 minutes, or until the mixture has become spongy.
3. Sift the flour, salt, and spices into a large bowl, blend in the butter, and add the sugar and fruit.
4. Add the beaten egg to the milk and yeast sponge, add this to the flour mixture, and mix to a soft dough. Cover and leave in a warm place for 40 minutes, when it should have doubled in bulk.
5. Turn onto a lightly floured board. Knead until the dough is smooth and elastic. Divide into 15 or 16 pieces and knead each into a round. Place about ½ inch apart on greased pans. Leave again in a warm place to rise for about 15 minutes.
6. Mix 2 tablespoons [1½ tbsp] flour with a little cold water to make a paste and, using a pastry bag with plain tube, pipe a cross on each bun.
7. Bake for 15–20 minutes. While still hot, brush with glaze, made by dissolving the sugar and gelatin in hot water.

Cinnamon Snails

 13:30
00:20 About 12 buns United States

American	Ingredients	Metric/Imperial
3 cups	Flour	350 g/12 oz
2 tbsp	Sugar	1½ tbsp
	A pinch of salt	
1 cup	Butter	225 g/8 oz
2 packages	Dry [dried] yeast	15 g/½ oz
½ cup	Lukewarm milk	125 ml/4 fl oz
3	Egg yolks	3
	Filling	
½ cup	Finely chopped walnuts	50 g/2 oz
1 cup	Sugar	225 g/8 oz
1 tbsp	Ground cinnamon	1 tbsp
1	Whole egg	1
2	Egg whites	2

1. Sift the flour, sugar, and salt into a bowl. Blend in the butter.
2. Crumble the yeast, mix with milk, and leave for 5 minutes. Add the egg yolks and beat for 3 minutes. Add to the flour mixture and mix to a soft dough. Wrap in waxed [greaseproof] paper or foil and refrigerate overnight.
3. Preheat the oven to 400°F/200°C/Gas Mark 6.
4. Remove from the refrigerator a half hour before the dough is to be used. Put on a lightly floured board and roll out about ¼ inch thick. Brush with a stiffly beaten egg white and sprinkle with walnut filling. Roll up and cut into ½ inch thick slices. Arrange close together in an 11 × 7 inch pan and leave to rise in a warm place for 30–40 minutes.
5. Bake for 20 minutes, or until browned. Then remove from the oven and brush with sugar glaze (see *Coffee Walnut Buns*, in Index).

Cornbread

 00:10
00:20 Serves 6 Mid Atlantic

American	Ingredients	Metric/Imperial
1 cup	Cornmeal	100 g//4 oz
1 cup	Flour	100 g/4 oz
1 tbsp	Baking powder	1 tbsp
½ tsp	Salt	½ tsp
2–4 tbsp	Sugar (optional)	1½–3½ tbsp
1	Egg	1
1 cup	Milk	250 ml/8 fl oz
¼ cup	Fat or oil, melted	60 ml/2 fl oz

1. Preheat the oven to 425°F/220°C/Gas Mark 7.
2. Mix the cornmeal, flour, baking powder, salt, and sugar. Set aside.
3. Beat the egg. Add the milk and fat. Add to the cornmeal mixture; stir just enough to mix. Fill a greased pan half full.
4. Bake 20–25 minutes, until lightly browned.

Cinnamon Snails

Drop Doughnuts 👨‍🍳

	00:15		
	00:20	36 doughnuts	New England

American	Ingredients	Metric/Imperial
¼ cup	Soft butter	50 g/2 oz
1 cup	Sugar	225 g/8 oz
2	Egg yolks, beaten	2
1	Whole egg, beaten	1
4 cups	Flour	450 g/1 lb
2 tsp	Baking powder	2 tsp
¼ tsp	Nutmeg	¼ tsp
½ tsp	Baking soda [bicarbonate of soda]	½ tsp
¾ cup	Buttermilk	175 ml/6 fl oz
	Confectioner's [icing] sugar	

1. Cream the butter and sugar. Stir in the egg yolks and whole egg; blend. In a separate bowl, sift all the dry ingredients together except the confectioners' sugar; add to the creamed mixture, alternating with buttermilk. Stir to mix all ingredients.
2. Cook by dropping spoonfuls of dough into 375°F/190°C deep fat. Fry a few at a time, to keep the fat temperature constant. Turn to brown on all sides. Drain on paper towels [kitchen paper]; sprinkle with confectioners' sugar.

Fourses 👨‍🍳👨‍🍳

	01:30		
	00:15	16 tea cakes	United States

American	Ingredients	Metric/Imperial
2 packages	Dry [dried] yeast	15 g/½ oz
1 tsp	Sugar	1 tsp
1 cup	Lukewarm milk	250 ml/8 fl oz
8 cups	Flour	900 g/2 lb
½ tsp	Salt	½ tsp
¼ cup	Lard	50 g/2 oz
¼ cup	Sugar	50 g/2 oz
5 tbsp	Raisins	4 tbsp
¼ tsp	Ground mixed spices	¼ tsp
3	Eggs	3
¾ cup	Butter	175 g/6 oz

1. Preheat the oven to 475°F/240°C/Gas Mark 9.
2. Cream the yeast with sugar and add milk.
3. Sift the flour and salt together; blend in the lard and add the sugar, raisins, and spices.
4. Beat the eggs, add melted butter, and stir into the warm milk mixture. Mix to a light dough; then cover and leave in a warm place until the dough has doubled in bulk.
5. Turn onto a floured board. Knead lightly. Then roll out to about ¾ inch thick and cut into 4-inch rounds. Put on greased baking sheets and leave until doubled in size.
6. Bake for 15 minutes. Then sprinkle with sugar and eat hot.

Light Dinner Bread (Food Processor Method)

Light Dinner Bread (Food Processor Method)

01:30
00:35
1 loaf
United States

American	Ingredients	Metric/Imperial
4 cups	Flour	450 g/1 lb
1 tsp	Salt	1 tsp
1½ tsp	Ground caraway	1½ tsp
1¾ tbsp	Margarine	25 g/1 oz
1⅔ cups	Milk	300 ml/11 fl oz
3½ packages	Dry [dried] yeast	25 g/1 oz

1. Place the flour, salt, and caraway in your food processor. Melt the margarine in a pan. Add the milk and heat to 98°F/37°C. Dissolve the yeast in the liquid mixture.
2. Using the plastic mixing attachment, start the food processor. Pour in the liquid mixture through the feeder funnel. Run the machine for 20–30 seconds. Take off the top and let the dough rise, covered with a baking cloth, for about 30 minutes.
3. Work the dough on a floured baking board. Shape it in an oval loaf and place it on a buttered baking sheet. Cut slits in the top of the bread with a sharp knife. Let the bread rise, covered, for about 30 minutes.
4. Preheat the oven to 400°F/200°C/Gas Mark 6.
5. Bake in the lower part of the oven for 30–35 minutes. Let the bread cool under a baking cloth.
6. The dough can also be rolled out into 24 buns. Bake them in the middle of the oven at 425°F/220°C/Gas Mark 7 for about 10 minutes.

Jam Slices

01:15
00:10
About 60 slices
United States

American	Ingredients	Metric/Imperial
1⅔ cups	Flour	200 g/7 oz
¼ cup	Sugar	50 g/2 oz
14 tbsp	Margarine or butter, at room temperature	200 g/7 oz
5 tbsp	Jam or applesauce	4 tbsp
⅔ cup	Confectioner's [icing] sugar	90 g/3½ oz
½ tbsp	Water	½ tbsp

1. Place the flour and sugar in a food processor. Divide the margarine or butter into 6–8 pieces and add to the flour and sugar. Using a plastic mixer attachment, start the machine; let the mixture blend for 20–30 seconds. Let the dough stand in a cold place for about an hour.
2. Preheat the oven to 400°F/200°C/Gas Mark 6.
3. Roll the dough out into 4, flat, long-shaped buns and place them on a baking sheet lined with baking paper. Make a depression down the middle of the buns; fill with jam or applesauce. Bake in the middle of the oven for about 10 minutes. Let the buns cool on the baking sheet.
4. Mix the confectioners' sugar and water together. Brush it over the buns and cut them into slanted slices.

Walnut Brown Bread

25:00
01:00
1 loaf
New England

American	Ingredients	Metric/Imperial
1 cup	All-purpose [plain] flour, sifted	100 g/4 oz
½ cup	Sugar	100 g/4 oz
2 tsp	Baking soda [bicarbonate of soda]	2 tsp
½ tsp	Salt	½ tsp
1½ cups	Graham flour [crushed digestive biscuits]	175 g/6 oz
1½ cups	Walnuts, coarsely chopped	175 g/6 oz
1 can (6 fl oz)	Evaporated milk	1 tin (175 ml/6 fl oz)
½ cup	Water	125 ml/4 fl oz
1 tbsp	Vinegar	1 tbsp
1	Egg, well beaten	1
1 cup	Dark molasses [black treacle]	250 ml/8 fl oz
	Maple syrup	

1. Preheat the oven to 325°F/160°C/Gas Mark 3.
2. Sift the flour, sugar, soda and salt together in a large mixing bowl, then stir in the graham flour and 1 cup [100 g/4 oz] of walnuts. Mix the milk and water, then stir in the vinegar; add to the flour mixture. Add the egg and molasses and beat until well mixed.
3. Place in a greased loaf pan. Bake for 1 hour and 15 minutes, or until the bread tests done. Cool for 10 minutes, then remove from the pan. Place on a wire rack and cool completely.
4. Brush the top lightly with maple syrup, then sprinkle the remaining walnuts over the syrup. Wrap in aluminum foil and store for at least 24 hours before serving.

Jam Slices

Different Kinds of Muffins

Boston Brown Bread

  00:10 / 02:00   1 loaf   New England

American	Ingredients	Metric/Imperial
½ cup	Yellow cornmeal	50 g/2 oz
½ cup	Rye flour	50 g/2 oz
½ cup	Graham flour	50 g/2 oz
1⅛ tsp	Baking soda [bicarbonate of soda]	1⅛ tsp
½ tsp	Salt	½ tsp
¾ cup	Milk	175 ml/6 fl oz
3 tbsp	Butter, melted	40 g/1½ oz
6 tbsp	Molasses	5 tbsp
½ cup	Currants	50 g/2 oz

1. Mix the dry ingredients together in a large bowl. Mix the milk, butter, molasses, and currants together in a separate bowl. Add the milk mixture to the dry ingredients and mix well.
2. Pour the batter into a buttered 1-quart [1 1/1¾ pint] mold that can be fitted into a steamer. Steam for 1½–2 hours, or until a cake tester inserted in the center comes out clean.

Pecan Whole-Wheat Muffins

  00:10 / 00:18   12 muffins   Mid Atlantic

American	Ingredients	Metric/Imperial
1 cup	Flour	100 g/4 oz
3 tsp	Baking powder	3 tsp
4 tbsp	Sugar	3½ tbsp
1 tsp	Salt	1 tsp
1 cup	Whole-wheat flour	100 g/4 oz
1 cup	Pecans, chopped	100 g/4 oz
4 tbsp	Butter, melted	50 g/2 oz
1 cup	Milk	250 ml/8 fl oz
2	Eggs	2

1. Preheat the oven to 375°F/190°C/Gas Mark 5.

2. Mix the flour, baking powder, sugar, and salt together in a medium-sized bowl. Stir in the whole-wheat flour and nuts.
3. Add the butter, milk, and eggs to the dry ingredients; blend until thoroughly moistened.
4. Spoon the batter into well-greased muffin tins. Bake for 15–18 minutes.

Blueberry Muffins

  00:15 / 00:30   12 muffins   New England

American	Ingredients	Metric/Imperial
½ cup	Butter	100 g/4 oz
1 cup plus 2 tsp	Sugar	225 g/8 oz plus 2 tsp
2	Eggs	2
2 cups	Flour	225 g/8 oz
2 tsp	Baking powder	2 tsp
½ tsp	Salt	½ tsp
½ cup	Milk	125 ml/4 fl oz
2 cups	Fresh or frozen blueberries	225 g/8 oz
1 tsp	Vanilla extract	1 tsp

1. Preheat the oven to 375°F/190°C/Gas Mark 5.
2. On the low speed of an electric mixer, cream the butter and 1 cup [225 g/8 oz] of the sugar until fluffy. Add the eggs, one at a time, and mix until blended. Sift the flour, baking powder, and salt together. Mix the dry ingredients with the butter mixture alternately with the milk. Add the blueberries and vanilla.
3. Grease a muffin tin, including the top of the muffin tin, or you can use paper cupcake liners. Pile the batter high in the tins and sprinkle with the remaining 2 teaspoons of sugar. Bake for 30 minutes.

Cranberry Muffins

  00:15 / 00:30   10 muffins   Mid Atlantic

American	Ingredients	Metric/Imperial
1¾ cups	Flour	200 g/7 oz
5 tbsp	Sugar	4 tbsp
2½ tsp	Baking powder	2½ tsp
¾ tsp	Salt	¾ tsp
1	Egg, well beaten	1
¾ cup	Milk	175 ml/6 fl oz
5 tbsp	Melted butter	65 g/2½ oz
1 cup	Cranberries, chopped	225 g/8 oz
3 tbsp	Sugar	2 tbsp

1. Preheat the oven to 400°F/200°C/Gas Mark 6.
2. Mix the flour with 2 tablespoons [1½ tbsp] of the sugar, the baking powder, and salt. Combine the egg and milk and add all at once to the flour mixture. Add the shortening and stir only until the dry ingredients are dampened. (Batter will be lumpy.)
3. Sprinkle the cranberries with the remaining 3 tablespoons [2 tbsp] of sugar and stir into the batter. Spoon into greased muffin pans, filling each about two thirds full. Bake for 25–30 minutes, or until done.

Hard Rye Bread Wafers

01:20
00:10   About 25 slices   United States

American	Ingredients	Metric/Imperial
1½	Cakes compressed [fresh] yeast	25 g/1 oz
2 cups	Lukewarm water	450 ml/¾ pint
3 cups	Coarse rye flour	350 g/12 oz
2 cups	All-purpose [plain] flour	225 g/8 oz
2½ tsp	Salt	2½ tsp
1 tsp	Sugar for the rising process	1 tsp
2 tsp	Caraway	2 tsp

1. Crumble the yeast into a large bowl and dissolve it in the water. Add the remaining ingredients and work together into a smooth dough. Sprinkle with a little flour, cover with a baking cloth, and let rise for about 30 minutes.

2. Knead the dough and roll it out so that it is very, very thin. Cut out large, round "cookies" with the help of a plate that is about 7 inches in diameter. Prick the dough with a fork, place the rounds on a baking sheet, spread a baking cloth over them, and let rise for about 20 minutes.

3. Preheat the oven to 400°F/200°C/Gas Mark 6 while the dough is rising. Bake for 5 minutes. Turn the slices over and bake for another 5 minutes.

Overnight Bread

Overnight Bread

13:00
01:30   4 loaves   Midwest

American	Ingredients	Metric/Imperial
1⅔ cups	Bran	150 g/5 oz
6⅓ cups	Water	1.5 l/2½ pints
6 packages	Dry [dried] yeast	50 g/1½ oz
2–2½ tbsp	Salt	1½–2 tbsp
2 tbsp	Oil	1½ tbsp
12 cups	Flour	1.5 kg/3 lb

1. Bring the crushed wheat to a boil in 2 cups [450 ml/¾ pint] water and then let it carefully simmer for 10 minutes. Pour into a bowl and add the remaining cold water. Let stand until cold.

2. Grease 4 9 × 5 × 3-inch loaf pans.

3. Crumble the yeast into the dough liquid, add the salt and oil, and work in the flour. Pour the dough out onto a baking board and knead well. Divide the dough into 4 parts and make loaves of each. Place in the refrigerator, covered with a cloth, and allow to stand until the next morning.

4. Preheat the oven to 400°F/200°C/Gas Mark 6.

5. Place the baking tins directly from the refrigerator into a warm oven for 45 minutes. Bake in 2 batches, allowing 2 of the tins to remain in the refrigerator while the other 2 are in the oven.

6. Cool the loaves on a rack, covered with a baking cloth.

Hard Rye Bread Wafers

Potato Bread

Potato Bread

	01:40		2 loaves	New England
	00:40			

American	Ingredients	Metric/Imperial
8	Medium-large potatoes	8
1 tsp	Salt	1 tsp
2½ cups	Skim [skimmed] milk	600 ml/1 pint
2 tbsp	Oil	1½ tbsp
3	Cakes compressed [fresh] yeast	50 g/2 oz
7 cups (about)	All-purpose [plain] flour	825 g/1¾ lb
¾ cup	Coarse rye flour	75 g/3 oz
1 tbsp	Ground fennel	1 tbsp

1. Peel the potatoes, boil them until soft, and mash them with the salt, a small amount of the milk, and the oil. Add the rest of the milk, warm to finger temperature (98°F/37°C). Stir the yeast into a small amount of the mixture, and pour into the dough.
2. Add most of the all-purpose flour, the rye flour, plus the fennel, and knead into a workable dough. Let rise until doubled in size (about 45 minutes), covered under a cloth.
3. Preheat the oven to 400°F/200°C/Gas Mark 6.
4. Knead the dough on a baking board and divide it into 2 parts. Form each part into 2 round rolls. Let rise until doubled in size, about 40 minutes. Cut a diamond pattern on the top of the loaves, using a sharp knife or a razor blade. Bake for about 40 minutes. Test for doneness, using a toothpick.

Country Rusks

	00:20		About 30	United States
	00:25			

American	Ingredients	Metric/Imperial
½ cup	Butter	50 g/2 oz
2 tbsp	Sugar	1½ tbsp
2 cups	All-purpose [plain] flour	225 g/8 oz
¼ tsp	Baking powder	¼ tsp
¼ tsp	Cream of tartar	¼ tsp
1	Egg	1

1. Preheat the oven to 350°F/180°C/Gas Mark 4.
2. Beat the butter and sugar until light and creamy.
3. Sift the flour, baking powder, and cream of tartar, and add to the creamed mixture alternately with the beaten egg. Add a little water if needed to make a fairly soft dough.
4. Roll out on a floured surface to ¼–½ inch thick. Cut into about 15 rounds with a 2-inch cookie cutter. Place on a baking sheet, and bake for 10 minutes.
5. Remove from the oven, slice through the center, return to the oven, and bake (cut side uppermost) for another 10–15 minutes, or until golden brown. Cool on a wire rack.

Roasting Pan Bread

	01:40		4 loaves	United States
	00:45			

American	Ingredients	Metric/Imperial
6	Cakes compressed [fresh] yeast	100 g/4 oz
7 tbsp	Butter or margarine	90 g/3½ oz
4 cups	Water	1 l/1¾ pint
1 (16 fl oz)	Bottle light beer [lager]	1 (475 ml/ 16 fl oz)
4 tsp	Salt	4 tsp
2 tbsp	Corn [golden] syrup	1½ tbsp
4 lb	Whole-wheat flour	1.75 kg/4 lb

1. Crumble the yeast into a large bread bowl. Melt the butter and pour in the water and the beer. Dissolve the yeast in a little of the lukewarm liquid mixture. Add the rest of the liquid, plus the salt, syrup, and most of the flour. Make into a workable dough.
2. Place the entire dough in a greased roasting pan, about 12 × 16 inches, and flatten it with a floured hand. Prick the surface with a fork. Let the dough rise, covered with a damp baking cloth, for about 1 hour.
3. Preheat the oven to 475°F/240°C/Gas Mark 9.
4. Bake for about 15 minutes, until the bread has become a golden brown. Decrease the heat to 400°F/200°C/Gas Mark 6 and bake for another 30 minutes.
5. Cut the bread into 4 loaves when it has become cold.

Spoon Bread

00:10
00:55   Serves 6–8   South

American	Ingredients	Metric/Imperial
10 oz	Sweetcorn	275 g/10 oz
3 cups	Milk	700 ml/1¼ pints
1 cup	Cornmeal	100 g/4 oz
2 tbsp	Butter	25 g/1 oz
	Salt	
1 tsp	Baking powder	1 tsp
3	Eggs, separated	3

1. Preheat the oven to 325°F/160°C/Gas Mark 3.
2. Cook the corn; drain and cool.
3. Heat 2 cups [450 ml/¾ pint] of milk. Mix the cornmeal with the remaining milk, then add to the hot milk. Cook until thick, stirring constantly. Add butter and salt, and let cool.
4. Then add the corn, baking powder, and slightly beaten egg yolks, mixing well. Beat the egg whites until stiff, fold into the cornmeal mixture, and pour it all into a greased casserole.
5. Bake in oven for about 45 minutes.

Spoon Bread 2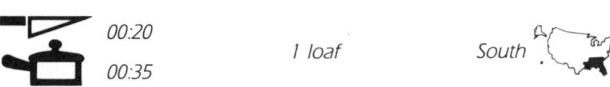

00:20
00:35   1 loaf   South

American	Ingredients	Metric/Imperial
2 cups	Milk	450 ml/¾ pint
¼ cup	Cornmeal	25 g/1 oz
3 tbsp	Butter	40 g/1½ oz
1 tsp	Salt	1 tsp
3	Eggs, separated	3

Roasting Pan Bread

Tea Bread

1. Preheat the oven to 350°F/180°C/Gas Mark 4.
2. Heat the milk in a double boiler, stir in the cornmeal, and cook slowly until thick and smooth. Remove from the heat and add the butter and salt. Let the mixture cool while you beat the egg whites stiff.
3. Beat the egg yolks and add to the cornmeal mixture; then fold in the egg whites and bake for 30 minutes in a buttered pan.

Tea Bread

01:20
00:15   16 small buns   New England

American	Ingredients	Metric/Imperial
⅔ cup	Milk	150 ml/¼ pint
1	Cake compressed [fresh] yeast	20 g/⅔ oz
1	Egg	1
1 tbsp	Sugar	1 tbsp
½ tsp	Salt	½ tsp
2 cups	Flour	225 g/8 oz
5 tbsp	Butter	65 g/2½ oz
1	Beaten egg	1
	Poppy seeds	

1. Heat the milk so that it is lukewarm (98°F/37°C). Dissolve the yeast in the milk. Add the egg, sugar, salt, and flour, and knead well. Let stand and rise in a warm place for about 20 minutes.
2. Preheat the oven to 400°F/200°C/Gas Mark 6.
3. Punch down the dough and knead again. Roll it out into a rectangle about 10 × 16 inches. Slice the butter with a cheese cutter and lay the slices out over half the dough. Fold the other half over the buttered half. Roll the dough and fold it together into 3 layers. Roll again and fold it together into 3 layers. Roll again and fold it again in the same way. Repeat 1 or 2 more times.
4. Finally, roll out the dough so that it is about 12 × 30 inches and fold it lengthwise into 3 layers. Cut the dough into 2-inch wide pieces and let it rise on a baking sheet for about 15 minutes. Brush with an egg and sprinkle with poppy seeds. Bake for about 15 minutes.

Whole-Wheat Bread in a Roasting Pan

Whole-Wheat Bread in a Roasting Pan

01:15
00:20   15 pieces   United States

American	Ingredients	Metric/Imperial
2¾ cups	Whole-wheat flour	300 g/11 oz
1⅔ cups	All-purpose [plain] flour	175 g/6½ oz
1 tsp	Salt	1 tsp
2 tsp	Ground bitter orange peel	2 tsp
2 tbsp	Margarine	25 g/1 oz
1⅔ cups	Water	400 ml/14 fl oz
¼ cup	Corn [golden] syrup	60 ml/2 fl oz
3	Cakes compressed [fresh] yeast	50 g/2 oz
1	Egg	1

1. Place the flour, salt, and the bitter orange peel in your food processor. Melt the margarine in a pan and pour in the water and corn syrup. Heat to 98°F/37°C. Dissolve the yeast in the liquid mixture.
2. Using the plastic mixer attachment, start the machine; pour in the liquid through the feeder funnel. Knead the dough quickly 20–30 seconds. Take off the lid and let the dough rise under a cloth for 30 minutes.
3. Preheat the oven to 425°F/220°C/Gas Mark 7.
4. Turn the dough out onto a baking board and work it lightly. Flatten the dough into a greased roasting pan. Cut the dough into 15 pieces with a floured dough cutter or knife. Cover and let the bread rise for about 30 minutes.
5. Brush the bread with the beaten egg. Bake in the middle of the oven for about 15 minutes. Break the bread into pieces when it has cooled.

Walnut Bread

02:00
00:40   3 small loaves   United States

American	Ingredients	Metric/Imperial
2 cups	Water	450 ml/¾ pint
2 tbsp	Oil	1½ tbsp
1	Cake compressed [fresh] yeast	20 g/⅔ oz
2 tsp	Salt	2 tsp
5 tbsp	Wheat bran	4 tbsp
3¼ cups	Flour	375 g/13 oz
2¾ cups	Light rye flour	300 g/11 oz
½ cup	Walnuts, chopped into large pieces	50 g/2 oz

1. Warm the water and the oil to 98°F/37°C. Dissolve the yeast in a little of the liquid, then add the rest of the liquid. Blend in the salt, wheat bran, flours, and nuts. Pour in the liquid and make into a workable dough; let the dough rise under a cloth for about 45 minutes.
2. Knead the dough and shape it into 3 small loaves or 2 larger loaves. Slash the top with a sharp knife, brush with water, and sprinkle with a little of the rye flour. Let rise until doubled in bulk.
3. Bake in the oven at 400°F/200°C/Gas Mark 6 for 30–40 minutes. Test with a toothpick to make sure the bread is done.

Popovers

00:10
00:35   Serves 4   New England

American	Ingredients	Metric/Imperial
1 cup	Flour	100 g/4 oz
¼ tsp	Salt	¼ tsp
2	Eggs	2
1 cup	Milk [scant measure]	250 ml/8 fl oz
1 tbsp	Shortening	1 tbsp

1. Preheat the oven to 450°F/230°C/Gas Mark 8.
2. Sift the flour and salt together. Mix the beaten eggs, milk, and melted shortening; add gradually to the flour. Beat until smooth with a whisk or use an electric mixer. This should only take about 1 minute.
3. Pour the mixture into greased popover tins or muffin pans, which should only be one third full. Bake for 20 minutes at the temperature given, then reduce the heat to 350°F/180°C/Gas Mark 4 and bake another 15 minutes, or until the popovers are firm.

Walnut Bread

Ginger Waffles

00:15
00:10   Serves 8   New England

American	Ingredients	Metric/Imperial
2 cups	Sifted flour	225 g/8 oz
¾ tsp	Baking soda [bicarbonate of soda]	¾ tsp
½ tsp	Salt	½ tsp
2 tsp	Ground ginger	2 tsp
2	Eggs	2
1 cup	Molasses	250 ml/8 fl oz
5 tbsp	Shortening [vegetable fat]	4 tbsp
½ cup	Buttermilk	125 ml/4 fl oz

1. Mix the flour, baking soda, salt, and ginger together.
2. Separate the eggs. Beat the yolks well with the molasses and add to the flour mixture alternately with buttermilk. Beat until smooth. Add melted shortening. Fold in stiffly beaten egg whites and bake in a hot waffle iron.
3. Serve with whipped cream flavored with molasses, or they are very good served hot with apple sauce and bacon.

Pecan Waffles

00:10
00:10   Serves 5–6   New England

American	Ingredients	Metric/Imperial
1½ cups	Flour	175 g/6 oz
1½ tbsp	Sugar	1¼ tbsp
2½ tsp	Baking powder	2½ tsp
½ tsp	Salt	½ tsp
3	Eggs, separated, whites beaten stiff	3
1½ cups	Milk	350 ml/12 fl oz
5 tbsp	Butter, melted	65 g/2½ oz
¼ cup	Pecans, chopped	25 g/1 oz

1. Measure the dry ingredients into a 4-cup [1 l/1¾ pint] measure; set aside.
2. Beat the egg yolks until thick; combine with the milk and butter. Add the dry ingredients. When the batter is well mixed, gently add the pecans. Fold in the egg whites. Bake in a hot waffle iron. Serve with syrup or cinnamon-sugar mixture.

Waffle Hermits

00:10
00:02   About 36   Mid Atlantic

American	Ingredients	Metric/Imperial
1 cup	Flour	100 g/4 oz
1½ tsp	Baking powder	1½ tsp
½ tsp	Salt	½ tsp
½ tsp	Ground cinnamon	½ tsp
½ tsp	Ground allspice	½ tsp
½ tsp	Ground cloves	½ tsp
½ tsp	Ground ginger	½ tsp
¼ tsp	Grated nutmeg	¼ tsp
½ cup	Butter	100 g/4 oz
½ cup	Sugar	100 g/4 oz
2	Eggs	2
1 tbsp	Molasses	1 tbsp
1 cup	Currants	175 g/6 oz

1. Sift the flour, baking powder, salt, and spices together three times.
2. Cream the butter; add the sugar and beat until light and fluffy. Add the beaten eggs, molasses, and currants.
3. Drop spoonfuls on each section of the heated waffle iron and cook for 2 minutes or until pale brown. Remove carefully with a fork.

Sour Cream Waffles

00:10
00:05   Serves 5   New England

American	Ingredients	Metric/Imperial
2 cups	Flour	225 g/8 oz
½ tsp	Baking soda [bicarbonate of soda]	½ tsp
½ tsp	Salt	½ tsp
1 tbsp	Sugar	1 tbsp
2	Eggs	2
2 cups	Sour cream	450 ml/¾ pint

1. Sift the flour, baking soda, salt, and sugar together.
2. Separate the eggs. Beat the yolks well with cream. Then add the flour and beat until smooth. Fold in the stiffly beaten egg whites, and bake in the waffle iron.

Griddlecakes or Pancakes

00:10
00:10   Serves 4   Mid Atlantic

American	Ingredients	Metric/Imperial
2 cups	Flour	225 g/8 oz
3 tsp	Baking powder	3 tsp
½ tsp	Salt	½ tsp
1 tbsp	Sugar	1 tbsp
2	Eggs	2
1¼ cups	Milk	300 ml/½ pint
2 tbsp	Melted butter	25 g/1 oz

1. Sift the flour, baking powder, salt, and sugar together. Beat the eggs well. Stir in the milk. Then add the flour mixture and beat until smooth. Add melted butter.
2. Pour by tablespoons onto the hot griddle (there is no need to grease it) and cook until golden brown, turning once only.

Oatmeal Griddle Cake

 00:10
00:10   *Serves 6*   *United States*

American	Ingredients	Metric/Imperial
½ cup	All-purpose [plain] flour	50 g/2 oz
1 tsp	Baking powder	1 tsp
½ tsp	Salt	½ tsp
1½ cups	Cold cooked oatmeal	350 g/12 oz
½ cup	Evaporated milk	125 ml/4 fl oz
¼ cup	Water	60 ml/2 fl oz
2 tbsp	Melted bacon fat or butter	1½ tbsp
1	Egg	1

1. Sift the flour, baking powder, and salt together.
2. Combine the oatmeal, evaporated milk, water, and melted fat. Add the beaten egg. Stir the oatmeal mixture into the flour, and combine well.
3. Drop in spoonfuls onto a hot griddle, and cook until brown on the underside. Then turn and complete the cooking.
4. Serve hot.

Blueberry-Sour Cream Pancakes

00:10
00:15   *Serves 4*   *New England*

American	Ingredients	Metric/Imperial
1 cup	Flour, sifted	100 g/4 oz
3 tsp	Baking powder	3 tsp
¼ tsp	Salt	¼ tsp
1 tbsp	Sugar	1 tbsp
1	Egg	1
1 cup	Milk	250 ml/8 fl oz
¼ cup	Sour cream	60 ml/2 fl oz
2 tbsp	Butter, melted	25 g/1 oz
½ cup	Blueberries	50 g/2 oz

1. Sift the dry ingredients together. Beat the egg, milk, and sour cream together. Pour the milk mixture over the dry ingredients and blend with a rotary beater until the batter is just smooth. Stir in the butter. Fold in the blueberries.
2. Pour 2 tablespoons [1½ tbsp] of batter onto a hot griddle for each cake. Brown on 1 side until golden. Turn and brown on the other side. If the cakes brown too fast, lower the heat. Serve them hot with butter and maple syrup.

Beverages, Sauces and Preserves

Boiled Berry Juice

Hot Apple Toddy

| | 00:05 | 4 pints | |
| | 00:05 | [1.75 l/3 pints] | Mid Atlantic |

American	Ingredients	Metric/Imperial
4 pints	Apple juice	1¾ l/3 pints
⅔ cup	Brown [demerara] sugar	150 g/5 oz
1	Lemon, cut into thin slices	1
	Angostura bitters	

1. Put the apple juice, sugar, and slices of lemon into a pot. Bring to a boil, and simmer for 5 minutes.
2. Add a dash or two of angostura bitters to taste.

Boiled Berry Juice Concentrate

|  | 00:30 | | |
| | 00:15 | Serves 8 | New England |

American	Ingredients	Metric/Imperial
2 quarts	Berries, well ripened, without any bad spots	900 g–2 kg/2–4 lb
1¼–1⅔ cups	Water	300–400 ml/½–⅔ pint
2⅓ cups	Sugar per quart drained juice	550 g/19 oz
¼ tsp	Sodium benzoate per quart juice	¼ tsp

1. Boil the water and the cleaned berries (currants do not need to be cleaned, just rinsed, and the pits do not need to be removed from cherries) until they become runny, about 10 minutes. Crush the berries against the side of the pot while boiling. Strain the mixture through a straining-cloth. Do not let it drain for more than 30 minutes.

2. Measure the juice and pour it back into the pot. Bring to a boil, add the sugar, and bring to a boil again. Skim the surface whenever necessary.
3. Add the sodium benzoate, which first has been stirred into a small amount of juice, and then fill warm, well-cleaned bottles up to the brims. Seal immediately.
4. It is a good idea to cover the bottle corks with paraffin. Do this by dipping them into melted paraffin. The bottles will then seal more tightly. Store the juice in a cold and dark place.
5. Dilute the concentrate with water before serving.

Champagne Punch

| | 00:05 | | |
| | 00:00 | Serves 15–20 | United States |

American	Ingredients	Metric/Imperial
	Juice of 12 lemons	
	Confectioners' [icing] sugar	
1 quart	Soda water	1 l/1¾ pints
1 cup	Maraschino	250 ml/8 fl oz
1 cup	Curaçao	250 ml/8 fl oz
1 pint	Brandy	450 ml/¾ pint
2 quarts	Champagne	2 l/3½ pints

1. Put the lemon juice in a large punch bowl. Add enough sugar to sweeten. Add soda water and plenty of ice cubes, and stir well. Then add maraschino, curacao, and brandy. Stir well.
2. Just before serving, add the champagne. Stir well. Decorate with fruits in season, and serve in small glasses.

Champagne Punch

Party Punch

| | 01:30 | About 6 pints | Pacific Southwest |
| | 00:05 | [3 1/5 pints] | |

American	Ingredients	Metric/Imperial
1 cup	Sugar	225 g/8 oz
4 cups	Water	1 1/1¾ pints
¼ cup	Strong tea	60 ml/2 fl oz
	Juice of 4 oranges	
	Juice of 4 lemons	
2 cups	Grape juice	450 ml/¾ pint
2 cups	Crushed pineapple	450 ml/¾ pint
1½ pints	Ginger ale	700 ml/1¼ pints
	Orange slices and maraschino cherries (optional)	

1. Combine the sugar and water in a pot. Stir over low heat until the sugar dissolves, bring to a boil, and simmer for 5 minutes. Add the strained tea and let cool.
2. Add the strained orange and lemon juice, grape juice, and contents of the can of pineapple. Refrigerate, and add ginger ale just before serving.
3. Orange slices and maraschino cherries can be used as a garnish, if desired.

Spicy Mocha Nightcap

| | 00:10 | Serves 5–6 | United States |
| | 00:15 | | |

American	Ingredients	Metric/Imperial
¼ cup	Sugar	50 g/2 oz
4 tsp	Instant coffee powder	4 tsp
2	Squares (50/2 oz) unsweetened baking chocolate	2
¾ tsp	Ground cinnamon	¾ tsp
¼ tsp	Grated nutmeg	¼ tsp
	A pinch of salt	
1 cup	Water	250 ml/8 fl oz
3 cups	Milk	700 ml/1¼ pints
	A little heavy [double] cream, whipped	

1. Put the sugar, coffee, chocolate, spices, salt, and water into the top of a double boiler over hot water. Stir over low heat until the chocolate has melted and the mixture is smooth. Bring to a boil, and cook for 5 minutes, stirring all the time.
2. Add the milk and heat well, stirring constantly.
3. When ready to serve, beat until frothy with a rotary beater, pour into serving cups, and top with whipped cream.

Port Sangria

| | 00:05 | About 2½ pints | United States |
| | 00:00 | [1¼ 1/2 pints] | |

American	Ingredients	Metric/Imperial
1	Bottle claret	1
½	Bottle port wine	½
1 cup	Marsala	250 ml/8 fl oz
¾ cup	Fresh orange juice	175 ml/6 fl oz
1 tbsp	Lemon juice	1 tbsp

1. Combine all the ingredients and refrigerate.

Party Punch, Port Sangria and Hot Chocolate

Hot Chocolate

| | 00:05 | About 4 cups | Midwest |
| | 00:10 | [1 1/1¾ pints] | |

American	Ingredients	Metric/Imperial
1½	Squares unsweetened baking chocolate (40 g/1½ oz)	1½
¼ cup	Sugar	50 g/2 oz
¼ tsp	Salt	¼ tsp
1 cup	Boiling water	250 ml/8 fl oz
3 cups	Hot milk	700 ml/1¼ pints
½ tsp	Vanilla extract	½ tsp
	Marshmallows	

1. Melt the chocolate in the top of a double boiler over hot water, stir in the sugar and salt, add boiling water gradually, and stir until smooth.
2. Add the hot milk, and cook for 2 minutes. Add vanilla.
3. To serve, put a marshmallow into each cup, and add the hot chocolate.

Fruity Wine Punch

Iced Coffee

02:00
00:00   Serves 8   United States

American	Ingredients	Metric/Imperial
5 tbsp	Instant coffee powder	4 tbsp
2 cups	Hot water	450 ml/¾ pint
6 cups	Cold water	1.5 l/2½ pints
	Sugar	
	Vanilla ice cream	
	Whipped cream	
	Grated chocolate	

1. Dissolve the coffee in the hot water; add cold water and sugar to taste. Refrigerate until ready to serve.
2. Put a scoop of ice cream into each glass, and fill with the iced coffee. Top with cream and a sprinkling of grated chocolate.

Hot Spicy Punch

00:00
00:05   About 3 pints [1.5 l/2½ pints]   United States

American	Ingredients	Metric/Imperial
2 pints	Cider or dry red wine	1 l/1¾ pints
1 cup	Orange juice	250 ml/8 fl oz
½ cup	Lemon juice	125 ml/4 fl oz
2	Sticks cinnamon	2
1 tsp	Whole cloves	1 tsp
2 tbsp	Chopped crystallized ginger	1½ tbsp

1. Put all the ingredients into a pot, and bring to a boil. Then simmer for 5 minutes.
2. Strain through cheesecloth and sweeten to taste.
3. Reheat as required.

Yule Egg Nog

12:00
00:00   Serves 20–25   New England

American	Ingredients	Metric/Imperial
12	Eggs	12
	A pinch of baking soda [bicarbonate of soda]	
¾ cup	Rum	175 ml/6 fl oz
4½ cups	Confectioners' [icing] sugar	675 g/1½ lb
1 quart	Milk	1 l/1¾ pints
1 quart	Cream	1 l/1¾ pints
2 quarts	Rye or bourbon	2 l/3½ pints
	Grated nutmeg	

Fruity Wine Punch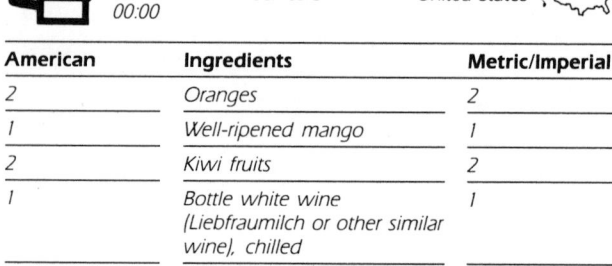

03:10
00:00   Serves 8   United States

American	Ingredients	Metric/Imperial
2	Oranges	2
1	Well-ripened mango	1
2	Kiwi fruits	2
1	Bottle white wine (Liebfraumilch or other similar wine), chilled	1
1¼ cups	Dry white vermouth	300 ml/½ pint
2 bottles	Clear tonic water, chilled	2
¾ cup	Orange juice (preferably frozen)	175 ml/6 fl oz
	Ice cubes	

1. Peel one of the oranges, removing as much of the white membrane as possible. Wash the other orange and the kiwi fruits, and cut these into thin slices. Peel the mango and cut it into small pieces. If you cannot find mango or kiwi fruits, use other fruits, such as several well-ripened pears, or cut grapes from which the seeds have been removed.
2. Place all the fruit, with the exception of the unpeeled orange, in a large bowl or pitcher. Pour in the wine and the vermouth, cover, and refrigerate for several hours so that the fruit draws in the flavor of the wine.
3. Right before serving, pour in the well-chilled tonic water and orange juice, and add the sliced unpeeled orange, plus ice cubes. Serve with a punch spoon in the glasses so the guests may taste the wine-soaked pieces of fruit.

1. Beat the egg yolks and whites separately. Pour together and add baking soda, rum, and sugar. Beat until thick.
2. Add the milk, cream, and rye or bourbon. Let stand in the refrigerator overnight.
3. Before serving, stir again, and serve in small glasses with a sprinkling of nutmeg on top.

Cranberry Punch

 02:00 / 00:00 — Serves 6–8 — Mid Atlantic

American	Ingredients	Metric/Imperial
½ cup	Sugar	100 g/4 oz
½ cup	Boiling water	125 ml/4 fl oz
2 cups	Bottled cranberry juice	450 ml/¾ pint
1 cup	Orange juice	250 ml/8 fl oz
¼ cup	Lemon juice	60 ml/2 fl oz
2 cups	Ginger ale	450 ml/¾ pint
	Orange slices and mint for garnish	

1. Dissolve the sugar in the boiling water, add the fruit juices, and set aside to chill.
2. To serve, put some crushed ice into glasses, half fill with the fruit juice, and top with chilled ginger ale. Put a slice of orange over the side of each glass and tuck a mint leaf underneath.

Spiced Tea

 02:05 / 00:05 — Serves 6–8 — United States

American	Ingredients	Metric/Imperial
6	Tea bags	6
¼ tsp	Allspice	¼ tsp
¼ tsp	Ground cinnamon	¼ tsp
¼ tsp	Grated nutmeg	¼ tsp
2½ cups	Boiling water	600 ml/1 pint
¾ cup	Sugar	175 g/6 oz
2 cups	Cranberry juice	450 ml/¾ pint
1½ cups	Water	350 ml/12 fl oz
½ cup	Orange juice	125 ml/4 fl oz
5 tbsp	Lemon juice	4 tbsp
	Lemon slices	

1. Put the tea bags into an earthenware or pottery pitcher, add the spices, and cover with boiling water. Cover, leave for 5 minutes. Then strain.
2. Add the sugar; stir until it has dissolved. Then add the other ingredients.
3. Chill thoroughly, and serve in glasses with a slice of lemon.

Summer Freshness

Summer Freshness

 00:10 / 00:00 — Serves 1 — South

American	Ingredients	Metric/Imperial
1–2	Slices kiwi fruit	1–2
1–2	Sliced strawberries	1–2
	Dab orange sherbet [sorbet]	
1 cup	Chilled bubbly cider or champagne	250 ml/8 fl oz

1. Cover the bottom of a glass with the kiwi slices and strawberries. Add a dab of sherbet.
2. Fill the glass with cider or champagne.

Grape Juice Cup

 02:00 / 00:05 — About 3 pints [1.5 l/2½ pints] — South

American	Ingredients	Metric/Imperial
2 cups	Grape juice	450 ml/¾ pint
2 cups	Apple juice	450 ml/¾ pint
	Soda water	
¼ cup	Sugar	50 g/2 oz
	Juice of 2 lemons	
1	Banana, sliced	1
1 cup	Grapes, peeled and seeded	100 g/4 oz

1. Mix the grape juice and apple juice with 2 cups [450 ml/¾ pint] of soda water and set aside to chill thoroughly.
2. Make a syrup with the sugar and ½ cup [125 ml/4 fl oz] of water. Boil for 5 minutes and let chill.
3. When ready to serve, mix all the ingredients together and top with more soda water.

Devil Baste

| | 00:05 | About ½ cup | | United States |
| | 00:00 | [125 ml/4 fl oz] | | |

American	Ingredients	Metric/Imperial
2 tbsp	Hot chutney	1½ tbsp
2 tbsp	Prepared mustard	1½ tbsp
1 tbsp	Anchovy paste	1 tbsp
4 tbsp	Oil	3½ tbsp
	Cayenne pepper	

1. Combine the chutney, mustard, and anchovy paste with the oil, and add cayenne pepper to taste.

Barbecue Baste

| | 00:02 | About ½ cup | | Southwest |
| | 00:00 | [125 ml/4 fl oz] | | |

American	Ingredients	Metric/Imperial
½ cup	Oil	125 ml/4 fl oz
2 tbsp	Worcestershire sauce	1½ tbsp
	A good pinch of salt	
	A dash of pepper	

1. Put all the ingredients in a screwtop jar, and shake well together.

Spicy Barbecue Sauce

| | 00:05 | About 2½ cups | | Southwest |
| | 00:25 | [600 ml/1 pint] | | |

American	Ingredients	Metric/Imperial
2 tbsp	Oil	1½ tbsp
¾ cup	Finely chopped onion	75 g/3 oz
¾ cup	Maple syrup	175 ml/6 fl oz
1 cup plus 2 tbsp	Vinegar	250 ml/8 fl oz plus 1½ tbsp
¾ cup	Water	175 ml/6 fl oz
3	Beef bouillon [stock] cubes	3
1½ tbsp	Worcestershire sauce	1¼ tbsp
2 tsp	Salt	2 tsp
¼ tsp	Pepper	¼ tsp
3	Drops Tabasco sauce	3

1. Heat the oil in a pan and sauté the onion until lightly browned.
2. Add all the other ingredients, bring slowly to boiling point, and simmer for 15 minutes, stirring frequently.

Tangy Barbecue Sauce

| | 12:00 | About ¾ cup | | Southwest  |
| | 00:00 | [175 ml/6 fl oz] | | |

American	Ingredients	Metric/Imperial
½	Small onion	½
1	Clove garlic	1
1	Sprig parsley	1
½ cup	Tomato ketchup	125 ml/4 fl oz
2 tbsp	Wine vinegar	1½ tbsp
2 tbsp	Oil	1½ tbsp
1 tsp	Worcestershire sauce	1 tsp
	A little sugar	

1. Mince the onion, garlic, and parsley and put into a screwtop jar with all the other ingredients.
2. Screw down tightly and shake well until all the ingredients are well blended.
3. Let stand before using, preferably overnight, shaking occasionally.

Barbecue Sauce 1

| | 00:05 | About 3½ cups | | Southwest |
| | 00:15 | [875 ml/1½ pints] | | |

American	Ingredients	Metric/Imperial
½ cup	Butter or margarine	100 g/4 oz
1 cup	Chopped onion	100 g/4 oz
1 can (10¾ oz)	Tomato soup	1 tin (300 g/10¾ oz)
1 cup	Water	250 ml/8 fl oz
2 tsp	Vinegar	2 tsp
1 tsp	Worcestershire sauce	1 tsp
¼ tsp	Salt	¼ tsp
⅛ tsp	Pepper	⅛ tsp
½ tsp	Dry mustard	½ tsp
½ tsp	Paprika	½ tsp
¼–½ tsp	Chili powder	¼–½ tsp

1. Heat the butter and sauté the onion until soft but not colored.
2. Add all the other ingredients, and simmer for 10 minutes.

Barbecue Sauce 2

| | 00:05 | About 3 cups | | Southwest  |
| | 00:05 | [700 ml/1¼ pints] | | |

American	Ingredients	Metric/Imperial
6 oz	Tomato paste	175 g/6 oz
1½ cups	Water	350 ml/12 fl oz
2 tsp	Lemon juice	2 tsp

American	Ingredients	Metric/Imperial
1	Onion, peeled and minced, or very finely chopped	1
1	Clove garlic, crushed	1
½ tsp	Celery salt	½ tsp
½ tsp	Onion salt	½ tsp
4 tsp	Worcestershire sauce	4 tsp
	Pinch of cayenne pepper	

1. Put all the ingredients together and simmer for 5 minutes.

Barbecue Sauce 3

 00:05
00:10
About 1½ cups
[350 ml/12 fl oz]
Southwest

American	Ingredients	Metric/Imperial
¼ cup	Butter or margarine	50 g/2 oz
¼ cup	Olive oil	125 ml/4 fl oz
½ cup	Vinegar	125 ml/4 fl oz
2 tbsp	Tomato ketchup	1½ tbsp
1 tsp	Grated lemon rind	1 tsp
4–5 tbsp	Lemon juice	3½–4 tbsp
1½ tbsp	Worcestershire sauce	1¼ tbsp
2 tsp	Salt	2 tsp
½ tsp	White pepper	½ tsp
½ tsp	Cayenne pepper	½ tsp
1	Clove garlic, crushed	1

1. Put the butter, oil, vinegar, and ketchup into a pan and stir over low heat until the butter has melted and the ingredients are well mixed.
2. Add all the other ingredients and bring slowly to a boil.
3. Remove from heat and let stand before using.

Barbecue Sauce 4

 00:08
00:00
About 2 cups
[450 ml/¾ pint]
Southwest

American	Ingredients	Metric/Imperial
1	Clove garlic	1
½ cup	Vinegar	125 ml/4 fl oz
1¼ cups	Tomato ketchup	300 ml/½ pint
2 tsp	Prepared mustard	2 tsp
1 tsp	Worcestershire sauce	1 tsp
½ tsp	Tabasco	½ tsp
2½ tbsp	Orange juice	1¾ tbsp
1 tsp	Sugar	1 tsp
	A good pinch of salt	

1. Crush the garlic very finely and put it into a bowl.
2. Add all the other ingredients and mix well.

Tangy Barbecue Sauce

Barbecue Sauce 5

 00:05
00:00
About 1 cup
[250 ml/8 fl oz]
Southwest

American	Ingredients	Metric/Imperial
2 tsp	Dry mustard	2 tsp
½ tsp	Curry powder	½ tsp
2 tbsp	White wine vinegar	1¼ tbsp
1 cup	Tomato ketchup	250 ml/8 fl oz
2 tsp	Prepared horseradish [relish]	2 tsp

1. Mix the mustard and curry powder into a smooth paste with the vinegar, and add to the ketchup and horseradish.

Sweet-sour Jelly Sauce

00:05
00:10
About 3 cups
[700 ml/1¼ pints]
Pacific Southwest

American	Ingredients	Metric/Imperial
½ cup	Brown [demerara] sugar	100 g/4 oz
½ cup plus 2 tbsp	White wine vinegar	125 ml/4 fl oz plus 1½ tbsp
1½ tsp	Dry mustard	1½ tsp
1 tbsp	Flour	1 tbsp
2	Eggs	2
1 cup	Currant jelly	225 g/8 oz

1. Heat the sugar and ½ cup [125 ml/4 fl oz] of vinegar in a double boiler until the sugar has melted.
2. Mix the flour and mustard smoothly with the 2 tablespoons [1½ tbsp] of vinegar and put into the pan together with the lightly beaten eggs and jelly. Stir continuously over low heat until the sauce thickens.

Tartare Sauce

00:10
00:00
About 2 cups
[450 ml/¾ pint]
Pacific Southwest

American	Ingredients	Metric/Imperial
1⅔ cups	Mayonnaise	375 ml/13 fl oz
3 tbsp	Chopped sweet pickle	2 tbsp
3 tbsp	Chopped stuffed olives	2 tbsp
1 tbsp	Chopped capers	1 tbsp
1 tbsp	Minced onion	1 tbsp
1 tbsp	Minced parsley	1 tbsp
1 tsp	Vinegar	1 tsp
1 tsp	Lemon juice	1 tsp

1. Combine all the ingredients, and taste for seasoning. A little extra vinegar or lemon juice and a pinch of salt may be required, depending on the kind of mayonnaise used.

Pineapple Glaze

00:05
00:05
About 1¼ cups
[300 ml/½ pint]
Pacific Northwest

American	Ingredients	Metric/Imperial
1 can (8 oz)	Crushed pineapple	1 tin (225 g/8 oz)
3 tbsp	Brown [demerara] sugar	2 tbsp
2 tbsp	Lemon juice	1½ tbsp
1 tbsp	Prepared mustard	1 tbsp

1. Drain the pineapple and put into a pan with 2 tablespoons [1½ tbsp] of the pineapple juice.
2. Add the remaining ingredients, and simmer for 5 minutes.

Blackberry Sauce

00:10
00:15
Serves 7–8
United States

American	Ingredients	Metric/Imperial
4 cups	Blackberries or blueberries	450 g/1 lb
¾ cup	Water	175 ml/6 fl oz
½ cup	Sugar	100 g/4 oz
1 tbsp	Cornstarch [cornflour]	1 tbsp
	Lemon juice	

1. Wash the berries, put into a pan with 3–4 [2–3½] tablespoons of water, and cook over low heat for 5–10 minutes.
2. Draw off the heat, add sugar, and stir until the sugar had dissolved. Then pass through a sieve. Return the purée to the pan.
3. Blend the cornstarch smoothly with the remaining water, and stir into the purée. Stir until boiling. Then boil for 2 minutes.
4. Take off the heat, add strained lemon juice to taste, cover, and let stand to get cold.

Medium Cream Sauce

00:05
00:10
About 1¼ cups
[300 ml/½ pint]
United States

American	Ingredients	Metric/Imperial
1 cup	Milk	250 ml/8 fl oz
1	Small onion	1
1	Sprig parsley	1
2 tbsp	Butter	25 g/1 oz
2 tbsp	Flour	1½ tbsp
	Salt and pepper	
2 tbsp	Heavy [double] cream	1½ tbsp

1. Place the milk in a pan with the onion and parsley; bring to a boil.
2. Melt the butter in a different pan; add the flour, stirring with a whisk. Strain the hot milk into the butter mixture, stirring constantly.
3. When the sauce has thickened, simmer gently for 4 minutes, stirring occasionally. If the sauce is too thick, add a little more milk.
4. Add salt and pepper, and the cream.

Honey Butter Syrup

00:05
00:00
About ¾ cup
[175 ml/6 fl oz]
Mid Atlantic

American	Ingredients	Metric/Imperial
½ cup	Butter	100 g/4 oz
½ cup	Honey	125 ml/4 fl oz

1. Cream butter until light and fluffy, then gradually beat in honey.

Mocha Syrup

00:10
00:05
1¼ cups
[300 ml/½ pint]
United States

American	Ingredients	Metric/Imperial
½ cup	Firmly packed brown [demerara] sugar	100 g/4 oz
3 tsp	Instant coffee powder	3 tsp
½ cup	Water	125 ml/4 fl oz
2 tbsp	Butter	25 g/1 oz
6 oz	Chocolate chips	175 g/6 oz
1 tsp	Vanilla extract	1 tsp

1. Put the sugar, coffee, water, and butter into a pan and stir over low heat until the mixture boils. Cook for 3 minutes, stirring all the time.
2. Remove from the stove, add the chocolate and vanilla, and stir until the chocolate has melted. Serve warm.

Pickled Pears

00:10 00:30 About 4 pints [1.75 1/3 pints] Mid Atlantic

American	Ingredients	Metric/Imperial
2 cups	Cider vinegar	450 ml/¾ pint
2 cups	Water	450 ml/¾ pint
4 cups	Sugar	900 g/2 lb
2	Sticks cinnamon	2
2	Small pieces root ginger	2
3 tbsp	Whole cloves	2 tbsp
	Red food coloring (optional)	
3 lb	Pears, peeled but with stem left on	1.5 kg/3 lb

1. Put the vinegar, water, and sugar into a saucepan; add the cinnamon sticks, ginger, and 1 tablespoon of cloves. Bring slowly to the boiling point, and boil for 5 minutes. Add a few drops of red food coloring, if desired.
2. Reduce the heat, and add the pears, each stuck with 2–3 cloves. Cook until the pears are tender and almost transparent.
3. Pack into hot sterilized jars, cover with the strained syrup, and seal at once.

Jelly Syrup

00:05 00:08 About 1 cup [250 ml/8 fl oz] United States

American	Ingredients	Metric/Imperial
1 cup	Cranberry jelly	225 g/8 oz
¼ cup	Water	60 ml/2 fl oz
3 tbsp	Butter	40 g/1½ oz

1. Put the cranberry (or other) jelly into a pan with the water. Stir over low heat until the jelly has melted. Then stir in the butter and serve warm.

Orange Syrup

00:10 00:15 1½ cups [350 ml/12 fl oz] United States

American	Ingredients	Metric/Imperial
1	Orange	1
¾ cup	Granulated sugar	175 g/6 oz
¾ cup	Brown [demerara] sugar	175 g/6 oz
1 cup	Orange juice	250 ml/8 fl oz
2 tbsp	Butter	25 g/1 oz

1. Wash and dry the orange but do not peel. Cut into thin slices; cut each slice in quarters and discard the seeds.
2. Put the granulated and brown sugar into a pan with the orange juice, and stir until boiling. Add the pieces of orange and cook over low heat for 10 minutes. Mix in butter and serve warm.

Pickled Pears

Orange Marmalade Syrup

00:05 00:08 About 1 cup [250 ml/8 fl oz] South

American	Ingredients	Metric/Imperial
¾ cup	Orange marmalade	350 g/12 oz
¾ cup	Water	175 ml/6 fl oz
2 tbsp	Butter	25 g/1 oz

1. Put the marmalade and water into a pan, and stir over low heat until the mixture is smooth. Stir in butter.

Brown Sugar Syrup

00:05 00:05 About 1 cup [250 ml/8 fl oz] United States

American	Ingredients	Metric/Imperial
1 cup	Brown [demerara] sugar	225 g/8 oz
⅛ tsp	Salt	⅛ tsp
¾ cup	Water	175 ml/6 fl oz
2 tbsp	Heavy [double] cream	1½ tbsp

1. Put the sugar, salt, and water into a pan, and stir over medium heat until the mixture boils. Cook for 5 minutes, stirring all the time. Cool a little, stir in the cream, and serve warm.

Cookies
and Cakes

Flaked Almond Cookies

Almond Drops

 00:15
00:10   36 cookies   Pacific Southwest

American	Ingredients	Metric/Imperial
3	Egg whites	3
4 tbsp	Sugar	3½ tbsp
2 tbsp	Grated lemon rind	1½ tbsp
2 cups	Ground almonds	225 g/8 oz

1. Preheat the oven to 350°F/180°C/Gas Mark 4.
2. Grease some baking sheets and sprinkle lightly with cornstarch [cornflour].
3. Beat the egg whites until stiff. Beat in the sugar gradually. Then add the grated lemon rind and ground almonds, and fold in carefully.
4. Drop by teaspoons onto the baking sheets or use a cookie press, and bake for about 10 minutes.
5. Remove carefully to cooling trays, and let cool before storing.

Flaked Almond Cookies

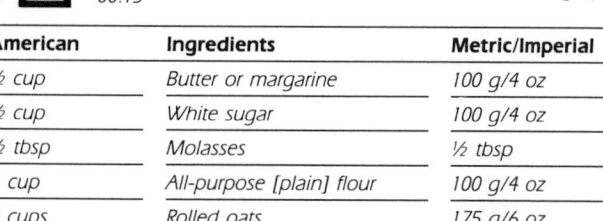 00:20
00:15   48 cookies   Pacific Southwest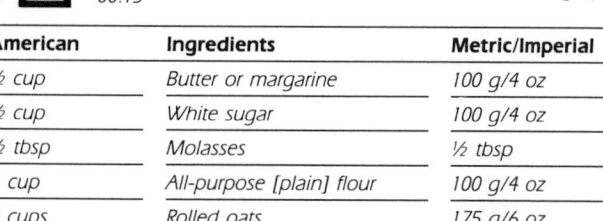

American	Ingredients	Metric/Imperial
½ cup	Butter or margarine	100 g/4 oz
½ cup	White sugar	100 g/4 oz
½ tbsp	Molasses	½ tbsp
1 cup	All-purpose [plain] flour	100 g/4 oz
2 cups	Rolled oats	175 g/6 oz
½ cup	Flaked almonds	50 g/12 oz
1 tsp	Baking soda [bicarbonate of soda]	1 tsp
¼ cup	Boiling water	60 ml/2 fl oz

1. Preheat the oven to 375°F/190°C/Gas Mark 5.
2. Cream the butter and sugar until creamy. Add the molasses and mix well. Stir in flour, rolled oats, and flaked almonds.
3. Dissolve the baking soda in boiling water and add to the mixture while hot. Mix to a stiff dough. Then roll teaspoons of the mixture into balls and place on greased baking pans, allowing room for them to spread. Press flat, decorate the top of each with a flaked almond. Then bake for 15 minutes. Remove to a cooling tray and store when quite cold.

Anzac Cookies

 00:15
00:20   36 cookies   Pacific Southwest

American	Ingredients	Metric/Imperial
1 cup	Flour	100 g/4 oz
1 cup	Rolled oats	75 g/3 oz
¼ cup	Finely shredded coconut	50 g/2 oz
1 cup	Sugar	100 g/4 oz
½ cup	Butter	100 g/4 oz
1 tbsp	Syrup	1 tbsp
1½ tsp	Baking soda [bicarbonate of soda]	1½ tsp
2 tbsp	Boiling water	1½ tbsp

1. Preheat the oven to 350°F/180°C/Gas Mark 4.
2. Sift the flour and add the rolled oats, coconut, and sugar.
3. Put the butter and syrup in a pan, and stir over low heat until melted. Mix the baking soda with boiling water, add to the melted butter, and stir all into the dry ingredients.
4. Put heaping teaspoons of the mixture on greased baking sheets, allowing room to spread. Bake for 20 minutes. Then remove to cooling racks.

Bright Eyed Susans

Bright Eyed Susans

00:25
00:15

48 cookies

Mid Atlantic

American	Ingredients	Metric/Imperial
2 cups	Flour	225 g/8 oz
½ tsp	Baking powder	½ tsp
1 cup	Butter or margarine	225 g/8 oz
½ cup	Sugar	100 g/4 oz
2 tbsp	Water	1½ tbsp
1 tsp	Vanilla extract	1 tsp
1	Egg	1
1¼ cups	Finely chopped nuts	150 g/5 oz
	A little jam or jelly	

1. Preheat the oven to 350°F/180°C/Gas Mark 4.
2. Sift the flour and baking powder twice. Cream the butter and sugar until light and fluffy. Add the water, vanilla, and egg yolk. Add the flour and mix well.
3. Form the dough into balls about the size of a walnut. Roll in the slightly beaten egg white and then in the nuts.
4. Place on lightly greased baking sheets and bake for 5 minutes. Remove from the oven and press your thumb print in each ball. Return to the oven and bake a further 8–10 minutes.
5. Remove to cooling trays and fill the center with bright jam or jelly.

Date and Almond Brownies

00:10
00:30

16–20 brownies

Pacific Southwest

American	Ingredients	Metric/Imperial
⅔ cup	Flour	65 g/2½ oz
½ tsp	Baking powder	½ tsp
¼ tsp	Salt	¼ tsp
⅓ cup	Butter or margarine	65 g/2½ oz
2	Squares (50 g/2 oz) unsweetened baking chocolate	2
1 cup	Sugar	225 g/8 oz
2	Eggs	2
½ cup	Chopped almonds	50 g/2 oz
½ cup	Chopped dates	100 g/4 oz
1 tsp	Vanilla extract	1 tsp

1. Preheat the oven to 350°F/180°C/Gas Mark 4.
2. Grease an 8-inch square pan. Sift the flour, baking powder, and salt together.
3. Melt the butter and chocolate in the top of a double boiler.
4. Add the sugar to the beaten eggs and beat well. Add the melted butter and chocolate. Then stir in the flour. Add the almonds, dates, and vanilla.
5. Turn into the prepared pan and bake for 25 minutes. Cool in the pan, then cut into squares or bars. The brownies can be decorated with a date or almond, if desired.

Date and Almond Brownies

Peanut Brownies

00:10
00:30

25 brownies

Southwest

American	Ingredients	Metric/Imperial
1 cup	Flour	100 g/4 oz
2 tsp	Baking powder	2 tsp
¼ tsp	Salt	¼ tsp
2 tbsp	Butter or margarine	25 g/1 oz
½ cup	Peanut butter	100 g/4 oz
1 cup	Sugar	225 g/8 oz
1	Egg	1
2	Squares (50 g/2 oz) unsweetened baking chocolate, melted	2
½ cup	Chopped peanuts	50 g/2 oz
¼ cup	Milk	60 ml/2 fl oz

1. Preheat the oven to 350°F/180°C/Gas Mark 4.
2. Grease a shallow 9-inch square pan.
3. Mix the flour, baking powder, and salt together.
4. Cream the butter, peanut butter, and sugar together until soft and creamy. Beat in the egg and melted chocolate. Add the sifted flour mixture alternately with milk. Mix well, and stir in the peanuts.
5. Turn into the prepared pan and bake for 25–30 minutes. Mark into squares while warm, and cut when cold.

Chocolate Fruit Squares

Chocolate Fruit Squares

01:10
00:05   18 squares   United States

American	Ingredients	Metric/Imperial
¼ cup	Instant cocoa	25 g/1 oz
1 cup	Shredded coconut	100 g/4 oz
5 tbsp	Raisins	4 tbsp
½ cup	Cornflakes or other breakfast cereal	15 g/½ oz
¼ cup	Chopped nuts	25 g/1 oz
1 tsp	Sherry or fruit juice	1 tsp
2 tbsp	Crushed vanilla wafer crumbs	1½ tbsp
4 tbsp	Condensed milk	3½ tbsp
3	Squares (75 g/3 oz) unsweetened baking chocolate	3

1. Lightly grease a 7-inch square pan [tin].
2. Put all the ingredients except the chocolate squares into a mixing bowl and mix well together. Press into the pan and smooth the surface.
3. Melt the chocolate in a double boiler and spread it evenly over the top of the mixture. Score with a fork and refrigerate until firm. Cut into small bars or squares.

Marble Brownies

00:15
00:30   16 brownies   United States

American	Ingredients	Metric/Imperial
¼ cup	Butter or margarine	50 g/2 oz
1 cup	Sugar	225 g/8 oz
2	Eggs	2
⅔ cup	Cake [pastry] flour	65 g/2½ oz
¼ tsp	Salt	¼ tsp
½ cup	Chopped nuts	50 g/2 oz
½ tsp	Vanilla extract	½ tsp
2	Squares (50 g/2 oz) unsweetened baking chocolate	2

1. Preheat the oven to 350°F/180°C/Gas Mark 4.
2. Grease an 8-inch baking pan.
3. Cream the butter; add the sugar and beat until light and fluffy. Add the eggs and beat until the mixture is smooth.
4. Gradually add the flour and salt sifted together. Then stir in the nuts and vanilla.
5. Pour half the batter into the prepared pan. Mix the melted chocolate with the other half, pour over the plain batter, and swirl it through with a spoon.
6. Bake for 30 minutes; cool, mark into squares or bars, and cut when cold.

Brown Sugar Brownies

00:45
00:30   16 brownies   United States

American	Ingredients	Metric/Imperial
1 cup	Cake [pastry] flour	100 g/4 oz
½ cup	Unsweetened cocoa	50 g/2 oz
½ cup	Butter or margarine	100 g/4 oz
1¼ cups	Firmly packed [demerara] sugar	275 g/10 oz
2	Eggs	2
½ cup	Milk	125 ml/4 fl oz
1 tsp	Vanilla extract	1 tsp
1 cup	Chopped pecan nuts	100 g/4 oz

1. Preheat the oven to 350°F/180°C/Gas Mark 4.
2. Grease an 8-inch baking pan [tin].
3. Sift the flour and cocoa together. Cream the butter; gradually add the sugar and beat together until light and fluffy. Add the beaten eggs, then the flour mixture alternately with the milk. Add the vanilla and pecans.
4. Pour into the prepared pan and bake for about 30 minutes. Mark into squares while hot, and cut when cold.

Marble Brownies

Fudge Brownies

 00:15
00:30

16 brownies

United States

American	Ingredients	Metric/Imperial
¾ cup	Flour	75 g/3 oz
½ tsp	Salt	½ tsp
1 cup	Coarsely chopped walnut meats	100 g/4 oz
2	Squares (50 g/2 oz) unsweetened baking chocolate	2
⅓ cup	Butter or margarine	65 g/2½ oz
1 cup	Sugar	225 g/8 oz
2	Eggs	2
½ tsp	Vanilla extract	½ tsp

1. Preheat the oven to 350°F/180°C/Gas Mark 4.
2. Grease an 8-inch square pan. Sift the flour and salt together and stir in the nuts.
3. Melt the chocolate in the top of a double boiler.
4. Cream the butter and sugar together until light and fluffy. Add eggs 1 at a time, beating well after each addition. Add the vanilla and cooled chocolate. Stir in the flour mixture and blend well.
5. Turn into the prepared pan and bake for about 30 minutes. Cut into squares when cool.

Butter Fingers

 00:15
00:50

24 cookies

United States

American	Ingredients	Metric/Imperial
1 cup	Butter	225 g/8 oz
1 cup	Light brown [demerara] sugar	225 g/8 oz
2 tsp	Grated lemon rind	2 tsp
1	Egg	1
2 cups	Flour	225 g/8 oz
5 tbsp	Blanched chopped almonds	4 tbsp

1. Preheat the oven to 375°F/190°C/Gas Mark 5.
2. Grease a shallow baking pan about 8 × 12 inches. Cream the butter, sugar, and grated lemon rind thoroughly. Then beat in the egg, and fold in the sifted flour.
3. Spread the mixture evenly in the prepared pan and sprinkle with chopped nuts. Bake in the center of the oven for 45–50 minutes.
4. Allow to cool a little in the pan—then cut into finger shapes, and remove when cold.

Cheese and Cranberry Cookies

Cheese and Cranberry Cookies

01:30
00:10   30 cookies   Mid Atlantic

American	Ingredients	Metric/Imperial
2 cups	Sifted flour	225 g/8 oz
2 cups	Grated Cheddar cheese	225 g/8 oz
½ tsp	Salt	½ tsp
½ cup	Shortening [vegetable fat]	100 g/4 oz
¼ cup	Milk	60 ml/2 fl oz
	Filling	
¾ cup	Cranberry jelly	175 g/6 oz
1½ cups	Chopped pecans	175 g/6 oz
½ tsp	Salt	½ tsp
2 tbsp	Brown [demerara] sugar	1½ tbsp
¼ tsp	Ground cinnamon	¼ tsp

1. Preheat the oven to 400°F/200°C/Gas Mark 6.
2. Mix the flour, cheese, and salt together. Cut in the shortening, using a pastry blender. Stir in the milk. Then roll the dough in foil and chill.
3. To make the filling, break up the jelly with a fork, add the other ingredients, and mix well.
4. Roll out thinly on a lightly floured board and cut into shapes as preferred—squares, fingers, etc. Spread half the shapes with the filling, cover with the remaining ones, and press the edges well together.
5. Place on ungreased baking sheets and bake about 10 minutes.

Cheese and Sesame Wafers

01:00
00:30   50 cookies   United States

American	Ingredients	Metric/Imperial
5 tbsp	Sesame seeds	4 tbsp
1 cup	Flour	100 g/4 oz
½ tsp	Salt	½ tsp
	A pinch of cayenne pepper	
½ tsp	Dry mustard	½ tsp
½ tsp	Ground ginger	½ tsp
½ tsp	Sugar	½ tsp
½ cup	Grated cheese	50 g/2 oz
1	Egg yolk	1
¼ cup	Butter	50 g/2 oz
1 tbsp	Water	1 tbsp

1. Preheat the oven to 375°F/190°C/Gas Mark 5.
2. Sprinkle the sesame seeds onto a baking tray and toast in the oven for about 15 minutes.
3. Sift the flour, salt, cayenne, mustard, ginger, and sugar together. Then sift again into a mixing bowl. Add the cheese and cooled toasted sesame seeds.
4. Beat the egg yolk; add the melted butter and water and stir into the dry ingredients. Blend well. Then form the dough into a ball, wrap it in waxed [greaseproof] paper and refrigerate for about a half hour or until firm.
5. Place on a lightly floured board, roll to about ⅛ inch and cut into 2-inch squares.
6. Place on ungreased baking sheets and bake for 15 minutes. Remove carefully to cooling trays.

Cream Cheese Cookies 🐾

01:30
00:06   40 cookies   United States

American	Ingredients	Metric/Imperial
1 cup	Cake [pastry] flour	100 g/4 oz
¼ tsp	Salt	¼ tsp
½ cup	Butter	100 g/4 oz
¼ cup	Sugar	50 g/2 oz
1 cup	Cream cheese	225 g/8 oz
1 tbsp	Caraway seeds	1 tbsp

1. Preheat the oven to 400°F/200°C/Gas Mark 6.
2. Sift the flour and salt together. Beat the butter and cheese together until creamy. Add the sugar and stir in the flour gradually.
3. Shape into 2-inch rolls, wrap each in waxed [greaseproof] paper, and chill thoroughly in the refrigerator.
4. Cut into thin slices, put on lightly greased baking sheets, and sprinkle lightly with caraway seeds.
5. Bake for about 6 minutes.

Chocolate Balls

01:30
00:20
40 small cookies   United States

American	Ingredients	Metric/Imperial
3	Squares (75 g/3 oz) unsweetened baking chocolate	3
1 tbsp	Strong black coffee	1 tbsp
1 cup	Butter or margarine	225 g/8 oz
¼ cup	Sugar	50 g/2 oz
1	Egg yolk	1
1 cup	Chopped walnuts or pecans	100 g/4 oz
1 tbsp	Rum	1 tbsp
2½ cups	Flour	275 g/10 oz

1. Preheat the oven to 350°F/180°C/Gas Mark 4.
2. Break up the chocolate into small pieces and put into a double boiler with the coffee. Stir until melted. Then let cool.
3. Cream the butter and sugar until light and fluffy. Beat in the egg yolk. Add the nuts and rum. Then stir in the cooled chocolate. Add the sifted flour, and blend to a smooth dough. Wrap in foil and chill for 1 hour.
4. Form teaspoons of the dough into balls, roll well in sugar, and arrange on well-greased baking sheets, leaving space between for them to spread.
5. Press half a nut into each ball and bake for about 15 minutes.

Chocolate Molasses Squares

00:15
00:30
24 squares   Mid Atlantic

American	Ingredients	Metric/Imperial
2	Squares (50 g/2 oz) unsweetened baking chocolate	2
1 cup	Flour	100 g/4 oz
½ tsp	Baking powder	½ tsp
¼ tsp	Baking soda [bicarbonate of soda]	¼ tsp
¼ tsp	Salt	¼ tsp
1 cup	Chopped walnuts	100 g/4 oz
½ cup	Sugar	100 g/4 oz
½ cup	Molasses	125 ml/4 fl oz
1	Egg	1

1. Preheat the oven to 350°F/180°C/Gas Mark 4.
2. Melt the chocolate over a double boiler; let cool.
3. Grease a shallow baking pan about 7 × 11 inches.
4. Sift the flour, baking powder, baking soda, and salt together. Stir in the nuts. Beat the butter, sugar, molasses, and egg well. Add the cooled melted chocolate. Then stir into the flour mixture.
5. Turn into the prepared pan and bake for about 30 minutes. Leave in the pan for a few minutes. Then cut into squares and remove to cooling trays.

Chocolate Balls

Chocolate Kisses

00:20
00:40
24 kisses   United States

American	Ingredients	Metric/Imperial
4	Squares (100 g/4 oz) unsweetened baking chocolate	4
½ cup	Cake [pastry] flour	50 g/2 oz
¾ cup	Confectioners' [icing] sugar	100 g/4 oz
4	Egg whites	4
¼ tsp	Salt	¼ tsp
½ tsp	Vanilla extract	½ tsp

1. Preheat the oven to 275°F/140°C/Gas Mark 1.
2. Melt the chocolate over a double boiler; let cool.
3. Cover an ungreased baking sheet with waxed [greaseproof] paper.
4. Sift the flour and ¼ cup [50 g/2 oz] of sugar together twice.
5. Beat the egg whites until frothy, sprinkle with the salt, and beat until stiff. Gradually beat in the other ½ cup [100 g/4 oz] of sugar, adding only about 2 tablespoons [1½ tbsp] at a time.
6. Fold in half the flour mixture; blend well. Then fold in the rest of the flour. Stir in the cooled melted chocolate and vanilla.
7. Drop in teaspoons onto the baking sheet and bake for about 40 minutes.

Chocolate Cherry Bars

Chocolate Cherry Bars

	12:45		
	00:25	24 bars	United States

American	Ingredients	Metric/Imperial
8	Squares (225 g/8 oz) unsweetened dark baking chocolate	8
2	Eggs	2
½ cup	Sugar	100 g/4 oz
1 cup	Finely shredded coconut	75 g/3 oz
½ cup	Candied [glacé] cherries	75 g/3 oz
	Confectioners' [icing] sugar	

1. Preheat the oven to 375°F/190°C/Gas Mark 5.
2. Break up the chocolate into pieces and melt in a double boiler. While the chocolate is melting, well grease an oblong shallow pan, about 11 × 7 inches. When the chocolate is ready, spread it over the base of the pan. Put it into the refrigerator and leave until set.
3. Beat the eggs and sugar together until light and frothy. Carefully fold in the coconut and cherries, cut into quarters. Spread this mixture over the chocolate and bake for about 15 minutes, or until the top is firm to the touch. Remove from the oven, let cool, and refrigerate overnight.
4. Cut into bars, remove from the pan, and sprinkle with confectioners' sugar, or sandwich 2 bars together with chocolate inside.

Date Cookies

	01:20		
	00:10	48 cookies	Pacific Southwest

American	Ingredients	Metric/Imperial
2 cups	Flour (approximately)	225 g/8 oz
1½ tsp	Baking powder	1½ tsp
½ tsp	Salt	½ tsp
1 tsp	Ground cinnamon	1 tsp
½ tsp	Ground ginger	½ tsp
¼ tsp	Ground cloves	¼ tsp
½ cup	Butter or margarine	100 g/4 oz
¾ cup	Sugar	175 g/6 oz
1	Egg	1
½ cup	Molasses	125 ml/4 fl oz
1 tbsp	Vinegar	1 tbsp
½ cup	Chopped dates	100 g/4 oz
	Walnuts	

1. Preheat the oven to 375°F/190°C/Gas Mark 5.
2. Sift 1½ cups [175 g/6 oz] of flour with baking powder, salt, and spices.
3. Cream the butter and beat in the sugar, egg, molasses, and vinegar. Stir in the flour mixture and chopped dates. Then add enough of the remaining flour to make a dough stiff enough to roll out.
4. Chill well, then place on a lightly floured board and roll about ⅛ inch thick. Cut into rounds with a plain floured cookie cutter and place on greased baking sheets.
5. Press half a walnut meat in the center of each and bake for about 10 minutes.

Date Munchies

	00:15		
	00:50	24 cookies	United States

American	Ingredients	Metric/Imperial
1 cup	All-purpose [plain] flour	100 g/4 oz
1 tsp	Baking powder	1 tsp
1½ tsp	Ground cinnamon	1½ tsp
¼ tsp	Salt	¼ tsp
1 cup	Pitted [stoned] dates, chopped	225 g/8 oz
¼ cup	Chopped walnuts	25 g/1 oz
2	Eggs	2
1 cup	Sugar	225 g/8 oz
2 tbsp	Melted margarine	25 g/1 oz
	Confectioners' [icing] sugar	

1. Preheat the oven to 350°F/180°C/Gas Mark 4.
2. Grease and line a square cake pan about 9 × 2 inches.
3. Sift the flour, baking powder, cinnamon, and salt together. Add the dates and nut meats.
4. Whisk the eggs and sugar until pale and frothy, stir in the melted margarine, add to the dry ingredients, and mix well.
5. Pour into the prepared pan, and bake for about 50 minutes. Cut into squares while still warm, and serve dusted with confectioners' sugar.

Chocolate Raisin Fingers

| | 02:00 | 12 fingers | Midwest  |
| | 00:00 | | |

American	Ingredients	Metric/Imperial
1 cup	Seedless raisins	100 g/4 oz
½ cup	Margarine	100 g/4 oz
1 cup	Roughly crumbled angel food or sponge cake	100 g/4 oz
4	Squares (100 g/4 oz) semi-sweet [plain] chocolate, melted	4
	Grated rind of 1 orange	
1 tbsp	Corn [golden] syrup	1 tbsp

1. Cover the raisins with boiling water, and leave for about 3 minutes to plump. Drain and dry.
2. Soften the margarine, and add to the cake crumbs with the melted chocolate, grated orange rind, and syrup.
3. Add the raisins, mix well, and press into an oblong shape—about ½ inch thick—onto greased paper. Chill until set. Then cut into fingers.

Christmas Cookies

Chocolate Raisin Fingers

Christmas Cookies

| | 00:30 | 24 cookies | United States |
| | 00:14 | | |

American	Ingredients	Metric/Imperial
2¾ cups	Flour	300 g/11 oz
½ tsp	Baking soda [bicarbonate of soda]	½ tsp
1 tsp	Ground cinnamom	1 tsp
½ tsp	Ground cloves	½ tsp
½ tsp	Grated nutmeg	½ tsp
¾ tsp	Powdered cardamom	¾ tsp
½ cup	Finely chopped mixed candied [glacé] fruits	75 g/3 oz
½ cup	Chopped nut meats	50 g/2 oz
1 cup	Corn [golden] syrup	250 ml/8 fl oz
¾ cup	Brown [demerara] sugar	175 g/6 oz
1 tbsp	Lemon juice	1 tbsp
1 tsp	Grated lemon rind	1 tsp
1	Egg	1

1. Preheat the oven to 400°F/200°C/Gas Mark 6.
2. Sift the flour, baking soda, and spices together, and stir in the candied fruits and nuts.
3. Add the corn syrup, lemon juice, and rind to the beaten egg and mix well. Add the flour and fruit mixture, and mix all well.
4. Cut out some rounds of waxed [greaseproof] paper about 4 inches in diameter, grease them, and put them onto greased baking sheets about 2 inches apart. Put a tablespoon of dough on each round of paper, and spread it to within ¼ inch of the outer edge of the paper.
5. Bake for 12–14 minutes, or until lightly browned and firm to the touch. When cold, decorate as desired with plain or chocolate glaze, cherries, nuts, etc.

Coconut Pecan Cookies

Coconut Pecan Cookies

| | 00:20 | | |
| | 00:35 | 16 cookies | United States |

American	Ingredients	Metric/Imperial
1¼ cups	Flour	150 g/5 oz
⅛ tsp	Salt	⅛ tsp
1¼ cups	Firmly packed brown [demerara] sugar	275 g/10 oz
5 tbsp	Melted butter	65 g/2½ oz
2	Eggs	2
½ tsp	Baking powder	½ tsp
½ tsp	Almond extract	½ tsp
1¼ cups	Flaked or shredded coconut	100 g/4 oz
1 cup	Chopped pecans	100 g/4 oz

1. Preheat the oven to 350°F/180°C/Gas Mark 4.
2. Lightly grease an 8-inch square pan.
3. Sift 1 cup [25 g/1 oz] of flour with salt and add ¼ cup [50 g/2 oz] of sugar. Add melted butter and mix until smooth. Then press the mixture into the bottom of the prepared pan. Bake for 15 minutes.
4. While this is cooking, prepare the topping: beat the eggs well, then gradually beat in the remaining sugar and beat together until the mixture is fluffy. Sift the remaining flour with baking powder, add to the creamed mixture, and beat well. Then add the almond extract, coconut, and nuts.
5. Spread this mixture quickly over the pastry, then return to the oven and bake for 20 minutes or until browned.
6. Mark into squares or triangles while still warm, and leave in the pan to cool.

Cinnamon Cookies

| | 00:20 | | |
| | 00:12 | 50 cookies | United States |

American	Ingredients	Metric/Imperial
2½ cups	Flour	275 g/10 oz
1½ tsp	Baking powder	1½ tsp
½ tsp	Salt	½ tsp
1 tsp	Ground cinnamon	1 tsp
1 cup	Sugar	225 g/8 oz
¾ cup	Oil	175 ml/6 fl oz
2	Eggs	2
1 tsp	Vanilla extract	1 tsp

1. Preheat the oven to 375°F/190°C/Gas Mark 5.
2. Sift the flour, baking powder, salt, and cinnamon together.
3. Put the sugar and oil together in a mixing bowl. Mix well. Add the beaten egg gradually, then add vanilla. Add the flour mixture all at once, and beat well.
4. Shape into ½-inch balls, roll in sugar, and place on lightly greased baking sheets. Flatten with a fork and sprinkle again with sugar. Bake for 10–12 minutes.
5. Remove to cooling trays.

Cinnamon Stars

| | 00:30 | | |
| | 00:20 | 24 cookies | United States |

American	Ingredients	Metric/Imperial
2 cups	Granulated sugar	450 g/1 lb
5 tsp	Ground cinnamon	4 tsp
7	Egg whites	7
2 cups	Finely crushed almonds	225 g/8 oz
1½ tsp	Grated lemon rind	1½ tsp
2 cups	Confectioners' [icing] sugar	275 g/10 oz

1. Preheat the oven to 350°F/180°C/Gas Mark 4.
2. Mix the granulated sugar and cinnamon well together.
3. Beat the egg whites until frothy. Gradually beat in the sugar and cinnamon, sprinkling only about ¼ cup [50 g/2 oz] at a time onto the egg whites. When all the sugar has been added, beat until the mixture becomes very thick (about 15 minutes in an electric mixer).
4. Set aside ½ cup of the mixture, add almonds and lemon rind to the rest, then knead in the confectioners' sugar.
5. Turn onto a well-sugared board and roll out about ½ inch thick. Cut with a star-shaped cutter and put on lightly oiled baking sheets. Brush the tops with the reserved mixture and bake for 20 minutes, or until lightly browned.

Florentines

Spicy Fruit Cookies

00:15
00:30   25 cookies   United States

American	Ingredients	Metric/Imperial
1 cup	Flour	100 g/4 oz
¼ tsp	Baking soda [bicarbonate of soda]	¼ tsp
¼ tsp	Salt	¼ tsp
½ tsp	Ground ginger	½ tsp
¼ tsp	Ground cinnamon	¼ tsp
¼ tsp	Grated nutmeg	¼ tsp
1 cup	Seedless raisins	100 g/4 oz
1 cup	Chopped nuts	100 g/4 oz
¼ cup	Butter or margarine	50 g/2 oz
¼ cup	Firmly packed brown [demerara] sugar	50 g/2 oz
2	Eggs	2
¼ tsp	Vanilla extract	¼ tsp
½ cup	Molasses	125 ml/4 fl oz

1. Preheat the oven to 350°F/180°C/Gas Mark 4.
2. Grease a shallow 9-inch square baking pan.
3. Sift the flour, baking soda, salt, and spices together twice. Add the raisins and nuts.
4. Cream the butter and sugar well. Beat in eggs, 1 at a time, beating well between each addition. Add the vanilla and molasses. Then stir in the flour, and mix well.
5. Turn into the prepared pan and bake for about 30 minutes. mark into squares while warm.

Florentines

00:25
00:20   30 cookies   South

American	Ingredients	Metric/Imperial
¾ cup	Raisins	75 g/3 oz
2 cups	Crushed cornflakes	175 g/6 oz
¾ cup	Peanuts	75 g/3 oz
½ cup	Candied [glacé] or maraschino cherries	50 g/2 oz
½ can (7 fl oz)	Condensed milk	½ tin (200 ml/ 7 fl oz)
3	Squares (75 g/3 oz) unsweetened baking chocolate	3

1. Preheat the oven to 375°F/190°C/Gas Mark 5.
2. Grease some baking sheets, line with greased paper, and dust lightly with cornstarch [cornflour].
3. Mix the raisins, cornflakes, peanuts, and cherries together in a mixing bowl. Add the condensed milk and blend well. Place 2 teaspoons of the mixture in small heaps on the sheets.
4. Bake for 15–20 minutes. Then leave on the sheets to cool. Using a spatula, remove to cooling trays.
5. Melt the chocolate in a double boiler, remove from the heat, and stir until slightly thickened. Then spread over the flat side of the cookie and mark with a fork. Allow the chocolate to set before storing.

Kitchells

Kitchells

  00:20 / 00:25   12 Kitchells   New England

American	Ingredients	Metric/Imperial
1 lb	Puff pastry	450 g/1 lb
¼ cup	Butter	50 g/2 oz
1 cup	Currants	100 g/4 oz
½ cup	Chopped candied peel	50 g/2 oz
5 tbsp	Ground almonds	4 tbsp
½ tsp	Ground cinnamon	½ tsp
1 tsp	Grated nutmeg	1 tsp

1. Preheat the oven to 450°F/230°C/Gas Mark 8.
2. Divide the pastry in 2 equal-sized pieces and roll each into a thin square.
3. Melt the butter; add the currants, candied peel, ground almonds, and spices and mix well.
4. Spread the mixture on 1 square of pastry to within ½ inch of the edge, and moisten the edges with water. Cover with the second square of pastry, and press the edges well together.
5. With the back of a knife, mark the top of the pastry into squares, without cutting through the filling. Put on a baking sheet and bake for about 25 minutes.
6. Sprinkle with sugar and divide into squares while still warm.

Ginger Cookies

  01:20 / 00:15   48 cookies   New England

American	Ingredients	Metric/Imperial
1 cup	Dark molasses [black treacle]	250 ml/8 fl oz
½ cup	Butter or margarine	100 g/4 oz
¼ cup	Milk	60 ml/2 fl oz
4 cups	Flour	450 g/1 lb
1½ tsp	Baking powder	1½ tsp
½ tsp	Baking soda [bicarbonate of soda]	½ tsp
½ tsp	Salt	½ tsp
1½ tsp	Ground ginger	1½ tsp

1. Preheat the oven to 350°F/180°C/Gas Mark 4.
2. Put the molasses and butter together in a pan and heat slowly to just below boiling point. Stir in the milk and let cool.
3. Mix the flour, baking powder, baking soda, salt, and ginger together and sift twice. Add all at once to the molasses mixture, mix well, and put aside to chill.
4. Put the dough on a lightly floured board and roll into a rectangular shape about ¼ inch thick. Place on a greased baking sheet. Rib the surface with a fork, then mark into squares or bars.
5. Sprinkle liberally with sugar and bake for 10–15 minutes.

Ginger Drops

00:15 / 00:15   40 cookies   New England

American	Ingredients	Metric/Imperial
2 cups	All-purpose [plain] flour	225 g/8 oz
1 tsp	Baking soda [bicarbonate of soda]	1 tsp
½ tsp	Ground ginger	½ tsp
2 tbsp	Corn [golden] syrup	1½ tbsp
4 tbsp	Chopped preserved ginger	3½ tbsp
½ cup	Margarine	100 g/4 oz
½ cup	Brown [demerara] sugar, lightly packed	100 g/4 oz
4 tbsp	Milk	3½ tbsp

1. Preheat the oven to 350°F/180°C/Gas Mark 4.
2. Sift the flour, baking soda, and ginger together.
3. Warm the corn syrup in a small pan with the preserved ginger. Cream the margarine and sugar. Add the warmed syrup and ginger, half of the flour, and 2 [1½] tablespoons milk. Beat well. Then add the remaining flour and milk.
4. Drop by spoonfuls onto greased baking sheets, allowing room for them to spread, and bake for about 15 minutes. Then cool on a wire rack before storing.

Gingersnaps

00:15 / 00:10   48 cookies   New England

American	Ingredients	Metric/Imperial
¾ cup	Shortening [vegetable fat]	175 g/6 oz
1 cup	Brown [demerara] sugar	225 g/8 oz
¾ cup	Molasses	175 ml/6 fl oz
1	Egg	1
2¼ cups	Flour	250 g/9 oz
2 tsp	Baking soda [bicarbonate of soda]	2 tsp
½ tsp	Salt	½ tsp
1 tsp	Ground ginger	1 tsp
1 tsp	Ground cinnamon	1 tsp
½ tsp	Ground cloves	½ tsp

1. Preheat the oven to 375°F/190°C/Gas Mark 5.

2. Put the shortening, sugar, molasses, and egg together in a mixing bowl and beat well until creamy.
3. Sift the flour, baking soda, salt, and spices together. Add to the creamed mixture and blend well.
4. Form into balls, roll in granulated sugar, and place about 2 inches apart on greased baking sheets. Bake for about 10 minutes and let cool a little before removing to cooling trays.

Melting Moments

 00:15
00:20   24 cookies   United States

American	Ingredients	Metric/Imperial
½ cup	Butter or margarine	100 g/4 oz
½ cup	Sugar	100 g/4 oz
1	Egg	1
1½ cups	All-purpose [plain] flour	175 g/6 oz
	Pinch salt	
	Rolled oats	
	Candied [glacé] or maraschino cherries	

1. Preheat the oven to 350°F/180°C/Gas Mark 4.
2. Cream the butter and sugar until soft and white, then beat in the egg. Add the flour and salt sifted together and mix to a firm dough. Dampen your hands, roll the dough into balls about the size of a walnut, and roll in the rolled oats.
3. Put on greased baking pans, allowing room for them to spread. Flatten a little and place a candied or maraschino cherry in the center of each cookie. Bake for 20 minutes.

Molasses Bites

 01:15
00:20   24 cookies   Mid Atlantic

American	Ingredients	Metric/Imperial
½ cup	All-purpose [plain] flour	50 g/2 oz
1 cup	Rolled oats	75 g/3 oz
3 tbsp	Finely shredded coconut	2 tbsp
½ cup	Butter	100 g/4 oz
½ cup	Sugar	100 g/4 oz
1½ tbsp	Molasses	1¼ tbsp
1 tsp	Baking soda [bicarbonate of soda]	1 tsp
1 tbsp	Milk	1 tbsp

1. Preheat the oven to 350°F/180°C/Gas Mark 4.
2. Mix the flour, rolled oats, and coconut together.
3. Put the butter, sugar, and molasses into a pan and bring very slowly to the boiling point, stirring all the time. Remove from the heat and add baking soda dissolved in milk. Pour this hot mixture into the dry ingredients and mix well.
4. Wrap in foil and refrigerate until firm, then roll into marbles and put on greased baking pans, allowing room for them to spread. Flatten a little and bake for 15 minutes. Remove carefully to cooling trays.

Melting Moments

Lunchbox Cookies

 00:15
00:15   Makes 40 cookies   United States

American	Ingredients	Metric/Imperial
¾ cup	Butter or margarine	175 g/6 oz
½ cup	Brown [demerara] sugar	100 g/4 oz
½ cup	Sugar	100 g/4 oz
1 tsp	Vanilla extract	1 tsp
1	Egg	1
1½ cups	Flour	175 g/6 oz
½ tsp	Baking powder	½ tsp
½ tsp	Baking soda [bicarbonate of soda]	½ tsp
½ tsp	Salt	½ tsp
½ tsp	Ground ginger	½ tsp
½ tsp	Ground cinnamon	½ tsp
1¼ cups	Rolled oats	100 g/4 oz
¼ cup	Marmalade	50 g/2 oz
1 cup	Chopped raisins	100 g/4 oz

1. Preheat the oven to 375°F/190°C/Gas Mark 5.
2. Cream the butter, brown sugar, and white sugar together until soft and creamy. Beat in the egg and vanilla.
3. Sift the flour, baking powder, baking soda, salt, ginger, and cinnamon together and add to the creamed mixture. Fold in the oats, marmalade, and raisins, and mix well.
4. Place in teaspoons on greased baking sheets, and bake for 15 minutes or until evenly browned.

Crispy Orange Cookies

Orange and Cinnamon Squares

	00:15		
	00:45	18 large squares	Pacific Southwest 

American	Ingredients	Metric/Imperial
2 cups	Flour	225 g/8 oz
1 tsp	Ground cinnamon	1 tsp
1 tsp	Baking soda [bicarbonate of soda]	1 tsp
	Grated rind and juice of 1 large orange	
½ cup	Butter or margarine	100 g/4 oz
5 tbsp	Corn [golden] syrup	4 tbsp
3 tbsp	Orange marmalade	2 tbsp
5 tbsp	Light brown [demerara] sugar	4 tbsp
½ cup	Milk	125 ml/4 fl oz
1	Egg	1

1. Preheat the oven to 350°F/180°C/Gas Mark 4.
2. Grease a shallow baking pan about 10 × 7 inches and line it with greased paper.
3. Sift the flour, cinnamon, and baking soda together twice. Then add the grated orange rind.
4. Put the butter, corn syrup, marmalade, sugar, and milk into a pan and stir over low heat until melted. Add the orange juice. Then stir all these liquid ingredients into the flour. Add the beaten egg and beat until smooth.
5. Pour into the prepared pan and bake for 40–45 minutes. Leave in the pan to cool a little. Then turn out on a cooling tray. When cold, cut into squares.

Molasses Drops

	02:15		
	00:10	36 cookies	Mid Atlantic

American	Ingredients	Metric/Imperial
1½ cups	Cake [pastry] flour	175 g/6 oz
¼ tsp	Salt	¼ tsp
¾ tsp	Baking soda [bicarbonate of soda]	¾ tsp
½ tsp	Ground cinnamon	½ tsp
¾ tsp	Ground ginger	¾ tsp
¼ tsp	Grated nutmeg	¼ tsp
¼ cup	Butter or margarine	50 g/2 oz
½ cup	Sugar	100 g/4 oz
1	Egg yolk	1
¼ cup	Molasses	60 ml/2 fl oz
½ cup	Buttermilk	125 ml/4 fl oz

1. Preheat the oven to 400°F/200°C/Gas Mark 6.
2. Sift the flour, salt, baking soda, cinnamon, ginger, and nutmeg together.
3. Cream the butter and sugar until light and fluffy. Beat in the egg yolk, then the molasses. Add the flour mixture alternately with the buttermilk, mixing well after each addition.
4. Chill for 1–2 hours, then place by teaspoons onto greased baking sheets, leaving about 2 inches between each cookie.
5. Bake for about 10 minutes or until lightly browned.

Nut and Raisin Squares

	00:10		
	00:30	25 squares	Southwest

American	Ingredients	Metric/Imperial
1 cup	Flour	100 g/4 oz
¼ tsp	Baking soda [bicarbonate of soda]	¼ tsp
¼ tsp	Salt	¼ tsp
½ tsp	Ground ginger	½ tsp
1 cup	Seedless raisins	100 g/4 oz
1 cup	Chopped nuts	100 g/4 oz
¼ cup	Shortening [vegetable fat]	50 g/2 oz
¼ cup	Firmly packed brown [demerara] sugar	50 g/2 oz
2	Eggs	2
¼ tsp	Vanilla extract	¼ tsp
½ cup	Molasses	125 ml/4 fl oz

1. Preheat the oven to 350°F/180°C/Gas Mark 4.
2. Grease a shallow 9-inch square pan.
3. Sift the flour, baking soda, salt, and ginger together. Stir in the raisins and nuts.
4. Cream the shortening and sugar. Beat in the eggs 1 at a time. Then add the vanilla and molasses. Add the flour and nut mixture and blend well.
5. Pour into the prepared pan and bake about 30 minutes. Mark into squares and allow to cool in the pan before removing.

Crispy Orange Cookies

 00:50 / 00:20   36 cookies   Pacific Southwest

American	Ingredients	Metric/Imperial
1¼ cups	Flour	150 g/5 oz
¼ cup	Ground rice	50 g/2 oz
½ cup	Butter or margarine	100 g/4 oz
⅜ cup	Sugar	75 g/3 oz
	Grated rind of 1 large orange	
1	Egg	1
½ cup	Brown [demerara] sugar	100 g/4 oz

1. Preheat the oven to 350°F/180°C/Gas Mark 4.
2. Sift the flour and ground rice into a bowl, and rub in the butter until the mixture resembles fine bread crumbs. Add the sugar, grated orange rind, and egg yolk; mix well, and knead until smooth. Wrap in foil and refrigerate for a half hour.
3. Roll out the dough to about 12 inches square, brush with lightly beaten egg white, and sprinkle with brown sugar.
4. Fold the corners of the dough to the center, form into a ball, and knead lightly. Cut in half and shape each half into a roll about 9 inches long. Cut the rolls into slices about ½ inch thick and place on greased baking sheets. Bake for about 20 minutes, then remove to cooling trays. Store when quite cold.

Peanut Cookies

 00:15 / 00:10   40 cookies   Southwest

American	Ingredients	Metric/Imperial
½ cup	Butter or margarine	100 g/4 oz
1 cup	Sugar	225 g/8 oz
1	Egg	1
1 cup	Flour	100 g/4 oz
½ tsp	Baking soda [bicarbonate of soda]	½ tsp
½ tsp	Baking powder	½ tsp
1 cup	Rolled oats	75 g/3 oz
½ cup	Chopped salted peanuts	50 g/2 oz
1 cup	Cornflakes	25 g/1 oz

1. Preheat the oven to 400°F/200°C/Gas Mark 6.
2. Cream the butter and sugar together. Add the egg and beat well.
3. Sift the flour, baking soda, and baking powder together, and fold into the creamed mixture. Add the rolled oats, peanuts, and cornflakes, and mix well.
4. Place by teaspoons on greased baking sheets, leaving room for them to spread. Bake for about 10 minutes.

Easy Orange Cookies

Easy Orange Cookies

 00:20 / 00:10   14 cookies   United States

American	Ingredients	Metric/Imperial
⅔ cup	Margarine	150 g/5 oz
2	Eggs	2
5 tbsp	Sugar	4 tbsp
	A little vanilla extract	
⅔ cup	Flour	75 g/3 oz
	Garnish	
3 tbsp	Confectioners' sugar [icing sugar]	2 tbsp
3–4 tsp	Orange juice	3–4 tsp
	Chopped candied orange peel	

1. Preheat the oven to 400°F/200°C/Gas Mark 6.
2. Melt the margarine. Let it cool. Beat in the eggs, sugar, vanilla, and flour. Spoon the batter onto a greased pancake iron. Bake for about 10 minutes.
3. Let the cookies cool slightly. Curl them around a greased, paper-covered, thin, cylindrical-shaped object.
4. Mix the confectioners' sugar with orange juice. Brush over the cookies when they have stiffened. Sprinkle with orange peel.

Paprika Cookies

Paprika Cookies

| | 00:15 | | |
| | 00:20 | 18 cookies | United States |

American	Ingredients	Metric/Imperial
½ cup	Butter or margarine	100 g/4 oz
¾ cup	Grated cheese	75 g/3 oz
1 cup	Flour	100 g/4 oz
1 tsp	Paprika	1 tsp
½ tsp	Salt	½ tsp
½ tsp	Dry mustard	½ tsp
½ tbsp	Poppy seeds	½ tbsp

1. Preheat the oven to 375°F/190°C/Gas Mark 5.
2. Mix the butter and cheese together until soft and creamy.
3. Sift the flour, paprika, salt, and mustard together, and add to the butter and cheese. Beat until well blended.
4. Flour the hands lightly and roll heaping teaspoons of the mixture into small balls. Place on greased baking sheets, flatten a little, and sprinkle with poppy seeds.
5. Bake for 15–20 minutes, or until golden brown. Loosen the cookies, but leave on the baking sheets to cool.

Peanut Butter Nuggets

| | 00:10 | | |
| | 00:10 | 36 cookies | Southwest |

American	Ingredients	Metric/Imperial
1 cup	Peanut butter	225 g/8 oz
1 tsp	Lemon juice	1 tsp
¼ tsp	Salt	¼ tsp
1½ cups	Condensed milk	375 ml/12 fl oz
1 cup	Chopped seedless raisins	100 g/4 oz

1. Preheat the oven to 375°F/190°C/Gas Mark 5.
2. Mix the peanut butter, lemon juice, and salt together. Gradually stir in the condensed milk. Then add the raisins.
3. Drop by teaspoons onto greased baking sheets, and bake for 10 minutes.

Peanut Butter Crisps

| | 00:15 | | |
| | 00:12 | 24 cookies | Southwest |

American	Ingredients	Metric/Imperial
½ cup	Flour	50 g/2 oz
¼ tsp	Baking soda [bicarbonate soda]	¼ tsp
¼ cup	Butter or margarine	50 g/2 oz
1 tbsp	Sugar	1 tbsp
¼ cup	Brown [demerara] sugar	50 g/2 oz
½ tsp	Vanilla extract	½ tsp
¼ cup	Peanut butter	50 g/2 oz
1	Egg	1

1. Preheat the oven to 350°F/180°C/Gas Mark 4.
2. Sift the flour and baking soda twice.
3. Cream the butter, white and brown sugar, vanilla, and peanut butter until quite soft and creamy. Beat in the egg; then stir in the flour and mix well.
4. Put on unbuttered baking pans by teaspoons about 1 inch apart. Bake for 10–12 minutes, then remove to cooling trays.

Peanut Butter Nuggets

Peppermint Chocolate Cookies

00:15
00:10 | 25 cookies | United States

American	Ingredients	Metric/Imperial
1 cup	Flour	100 g/4 oz
1 tsp	Baking powder	1 tsp
¼ tsp	Salt	¼ tsp
½ cup	Shortening [vegetable fat]	100 g/4 oz
½ cup	Sugar	100 g/4 oz
1	Square [25 g/1 oz] unsweetened baking chocolate, melted	1
	A few drops oil of peppermint or ⅛ tsp peppermint extract	

1. Preheat the oven to 400°F/200°C/Gas Mark 6.
2. Sift the flour, baking powder, and salt together.
3. Cream the shortening, add the sugar, and beat until light and fluffy. Add the melted chocolate and peppermint flavoring. Then add the beaten egg. Add the flour alternately with the milk.
4. Mix well. Then drop by teaspoons onto an ungreased baking sheet. Flatten with a knife dipped in cold water, and place a pecan or blanched almond in the center.
5. Bake for 8–10 minutes.

Pretzel Cookies

03:20
00:12 | 36 cookies | New England

American	Ingredients	Metric/Imperial
½ cup	Butter or margarine	100 g/4 oz
¾ cup	Granulated sugar	175 g/6 oz
2	Eggs	2
2 tbsp	Milk	1½ tbsp
1 cup	Flour	100 g/4 oz
¼ tsp	Salt	¼ tsp
½ cup	Brown [demerara] sugar	100 g/4 oz
2 tbsp	Ground cinnamon	1½ tbsp

1. Cream the butter with ¼ cup [50 g/2 oz] of the measured granulated sugar. Add the beaten eggs and milk, and beat until smooth. Add the flour and salt sifted together, and mix to a smooth dough. Wrap in foil and chill for 2–3 hours.
2. Preheat the oven to 375°F/190°C/Gas Mark 5.
3. Mix the brown sugar, cinnamon, and remaining granulated sugar together, and sprinkle the mixture onto a pastry board. Put the dough on the board and roll out to about ¼ inch thick. Cut the dough into strips about ½ inch wide and form into twists.
4. Sprinkle well with the sugar mixture and arrange on greased and floured baking sheets.
5. Bake for 12 minutes or until just delicately browned.

Pretzel Cookies

Sour Cream Cookies

02:15
00:10 | 48 cookies | Midwest

American	Ingredients	Metric/Imperial
1½ cups	Flour	175 g/6 oz
½ tsp	Baking powder	½ tsp
⅛ tsp	Baking soda [bicarbonate of soda]	⅛ tsp
½ tsp	Salt	½ tsp
½ cup	Butter	100 g/4 oz
½ cup	Granulated sugar	100 g/4 oz
⅛ cup	Firmly packed brown [demerara] sugar	25 g/1 oz
1	Egg	1
½ tsp	Vanilla extract	½ tsp
¼ cup	Sour cream	60 ml/2 fl oz

1. Sift the flour, baking powder, baking soda, and salt together. Cream the butter. Add the granulated and brown sugar, and beat until all is soft and creamy. Add the beaten egg and vanilla.
2. Add the flour mixture alternately with the sour cream. Set aside to chill. Then divide into rolls about 2 inches in diameter and wrap each in waxed [greaseproof] paper. Put in the refrigerator and leave until thoroughly chilled.
3. Preheat the oven to 400°F/200°C/Gas Mark 6.
4. Cut the dough into slices about ⅛ inch thick. Place on ungreased baking sheets, and bake for about 8–10 minutes.

Sugar Cookies

Vanillekipferl

01:00
00:10
24 cookies
United States

American	Ingredients	Metric/Imperial
1 cup	Flour	100 g/4 oz
	A pinch of salt	
¼ cup	Butter or margarine	50 g/2 oz
¼ cup	Ground almonds	25 g/1 oz
1 cup	Vanilla-flavored sugar or 1 cup [225 g/8 oz] white sugar and ¼ tsp vanilla extract	225 g/8 oz

1. Sift the flour and salt onto a board, add the butter (cut into small pieces) ground almonds, and 3 [2] tablespoons of the flavored sugar. Using the hand, work all together to a smooth paste. Cover, and leave in a cool place for at least a half hour.
2. Preheat the oven to 350°F/180°C/Gas Mark 4.
3. Put onto a board (do not add any flour) and roll with the palm of the hand into a long sausage shape. Cut into 24 equal pieces. Roll each piece into a sausage, keeping the middle a little thicker than the ends. Then twist into a crescent shape.
4. Put onto baking sheets (not greased or floured) and bake until a pale golden color, about 10 minutes. Put the remaining sugar onto a large dish; when the cookies are done, put 1 at a time into the sugar and coat thoroughly. At this stage, they are very fragile and need to be handled carefully.
5. When quite cold, store in an airtight jar.

Sugar Cookies

01:20
00:10
50–60 cookies
United States

American	Ingredients	Metric/Imperial
2 cups	Flour (approximately)	225 g/8 oz
1½ tsp	Baking powder	1½ tsp
½ tsp	Salt	½ tsp
½ cup	Butter	100 g/4 oz
1 cup	Sugar	225 g/8 oz
1	Egg	1
1 tsp	Vanilla extract	1 tsp
1 tbsp	Cream or milk	1 tbsp

1. Sift 1½ cups [175 g/6 oz] of flour with baking powder and salt.
2. Cream the butter until soft. Beat in the sugar, egg, vanilla, and cream. Stir in the flour mixture. Then add enough of the remaining flour to make a dough stiff enough to roll out. Refrigerate until well chilled.
3. Preheat the oven to 375°F/190°C/Gas Mark 5.
4. Place the dough on a lightly floured board and roll about ⅛ inch thick. Cut into shapes as liked with a floured cutter or use a cookie press. Place on ungreased baking sheets, sprinkle with sugar, and bake for 8–10 minutes. Remove to cooling trays. The cookies can be served plain or decorated in a variety of ways.

Spritz Cookies

00:20
00:08
30 cookies
United States

American	Ingredients	Metric/Imperial
½ cup	Shortening [vegetable fat]	100 g/4 oz
½ cup	Confectioners' [icing] sugar	65 g/2½ oz
½ tsp	Almond extract	½ tsp
1	Egg yolk	1
1¼ cups	Cake [pastry] flour	150 g/5 oz
¼ tsp	Salt	¼ tsp
1	Egg white	1
	Colored coarse sugar crystals	

1. Preheat the oven to 400°F/200°C/Gas Mark 6.
2. Cream the shortening; add the confectioners' sugar and beat well until soft and creamy. Add the almond extract and beaten egg yolk. Then gradually stir in the sifted flour and salt.
3. Put the mixture into a cookie press. Using various forms of nozzles as available, press out shapes onto an ungreased baking sheet.
4. Brush over with egg white beaten until frothy with a few drops of water, and sprinkle with colored coarse sugar crystals or with chopped nuts.
5. Bake for about 8 minutes, or until very lightly browned.

Angel Cake

01:45
01:00   Serves 8–10   South

American	Ingredients	Metric/Imperial
1 cup	Sifted cake [pastry] flour	100 g/4 oz
8–9	Egg whites	8–9
¼ tsp	Salt	¼ tsp
1 tsp	Cream of tartar	1 tsp
1¼ cups	Sifted white sugar	275 g/10 oz
¾ tsp	Vanilla extract	¾ tsp
½ tsp	Almond extract	½ tsp

1. Preheat the oven to 325°F/160°C/Gas Mark 3.
2. Sift the flour 3 or 4 times.
3. Beat the egg whites until frothy, sprinkle salt and cream of tartar over the top, and continue to beat until the whites stand in peaks but are not dry.
4. Fold in the sugar about 2 tablespoons [1½ tbsp] at a time. Then fold in the vanilla and almond extract. Fold in the flour, sifting about ¼ cup [25 g/1 oz] at a time over the surface. Pour into a 9-inch tube pan [ring tin] and bake for about 1 hour.
5. Invert the pan until the cake is cold, and do not remove it for at least 1½ hours.

Apple Cake

00:15
00:45   Serves 10   United States

American	Ingredients	Metric/Imperial
1⅔ cups	All-purpose [plain] flour	175 g/6 oz
¾ cup	Sugar	175 g/6 oz
2 tsp	Baking powder	2 tsp
3½ tbsp	Butter	45 g/1¾ oz
¾ cup	Milk	175 ml/6 fl oz
2 or 3	Sliced apples	2 or 3
	1 tsp cinnamon and 1½ tbsp sugar, mixed together	

1. Preheat the oven to 350°F/180°C/Gas Mark 4.
2. Grease a 9½-inch round cake pan [tin]. Dust it with bread crumbs or flour.
3. Mix the flour, sugar, and baking powder.
4. Finely chop the butter into the flour mixture. Crumble it with your fingertips. Add the milk. Quickly mix into a batter.
5. Pour the batter into the greased pan. Press the apple slices down into the cake. Make a decorative sun-ray pattern. Sprinkle the cinnamon and sugar mixture over the cake. Bake for 40–45 minutes.
6. Turn the cake out of the pan and tip it right side up again onto the plate from which it is to be served.

Almond Gateaux

Almond Gateaux

00:20
00:45   Serves 6–8   South

American	Ingredients	Metric/Imperial
½ cup	Butter	100 g/4 oz
¼ cup	Brown [demerara] sugar	50 g/2 oz
2 tbsp	Thick honey	1½ tbsp
1½ cups	Cake [pastry] flour	175 g/6 oz
2	Eggs	2
4 tbsp	Milk	3½ tbsp
1 tsp	Almond extract	1 tsp
	Filling	
⅓ cup	Butter	65 g/2½ oz
1½ tbsp	Thick honey	1¼ tbsp
⅔ cup	Sifted confectioners' [icing] sugar	100 g/4 oz
	Flaked toasted almonds	

1. Preheat the oven to 350°F/180°C/Gas Mark 4.
2. Line a 7-inch round cake pan [tin] with greased waxed [greaseproof] paper and grease the rest of the pan.
3. Cream the butter, sugar, and honey together until soft and light. Gradually beat in the eggs, adding a spoonful of flour between each one.
4. Fold in the sifted flour, then the milk and almond extract. Turn into the prepared pan and bake for 45 minutes.
5. To make the topping and filling; cream the butter well; add honey and sugar, and beat well together.
6. Fill and cover the top of the cake and sprinkle liberally with the almonds.

Dutch Apple Cake

Fluffy Cheesecake

 00:50
01:00

Serves 10–12

United States

American	Ingredients	Metric/Imperial
16	Graham crackers [digestive biscuits], crushed finely	16
2 tsp	Ground cinnamon	2 tsp
1 cup plus 2 tsp	Sugar	225 g/8 oz plus 2 tsp
3 tbsp	Butter	40 g/1½ oz
4 cups	Cream cheese	900 g/2 lb
¼ tsp	Salt	¼ tsp
4	Eggs	4
1½ tbsp	Lemon juice	1¼ tbsp
2 tsp	Grated lemon rind	2 tsp
1½ tsp	Vanilla extract	1½ tsp
2 cups	Heavy [double] cream	450 ml/¾ pint

1. Preheat the oven to 350°F/180°C/Gas Mark 4.
2. Grease the bottom and sides of a 9-inch springform pan [tin].
3. Mix the cracker crumbs and cinnamon with 2 teaspoons of sugar and press half the mixture into the prepared pan.
4. Beat the cream cheese until smooth. Add the remaining sugar, salt, egg yolks, lemon juice, lemon rind, and vanilla. Beat well and blend in the cream. Beat the egg whites until stiff but not dry. Then fold lightly, but thoroughly, into the cheese mixture.
5. Turn into the prepared pan and sprinkle the remaining crumbs on top.
6. Bake for 1 hour or until set. Then turn off the heat and leave cake in the oven for 5 minutes. Remove and cool on a rack away from drafts.

Dutch Apple Cake

00:25
00:45

Serves 6

Mid Atlantic

American	Ingredients	Metric/Imperial
1⅓ cups	Cake flour	150 g/5 oz
½ tsp	Salt	½ tsp
1 tsp	Baking powder	1 tsp
¾ cup	Butter	175 g/6 oz
¾ cup	Sugar	175 g/6 oz
2	Egg yolks	2
3 tbsp	Milk	2 tbsp
1 lb	Tart apples, peeled, cored, and sliced	450 g/1 lb
1 tsp	Ground cinnamon	1 tsp

1. Preheat the oven to 375°F/190°C/Gas Mark 5.
2. Grease an 8-inch square cake pan [tin].
3. Reserve 2 tablespoons [1½ tbsp] of the flour; sift the rest with the salt and baking powder.
4. Cream ½ cup [100 g/4 oz] of the butter with 1 tablespoon of the sugar. Add the egg yolks and milk, and beat until light and fluffy. Blend in the flour mixture and stir until smooth. Then spread in the prepared pan. Arrange the apples on top.
5. Combine the reserved 2 tablespoons [1½ tbsp] of flour with the remaining butter, sugar, and cinnamon. Rub with your fingertips until the mixture is like coarse crumbs. Then sprinkle over the apples, and bake for 45 minutes or until well browned.

Chiffon Cake

01:15
01:10

Serves 10

United States

American	Ingredients	Metric/Imperial
2¼ cups	Cake [pastry] flour	250 g/9 oz
1 tsp	Salt	1 tsp
1½ cups	Sugar	350 g/12 oz
1 tbsp	Baking powder	1 tbsp
½ cup	Corn oil	125 ml/4 fl oz
6	Eggs	6
¾ cup	Water	175 ml/6 fl oz
1 tsp	Grated lemon rind	1 tsp
2 tsp	Vanilla extract	2 tsp
½ tsp	Cream of tartar	½ tsp

1. Preheat the oven to 325°F/160°C/Gas Mark 3.
2. Sift the flour, salt, sugar, and baking powder 3 times. Make a well in the center and add the oil, egg yolks, water, lemon rind, and vanilla. Beat until very smooth.
3. Beat the egg whites and cream of tartar until stiff enough to stand in peaks. Then fold carefully into the cake mixture.
4. Put into an ungreased 10-inch tube pan [ring tin] and bake for 1 hour and 10 minutes.
5. Invert the pan and let cool before removing.

Chocolate Chiffon Cake

 01:20
01:10
Serves 10
United States

American	Ingredients	Metric/Imperial
1¾ cups	Sifted cake [pastry] flour	200 g/7 oz
1 tsp	Baking soda [bicarbonate of soda]	1 tsp
2½ tsp	Cream of tartar	2½ tsp
2 cups	Sugar	450 g/1 lb
⅔ cup	Unsweetened cocoa	65 g/2½ oz
½ cup	Corn oil	125 ml/4 fl oz
7	Egg yolks	7
¾ cup	Cold water	175 ml/6 fl oz
1 tsp	Vanilla extract	1 tsp
8-9	Egg whites	8-9
1 tsp	Salt	1 tsp

1. Preheat the oven to 350°F/180°C/Gas Mark 4.
2. Sift the flour, baking soda, 2 teaspoons of cream of tartar, sugar, and cocoa together 3 times. Make a well in the center and pour in the oil, egg yolks, water, and vanilla. Beat until the mixture is quite smooth.
3. Beat the egg whites with salt and the remaining ½ teaspoon cream of tartar until it stands in peaks. Then fold carefully into the cake mixture.
4. Put into a 10-inch ungreased tube pan [ring mold] and bake for about 1 hour and 10 minutes.
5. Invert the pan and leave to get cold before removing.

Mock Cheesecake

 00:35
00:25
Serves 10-12
United States

American	Ingredients	Metric/Imperial
2 cups	Cookie crumbs	100 g/4 oz
½ cup	Melted butter	100 g/4 oz
6	Eggs	6
½ cup	Condensed milk	125 ml/4 fl oz
¼ cup	Lemon juice	60 ml/2 fl oz
1 tbsp	Grated lemon rind	1 tbsp

1. Preheat the oven to 350°F/180°C/Gas Mark 4.
2. Grease a 9-inch pie plate.
3. Mix the cookie crumbs and melted butter, and reserve 3 tablespoons [2 tbsp] of the mixture. Pat the rest into the pie plate.
4. Beat the egg yolks. Stir in the condensed milk, lemon juice, and lemon rind. Beat the egg whites stiffly and fold them into the egg yolk mixture.
5. Turn into a pie shell and sprinkle reserved crumbs on top. Bake for about 25 minutes. Then let cool.

Orange Cheesecake

Orange Cheesecake

 12:15
00:02
Serves 6-8
Pacific Southwest

American	Ingredients	Metric/Imperial
4 tbsp	Cold water	3½ tbsp
4 envelopes	Unflavored gelatin [gelatine]	4 sachets
3	Eggs	3
½ cup	Sugar	100 g/4 oz
	Juice and grated rind of 2 oranges	
	Juice and grated rind of ½ lemon	
1½ cups	Cottage cheese, sieved	350 g/12 oz
1 cup	Heavy [double] cream, whipped	250 ml/8 fl oz
	Crumb Base	
1¼ cups	Graham crackers [digestive biscuit] or Zwieback crumbs	175 g/6 oz
¼ cup	Sugar	50 g/2 oz
6 tbsp	Melted butter or margarine	75 g/3 oz

1. Line the bottom and sides of an 8-inch round cake pan [tin] with waxed [greaseproof] paper.
2. Put the water into a small pan, sprinkle in the gelatin, and set aside to soak.
3. Break the eggs into a warmed bowl, add the sugar and a pinch of salt, and whisk until thick and pale in color.
4. Dissolve the soaked gelatin over low heat, add the strained orange and lemon juice, and beat into the egg mixture. Fold in the cottage cheese, grated orange and lemon rind and, finally, lightly whipped cream. Pour into the prepared cake pan.
5. Mix the cracker crumbs and sugar together, add melted butter, and mix well. Sprinkle evenly over the top of the cheesecake and let chill overnight. Invert to serve.

Glazed Cherry Cake

Glazed Cherry Cake

01:20
01:00
Serves 8
United States

American	Ingredients	Metric/Imperial
½ cup	Butter	100 g/4 oz
5 tbsp	Brown [demerara] sugar	4 tbsp
1 tbsp	Molasses	1 tbsp
2	Eggs	2
1½ cups	All-purpose [plain] flour	175 g/6 oz
½ tsp	Ground mixed spices	½ tsp
½ cup	Raisins	50 g/2 oz
½ cup	Candied [glacé] cherries	50 g/2 oz
3 tbsp	Milk	2 tbsp
	Topping	
4 tbsp	Warmed sieved apricot jam	3½ tbsp
	Flaked toasted almonds	
	Maraschino or candied [glacé] cherries	

1. Preheat the oven to 300°F/150°C/Gas Mark 2.
2. Line a round 7-inch cake pan [tin] with greased waxed [greaseproof] paper and grease the rest of the pan.
3. Beat the butter, sugar, and molasses together until soft and creamy. Gradually add the well-beaten eggs. Fold in the flour and spices sifted together; add the raisins and chopped cherries, and finally the milk.
4. Put into the prepared pan and bake for about 1 hour. Let cool in the pan before turning out on a cooling rack.
5. To finish the cake, brush the sides with apricot jam and coat with nuts. Arrange half cherries all over the top and brush thickly with apricot glaze.

Mocha Cake

01:15
01:05
Serves 6
United States

American	Ingredients	Metric/Imperial
½ cup	Hot coffee	125 ml/4 fl oz
2	Squares (50 g/2 oz) Unsweetened baking chocolate, chopped	2
½ cup	Margarine	100 g/4 oz
2 cups	Brown [demerara] sugar, lightly packed	450 g/1 lb
2	Eggs	2
2 cups	Cake [pastry] flour	225 g/8 oz
1 tsp	Baking soda [bicarbonate of soda]	1 tsp
1 tsp	Salt	1 tsp
½ cup	Buttermilk	125 ml/4 fl oz
1 tsp	Vanilla extract	1 tsp

1. Preheat the oven to 325°F/160°C/Gas Mark 3.
2. Grease and line a baking pan about 8 × 8 × 2 inches with waxed [greaseproof] paper.
3. Pour the hot coffee over the chocolate, and stir until the chocolate has melted.
4. Cream the margarine and sugar, and beat until light and fluffy. Add the eggs, 1 at a time, beating well after each addition.
5. Sift the flour, baking soda, and salt together. Add to the creamed mixture alternately with the milk. Add the melted chocolate and coffee and vanilla, and mix well.
6. Pour into the prepared pan, and bake for about 1 hour. Let cool in the pan for a few minutes. Then turn out on a cooling rack. Remove the paper, and when quite cold, frost with your favorite frosting.

Fudge Cake

01:25
00:35
Serves 10-12
United States

American	Ingredients	Metric/Imperial
4	Squares (100 g/4 oz) unsweetened baking chocolate	4
½ cup	Hot water	125 ml/4 fl oz
1¾ cups	Sugar	400 g/14 oz
2 cups	Cake [pastry] flour	225 g/8 oz
1 tsp	Baking soda [bicarbonate of soda]	1 tsp
1 tsp	Salt	1 tsp
½ cup	Butter	100 g/4 oz
3	Eggs	3
⅔ cup	Milk	150 ml/¼ pint
1 tsp	Vanilla extract	1 tsp

1. Preheat the oven to 350°F/180°C/Gas Mark 4.
2. Grease 2, 9-inch layer pans [sandwich tins] and put a piece of greased waxed [greaseproof] paper in the bottom.

3. Put the chocolate and water into the top of a double boiler, and stir over warm water until the chocolate has melted and the mixture has thickened. Add ½ cup [100 g/4 oz] of sugar, stir for 2 minutes, and leave until lukewarm.
4. Sift the flour, baking soda, and salt together 3 times.
5. Cream the butter; add the remaining sugar, and beat until light and fluffy. Add the eggs, 1 at a time, beating well between each addition. Add the flour alternately with the milk, beating after each addition of milk until the mixture is smooth. Stir in the vanilla and chocolate.
6. Pour into the prepared pans and bake for 30 minutes.
7. When cold, fill and frost with Butterscotch Fudge Frosting (see Index).

Chocolate Dessert

 00:35
00:30   Serves 8–10   United States

American	Ingredients	Metric/Imperial
2	Squares (50 g/2 oz) unsweetened baking chocolate	2
2 cups	All-purpose [plain] flour	225 g/8 oz
¼ tsp	Salt	¼ tsp
1 tsp	Baking powder	1 tsp
¼ tsp	Baking soda [bicarbonate of soda]	¼ tsp
½ cup	Butter or margarine	100 g/4 oz
¾ cup	Sugar	175 g/6 oz
2	Eggs	2
1 cup	Lager or ale	250 ml/8 fl oz
½ cup	Coarsely chopped pecans	50 g/2 oz
	Filling	
¼ cup	Softened butter	50 g/2 oz
¾ cup	Confectioners' [icing] sugar	100 g/4 oz
1 tbsp	Lager or ale	1 tbsp
2	Squares (50 g/2 oz) unsweetened baking chocolate	2

1. Preheat the oven to 350°F/180°C/Gas Mark 4.
2. Line 2, 8-inch cake pans [tins] with greased wax [greaseproof] paper and grease the rest of the pan.
3. Melt the chocolate and let cool.
4. Sift the flour, salt, baking powder, and bicarbonate together.
5. Beat the butter and sugar together until light and creamy. Beat in the eggs, 1 at a time. Then add the melted chocolate and flour mixture alternately with the lager. Beat well. Then fold in the pecans.
6. Put into the prepared pans and bake for 25–30 minutes. Leave in the pans to cool for 5 minutes before turning out.
7. To make the filling: beat the butter and sugar until creamy; add lager and melted chocolate, beat well, and chill until required.
8. To finish: sandwich the cakes with half of the filling, and spread the rest on top. Decorate with extra pecans or whipped cream if desired.

Chocolate Dessert

Devil's Food Cake

 00:20
00:25   Serves 10-12   United States

American	Ingredients	Metric/Imperial
¼ cup	Butter	50 g/2 oz
1 cup	Sugar	225 g/8 oz
2	Eggs	2
1½ cups	Cake [pastry] flour	175 g/6 oz
4 tbsp	Buttermilk	3½ tbsp
6 tbsp	Strong black coffee	5 tbsp
2	Squares (50 g/2 oz) unsweetened baking chocolate, melted	2
1 tsp	Baking soda [bicarbonate of soda]	1 tsp
1 tsp	Vanilla extract	1 tsp
	Frosting	
1	Egg white	1
3 tsp	Water	3 tsp
1 cup	Sugar	225 g/8 oz
¼ tsp	Cream of tartar	¼ tsp
½ tsp	Vanilla extract	½ tsp
About 1 oz	Unsweetened baking chocolate	About 25 g/1 oz

1. Preheat the oven to 375°F/190°C/Gas Mark 5.
2. Line 2 round 9-inch pans with greased waxed [greaseproof] paper and grease the rest of the pan.
3. Cream the butter and sugar until light and frothy. Beat in the eggs gradually. Add sifted flour alternately with milk, finishing with flour.
4. Boil the coffee, pour onto the melted chocolate, and add baking soda. Cool, then add to the cake mixture. Add vanilla.
5. Put into the prepared pans and bake for 25 minutes.
6. To make the frosting, put the egg white, water, sugar, and cream of tartar into a bowl and whisk over hot water until the mixture stands in peaks. Add the vanilla. Use for the filling and frosting, and dribble the chocolate on the top.

Chocolate Layer Cake

Chocolate Layer Cake

	00:45		
	01:30	Serves 8–10	United States

American	Ingredients	Metric/Imperial
½ cup	Butter	100 g/4 oz
	Grated rind of 1 orange	
	Grated rind of 1 lemon	
1 cup	Sugar	225 g/8 oz
4	Eggs	4
2 cups	Cake [pastry] flour	225 g/8 oz
1 tsp	Cream of tartar	1 tsp
1 tsp	Baking soda [bicarbonate of soda]	1 tsp
¼ cup	Cornstarch [cornflour]	25 g/1 oz
Scant ½ cup	Milk	Scant 125 ml/ 4 fl oz
	Chocolate frosting (see Index)	

1. Preheat the oven to 350°F/180°C/Gas Mark 4.
2. Line an 8-inch round cake pan [tin] with greased waxed [greaseproof] paper and grease the rest of the pan.
3. Beat the butter until soft and creamy. Add the grated orange and lemon rind and sugar, and beat well together. Beat in egg yolks 1 at a time, adding 1 spoonful of flour with each.
4. Sift the rest of the flour, cream of tartar, baking soda, and cornstarch together 3 times. Then add gradually to the creamed mixture alternately with the milk. Beat the egg whites until frothy and fold lightly into the mixture.
5. Put into the prepared pan and bake for 1¼–1½ hours, or until it is firm to the touch.
6. Let cool a little in the pan before turning out on a cooling rack. Cut into 3 or 4 layers; spread with chocolate frosting. Reassemble the cake and cover the top with frosting.

Marbled Chocolate Loaf

	01:20		
	00:45	Serves 8	United States

American	Ingredients	Metric/Imperial
⅓ cup	Shortening [vegetable fat]	65 g/2½ oz
1 cup	Sugar	225 g/8 oz
1 tsp	Vanilla extract	1 tsp
2 cups	Cake [pastry] flour	225 g/8 oz
2½ tsp	Baking powder	2½ tsp
¼ tsp	Salt	¼ tsp
⅔ cup	Milk	150 ml/¼ pint
3	Egg whites	3
1	Square [25 g/1 oz] unsweetened baking chocolate, melted	1
2 tbsp	Hot water	1½ tbsp
¼ tsp	Baking soda [bicarbonate of soda]	¼ tsp

1. Preheat the oven to 350°F/180°C/Gas Mark 4.
2. Beat the shortening and sugar until light and fluffy. Add the vanilla.
3. Sift the flour, baking powder, and salt together, and add to the creamed mixture alternately with the milk. Beat well with each addition. Beat the egg whites stiffly and fold into the mixture.
4. Mix the melted chocolate with water and baking soda. Add this mixture to half of the cake batter.
5. Alternate light and dark batters by spoonfuls in a greased and lined loaf pan [tin] about 9½ × 5 × 3 inches. Then bake for 40–50 minutes.
6. When cold, frost with Creamy Chocolate Frosting (see Index).

Cupcakes

	00:45		
	00:20	24 cupcakes	United States 

American	Ingredients	Metric/Imperial
2 cups	Sifted all-purpose [plain] flour	225 g/8 oz
½ tsp	Salt	½ tsp
2 tsp	Baking powder	2 tsp
½ cup	Butter	100 g/4 oz
1¼ cups	Sugar	275 g/10 oz
2	Eggs	2
1 cup	Milk	250 ml/8 fl oz
1 tsp	Vanilla extract	1 tsp

1. Preheat the oven to 375°F/190°C/Gas Mark 5.
2. Line 24 muffin pans [patty tins] with paper liners or grease the pans and sprinkle them lightly with flour.
3. Sift the flour, salt, and baking powder together.
4. Cream the butter; add the sugar and beat until light and fluffy. Beat in the eggs, 1 at a time. Add the flour mixture alternately with the milk, beating well after each addition. Stir in the vanilla.
5. Put into the prepared pans and bake for about 20 minutes.
6. When cool, sprinkle with confectioners' [icing] sugar or cover with frosting.

Marbled Chocolate Loaf

Butterscotch Coffee Cake

Butterscotch Coffee Cake

01:20
00:50
Serves 6-8
United States

American	Ingredients	Metric/Imperial
½ cup	Butter	100 g/4 oz
1 cup	Lightly packed brown [demerara] sugar	225 g/8 oz
1	Egg	1
2 cups	All-purpose [plain] flour	225 g/8 oz
3 tsp	Baking powder	3 tsp
½ cup	Milk	125 ml/4 fl oz
	Frosting	
¾ cup	Lightly packed brown [demerara] sugar	175 g/6 oz
2 tbsp	Milk	1½ tbsp
	A pinch of salt	
2 tbsp	Butter	25 g/1 oz
½ cup	Confectioners' [icing] sugar	65 g/2½ oz
	Chopped browned almonds	

1. Preheat the oven to 375°F/190°C/Gas Mark 5.
2. Grease an 8-inch layer pan [sandwich tin]. Cream the butter and sugar until light and fluffy; beat in the egg. Fold in the sifted flour and baking powder alternately with the milk. Turn into the prepared pan and bake for 40–45 minutes.
3. Turn out onto a cooling rack and, when cold, top with butterscotch frosting.
4. To make the frosting; put brown sugar, milk, salt, and butter into a pan and stir over low heat until the mixture boils. Cook steadily, without stirring, for 5 minutes. Remove from the stove. While still just warm, beat in sifted confectioners' sugar, adding extra, if necessary, to give a spreading consistency.
5. Spread over the cake and arrange the chopped almonds around the edge.

Crumble Coffee Cake

00:15
00:30
Serves 8
United States

American	Ingredients	Metric/Imperial
2⅔ cups	All-purpose [plain] flour	300 g/11 oz
1 tsp	Baking soda [bicarbonate of soda]	1 tsp
2 tsp	Baking powder	2 tsp
⅛ tsp	Salt	⅛
⅔ cup	Shortening [vegetable fat]	150 g/5 oz
1 cup	Sugar	225 g/8 oz
2	Eggs	2
1 cup	Buttermilk	250 ml/8 fl oz
	Crumble	
2 tbsp	Butter	25 g/1 oz
2 tbsp	Brown [demerara] sugar	1½ tbsp
2 tsp	Ground cinnamon	2 tsp

1. Preheat the oven to 350°F/180°C/Gas Mark 4.
2. Grease a 9 × 13-inch baking pan [tin].
3. Sift 2½ cups [275 g/10 oz] of flour, baking soda, baking powder, and salt together.
4. Cream the shortening and sugar until light and creamy. Add the eggs and beat well. Add the flour alternately with the buttermilk, and put into the prepared pan.
5. For the crumble, cream the butter and beat in the brown sugar, cinnamon, and remaining flour. Sprinkle over the top of the cake batter, and bake for 30 minutes or until nicely browned.

Date and Walnut Cake

00:25
00:40
Serves 10
United States

American	Ingredients	Metric/Imperial
1 cup	Chopped dates	175 g/6 oz
1 cup	Boiling water	250 ml/8 fl oz
½ cup	Butter	100 g/4 oz
1 cup	Sugar	225 g/8 oz
1 tsp	Vanilla extract	1 tsp
1	Egg	1
1⅔ cups	Cake [pastry] flour	225 g/7 oz
1 tsp	Baking soda [bicarbonate of soda]	1 tsp
¼ tsp	Salt	¼ tsp
½ cup	Chopped walnuts	50 g/2 oz

1. Preheat the oven to 350°F/180°C/Gas Mark 4.
2. Line a cake pan [tin] about 9×9×2 inches with greased waxed [greaseproof] paper and grease the rest of the pan.
3. Pour water over the dates and let cool to room temperature.
4. Cream the butter and sugar until light and fluffy. Beat in the egg and vanilla. Sift the flour, baking soda, and salt together twice. Then add to the creamed mixture alternately with the dates and water, beating well after each addition. Stir in the walnuts.
5. Put into the prepared pan and bake for 35–40 minutes.

Galette De Mange

01:00
00:30

Serves 6–8

South

American	Ingredients	Metric/Imperial
2 cups	All-purpose [plain] flour	225 g/8 oz
1 tbsp	Sugar	1 tbsp
½ tsp	Salt	½ tsp
½ cup	Warm milk	125 ml/4 fl oz
¾ cup	Softened butter	175 g/6 oz
1	Egg yolk	1
1 tbsp	Water	1 tbsp

1. Preheat the oven to 450°F/230°C/Gas Mark 8.
2. Sift the flour onto a pastry board and make a well in the center. Put the sugar, salt, milk, and softened butter into the well and work the flour into it with your fingertips until the dough forms a smooth ball. Let stand in a cool place for about 45 minutes.
3. Roll into a round about ½ inch thick and place on a buttered and floured baking sheet. Trace patterns of vertical and horizontal lines over the surface with a sharp knife, but be careful not to cut into the dough.
4. Brush with egg yolk and water, and bake for about 30 minutes.

Gingerbread

00:45
00:55

16–20 squares

New England

American	Ingredients	Metric/Imperial
3 cups	All-purpose [plain] flour	350 g/12 oz
¼ tsp	Salt	¼ tsp
2 tbsp	Ground ginger	1½ tbsp
2 tsp	Mixed spice	2 tsp
2 tsp	Ground cinnamon	2 tsp
½ cup	Brown [demerara] sugar, tightly packed	100 g/4 oz
4 tbsp	Milk	3½ tbsp
½ cup	Light molasses	125 ml/4 fl oz
2 tbsp	Dark molasses [black treacle]	1½ tbsp
½ cup	Lard and margarine mixed	100 g/4 oz
3	Eggs	3
2 tsp	Baking soda [bicarbonate of soda]	2 tsp

1. Preheat the oven to 375°F/190°C/Gas Mark 5.
2. Line a baking pan [tin] about 10 × 7 × 2½ inches with greased waxed [greaseproof] paper and grease the rest of the pan.
3. Sift the flour, salt, and spices together. Add the sugar.
4. Put 3 [2] tablespoons of milk into a small pan with the molasses and fat, and melt over a low heat. Add the beaten egg, and stir all into the flour mixture. Beat well. Dissolve the soda in the remaining 1 tablespoon warm milk, and beat into the mixture.
5. Spread evenly in the prepared pan, and bake for about 50 minutes. Cool in the pan and cut into squares.

Gingerbread

Lemon Spice Dessert

01:15
00:50

Serves 6

United States

American	Ingredients	Metric/Imperial
⅓ cup	Margarine	65 g/2½ oz
¾ cup	Sugar	175 g/6 oz
1	Egg	1
1½ cups	Cake [pastry] flour	175 g/6 oz
½ tsp	Salt	½ tsp
¼ tsp	Grated nutmeg	¼ tsp
¼ tsp	Ground cinnamon	¼ tsp
¼ tsp	Ground ginger	¼ tsp
2 tsp	Baking powder	2 tsp
4 tbsp	Water	3½ tbsp
4 tbsp	Lemon juice	3½ tbsp
½ cup	Seedless raisins	50 g/2 oz
1 tsp	Grated lemon rind	1 tsp
	Topping	
2 tbsp	Soft butter or margarine	25 g/1 oz
½ cup	Light brown [demerara] sugar	100 g/4 oz
¼ tsp	Grated nutmeg	¼ tsp
¼ tsp	Ground cinnamon	¼ tsp
¼ tsp	Ground ginger	¼ tsp
⅛ tsp	Salt	⅛ tsp
2 tbsp	All-purpose [plain] flour	1½ tbsp

1. Preheat the oven to 350°F/180°C/Gas Mark 4.
2. Grease and flour a cake pan [tin] about 8 × 8 × 2 inches.
3. Cream the margarine and sugar until light and fluffy. Add the egg and beat well.
4. Set aside 2 [1½] tablespoons of the flour; sift the rest with the salt, spices, and baking powder. Add to the creamed mixture alternately with the water and lemon juice mixed together.
5. Dredge the raisins with the reserved flour, and stir into the cake mixture with the lemon rind. Pour into the prepared pan.
6. Toss all the ingredients for the topping together with a fork, and sprinkle over the cake batter. Bake for 45–50 minutes. Leave in the pan until cold. Then cut into squares.

Christmas Fruit Loaf

Christmas Fruit Loaf

 00:25
04:00

Serves 24

United States

American	Ingredients	Metric/Imperial
4 cups	Cake [pastry] flour	450 g/1 lb
1 tsp	Double-acting baking powder	1 tsp
½ tsp	Powdered cloves	½ tsp
½ tsp	Ground cinnamon	½ tsp
¼ tsp	Ground nutmeg	¼ tsp
¼ tsp	Ground mace	¼ tsp
2 cups	Butter	450 g/1 lb
2¼ cups	Brown [demerara] sugar	500 g/18 oz
10	Eggs	10
1½ cups	Candied [glacé] or maraschino cherries	175 g/6 oz
1½ cups	Candied [glacé] pineapple	75 g/6 oz
2½ cups	Chopped dates	425 g/15 oz
2½ cups	Seedless raisins	275 g/10 oz
2½ cups	Currants	275 g/10 oz
2 cups	Candied orange and lemon peel	225 g/8 oz
1¼ cups	Chopped nuts	150 g/5 oz
1 cup	Honey	250 ml/8 fl oz
1 cup	Molasses	250 ml/8 fl oz
¼ cup	Brandy or rum	60 ml/2 fl oz
¼ cup	Cider	60 ml/2 fl oz

1. Preheat the oven to 250°F/130°C/Gas Mark ½.
2. Grease 3, 10 × 5 × 3-inch loaf pans [tins]; line with greased waxed [greaseproof] paper.
3. Sift the flour, baking powder, and spices 3 times.
4. Cream the butter; gradually add the sugar and beat together until light and fluffy. Add the beaten eggs, fruit, candied peel, nuts, honey, molasses, cider, and brandy or rum.
5. Add the flour gradually, beating after each addition.
6. Place in the prepared loaf pans and bake for 3½–4 hours.

Lemon Syrup Cake

00:15
00:30

Serves 8

United States

American	Ingredients	Metric/Imperial
1½ cups	Cake [pastry] flour	175 g/6 oz
⅛ tsp	Salt	⅛ tsp
1 tsp	Baking soda [bicarbonate of soda]	1 tsp
¼ cup	Butter	50 g/2 oz
1¼ cups	Brown [demerara] sugar	275 g/10 oz
1	Egg	1
¾ cup	Buttermilk	175 ml/6 fl oz
¼ cup	Seedless raisins	25 g/1 oz
2 tsp	Grated lemon rind	2 tsp
1 tbsp	Rum	1 tbsp
3 tbsp	Lemon juice	2 tbsp

1. Preheat the oven to 350°F/180°C/Gas Mark 4.
2. Sift the flour, salt, and baking soda together.
3. Cream the butter. Then gradually beat in 1 cup [225 g/8 oz] of the sugar, until light and fluffy. Beat in the egg. Add the flour alternately with the buttermilk, beating well after each addition. Stir in the raisins and lemon rind.
4. Put into a greased 8-inch square pan [tin] and bake for 30 minutes, or until the cake begins to shrink away from the sides of the pan.
5. While the cake is baking, prepare the syrup. Put the rum, lemon juice, and remaining ¼ cup [50 g/2 oz] of sugar into a saucepan over low heat. Stir until the sugar dissolves. Then bring to a boil. Cool a little.
6. When the cake is baked, remove to a cooling rack, standing over a plate, and pour the syrup over at once. Serve warm or cold.

Lemon Tea Cake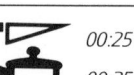

00:25
00:25

Serves 6

United States

American	Ingredients	Metric/Imperial
½ cup	Shortening [vegetable fat]	100 g/4 oz
½ cup plus 2 tsp	Sugar	100 g/4 oz plus 2 tsp
2	Eggs (separated)	2
	Grated rind of 1 lemon	
¾ cup	All-purpose [plain] flour	75 g/3 oz
1 tsp	Baking powder	1 tsp
¼ tsp	Salt	¼ tsp
2 tbsp	Soft butter or margarine	25 g/1 oz
1 tsp	Lemon juice	1 tsp
	Confectioners' [icing] sugar	

1. Preheat the oven to 400°F/200°C/Gas Mark 6.

2. Line an 8-inch layer cake pan [sandwich tin] with waxed [greaseproof] paper and grease the rest of the pan.

3. Cream the shortening and ½ cup [100 g/4 oz] of sugar until light and fluffy. Add the beaten egg yolks and lemon rind, and beat well.

4. Sift the flour, baking powder, and salt together, and add to the creamed mixture. Beat until well blended. Whip the egg whites until stiff and fold lightly into the mixture.

5. Pour into the prepared pan and bake for 25 minutes.

6. Turn out on a rack, remove the paper, and split the cake through the center. Spread with the butter, creamed with the remaining 2 teaspoons of sugar, and lemon juice. Put the halves together again, sprinkle with confectioners' sugar, and serve cut into portions.

Orange Cream Roll

Peach Marshmallow Dessert

·00:55
00:30   Serves 6–8   United States

American	Ingredients	Metric/Imperial
⅔ cup	Cake [pastry] flour	65 g/2½ oz
1 tsp	Baking powder	1 tsp
¼ tsp	Salt	¼ tsp
3	Eggs	3
¾ cup	Sugar	175 g/6 oz
1 tbsp	Cold water	1 tbsp
½ tsp	Grated lemon rind	½ tsp
1 tbsp	Lemon juice	1 tbsp
	Orange Cream Filling	
½ cup	Sugar	100 g/4 oz
2½ tbsp	Cornstarch [cornflour]	2 tbsp
	A pinch of salt	
1	Egg yolk	1
½ cup	Orange juice	125 ml/4 fl oz
1 tbsp	Lemon juice	1 tbsp
½ cup	Water	125 ml/4 fl oz
1 tsp	Grated orange rind	1 tsp
1 tbsp	Butter	15 g/½ oz

1. Preheat the oven to 350°F/180°C/Gas Mark 4.

2. Grease a baking pan [tin], about 9 × 13 × 1 inch and line with greased waxed [greaseproof] paper.

3. Sift the flour, baking powder, and salt together.

4. Beat the egg yolks until thick and honey colored. Beat in the sugar gradually. Then add water, lemon rind, and lemon juice. Fold in half of the stiffly beaten egg whites. Then fold in the flour very gradually, adding only about 3 tablespoons [2 tbsp] at a time. Fold in the remaining egg whites.

5. Pour into the prepared pan and bake for 20 minutes.

6. Turn out on a cloth sprinkled with confectioners' [icing] sugar, cut off the crisp edges, remove the paper, and spread with filling. Roll up, wrap in the cloth, and cool on a cooling rack.

7. Make the filling: Mix the sugar, cornstarch, and salt with lightly beaten egg yolk. Add the orange juice, lemon juice, and water. Cook over low heat, stirring all the time until the mixture thickens. Then reduce the heat and cook a few minutes longer. Add the grated orange rind and butter, and use when cool.

Peach Marshmallow Dessert

00:15
00:45   Serves 8   United States

American	Ingredients	Metric/Imperial
2 tbsp	Butter	25 g/1 oz
¼ cup	Sugar	50 g/2 oz
½ cup	Corn [golden] syrup	125 ml/4 fl oz
1	Egg	1
2 cups	Cake [pastry] flour	225 g/8 oz
2 tsp	Baking powder	2 tsp
¼ tsp	Salt	¼ tsp
½ cup	Milk	125 ml/4 fl oz
8	Peach halves	8
1 tbsp	Butter	15 g/½ oz
1⅓ cups	Brown [demerara] sugar	300 g/11 oz
1 tsp	Ground cinnamon	1 tsp
8	Marshmallows	8

1. Preheat the oven to 350°F/180°C/Gas Mark 4.

2. Grease a baking pan [tin] 8 × 12 inches.

3. Cream the butter, sugar, and corn syrup together. Add the egg and beat well. Sift the flour, baking powder, and salt and add to the creamed mixture alternately with the milk. Pour into the prepared pan and arrange the peach halves on top.

4. Cream 1 tablespoon [15 g/½ oz] of butter with brown sugar and cinnamon, and sprinkle over the peaches.

5. Bake for 40 minutes. Then place marshmallows on top of each peach half and return to the oven to brown.

Peanut Butter Layer Cake

Peanut Butter Layer Cake

00:40

00:35

Serves 10   Southwest

American	Ingredients	Metric/Imperial
2	Eggs	2
½ cup	Granulated sugar	100 g/4 oz
2¼ cups	Cake [pastry] flour	250 g/9 oz
3 tsp	Baking powder	3 tsp
1 tsp	Salt	1 tsp
¼ tsp	Baking soda [bicarbonate of soda]	¼ tsp
1 cup	Brown [demerara] sugar, well packed	225 g/8 oz
5 tbsp	Peanut butter	4 tbsp
5 tbsp	Vegetable oil	4 tbsp
1¼ cups	Milk	300 ml/½ pint
	Peanut Butter Frosting	
¼ cup	Peanut butter	50 g/2 oz
3 cups	Sifted confectioners' [icing] sugar	450 g/1 lb
4–5 tbsp	Milk	3½–4 tbsp

1. Preheat the oven to 350°F/180°C/Gas Mark 4.
2. Grease and flour 2, 8 × 9 × 1½-inch layer cake pans [sandwich tins].
3. Separate the eggs, beat the whites until fluffy, add the granulated sugar, and continue beating until stiff and glossy.
4. Sift the flour, baking powder, salt, and baking soda together into a bowl. Add the brown sugar, peanut butter, oil, and half of the milk. Beat well. Then add the remaining milk and egg yolks, and beat again. (If using a mixer, beat for 1 minute each time at medium speed.) Fold in the egg white mixture lightly.
5. Put into the prepared pans and bake 30–35 minutes. Leave in the pans to cool a little. Then turn out on a rack.
6. Blend the peanut butter with the sugar, and add enough milk to make a creamy consistency. Use it to sandwich the layers together, and spread the rest over the top.

Pecan Spice Cake

00:20

00:50

Serves 12   New England

American	Ingredients	Metric/Imperial
2 cups	All-purpose [plain] flour	225 g/8 oz
1 tsp	Baking powder	1 tsp
½ tsp	Baking soda [bicarbonate of soda]	½ tsp
¾ tsp	Salt	¾ tsp
1 tsp	Ground cinnamon	1 tsp
½ tsp	Ground mace	½ tsp
1½ tsp	Ground cloves	1½ tsp
½ cup	Butter	100 g/4 oz
1 cup	Sugar	225 g/8 oz
3	Eggs	3
½ cup	Chopped pecans	50 g/2 oz
¼ cup	Molasses	60 ml/2 fl oz
1 cup	Milk	250 ml/8 fl oz

1. Preheat the oven to 350°F/180°C/Gas Mark 4.
2. Grease a square 8-inch baking pan [tin].
3. Sift the flour, baking powder, baking soda, salt, and spices together.
4. Cream the butter until soft and creamy. Gradually beat in the sugar and then eggs. Stir in the chopped pecans. Add the flour mixture alternately with molasses and milk, beating well after each addition.
5. Turn into the prepared pan and bake for 40–50 minutes.

Pecan and Raisin Cake

00:25

00:40

Serves 8–10   New England

American	Ingredients	Metric/Imperial
2 cups	Cake [pastry] flour	225 g/8 oz
½ tsp	Salt	½ tsp
1½ tsp	Baking powder	1½ tsp
½ cup	Butter	100 g/4 oz
1 cup	Sugar	225 g/8 oz
1 tsp	Vanilla extract	1 tsp
½ cup	Milk	125 ml/4 fl oz
4	Egg whites	4
	Filling	
4	Egg yolks	4
½ cup	Sugar	100 g/4 oz
4 tbsp	Butter	50 g/2 oz
½ cup	Chopped pecans	50 g/2 oz
½ cup	Chopped seedless raisins	50 g/2 oz
3 tbsp	Sherry or bourbon	2 tbsp

1. Preheat the oven to 375°F/190°C/Gas Mark 5.
2. Grease 2, 8-inch layer pans [sandwich tins] and dust lightly with flour.
3. Sift the flour, salt, and baking powder twice.

4. Cream the butter, gradually add sugar, and beat until light and fluffy. Stir in the vanilla. Add the flour alternately with milk, beating well between each addition. Fold in stiffly beaten egg whites.

5. Put into the prepared pans and bake for 25 minutes, or until firm to the touch. Let cool in the pans for 10 minutes before turning out.

6. To make the filling: Stir the egg yolks in the top of a double boiler until thick. Add the sugar and butter. Place over hot water and cook, stirring constantly until thick (about 10 minutes). Add nuts, raisins, and sherry, and cook for 1 minute longer. Cool and spread between the layers.

7. This cake is best if served the following day.

Pineapple Fruit Cake

 00:40 / 01:55   Serves 12   United States

American	Ingredients	Metric/Imperial
1 cup	Sugar	225 g/8 oz
1½ cups	Crushed pineapple	250 g/9 oz
2½ cups	Mixed dried fruits	425 g/15 oz
1 tsp	Baking soda [bicarbonate of soda]	1 tsp
½ cup	Butter or margarine	100 g/4 oz
2 cups	All-purpose [plain] flour	225 g/8 oz
1 tsp	Mixed spice	1 tsp
2	Eggs	2

1. Preheat the oven to 350°F/180°C/Gas Mark 4.
2. Grease and line an 8-inch round cake pan [tin] with waxed [greaseproof] paper.
3. Put the sugar, pineapple, dried fruits, baking soda, and butter into a pan. Heat to the boiling point, and boil for 3 minutes. Let stand until quite cold.
4. Sift the flour and spice and stir into the cold fruit mixture with the well-beaten eggs.
5. Put into the prepared pan, and bake about 1½ hours. Then reduce the heat to 325°F/160°C/Gas Mark 3, and cook another 20 minutes or until the cake feels firm to the touch.
6. Cool a little. Then turn out on a cooling rack.

Rice Cake

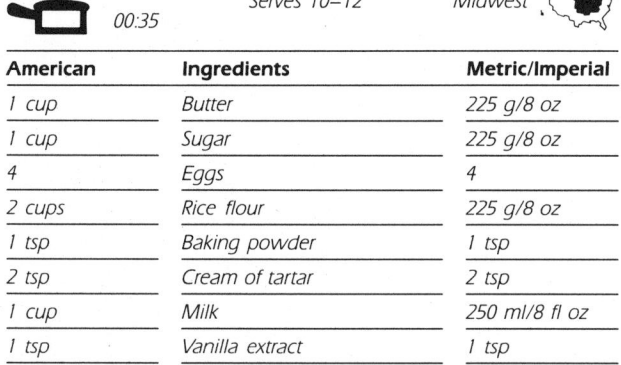 00:15 / 00:35   Serves 10–12   Midwest

American	Ingredients	Metric/Imperial
1 cup	Butter	225 g/8 oz
1 cup	Sugar	225 g/8 oz
4	Eggs	4
2 cups	Rice flour	225 g/8 oz
1 tsp	Baking powder	1 tsp
2 tsp	Cream of tartar	2 tsp
1 cup	Milk	250 ml/8 fl oz
1 tsp	Vanilla extract	1 tsp
½ tsp	Grated nutmeg	½ tsp

Pineapple Fruit Cake

1. Preheat the oven to 325°F/160°C/Gas Mark 3.
2. Grease a 12-inch loaf pan [tin].
3. Cream the butter, add the sugar gradually, and beat until light and fluffy. Add the eggs and beat well.
4. Sift the rice flour with baking powder and cream of tartar. Add to the creamed mixture alternately with the milk, beating constantly. Add the vanilla and nutmeg.
5. Pour into the prepared pan and bake for about 35 minutes.

Eggless Spice and Raisin Cake

00:10 / 01:05   Serves 8   United States

American	Ingredients	Metric/Imperial
1 cup	Beer (or water)	250 ml/8 fl oz
2 cups	Seedless raisins	225 g/8 oz
1 cup	Brown [demerara] sugar, tightly packed	225 g/8 oz
⅓ cup	Butter	65 g/2½ oz
½ tsp	Salt	½ tsp
2 cups	Cake [pastry] flour	225 g/8 oz
1 tsp	Baking powder	1 tsp
1 tsp	Baking soda [bicarbonate of soda]	1 tsp
½ tsp	Cinnamon	½ tsp
½ tsp	Mixed spice	½ tsp
⅛ tsp	Grated nutmeg	⅛ tsp

1. Preheat the oven to 325°F/160°C/Gas Mark 3.
2. Grease a 7-inch tube cake pan [ring tin].
3. Put the beer (or water), raisins, sugar, butter, and salt into a pan. Bring to the boiling point, and boil for 3 minutes. Then let cool.
4. Sift the flour, baking powder, baking soda, and spices together, and add to the cooled mixture. Stir until quite smooth.
5. Pour into the prepared pan and bake for about 1 hour. Serve plain or covered with a frosting, if desired.

Pineapple Meringue Dessert Cake

Pineapple Meringue Dessert Cake

| | 02:30 | | |
| | 00:50 | Serves 8 | United States |

American	Ingredients	Metric/Imperial
½ cup	Cake [pastry] flour	50 g/2 oz
¾ tsp	Baking powder	¾ tsp
	Pinch of salt	
2	Eggs	2
¾ cup	Sugar	175 g/6 oz
¼ cup	Shortening [vegetable fat]	50 g/2 oz
½ tsp	Vanilla extract	½ tsp
3½ tbsp	Milk	3 tbsp
	Chopped blanched almonds	
1 cup	Drained crushed pineapple	225 g/8 oz
½ cup	Heavy [double] cream, whipped	125 ml/4 fl oz

1. Preheat the oven to 300°F/150°C/Gas Mark 2.
2. Grease 2, 8-inch layer pans [sandwich tins].
3. Sift the flour, baking powder, and salt together.
4. Beat the egg yolks until thick and honey colored. Then gradually beat in ¼ cup [50 g/2 oz] of the sugar. Add the well-creamed shortening and vanilla. Mix well. Then beat in the flour and milk. Spread the mixture evenly between the 2 layer pans and chill.
5. Beat the egg whites stiffly, fold in the remaining ½ cup [100 g/4 oz] of sugar and spread on top of each cake. Sprinkle thickly with chopped almonds, pressing them into the surface of the cakes.
6. Bake for about 50 minutes.
7. When cold, sandwich the layers with a little pineapple and whipped cream mixed together, and cover the top with the remaining pineapple and whipped cream.

Pound Cake

| | 00:35 | | |
| | 00:45 | Serves 10 | South |

American	Ingredients	Metric/Imperial
1 cup	Butter	225 g/8 oz
1 cup	Sugar	225 g/8 oz
6	Eggs	6
1 tsp	Vanilla extract	1 tsp
2 cups	Cake [pastry] flour	225 g/8 oz
⅛ tsp	Salt	⅛ tsp

1. Preheat the oven to 350°F/180°C/Gas Mark 4.
2. Grease a 9-inch tube pan [ring tin] and dust it lightly with flour.
3. Cream the butter, add half the sugar, and beat until light and fluffy. Add the egg yolks 1 at a time, beating well after each addition. Add the vanilla.
4. Beat the egg whites until soft peaks form. Then beat in the remaining sugar, 1 tablespoon at a time. Continue beating until very stiff. Pile the egg whites on top of the butter mixture. Then sprinkle sifted flour and salt over the egg whites. Fold together carefully but thoroughly.
5. Put into the prepared pan and bake for 45 minutes, or until slightly shrunk away from the sides of the pan.
6. Let cool for about 20 minutes. Then turn out onto a cooling rack. Before serving, sprinkle thickly with confectioners' [icing] sugar.

Butter Sponge Cake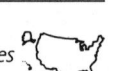

| | 00:20 | | |
| | 00:30 | Serves 8–10 | United States |

American	Ingredients	Metric/Imperial
4	Egg yolks	4
¾ cup	Sugar	175 g/6 oz
1¼ cups	Cake [pastry] flour	150 g/5 oz
4	Egg whites	4
⅛ tsp	Salt	⅛ tsp
¼ cup	Cool melted butter	50 g/2 oz
1 tsp	Vanilla extract or other flavoring	1 tsp

1. Preheat the oven to 350°F/180°C/Gas Mark 4.
2. Grease a 9-inch layer cake pan [sandwich tin] and dust it lightly with flour.
3. Beat the egg yolks. Then gradually add all but 2 tablespoons [1½ tbsp] of the sifted sugar, beating until the mixture is thick and pale in color. Fold in the sifted flour very lightly. (If you use an electric mixer for beating the eggs, remember to fold in the flour by hand.)
4. Beat the egg whites and salt until soft peaks form. Then add the remaining 2 tablespoons [1½ tbsp] of sugar and beat until stiff but not dry. Fold half the egg whites into the cake mixture. Blend carefully. Then add the remaining egg whites. Fold in the melted butter and flavoring.
5. Turn into the prepared pan and bake for 30 minutes, or until the top is firm to the touch and the cake shrinks slightly from the sides of the pan.
6. Cool in the pan for 5 minutes, then turn, right side up, onto a cooling rack. (If to be served plain, sprinkle with confectioners' [icing] sugar.)

Lemon Sponge Cake

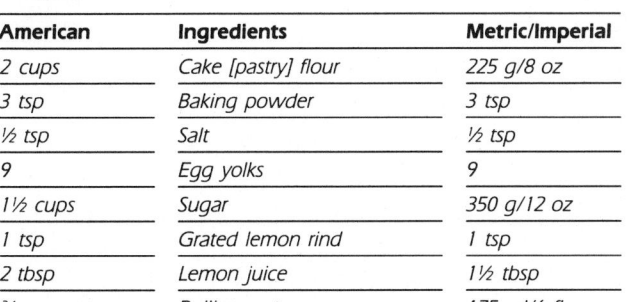
01:15
01:00   Serves 10   United States

American	Ingredients	Metric/Imperial
2 cups	Cake [pastry] flour	225 g/8 oz
3 tsp	Baking powder	3 tsp
½ tsp	Salt	½ tsp
9	Egg yolks	9
1½ cups	Sugar	350 g/12 oz
1 tsp	Grated lemon rind	1 tsp
2 tbsp	Lemon juice	1½ tbsp
¾ cup	Boiling water	175 ml/6 fl oz

1. Preheat the oven to 350°F/180°C/Gas Mark 4.
2. Sift the flour, baking powder, and salt together 3 times.
3. Beat the egg yolks until thick and pale in color, then add the sugar gradually and beat again until quite thick. Stir in the lemon rind, lemon juice, and boiling water.
4. Fold the flour in carefully and turn the mixture into a large tube pan [ring tin].
5. Bake for about 1 hour. Invert the pan and leave to get cold before turning out.

Chocolate Sponge Roll

01:30
00:13   Serves 6–8   United States

American	Ingredients	Metric/Imperial
3 tbsp	Cake [pastry] flour	2 tbsp
5 tbsp	Cocoa	4 tbsp
½ tsp	Baking powder	½ tsp
¼ tsp	Salt	¼ tsp
3	Eggs	3
4 tbsp	Confectioners' [icing] sugar	3½ tbsp
½ tsp	Vanilla extract	½ tsp
1 cup	Heavy [double] cream, whipped	250 ml/8 fl oz
	Sugar	

1. Preheat the oven to 350°F/180°C/Gas Mark 4.
2. Grease a baking pan [tin] about 9 × 13 × 1 inch and line with greased waxed [greaseproof] paper.
3. Sift the flour, cocoa, baking powder, and salt together.
4. Beat the egg yolks until thick and honey colored. Gradually beat in the sugar. Add the vanilla. Fold the flour in gradually, adding 1 tablespoon at a time. Then fold in the stiffly beaten egg whites.
5. Pour into the prepared pan and bake for 13 minutes.
6. Turn out immediately onto a cloth sprinkled with sugar, cut off the crisp edges, remove the paper, and roll up.
7. When cold, remove the paper, unroll carefully, and spread with sweetened whipped cream; then re-roll. Frost, if desired.

Lemon Sponge Cake

Marmalade Sponge Roll

00:20
00:20   Serves 8   Mid Atlantic

American	Ingredients	Metric/Imperial
⅔ cup	Cake [pastry] flour	65 g/2½ oz
1 tsp	Baking powder	1 tsp
¼ tsp	Salt	¼ tsp
3	Eggs	3
¾ cup	Sugar	175 g/6 oz
1 tbsp	Water	1 tbsp
1 tsp	Grated orange rind	1 tsp
1 tbsp	Orange juice	1 tbsp
	Marmalade	

1. Preheat the oven to 350°F/180°C/Gas Mark 4.
2. Prepare a baking pan [tin] about 9 × 13½ × 1 inch by greasing and lining with greased waxed [greaseproof] paper.
3. Sift the flour, baking powder, and salt together.
4. Beat the egg yolks until thick and pale in color. Beat in the sugar. Then add the water, orange rind, and orange juice. Fold in half of the stiffly beaten egg whites gradually. Then fold in the flour, adding about 3 [2] tablespoons at a time and sifting it over the surface. Fold in the remaining egg whites.
5. Spread the mixture into the prepared pan and bake for 20 minutes.
6. Turn quickly onto a damp cloth sprinkled with confectioners' [icing] sugar, trim the edges, and remove the paper. Spread with warmed marmalade and roll up.

Sunflower Cake

| | 01:20 | | |
| | 01:25 | Serves 10 | United States |

American	Ingredients	Metric/Imperial
1 cup	Sifted cake [pastry] flour	100 g/4 oz
1½ cups	Sugar	350 g/12 oz
10–12	Egg whites	10–12
½ tsp	Salt	½ tsp
1 tsp	Cream of tartar	1 tsp
½ tsp	Vanilla extract	½ tsp
4	Egg yolks	4
½ tsp	Grated orange rind	½ tsp

1. Preheat the oven to 325°F/160°C/Gas Mark 3.
2. Mix the flour and ½ cup [100 g/4 oz] of sugar and sift 3 times.
3. Beat the egg whites until frothy, sprinkle with salt and cream of tartar, and continue to beat until stiff enough to stand in peaks but not dry. Gradually beat in the remaining cup [225 g/8 oz] of sugar. Then fold in the flour and sugar mixture, carefully sprinkling about ¼ cup [40 g/1½ oz] at a time over the surface.
4. Divide the batter into 2 parts. Add vanilla to 1 part, and fold well-beaten egg yolks and orange rind into the other. Put alternate spoonfuls into a large, ungreased tube pan [ring tin] and bake for about 1¼ hours.
5. Invert the pan until the cake is cold before removing.

Butterscotch Fudge Frosting

| | 00:20 | | |
| | 00:10 | Frosts 1 layer cake | United States |

American	Ingredients	Metric/Imperial
2 cups	Firmly packed brown [demerara] sugar	450 g/ 1 lb
½ cup	Butter	100 g/4 oz
1¼ cups	White sugar	275 g/10 oz
¾ cup	Milk	175 ml/6 fl oz
½ cup	Water	125 ml/4 fl oz
½ cup	Chopped pecans	50 g/2 oz

1. Put the brown sugar and butter into a saucepan and stir over low heat for about 5 minutes, or until the mixture darkens slightly. Remove from the heat. Add the white sugar, milk, and water. Then return to the heat and boil without stirring until a little syrup forms a soft ball when dropped into cold water. Remove from the heat, cool until lukewarm, and beat until the mixture is a spreading consistency.
2. Add the pecans to half of the mixture and use as a filling. Spread the remainder on top of the cake and decorate with pecan halves. If the frosting hardens while spreading, stir it over hot water.

Butter Cream Frosting

| | 00:10 | | |
| | 00:00 | Frosts 1 layer cake | South |

American	Ingredients	Metric/Imperial
½ cup	Butter	100 g/4 oz
4 cups	Confectioners' [icing] sugar	625 g/1 lb 6 oz
1	Egg	1
⅛ tsp	Salt	⅛ tsp
1 tsp	Vanilla extract	1 tsp
2 tbsp	Light [single] cream	1½ tbsp

1. Cream the butter until light and fluffy. Gradually add half the sifted sugar, beating well after each addition.
2. Blend in the egg, salt, and vanilla. Then add the remaining sugar alternately with the cream. Beat until smooth after each addition.

Butterscotch Frosting

| | 00:05 | | |
| | 00:02 | Frosts 1 layer cake | United States |

American	Ingredients	Metric/Imperial
3 tbsp	Sweet (unsalted) butter	40 g/1½ oz
2 cups	Confectioners' sugar [icing sugar]	300 g/11 oz
1½ tbsp	Milk	1¼ tbsp
½ tsp	Vanilla extract	½ tsp
½ cup	Ground pecans	50 g/2 oz

1. Put the butter into a pan and heat carefully until it just begins to brown. Then stir in the sugar.
2. Remove from the stove, add the milk and vanilla, and stir until smooth.
3. Add the ground pecan nuts.

Cream Frosting

| | 00:05 | | |
| | 00:00 | Frosts 1 layer cake | United States |

American	Ingredients	Metric/Imperial
4 cups	Confectioners' [icing] sugar	600 g/21 oz
½ cup	Melted butter	100 g/4 oz
1 tsp	Vanilla extract	1 tsp
1½ cups	Heavy [double] cream	350 ml/12 fl oz

1. Sift the sugar; add the melted butter and vanilla, and beat well.
2. Gradually mix in enough cream to make a spreadable mixture.

Quick Chocolate Frosting

	00:10		
	00:05	Frosts 1 layer cake	United States

American	Ingredients	Metric/Imperial
2	Squares (50 g/2 oz) unsweetened baking chocolate	2
1⅓ cups	Sweetened condensed milk	325 ml/11 fl oz
1 tbsp	Water	1 tbsp
	Flavoring as desired	

1. Put the chocolate and condensed milk in the top of a double boiler, and heat until the mixture thickens and the chocolate has melted.
2. Add the water and let cool. Add the extra flavoring as required.

Fudge Frosting

	00:15		
	00:15	Frosts 1½ layer cakes	United States

American	Ingredients	Metric/Imperial
4	Squares (100 g/4 oz) unsweetened baking chocolate	4
1⅓ cups	Milk	325 ml/11 fl oz
4 cups	Sugar	900 g/2 lb
½ tsp	Salt	½ tsp
2 tbsp	Light corn [golden] syrup	1½ tbsp
2 tbsp	Butter	25 g/1 oz
1 tsp	Vanilla extract	1 tsp

1. Put the chocolate and milk into a pan and stir over low heat until melted. Add the sugar, salt, and corn syrup; stir until the sugar has melted, then bring to a boil. Cover, and boil for 3 minutes. Then uncover and cook until a little will form a soft ball when dropped into cold water.
2. Remove from the heat, add the butter and vanilla, and let cool. When lukewarm, beat until the mixture is creamy and thick enough to spread.

Lemon Frosting

	00:05		
	00:00	Frosts 1 layer cake	United States

American	Ingredients	Metric/Imperial
1	Egg yolk	1
1 tbsp	Grated orange rind	1 tbsp
1½ tbsp	Lemon juice	1¼ tbsp
	A pinch of salt	
2 cups	Confectioners' [icing] sugar	300 g/11 oz

Sunflower Cake

1. Mix the egg yolk, orange rind, lemon juice, and salt. Gradually stir in enough sugar to give a spreading consistency.
2. To make orange frosting, substitute 2 [1½] tablespoons of orange juice for the lemon juice.

Seven Minute Frosting

	00:15		
	00:07	Frosts 1 layer cake	United States

American	Ingredients	Metric/Imperial
2	Egg whites	2
⅛ tsp	Salt	⅛ tsp
1½ cups	Sugar	350 g/12 oz
½ cup	Cold water	125 ml/4 fl oz
1 tbsp	Light corn [golden] syrup	1 tbsp
1½ tsp	Vanilla extract	1½ tsp

1. Put the egg whites, salt, sugar, and water in the top of a double boiler and add the corn syrup. Have the water in the lower pan just below boiling. Beat with an electric or rotary beater for 7 minutes, or until the frosting thickens and holds its shape when dropped from the beater.
2. Turn into a bowl; add the vanilla and continue beating until thick enough to spread. Cool the frosting for a few minutes before using, so that it does not sink into the cake.
3. Note: To make a successful cooked frosting, separate the eggs carefully and be sure there is no speck of egg yolk in with the whites. Eggs should not be used directly from the refrigerator. Allow the whites to be at room temperature before starting to whip them. Use clean dry bowls, pan, and beater.
4. To make chocolate frosting, melt 3 squares (75 g/3 oz) of unsweetened baking chocolate and stir into the frosting just before spreading on the cake.

Creamy Chocolate Frosting

	00:10		
	00:15	Frosts 1 layer cake	United States

American	Ingredients	Metric/Imperial
2	Squares (50 g/2 oz) unsweetened baking chocolate	2
½ cup	Milk	125 ml/4 fl oz
1½ cups	Sugar	350 g/12 oz
2	Egg yolks	2
1 tbsp	Butter	15 g/½ oz
1 tsp	Vanilla extract	1 tsp

1. Put the chocolate and milk into a pan and stir over low heat until the chocolate has melted.
2. Mix the sugar with beaten egg yolks; add to the chocolate milk mixture and cook gently for 10 minutes, stirring frequently.
3. Add the butter and vanilla, and leave until lukewarm. Then beat until thick enough to spread.

Mocha Glaze

	00:05		
	00:05	Covers 1 layer cake	South 

American	Ingredients	Metric/Imperial
2 tbsp	Cocoa	1½ tbsp
1 tsp	Instant coffee powder	1 tsp
3 tbsp	Hot water	2 tbsp
2 tbsp	Butter	25 g/1 oz
1½ cups	Confectioners' [icing] sugar	225 g/8 oz

1. Put the cocoa, coffee, water, and butter together in a pan and stir over very low heat until smooth.
2. Remove from the stove and gradually beat in the sifted sugar until smooth and a spreading consistency.

Orange Glaze

	00:10		
	00:05	Covers 1 layer cake	South

American	Ingredients	Metric/Imperial
1 tbsp	Butter	15 g/½ oz
1 tbsp	Milk	1 tbsp
1¾ cups	Sifted confectioners' [icing] sugar	250 g/9 oz
1½ tbsp	Orange juice	1¼ tbsp
2 tsp	Grated orange rind	2 tsp

1. Warm the butter and milk in a saucepan over low heat until the butter melts. Add the sugar and stir until smooth.

2. Beat in the orange juice and rind. Then let cool until thick enough to spread.
3. To make lemon glaze, substitute lemon juice and rind for the orange juice and rind.

Chocolate Glaze

	00:15		
	00:05	Covers 1 layer cake	United States

American	Ingredients	Metric/Imperial
4	Squares (100 g/4 oz) sweet chocolate	4
3 tbsp	Water	2 tbsp
1 tbsp	Butter	15 g/½ oz
1 cup	Confectioners' [icing] sugar	165 g/5½ oz
⅛ tsp	Salt	⅛ tsp
½ tsp	Vanilla extract	½ tsp

1. Break the chocolate up into small pieces and put into a pan with the water and butter. Stir over low heat until melted and smooth.
2. Sift the sugar and salt into a bowl and gradually mix in the melted chocolate. Add the vanilla and cool until thick enough to spread.

Basic Custard Cream Filling

	00:15		
	00:15	About 2½ cups [600 ml/1 pint]	South

American	Ingredients	Metric/Imperial
¾ cup	Sugar	175 g/6 oz
5 tbsp	Cornstarch [cornflour]	4 tbsp
¼ tsp	Salt	¼ tsp
4	Egg yolks	4
2 cups	Scalded milk	450 ml/¾ pint
1 tsp	Vanilla extract	1 tsp
2 tbsp	Butter	25 g/1 oz

1. Mix the sugar, cornstarch, and salt together and stir in the lightly beaten egg yolks. Add enough hot milk to make a thin paste.
2. Add this to the remaining hot milk and cook in a double boiler for 5 minutes, stirring all the time.
3. Reduce the heat and cook, stirring frequently, for 10 minutes, or until the mixture has thickened.
4. Remove from the stove. Add the vanilla and butter. Let cool.
5. Variation: To make Chocolate Cream Filling, heat 2 squares (50 g/2 oz) of unsweetened baking chocolate with milk. When melted, beat with a rotary beater until smooth. Increase the sugar to 1 cup [225 g/8 oz].

Creamy Chocolate Frosting

Lemon Cream Filling

	00:15	About 1¼ cups [300 ml/½ pint]	United States
	00:15		

American	Ingredients	Metric/Imperial
¾ cup	Sugar	175 g/6 oz
2 tbsp	Cornstarch [cornflour]	1½ tbsp
	A pinch of salt	
1	Egg yolk	1
¾ cup	Water	175 ml/6 fl oz
3 tbsp	Lemon juice	2 tbsp
1 tsp	Grated lemon rind	1 tsp
1 tbsp	Butter	15 g/½ oz

1. Put the sugar, cornstarch, and salt in the top of a double boiler; add the beaten egg yolk, water, and lemon juice. Cook over boiling water for 5 minutes, stirring all the time. Reduce the heat and cook for 10 minutes, or until the mixture is thick, stirring frequently.
2. Remove from the stove, add the grated lemon rind and butter, and let cool.

Mock Cream

	12:00	About 1¼ cups [300 ml/½ pint]	United States
	00:10		

American	Ingredients	Metric/Imperial
1½ cups	Evaporated milk	350 ml/12 fl oz
1 tbsp	Confectioners' [icing] sugar	1 tbsp
½ tsp	Vanilla extract or other flavoring	½ tsp
2 envelopes	Unflavored gelatin [gelatine]	2 sachets
2 tbsp	Warm water	1½ tbsp

1. Put the unopened can of milk into a pan, and cover with cold water. Bring to the boiling point, and boil for 10 minutes. Then refrigerate overnight.
2. Pour the milk into a bowl, and whisk until stiff. Add the sugar and flavoring.
3. Soften the gelatin in the warm water. Then dissolve over hot water, and stir into the cream. Refrigerate until required.

Desserts

Apricot Cheese Pie

Pastry for 8-Inch, 2-Crust Pie

01:10
00:00   2 crusts   United States

American	Ingredients	Metric/Imperial
1½ cups	All-purpose [plain] flour	175 g/6 oz
¾ tsp	Salt	¾ tsp
½ cup	Shortening [vegetable fat]	100 g/4 oz
3 tbsp	Water	2 tbsp

1. Sift the flour and salt into a bowl. Cut in the shortening with a pastry blender until the particles are the size of peas.
2. Sprinkle with water, 1 teaspoon at a time, and mix lightly with a fork.
3. Gather the dough together with the fingers and press into a ball. Refrigerate until required, at least 1 hour.

Pastry for 9-Inch, 2-Crust Pie

01:10
00:00   2 crusts   United States

American	Ingredients	Metric/Imperial
2 cups	All-purpose [plain] flour	225 g/8 oz
1 tsp	Salt	1 tsp
⅔ cup	Shortening [vegetable fat]	150 g/5 oz
¼ cup	Water	60 ml/2 fl oz

1. Sift the flour and salt into a bowl. Cut in the shortening with a pastry blender until the particles are the size of peas.
2. Sprinkle with water, 1 teaspoon at a time, and mix lightly with a fork.
3. Gather the dough together with the fingers and press into a ball. Refrigerate until required, at least 1 hour.

Pastry for 8–9 Inch, 1-Crust Pie

01:10
00:00   1 crust   United States

American	Ingredients	Metric/Imperial
1 cup	All-purpose [plain] flour	100 g/4 oz
½ tsp	Salt	½ tsp
⅓ cup	Shortening [vegetable fat]	65 g/2½ oz
2 tbsp	Water	1½ tbsp

1. Sift the flour and salt into a bowl. Cut in the shortening with a pastry blender until the particles are the size of peas.
2. Sprinkle with water, 1 teaspoon at a time, and mix lightly with a fork.
3. Gather the dough together with the fingers and press into a ball. Refrigerate until required, at least 1 hour.
4. Note: If a pie shell is baked without a filling, it is referred to as being baked "blind." Line the pie plate with the pastry, prick the bottom with a fork or put a piece of greased paper (greased-side downwards) in the bottom and fill with rice or beans, or crusts of bread. This can then be stored for future use. Remove the paper and beans a few minutes before the end of the cooking.

Apricot Cheese Pie

04:30
00:05   Serves 6–8   United States

American	Ingredients	Metric/Imperial
3 cups	Crushed sweet cracker crumbs	175 g/6 oz
½ cup	Butter	100 g/4 oz
½ tsp	Grated nutmeg	½ tsp
1½ cups	Cream cheese	350 g/12 oz
½ cup	Sweetened condensed milk	125 ml/4 fl oz
4 tsp	Lemon juice	4 tsp
½ cup	Heavy [double] cream	125 ml/4 fl oz
	Topping	
1 tsp	Gelatin [gelatine]	1 tsp
2 tbsp	Water	1½ tbsp
1 cup	Apricot jam	225 g/8 oz
2 tbsp	Sugar	1½ tbsp

1. Butter a 9-inch pie plate.
2. Put the crumbs in a bowl with the nutmeg. Melt the butter and add enough to the crumbs so that when squeezed in the hands, the mixture will form a firm ball. Press the mixture firmly around the sides and bottom of a pie plate. Refrigerate while preparing the filling.
3. Sieve the cheese, add the condensed milk and lemon juice, and beat until smooth. Whip the cream and fold into the cheese mixture. Pour into the crumb case and refrigerate while preparing the topping.
4. Topping: Soften the gelatin in 1 tablespoon of water. Sieve the jam. Add the sugar and remaining water. Stir over low heat until the sugar has dissolved. Then boil, without stirring, for 2 minutes. Remove from the heat, add the gelatin, and stir until dissolved. Let cool a little and spoon over the cream cheese filling. Refrigerate well before serving.

Pâté Brisée

	01:10		
	00:00	2 crusts	South

American	Ingredients	Metric/Imperial
2 cups	All-purpose [plain] flour	225 g/8 oz
½ tsp	Salt	½ tsp
½ cup	Butter	100 g/4 oz
½–¾ cup	Water	125–175 ml/4–6 fl oz

1. Sift the flour and salt; rub in the butter with your fingertips.
2. Make a well in the center, and add the water a little at a time. The index finger is really best to do this, or use a fork and stir in spiral fashion, beginning at the inside of the well and gradually moving to the outer edge. The dough should be soft enough to gather up into a ball, but not sticky.
3. Roll in foil and refrigerate for as long as possible before using, at least 1 hour.

Graham Cracker Pie Crust

	00:20		
	00:08	1 crust	United States

American	Ingredients	Metric/Imperial
20	Graham crackers [digestive biscuits]	20
¼ cup	Sugar	50 g/2 oz
¼ cup	Softened butter	50 g/2 oz

1. Roll the crackers into fine crumbs. (The best way is to put the crackers into a plastic bag, and crush them with a rolling pin.)
2. Add the sugar and butter, and mix well with a pastry blender.
3. Put the crumbs into a 9-inch pie pan. Then put an 8-inch pie pan on top, and press down firmly into an even layer on the bottom and sides. Remove the pie pan, and bake for about 8 minutes.
4. Let cool before using.

Hot Water Pastry

	00:45		
	00:08	2 crusts	United States

American	Ingredients	Metric/Imperial
2½ cups	Cake flour	275 g/10 oz
½ tsp	Salt	½ tsp
1	Egg yolk	1
¼ cup plus 2 tbsp	Lard	75 g/3 oz
½ cup	Water	125 ml/4 fl oz

1. Sift the flour and salt into a bowl and make a well in the center. Drop in the egg yolk and cover with some of the flour.
2. Put the lard and water into a small pan; heat slowly until the lard melts, then increase the heat and bring to the boiling point.

Blueberry Custard Cream Pie

3. Pour all of the liquid into the flour and mix with a wooden spoon until the pastry is cool enough to handle; then use the hand and knead until the dough is smooth.
4. Leave to rest in a warm place for 20–30 minutes and use warm. This is good for cold meat and game pies.

Blueberry Custard Cream Pie

	01:00		
	00:20	Serves 8	United States

American	Ingredients	Metric/Imperial
	Crust	
7 tbsp	Butter or margarine	90 g/3½ oz
3 tbsp	Confectioners' [icing] sugar	2 tbsp
1 cup	All-purpose [plain] flour	100 g/4 oz
	Filling	
1 package	Vanilla pudding [canned custard]	450 ml/¾ pint
⅓ cup	Heavy [double] cream, whipped	75 ml/2½ fl oz
2 envelopes	Unflavored gelatin [gelatine]	2 sachets
1¼ cups	Blueberries	150 g/5 oz
¾ cup	Currant juice or blueberry juice	175 ml/6 fl oz

1. Preheat the oven to 400°F/200°C/Gas Mark 6.
2. Mix all the ingredients for the crust together and let stand in a cool place. Line a lightly buttered cake pan with a detachable bottom with the crust. Fasten a strip of foil around the edge so that the crust does not slide down during baking. Bake for about 20 minutes.
3. Make the vanilla pudding according to the directions on the package. Soak 1 tablespoon of gelatin in a little water, then stir into the warm pudding [or custard] and mix so that it melts. When the pudding has cooled, add the whipped cream.
4. Take the pie shell out of the pan and fill it with pudding. Place the blueberries on top. Dissolve the remaining gelatin and blend with the juice. Pour jelly over the berries when it starts to harden.
5. Serve with a dab of whipped cream.

Cherry Pie

Pastry Made With Oil

00:10		
00:00	1 or 2 crusts	United States

American	Ingredients	Metric/Imperial
	For 8–9 Inch, 1-Crust Pie	
1⅔ cups	All-purpose [plain] flour	200 g/7 oz
½ tsp	Salt	½ tsp
5 tbsp	Vegetable oil	4 tbsp
2 tbsp	Cold water	1½ tbsp
	For 8–9 Inch, 2-Crust Pie	
2 cups	All-purpose [plain] flour	225 g/8 oz
1 tsp	Salt	1 tsp
½ cup	Vegetable oil	125 ml/4 fl oz
3 tbsp	Cold water	2 tbsp

1. Sift the flour and salt into a bowl. Add the oil and mix with a pastry blender or fork until the mixture looks like fine bread crumbs.
2. Sprinkle with water and mix with a fork. Gather the dough together with the fingers and press into a ball. Add a little more oil if too dry. This pastry is best rolled out between waxed [greaseproof] paper.
3. Use at once; do not store in the refrigerator.

Flaky Pastry

01:45		
00:00	1 crust	United States

American	Ingredients	Metric/Imperial
1 cup	All-purpose [plain] flour	100 g/4 oz
½ tsp	Salt	½ tsp
⅔ cup	Shortening [vegetable fat]	150 g/5 oz
2 tbsp	Water	1½ tbsp

1. Sift the flour and salt into a bowl. Cut in ⅓ cup [65 g/2½ oz] of the shortening with a pastry blender until the particles are the size of peas.
2. Sprinkle with water, 1 teaspoon at a time, and mix lightly with a fork.
3. Gather the dough together with the fingers and press into a ball. Refrigerate until chilled.
4. Roll out the pastry into a square about ½ inch thick. Place the rest of the shortening in the center of the upper half of the square. Fold the pastry over, enclosing the shortening. Fold in thirds, roll again into a square about ¼ inch thick. Fold a second time in half and then in quarters.
5. Repeat this once more, then wrap in waxed [greaseproof] paper or foil, and refrigerate until required.

Cherry Pie

01:00		
00:30	Serves 8	South 

American	Ingredients	Metric/Imperial
	Crust	
1 cup	All-purpose [plain] flour	100 g/4 oz
2–3 tbsp	Sugar (optional)	1½–2 tbsp
10½ tbsp	Butter or margarine	150 g/5¼ oz
2 tbsp	Water or cream	1½ tbsp
	Filling	
2–3 cups	Pitted [stoned] cherries	225–350 g/ 8–12 oz
¼ cup	Sugar	50 g/2 oz

1. Mix the flour and sugar together and place in a pile on a baking board. Slice the butter and place on top. Chop the butter and flour together using a long knife until the mixture becomes crumb-like. Pour the water or cream on top and quickly work into a dough. Refrigerate for a half hour. Roll out two thirds of the dough, and cover a 9-inch pie plate on both the bottom and sides. Alternate the cherries and sugar in the pie crust.
2. Preheat the oven to 425°F/220°C/Gas Mark 7.
3. Make strips from the dough, and make a lattice pattern on top of the cherries. Bake for about 30 minutes, until the surface has become golden brown.
4. Serve warm or cold, with whipped cream, if desired.

Chocolate Marshmallow Pie

01:10
00:05
Serves 6
United States

American	Ingredients	Metric/Imperial
1 (8-inch)	Baked pastry shell	1 (8-inch)
2	Squares (350 g/2 oz) unsweetened baking chocolate	2
2 tbsp	Sugar	1½ tbsp
½ cup	Milk	125 ml/4 fl oz
12	Marshmallows	12
1½ cups	Heavy [double] cream	350 ml/12 fl oz
½ cup	Chopped toasted almonds	50 g/2 oz

1. Put the chocolate, sugar, milk, and marshmallows into the top of a double boiler, and stir over hot water until melted. Let cool, stirring frequently.
2. Whip the cream and fold into the mixture.
3. Pour into the pastry shell, sprinkle with almonds, and chill thoroughly before serving.

Chocolate Marshmallow Pie

Pineapple Chiffon Pie

02:20
00:05
Serves 8
United States

American	Ingredients	Metric/Imperial
1 envelope	Unflavored gelatin [gelatine]	1 sachet
3	Eggs	3
¾ cup	Sugar	175 g/6 oz
1 cup	Crushed pineapple	225 g/8 oz
3 tbsp	Lemon juice	2 tbsp
1 tbsp	Grated lemon rind	1 tbsp
½ cup	Heavy [double] cream, whipped	125 ml/4 fl oz
1 (9-inch)	Baked pastry shell	1 (9-inch)

Apple Rice

1. Soften the gelatin in ¼ cup cold water.
2. Separate the eggs, and put the yolks into the top of a double boiler with ¼ cup [50 g/2 oz] of the sugar, undrained crushed pineapple, lemon juice, and lemon rind. Stir over hot water until the mixture thickens. Then add the gelatin and stir until dissolved. Pour the mixture into a bowl, and refrigerate until it begins to set.
3. Add a pinch of salt to the egg whites, and beat until stiff. Gradually beat in the remaining ½ cup [100 g/4 oz] of sugar, and beat until the mixture is smooth and glossy.
4. Fold the egg whites and whipped cream into the pineapple mixture, and pour it into the pastry shell.
5. Chill thoroughly before serving.

Apple Rice

00:20
00:20
Serves 4
New England

American	Ingredients	Metric/Imperial
½ cup	Round-grained rice	100 g/4 oz
1 cup	Water	250 ml/8 fl oz
½ tsp	Salt	½ tsp
3	Sour apples	3
2 tbsp	Sugar	1½ tbsp
½ cup	Heavy [double] cream, whipped (can be omitted if the rice is to be eaten warm)	125 ml/4 fl oz
1 oz	Roasted sliced almonds	25 g/1 oz

1. Boil the rice in the water, into which the salt has been added, for about 10 minutes.
2. Peel the apples, if you wish, and carefully remove all of the core. Cut the apples into small cubes. Stir the fruit into the rice together with the sugar. Boil for 5 minutes, then let stand for 5 minutes. Let the rice cool.
3. Whip the cream and stir it into the apple rice, if desired. Add the roasted almonds or sprinkle them on top of the rice. Serve with cinnamon or ginger, or with milk if the rice is warm.

Fruity Squares

Barbecued Fruit Dessert

| | 01:45 | | |
| | 00:20 | Serves 6 | United States |

American	Ingredients	Metric/Imperial
2	Bananas	2
2	Pears	2
	Juice of 2 lemons	
2	Oranges	2
2	Peaches	2
	Other fruit according to your taste and the season	
½ cup	Sugar	100 g/4 oz
2 tsp	Ground cinnamon	2 tsp
	Grand Marnier or liqueur, if desired	

1. Peel and cut the bananas into 3 pieces; peel and core the pears and cut into quarters. Put into a bowl, and add the lemon juice, covering as much of the fruit as possible.

2. Peel the oranges, removing all the white pith, divide into 3–4 sections, and put with the other fruit. Prepare the peaches and any other fruit in a similar way. Sprinkle all with sugar and cinnamon, and toss lightly. Cover tightly, and leave the fruit to soften for an hour or more.

3. Heat the coals in an outdoor grill until hot, about 30 minutes, or preheat the broiler [grill].

4. Drain the fruit well and reserve the juice. Divide evenly on 6 skewers. Wrap each skewer in a rectangular piece of heavy duty or double thickness foil, and seal carefully. Cook on the grid or broiler pan for 10–15 minutes, turning occasionally.

5. Meanwhile, pour the juices into a small pan, and boil gently until reduced almost by half. Remove from the heat; add a few drops of liqueur if desired.

6. When ready to serve, fold back the foil wrapping, and spoon a little sauce over each parcel of fruit. Serve in the foil.

Fruity Squares

| | 00:45 | | |
| | 00:30 | 12 squares | Midwest |

American	Ingredients	Metric/Imperial
	Pastry for 8-inch, 2-crust pie (see Index)	
¼ cup	Butter or margarine	50 g/2 oz
½ cup	Currants	50 g/2 oz
½ cup	Seedless raisins	50 g/2 oz
½ cup	Chopped candied peel (orange or lemon)	50 g/2 oz
¼ cup	Chopped blanched almonds	25 g/1 oz
½ tsp	Cinnamon	½ tsp
1 tsp	Ground nutmeg	1 tsp

1. Preheat the oven to 450°F/230°C/Gas Mark 8.

2. Divide the pastry in half, and roll each half thinly into a square. Place 1 square on a baking sheet.

3. Melt the butter in a pan, add all the other ingredients, and mix well.

4. Spread evenly on the pastry square to within ¾ inch of the edge. Moisten the edge and place the second square of pastry on top, pressing the edges well together.

5. Using the back of a knife, mark the pastry into squares without cutting through. Brush with water and sprinkle with sugar.

6. Bake for 25–30 minutes. Let cool and cut into squares when ready to serve.

Butterscotch Pie

| | 01:10 | | |
| | 00:10 | Serves 8 | United States |

American	Ingredients	Metric/Imperial
2 cups	Milk	450 ml/¾ pint
1 cup	Firmly packed dark brown [demerara] sugar	225 g/8 oz
3 tbsp	Cornstarch [cornflour]	2 tbsp
2	Egg yolks	2
3 tbsp	Butter	40 g/1½ oz
1 (9-inch)	Baked pastry shell or graham cracker [digestive biscuit] crust	1 (9-inch)
	Heavy [double] cream, whipped	

1. Preheat the oven to 350°F/180°C/Gas Mark 4.

2. Put ½ cup [125 ml/4 fl oz] of the milk and the sugar in the top of a double boiler, and heat until the sugar has dissolved.

3. Blend the cornstarch smoothly with the remaining milk, add the beaten egg yolks, and stir this into the pan. Continue stirring, until the mixture thickens. Then cook for 5 minutes, stirring constantly.

4. Remove from the heat, stir in the butter, and pour into the pastry shell. Chill thoroughly and serve with whipped cream.

Fruit Savarin

Fruit Savarin

01:45 01:10	Serves 6–8	South

American	Ingredients	Metric/Imperial
5 tbsp	Blanched flaked almonds	4 tbsp
1 cup	Milk	250 ml/8 fl oz
3 cakes	Compressed [fresh] yeast	50 g/2 oz
4 cups	All-purpose [plain] flour	450 g/1 lb
1 cup	Butter or margarine	225 g/8 oz
¾ cup	Sugar	175 g/6 oz
5	Eggs	5
1 tsp	Salt	1 tsp
	Filling	
1 cup	Peach slices	225 g/8 oz
1 cup	Apricots	225 g/8 oz
1 cup	Pineapple rings	225 g/8 oz
1 cup	Cherries, pitted [stoned]	225 g/8 oz
	Juice ½ lemon	
4 tbsp	Clear honey	3½ tbsp
2–3 tbsp	Rum	1½–2 tbsp

1. Preheat the oven to 400°F/200°C/Gas Mark 6.

2. Grease a 9-inch fluted tube pan [ring tin] and sprinkle with flaked almonds.

3. Scald the milk, leave to cool slightly, then pour over the crumbled yeast. Stir until dissolved. Sift in 1 cup [100 g/4 oz] of the flour, beat well, and leave in a warm place until doubled in size.

4. Beat the butter until soft, add the sugar, and beat again. Beat in eggs, 1 at a time. Add the remaining flour and salt, then add to the yeast mixture. Beat all well together and put into the prepared pan. Leave in a warm place until almost doubled in bulk; then bake for 50–60 minutes.

5. To make the syrup: Drain the fruits and put 1½ cups [350 ml/12 fl oz] of the syrup into a pan with lemon juice and honey. Boil for 5 minutes; add rum to taste.

6. When the savarin is done, turn out onto a rack standing over a dish. Prick all over with a fine skewer, then pour the hot syrup over, leaving about ¼ cup [60 ml/2 fl oz]. Spoon over any syrup that runs onto the dish, until all has been absorbed and the savarin is well soaked.

7. Fill the center with the fruit. Boil the remaining syrup until reduced and thick, then pour over the fruit.

Baked Nut Apples

00:10 00:20	Serves 6	Mid Atlantic

American	Ingredients	Metric/Imperial
6	Fine apples	6
3 tbsp	Butter or margarine	40 g/1½ oz
1½–2 oz	Chopped nuts	40–50 g/ 1½–2 oz
2 tbsp	Sugar	1½ tbsp

1. Preheat the oven to 425°F/220°C/Gas Mark 7.

2. Core the apples. Cut off a piece of the core and place it back in the bottom. This is so the filling does not run out as easily. Place the apples in a greased, ovenproof dish.

3. Mix the butter, nuts, and sugar together. Fill the holes in the apples with the mixture. Bake until the apples are soft, about 20 minutes.

4. Serve with lightly whipped cream, vanilla custard sauce, or ice cream.

Baked Nut Apples

Barbecued Apples

00:10 00:12	Serves 4	Mid Atlantic

American	Ingredients	Metric/Imperial
4	Eating apples	4
	Soft dark brown [demerara] sugar	

1. Heat the coals in an outdoor grill until hot, about 30 minutes, or preheat the broiler [grill].

2. Choose hard, crisp eating apples and impale them on the end of a thick metal skewer.

3. Turn slowly over the hot coals or in the broiler until the skin bursts and begins to peel away (this will take about 10 minutes).

4. Pull off the skin with your fingers, roll the apples in soft dark brown sugar, and then put them back over the hot coals for a minute or two longer until the sugar just melts.

5. Don't forget the sugar will be hot—let the apples cool before eating.

Apple John

Apple Crumble

00:20
00:45

Serves 5–6

Mid Atlantic

American	Ingredients	Metric/Imperial
2 lb	Cooking apples, peeled, cored, and sliced	900 g/2 lb
2 tsp	Lemon juice	2 tsp
¼ tsp	Grated nutmeg	¼ tsp
½ tsp	Ground cinnamon	½ tsp
1 cup	Sugar	225 g/8 oz
¾ cup	All-purpose [plain] flour	75 g/3 oz
¼ cup	Butter	50 g/2 oz
¼ cup	Chopped nuts, optional	25 g/1 oz

1. Preheat the oven to 350°F/180°C/Gas Mark 4.
2. Combine the apples, lemon juice, spices, and half of the sugar. Toss together, and put into a greased baking dish. Add 1–2 tablespoons [1–1½ tbsp] of water.
3. Sift the flour with a good pinch of salt into a bowl, cut in the butter, add the remaining sugar and the nut meats, and sprinkle over the apples.
4. Bake for about 45 minutes.

Apple John

00:30
00:45

Serves 5–6

Mid Atlantic

American	Ingredients	Metric/Imperial
1½ lb	Cooking apples, peeled, cored, and sliced	675 g/1½ lb
¾ cup	Sugar	175 g/6 oz
½ tsp	Ground cinnamon	½ tsp
1 tsp	Grated nutmeg	1 tsp
2 tbsp	Margarine	25 g/1 oz

	Pastry	
2 cups	All-purpose [plain] flour	225 g/8 oz
½ tsp	Salt	½ tsp
1 tsp	Baking powder	1 tsp
½ cup	Shortening [vegetable fat]	100 g/4 oz
⅔ cup	Milk	150 ml/¼ pint

1. Preheat the oven to 425°F/220°C/Gas Mark 7.
2. Put the apples into a baking dish. Mix the sugar with the spices, and sprinkle on top. Dot with the margarine.
3. Sift the flour, salt, and baking powder together, and cut in the shortening. Add the milk, and mix with a fork until the ingredients are just blended. Knead lightly on a floured surface. Roll out, cut into 2-inch rounds and arrange on top of the apples, pressing the sides down well.
4. Brush lightly with milk and bake for 25 minutes. Then reduce the heat to 350°F/180°C/Gas Mark 4, and cook for 20 minutes longer.

Apple-Filled Puff Pastries

00:45
00:20

Serves 10

United States

American	Ingredients	Metric/Imperial
1 (17¼-oz)	Package frozen puff pastry	1 (475 g/17¼ oz)
5 tbsp	Sugar	4 tbsp
1–2 tsp	Cinnamon	1–2 tsp
4–6	Apples, depending on size, sliced	4–6
1	Egg, beaten	1
	Baking paper for 2 baking sheets	

1. Take the puff pastry out of the freezer and let the pieces defrost for about 15 minutes. It can defrost longer.
2. Roll the pastry into 5, 4-inch long rectangles.
3. Mix the sugar and cinnamon together. Sprinkle ½ tablespoon of the mixture evenly over each piece of puff pastry. Press the mixture into each rectangle. Turn over the rectangles so that the sugar-cinnamon mixture is on the bottom.
4. Place the apple slices (close together) in 2 rows across, with a slight space between the 2 rows, on half of the rectangle. Sprinkle ½ tablespoon of sugar-cinnamon on each. Brush with the beaten egg along the edges and between the 2 apple rows.
5. Fold half of the pastry over the apple-covered half. Cut between the rows of apples. Press the edges together with a fork. Two pastries are made from each pastry rectangle. Place them on baking sheets that have been covered with baking paper. They can stay like this until it is time to bake them.
6. Brush with egg. Bake in the center of a preheated 400°F/200°C/Gas Mark 6 oven for 15–20 minutes.
7. These taste best when just made, but they are also good when reheated.

Apricot Charlotte

06:00
00:05   Serves 6–8   United States

American	Ingredients	Metric/Imperial
	Lady fingers [sponge fingers] or sponge cake	
1 large can (1 lb 13 oz)	Apricots	1 large tin (800 g/1 lb 13 oz)
2 envelopes	Unflavored gelatin [gelatine]	2 sachets
1 cup	Water	250 ml/8 fl oz
2 cups	Heavy [double] cream	450 ml/¾ pint
½ cup	Sugar	100 g/4 oz
	Grated rind of ½ lemon	
	Extra cream for decorating	

1. Line a 10-inch spring mold [tin] with lady fingers (round side out) or fingers of sponge cake.
2. Drain and purée the apricots, reserving ½ cup [125 ml/4 fl oz] of the syrup.
3. Soften the gelatin in the water and syrup, then heat until the gelatin has dissolved. Remove from the heat; leave until the mixture begins to thicken, then beat in the apricot purée; (there should be 1 cup [250 ml/8 fl oz].
4. Whip the cream, sugar, and lemon rind together, and fold into the apricot mixture.
5. Turn carefully into the prepared mold and refrigerate until completely firm and set.
6. Unmold onto a serving platter, decorate with whipped cream, and tie a piece of ribbon around the middle.

Apricot Charlotte

Apple-Filled Puff Pastries

Brown Betty

00:15
00:30   Serves 4   Mid Atlantic

American	Ingredients	Metric/Imperial
4	Slices stale bread	4
¼ cup	Melted margarine	50 g/2 oz
1½ lb	Rhubarb, wiped and cut into about 2-inch lengths	675 g/1½ lb
⅔ cup	Brown [demerara] sugar	150 g/5 oz
¼ tsp	Grated nutmeg	¼ tsp
¼ tsp	Ground cinnamon	¼ tsp
1 tbsp	Lemon juice	1 tbsp

1. Preheat the oven to 375°F/190°C/Gas Mark 5.
2. Cut the bread into small cubes, and toss in the melted margarine. Put about one third into a greased, shallow baking dish.
3. Cover with half of the rhubarb and half of the other ingredients. Repeat, and top with the remaining cubes of bread.
4. Bake for about 30 minutes, or until the rhubarb is cooked and the top is crisp and brown.

Barbecued Bananas

00:35
00:05   Serves 4   Pacific Northwest

American	Ingredients	Metric/Imperial
4	Ripe bananas	4
	Cinnamon	
	Sugar	

1. Preheat the coals in an outdoor grill until hot, about 30 minutes, or preheat the broiler [grill].
2. Choose firm ripe bananas and do not peel them.
3. Place the bananas on the barbecue or broiler pan and leave them until the skins turn black, turning occasionally.
4. Remove from the heat with tongs, and peel back the top layer of skin.
5. Dip the bananas in a mixture of ground cinnamon and sugar.

Coffee Dessert

Coffee Dessert

05:00
00:10 — Serves 6 — United States

American	Ingredients	Metric/Imperial
1½ envelopes	Unflavored gelatin [gelatine]	1½ sachets
1½ cups	Water	350 ml/12 fl oz
1 cup	Milk	250 ml/8 fl oz
¾ cup	Sugar	175 g/6 oz
¼ tsp	Salt	¼ tsp
2 tbsp	Instant coffee powder	1½ tbsp
3	Eggs (separated)	3
1 tsp	Vanilla extract	1 tsp

1. Put the gelatin, water, milk, sugar, salt, and coffee together in a double boiler. Stir until the gelatin has melted and the mixture just reaches the boiling point.
2. Add the egg yolks, and stir over low heat until the mixture is thick enough to coat the back of the spoon.
3. Remove from the heat, add the vanilla, and chill until the mixture thickens to a syrupy consistency.
4. Beat the egg whites until stiff, and fold into the mixture. Pour into sherbet glasses, chill until firm, and decorate as desired.

Coffee Jelly Whip

06:00
00:12 — Serves 7–8 — United States

American	Ingredients	Metric/Imperial
3 envelopes	Unflavored gelatin [gelatine]	3 sachets
½ cup	Water	125 ml/4 fl oz
6 cups	Very strong coffee	1.5 l/2½ pints
3	Cloves	3
1½	Sticks cinnamon	1½
1 cup	Sugar	225 g/8 oz
1 tbsp	Finely chopped preserved ginger	1 tbsp

1. Soften the gelatin in the water.
2. Put the coffee into a pan with the cloves and cinnamon, and simmer for 10 minutes.
3. Add the sugar and softened gelatin, and stir until the gelatin has melted. Then strain into a bowl, and chill until the gelatin begins to set. Stir in the ginger and chill until firm.
4. Break up with a fork until the gelatin is foamy. Then pile into a glass serving bowl (a few drops of cold water sprinkled over the gelatin will make it sparkle) and serve with whipped cream, if desired.

Butterscotch Ice Cream with Raspberry Liqueur

01:00
00:10 — Serves 5 — New England

American	Ingredients	Metric/Imperial
¼ cup	Sugar	50 g/2 oz
5 tbsp	Hot water	4 tbsp
⅔ cup	Heavy [double] cream	150 ml/¼ pint
2 cups	Vanilla ice cream	450 ml/¾ pint
	Raspberry liqueur	

1. Melt the sugar in a dry, clean frying pan. Remove the pan from the heat when the sugar has melted. Add the hot water. Beat and stir over heat until the sugar melts again. Then boil into a rich, thick sauce. Cool.
2. Beat the cream. Stir the cooled butterscotch sauce into the cream. Refrigerate the cream while cutting the ice cream into cubes. This can be done in the ice-cream package so as not to make too much of a mess.
3. Quickly, partially mix the ice cream and cream together. Place it in a 7-inch ring mold or in individual glasses. Freeze for at least a half hour or more.
4. Dip the mold into hot water before turning the ice cream out onto a serving plate. Serve with raspberry liqueur.

Butterscotch Ice Cream with Raspberry Liqueur

Ice-Cream-Filled Oranges

	03:20		
	00:04	Serves 4	South

American	Ingredients	Metric/Imperial
4	Oranges	4
	Vanilla ice cream	
2–3 tbsp	Frozen orange juice	1½–2 tbsp
2	Egg whites	2
¼ cup	Sugar	50 g/2 oz
	Several drops of rum, brandy, or orange liqueur	

1. Cut a lid off the oranges. Spoon out the fruit. (Save the juice to drink.)
2. Beat the ice cream until soft. Flavor with the frozen orange juice. Fill the orange peels with the ice cream. Place in the freezer for several hours so that the ice cream becomes frozen again.
3. Beat the egg whites until stiff. Stir in the sugar and liqueur. Top the oranges with the meringue batter. Bake for about 4 minutes in a very hot oven, until the meringue has become a golden brown. Serve immediately.

Strawberry Frappé with Almond Crisps

	00:20		
	00:10	Serves 8	South

American	Ingredients	Metric/Imperial
1 quart	Strawberry ice cream	1 l/1¾ pints
2 quarts	Fresh strawberries	2 l/3½ pints
⅓ cup	Milk	75 ml/3 fl oz
1 quart	Vanilla ice cream	1 l/1¾ pints
2	Kiwi fruits	2
8	Strawberries as decoration	8
	Almond Crisps	
½ cup	Sliced almonds	50 g/2 oz
4 tbsp	Flour	3½ tbsp
½ cup	Sugar	100 g/4 oz
9 tbsp	Melted butter	115 g/4½ oz
2 tbsp	Heavy [double] cream	1½ tbsp

1. Prepare immediately before serving.
2. Remove the strawberry ice cream from the freezer and divide it into pieces.
3. Mix the strawberries in several batches in a blender or food processor together with the strawberry ice cream and a little milk. Pour into large coupé glasses or into small bowls. Place a dab or ball of vanilla ice cream in the middle of the glass. Place a slice of kiwi on top of the ice-cream ball. Top with a strawberry. Serve with almond crisp.
4. To make almond crisps, mix all the listed ingredients together. Drop the batter onto a greased baking sheet, using a dessert spoon. Allow for ample space between the dabs. Bake the

Strawberry Frappé with Almond Crisps

cookies in a preheated 400°F/200°C/Gas Mark 6 oven for about 10 minutes, until they have become a pretty golden brown. Let them cool somewhat before carefully removing them from the baking sheet with a thin spatula. Place on a flat surface until cold.

Ice-Cream-Filled Pineapple

	00:15		
	00:00	Serves 4	Pacific Southwest

American	Ingredients	Metric/Imperial
2	Small pineapples, divided lengthwise	2
2 tbsp	Grand Marnier or other liqueur	1½ tbsp
1¼ cups	Vanilla ice cream	300 ml/½ pint
¾ cup	Heavy [double] cream, whipped	175 ml/6 fl oz
8–10	Crushed walnuts	8–10

1. Cut out the pineapple flesh. Cut it into cubes. Place the cubes into the pineapple shell. Drip Grand Marnier over the cubes.
2. Fill with vanilla ice cream. Decorate with whipped cream and walnuts.

Ice-Cream-Filled Pineapple

Lemon Sherbet

Lemon Sherbet

	03:00	Serves 4	South
	00:00		

American	Ingredients	Metric/Imperial
3	Lemons	3
¾ cup	Confectioners' [icing] sugar	100 g/4 oz
1 cup	Water	250 ml/8 fl oz
2	Egg whites	2
	Strawberries for decoration	

1. Peel the lemons with a knife. Remove even the white part of the peel. Halve the lemons and remove the seeds. Mix the lemons in a blender or food processor until they become a smooth mass. Add the confectioners' sugar and water. Freeze the sherbet halfway. Beat the mixture several times while it is freezing.
2. Beat the egg whites into dry, stiff peaks. Mix them into the half-frozen sherbet. Continue to freeze.
3. When it is time to serve the sherbet, beat it until smooth, then spoon it into glasses or a bowl. Decorate with strawberries. Eat immediately with small cookies.

Melon à la Mode

	00:05	Serves 4	Pacific Southwest
	00:00		

American	Ingredients	Metric/Imperial
2	Canteloupes	2
8 tbsp	Nougat ice-cream	7 tbsp
4 tbsp	Good brandy	3½ tbsp

1. Wash the melons, cut them in half, and remove the seeds. Put the melon halves on serving plates.
2. Just before serving, place 2 spoonfuls of the ice cream in each melon half, and pour a tablespoon of brandy on top.

Barbecued Pineapple

	00:40	Serves 6	Pacific Northwest 
	00:05		

American	Ingredients	Metric/Imperial
1	Large ripe pineapple	1
	Melted butter	
	Sugar, as desired	
	Cream, as desired	

1. Heat the coals in an outdoor grill until hot, about 30 minutes, or preheat the broiler [grill].
2. Choose a large ripe one and cut it into 6–8 wedges, without peeling it. Remove the core from each wedge.
3. Brush the cut sides generously with melted butter, and leave on the barbecue until each wedge is lightly browned on the under side. Turn, spread again with butter, and brown the other side.
4. Serve warm, sprinkled with sugar and with cream, if desired. The skin will come away easily as the slices are eaten.

Melon à la Mode

Raspberry-Cream Cookie Bowls

	00:25	About 10 cookies	Mid Atlantic 
	00:05		

American	Ingredients	Metric/Imperial
1	Egg	1
¼ cup	Sugar	50 g/2 oz
¼ cup	Flour	25 g/1 oz
1 tbsp	Melted butter or margarine	15 g/½ oz

Raspberry-Cream Cookie Bowls

	Filling	
	Whipped cream	
	Raspberries	

1. Preheat the oven to 400°F/200°C/Gas Mark 6.
2. Beat together the egg and sugar. Stir in the flour and butter. Onto a well-greased baking sheet, spread the batter into thin, round cookies with ample space between them.
3. Bake for about 5 minutes. Loosen them immediately from the baking sheet.
4. Shape them into bowls, using a cup or a glass; or form them into cones by rolling them up. The cookies harden quickly, so do not make too many at a time. If the cookies become hard before you have shaped them, just place them back into the oven for a few minutes.
5. Whip the cream and stir in a small amount of raspberries. Fill the bowls. Decorate with a raspberry. Serve immediately.
6. Unfilled cookies can be stored in a dry place.

Christmas Snowballs

	00:45 00:20	Serves 6	United States 

American	Ingredients	Metric/Imperial
6	Medium-sized cooking apples, cored	6
6 tbsp	Mincemeat or cranberry jelly	5 tbsp
	Butter Cream	
½ cup	Butter	100 g/4 oz
1 cup	Sieved confectioners' [icing] sugar	150 g/5 oz
	Grated rind and juice of 1 lemon	
	Decoration	
2 cups	Shredded coconut	225 g/8 oz
	Sprigs of holly	
6	Short red candles	6

1. Preheat the oven to 375°F/190°C/Gas Mark 5.
2. Wipe the apples and score around the center, as this will prevent them from breaking. Put the apples into a baking dish with 3–4 tablespoons [2–3½ tbsp] of water.
3. Fill the centers with mincemeat or jelly and cook for about 20 minutes. Remove from the oven and allow to get quite cold.
4. Cover carefully with butter cream and sprinkle thickly with coconut.
5. Just before serving, put a short red candle in the center and arrange a sprig of holly at the bottom of the candle. Light the candles at the last minute.

Christmas Snowballs

Honey Rice Pudding

	00:10 01:00	Serves 4	Midwest

American	Ingredients	Metric/Imperial
1 cup	Rice	225 g/8 oz
¾ cup	Honey	175 ml/6 fl oz
¼ cup	Seedless raisins	25 g/1 oz
1¾ cups	Evaporated milk	425 ml/14 fl oz
2 tbsp	Butter	25 g/1 oz
½ tsp	Ground cinnamon	½ tsp
¼ cup	Chopped nuts	25 g/1 oz
	Juice of ½ lemon	

1. Preheat the oven to 375°F/190°C/Gas Mark 5.
2. Cook the rice in the usual way.
3. Put the honey in a frying pan, and heat very slowly until light brown. Add the raisins, evaporated milk, butter, cinnamon, and nuts, and mix well.
4. Turn the rice and honey mixture into a greased baking dish or casserole and bake for 20 minutes.
5. Stir in the lemon juice and cook for 15 minutes longer.

Apple Pudding

Apple Pudding

 00:20
00:40　　　Serves 5–6　　　Mid Atlantic

American	Ingredients	Metric/Imperial
5–6	Good-sized cooking apples, peeled, cored, and sliced	5–6
¼ cup	Sugar	50 g/2 oz
½ tsp	Ground cinnamon	½ tsp
½ tsp	Ground nutmeg	½ tsp
2 tbsp	Butter	25 g/1 oz
4 tbsp	Hot water	3½ tbsp
	Batter	
1	Egg	1
½ cup	Sugar	100 g/4 oz
2 tbsp	Melted butter	25 g/1 oz
1 cup	All-purpose [plain] flour	100 g/4 oz
1 tsp	Baking powder	1 tsp
	A pinch of salt	

1. Preheat the oven to 375°F/190°C/Gas Mark 5.
2. Put the apples into a baking dish, sprinkle with sugar and spices, dot with butter, and add the hot water.
3. Beat the egg and sugar together until thick. Then stir in the melted butter.
4. Sift the flour, baking powder, and salt together, and fold into the egg mixture. Spread on top of the apples, and bake for 25 minutes. Then reduce the heat to 350°F/180°C/Gas Mark 4, and bake for 10–15 minutes longer.

Butterscotch Bread Pudding

 00:15
00:45　　　Serves 6　　　Mid Atlantic

American	Ingredients	Metric/Imperial
3 tbsp	Butter	40 g/1½ oz
½ cup	Brown [demerara] sugar	100 g/4 oz
¼ tsp	Baking soda [bicarbonate of soda]	¼ tsp
2 cups	Milk	450 ml/¾ pint
2	Eggs	2
	A pinch of salt	
2 cups	Stale bread cubes (about ½-inch cubes)	25 g/1 oz

1. Preheat the oven to 350°F/180°C/Gas Mark 4.
2. Melt the butter in a pan, add the sugar, and heat until well blended.
3. Dissolve the baking soda in the milk. Add gradually to the sugar mixture, stir until well blended, and set aside to cool.
4. Beat the eggs lightly. Then add the salt and the cooled milk and sugar mixture.
5. Put the bread cubes into a greased baking dish, pour the custard over, and bake for about 45 minutes.

Cranberry Pudding

 00:20
01:15　　　Serves 6　　　Mid Atlantic

American	Ingredients	Metric/Imperial
1½ cups	Cranberries	350 g/12 oz
1½ cups	All-purpose [plain] flour	175 g/6 oz
½ tsp	Salt	½ tsp
1 tsp	Baking powder	1 tsp
¼ cup	Butter	50 g/2 oz
¾ cup	Sugar	175 g/6 oz
1	Egg	1
⅔ cup	Milk	150 ml/¼ pint
1 tsp	Vanilla extract	1 tsp

1. Pick over, wash, and dry the cranberries; chop coarsely.
2. Sift the flour, salt, and baking powder together.
3. Cream the butter, add the sugar, and beat until light and fluffy. Then beat in the egg and stir in the cranberries.
4. Mix the milk and vanilla, and add to the creamed mixture alternately with the flour. Combine all together.
5. Turn into a greased 2-pint [1 1/1¾-pint] mold or heatproof bowl, and cover securely with foil. Place on a rack in a deep pan. Add boiling water to halfway up the bowl. Cover the pan, and cook over low heat for about 1¼ hours. (Check that the water is simmering gently throughout the cooking.)

Special Christmas Pudding

00:15
05:30
Serves 5–6
United States

American	Ingredients	Metric/Imperial
1 cup	All-purpose [plain] flour	100 g/4 oz
1 tsp	Baking powder	1 tsp
1 tsp	Pudding spice	1 tsp
	A pinch of salt	
¾ cup	Soft bread crumbs	40 g/1½ oz
¾ cup	Chopped suet	175 g/6 oz
½ cup	Brown [demerara] sugar	100 g/4 oz
5 tbsp	Seeded raisins	4 tbsp
5 tbsp	Currants	4 tbsp
2	Apples, peeled, cored, and finely chopped	2
5 tbsp	Chopped candied peel	4 tbsp
¼ cup	Molasses	60 ml/2 fl oz
½ cup	Milk	125 ml/4 fl oz
2 tbsp	Brandy or rum	1½ tbsp

1. Butter a 1½-pint [700 ml/1¼ pint] ring mold and sprinkle with brown sugar.
2. Sift the flour, baking powder, spice, and salt together into a bowl. Stir in bread crumbs, suet, sugar, and fruits.
3. Mix the molasses with the milk and brandy; stir into the pudding and mix well.
4. Turn into the prepared mold, cover with buttered paper and then with foil, and steam for 4 hours.
5. Remove the paper, re-cover, and store in a dry place.
6. When required for use, steam a further 1½ hours.

Special Christmas Pudding

Bread and Almond Pudding

Bread and Almond Pudding

00:45
00:25
Serves 4–6
New England

American	Ingredients	Metric/Imperial
¼ cup	Raisins	25 g/1 oz
About ⅓ cup	Sweet white wine	About 75 ml/3 fl oz
¾ cup	Almonds	75 g/3 oz
2	Eggs	2
⅔ cup	Sugar	150 g/5 oz
¾ cup	Milk	175 ml/6 fl oz
¾ cup	Heavy [double] cream	175 ml/6 fl oz
About ¾ cup	White bread, crust removed, cut into cubes	About 40 g/1½ oz
1½ tsp	Cinnamon	1½ tsp
1 tsp	Nutmeg	1 tsp

1. Preheat the oven to 350°F/180°C/Gas Mark 4.
2. Soak the raisins for about 30 minutes in the wine. If the raisins are dry, warm the mixture slightly. Strain away the wine (save this for another recipe).
3. Scald, peel, dry, and grind the almonds.
4. Beat the eggs and sugar together until white and light. Add the milk, cream, and remaining ingredients. Blend well. Pour into a greased round dish or into individual dishes. Stir with a fork so the raisins do not sink to the bottom.
5. Bake in a pan of water in the oven for about 25 minutes, or until the pudding has become firm and has a golden brown crust on the top.
6. Serve hot or warm with chilled whipped cream, grated orange peel, and a dash of orange liqueur.

Index

A TASTE OF
AMERICA

A TASTE OF
AMERICA

THE COMPLETE BOOK OF
AMERICAN REGIONAL COOKING

Edited and adapted by
MARIAN HOFFMAN

GALLERY BOOKS

A *Macdonald Orbis* BOOK

Created and manufactured by arrangement with
Ottenheimer Publishers, Inc.

Copyright © 1988, Ottenheimer Publishers, Inc.

First published in Great Britain in 1988
by Macdonald & Co (Publishers) Ltd
London & Sydney

A member of Maxwell Pergamon Publishing Corporation plc

British Library Cataloging in Publication Data

Hoffman, Marian
    A taste of America.
1. Food: American dishes—Recipes
    I. Title
    641.5973

ISBN 0-8317-8652-3

Text edited by Marian Hoffman

Printed in the United States of America

Macdonald & Co (Publishers) Ltd
Greater London House
Hampstead Road
London NW1 7QX

Contents

Symbols

The symbols will enable you to see at a glance how easy a recipe is, the preparation and cooking times, and from which region of the United States the recipe originated.

 easy

 more difficult

 for experienced cooks

 preparation time

 cooking time

 region

When using the recipes in this book remember the following points:

Cooking and preparation times are approximate and will vary according to the type of equipment used, the experience of the cook, and the number of convenience foods used.

Use only one set of measurements for the recipes, since American, imperial, and metric measurements are not exact equivalents.

In the text of the recipes, American quantities and ingredients are listed first, with the British equivalents in brackets. The British equivalent to an American ingredient only appears after the first mention of that ingredient.

Introduction

Just what constitutes American cuisine is difficult to define. Many "American" recipes are versions of traditional dishes brought over from the Old World, reflecting the ethnic heritage of many Americans. Other recipes reflect the foods and innovations of the New World. Each region of the United States has its own specialties depending on which crops grow in that climate, how close it is to the coast, and which ethnic groups have settled in that area.

A Taste of America is a comprehensive collection of over 1,000 recipes culled from the different regions of the United States. Each recipe has been labeled according to region; there are recipes from New England, the Mid Atlantic, the South, the Midwest, the Pacific Southwest, and the Pacific Northwest. Some recipes, however, are found so commonly throughout the country that they have simply been labeled "United States."

The recipes, many of which are illustrated by full color photographs, include preparation and cooking times and are ranked according to degree of difficulty. These features, plus step-by-step instructions, make this book an easy-to-use as well as comprehensive collection of American cookery.

Appetizers and First Courses

Stuffed Mushrooms

Stuffed Mushrooms

| | 00:20 | Serves 4 | United States |
| | 00:40 | | |

American	Ingredients	Metric/Imperial
4	Large (or 8 smaller mushrooms)	4
4 tbsp	Margarine	50 g/2 oz
1	Small onion, chopped	1
1 tbsp	Flour	1 tbsp
½ cup	Milk	125 ml/4 fl oz
½	Small red pepper	½
¼ cup	Cooked ham, chopped	50 g/2 oz
1 tbsp	Parsley, chopped	1 tbsp
	Salt and pepper	
5 tbsp	Fresh bread crumbs	4 tbsp

1. Preheat oven to 350°F/180°C/Gas Mark 4.
2. Wipe the mushrooms, remove the stalks, and reserve. Put mushroom caps, upside down, in a shallow, greased, ovenproof dish. Dot with 2 tablespoons [25g/1oz] of margarine and bake in oven for 10 minutes.
3. Meanwhile, heat the remaining margarine in a saucepan and fry the onion until softened. Stir in the flour and cook, stirring, for 2 to 3 minutes. Blend in the milk and bring to a boil, stirring all the time. Boil for 2 minutes.
4. Chop the reserved mushroom stalks and half the pepper (slice remainder of the pepper for garnish). Add the pepper, mushroom stalks, ham, parsley, salt, pepper, and bread crumbs to the sauce. Pile some stuffing into each mushroom cap.
5. Return to the oven and bake for a further 15 to 20 minutes. Serve hot, garnished with strips of red pepper.

Stuffed Artichokes

| | 00:30 | Serves 4 | Pacific Southwest |
| | 00:50 | | |

American	Ingredients	Metric/Imperial
4	Medium globe artichokes	4
¾ cup	Dry bread crumbs	40 g/1½ oz
3 tbsp	Parmesan cheese, grated	2 tbsp
1 tbsp	Parsley, chopped	1 tbsp
½ tsp	Garlic salt	½ tsp
¼ tsp	Dried oregano, crumbled	¼ tsp
¼ tsp	Pepper	¼ tsp
2 tbsp	Butter	25 g/1 oz
2 tbsp	Olive oil	1½ tbsp
1 cup	Boiling water	250 ml/8 fl oz

1. Remove stems from the artichokes. Cut about ½ inch from the tips of the leaves, using kitchen scissors. Drop into boiling salted water: cook 5 minutes. Drain; shake to remove water; cool.
2. Combine the bread crumbs, cheese, parsley, garlic salt, oregano, and pepper. Mix well.
3. Tap the base of the artichokes on a flat surface to spread the leaves. Stuff each artichoke with one quarter of the bread-crumb mixture; spoon it between the leaves. Put the artichokes into a saucepan or stove-top [flame-proof] casserole; place them close together so they do not tip over. Top each artichoke with ½ tablespoon [7½ g/¼ oz] butter and ½ tablespoon oil. Pour in boiling water and cover. Cook over low heat 35 to 45 minutes or until the artichokes are tender.

Stuffed Tomatoes

| | 02:15 | Serves 4 | United States |
| | 00:00 | | |

American	Ingredients	Metric/Imperial
4	Medium tomatoes, peeled	4
	Cream-Cheese Stuffing	
4 oz	Cream cheese, softened	100 g/4oz
2 tbsp	Light [single] cream	1½ tbsp
1 tsp	Chopped chives	1 tsp
	Dressing	
2 tbsp	Wine vinegar	1½ tbsp
6 tbsp	Vegetable oil	5 tbsp
¼ tsp	Salt	¼ tsp
	Pepper to taste	
1 tsp	Chopped chives	1 tsp

1. Cut a thin slice from the bottom of each tomato. Reserve the slices. From stem ends, scoop out the seeds and pulp with a spoon. Mix the cream cheese, cream, and 1 teaspoon chives. Fill the tomatoes with cream-cheese stuffing.
2. Mix the vinegar, oil, salt, pepper, and 1 teaspoon chives. Pour the dressing over the tomatoes. Chill up to 2 hours. Serve on salad greens. Use reserved tomato slices as hats for tomatoes.
3. Note: To peel tomatoes, dip in boiling water 30 seconds, then rinse with cold water. Skins will slip off.

Sweet-Potato Fingers

	00:15		
	00:20	Serves 10	South

American	Ingredients	Metric/Imperial
4-6	Cooked sweet potatoes	4-6
¼ cup	Flour	25 g/1 oz
	Fat for deep frying	
½ cup	Brown [demerara] sugar	100 g/4 oz
1 tsp	Salt	1 tsp
½ tsp	Nutmeg	½ tsp

1. Cut the sweet potatoes into strips or fingers. Score lightly with a fork. Dip each finger into flour until well coated.
2. Heat the fat in a medium frying pan. Fry the potato fingers until golden brown. Drain on paper towels [kitchen paper]. Sprinkle with a mixture of brown sugar, salt, and nutmeg. Makes about 40 fingers.

Toasted Pecans

	00:05		
	01:30	Serves 24	South

American	Ingredients	Metric/Imperial
12 cups	Pecans	1.5 kg/3¼ lb
¼ lb	Butter	100 g/4 oz
	Salt	

1. Preheat oven to 250°F/130°C/Gas Mark ½.
2. Place the pecans in a rectangular oven dish. Toast in the oven 30 minutes. Add butter over all by slicing or dotting it over nuts. Stir once or twice, until the pecans and butter have mixed well. The nuts will be greasy at this point.
3. Sprinkle with salt to taste. Toast the pecans 1 hour; salt again several times. Stir as you go. When done, the butter will be completely absorbed and nuts crisp.

Roasted Chestnuts

	00:15		
	00:30	Serves 4	New England 

American	Ingredients	Metric/Imperial
24	Chestnuts	24

1. Using a sharp knife, make two diagonal slits on the flat side of each chestnut.
2. Heat charcoal grill. If you don't have a charcoal grill, cook the chestnuts in an open fire.
3. Put 6 chestnuts on a square of foil and wrap up into a neat parcel—one for each person. Put directly on the hot coals and leave for about 30 minutes.
4. Remember to let the nuts cool a little before eating.

Vegetable Fritters

Vegetable Fritters

	01:00		
	00:20	Serves 6	United States

American	Ingredients	Metric/Imperial
1	Small eggplant [aubergine]	1
	Salt	
1	Large zucchini [courgette]	1
½	Small cauliflower	½
¾ cup	Flour	75 g/3 oz
2	Eggs	2
4 tbsp	Milk	3½ tbsp
	Oil for deep-frying	

1. Slice the eggplant into thin rounds. Place the slices in a colander and sprinkle with salt. Cover with a plate and put aside for 30 minutes. Slice the zucchini. Divide the cauliflower into flowerets.
2. Sift the flour into a mixing bowl with a pinch of salt. Make a well in the center and add the eggs. Mix the eggs into the flour; gradually add milk, beating well until the batter is smooth. Rinse then drain the eggplant and pat dry with paper towels [kitchen paper]. Fill a deep frying pan half full of oil. When the fat is hot, dip the vegetables into batter and fry individual pieces until golden all over. Drain on paper towels [kitchen paper] and serve as soon as possible.

Avocado Cream

Potato Skins

| | 00:30 | Serves 8 | New England |
| | 01:15 | | |

American	Ingredients	Metric/Imperial
8	Medium-sized potatoes	8
¼ cup	Flour	50 g/2 oz
	Cooking oil	
	Seasoned salt	

1. Preheat oven to 400°F/200°C/Gas Mark 6.
2. Scrub the potatoes and pierce with a fork. Rub lightly with oil and bake for about 50 to 60 minutes, or until tender. Cool.
3. Cut the potatoes in half lengthwise and scoop out most of the white part, leaving about a ¼-inch shell. Cut the shells in half lengthwise, then in half cross-wise, which will give you eight pieces from each potato. Dip in flour and shake off excess, then deep fry in oil heated to 375°F [190°C] for about 2 minutes or until lightly browned.
4. Drain on a paper towel [kitchen paper]. Sprinkle with seasoned salt, and serve. Makes about 64 potato skins.
5. These may be made ahead of time and reheated by placing on baking sheet in 375°F/190°C/Gas Mark 5 oven for about 10 minutes.

Avocado Cream

| | 01:15 | Serves 4 | Pacific Southwest |
| | 00:00 | | |

American	Ingredients	Metric/Imperial
2	Ripe avocado	2
1 tbsp	White wine vinegar	1 tbsp
4	Anchovy fillets, finely chopped	4
2 tsp	Finely chopped onion	2 tsp
	Salt	
	Cayenne pepper	
1 tsp	Sugar	1 tsp
½ cup	Heavy [double] cream, whipped	125 ml/4 fl oz
	Paprika	

1. Cut the avocados in half and remove the seed.
2. Scrape out all the flesh, being careful not to break the skin. Reserve the empty shells, adding lemon juice to prevent discoloring. Put the flesh into a bowl and mash well. Add vinegar, anchovy, and onion. Season with salt, cayenne pepper, and sugar.
3. Chill for at least an hour; just before serving, fold in the whipped cream. Fill the avocados shells and sprinkle with paprika.

Quiche Lorraine

| | 01:40 | Serves 6 | South |
| | 00:50 | | |

American	Ingredients	Metric/Imperial
1	Recipe Pâte Brisée (see Index)	1
6 oz	Gruyère cheese	175 g/6 oz
4 slices	Bacon	4 rashers
3	Eggs	3
¾ cup	Light [single] cream	175 ml/6 fl oz
1	Small onion, peeled and finely chopped	1
¼ tsp	Nutmeg	¼ tsp

1. Preheat oven to 450°F/230°C/Gas Mark 8.
2. Line a deep 8-inch pie plate with the pastry, and refrigerate while preparing the filling. Rest for 1 hour.
3. Cut the cheese into thin slices, or use packaged cheese slices, and cut into 2-inch strips.
4. Cut the bacon into small pieces. Fry until crisp and then drain.
5. Arrange alternate layers of cheese and bacon in the pie shell and sprinkle with chopped sautéed onion.
6. Beat the eggs lightly. Combine with the cream, nutmeg, and seasoning and pour over the bacon and cheese.
7. Bake for 10 minutes; then reduce heat to 300°F/150°C/Gas Mark 2 and bake for 30 minutes, or until the custard is set and pastry is cooked.

Cucumber Boats

Cucumber Boats

 00:30
00:00

Serves 8

United States

American	Ingredients	Metric/Imperial
1	Cucumber	1
1 (4½-oz) can	Sardines	1 (125 g/4½ oz) tin
½ cup	Mayonnaise	125 ml/4 fl oz
2 tsp	Lemon juice	2 tsp
1 tbsp	Parsley, chopped	1 tbsp
2	Hard-boiled eggs	2
1 tsp	Salt	1 tsp
½ tsp	Pepper	½ tsp
1	Lettuce	1
½	Head celery	½
2	Large carrots	2

1. Cut the cucumber into 2½-inch lengths. Cut in half length-wise, remove ½ inch strip of skin underneath cucumber pieces to make them stand up. Cut each strip into 2 triangles to make sails. Remove the soft center from each piece of cucumber.

2. Drain the sardines and mash them in a bowl with mayonnaise and lemon juice. Chop the parsley and hard-boiled eggs; add them to the sardine mixture with salt and pepper. Fill the cucumber pieces with the mixture.

3. Arrange the cucumbers on a serving plate. Shred the lettuce; cut the celery into 1-inch pieces and the carrot into wedges. Arrange these vegetables on a serving plate in between the cucumber boats. Secure sails by pushing the narrow end of the sail into the filling and propping it up with a cocktail stick if necessary.

Party Croissant

Party Croissant

| | 01:30 | | | | |
| 00:20 | Serves 8 | United States | |

American	Ingredients	Metric/Imperial
1 oz	Yeast	25 g/1 oz
5 tbsp	Butter or margarine	65 g/2½ oz
⅔ cup	Lukewarm water	150 ml/¼ pt
	Salt	
½ tsp	Sugar	½ tsp
2	Eggs	2
1 tbsp	Sesame seeds, without skins, plus more to sprinkle over croissant	1 tbsp
2 cups	Flour	225 g/8 oz
	Filling	
5 oz	Garlic cheese	150 g/5 oz
¼ lb	Smoked ham, in thin slices	100 g/4 oz
18-20	Pimento-filled olives	18-20

1. Crumble the yeast in a large bowl. Melt the butter in a pan and add water. Pour a little of the warm liquid over the yeast and stir. Pour in the rest of the liquid. Add salt, sugar, 1 egg, and sesame seeds. Add nearly all of the flour and work until the dough becomes smooth and shiny. Let it rise under a cloth for about 30 minutes.

2. Place the dough onto a lightly floured baking board and knead it until it stops sticking to the board. Roll out the dough into a triangle. Lay the filling in an even strip across the widest part of the triangle. Roll together toward the point. Form into a croissant.

3. Preheat oven to 400°F/200°C/Gas Mark 6.

4. Place the croissant on a prepared baking sheet and let it rise for approximately 20 minutes. Brush with second egg and sprinkle some sesame seeds over croissant. Bake on the lowest rack in the oven for about 20 minutes. Test with a toothpick.

Mushroom Rolls

| | 00:30 | | | | |
| 00:15 | Serves 15-20 | United States | |

American	Ingredients	Metric/Imperial
½ lb	Mushrooms	225 g/8oz
¼ cup	Butter	50 g/2oz
3 tbsp	Flour	2 tbsp
¾ tsp	Salt	¾ tsp
1 cup	Light [single] cream	250 ml/8 fl oz
2 tsp	Chives, minced	2 tsp
1 tsp	Lemon juice	1 tsp
1	Family-sized loaf sliced fresh white bread	1

1. Clean and finely chop the mushrooms. Sauté for 5 minutes in butter. Blend in flour and salt. Stir in the light cream. Cook until thick.

2. Add the chives and lemon juice; cool. Remove the crust from the white bread. Roll slices thin and spread with the mixture. Roll up. Pack and freeze, if desired.

3. When ready to serve, defrost, cut each roll in half, and toast on all sides in 400°F/200°C/Gas Mark 6 oven. Makes 3½ dozen.

Cheese and Anchovy Snack

| | 00:15 | | | | |
| 00:15 | Serves 4 | United States |  |

American	Ingredients	Metric/Imperial
¼	Loaf French bread	¼
	Bel Paese or Cheddar cheese	
1 can (2 oz)	Anchovy fillets	1 tin (50 g/2 oz)
½ cup	Butter	50 g/2 oz

1. Preheat oven to 400°F/200°C/Gas Mark 6.

2. Cut the bread into slanting slices about ¼ inch thick. Place a slice of cheese on each and arrange in a baking pan, slightly overlapping. Put into a moderately hot oven until the cheese has melted and the bread is crisp.

3. Mash the anchovy fillets and mix with the butter. Spread over the bread and return to the oven for a few minutes to heat through.

4. If you find anchovies a little too salty for your taste, soak them for 10-15 minutes in a little milk and then pat dry before using.

Stuffed Eggs

| | 00:25 | | |
| | 00:15 | Serves 4 | United States  |

American	Ingredients	Metric/Imperial
4	Eggs	4
½ tsp dried or ½ tbsp fresh	Parsley	½ tsp dried or ½ tbsp fresh
	Salt and pepper	
4 tbsp	Mayonnaise	3½ tbsp

1. Hard-boil the eggs in boiling water to cover for 10-15 minutes. Stir cooking eggs for the first 2 minutes to help keep the yolks in the middle. Drain and cool the eggs in cold water.
2. Shell and cut each egg in half lengthwise. Scoop out the yolks into a bowl; add parsley, salt and pepper, and mayonnaise. Beat until smooth. Pile the yolks back into the whites or pipe them with a large star pipe.

Swiss Cheese Snack

| | 00:05 | | |
| | 00:10 | Serves 4 | Midwest  |

American	Ingredients	Metric/Imperial
8	Slices bread	8
	Butter	
	Prepared mustard	
4	Slices Swiss cheese	4
4	Thin slices cooked ham	4

1. Cut the crusts from the bread and spread with butter.
2. Spread a little mustard on half the slices; put a slice of cheese and a slice of ham on top. Cover with the remaining slices of bread and press down firmly.
3. Cut in half crosswise and fry in hot butter, turning once.

Cheese Fingers

| | 00:15 | | |
| | 00:15 | Serves 9 | Midwest |

American	Ingredients	Metric/Imperial
9	Bread slices	9
	Butter	
½ cup	Grated cheese	50 g/2 oz
2	Eggs	2
2 tbsp	Milk	1½ tbsp

1. Remove the crusts from the bread, spread with butter, and make into sandwiches with the grated cheese. (Spread a little prepared mustard or chopped pickle on one side of the bread if desired.)
2. Cut into neat fingers.
3. Beat the eggs; add milk and seasoning.
4. Dip the fingers quickly in and out of the egg and fry in hot butter until crisp and golden.

Stuffed Eggs

Cheese Pastries

| | 01:30 | | |
| | 00:15 | Serves 4 | United States |

American	Ingredients	Metric/Imperial
	Pasta Pastry	
2 cups	Flour	225 g/8 oz
½ tsp	Salt	½ tsp
¼ cup	Butter or margarine	50 g/2 oz
	Lukewarm water to mix	
	Filling	
¼ cup	Butter or margarine	50 g/2 oz
1½ cups	Grated cheese	175 g/6 oz
1	Egg	1

1. To make the pastry, sift the flour and salt, rub in the butter, and add enough water to make a soft but not sticky dough. Knead into a ball, cover, and leave for about 1 hour.
2. To make the filling, beat the butter until soft. Then beat in most of the cheese, beaten egg, and seasoning.
3. Roll out the dough very thinly, cut into rounds with a serrated cutter, about 2½ inches in diameter.
4. Put a little of the cheese mixture on each round of dough, dampen the edge and fold over, pressing the edges well together.
5. Fry in deep fat until well browned. Drain and serve sprinkled with the remaining cheese.

Melon Shrimp

Cheese Straws

	00:50			
	00:10	Serves 4	Mid Atlantic	

American	Ingredients	Metric/Imperial
½ cup	Butter or 1 stick	100 g/4 oz
1 cup	All-purpose [plain] flour	100 g/4 oz
1 cup	Grated cheese	100 g/4 oz
1 tsp	Dry mustard	1 tsp
	Cayenne pepper and salt to taste	

1. Cut the butter into the flour, which has been sifted into a bowl. Blend well. Add the grated cheese, dry mustard, pepper, cayenne pepper, and salt if necessary. Shape the paste into a ball, wrap well, and refrigerate for at least 30 minutes.
2. Preheat oven to 400°F/200°C/Gas Mark 6.
3. Roll out paste on a floured board and cut into strips or rounds. Bake in an oven for 6–10 minutes or until golden brown and crisp.

Melon Shrimp

	00:15			
	00:00	Serves 4-6	Pacific Southwest	

American	Ingredients	Metric/Imperial
1	Honeydew melon (or watermelon)	1
1 can (4½ oz)	Shrimp [prawns]	1 tin (125 g/4½ oz)
	A little mayonnaise, tomato purée and cream	

1. Using a vegetable ball cutter, cut some balls from a honeydew or watermelon and mix with the shrimp.
2. Put into dishes and coat with mayonnaise to which a little tomato purée and cream has been added.

Peaches Filled with Cheese

	00:15			
	00:00	Serves 4-5	Midwest	

American	Ingredients	Metric/Imperial
1 can (about 30 oz)	Peach halves	1 tin (850 g/ 30 oz)
3 tbsp	Grated Cheddar cheese	2 tbsp
1 tbsp	Grated Parmesan cheese	1 tbsp
1 tbsp	Softened butter	15 g/½ oz
	Cayenne pepper	
	Lettuce	
3 oz	Cream cheese	75 g/3 oz
5-6 tbsp	Light [single] cream	4-5 tbsp
	Paprika	

1. Drain the peaches.
2. Mix the cheese with the butter, season to taste with salt and cayenne pepper, and fill the peach halves.
3. Arrange them on a platter, or on individual dishes, on a bed of lettuce.
4. Beat the cream cheese and cream together, and spoon over the peaches. Sprinkle with paprika.

Piroshki

	00:40			
	00:55	Serves 4	Pacific Northwest	

American	Ingredients	Metric/Imperial
2 tbsp	Butter	25 g/1 oz
1	Small onion, finely chopped	1
4-6	Mushrooms	4-6
2–3 tbsp	Cooked rice	1½–2 tbsp
2 tbsp	Cooked chopped ham	1½ tbsp
1 tbsp	Chopped parsley	1 tbsp
1 (8-oz)	Package frozen flaky pastry, thawed	1 (225 g/8 oz)
1	Beaten egg	1

1. Melt the butter and cook finely chopped onion for 2–3 minutes to soften; then add the mushrooms and cook for 4 more minutes. Add the cooked rice and ham. Season with salt and pepper, and add chopped parsley. Cool before using.
2. Roll out the puff pastry into a long strip about 1½ inches in width or wider if larger piroshki are desired. Using a 1½-inch cutter, cut out as many rounds as possible.
3. Put a teaspoon of the cooled filling into the center of each pastry circle. Moisten the edges and press together to form a crescent-shaped pie. Brush the top with a beaten egg and bake in a hot oven for 10–15 minutes until golden brown and crisp. Serve hot.
4. Other ingredients can be used in piroshki such as smoked salmon, diced chicken, or small quantities of leftover meat.

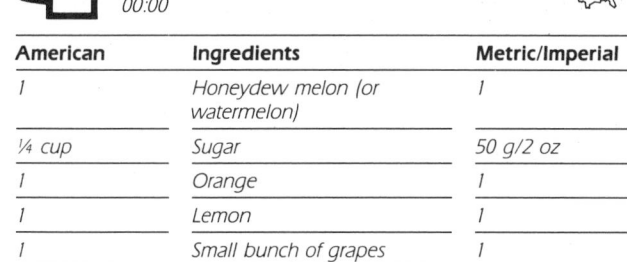

Peaches Filled with Cheese

Meatball Appetizers 🍴

| 00:20 | | | |
| 00:20 | Serves 4 | Midwest | |

American	Ingredients	Metric/Imperial
1 lb	Ground [minced] beef	450 g/1 lb
5 tbsp	Dry bread crumbs	4 tbsp
1	Egg	1
⅓ cup plus 2 tbsp	Steak sauce	75 ml/3 fl oz plus 1½ tbsp
2 tbsp	Oil	2 tbsp
2 tbsp	Light brown sugar	2 tbsp
2 tbsp	Butter	25 g/1 oz

1. Combine the beef, bread crumbs, egg, and 2 tablespoons [1½ tbsp] steak sauce. Mix and shape into 1-inch meatballs. Brown in the oil in a frying pan. Drain fat from the pan.
2. Add ⅓ cup [75 ml/3 fl oz] steak sauce, brown sugar, and butter to the meatballs in the pan. Simmer for 15 minutes until done. Makes 2 dozen meatballs.

Melon and Grape Cocktail 🍴🍴

| 00:15 | | | |
| 00:00 | Serves 4-6 | Pacific Southwest | |

American	Ingredients	Metric/Imperial
1	Honeydew melon (or watermelon)	1
¼ cup	Sugar	50 g/2 oz
1	Orange	1
1	Lemon	1
1	Small bunch of grapes	1
1	Sprig mint	1

1. Using a vegetable ball cutter, cut some balls from a honey-dew or watermelon. Half fill some glasses with the melon balls.
2. Dissolve sugar in juice of 1 orange and 1 lemon, and pour over melon.
3. Peel and seed some grapes, and put them on top of the melon. Do not mix them at this stage. Cover and leave for several hours.
4. When ready to serve, mix the fruit and garnish with a sprig of mint.

Beef Tartare

Beef Tartare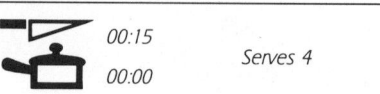

	00:15	Serves 4	New England
	00:00		

American	Ingredients	Metric/Imperial
1 lb	Chuck, round sirloin or tenderloin [fillet] steak	450 g/1 lb
4	Large rings raw onion	4
4	Raw egg yolks	4
4	Anchovy fillets	4
2 tsp	Capers	2 tsp
	Fresh horseradish, if available (optional)	
4	Quarters lemon	4
	Freshly ground black pepper	

1. Buy and grind [mince] the steak as near to serving time as possible, as the meat becomes dark in color if left standing. Only add pepper to the meat.
2. Shape the meat into 4 equal-sized cakes and make a depression in the center of each with a spoon. Place an onion ring around this depression and put an egg yolk into the center of each. Sprinkle a few capers on top of the egg yolk and lay one curled anchovy fillet on top of each yolk. Garnish with a few chives or fresh horseradish if available.
3. Serve with rye bread and butter, or French bread and lemon quarters.

Baked Spareribs

	12:00	Serves 4-6	Pacific Southwest
	01:30		

American	Ingredients	Metric/Imperial
3–4 lb	Pork spareribs	1.25–1.75 kg/ 3–4 lb
½	Clove garlic	½
¼ cup	Soy sauce	60 ml/2 fl oz
¼ cup	Sherry	60 ml/2 fl oz
3 tbsp	Honey	2 tbsp
¼ tsp	Ginger	¼ tsp

1. Preheat oven to 350°F/180°C/Gas Mark 4.
2. Crush the garlic. Mix the ingredients together and add seasoning. Pour this mixture over the spareribs. Leave to marinate overnight or longer, turning as often as possible.
3. Bake the spareribs for 1¼–1½ hours, basting every 15 minutes with marinade. The ribs should be well browned and the meat tender.
4. Serve with rice and salad.

Sausage Biscuits

	00:15	Serves 12	South
	00:15		

American	Ingredients	Metric/Imperial
8 oz	Sharp Cheddar cheese, grated	225 g/8 oz
1 lb	Hot [spicy] pork sausage meat	450 g/1 lb
2 cups	Biscuit mix [biscuit dough]	225 g/8 oz

1. Preheat oven to 400° F/200°/C Gas Mark 6.
2. Mix everything together in a bowl, working in the sausage and cheese well. Drop onto ungreased cookie [baking] sheets; shape slightly with your fingers if you wish. Bake about 15 minutes or until nicely browned.
3. Serve the biscuits piping hot. Makes about 3 dozen biscuits.

Herb Cheese Dip

	00.05	About 1½ cups [375 ml/12 fl oz]	Mid Atlantic
	00.00		

American	Ingredients	Metric/Imperial
3 pkg (3 oz each)	Cream cheese	250 g/9 oz
4 tbsp	Heavy [double] cream	3½ tbsp
2 tsp	Lemon juice	2 tsp
½	Clove garlic, crushed	½
1–2 tbsp	Milk	1–2 tbsp
2 tbsp	Freshly chopped parsley	2 tbsp

1. Mix all the ingredients well, adding seasoning to taste.
2. Serve slightly chilled.

Ham Appetizer

Mexican Dip

	00:10		
	00:15	Serves 4	Southwest

American	Ingredients	Metric/Imperial
3 tbsp	Ground or very finely chopped onion	2 tbsp
3 tbsp	White wine vinegar	2 tbsp
½ cup	Tomato ketchup	125 ml/4 fl oz
1 tsp	Worcestershire sauce	1 tsp
	Juice of ½ lemon	
½ tsp	Paprika pepper	½ tsp
	Black pepper, salt, sugar	
6–8	Frankfurters	6–8

1. Put the onion and vinegar into a pan, and simmer for 5 minutes.
2. Add tomato ketchup, Worcestershire sauce, and lemon juice. Simmer for a few minutes longer, then add paprika, pepper, salt, and sugar to taste.
3. Cut some frankfurters into 2–3 pieces and heat in the dip.
4. Serve with crusty bread.

Ham Appetizer

	00:20		
	00:00	Serves 4	Mid Atlantic

American	Ingredients	Metric/Imperial
2 tbsp	Finely chopped green pepper	1½ tbsp
2 tbsp	Finely chopped celery	1½ tbsp
2 tbsp	Finely chopped pimento	1½ tbsp
¼ tsp	Dijon mustard	¼ tsp
2 tsp	Lemon juice	2 tsp
2 tsp	Olive oil	2 tsp
4	Slices cooked ham	4
	Stuffed olives or gherkins for garnish	

1. Mix the green pepper, celery, and pimento together.
2. Mix the mustard with the lemon juice and oil. Add salt and pepper to taste. Pour over the vegetables, and mix well.
3. Divide equally between the four slices of ham, fold over, and secure with toothpicks.
4. Arrange on a serving dish, and garnish with stuffed olives or gherkins cut into fan shapes.

Shrimp Dip

| | 00:05 | About 1¾ cups [425 ml/14 fl oz] | South  |
| | 00:00 | | |

American	Ingredients	Metric/Imperial
¼ cup	Chili sauce	60 ml/2 fl oz
2 tsp	Lemon juice	2 tsp
1 tsp	Prepared horseradish [relish]	1 tsp
¼ tsp	Salt	¼ tsp
4	Drops hot-pepper sauce	4
1 cup	Sour cream	250 ml/8 fl oz
1 (4½-oz) can	Shrimp [prawns], drained and chopped	1 (125g/4½ oz) tin

1. Combine the chili sauce, lemon juice, horseradish, salt, and hot-pepper sauce. Fold in sour cream; add chopped shrimp. Chill.
2. Serve dip with crisp vegetables.

Garlic Butter Chips

| | 00:10 | Serves 8 | United States |
| | 00:08 | | |

American	Ingredients	Metric/Imperial
¾ cup	Butter or margarine	175 g/6 oz
2–3 cloves	Garlic, cut into slivers	2–3
1 bag (7½ oz)	Potato chips [crisps]	1 bag (200 g/7½ oz)

1. Preheat oven to 350°F/180°C/Gas Mark 4.
2. Heat the butter with the garlic for a few minutes, then remove the garlic.
3. Brush the potato chips with the garlic butter and place on baking sheets lined with paper towels [kitchen paper]. Heat for 5 minutes, then drain on clean paper towels.

Avocado Spread

| | 00:05 | About ½ cup [125 ml/4 fl oz] | Pacific Southwest |
| | 00:00 | | |

American	Ingredients	Metric/Imperial
4 oz	Mashed avocado	100 g/4 oz
2 tsp	Ground onion	2 tsp
1 tbsp	Lemon juice	1 tbsp
1 tbsp	Mayonnaise	1 tbsp
	Pinch of cayenne pepper	
	Dash of Tabasco	

1. Combine all the ingredients and beat until smooth.

Avocado Dip

| | 00:10 | About 1 cup [250 ml/8 fl oz] | Pacific Southwest  |
| | 00.00 | | |

American	Ingredients	Metric/Imperial
1	Cut clove garlic	1
3	Ripe avocado pears	3
	Pinch of cayenne pepper	
1 tbsp	Finely chopped onion	1 tbsp
1 tbsp	Olive oil	1 tbsp
1 tbsp	Lemon juice	1 tbsp
	A few drops of Tabasco sauce	

1. Rub the sides of a bowl with the garlic.
2. Remove the seeds and scoop out all the flesh from the pears and put it into the bowl.
3. Add all the other ingredients and mix well. Season to taste and chill before serving.

Chili Dip

| | 00:05 | About 2½ cups | South  |
| | 00:00 | | |

American	Ingredients	Metric/Imperial
4 pkg (3 oz each)	Cream cheese	350 g/12 oz
½ cup	Mayonnaise	125 ml/4 fl oz
½ cup	Chili sauce	125 ml/4 fl oz
3 tbsp	Prepared horseradish	2 tbsp
2 tbsp	Pickle relish	1½ tbsp

1. Beat the cream cheese with the mayonnaise until smooth and creamy.
2. Add the other ingredients and mix well.

Mustard Dip

| | 00:10 | About 1 cup [250 ml/8 fl oz] | Midwest |
| | 00:00 | | |

American	Ingredients	Metric/Imperial
4 tbsp	Prepared mustard	3½ tbsp
1 tbsp	Vinegar	1 tbsp
2 tsp	Ketchup	2 tsp
2 tsp	Prepared horseradish	2 tsp
1	Small onion, peeled and finely chopped	1
½ cup	Heavy [double] cream, whipped	125 ml/4 fl oz

1. Combine the mustard, vinegar, ketchup, horseradish, and onion.
2. Whip the cream lightly, and mix with the other ingredients.

Cream Cheese and Orange Spread

 00.05 / 00.00 — About ½ cup [125 ml/4 fl oz] — Pacific Southwest

American	Ingredients	Metric/Imperial
3 oz	Cream cheese	75 g/3 oz
2 tbsp	Finely chopped crystallized or preserved ginger	1½ tbsp
2 tsp	Grated orange rind	2 tsp
3 tbsp	Orange juice	2 tbsp

1. Beat the cream cheese until soft and smooth.
2. Add the ginger and orange rind, and mix in the orange juice.

Blue Cheese Spread

  00:10 / 00:10 — About 1 cup [250 ml/8 fl oz] — Midwest

American	Ingredients	Metric/Imperial
¼ lb	Blue cheese	100 g/4 oz
2 pkg (3 oz)	Cream cheese	175 g/6 oz)
2 tbsp	Mayonnaise	1½ tbsp
2 tbsp	Crisply cooked diced bacon	1½ tbsp

1. Combine the cheeses, and blend until creamy and smooth.
2. Add the mayonnaise and bacon.

Cheese and Pimento Spread

01.05 / 00.00 — About 1¼ cups [300 ml/10 fl oz] — Pacific Southwest

American	Ingredients	Metric/Imperial
1 cup	Grated Cheddar cheese	100 g/4 oz
1 jar (4 oz)	Pimento, drained and chopped	1 jar (100 g/4 oz)
3–4 tbsp	Mayonnaise	2–3½ tbsp
	Pinch of paprika	

1. Blend the ingredients together to form a spreadable paste.

Garlic Butter Chips and Chili Dip

Cheese and Chive Dip

 01:05 / 00:00 — About 2 cups [450 ml/¾ pint] — Midwest

American	Ingredients	Metric/Imperial
2 cups	Sour cream	450 ml/¾ pint
1 envelope	Garlic salad dressing mix	1 sachet
1 tbsp	Vinegar	1 tbsp
½ cup	Crumbled blue cheese	100 g/4 oz
4 tbsp	Finely chopped chives	3½ tbsp

1. Combine all the ingredients and let chill for at least 1 hour before using. The flavors will then be well blended.

Onion Dip

	01:10	3 cups	
	00:00	[750 ml/1¼ pints]	United States

American	Ingredients	Metric/Imperial
1 cup	Sour cream or yogurt	250 ml/8 fl oz
2 cups	Cottage cheese	450 g/1 lb
½ cup	Mayonnaise	125 ml/4 fl oz
1	Package onion soup mix	1
2 tbsp	Chopped parsley	1½ tbsp

1. Combine the sour cream or yogurt with the cottage cheese and beat until smooth.
2. Stir in the mayonnaise. When well mixed, add the onion soup mix and parsley. Blend well, and chill before serving.

Curried Cheese Dip

	00:05	2½ cups	
	00:00	[600 ml/1 pint]	South

American	Ingredients	Metric/Imperial
2 cups	Cottage cheese	450 g/1 lb
¼ cup	Evaporated milk	4 tbsp
1 tbsp	Worcestershire sauce	1 tbsp
	A few drops of hot pepper sauce	
½ tsp	Salt	½ tsp
1 tbsp	Curry powder	1 tbsp
1 tbsp	Minced onion	1 tbsp

1. Beat the cheese with the evaporated milk until smooth and creamy.
2. Add the other ingredients, and taste for seasoning.

Apple-Nut Horseradish Dip

	00:10	1 cup	
	00:00	[250 ml/8 fl oz]	New England

American	Ingredients	Metric/Imperial
2	Apples, peeled and cored	2
1 tbsp	Lemon juice	1 tbsp
¼ cup	Yogurt	125 ml/4 fl oz
1 tbsp	Prepared horseradish	1 tbsp
2 tbsp	Walnuts, minced or ground	1½ tbsp

1. Grate the apples; immediately combine with lemon juice to prevent discoloration. Blend in the remaining ingredients.
2. Serve the dip at once with chips [crisps], crackers, or vegetable dippers.

Creamy Curry Dip

	00:15		
	00:05	Serves 8	United States

American	Ingredients	Metric/Imperial
1 tbsp	Margarine	15 g/½ oz
1	Onion, finely chopped	1
1 tsp	Curry powder	1 tsp
½ cup	Cheddar cheese, grated	50 /2 oz
½ cup	Cottage cheese, sieved	100 g/4 oz
2 tbsp	Lemon juice	2 tbsp
4 tbsp	Milk	3½ tbsp

1. Heat the margarine in a frying pan. Add the onion and fry until soft (about 5 minutes). Stir in the curry powder, then put aside to cool.
2. Stir the grated cheese into the cottage cheese with a tablespoon, then beat in the lemon juice, milk, and cold onion mixture until all are thoroughly combined.

Blue Cheese Dip

	00:05	About 1 cup	
	00:00	[250 ml/8 fl oz]	Midwest

American	Ingredients	Metric/Imperial
3 tbsp	Blue cheese	2 tbsp
2 tbsp	Chili sauce	1½ tbsp
1 tbsp	Dry vermouth	1 tbsp
½ cup	Sour cream	125 ml/4 fl oz

1. Soften the cheese. Add the other ingredients and beat until smooth and creamy.

Appetizer Franks

	00:10		
	00:25	Serves 10	Midwest

American	Ingredients	Metric/Imperial
1 cup	Tomato ketchup	250 ml/8 fl oz
¼ cup	Steak sauce	60 ml/2 fl oz
¼ cup	Brown [demerara] sugar, packed	50 g/2 oz
2 tbsp	Vinegar	1½ tbsp
1 lb	Hot dogs, cut in 1-inch pieces	450 g/1 lb

1. In a medium saucepan, combine all the ingredients except the hot dogs; simmer 10 minutes. Add hot dogs; simmer 15 minutes longer.
2. To serve, keep warm in a chafing dish or fondue pot. Makes about 50.

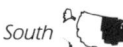

Creamy Curry Dip

Sausage and Apple Snack

Sausage and Apple Snack

| | 00:25 | | |
| | 00:20 | Serves 6 | Mid Atlantic |

American	Ingredients	Metric/Imperial
1 lb	Sausage meat	450 g/1 lb
2 tbsp	Chopped parsley	1½ tbsp
½ tsp	Curry powder	½ tsp
½ tsp	Mixed herbs	½ tsp
	Butter	
2	Dessert apples	2
6 thin slices	Bacon	6 thin rashers
	A few sprigs of parsley	
	Toast	

1. Combine the sausage meat, parsley, curry powder, herbs, and seasoning. Shape into 6 patties.
2. Sauté for about 5 minutes on each side. Remove from the pan and keep hot.
3. Core but do not peel the apples, cut each into three slices and sauté for about 2 minutes on each side.
4. Roll up the bacon, put onto a skewer, and fry or broil [grill].
5. Put the sausage patties on a serving dish with an apple ring on the bottom. Arrange the bacon rolls in the center and garnish with parsley. Serve with hot toast.

Pigs in Blankets

| | 00:30 | | |
| | 00:20 | Serves 6 | United States  |

American	Ingredients	Metric/Imperial
6	Frankfurters	6
	Prepared mustard	
6	Thin fingers cheese	6
	Flaky pastry (see Index)	
	Egg or milk to glaze	

1. Preheat oven to 450°F/230°C/Gas Mark 8.
2. Split the frankfurters, spread very lightly with mustard, and insert a finger of cheese in each.
3. Roll the pastry thinly and cut into 6-inch squares. Place 1 frankfurter diagonally on each square, and bring together the other two diagonal corners of the pastry, so that the ends of the frankfurters are exposed.
4. Put onto a baking sheet, glaze with egg or milk, and bake for 20 minutes.
5. Serve hot with broiled [grilled] tomatoes or cold with salad.

Chicken Liver Paté

| | 08:30 | | |
| | 00:10 | Serves 8-10 | United States |

American	Ingredients	Metric/Imperial
1 lb	Chicken livers (fresh or frozen)	450 g/1 lb
1 cup	Butter	225 g/8 oz
2	Onions	2
1	Large clove garlic (optional)	1
1	Small glass sherry or brandy	1
1 tbsp	Fresh mixed herbs: parsley, lemon thyme, basil, marjoram, and summer savory (or 2 tsp dried herbs)	1 tbsp
	Pinch of dried mace (optional)	
	Garnish	
1 can (14 fl oz)	Consomme, chilled	1 tin (400 ml/14 fl oz)
1 cup	Button mushrooms	125 g/4 oz
1	Bunch watercress	1

1. Fry the finely chopped onions and crushed garlic gently in ⅓ cup [75 g/3 oz] of butter for a few minutes. Do not allow it to brown. Remove garlic. Add the chicken livers and cook for 3–4 minutes. Then add the mixed herbs, mace, and seasoning. Cook for 1 minute. Remove from the stove and let cool.
2. Mash the livers to a soft pulp in a electric blender, stirring in ⅓ cup [75 g/3 oz] of melted butter. Add the sherry or brandy. Put the pâté into a serving dish or a lightly oiled mold so that it can be turned out after chilling. It can be made several days before a party if kept in the refrigerator, and should be a delicate pink inside when cut.
3. Make the garnish: Chop the chilled consomme and place it around the pâté. Cook the mushrooms gently for a few minutes in the remaining melted butter until completely absorbed. Drain on paper towel [kitchen paper]. Let cool. Garnish the top of the pâté with mushrooms and surround with watercress.

Duck Paté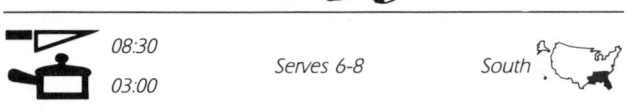

08:30
03:00

Serves 6-8

South

American	Ingredients	Metric/Imperial
4 cups	Cooked duck	900 g/2 lb
1 cup	Chopped duck and lamb liver	225 g/8 oz
1 cup	Chopped lean raw pork or veal	100 g/4 oz
1 cup	Chopped fat bacon, blanched	175 g/6 oz
1	Onion	1
½	Clove garlic	½
4 tbsp	Bread crumbs soaked in cream	3 tbsp
1	Small egg	1
1 tbsp	Chopped parsley and thyme	1 tbsp
2 tsp	Grated orange rind	2 tsp
¼–½ cup	Brandy	60–125 ml/ 2–4 fl oz
	Pinch of mace	
10–12 slices	Fat bacon	10-12 rashers
4	Slices orange	4
½ can (7 fl oz)	Consomme	½ tin (200 ml/7 fl oz)
3 tsp	Gelatin [gelatine]	3 tsp
1–2 tbsp	Brandy (or sherry)	1-2 tbsp

1. Preheat oven to 325°F/160°C/Gas Mark 3.
2. Grind the livers, pork or veal, fat bacon, finely chopped onions, and crushed garlic together. Mix in the bread crumbs, beaten egg, chopped herbs, orange rind, and brandy (or sherry). Add seasoning and mace.
3. With a knife, stretch the bacon slices by scraping them; line a loaf or pâté pan completely with them. Cut cooked duck into strips and sprinkle half into the loaf pan; season, then cover with half the meat mixture. Put in the rest of the duck, then the remaining mixture. Fold over any overlapping pieces of bacon. Cover the whole pan carefully with foil. Put in a baking pan of water [bain-marie] and bake in the oven for 2–3 hours.
4. Half an hour before the pâté is done, remove the foil and place 4 slices of orange down the center; recover and continue cooking. When done, remove from the oven and let cool. Put a double layer of greaseproof paper on top, then weights to press the pâté and make it firm.
5. Dissolve 3 teaspoons of gelatin in half a can of consomme; let cool and add 1–2 tablespoons of brandy (or sherry). When nearly set, turn the pâté out onto a wire rack and spoon jelly consomme over it. Let set. Serve on a salad-lined plate with orange segments for flavor and color.

Duck Paté

Tuna Fish Paté

08:30
00:00

Serves 8

Pacific Southwest

American	Ingredients	Metric/Imperial
2 cans (about 7 oz)	Tuna fish	2 tins (200 g/7 oz)
1 cup	Butter	225 g/8 oz
4 tbsp	Olive oil	3½ tbsp
2 tbsp	Lemon juice	1½ tbsp
1 tsp	Dijon mustard	1 tsp
2 tbsp	Grated onion	1½ tbsp
2 tbsp	Brandy	1½ tbsp

1. Drain the fish, soften the butter, and then pound all the ingredients together, seasoning to taste with salt and freshly ground black pepper.
2. Pack into dishes and chill well before serving.

Grapefruit with Crab

1. Preheat the broiler [grill].
2. Remove the crusts from the bread and toast on one side only. Lightly butter the untoasted side.
3. Flake the crabmeat, combine with the mayonnaise and onion, and spread on the buttered side of the toast. Sprinkle generously with cheese.
4. Put under a hot broiler [grill] for 1–2 minutes until the cheese melts and is lightly browned. Serve at once.

Party Crabmeat

	00:20	Serves 50	Mid Atlantic
	00:10		

American	Ingredients	Metric/Imperial
1 cup	Butter	225 g/8 oz
1½ cups	Flour	175 g/6 oz
2 qts	Milk	2 l/3½ pint
3 lb	Crabmeat, picked over	1.25 kg/3 lb
1 lb	Mushrooms, sliced and sautéed	450 g/1 lb
1 cup	Dry sherry	250 ml/8 fl oz
	Hearty dash lemon juice	
	Hearty dash Worcestershire sauce	
	Dash nutmeg	
	Parsley	

1. In a large pan, melt the butter, stir in the flour, and then add the milk. Stir constantly until the white sauce is thick.
2. Add all the remaining ingredients and heat until the mixture is hot. (Be careful the mixture does not scorch). Serve from the chafing dish with toast rounds or favorite crackers.

Grapefruit with Crab

	00:15	Serves 4	Pacific Southwest
	00:00		

American	Ingredients	Metric/Imperial
2	Grapefruit	2
1 cup	Crabmeat	225 g/8 oz
	A little mayonnaise	
	Parsley or lemon slices for garnish	

1. Mix the flesh from the grapefruit with the crabmeat.
2. Bind with a little mayonnaise, season to taste, and serve in the grapefruit shells, garnished with parsley or lemon slices.

Clam Puffs

	00:20	Serves 4-6	South
	00:04		

American	Ingredients	Metric/Imperial
½ lb	Minced clams, drained and chopped	225 g/8 oz
¼ cup	Swiss cheese, freshly grated	25 g/1 oz
1	Clove garlic, mashed or put through garlic press	1
1 tbsp	Mayonnaise	1 tbsp
	Salt	
	White pepper	
	Cayenne pepper	

1. Mix all the ingredients, adding enough mayonnaise to bind. Add salt and white pepper to taste and a light dash of cayenne. All this may be mixed together ahead of time.
2. Preheat the broiler [grill]. Spread the mixture, forming a crown, on toasted rounds of white bread. Broil [grill] for 3-4 minutes, watching carefully so they don't burn. Remove when golden and serve hot. Makes 16 to 18.

Crabmeat Nippies

	00:10	Serves 4	Mid Atlantic
	00:04		

American	Ingredients	Metric/Imperial
4	Slices bread	4
	Butter	
1 can (6 oz)	Crabmeat	1 tin (175 g/6 oz)
2 tsp	Mayonnaise	2 tsp
1 tsp	Grated onion	1 tsp
½ cup	Grated Cheddar or American cheese	50 g/2 oz

Clam Savory

Clam Savory

 00:10 / 00:05   Serves 4-5   New England

American	Ingredients	Metric/Imperial
3 tbsp	Butter	40 g/1½ oz
1	Small onion, peeled and finely chopped	1
½	Green pepper, finely chopped	½
1 can (7½ oz)	Clams, drained and chopped	1 tin (200 g/7½ oz)
1 cup	Grated cheese	100 g/4 oz
1 tbsp	Tomato purée	1 tbsp
1 tbsp	Worcestershire sauce	1 tbsp
1 tbsp	Sherry	1 tbsp
⅛ tsp	Cayenne pepper	⅛ tsp
	Dill pickle (optional)	
4-5	Slices hot buttered toast	4-5

1. Heat the butter in a sauté pan, add onion and green pepper, and sauté for 3 minutes.
2. Add the clams, cheese, tomato purée, Worcestershire sauce, sherry, and cayenne pepper. Cook for a few minutes until the cheese has melted, stirring all the time.
3. Put a thin slice of dill pickle on each slice of toast and serve the clam mixture on top.

Fish and Mushroom Bundles

Fish and Mushroom Bundles

	00:45	Serves 4	United States
	01:00		

American	Ingredients	Metric/Imperial
¼ lb	White fish	100 g/4 oz
	Salt and pepper to taste	
½ cup	Milk	125 ml/4 fl oz
3 tbsp	Margarine	40 g/1½ oz
2 tbsp	Flour	1½ tbsp
2 tbsp	Mushrooms, chopped	1½ tbsp
1 tbsp	Parsley, chopped	1 tbsp
1 tsp	Lemon juice	1 tsp
1 (8-oz)	Package frozen puff pastry, thawed	1 (225 g/8 oz)
	Extra milk for glazing	

1. Put the fish into a saucepan, season well with salt and pepper, then add the milk. Bring to a boil, then simmer for 15 to 20 minutes or until the fish flakes easily. Drain and reserve the cooking liquid.
2. Heat 2 tablespoons [25 g/1 oz] of margarine in a saucepan, stir in flour and cook, stirring, for 2 minutes. Add the reserved cooking liquid and bring to a boil, stirring all the time. Cook for 2 minutes.
3. Melt the remaining margarine in a frying pan and fry the mushrooms until cooked. Flake the cooked fish, removing all skin and bones. Add the fish to the sauce with mushrooms, parsley, and lemon juice. Allow the mixture to become cold.
4. Preheat oven to 450°F/230°C/Gas Mark 8.
5. Roll out the pastry on a lightly floured surface. Cut into 8, 5-inch circles. Place each pastry circle in a muffin tin (the pastry should stand well above the edges of the tin). Put a spoonful of fish mixture into each circle. Dampen the inside edges of the pastry, bring them to the center, and press them firmly together to seal. Make a small slit in the top of each bundle. Brush with milk and bake for 20 to 25 minutes or until golden. Serve the hot bundles, 2 per person, with salad.

Oysters Baltimore

	00:10	Serves 4-6	Mid Atlantic
	00:20		

American	Ingredients	Metric/Imperial
4 slices	Bacon	4 rashers
18	Oysters	18
3 tbsp	Chili sauce	2 tbsp
1 tbsp	Worcestershire sauce	1 tbsp
6 tbsp	Heavy [double] cream	5 tbsp
½ tsp	Tarragon	½ tsp
2 tbsp	Lemon juice	2 tbsp
1 tsp	Salt	1 tsp
¼ tsp	Pepper	¼ tsp

1. In a medium-sized frying pan, fry the bacon until crisp. Set the bacon aside to drain, then crumble into bits for garnish. Pour off all but 1 tablespoon of fat from the pan. Add the oysters with their liquid. Cook uncovered over medium heat until most of the pan juices are absorbed.
2. Mix the remaining ingredients; add to the oysters. Simmer no more than 5 minutes to blend all flavors. Add extra seasonings if desired. These oysters are delicious served over hot buttered toast. Garnish with crumbled bacon.

Shrimp Mold

	08:30	Serves 12-16	South
	00:00		

American	Ingredients	Metric/Imperial
¼ cup	Water	60 ml/2 fl oz
1 envelope	Gelatin [gelatine]	1 sachet
1 can (10¾ oz)	Tomato soup	1 tin (300 g/10¾ oz)
8 oz	Cream cheese	225 g/8 oz
½ cup	Onion, chopped	100 g/4 oz
1 cup	Celery, chopped	225 g/8 oz
1 cup	Mayonnaise	250 ml/8 fl oz
1 lb	Cooked shrimp [prawns], chopped	450 g/1 lb

1. Soften the gelatin in water. Warm the soup and add gelatin and cream cheese. Mix well. Add the other ingredients.
2. Pour into an oiled 6-cup [1.5 l/2½ pint] mold. Refrigerate until firm. Unmold to serve. Serve with light and dark cocktail rye bread.